PERGAMON INTERNATIONAL LIBRARY
of Science, Technology, Engineering and Social Studies
*The 1000-volume original paperback library in aid of education,
industrial training and the enjoyment of leisure*
Publisher: Robert Maxwell, M.C.

PLANKTON AND PRODUCTIVITY
IN THE OCEANS

_____ **Publisher's Notice to Educators** _____

THE PERGAMON TEXTBOOK
INSPECTION COPY SERVICE

An inspection copy of any book published in the Pergamon International Library
will gladly be sent without obligation for consideration for course adoption or
recommendation. Copies may be retained for a period of 60 days from receipt and
returned if not suitable. When a particular title is adopted or recommended for
adoption for class use and the recommendation results in a sale of 12 or more copies,
the inspection copy may be retained with our compliments. If after examination
the lecturer decides that the book is not suitable for adoption but would like to
retain it for his personal library, then our Educators' Discount of 10% is allowed on
the invoiced price. The Publishers will be pleased to receive suggestions for revised
editions and new titles to be published in this important International Library.

Other books of interest

BACQ & ALEXANDER
Fundamentals of Radiobiology

BELFIELD & DEARDEN
A Practical Course in Biology

BOYDEN
Perspectives in Zoology

CAMPBELL
The Structure and Functions of Animal Cell Components

CLEGG
General Science: Biology

CLOUDESLEY-THOMPSON
Desert Life
Spiders, Scorpions, Centipedes and Mites

COHEN
Living Embryos

DEARDEN & DEARDEN
A Modern Course in Biology

FAHN
Plant Anatomy

GOODWIN & MERCER
Introduction to Plant Biochemistry

GOSS
Physiology of Plants and their Cells

JAMIESON & REYNOLDS
Tropical Plant Types

KOREN
Environmental Health and Safety

McMILLAN
An Introduction to Biochemistry

MARSHALL
The Development of Modern Biology

MORGAN
Environmental Biology, Volumes 1, 2, 3, 4

PANTELOURIS
Introduction to Animal Physiology and Physiological Genetics

PARSONS & TAKAHASHI
Biological Oceanographic Processes

PERCIVAL
Floral Biology

SCORER
Air Pollution

STREET & COCKBURN
Plant Metabolism

THREADGOLD
The Ultrastructure of the Animal Cell

WAREING & PHILLIPS
The Control of Growth and Differentiation in Plants

WISCHNITZER
Introduction to Electron Microscopy

The terms of our inspection copy service apply to all the above books. Full details of all books listed and specimen copies of journals listed will gladly be sent upon request.

PLANKTON
and
PRODUCTIVITY
in the
OCEANS

JOHN E. G. RAYMONT

DEPARTMENT OF OCEANOGRAPHY
IN THE
UNIVERSITY OF SOUTHAMPTON

PERGAMON PRESS

OXFORD · NEW YORK · TORONTO
SYDNEY · PARIS · BRAUNSCHWEIG

U.K.	Pergamon Press Ltd., Headington Hill Hall, Oxford OX3 0BW, England
U.S.A.	Pergamon Press Inc., Maxwell House, Fairview Park, Elmsford, New York 10523, U.S.A.
CANADA	Pergamon of Canada Ltd., 207 Queen's Quay West, Toronto 1, Canada
AUSTRALIA	Pergamon Press (Aust.) Pty. Ltd., 19a Boundary Street, Rushcutters Bay, N.S.W. 2011, Australia
FRANCE	Pergamon Press SARL, 24 rue des Ecoles, 75240 Paris, Cedex 05, France
WEST GERMANY	Pergamon Press GmbH, D-3300 Braunschweig, Postfach 2923, Burgplatz 1, West Germany

First edition 1963
Reprinted 1967, 1972 and 1976
Library of Congress Catalog Card No. 62–11561

Printed in Great Britain by A. Wheaton & Co., Exeter
0 08 010185 2 (Hard cover)
0 08 019009 X (Flexi cover)

CONTENTS

FOREWORD

THE SEAS of the world are so vast and complex, and the assemblages of plants and animals so diverse that one brief book must necessarily give only an incomplete picture of marine science. One might attempt a superficial coverage of the main aspects of marine biology, or instead concentrate on a treatment of certain basic problems in the marine environment. Among these, one of the most challenging is surely the concept of basic production, by which is implied the synthesis of organic material from inorganic substances, such a synthesis being effected almost entirely by the photosynthetic activity of green plants. Consideration of the conditions limiting this basic production both in space and time, leads inevitably to a study of the physics and chemistry of seawater. Having traced the production of organic matter by plants, we may then follow the fate of this material through the animals of the plankton community, and then through the animals on the sea bottom and those actively swimming animals such as fishes and whales which make up the nekton. Finally, we may see the return of materials to the seawater as inorganic substances, due mainly to the activities of bacteria.

Even this cycle is too extensive and complex for us to survey adequately. We shall therefore concentrate first on those conditions which are important in primary production, and then deal with the biology of the plankton community. The role of the benthos and the nekton will be examined but briefly. Interesting and important aspects of marine investigations such as the biology of inter-tidal areas, life in abyssal depths, studies of estuarine waters and much of fisheries science must unfortunately be largely neglected. Nevertheless, it would seem highly desirable to gain some appreciation first of a few of the basic problems in the open sea before attempting to examine particular aspects or more specialised marine environments. The concept of productivity is so much at the very heart of any ecological problem, and the physical and chemical factors related to productivity so all-important, that these aspects of oceanography must surely be studied early. Moreover, basic production in the sea is not only of academic interest since to a large extent it determines the siting of the world's commercial fisheries. Before long, also, the acute need of the increasing world population for foodstuffs may make it necessary to look for a greater contribution from the vast organic production of the oceans.

This book is intended primarily for students in their latter years of a university course who are becoming interested in oceanography mainly after training in biological science. It may be of some assistance to workers who are beginning investigations in the marine field, but it is not intended to be an exhaustive review of plankton research. The author realises that much of the chemistry and physics of sea-water has been dealt with somewhat cursorily, and he has borrowed consciously from such excellent works as *The Oceans. Their Physics, Chemistry, and General Biology*, by Sverdrup, Johnson and Fleming, and *Treatise on Marine Ecology and Paleoecology*. (Volume 1) *Ecology*. Edited by Hedgpeth, and from the reviews of Harvey, especially *The Chemistry and Fertility of Seawaters*. No claim is made that in the various sections of the book all the relevant literature has been mentioned, since a student approaching oceanography for the first time may be dismayed by the width of the subject. Reviews have been extensively used; nevertheless it is hoped that the considerable number of references quoted will induce students to refer to original papers. To a large extent these are in the English language, but readers who are beginning to study marine science may be encouraged to consult some of the outstanding foreign literature. Usually, when reference is made in the text to a particular species, the nomenclature used by the author of the paper consulted has been followed; sometimes an alternative, commonly used, specific name has also been quoted.

One of the chief aims of this volume is to demonstrate that although one may approach the study of oceanography through biological science, some knowledge of the other closely related disciplines of oceanography soon becomes essential for a proper understanding. On the other hand, it may become apparent that to concentrate entirely on physical oceanography is equally dangerous, since the diverse roles of living organisms are fundamental to our knowledge of the seas.

My sincere thanks are due to my publishers for their ready help, and to the editors of many journals and to the authors of books and scientific papers for permission to include a large number of original figures and other illustrations in this volume. Detailed references to the sources of illustrations are included in the general bibliography. I am deeply grateful to Dr. H. G. Stubbings and to Dr. L. H. N. Cooper, who have read the whole manuscript of this book, and to Dr. F. S. Russell, F.R.S., and Dr. M. Parke, who have read many of the chapters. Their ready advice and helpful criticisms have greatly encouraged and assisted me. Other friends and colleagues, including Dr. Carruthers, and many of my former research students, have helped me in discussing particular problems.

Finally, I am greatly indebted to my wife who has been always ready to read and criticise the manuscript, and who has undertaken the laborious tasks of proof-reading and preparation of the index. The guidance of all these friends has enabled me to complete this volume and saved me from many errors; for the faults which remain I must be held solely responsible.

CHAPTER I

THE AQUATIC ENVIRONMENT—
TEMPERATURE

ANY CONSIDERATION of the ecology of aquatic organisms, that is to say the relationship between these organisms and their physico-chemical and biological environment, must almost inevitably lead to a comparison between the aquatic and the terrestrial environments. On even a somewhat superficial view it would seem that life in an aquatic medium is much easier than life on land. Protoplasm is a complex colloidal mixture of sols and gels and the intercellular fluids are largely water. Thus water makes up something like 70%, or in some organisms like jelly fish more than 95%, of the body weight. But water not only enters into the composition of animals; all the complex chemical reactions in the living organism proceed in a watery medium. The constant tendency to desiccation, which occurs with existence on land, will have a profound influence on the surfaces of cells, and on mucous membranes. Morphological and physiological adaptations appear concerned with direct water loss itself, and with the flow of urine, the form of nitrogenous excretion, with respiration, and with other functions in which water plays a significant role.

While, therefore, the inhabiting of the aquatic environment is clearly easier in many ways, there are certain particular and somewhat less immediately obvious properties of water which render it especially fitting for life. Water is a rather peculiar fluid in many of its physical and chemical characteristics. Two of its properties which are of great significance for life are its high specific heat and transparency to radiation. The specific heat of water is very high indeed; among the commoner liquids only liquid ammonia exceeds it. As compared with the specific heat of a gas the specific heat of water is thus extraordinarily great. Seawater, for example, has something like three thousand times the specific heat of air.

These differences in specific heat are of considerable importance. The primary effect is to prevent any extreme range in temperature and to smooth out changes in temperature in temperate and high latitudes where seasons are marked. Freshwater and particularly marine habitats will therefore tend to have much more constant temperature conditions than terrestrial environments. The high specific heat also permits large quantities of heat to be transferred by moving water masses.

Water is a fairly transparent substance in comparison with other fluids. At the same time it is vastly less transparent than air. Water

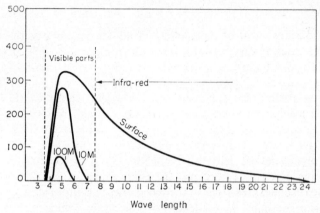

FIG. 1.1 Incident solar radiation falling on the sea surface, and the amounts remaining at 10 and 100 m. Visible wave lengths and especially infra-red rays are very rapidly absorbed. (Energy units along ordinate are arbitrary.) (Slightly altered from Sverdrup *et al.*, 1946.)

is reasonably transparent in the visible portion of the solar energy spectrum, but of the energy falling on the surface of the earth, more than 50%, is in the infra-red (the "heat rays") (Fig. 1.1). It happens that water is particularly opaque to infra red rays so that even in the first couple of metres of water, about 98% of the total infra red radiation reaching the earth is absorbed. Even much of the visible portion of the energy spectrum is absorbed in the first ten metres of water (Fig. 1.1), so that of the whole radiation received on the earth's surface more than half is absorbed in the first metre of water, and only about 5% remains at a depth of 20 m though the degree of penetration varies with the type of ocean water (cf. Fig. 1.2). The heating effect of solar radiation is therefore confined to the few upper metres of water. This is one of the most important aspects of temperature

relations in the aquatic environment, whether it be in bodies of freshwater or in the oceans.

Although the common physical properties of water permit us to
draw many parallels between life in freshwaters and life in the marine
habitat, it is necessary to distinguish certain characteristics of the two

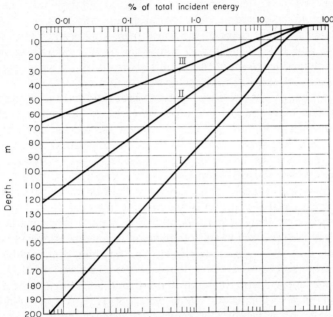

Fig. 1.2 Percentage of total incident energy reaching various depths in
three types of ocean water. (From Jerlov, 1951.)

environments. There are approximately 140 million square miles
of ocean out of roughly 200 million square miles of earth's surface.
In other words about seven tenths of the earth's surface is covered
with sea. And this seawater has probably changed very little in composition through the aeons of time (cf. Robertson, 1957), and has
been more or less continuous in space and time despite all the upheavals
of the earth's surface. By contrast, freshwaters cover a very much
smaller fraction, about 1/50 of the earth, and they are much more
transient. Very few of our great lakes (Tanganyika is one of the exceptions), extend back to Tertiary times; many of the ponds and smaller
lakes are becoming shallower owing to sedimentation, and will,
in the not too distant future, be converted to land.

Even more obvious is the difference between the seas and freshwaters when we consider depth. It is somewhat surprising that the average depth of the oceans exceeds 3500 m. Some enormously deep trenches exist in the oceans; for example, the Sunda and Weber deeps exceed 7000 m, and the Bougainville, Mariana and Kermadec trenches 9000 m. The Japan and Mindanao (Philippines) trenches have soundings exceeding 10,000 m, i.e. greater depth than the highest mountains. Of the lakes of the world there are very few (e.g. Lake Baikal and Lake Tanganyika) which are more than 1500 m deep. The volume, therefore, of the world's oceans is out of all proportion vastly greater than the total volume of freshwaters.

The effect of the opacity of water to heat rays and the consequent restriction of heating to the upper water layers is, therefore, going to be much more strongly experienced in the marine environment (because of the vastly greater depth of water) than in freshwaters. How may heat be transmitted to the deeper layers? Here again the physical characteristics of water must be considered. Conduction of heat by water, though high for liquids, is almost a negligible quantity. This means that conduction is not effective in transporting heat from the surface to the lower layers, and this is particularly marked in the deep oceans. Even in lakes conduction is quite ineffective in transferring heat. It has been calculated, for example, for a freshwater body such as Lake Constance, that if all the lake were cooled to 0 °C and the upper metre subsequently warmed to 30 °C by the sun's action, then if conduction alone were operative, 100 yr would be necessary for a measurable amount of heat to reach the bottom (Clarke, 1954).

Of other heating factors which might play a part in the heat budget of bodies of water, heating through the earth's crust has been shown to be practically negligible in the oceans, amounting to about 1/10,000 of the solar surface radiation. As regards the freshwater environment, certain peculiar lakes are fed by hot springs, and obviously some of the heat there is derived from the terrestrial crust, but in normal large lakes, as with the seas, no appreciable contribution of heat comes from the earth. Adiabatic changes and the transformation of kinetic energy (due to wind on the surface) into heat are also negligible in both the freshwater and marine habitats. A certain amount of heat will be added to fresh and marine waters by condensation of water vapour if warm moist air passes over a colder water surface. However, the amount of this condensation over the oceans is small, so that very little heat is added to the water by this means. As regards heating processes in the oceans, therefore, the absorption of heat from solar radiation is really the only significant factor, and this is essentially a surface effect.

We must now consider those factors which are responsible for cooling the oceans. Of these, cold air may be important. If the sea surface is warmer than the overlying air, heat will be transported from the sea, and warmed air leads to considerable turbulence of the air layers. Heat is lost in this way, and in particular, chilling of seas off the great land masses can occur from outflowing continental cold air streams. Similarly, very marked chilling of freshwaters may occur, especially in great continents. The greatest cooling factor in the oceans is, however, evaporation. Here again a physical characteristic of water is significant. The latent heat of evaporation of water is the highest of all liquids, so that when water evaporates there must be a very marked cooling effect at the surface. While this is true for both the freshwater and marine environments, it is particularly important in the open oceans, where it accounts for about 90% of the total heat surplus. Bigelow estimates that for the Gulf of Maine, off the north-east coast of America, the amount of evaporation yearly would cool the first 50 m of water over the whole Gulf through about 5 °C.

In middle and higher latitudes evaporation is rather greater in winter than in summer. This is partly due to the high specific heat of water maintaining water temperatures in those latitudes above that of the over-lying air. As regards the annual amount of evaporation, the maximum zone lies a little north and south of the equator (Fig. 1.3), i.e. evaporation is rather less in the equatorial regions than it is in the sub-tropical areas. This is probably associated with the high humidity and to the rather low velocity of the wind in equatorial as compared with sub-equatorial regions. Outside the sub-tropical areas the amount of evaporation drops off fairly steadily towards the north and south (Fig. 1.3). The overall extent of evaporation is really surprising. Wust has calculated that some 334,000 km³ of water are evaporated every year from the oceans. By contrast, the total amount of precipitation falling on the whole of the land areas of the world in a year is less that one third of this – about 99,000 km³. The importance of evaporation in cooling the oceans is thus obvious.

A further potent agent in the cooling of fresh and marine waters is the melting of ice. Water has a very high latent heat of fusion, exceeded only by ammonia, and therefore there is a marked thermostatic effect at the freezing point. Freshwater bodies in temperate regions are frequently ice-covered during the winter season, and during melting in the spring the water layers below will be cooled. In the oceans the amount of ice in the polar regions is well worthy of our consideration. One estimate states that in the North Atlantic alone approximately 1000 cubic miles of ice are melted every year. But apart from the North Atlantic and North Pacific polar regions,

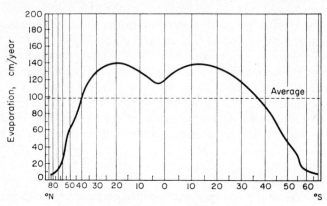

FIG. 1.3 Average annual evaporation from the oceans at various latitudes (after Wust *et al.*, 1954).

by far the greatest ice front is round the vast Antarctic continent. Cooling due to ice is a very important agent in changes of temperature in the seas, but for the oceans as a whole, evaporation is a more potent factor. Since ice is floating, any cooling due to melting of ice is essentially a surface effect in the first place.

Clearly, the various heating and cooling factors considered so far are all primarily surface phenomena, and the surface of the oceans will tend to lose heat at the polar regions and to gain heat at the tropics. A new factor, however, must be considered. Once water is cooled, whether by evaporation or by melting of ice, it will become denser and will tend to sink. In this way the cooling effect may be transmitted to lower levels, and, equally important, there will be a certain degree of mixing of water layers. Once water layers are in movement. transference of heat between the layers becomes possible, especially since the heat capacity of water is so large.

Presumably, since at the surface the heating effect is most intense at the tropics and the cooling effect at the surface is most marked

near the poles, the surface of the oceans should show the most extreme
conditions of temperature. In equatorial regions of the oceans the
surface temperature is a little below 30 °C. Towards the Arctic the
surface summer temperature may be as high as 5 °C (Fig. 1.4) falling
to the freezing point of seawater (− 1.9 °C) in winter. Towards the
South Pole temperatures are rather lower than in corresponding

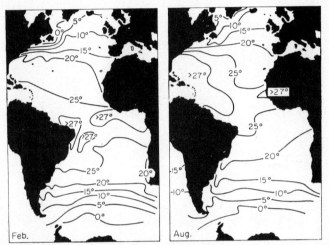

FIG. 1.4 Summer and winter surface temperatures in the Atlantic Ocean
(Harvey, 1955).

northern latitudes; much of the Antarctic seas are always below 0 °C
(Fig. 1.5). There is then a total range between the poles and the equator
for the surface of the ocean of about 30 °C. There are one or two
more enclosed warm seas, such as the Red Sea and the Persian
Gulf, where temperatures exceed 30 °C. Even in temperate areas,
for example over mud flats exposed at low tide, relatively high temperatures may be experienced for a short period of the day. But over
the open oceans as a whole the surface temperature approaches 30 °C,
and at the other extreme reaches the freezing point of seawater.

The effects of temperature upon animals, both terrestrial and
aquatic, have perhaps been more fully investigated than other physical
and chemical factors (cf. Heilbrunn, 1952). In general, if we omit from
consideration certain resting stages, and organisms such as bacteria
tardigrades and rotifers, which can withstand remarkably low temperatures, and blue-green algae which live in hot springs, most

organisms live in the temperature range from *ca.* 45 °C to a little below 0 °C (Fig. 1.6). Most marine animals, however, will not survive temperatures exceeding 35 °C, except for some marine species which live between tide marks and are specially adapted to the somewhat higher temperatures. Thus Evans (1948) has shown that some species of *Littorina* are killed only when the temperature approaches 45 °C and *Patella* can survive up to 42 °C.

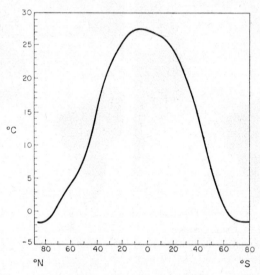

FIG. 1.5   The average surface temperature for all oceans as a function of latitude (after Wust *et al.*, 1954).

The temperatures at which death results from both heat and cold in various animals are given by Prosser (1950); the lower limit is usually less precise since many animals can withstand lowered temperatures, at least for some time, in a more or less dormant condition. If the temperature is then raised slowly, the animals may survive. To some extent this is true of "heat death" also; that is to say, animals pass into a state of coma at temperatures below the thermal death point, but more usually the animals die in a comatose condition even though the temperature is lowered again. Death at high temperatures may be due to a coagulation of the protoplasm, but death at both the higher and lower limits frequently occurs owing to interference with metabolic activities (e.g. respiration) before any general deterioration of the body protoplasm occurs.

There is no doubt that many marine animals in particular are acclimatized to the temperature range which they normally experience. Thus Arctic and Antarctic zooplankton living at about 0 °C may not survive an upper temperature limit even as low as 10 °C. On the other hand Gunter (1957) lists warm water marine animals which

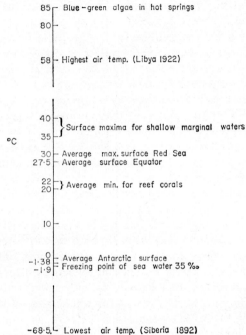

°C

85 — Blue–green algae in hot springs

80 —

58 — Highest air temp. (Libya 1922)

40 —⎫
      ⎬ Surface maxima for shallow marginal waters
35 —⎭

30 — Average max. surface Red Sea
27·5 — Average surface Equator

22 —⎫
20 —⎭ Average min. for reef corals

10 —

0 — Average Antarctic surface
−1·38 —
−1·9 — Freezing point of sea water 35 ‰

−68·5 — Lowest air temp. (Siberia 1892)

FIG. 1.6 Range of temperature in the terrestrial and marine environment (adapted from Gunter, 1957).

were killed by cold off Bermuda at a temperature of 7 °C, and other species in Texas waters at 4 °C.

Between those upper and lower temperature limits where in-activity of an animal sets in, lies the normal physiological range for a species. We are very familiar with the observation that within this range an increase in temperature results in an increase in the rate of various physiological processes (e.g. enzyme activity, heart beat, oxygen uptake, etc.) until an optimum is reached. For some processes the rate is approximately doubled or trebled for a rise of 10 °C (van't Hoff's rule), though this must be regarded only as a broad generalization as applied to animals; there are numerous exceptions.

Beyond the optimum, activity declines, and usually a further rise in temperature soon induces heat coma. Although marine animals are profoundly affected by changes in temperature, relatively rapid, large-scale changes are unlikely to occur in the marine environment, and certainly few marine animals would survive such changes. But the rates of all the varied activities of marine organisms (breathing rate, O_2 uptake, nerve conduction, general activity, photosynthesis) will depend on the temperature level. The rate of development of many marine species (e.g. fishes, bivalves and crustaceans) has been shown to be temperature dependent. Nevertheless, marine animals show marked adaptations in their temperature range. Thus, while cod may develop successfully up to *ca.* 15 °C, oysters require temperatures exceeding 16 °C. Orton observed that the oxygen uptake of arctic, boreal and tropical lamellibranchs was approximately the same though the water temperatures were *ca.* 0, 8 and 30 °C respectively. Thorson (1958) in considering parallel communities of benthic animals existing in cold, temperate and warm waters, also states that marked temperature adaptations are exhibited in the metabolic growth rates. Scholander and his coworkers (1957) have recently demonstrated an adaptation in the body fluids of marine teleosts living at shallow depths in the coldest icebound seas, such that the osmotic pressure of the blood becomes raised during winter and freezing is prevented.

Temperature thus exerts a profound influence on marine species, and many are adapted to live within only comparatively narrow temperature limits. Nevertheless, at the whole range of temperatures experienced in the world's oceans (i.e. − 1.9–30 °C) some species can exist. Exceedingly few species are sufficiently cosmopolitan to live throughout most of this range, but the cold-loving species not only exist but flourish in the colder waters, and the warm species breed and live successfully in the warmer seas. The species peculiar to a marine area have become adapted so that their physiological processes work most efficiently at the temperature levels normally experienced in the particular marine environment. In other words, the regional variation in temperature in the whole oceans is such that certain organisms can live successfully in each area. This is in contrast to life on land, where, for example, parts of deserts are too hot at times for living organisms, and where also the extreme cold of a terrestrial polar winter does not permit active life (cf. Fig. 1.6).

In the sea, even the range of 30 °C which occurs between the poles and the tropics, decreases rapidly with depth. This is partly due to the high specific heat of water and in part to its relative opacity (cf. Fig. 1.2). The difference in temperature between the tropics and the poles, for instance at 1000 m depth, is only of the order of 5 °C, and below 2000 m the difference is usually less than 2 °C. A diagrammatic representation of the temperature conditions with regard to depth and latitude in a typical ocean is shown in Fig. 1.7. This may

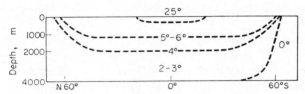

FIG. 1.7 A diagram of the range in temperature with depth and with latitude in an idealized ocean.

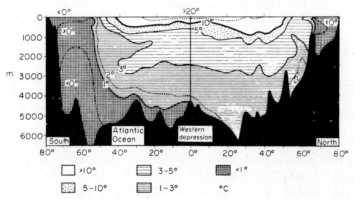

FIG. 1.8 Temperature in the Atlantic Ocean as a function of depth and latitude (from Wust, 1930).

be compared with the profile of temperature in the Atlantic Ocean (Fig. 1.8). In as far as geographical distribution is determined by temperature, there would seem to be very little barrier to distribution of marine animals below a depth of about 2000 m. Moreover, since the average depth of the ocean approaches 4000 m, the uniformity of temperature over the vast areas of great depth is really quite astonishing. The whole of the really deep water in the tropical, sub-tropical and temperate regions does not vary much from 2–3 °C and only towards the poles does it get slightly colder (cf. Table 1.1 and Fig. 1.8). The small regional range in temperature of deep ocean water, is reflected in a wide zoogeographical distribution of many pelagic species. Some bottom-living animals are also widely distributed, but Vinogradova (1959) has shown that the bottom fauna in abyssal depths shows a high degree of endemism. Thus of more than 1000 deep-living bottom species, only 4% occur in all three oceans. Although temperature is not a barrier in distribution, other factors including the bottom topography limit the spread of deep sea bottom species.

The contrast between the terrestrial and the marine environment in temperature conditions can be seen equally clearly in the daily and seasonal temperature changes. On land the difference in temperature due to day and night can be very considerable. Even in temperate climates a drop of more than 5 °C is not unusual, and in high latitudes there may be a change of even 15 or 20 °C, the most extreme cases occurring in deserts. By contrast, at the surface of the sea over the great oceans the difference between day and night is usually less than 0.5 °C, though slightly greater values exceeding 1 °C are quoted for the tropics by Sverdrup et al. (1946). Immediately beneath the surface of the sea even this minute change is ironed out, so that below a depth of some 10 to 15 m there is no detectable diurnal variation in sea temperature anywhere over the world.

Seasonal changes on land tend to be large. Even in the fairly mild climate of our own country the winter average temperature is about 5 °C as compared with some 18 °C in summer—a range of about 13°. But in the interior of continents an average range of 30 °C is by no means unusual. There are, of course, even more extreme cases, as in the heart of Siberia, where the range can be as much as 50 °C.

In the oceans the seasonal temperature variation, though more noticeable than daily changes, is very small indeed. At the tropics and towards the poles the difference between summer and winter is less than 5 °C; in temperate zones there may be as much as a 10 °C range, with an even greater difference in shallow water (cf. Figs. 1.8.1 A and B). Generally off the east coast of a continent there may be a variation in sea temperature between summer and winter of approximately 15 °C, but even here the changes are virtually confined to the surface. The annual variation in temperature is extraordinarily rapidly wiped out with depth. An investigation made in the Bay of Biscay, for example, where the annual surface range was nearly 8 °C showed that at 50 m the seasonal range was only ca. 2 °C and at 100 m less than 1 °C

(Fig. 1.8.2). Even comparatively close to coasts, below 100 m depth the range throughout a year is seldom more than 3 °C. It may fairly be claimed for the seas as a whole that below 200 m there is virtually no seasonal temperature fluctuation. Not only, therefore, are temperatures in the oceans such that life can exist everywhere, but there

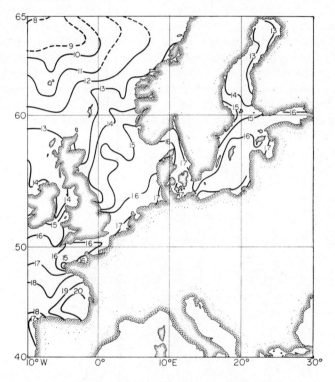

FIG. 1.8.1 (A) Summer surface temperatures in the N.W. Atlantic (from Bruns, 1958).

is so little variation in temperature, that rapid adaptation by the organisms to resist temperature change is unnecessary.

Often in a temperate sea area, however, where there is some range in temperature between summer and winter, different species will breed at different times of the year. For example, in British seas some fishes like plaice and cod tend to breed about February or March whereas other fish, such as blennies and gobies, will breed in summer.

Similarly, among the barnacles, *Balanus balanoides* has a very sharply defined breeding time during the coldest period of the year, whilst the warmer water *Balanus improvisus* is mainly a summer spawner (cf. Chap. XII).

In the sea maximum and minimum temperatures occur at different months as compared with land in the same region. Thus, in northern latitudes the temperature maximum on land is usually in July, and the minimum about January. In the sea the seasons tend to be later, so that the maximum surface temperature occurs about August, and the minimum about February. At greater depths in the seas, the temperature range becomes much smaller, but also the seasons become even later. For example, at 50 m depth in northern latitudes the maximum occurs in autumn, in October or November, and the minimum as late as April (Fig. 1.8.2).

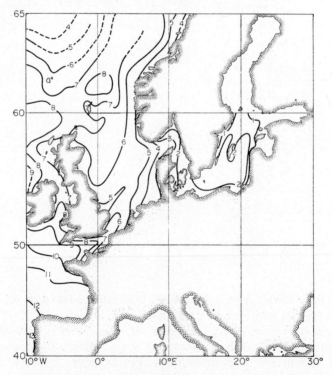

FIG. 1.8.1 (B) Winter surface temperatures in the N.W. Atlantic (from Bruns, 1958).

If we turn from the sea for a moment and consider a freshwater lake, in any temperate region during the summer the water on the surface will warm considerably and this warmer surface water, being less dense, will tend to remain on the surface. In autumn, as the surface water becomes progressively cooler, it increases in density until eventually it becomes dense enough to sink downwards, even reaching the bottom of the lake. This is often known as the "autumn

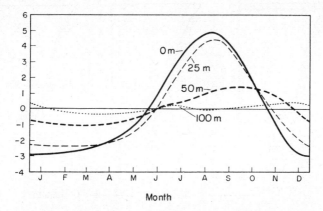

FIG. 1.8.2 Annual variation of temperature of different depths off the Bay of Biscay (approximately 47° N, 12° W) (from Sverdrup *et al.*, 1946).

(or fall) overturn" and it will lead eventually to the establishment of a homogeneous column of water, that is the whole lake waters will come to be at the same temperature, and there will be no temperature stratification (Fig. 1.9). During winter the temperature may have dropped sufficiently, depending on the latitude, for freezing to occur. But water (i.e. freshwater), has a peculiarity that at 4 °C the density reaches its maximum; cooling below 4 °C means that the colder water becomes lighter and lies at the surface. For this reason the freezing of freshwater begins on the surface, and below the ice there will be a layer of water of slightly higher temperature up to 4 °C. In this way life in a temperate lake can persist under ice. In spring, with the melting of the ice, the surface water gradually warms until it reaches 4 °C, when again there is a mass mixing of water, dense water dropping down to the bottom. This is known as the "spring overturn" (Fig. 1.9). Winds, of course, assist in the mixing process.

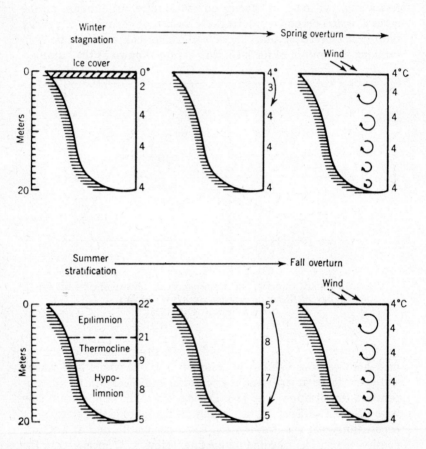

FIG. 1.9 A diagram illustrating the changes in temperature and the consequent formation and destruction of a thermocline in a typical temperate lake (from Clarke, 1954).

As the temperature increases at the surface with solar radiation, the surface waters become lighter and the density difference may be so great as virtually to cut off the upper from the lower layers. Thus is established a more or less homogeneous upper region of the lake, mixed by the winds, termed the epilimnion, which is succeeded by a layer where the temperature changes relatively rapidly with depth. Then follows a lower part, the hypolimnion, where the temperature is generally lower and changes only slowly with depth, but these hypolimnion waters are practically isolated from the upper regions. The zone in the lake where the temperature changes rapidly with depth is usually referred to as the thermocline, or discontinuity layer (Fig. 1.9). Freshwater ecologists define a thermocline as a layer of water where the change of temperature with depth is not less than 1 °C per metre. Sometimes the change in temperature with depth is much more rapid, as much as 4 °C or more per metre. It is clear that during the summer the epilimnion layers will be largely cut off from the lower hypolimnion layers. Admittedly, winds blowing on the surface can stir the water to some degree, piling up the water at one end of the lake and causing reverse currents. But while the waters of the epilimnion are kept circulating, they are almost shut off from the lower layers, except for a very slight degree of mixing. The breakdown of the thermocline will not normally occur until the autumn cooling.

In the sea something approaching the same condition may occur. In temperate waters and at high latitudes during the summer there is a warming of the surface layers, but these are kept mixed by winds and waves. With evaporation causing local cooling, small convection currents are also set up in the near surface layers. Below this homogeneous layer, however, the increase in density of the water tends to isolate the upper, warmer, less dense layers from the lower colder layers of the ocean. This is what might be termed the region of the thermocline (Fig. 1.10). But in the oceans temperature does not change nearly so rapidly with depth as in most freshwaters. The oceanographer and marine ecologist cannot limit the term thermocline to so steep a change (1 °C/m) as the freshwater ecologist; a thermocline can exist, but it is less obvious. In the sea, beneath the thermocline, the temperature changes very slowly indeed. In the eastern North Atlantic the depth-temperature pattern is exceptional in that between 100 and 1000 m the fall in temperature amounts to only 2 °C (cf. Cooper 1952c). This occurrence of comparatively warm water at considerable depth, is associated with the warm saline Gibraltar outflow (cf. Chapter IV). However, the broad picture of temperature conditions in an ocean in middle latitude usually shows a homogeneous layer of water down to perhaps 50 or 100 m depth, then a zone exhibiting relatively rapid change of temperature with depth — a thermocline — which may be several hundred metres thick. The deeper water shows only a very slow decrease in temperature, until

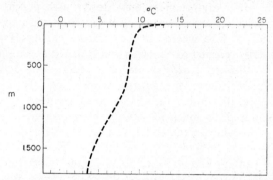

FIG. 1.10 Occurrence of a thermocline in oceanic waters. Station east of Rockall (altered from Murray and Hjort, 1912).

finally in really great depths, of several thousand metres, the temperature change is so gradual as to be almost imperceptible (Figs. 1.11 and 1.12). A most important difference in the marine environment, however, is that whereas cooling does take place in winter in temperate latitudes, and therefore some degree of mixing occurs, the autumn and spring over-turns never occur, except in very shallow waters, to the extent that they do in the freshwater environment. The difference arises because seawater, in contrast to freshwater, does not reach a maximum density at 4 °C. The density of seawater continues to increase right to the freezing point, viz. − 1.9 °C. Therefore, in temperate latitudes, as the seawater cools in the winter and becomes dense, it must sink to some extent, but finally it is limited by the very cold and dense waters of the great depths. In the Atlantic Ocean these deepest waters are permanently at a temperature of about 3 °C; in the other oceans the deepest waters are some 2 °C colder. In winter, therefore, in temperate latitudes there is usually still a gradual decrease in temperature with depth.

The occurrence of a thermocline is clearest in tropical and sub-tropical seas. There the surface waters are always relatively warm, and therefore light. Complete mixing occurs to a depth of 100 m, or more, but below that depth a very clear thermocline exists where the temperature drops fairly rapidly. Below this zone the drop in temperature becomes much slower and from 1000 m depth or so the change with depth is extremely slow (c.f. Table 1.1). In the tropics, surface cooling hardly occurs, and therefore a permanent thermocline exists (cf. Fig. 1.11 B and C; Fig. 1.12A).

TABLE 1.1 Change in temperature (°C) with latitude and with depth. (Adapted from Sverdrup *et al.*, 1946.)

Month Latitude Depth m	MARCH 59° 38′ N.	JUNE 52° 37′ N.	MARCH 26° 21′ N.	MAY 15° 22′ N.
0	4.1	6.6	16.0	29.5
50	4.1	3.9	15.3	24.1
100	4.1	3.5	13.4	18.7
400	—	3.4	9.6	9.9
1000	3.3	2.9	4.5	4.4
1500	3.3	2.3	2.9	—
2000	2.8	1.9	2.5	2.5
2500	—	1.7	2.6	—
3000	—	1.6	—	2.4

In more temperate waters the warmer upper layers are marked off from the deeper water by a thermocline during the summer. This thermocline is limited to shallow depths approaching 50 m. During winter, cooling produces a mixing of these upper layers and the seasonal thermocline is therefore destroyed. But beneath this seasonal thermocline there is a decrease in temperature, and thus an increase in density as one goes deeper, leading to the establishment of a less steep thermocline at depths of around 1000 m. This thermocline is permanent in that it is not affected by any seasonal change in temperature. Below the permanent thermocline, as in tropical seas, the change of temperature with depth is exceedingly slow. In higher latitudes the decrease in temperature below the comparatively shallow seasonal thermocline zone is more gradual, so that a thermocline may hardly be said to exist. As we have seen, however, complete homogeneity is never established, as it is in freshwaters, except in special areas. Such special areas include relatively very shallow temperate waters (e.g. English Channel) where the bottom water is at a temperature such that mixing and complete homogeneity can be

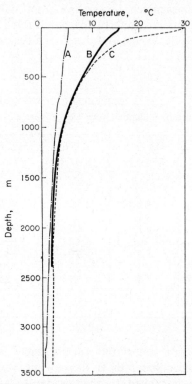

FIG. 1.11 Variation of temperature with depth in several seas.
A = *Discovery II* Stat. 385. 58° 41′ S, 64° 43′ W (Antarctic Ocean).
B = E. W. Scripps Stat. VII-27. 26° 21′ N, 110° 46′ W (Gulf of California).
C = Dana Stat. 3714. 15° 22′ N, 115° 20′ E (South China Sea).
Note the very marked thermocline in C and its complete absence in A. (Data for A from *Discovery Reports*, Vol. 4, 1932; for B and C from Sverdrup *et al.*, 1946.)

established during autumn cooling. In such shallow seas as the English Channel and parts of the North Sea a thermocline exists in summer, though winds tend to break it down or force it deeper, but during autumn, with cooling assisting the effects of gales, the thermocline disappears completely (Fig. 1.13). Another type of special area occurs

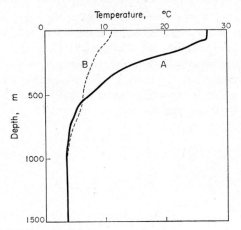

FIG. 1.12 Variation of temperature with depth.
A = *Discovery* II Stat. 684. 15° 38′ S, 29° 50′ W (South Atlantic).
B = *William Scoresby* Stat. WS. 438. 39° 18′ S, 1° 59′ E (South Atlantic).
(Data from *Discovery Reports*, Vol. 4. 1932.)

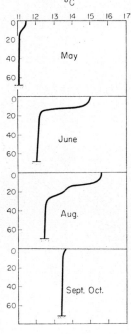

FIG. 1.13 Formation of a thermocline and its complete destruction in the shallow waters of the English Channel (from Harvey, 1955).

in high northern latitudes, where the winter cooling may be so extreme that the surface water acquires sufficient density to sink to the bottom even at considerable depths (cf. Chapter IV). Complete homogeneity is therefore established with very low temperature of the whole water column (cf. results for latitude 59° 38′ N. – Table 1.1). Constant mixing also occurs in Antarctic waters resulting in uniformly low temperatures from the surface to great depths (Fig. 1.11).

CHAPTER II

GASES OF BIOLOGICAL IMPORTANCE
IN THE OCEANS

OF THE more common gases that are dissolved in natural waters two, oxygen and carbon dioxide, are of profound significance since they enter into the normal biological cycle.

Oxygen

The maximum amount of gas which can be dissolved in water depends on the partial pressure of the gas in the air and on a constant which varies with temperature and salinity. The amount of oxygen in the air, is almost invariable, amounting to something approaching 210 c.c. of oxygen per l. The partial pressure of oxygen is therefore fixed, leaving aside small variations due to the variable water content of the air, and thus the amount of gas which can be dissolved in water will clearly depend on the two major factors, temperature and salinity.

Oxygen is only moderately soluble in water. For pure water approximately 10 c.c. per l. will dissolve at 0 °C, and with rise in temperature the saturation value decreases so that, for example, at 30 °C the value is only 5.6 c.c. per l. (Table 2.1). The effect of salts dissolved in water is to decrease the amount of gas dissolved. Some indication of the variation in oxygen saturation values with salinity is seen in Table 2.1. For example, the saturation value at 0 °C is only 8 c.c. oxygen per l. for $35^0/_{00}$ seawater; 8.6 c.c. per l. for seawater of reduced salinity ($27^0/_{00}$), and 10.3 c.c. per l. for pure water. At 20 °C pure water when saturated with oxygen has 6.6 c.c. O_2 per l. as compared with 5.3 c.c. for full seawater (Table 2.1).

At first sight the terrestrial environment would appear to be distinctly more favourable for life, as regards oxygen content, than the aquatic medium: air contains approximately 210 c.c. oxygen per l. as compared with a maximum of about 10 c.c. per l. for water. However, the respiratory mechanisms of many aquatic organisms,

23

display an efficiency such that the amount of oxygen in fully saturated water is more than sufficient for their metabolic needs. The constant supply of seawater bathing the respiratory surfaces of marine animals is an important factor allowing efficient uptake of oxygen, even at considerably lowered tensions. Many aquatic organisms in fact

TABLE 2.1 The amounts of oxygen dissolved in freshwater and seawater at different temperatures, when saturated with air (from Fox's data).

Temperature	c.c. O_2 per litre		
		Seawater	
°C	Freshwater	(ca. $27\,^0/_{00}$)	(ca. $35\,^0/_{40}$)
0	10.3	8.6	8.0
5	9.0	7.6	7.1
10	8.0	6.8	6.4
15	7.2	6.1	5.8
20	6.6	5.6	5.3
25	6.0	5.2	4.9
30	5.6	4.7	4.5

respire efficiently, even though the oxygen tension may drop considerably below saturation values. Marshall, Nicholls and Orr (1935) showed that the respiration of *Calanus* was unaffected by reductions in oxygen concentration down to about 3 c.c. O_2 per l., and that respiration continued at dissolved oxygen concentrations below this level. At concentrations of 1.2 c.c. O_2 per l. the *Calanus* were killed, but even at these low oxygen tensions some copepods survived provided that the temperature was lowered. Banse (1956) suggested from the vertical distribution of zooplankton off Kiel that the animals were little affected by considerably lowered oxygen tensions. Although planktonic polychaete larvae were mainly represented, some holoplanktonic animals (*Sagitta* and *Oikopleura*) also occurred in strata of low oxygen. The fact that relatively large populations of zooplankton can apparently live in oxygen-poor layers in the open oceans also suggests that oxygen is probably seldom a limiting factor in the sea (cf. Chapter XVII).

Similarly, many benthic invertebrates have relatively low oxygen demands. The respiration of some corals is apparently not affected, even if the oxygen content is reduced to 40% or 50% of its original

value; indeed corals seem to be very variable in their oxygen requirements (Yonge, Yonge and Nicholls, 1932). On the other hand, it
is true that some fishes must live in fully oxygenated water, at least
for full activity (cf. Brown, 1957).

The seas of the world would appear to have sufficient oxygen for
life everywhere, provided the water is saturated at all temperatures
which are experienced in the oceans. This temperature range as we
have seen, is from < 0 °C to > 30 °C. Oxygen is, however, being
abstracted from the water continually owing to the respiration of
animals and plants, and by bacterial decomposition. The degree of
saturation of seawater thus depends on the balance between the
respiratory demands of the organisms present in the water and the
addition of oxygen from other sources.

The main source of oxygen is the atmosphere. Oxygen can enter
an ocean or a freshwater lake only at the surface. The rate of invasion
of the gas from the air depends, among other factors, upon the degree
of under-saturation of the water, upon temperature, and also to a
very great extent upon the movement of air and water. Harvey (1945)
states that under quiescent conditions as in the laboratory the rate
of invasion of oxygen may be 100 times less than if the water is kept
moving by air currents above. Normally under natural conditions
over lakes or oceans, the air and water are in a continual state of
motion, and the rate of invasion will be relatively high. The second
source of oxygen in the aquatic medium is from the photosynthetic
activity of plants. This addition of oxygen will obviously be limited
to the light periods of the day, when alone photosynthesis can
proceed, and also must be restricted to the shallow upper zones
of water which receive sufficient light for active photosynthesis.

Since oxygen can be added only at the surface, or relatively near
to the surface, whether it is added by invasion from the air or by
photosynthesis, we are faced with the problem, of how the great
depths of the ocean receive an oxygen supply. As life is present in
the great depths, then by animal respiration and bacterial decomposition a continual loss of oxygen must occur. Unless a continuous
supply is in some way brought from the upper layers, these great
depths must become rapidly and completely de-oxygenated, i.e. they
would become a vast azoic zone. The only organisms which could
persist under such circumstances would be anaerobic bacteria. Such
a condition does in fact sometimes obtain in certain isolated basins
which are more or less cut off from the general circulation of the seas,

especially where low salinity water lies on the surface. On a small scale such basins ("polls") occur at the heads of some of the Norwegian fjords. The deeper parts of these polls have either a much lowered oxygen tension or they are completely lacking in oxygen, and life is restricted to the oxygenated upper layers. Strøm (1936) investigated a large number of these incompletely ventilated fjords in Norway, and claimed that any basins with shallow outlets to the sea, especially those relatively small in area, may be liable to stagnation near the bottom. In Norwegian fjords the small tidal range accentuates the effect, and marked freshening of the surface will tend to stabilize the water layers, augmenting stagnation. Strøm considers that such basins occurring in tropical regions will become stagnant much more easily than those in temperate areas, where they must experience marked seasonal climatic change. Basins differ in the frequency of renewal of the waters. This may occur at intervals depending on the topography of the bottom of the basin and its nearest sea area, on hydrological conditions, and indirectly upon climatic changes as far as these influence the stability of the water column. If total renewal of the bottom waters should take place, the layers containing hydrogen sulphide may approach so close to the surface that a catastrophic mortality of the fauna living in the upper waters may follow. Outside landlocked waters, Richards and Vaccaro (1956) have demonstrated that anaerobic conditions are found in the Cariaco Trench in the Caribbean. A marked sill shuts off the trench from the surrounding ocean, and there appear to be no currents mixing the deeper layers. From a depth of *ca.* 250 m the temperature is uniform (17 °C) suggesting that the trench is cut off from general circulation, and from about 400 m depth to the bottom at 1400 m anaerobic conditions prevail.

On a grander scale widespread de-oxygenation is known in the Black Sea. Owing to the peculiar configuration of the sea bottom across the Straits of Marmora and to the generally lower salinity of the Black Sea water, the deeper levels of the Black Sea are almost cut off from the general circulation of the Mediterranean and from upper convection currents. As a result, the deeper levels of the Black Sea show a rapid decrease in oxygen tension until zero oxygen values are reached at about 200 m (Table 2.2). Owing to the lack of oxygen the Black Sea shows no life in the deeper layers whatsoever, with the the exception of anaerobic bacteria which produce an abundance of sulphuretted hydrogen. Ekman states that only about 23% of the floor of the Black Sea is habitable by benthic animals (cf. Chapter XVIII Fig. 18.22). Plankton is limited to a depth of *ca.* 150–175 m (Fig. 2.1).

In the great oceans of the world, however, oxygen is present in the water at all depths (cf. Figs. 2.2 and 2.3). The occurrence of oxygen is intimately bound up with the mixing processes, above all with

TABLE 2.2 Hydrographic conditions in the Black Sea
(adapted from Sverdrup *et al.*, 1946).

Depth (m)	Temperature (°C)	Salinity ($^0/_{00}$)	O_2 (c.c./l.)	H_2S (c.c./l.)
0	24.1	17.59	5.14	
10	24.1	17.59	5.14	
25	12.73	18.22	7.40	
50	8.22	18.30	6.71	
75	7.44	18.69	5.51	
100	7.61	19.65	2.33	
150	8.31	20.75	0.17	
200	8.54	21.29		0.90
300	8.68	21.71		2.34
400	8.72	21.91		4.17
600	8.76	22.16		4.96
800	8.80	22.21		6.06
1000	8.85	22.27		6.04

the deep ocean currents which occur in all the major seas. The concentration of oxygen in any deep layer of an ocean depends on the previous history of the water, in particular when such water was in contact with the air, and also on what has been its subsequent biological history. If, for example, this water has descended to moderate depths where considerable animal populations are present, then because of the continual use of oxygen by animals and bacteria its oxygen tension will clearly show a progressive decline.

Even at the surface of the oceans there will be considerable differences in the oxygen tension of seawater from different areas. Owing to the temperature difference between water near the poles and near the equator the *maximum* concentration of oxygen for seawater near the tropics will be only about 4.5 c.c. oxygen per l., whereas near the poles approximately 8 c.c. oxygen per l. can occur. These, of course, represent saturation values which should hold for surface water in equilibrium with the atmosphere. In the oceanic depths the amount of oxygen is still relatively high, often exceeding 5 c.c. per 1. (Fig. 2.2). It must be remembered that these great depths in temperate and tropical latitudes are all at a low temperature (approximately 3 °C) and they are in communication with cold surface water at the poles. Deep ocean water which has only recently descended from the surface retains the relatively high oxygen content of surface water.

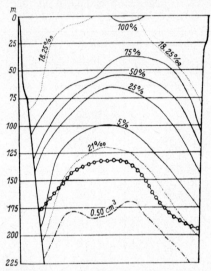

FIG. 2.1 Oxygen concentration as percentage saturation at various depths in the Black Sea. Two salinity layers are also shown. The lower limit of zooplankton is indicated and the depth at which the concentration of H₂S reaches 0.5 c.c./l. (from Ekman, 1953).

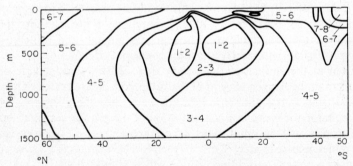

FIG. 2.2 Oxygen concentrations in the Atlantic Ocean as c.c. O₂/l. (from Murray and Hjort, 1912).

Where steady vertical mixing occurs as, for instance, in the Irminger Sea, South-east of Greenland, the whole water column to about

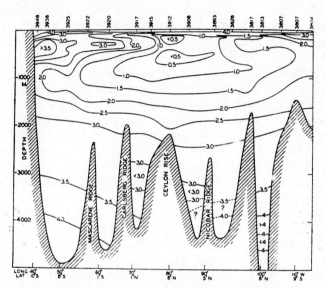

FIG. 2.3 The distribution of oxygen in the Indian Ocean (values in c.c. O_2/l.) (from Sverdrup *et al.* 1946).

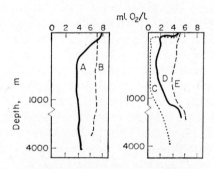

FIG. 2.4 Variation in oxygen content with depth in various seas

A = Antarctic Convergence, 50°08′ S, 35°49′ W.
B = North Polar Front, 55°03′ N, 44°46′ W.
C = E. Tropical Pacific, 11°39′ N, 114°15′ W.
D = E. Tropical Atlantic, 12°53′ N, 22°59′ W.
E = S. E. North Atlantic, 29°52′ N, 30°12′ W.
     (modified from Richards, 1957).

2000 m depth is homogeneous, with an oxygen content of 6–7 c.c. O_2 per l. (cf. Fig. 2.4). The water flows in the depths as slow ocean currents. Our knowledge of the speeds of deep currents is limited; from calculations of the time required to replace the water in the oceans, speeds of some 5 miles per year have been suggested for the North Atlantic. Recent current measurements, however, indicate that at least some deep currents may flow at speeds approaching three hundred times this value. Swallow (1957) found speeds of up to 11 miles per day for comparatively shallow waters (350–500 m) in the Faroe-Shetland Channel area. Even at > 800 m depth a current speed of 7 miles per day was recorded. In deeper water off Gibraltar, speeds of up to 5 miles per day were found at depths of approximately 1000 to 3000 m. Later investigations in the eastern North Atlantic suggested that deep currents were weak, and variable in direction and in speed (maximum *ca.* 3 miles per day); but in the western North Atlantic the recent work of Swallow and Worthington (1961) has demonstrated that deep waters (2500–3000 m) may flow constantly in direction at comparatively high velocities (5–10 miles per day). Even so, deep current speeds may be comparatively low over much of the oceans, and the oxygen content of the water tends to fall gradually in the direction of the current. In even the deepest parts of the oceans, however, an appreciable quantity of oxygen remains, often exceeding 4 c.c. O_2 per l. But it must be realized that such water, at the low temperatures of deep oceans, is much undersaturated. In certain deep basins as off California, where sills impede circulation, the oxygen content of the deeper layers may be lower than the average. Nevertheless, even deep trenches in the oceans are not de-oxygenated, except for the anaerobic Cariaco Trench (see p. 26). Low oxygen concentrations may however be encountered in many seas very close to the bottom deposit. In really cold seas, owing to the fairly continuous circulation, there may be only a very small fall in oxygen from the surface to the depths (cf. Fig. 2.4), but normally any sub-surface water is undersaturated, as may be seen in upwelling areas when sub-surface water reaches the surface (e.g. off California and in the Benguela Current).

Although, in warm and temperate oceans as in cold seas, there is a fairly abundant oxygen supply in the great depths, there is a zone which varies in depth from as little as 150 m in some seas to approximately 1000 m in other oceans, where the amount of oxygen tends to be low (Fig. 2.5 and 2.7). In tropical and sub-tropical regions, the surface

layers in contact with the air and with marked photosynthetic activity
will show saturation values amounting to some 4–5 c.c. O_2 per l.
Beneath the surface, however, there is a very rapid reduction of
oxygen with depth, and at intermediate depths oxygen tensions even
less than 1 c.c. per l. may be encountered (cf. Fig. 2.4 C and D).

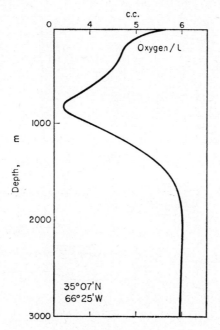

FIG. 2.5 The minimal oxygen zone in sub-tropical waters
(from Harvey, 1955).

This is the so-called "minimum oxygen zone" which appears to occur
generally in temperate and tropical oceans, but especially at lower
latitudes.

Below the minimum oxygen layer, a rise in oxygen value occurs
with increasing depth so that, as has already been stressed, the cold
depths of all oceans have fairly high oxygen tensions. The extreme
condition in the minimum oxygen zone appears to be reached in
parts of the eastern Pacific (Fig. 2.4 C). Brandhorst (1959) has referred
recently to values as low as less than 0.1 c.c. O_2 per l., occurring at
depths of 150–500 m off the west coast of Central and South America

(Fig. 2.6). On the whole, the values for oxygen in the minimal oxygen layer in the Atlantic Ocean tend to be somewhat higher than in the Pacific (cf. Fig. 2.7).

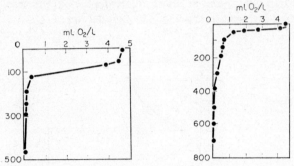

FIG. 2.6 Oxygen-deficient water in the Eastern Pacific (modified from Brandhorst, 1959).

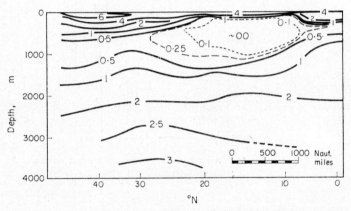

FIG. 2.7 Distribution of oxygen in the Northern Pacific showing minimal oxygen layer (from Sverdrup *et al.*, 1946).

It would appear that the occurrence of this minimal oxygen layer is the result of several factors. To some degree the circulating ocean currents are reaching their minimal force around this zone. To this must be added the relatively large increase in water density which occurs at about this level, which marks the thermocline in these tropical and sub-tropical seas. The occurrence of this relatively stable water layer of rapidly increasing density appears to result in a slowing down of the sinking of detritus produced from dead and dying plankton. Seiwell and Redfield have suggested that a temporary accumulation of detritus occurs about this region, some of the material probably coming from higher latitudes, but slowly drifting at intermediate depths towards the tropics. The bacterial decomposition which occurs owing to this detritus results in a lowering of the oxygen content. Often also, there is a large population of zooplankton near this minimum layer which will make further demands on the oxygen available (cf. Sewell, 1948). More recent studies by Miyake and Saruhashi (1956) in the northern Pacific have emphasized the productivity of a sea area and the vertical distribution of density of the subsurface waters as two major factors affecting the occurrence of the oxygen minimum layer. Where slowing in the sinking of dead plankton occurs, the increased demand for oxygen in the decomposition process can lead to a marked reduction of oxygen.

As well as under-saturation which may be seen in certain upwelling regions in the world's oceans, the phenomenon of super-saturation is also known. This occurs in freshwater lakes and ponds, as well as in the oceans. Super-saturation is essentially a result of the marked photosynthetic activity of plants, which occur in the upper layers of the seas. With very strong solar radiation during the day, the rate of oxygen production due to photosynthesis may exceed the giving off of oxygen from the surface, and temporary super-saturation may occur. Marshall and Orr (1927) found appreciable super-saturation during the spring increase of diatoms in Loch Striven, even down to 10 and 20 m depth. Fig. 2.8 taken from Richards (1957a) shows high super-saturation in oxygen values during summer in East Greenland waters. In the region of coral reefs super-saturation has been noted as a result of strong photosynthetic activity of the symbiotic zooxanthellae in the corals (cf. Orr and Moorhouse, 1933). Recent studies from certain Pacific coral reefs (Kohn and Helfrich, 1957) have suggested that super-saturation may also be largely due to benthic algae which occur in profusion on certain of these reefs.

Nitrogen

Of inert gases which may be present in both fresh and marine waters, nitrogen is the commonest. The amount of nitrogen dissolved in water will depend on the same factors as in the case of oxygen, and with the large partial pressure of nitrogen in the air it is not surprising that the amount of dissolved nitrogen will exceed the amount of oxygen. In the sea, for example, depending on temperature and salinity, the amount of dissolved nitrogen may vary between 8 and 14 c.c. of N_2 per l. Nitrogen, however, is an entirely inert gas, and is of little biological significance. The possibility of nitrogen fixation will be discussed in a later chapter.

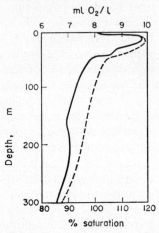

FIG. 2.8 Oxygen super-saturation. Hatched line indicates O_2 concentration. Full line represents percent saturation (slightly modified from Richards, 1957).

Carbon dioxide

The amount of carbon dioxide present normally in the atmosphere is only of the order of 0.03%. It is clear that if carbon dioxide dissolved in water solely in the way that an inert gas, such as nitrogen dissolves, then the amount of carbon dioxide present in any natural water would be exceedingly small. Nevertheless, the first stage in the solution of carbon dioxide in water will depend on the same factors as for oxygen, i.e. on temperature and salinity of the water and on the partial pressure of the gas. The rate of exchange of carbon dioxide between the atmosphere and the water is comparatively slow, but the upper layers of the water are more or less in equilibrium with the air. Owing to the differences in temperature and salinity of the seas at the poles and at the equator, a slightly unstable position obtains as regards carbon dioxide for the oceans of the world. At the poles the water is not fully saturated with carbon dioxide, and there is a tendency for carbon dioxide to pass into solution from the air into the ocean. Conversely, at the equator the warm saline water becomes over-saturated with carbon dioxide, and there is a passage of carbon dioxide from the ocean into the air. Thus a slow, but gigantic, circulation of carbon dioxide occurs, with carbon dioxide entering the water at the poles and passing from the water at the equator (cf. Cooper, 1956).

Carbon dioxide is more soluble in water than either oxygen or nitrogen, but with the very low partial pressure of carbon dioxide in the air, the amount dissolved in seawater or freshwater would, in the absence of any other factor than simple solution, be excessively small. Carbon dioxide, however, forms the compound carbonic acid with water, and this acid ionizes to a small degree. The content of free dissolved carbon dioxide and carbonic acid decreases with temperature and salinity as for inert gases. But in what are referred to as "hard" freshwaters, and above all in seawater, the content of carbon dioxide is vastly increased by its presence in the form of carbonates and bicarbonates. The amount of carbonate and bicarbonate together is referred to as the "bound CO_2". By far the greater proportion of carbon dioxide in seawater is in the bound condition. It is essential to realize that an equilibrium exists in seawater as regards carbon dioxide:

$$\begin{array}{c} CO_2 \\ \uparrow\downarrow \\ H_2CO_3 \end{array} \rightleftharpoons H^+ + HCO_3^- \rightleftharpoons H^+ + CO_3^{--}.$$

Carbon dioxide is a gas of great biological significance; it is essential of course in photosynthesis. But the CO_2 in solution which is abstracted by plants merely causes a shift in the equilibrium shown, so that more bicarbonate is drawn upon to supply the CO_2 which has been removed.

There is a further characteristic of seawater which increases greatly the availability of carbon dioxide. By virtue of its contained salts seawater has an excess of bases over strong acid radicles, the excess base being equivalent mainly to bicarbonate ion, and to some extent to carbonate and borate ions. This excess base is also referred to as the "alkali reserve" or the "alkalinity" of seawater. If seawater were neutral, approximately only 0.5 c.c. of CO_2 per l. would be dissolved in it. Owing to the excess base, however, a total of about 45 c.c. CO_2 per l. are present in seawater, i.e. this is the total amount of carbon dioxide which would be collected if the seawater were acidified and then boiled to drive off all the contained carbon dioxide.

Normal seawater has a pH of approximately 8.0 and at this pH the amount of CO_2 which exists as dissolved carbon dioxide and as

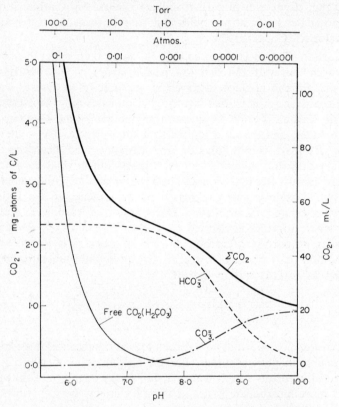

FIG. 2.9 Variations in total CO_2, free CO_2, HCO_3^- and CO_3^{--} with hydrogen ion concentration in seawater (from Sverdrup *et al.*, 1946).

H_2CO_3 is very small. Of this very small quantity of total free CO_2 almost all exists as dissolved carbon dioxide. According to Harvey (1945) H_2CO_3 amounts to only about 1% of the total free carbon dioxide. At normal pH the vast amount of the CO_2 present in seawater occurs in the bound condition, and of this by far the greatest amount is bicarbonate ion (Fig. 2.9). Carbonate ions do, in fact, exist, though the amount at pH 8 is so small as to be almost undetectable. It has been shown, however, that the relative amounts of carbonate and bicarbonate ion, and of free CO_2, vary with the pH of the water. A shift towards the alkaline range, for example, with a fall in the total amount of CO_2 in solution results in an increase of carbonate ions and a progressive loss of bicarbonate ions. Conversely, as the total amount of CO_2 in solution rises and the pH is reduced from pH 8, the relative amount of free CO_2 increases greatly (Fig. 2.9). Such a rise in total CO_2 might cause a loss of free CO_2 to the atmosphere, but the actual transference of gas between the water and air is slow. With strong photosynthetic activity, and with relatively high temperature, the rise in pH and production of carbonate ion may be sufficiently great to promote precipitation of $CaCO_3$, as in coral lagoons (cf. Chapter III).

The waters of the oceans are, however, relatively very constant in pH. Seawater containing weak acids, such as carbonic acid and, to a lesser extent, boric acid, has a very strong buffering action as compared with pure water. Thus the addition of acid to the system:

$$CO_2 + H_2O \rightleftarrows H_2CO_3 \rightleftarrows H^+ + HCO_3^- \rightleftarrows H^+ + CO_3^{--}$$

tends to shift the equilibrium to the left, the resulting carbonic acid ionizes to a very limited extent so that the pH remains relatively stable. This buffering action of seawater is of enormous importance biologically, in that the constancy of the environment is maintained to a very high degree. Thus respiration and decomposition processes producing CO_2 normally affect the pH of seawater very little. Similarly, the removal of CO_2, even in considerable amounts, in photosynthesis, affects the pH of the water only to a limited extent. Seawater is also doubly favourable for photosynthetic activity, since not only is the pH relatively stable, but large quantities of CO_2 are available to plants. Though a rise in temperature does cause a fall in pH, the effect is slight. With seawater of salinity ca. $35^0/_{00}$, and of pH 7.8–8.0, a rise in temperature of 1 °C produces a reduction in pH of the order of 0.01 pH unit. The upper waters of the open oceans in fact rarely vary more than from pH 8.1 to 8.3 (Fig. 2.10). Marine animals do not need therefore complex physiological mechanisms preserving the body against external fluctuations in acidity and alkalinity.

For the seas as a whole the range in pH is greater, varying from pH 7.5 to approximately pH 8.4 (Fig. 2.10). In the surface layers there will be a tendency to increase pH by photosynthesis, and to lower pH due to animal respiration and bacterial decomposition. Below the photosynthetic zone the general tendency will be towards a reduction of pH with respiration.

In general below the surface in moderate depths, especially in the sub-tropics and tropical areas, where we have already noted the presence of a pronounced minimal oxygen zone, the pH drops to

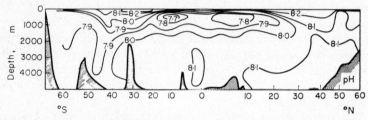

FIG. 2.10 Variation in pH in the Atlantic Ocean (from Sverdrup *et al.*, 1946).

values which are lower than are normally experienced in the sea. In this zone pH values of the order of 7.7 occur (Fig. 2.10). Beneath this minimum oxygen layer the pH tends to rise again, and in the comparatively well oxygenated waters of the ocean depths the pH approaches 8.0. However, the enormous pressures at the greatest depths cause a very slight fall in pH to values of about 7.9. The very low oxygen minimum which has been referred to already in the Pacific region is accompanied by an exceptionally low pH of about 7.5.

Once again, in isolated basins cut off from the general circulation of the seas, with complete de-oxygenation, the production of hydrogen sulphide may take place. At the bottom of such an isolated basin the pH may fall to values nearer 7. In a marine pond, Loch Craiglin, with very marked stratification, Marshall and Orr (1947 and 1948) found that photosynthetic activity at the surface caused a rise in pH to values approaching pH 9, whereas at the bottom, although only at a depth of a few metres, there was a lack of oxygen and the pH could reach 7.4; on a few occasions falling even to 7.0 (Fig. 2.11). Similar or even much more extreme conditions may obtain in fresh-waters where buffering action may be absent.

Because of the exact physical relationship which exists in the sea between pH and total CO_2, it is possible to calculate the amount of photosynthesis from the change in pH value. For example, a rise in pH from 8.16 to 8.31 at 15 °C, due to photosynthetic activity, would

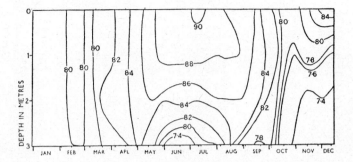

Fig. 2.11 Variations in pH with depth and seasons in Loch Craiglin
(from Orr, 1947).

mean the abstraction of 2.24 c.c. of CO_2 per l. Since one mole of a
gas at N.T.P. occupies 22.4 l., the 2.24 c.c. of CO_2 abstracted would
correspond to 0.0001 mole of CO_2, and since 1 mole of CO_2 has
12 g of carbon, this is equivalent to 0.0012 g (i.e. 1.2 mg) of carbon.
If, therefore, we assume that in taking up this amount of CO_2 the
plant cells convert all the carbon into organic matter, we may say
that a rise in pH of 0.15 is equivalent to the synthesis of 1.2 mg
of carbon material (cf. Raymont and Adams, 1958).

CHAPTER III

SALINITY

WATER is one of the best known of solvents and it is not surprising that seawater contains so many elements. Although some have not yet been detected in seawater, it is likely that almost all elements of the periodic table are represented. From the nutritional point of view seawater is a very suitable medium since, apart from water itself being an essential raw material, the varied requirements, especially in minerals, of the numerous species of animals and plants occurring in the oceans, can all be met from the variety of substances dissolved in the sea.

The salts dissolved in seawater, however, confer numerous other advantages. Pure water has a relatively very high density as compared with air, and as has frequently been observed, water thus supports the bodies of the animals floating in it. The increased density of seawater as compared with that of freshwater further assists in the flotation of marine, as compared with freshwater organisms. To some extent the buoyancy of seawater lessens the need for skeletal structures in marine animals. For example, some giant squids present in the seas have only a relatively small skeleton represented by a horny rod. Large jelly fish 2 or 3 feet in diameter can occur in seawater, yet these animals have no support apart from the hydrostatic skeleton typical of coelenterates. Certainly the largest mammals, the whales, must of necessity be aquatic. The blue whale, for example, is of the order of 100 tons, and this weight could never be supported on land. By contrast, one of the largest of terrestrial animals, the elephant, weighs only about 6 tons.

The composition and especially the relatively constant composition of seawater also confers a great benefit on marine organisms in that the sea has a constant osmotic pressure, practically equal to the osmotic pressure of the body fluids of organisms. This applies particularly to marine invertebrates. The osmotic pressure of the body fluids of the marine representatives of all the invertebrate phyla corresponds almost exactly to the osmotic pressure of seawater. It is true that the ionic composition of the body fluids of certain invertebrates may differ. For example, in many crustaceans the amounts of magnesium and of sulphate are lower than in the surrounding water; by contrast the concentration of potassium tends to be higher than in the sea (Table 3.1). Similar differences in ionic composition are known for such widely different groups as coelenterates and molluscs (Krogh, 1939; Robertson, 1957). However, the suggestion that the total osmotic concentration is isotonic with seawater still holds. Marine organisms have thus no need for regulatory mechanisms for maintaining a constant internal osmotic pressure in the face of osmotic unbalance. This constancy of conditions in the seas is probably of particular significance in the early development of organisms. The constancy of osmotic pressure, of temperature and

TABLE 3.1 Ionic regulation in some marine invertebrates (from Robertson, 1957).

	Concentrations in plasma or coelomic fluid as percentage of concentration in body fluid dialysed against seawater					
	Na	K	Ca	Mg	Cl	SO$_4$
COELENTERATA						
Aurelia aurita	99	106	96	97	104	47
ECHINODERMATA						
Marthasterias glacialis	100	111	101	98	101	100
TUNICATA						
Salpa maxima	100	113	96	95	102	65
ANNELIDA						
Arenicola marina	100	104	100	100	100	92
SIPUNCULOIDEA						
Phascolosoma vulgare	104	110	104	69	99	91
ARTHROPODA						
Maia squinado	100	125	122	81	102	66
Dromia vulgaris	97	120	84	99	103	53
Carcinus maenas	110	118	108	34	104	61
Pachygrapsus marmoratus	94	95	92	24	87	46
Nephrops norvegicus	113	77	124	17	99	69
MOLLUSCA						
Pecten maximum	100	130	103	97	100	97
Neptunea antiqua	101	114	102	101	101	98
Sepia officinalis	93	205	91	98	105	22

of pH, to take merely some of the factors, permits conditions which
are very favourable to the early development of organisms which
have not yet developed regulatory processes. It is noticeable that many
terrestrial animals have either to return to the aquatic medium for
the development of their young, or they have evolved relatively
complex mechanisms, such as the amnion of terrestrial vertebrates
which, of course, simulates the ancestral aquatic conditions for the
early development of the embryo.

Seawater contains a most impressive array of salts or, more strictly
speaking, of ions. But included in seawater is organic matter in the
dissolved state, and also very finely divided particulate matter.
Some determinations have been made of the amounts of carbon
and nitrogen present as dissolved organic matter in seawater, and the
amounts are by no means negligible. Keys, Christensen and Krogh
(1935) state that some 1200–2000 mg per m^3 of carbon occur in the
sea; of the organic matter some 200 mg per m^3 is present as organic-
ally combined nitrogen. More details of the amounts of organic
material in seawater are given in Chapter XVI.

Some of the material present in seawater is in the colloidal state.
For example, iron does not occur mainly in solution but as colloidal
particles of ferric hydroxide (cf. Chapter VII). Fox, Isaacs and Corcoran (1952) have also drawn attention to the presence of organic
material, partly colloidal, which they term, "leptopel", and which,
they believe, is important in the nutrition of some marine organisms.
It is admittedly difficult to delimit strictly dissolved organic material,
colloidal matter, and particulate inorganic and organic material of
excessively small dimensions. Considerable amounts of organic
matter, sufficiently fine to pass through the very finest filters, occur
widely in seawater, and Goldberg, Baker and Fox (1952) have shown
the presence of excessively fine inorganic as well as organic matter.
Armstrong (1958) has investigated the occurrence of fine particles
of inorganic material, using filters down to 0.1μ porosity. Very
fine particles of clay-like nature, containing silica, iron and alumina,
are apparently widely distributed in the sea, though the amount in
deeper waters (maximum 1 mg/l.) appears to be somewhat less than
in the shallow English Channel. Suspended particulate matter of
larger dimensions is also present in the sea. Living matter, especially
plankton, and the dead and decomposing remains of plankton and
nekton, as well as faecal pellets, are all to be included. To this is
added material which is carried out from the land, the whole of which

may be termed detritus. Murray and Hjort (1912) were among the first oceanographers to demonstrate how far fine detritus may be carried from the land.

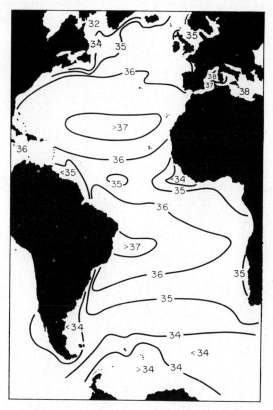

FIG. 3.1 Distribution of surface salinities in the Atlantic Ocean (from Harvey, 1955).

The term salinity deals *only* with the dissolved inorganic salts present in seawater. The total salt content of seawater, excluding those seas which are very close to the outflow of large rivers and those close to melting ice, varies very little over the oceans of the world. The range is from $38^0/_{00}$ to about $32^0/_{00}$ (Figs. 3.1; 3.1.1; 3.2). The Red Sea, with the intense evaporation in that area, is a little higher than the quoted range, the salinity amounting to just over $40^0/_{00}$.

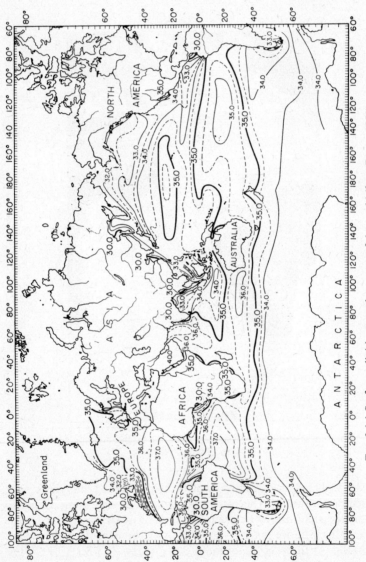

FIG. 3.1.1 Surface salinities over the oceans of the world (from Bruns, 1958).

On the other hand, the Baltic Sea is brackish, the surface varying from 15–20$^0/_{00}$ in the more western regions to less than 5$^0/_{00}$ at the eastern end (Fig. 3.3.). In estuaries, the salinity may be much lower and there are marked salinity changes with the tides each day. Apart

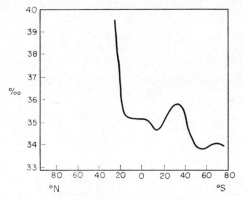

FIG. 3.2 Variation in surface salinity in the Indian Ocean
(from Wust *et al.*, 1954).

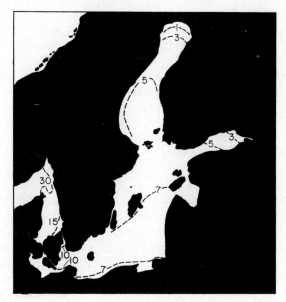

FIG. 3.3 Surface salinities in the Baltic Sea.

from the general fairly rapid reduction in salinity which is encountered on passing up an estuary, there occurs in many estuaries a marked layering of the water, so that the fresher water from the river flows out superficially over the more saline layers. Where this occurs, water is picked up from the deeper layers by the upper outflow and this

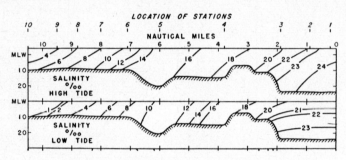

FIG. 3.4 The effect of tides on the distribution of salinity in the estuary of the Raritan River (from Ketchum, Ayers and Vaccaro, 1952).

may lead to a countercurrent nearer the bottom. The distribution of the water layers changes with the tide. The ebb is most marked at the surface while flooding of the tide is strongest in the deeper layers. The slope of the lines of equal salinity also changes with the tides (Fig. 3.4). These changes have been followed, for example, by Alexander, Southgate and Bassindale (1935) for the Tees Estuary, and by Ketchum, Ayers and Vaccaro (1952) for the Raritan River. The actual distribution of salinity layers varies greatly with the amount of run-off from the land. For example, Figs. 3.5 and 3.6 show the results of two salinity surveys carried out over a tidal cycle in the same area of Southampton Water, one after a long period of heavy rainfall and the other after a long dry spell. The marked freshening of the upper layers during the time of heavy rainfall is obvious, the effect being clearest at the ebb.

The variations in surface salinity in the open oceans may be correlated with the relative intensities of precipitation and evaporation. Wust *et al.* (1954) give data showing that an excess of precipitation over evaporation occurs, as might be expected, in high latitudes, where salinities are generally lower. In the regions of the Trade Winds there is an excess of evaporation and salinity is about maximal, but just near the equator, especially in the areas immediately north of the equator, precipitation is again high, so that the surface salinity is not quite as high as to the north and south (cf. Table 3.2) (Figs. 3.7, 3.8 and 3.10). Near polar areas the melting of ice and the run-off from land causes greater dilution than over the oceans as a whole. Run-off is especially marked in the high latitudes of the northern hemisphere, owing to the relatively large land masses surrounding the North Polar Seas (Figs. 3.9 and 3.10). At any place in the oceans some changes in the surface salinity might be expected owing to

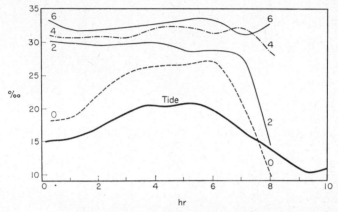

FIG. 3.5 Variations in salinity over a tidal cycle at Marchwood in the upper part of Southampton Water, after prolonged heavy rainfall. Salinities are given at four depths: 0, 2, 4 and 6 m.

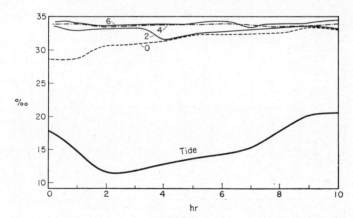

FIG. 3.6 Variations in salinity over a tidal cycle at Marchwood, Southampton Water after prolonged dry weather. Salinities at four depths: 0, 2, 4 and 6 m.

TABLE 3.2 Average values of salinity at different
latitudes for the Atlantic and for all Oceans
(after Wust, modified after Sverdrup *et al*, 1946)

Latitude	Salinity ($^0/_{00}$)	
	Atlantic Ocean	All Oceans
40 °N	35.80	34.54
35	36.46	35.05
30	36.79	35.56
25	36.87	35.79
20	36.47	35.44
15	35.92	35.09
10	35.62	34.72
5	34.98	34.54
0	35.67	35.08
5 °S	35.77	35.20
10	36.45	35.34
15	36.79	35.54
20	36.54	35.69
25	36.20	35.69
30	35.72	35.62
35	35.35	35.32
40	34.65	34.79
45	34.19	34.14
50	33.94	33.99

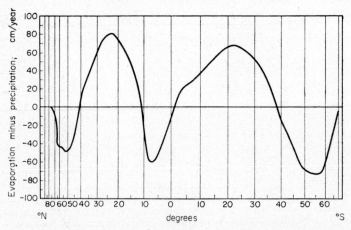

FIG. 3.7 The effect of latitude on the excess evaporation over precipitation
(from Wust *et al.*, 1954).

variations seasonally, or even diurnally, between evaporation and precipitation. On the whole, however, such variations are exceptionally small. Deacon (1933) found a total annual variation for surface waters north of South Georgia of just over $0.3^0/_{00}$. At 100 m depth in the same area, the annual variation was $< 0.1^0/_{00}$. Sewell (1929, 1948) recorded greater diurnal variations in surface Indian waters, in extreme cases amounting to as much as $0.7^0/_{00}$, but these waters are more coastal in character.

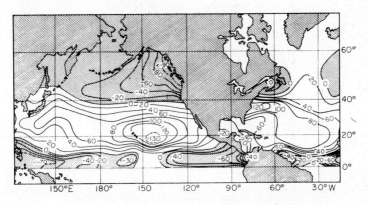

FIG. 3.8 The oceans showing areas of excessive dilution (shaded) just north of the equator and at high latitudes. A zone of excess evaporation lies at about 20 °N (from Fleming, 1957).

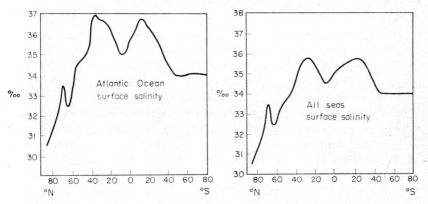

FIG. 3.9 Variation of surface salinity with latitude in the Atlantic Ocean and for all oceans combined (from Wust *et al.*, 1954).

Greater differences may occur in inshore waters, both from place to place and seasonally. Jones (1950) suggests a range of even as much as $23^0/_{00}$–$35^0/_{00}$ for shallow shores below low water springs. As regards seasonal fluctuations in inshore waters, Stubbings (personal communication) has investigated over a period of several years, the salinity changes in Chichester Harbour on the south coast

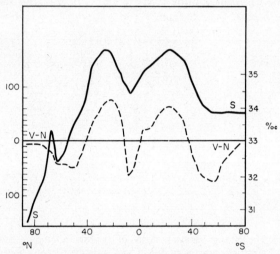

Fig. 3.10 The relation between surface salinity in the Atlantic Ocean and the excess of evaporation over precipitation (V–N).
The very low salinity at high northern latitudes is related to excessive run-off from the land (from Wust et al., 1954).

of England. During 1953 and 1954, for instance, the surface salinity about the time of high water (H.W. ± 3 hr) ranged from 34.8–$32.2^0/_{00}$ (Fig. 3.10.1). The seasonal variation presumably is mainly attributable to the amount of run-off from the land. Considerably greater fluctuations would be evident if observations on salinity at low tide were also included. In even shallower waters, between tide marks, there will be a very much greater salinity range; not only can very considerable dilution occur with heavy rainfall, but excessively high salinities can be encountered in rock pools and on exposed mudflats, especially in tropical countries.

If we confine our attention, however, to the open seas, the range in salinity is comparatively small (32–$38^0/_{00}$), and even this variation applies to the surface waters only. Over the vast areas of the deeper

oceans, where temperature is low and constant, the salinity
is also incredibly uniform and unchanging. The overall regional
range for deeper water is usually only 34.5–35.0$^0/_{00}$ (Figs. 3.11 and
3.12). However, even relatively minor differences in salinity can have
far-reaching effects. Since the density of seawater decreases with a

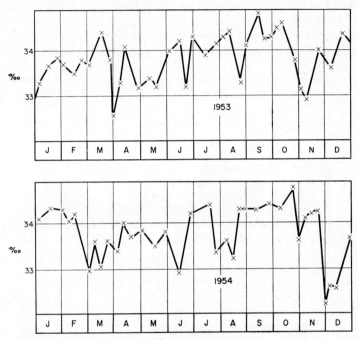

Fig. 3.10.1 Surface salinities in Chichester Harbour. All observations
near highwater (H.W. ± 3 hrs) (from Stubbings, unpublished).

reduction in salinity, the occurrence of a surface layer of slightly
lowered salinity will tend to increase the stability of the water column.
Among other effects this may act as a barrier to mixing of the water.

Over the oceans in general not only is the range in salinity small,
but the actual composition of the seawater, that is to say the relative
amounts of the various ions, is remarkably constant. The average
salinity of seawater amounts to 35$^0/_{00}$, and of the contained salts
sodium chloride accounts for approximately 30$^0/_{00}$ of this total.
It is necessary to stress again that both sodium and chlorine will
occur as ions. Apart from sodium the other commonest cations

are magnesium, calcium and potassium. Chloride is markedly predominant among the anions, but also occurring in fair quantities are sulphate, bicarbonate, bromide and, to a lesser extent, borate. Although sodium and chloride are overwhelmingly important in seawater, these other seven ions occur in reasonably high concentrations, so that they can be measured at least in parts per thousand. The nine ions together, in fact, make up about 99.5% of the total salt content of seawater (Table 3.3). By contrast, therefore, the large number of other ions which are also represented in seawater occur

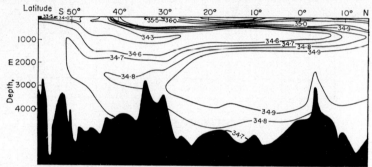

FIG. 3.11 Salinities in the South Atlantic Ocean. The low salinity Antarctic surface water is seen descending at the Antarctic Convergence and proceeding north as the Antarctic Intermediate Water (from Deacon, 1933).

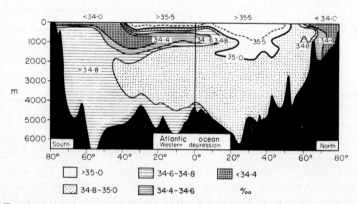

FIG. 3.12 Salinity in the Atlantic Ocean as a function of depth and of latitude. Note the very small range in deep water. (From Wust, 1930.)

at incredibly great dilutions; some, such as gold and radium, in such fantastically low concentrations that they have to be reckoned at dilutions of the order of 10^{-12} or 10^{-16} (cf. Sverdrup *et al.*, 1946; Goldberg, 1957).

The constancy in composition of seawater has already been stressed. In fact, the relative proportions of the major ions are so remarkably fixed that a determination of the amount of chloride in

TABLE 3.3 The constituents in solution in an ocean water having a salinity of 35.00 $^0/_{00}$ (from Harvey, 1955).

Ion.	Grams per kilo
Sodium	10.77
Magnesium	1.30
Calcium	0.409
Potassium	0.388
Chloride	19.37
Sulphate	2.71
Bicarbonate	0.14
Bromide	0.065
Boric acid (as H_3BO_3)	0.026

seawater is sufficiently accurate to permit the calculation of total salinity. Determination of the chloride content (or chlorinity as it is termed) of seawater involves the precipitation of silver chloride (together with a certain amount of silver bromide) by titrating seawater against silver nitrate. This method allows a fairly accurate and rapid determination, and the total salt content (or salinity) may be determined then according to the formula:

$$\text{Salinity } (^0/_{00}) = 0.030 + 1.8050 \times \text{chlorinity } (^0/_{00}).$$

The relatively high constancy in composition of seawater arises partly from the fact that, although most of the ions which have been quoted enter the composition of marine organisms and may be abstracted from the water, nevertheless, with the vast volume of the seas, the amounts of the various ions present are enormous. Further, organisms are constantly dying, so that minerals are being regenerated and returned to the seawater in an everlasting cycle. Moreover, the oceans are in a constant state of mixing, due mainly to slow ocean currents, and therefore no part of the sea apart from certain isolated basins is cut off from circulation and exchange. In this way mixing ensures constancy in composition. Take, for example, a substance like calcium which is extracted and stored by a number of plants, and especially by animals in shells and skeletons. The large amount extracted by populations of these organisms at any one period is still small in comparison with the total amount of calcium present in the seas. Furthermore, the death of the organisms and the regeneration and solution of the calcium, together with the constant mixing of ocean waters will keep the amount constant. This is, perhaps, at first sight even more remarkable when we realize that calcium, mostly in the form of calcium carbonate, is being poured into the seas from the rivers of the world. One estimate states that the rate of addition of calcium carbonate to the oceans is so high that in about one million years the calcium content of the seas would be doubled. In fact, the seas of the world are roughly saturated with calcium carbonate, so that deposition of this mineral as marine sediments must be constantly occurring, apart from the cycle through marine plants and animals. However, different conditions in the seas favour or suppress deposition of calcium carbonate. Thus, while sedimentation occurs in moderately great depths of up to ca. 5000 m, re-solution tends to occur in the greatest depths. Again photosynthetic activity, evaporation and rise in temperature favour precipitation of carbonate, and this may be frequently seen in coral lagoons. Low temperature and carbon dioxide production with bacterial decomposition and respiration will tend to promote solution of calcium carbonate.

Similar cycles, often involving biological activity, may hold for other minerals, but the composition of seawater remains amazingly constant, so that the ratios of the major constituents hardly vary. Certain minor exceptions may be cited; for instance the SO_4^{--}/Cl^- ratio may show some slight variation where freezing of seawater takes place and also where stagnant conditions promote a reduction of sulphate to sulphide. The ratio of strontium to calcium may also reveal very slight local differences since both ions can take part in the skeleton and shell formation of some animals (cf. Richards, 1957b). Such anomalies are far too small in general considerations of salinity, though where exceptionally accurate determinations of ions are required, they must be taken into account. Only far up estuaries there may be a slow change in relative composition of ions owing to the different ionic balance in freshwaters. Apart from the generally much lower salt content of freshwater, this uniformity of the composition of seawater may be contrasted with the very great variability which occurs in the ionic composition of bodies of freshwater. Despite the variable composition of freshwater it is possible to suggest very generally that whereas in seawater sodium is the most abundant of the cations, followed by magnesium and then calcium, in "hard" fresh waters calcium is most abundant and sodium relatively small in amount. In a similar manner, in seawater chloride is much more abundant than sulphate or bicarbonate, whereas in "hard" freshwaters bicarbonate is the most important of the anions. It is also worth recalling that although usually the total amount of salts in seawater is vastly greater than in freshwaters, special salt lakes exist in the world with their own individual, and often large, salt contents.

It is a remarkable fact that although some elements are present in seawater only at extraordinarily high dilutions, certain marine organisms can concentrate specific elements in their bodies. One of the best known examples is the occurrence of appreciable quantities of vanadium in the blood and tissues of some species of ascidians. Webb (1939) showed that vanadium could account for almost 0.2% of the dry organic weight of *Ascidia* spp. Goldberg, McBlair and Taylor (1951) found that a specimen of *Ciona intestinalis* having a wet weight of 20 g might contain nearly 100 μg of vanadium. However, the species *Euherdmania claviformis* on analysis showed a total vanadium content of 475 parts per million. This concentration (4.75×10^{-4}) may be compared with that in seawater which is of the order of 10^{-9}. Other ions which occur in seawater in very low concentrations may be accumulated to a remarkable extent by various marine organisms. Bowen and Sutton (1951), for example, have noted marked differences between species of sponges in their powers of concentrating such elements as copper, titanium, zinc and nickel (cf. also Chapter VII). A more familiar case is the accumulation by many large seaweeds of iodine, which is present in seawater in concentrations of the order of 10^{-7}. Seaweeds, particularly fucoids, can have such quantities of iodine stored in their thalli that these at one time were collected and burnt for the commercial production of this element. For a comparison of the concentrations of elements in the sea and in the bodies of a variety of marine organisms, the reader is referred to the volume by Vinogradov (1953) and to the paper by Goldberg (1957) (cf. Table 3.4). Many of the elements present in seawater are in such very low concentrations that, although their presence is detectable, the range of concentration is practically unknown. The amounts are often not detectable by ordinary classical chemical analytical methods. Some recent investigations of some of

TABLE 3.4 Trace elements in seawater
(after Goldberg 1957)

Element	mg/l.	Enrichment factor
Ti	0.001	> 10,000
V	0.002	> 280,000
Cr	0.00005	1400
Mo	0.01	6000
Mn	0.002	41,000
Fe	0.01	86,000
Co	0.0005	21,000
Ni	0.0005	41,000
Cu	0.003	7500
Ag	0.0003	22,000
Au	0.000004	1400
Zn	0.01	32,500
Cd	0.0001	> 4500
Ga	0.0005	800
Tl	< 0.00001	> 700
Ge	< 0.0001	> 7600
Sn	0.003	2700
Pb	0.003	2600
As	0.003	3300
Sb	< 0.0005	> 300
Bi	0.0002	1000

the lesser known elements such as yttrium, caesium and zirconium are summarized by Goldberg; the work has been stimulated by the problem of radio-active elements in seawater.

Some ions present in seawater in very low concentrations are actively absorbed by organisms, especially plants, in the normal biological cycle. It is possible that variations in concentration of these biologically important substances may occur, and although both maximum and minimum amounts are so small as to have no effect whatsoever on total salinity, nevertheless the variations in concentration may be of profound significance from a biological standpoint. Elements essential for plant growth are now fairly well known, and of these nitrogen and phosphorus are of the greatest significance. Other elements, such as iron and manganese, are also well known to be essential for the continued and healthy growth of plants. The amounts of these four substances in seawater are remarkably small. Phosphorus, for example, occurs as orthophosphate to the extent of about 1 to 100 mg/m^3, i.e. $1-100 \times 10^{-9}$. Manganese occurs at similar dilutions (about 1–10 mg/m^3). Nitrogen as nitrate occurs usually in somewhat greater concentrations than phosphate, but must still be reckoned in milligrammes per cubic metre. It will be noticed that not only are these essential plant nutrients present in extraordinarily low concentrations, but that the amounts vary both from place to place in the seas, and with time. Although, therefore, we must appreciate that the amounts of such elements are so very small that they cannot affect the overall salinity of the seawater, nevertheless the varying concentrations of these elements essential for plant growth may be of profound significance in temporarily slowing or limiting plant growth altogether. This will be discussed further in a later chapter.

CHAPTER IV

MIXING PROCESSES IN THE OCEANS

IN EARLIER chapters we have suggested that mixing processes occur in the oceans of the world, this mixing of the seawater being due to such different influences as waves, tides and ocean currents. The diverse factors which together ensure the thorough mixing and circulation of ocean waters are of tremendous significance, since they are responsible, among other things, for preserving the constancy of temperature in the oceans despite the heating and cooling processes which are confined mainly to the surface. Equally important, the mixing processes are responsible for the transport of oxygen to the depths of the oceans, and for maintaining the constancy of the salinity of the seas. A number of factors are together concerned with the circulation of water in the oceans.

1. *Wave action*

If we watch a cork floating on the sea when the sea surface is disturbed by a series of fairly regular waves, it is obvious that the cork rises and falls with each wave, but after a wave passes, the cork is returned practically to its same position. This leads us to consider not only the progress of waves in the sea, but also the movements of the individual water particles. It would appear from what we can see of the movements of the cork that the water particles do not move far; in fact each follows approximately a circular path.

If ocean waves have the physical characteristics of perfect wave motion, then we should be able to relate fairly simply the wave length (Fig. 4.1), velocity and the wave period. This last parameter may be defined as the time interval between the occurrence of one wave crest and the next. In point of fact the waves of the open ocean very rarely, if ever, show a perfect pattern. The waves are, of course, created by the wind, but at best, even with a fairly steady blow, there appears only a reasonably regular series of waves and these vary in height. Moreover, there appear even in this series quite irregular

58

waves. Variations in the strength and direction of wind will still further complicate the pattern on the sea surface. Nevertheless, the general physical laws governing wave motion may be usefully applied to ocean waves.

We shall first consider the most common waves in the open ocean, that is progressive surface waves where the wavelength, though it may be quite large, is very small compared with the total depth of water. In this case the velocity of the wave is independent of the depth. Wave lengths exceeding 100 m are known in the open sea,

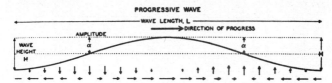

Fig. 4.1 Diagram of a progressive wave (from Sverdrup *et al.*, 1946).

though usually the waves are much shorter. Similarly, the wave period is rarely more than 10 sec, though some great ocean waves exceed 13 sec, and with big swells approaching the shore the period may be even longer. Some idea of the velocity of the greater waves in the open oceans may be appreciated from Table 4.1, which shows the relation between velocity, wave length and wave period. These figures are approximations taken both from actual observations at sea, and also from computations where velocity, wave length and wave period are related according to the physical laws governing wave motion. In general, good agreement is obtained between the observed and calculated values.

It is not possible to relate wave height (Fig. 4.1), nor for that matter other characteristics of waves, directly to the wind force, since the duration for which the wind blows and the width of water over which the waves are passing (the fetch) modify the wave form in addition to the wind force. On the whole, the height of waves has usually been greatly over-estimated. Cornish (1910), one of the few observers who has catalogued wave action very carefully, states that the greatest height observed in most oceans is not above 12 m, although it is true that in one or two exceptional storms and in hurricanes, wave heights probably approximating to twice this value have been recorded. In general, the height of waves is far less than the maximum quoted: even for fairly large waves a height of only 2–4 m is common.

TABLE 4.1 Observed and computed values of velocities, lengths, and periods of surface waves (From Sverdrup et al., 1946).

Region	Wave velocity, m/sec			Wave length, m			Wave period, sec		
	Observed	Computed from		Observed	Computed from		Observed	Computed from	
		$\sqrt{g\dfrac{L}{2\pi}}$	$g\dfrac{T}{2\pi}$		$\dfrac{2\pi c^2}{g}$	$g\dfrac{T^2}{2\pi}$		$\sqrt{\dfrac{2\pi L}{g}}$	$\dfrac{2\pi c}{g}$
Atlantic Ocean Trade wind region	11.2	10.8	10.5	65	70	61	5.8	6.0	6.2
Indian Ocean Trade wind region	12.6	13.1	13.7	96	88	104	7.6	7.3	6.9
South Atlantic Ocean West wind region	14.0	15.5	17.1	133	109	163	9.5	8.6	7.8
Indian Ocean West wind region	15.0	15.2	13.7	114	125	104	7.6	8.0	8.3
China Sea	11.4	11.9	12.4	79	72	86	6.9	6.6	6.3
Western Pacific Ocean	12.4	13.6	14.7	102	85	121	8.2	7.5	6.9

Where L = wave length
c = wave velocity
T = wave period

From the biological point of view one of the most important considerations in progressive surface waves is how far the movement of water particles varies with depth. In this type of wave the water particles move in circles, but the extent of displacement of the individual particles decreases very rapidly indeed with depth. From the surface down the motion of the water particles may be thought of

TABLE 4.2 Velocities of water particles at different depths in surface waves of different periods, lengths, and heights (From Sverdrup et al., 1946).

Wave characteristics				Velocity of particles in cm/sec at stated depths			
Period length (sec)	Velocity of progress (cm/sec)	Length (m)	Height (m)	0 m	2 m	20 m	100 m
2	312	6.2	0.25	39	5.2	0.0	0.0
4	624	25	1.00	79	49	0.5	0.0
6	937	56	2.00	105	85	11.3	0.0
8	1249	100	5.00	196	173	55.6	0.4
10	1561	156	7.00	220	203	99.0	4.2
12	1873	225	10.00	211	199	114.0	12.9
14	2185	306	12.00	273	262	180.0	35.0
16	2498	396	10.00	197	196	143.0	40.6
18	2810	506	8.00	140	136	109.0	40.5
20	3122	624	5.00	78	76	63.0	28.4

as a series of orbits, the radii of which decrease very rapidly. One calculation states that at a depth equal to the wave length of the wave the amplitude of displacement of the water particles is less than one five-hundredth of that observed at the surface. Roughly speaking one can say that motion is almost imperceptible for progressive surface waves at a depth equal to the wave length. Table 4.2 shows the velocity of water particles at different depths down to 100 m for waves of varying dimensions. It will be seen that for waves of less than 10 sec period (which covers the vast majority of ocean waves) the motion of water particles is negligible below 100 m. It is true that waves of greater wave length and of longer period (swells) may have an appreciable velocity somewhat below 100 m (cf. Table 4.2), but from the point of view of mixing of ocean waters it is clear that wave action cannot be effective, certainly below 200 m. It should be emphasized that these values for the movement of water particles at various depths are based on calculations, and that actual observations are very few. Nevertheless, experience from submarines tends to show that water movements due to surface waves disappear very rapidly with depth.

There is another type of wave, perhaps rather confusingly described as a "long wave", in which the wave length is not small as compared with the depth of water. This type mainly concerns us when we consider ocean waves which are approaching the coasts. In this case, as the depth of water rapidly shallows, a typical ocean wave of, say, wave length 100 m and wave period 10 sec will change in character as it approaches the shore. In long waves no vertical motion of water particles can exist at the bottom. Thus the motion of the water particles is modified in that instead of moving in circular orbits they tend to move in flat ellipses. These ellipses become practically horizontal lines the nearer the water particles approach the bottom, and the vertical displacement of the particles obviously decreases from surface to bottom. However, this type of wave causes considerable movement of water particles, and therefore greatly assists in mixing processes in shallow waters near the coast. Waves indeed assist to some extent in the breaking down of thermoclines in shallow water so that, as we have seen, shallow waters may become almost homogeneous during the colder season of the year.

As waves come further and further towards the shore the depth of water may be so small that the frictional drag due to the bottom may cause the wave to become unstable. In this case we have the familiar sight of waves "breaking" on the shore. It is perhaps unnecessary to emphasize that such tremendous disturbance of the water stirs up the whole water mass to a remarkable degree. Although, then, over the great oceans the stirring effect of waves is greatly limited in depth, it is still of very considerable significance in helping to render the uppermost layers of water reasonably homogeneous; in shallow waters the effect of wave action becomes increasingly important until in the inter-tidal zone, wave action is one of the chief factors to be considered. Wave action may have both positive and negative biological effects. For example, it can help in the oxygenation of water and in the replenishing of nutrients; at the same time it can tear away both animals and plants by its action, and cause severe abrasion by the movement of sand. The stirring of silt and debris by waves may provide food particles for filter feeding animals, but it also causes a reduction of light, thus reducing photosynthesis.

A word should perhaps be added on standing waves (Fig. 4.2) which theoretically may be thought of as two progressive waves passing in opposite directions and inter-acting. In such standing waves nodes appear where the vertical motion of particles is zero, but where there is the maximum horizontal displacement of particles. By contrast, at the internodes (i.e. the crests and troughs) the horizontal velocity of water particles is zero, but there is maximum vertical displacement (Fig. 4.2). Standing waves are well known in fresh-waters, especially in ponds and lakes, where they appear particularly

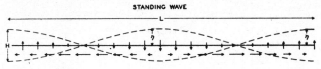

FIG. 4.2 Diagram of a standing wave (from Sverdrup *et al.*, 1946).

in the form of seiches. In the marine environment, standing waves of very considerable wave length may occur in bays, and perhaps along the length of some coasts where there are wide embayments. Such standing oscillations are of importance in that they require only relatively small expenditure of energy to maintain them in motion, and they will again assist in the mixing of the water layers.

2. *Internal waves*

It is known that just as surface waves occur at the air/water boundary, if a relatively low density layer is present on the surface of the sea, a considerable displacement, or internal wave, can occur at the junction of the lighter and the deeper, denser water. With excessive precipitation or with ice melting at higher latitudes, for example, a thin surface layer of lower salinity may be present and a small internal wave may occur at the boundary of the two layers. Sailing vessels moving in such waters may encounter some resistance to movement ("dead water") at low velocities, though the effect is overcome at higher speeds. Fig. 4.3 indicates an internal wave occurring at the boundary of two water layers of different densities $(\varrho^1 + \varrho)$. The free surface also shows some vertical displacement but this is grossly exaggerated. At (a) the boundary surface will rise and at (b) it will sink so that the wave progresses from left to right. On a much larger scale in the open oceans it is now known that where different water layers exist with their own particular characteristics of temperature and salinity and thus of density, considerable internal waves exist, especially at the boundary surfaces. The greatest vertical displacement appears to occur at those boundary surfaces at intermediate depths, and the amplitude may then be far greater than the largest surface waves with which we are familiar. In the open oceans the wave length of these internal waves tends to be very

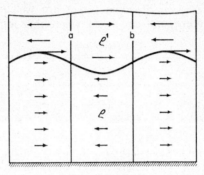

FIG. 4.3 An internal wave at a boundary between density layers ϱ^1 and $\varrho-$ see text (from Sverdrup *et al.*, 1946).

considerable, and the displacement can be 50 m or more. Seiwell (1939) showed off Bermuda that a series of internal waves was present, certainly from 50–1300 m depth, presumably corresponding with various water layers of differing densities. These internal waves had a minimum displacement, over a 24 hr period, of 5 to > 50 m, but Seiwell showed that their amplitude varied from day to day, the maximum displacement ranging up to 160 m. In a later study at another station in the North Atlantic, Seiwell (1942) showed that various internal waves existed with amplitudes of the order of 50 m. As with standing waves in bays, comparatively small variations in forces of a periodic nature are sufficient to maintain such internal waves, and from a biological point of view they are of importance in that they assist in the mixing of ocean waters at considerable depths. Emery (1956) has shown the presence of periodic temperature variations during the day in one of the deep basins off Southern California. These fluctuations can occur to considerable depths, even down to 1000 m. Emery suggests that the results are most consistent with the theory that standing internal waves exist in the basin in deep water and that these waves may have an amplitude of 130–200 m.

The existence of bottom currents of some velocity and the presence of a concentration of suspended particles in bottom water confirm the idea that strong water movements are occurring near the bottom of the deep sea basin. The importance of the internal waves in the processes of mixing is demonstrated by the presence of oxygen in the basin and the absence of gradients in oxygen and in nutrients near the bottom.

3. *Tides*

The actual rise and fall of water seen in intertidal areas as well as the tidal currents which may sometimes be of considerable velocity in straits are all part of the same tidal phenomenon. The tide producing

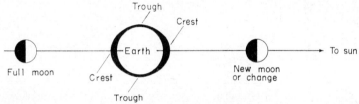

FIG. 4.4 A simplified representation of the forces involved in the lunar tidal cycle (from Harvey, 1928).

forces are complex, but as is well known the main force is the mutual attraction of earth and moon. The attraction of the moon is balanced by the centrifugal force of the earth. If we consider particles spread over the earth's surface, while the centrifugal force is the same everywhere, the attraction of the moon varies owing to the distance of various parts of the earth's surface in relation to the moon. It is thus possible to show that the acceleration due to gravity is reduced at points directly in line with the mid-point of the moon, and correspondingly, that there is an increase in the acceleration due to gravity at points which are at right angles to this line (Fig. 4.4). Thus a tide producing force can be set up by the moon, and since there is a relative rotation of earth and moon in 24.8 hr, the occurrence of two high and two low tides in just over 24 hr follows as a reasonable conclusion. This regular rhythm of two high and two low tides in a day is known as the lunar semidiurnal rhythm, and represents the main tides. The occurrence of these tides may most easily be pictured in the continuous Southern Ocean, and such forces would cause tidal currents to flow northwards into the main oceans.

Such a vertical heaping up of flood water is a useful conception of the tide which was first advanced by Newton as the equilibrium theory. It has now been superseded by the dynamic theory of tides, since the actual movement of the waters under such forces is the true consideration. It is the horizontal movements of the waters under the influence of the tidal forces which are the concern of modern tidal theory.

Variations in the declination of the moon during a lunar month will obviously cause variations in tidal forces so that different strengths

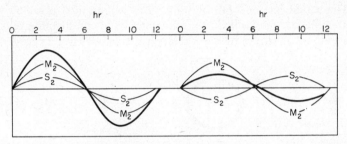

FIG. 4.5 The solar (S) and lunar (M) tides showing how they produce spring tides (left hand diagram) when in phase, and neap tides (right hand diagram) when out of phase
(from Sverdrup *et al.*, 1946).

of tides will occur with regularity. We have also disregarded so far the effect of heavenly bodies other than the moon in producing tidal forces on the earth. The sun, though of far greater mass than the moon, is so far away that the solar tidal force exerted on the earth is very much less than the lunar force. Nevertheless, there are solar tidal forces, and these working with the lunar forces complicate the actual tides during any one period. A clear and very well known example is the occurrence of spring and neap tides once a fortnight in regular succession. Springs occur during the new and full moons, and are unusually high (and low) tides due to the fact that the sun and moon tidal forces are exactly in phase, and therefore assist each other. On the other hand, at neaps, at the alternate quarters of the moon, the sun and moon are directly out of phase, and as a result unusually small tidal displacements occur (Fig. 4.5). The modern dynamic theory of tides is extremely complicated. Such considerations as the natural resonance of areas in which the tide is occurring must be brought into account, as well as frictional and other forces. For a detailed analysis the reader is referred to books such as those of Russell and Macmillan, (1952) and of Sverdrup et al., (1946).

From the biologist's point of view, one of the main effects of tides is in relation to mixing processes. Although relatively high tidal velocities are seen in narrow sounds, in the open oceans the tidal flow is usually of low velocity. However, such tidal currents can impinge on submarine plateaux and peaks, and they can assist in breaking down stratification, since although the tidal current will tend to flow around such a peak and will be deflected mainly horizontally, nevertheless there may be some degree of vertical mixing. Submarine peaks are found to be nearly always free of sediment, and this is partly due to the deflection of tidal currents. Regular tidal currents will then assist in the mixing of the layers of the ocean. At the same time it must be remembered that they are of a cyclical nature in that a reversal of tidal flow occurs during the 24 hr (Fig. 4.6). In this way tidal currents cannot effect the transport of large masses of water in the great oceans over vast distances. The overall circulation of the great oceans is not due to tidal causes.

4. *Eddy diffusion*

Under experimental conditions in the laboratory it is possible to have water layers moving at a given velocity in a perfectly orderly manner, so that local random fluctuations in velocity do not occur. This is sometimes known as laminar flow. Exchange of materials carried by the various water layers, such as oxygen, or nutrient salts, would then be extremely slow, since the exchange would have to rely on molecular diffusion alone. Even in the laboratory perfect laminar flow is difficult to achieve, as slight variations in the velocities of different layers will cause the appearance of eddies. In non-laminar flow (Fig. 4.7) the water layers are moving with different velocities, and thus there is a constant formation of eddies. This is the normal pattern in the seas where also the various water layers may even be moving in somewhat different directions. Any factor which increases turbulent flow, especially currents with their varying speeds, currents impinging on submarine obstacles, wave motion at the surface and convection currents promotes the formation of eddies and the rate of diffusion of materials. This new factor is known as eddy diffusion.

Eddies will be formed randomly in all directions, and the physical and chemical characters of the water mass (e.g. temperature, oxygen.

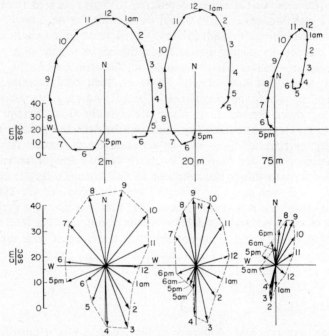

FIG. 4.6 The change in the tidal flow with time at 3 depths 2, 20 and 75 m. Lower figures show the speed and direction of flow at hourly intervals. Upper figures indicate approximate movement of the water for a 13-hr period (from Murray and Hjort, 1912).

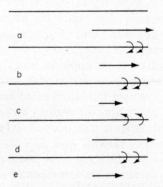

FIG. 4.7 Non-laminar flow. A diagram showing water layers a–e flowing at different speeds indicated by lengths of arrows. The occurrence of eddies is shown by curved arrows.

nutrient salts, salinity) can be transferred from one water layer to another. In this way eddy diffusion can vastly increase the rate of transference of a substance as compared with mere molecular diffusion. With such random formation of eddies, mixing can occur in all directions, but it is the vertical component of such mixing which is of particular importance in transferring heat and solutes from the surface to the deeper layers and vice versa. The vertical component of eddy diffusion (often designated as A) is not a fixed quantity for a particular water mass of given salinity and temperature. It will be damped down by conditions which lead to stability of the water column, as when the density of the water increases rapidly with depth due to an increase in salinity or to decreasing temperature. The rate of transfer of a solute must also vary according to the concentration gradient of the particular substance. But, given the concentration gradient, the vertical component of eddy diffusion, or eddy conductivity as it is sometimes termed, can be measured as the quantity of a substance passing vertically across a horizontal surface of one square cm in one second. Values of A vary considerably from < 1 to > 100 (cf. Sverdrup *et al.*, 1946). From the point of view of the marine ecologist, however, the precise numerical values are less important than the general thesis that eddy diffusion greatly increases the transport of materials in the sea over and above molecular diffusion which is extremely slow.

5. Ocean currents

By far the most potent factor in the mixing of the waters of the ocean has been left till last, namely the ocean currents. These, in fact, are responsible for the great though slow circulation of the oceans. They are in part due to wind, surface and sub-surface currents being set up where winds blow fairly constantly. But ocean currents also depend on many other factors; of these the most important are, the overall difference in temperature between the equator and the poles, the greater degree of evaporation near the equator, and the excess of precipitation towards the poles. These together lead to differences in density of the seawater. Wyrtki (1961) has recently discussed the relative roles of density differences and of winds in maintaining oceanic circulation.

Figure 4.8 shows the density of surface water in the Atlantic Ocean at various latitudes. The variations in mean surface temperature with latitude for the Atlantic are also given in Fig. 4.9. The most obvious correlation is the marked lowering of water density in tropical regions with the relatively high surface temperature, and the high

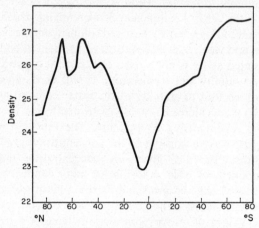

FIG. 4.8 Density of surface water as a function of latitude in the Atlantic Ocean. Density values (σ) are calculated according to the formula: $\sigma = (\text{density} - 1)\ 1000$ (after Wust *et al.*, 1954).

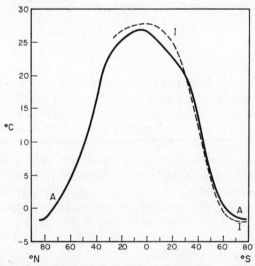

FIG. 4.9 Temperature of surface water as a function of latitude for the Atlantic (A) and Indian Oceans (I) (after Wust *et al.*, 1954).

density of the Antarctic waters in relation to the prevailing low temperature. In the northern hemisphere, however, while the surface density increases with decreasing temperature on passing north from the tropics, at really high latitudes there is a sharp decline in density owing to the low salinity in relation to excessive run-off. (The drop in density at latitudes about 55–65 °N is associated with the outflow of low salinity areas such as the Baltic.) Since lowered temperature causes an increase in density of seawater, this could presumably lead to mass vertical movements. It has been shown, however, (p. 16.) that whereas in freshwater lakes such mass movements can effect complete mixing to the bottom, in the sea there is generally a barrier; really deep ocean water being very cold is very dense, and thus mixing of surface water proceeds only to a limited depth.

Nevertheless, water from low latitudes of relatively high salinity may be carried on the surface partly as a wind driven current to high latitudes, where it becomes progressively cooled. Under these special circumstances the surface water, when sufficiently cold, may reach such a very high density that it can sink even to the bottom of the ocean (cf. p. 22.). This will occur when the local surface water in these high latitudes is of somewhat lowered salinity, owing to excessive precipitation, and thus is reduced in density. In certain regions of the Norwegian Sea, in the Irminger Sea (south east of Greenland), and off Labrador, currents bring high salinity water originating from low latitudes in the Atlantic (Fig. 4.10). This water as it cools becomes so dense that it drops to the bottom, giving complete homogeneity of the water layers over at least a considerable period of the year (cf. Table 1.1). These movements of deeper water assist in the deep circulation of the oceans, forming part of the complex pattern of ocean currents which is the most important factor in the mixing of the seas. Wind is one of the major forces maintaining surface ocean currents, and since the winds over the surface of the earth fall into a fairly regular pattern (cf. Fig. 4.11), it is possible to expect a similar broad picture of surface currents in the main oceans.

In the open oceans the surface water does not flow parallel to the direction of the prevailing wind, but at an angle. Ekman investigated the currents set up by wind stress in a homogeneous body of water of unlimited extent and infinite depth. He demonstrated that the surface current should flow at an angle of 45° to the wind direction, to the right in the northern hemisphere and to the left in the southern hemisphere. The stress of this surface current in turn sets up a current in a lower layer of water but the direction of this current is still further deflected from the direction of the wind. Thus the deviation of the currents set up by the wind increases regularly with depth (to the right in

FIG. 4.10 Surface currents in the Norwegian Sea and adjoining areas (from Murray and Hjort, 1912).

the northern hemisphere), until in the deeper layers the current is completely reversed and flows in a direction opposite to that of the wind. Ekman showed however that the speeds of the subsurface currents were much less; velocity decreased logarithmically with depth. At a depth where the current was opposite in direction to that at the surface, the speed was almost negligible (*ca.* 4%) (Fig. 4.12). The deviation of the wind driven surface current from the wind direction is independent of latitude, being always 45°, so that theoretically there should be an abrupt change in deflection in passing across the equator. In point of fact, since oceans are not limitless, this does

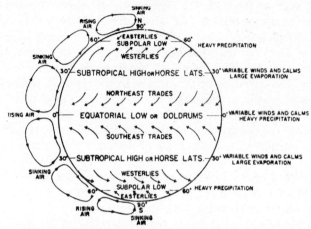

FIG. 4.11 Diagrammatic representation of wind systems over the world (from Fleming, 1957).

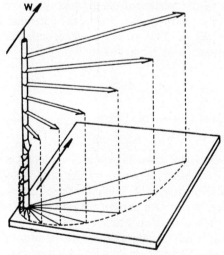

FIG. 4.12 The Ekman Spiral showing the wind direction (W) and the direction and speed of currents from the surface downwards (from Sverdrup *et al.*, 1946).

not hold. The angle of deflection would begin to decrease near the equator and would become zero at the equator before increasing again. Since also oceans are not infinitely deep, a correction for depth may need to be applied to the current direction. The presence of other currents such as those due to distribution of mass or to tides also affect the direction of a surface wind current. Nevertheless in open oceans, Ekman's theory that surface currents should show an average deflection of 45° to the wind has been shown to be correct. Nearer the coast the decreased depth of water markedly affects current direction. The deviation of the current to the right (in the northern hemisphere) is still recognizable, but the angle is less than 45°, until in very shallow seas the current flows in practically the same direction as the wind. The configuration of the coastline itself may also influence current direction so that the angle of deviation from the wind may vary from 0 to > 50°. It is worth noting that if an ocean current in the northern hemisphere moves over a submarine plateau it will tend to be deflected more to the right, and on moving over deeper water again it will tend to swing back in direction.

The velocity of a wind driven current depends on the wind stress, which in turn is proportional to the square of the wind velocity. Coriolis force also affects the current velocity. The deflective force is proportional to the tangential component of the centrifugal force due to the earth's rotation, and is thus proportional to the sine of the latitude (Φ) (Fig. 4.12.1). An empirical formula derived by Ekman for a wind current in an open ocean is:

$$\frac{v}{w} = \frac{0.0127}{\sqrt{\sin \Phi}}$$

where v = surface velocity of current

w = wind velocity.

However, the velocity of a wind current in an actual ocean is affected by the presence of other currents, by the land masses and by the bottom configuration, just as we found for the direction of the current. Moreover, no known surface current may be rightly regarded as due to wind alone. The characterization of particular ocean currents as due primarily to wind, or alternatively to density differences, is an over-simplification. Density differences, wind stress, bottom topography, the effect of other water masses, and many other factors, all play a part in contributing to and modifying the world's ocean currents. More precise details of the forces involved indeed still await elucidation. It is useful, however, to examine the more obvious effects of prevailing winds in contributing to the world's ocean currents, since in the main oceans of the world a common pattern of surface currents may be seen (Fig. 4.13).

In the Atlantic Ocean, which is perhaps best known, the trade winds will cause westerly flowing currents in the equatorial region,

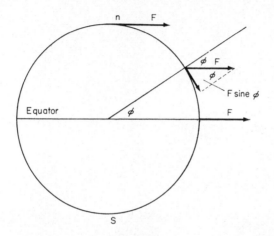

FIG. 4.12.1 Figure to show forces acting on a surface current
(from Harvey, 1928).

the well known North Equatorial and South Equatorial currents (Fig. 4.13). A compensating counter current is set up lying between these two major surface streams, which in the Atlantic appears off Africa as the Guinea Current. The flow of the North Equatorial current and part of the South Equatorial current towards the coast of South America is deflected north off the Brazilian coast. The majority of this water is driven into the Caribbean and eventually into the almost land-locked Gulf of Mexico. It thus emerges as a current of high velocity round the tip of Florida where it is joined by further water, the Antilles Current, travelling to the east of the West Indies (Fig. 4.13). Together these streams give rise to what is probably the best known of all currents in the world, the Gulf Stream, which flows with a very high velocity for an ocean current — its speed approaches some 9 knots off the south-east coasts of Florida.

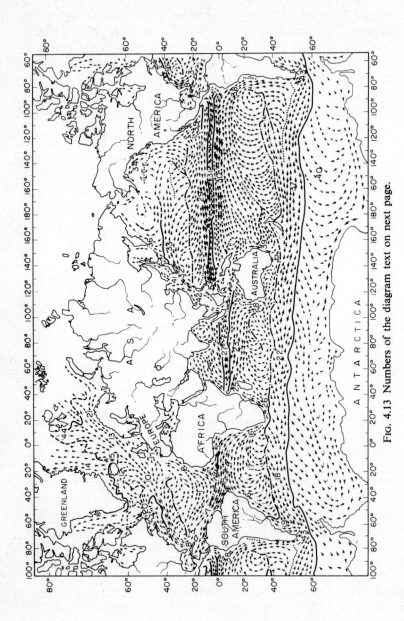

Fig. 4.13 Numbers of the diagram text on next page.

The main Florida Current as it emerges from the Gulf and is deflected north is kept close to the American coast by the shallow Bahama Bank. However the Gulf Stream is deflected more and more to the right by the coastline as it moves north and this, together with the effect of the prevailing westerly winds at higher latitudes, causes it to flow across the Atlantic Ocean (Fig. 4.13). Its speed has now decreased considerably, and the current is now normally spoken of as the North Atlantic Drift. A part of this drift turns south off the coast of Spain as the Canary Current, so that an enormous clockwise circulation is typical of the North Atlantic Ocean, in the middle of which lies the well-known Sargasso Sea area (Fig. 4.14).

A large part of the North Atlantic Drift water, however, is deflected north-eastwards, and flows north off the continental shelf to the west of the British Isles, proceeding further along the coast of Norway, and eventually reaching sub-arctic areas. Part of the flow

FIG. 4.13 Surface ocean currents.

Atlantic Ocean

1. North Equatorial current
2. Canaries current
3. Antillies current
4. South Equatorial current
5. Guinea current
6. Brazil current
7. Guiana current
8. Florida current
9. Gulf Stream
10. North Atlantic drift
11. English Channel flow
12. Irminger current
13. Norwegian current
14. East Greenland current
15. East Iceland current
16. Benguela current
17. South Atlantic drift
18. West wind drift
19. Falkland current
20. Labrador current
21. North Cape current

Indian Ocean

22. West wind drift
23. South Equatorial current

24. North-east Monsoon drift
25. Mozambique current
26. Agulhas current
27. Equatorial counter current
28. West Australian current

Pacific Ocean

29. North Equatorial current
30. South Equatorial current
31. Equatorial counter current
32. Kuroshio current
33. Kuroshio drift
34. Alaska current
35. California current
36. Oyashio current
37. West wind drift
38. Peru (Humboldt) current
39. East Australia current
40. South Polar drift
41. Tsushima current
42. North-east Monsoon drift
43. Cape Horn current

North Polar Sea

44. West Spitzbergen current
(from Bruns, 1958).

off Britain is deflected to the west by the extensive Shetland-Faroe-Iceland ridge which almost shuts off the deep Arctic Ocean from the Atlantic. This part of the North Atlantic Drift water proceeds to the north west, forming complicated current patterns off the coasts of Iceland and Greenland (Fig. 4.10). This water, originating in low latitudes, we have already referred to; it eventually attains such a high density, as it is progressively cooled, that it sinks in areas of the Irminger, Norwegian and Labrador seas, and contributes to deep currents.

In the South Atlantic region comparable wind systems are primarily responsible for a flow towards South America, which turns south off the coast as the Brazil Current, and then becomes deflected to the east by the prevailing "Westerlies". Off the west coast of Africa a main northerly current (the Benguela Current) completes an anti-clockwise circulation, which is set up in the South Atlantic (Figs. 4.13 and 4.14).

Similar surface current systems are known in the other oceans. In the Indian Ocean only the equatorial and counter-equatorial currents and the southerly anti-clockwise circulation can exist (Fig. 4.13). But in the Pacific Ocean a vast clockwise circulation occurs in the North Pacific, appearing as the north-easterly warm Kuroshio Current off the coast of Japan, and as a colder southerly Californian Current off the west coast of North America. Similarly in the South Pacific an anti-clockwise current system of enormous magnitude exists (Figs. 4.13, 4.14): the Humboldt Current proceeds north and then turns west off the coast of Chile and Peru as the Peru Current, merging into the Pacific South Equatorial current. This proceeds across the Pacific Ocean and is deflected as several southerly directed currents off the coasts of Australasia, finally merging into the easterly flow of the West Wind drift north of Antarctica (Figs. 4.13 and 4.14).

The tremendous effect of currents on temperature is of course well known. Thus the warm Gulf Stream water is carried along the east coast of the southern American states, but then passes across the Atlantic giving the relatively temperate climate of north west Europe. By contrast, the very cold Labrador Current originating off Baffinland and Greenland proceeds south fairly close to the eastern coasts of Canada and Newfoundland, and gives very different climatic conditions to the north east states of America (Fig. 4.14.1). A similar cold current proceeding southwards along the east side of the Asian Continent from the region of Kamchatka passes to the northern islands of Japan as the Oyashio Current (Fig. 4.14). The meeting of such warm and cold currents usually marks sharp faunistic boundaries. The effect of the meeting of warm and cold currents in causing fogs, as off Newfoundland, is also well known.

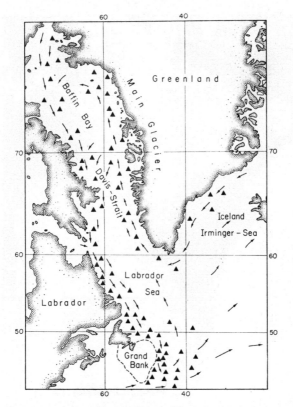

Fig. 4.14.1 Currents in Labrador Sea area showing main routes of glaciers (after Bruns, 1958).

As surface currents move away from coasts they cause a movement of deeper waters towards the surface. This is known as upwelling and occurs, for example, off the West coast of Africa where the Benguela Current begins to move west out across the Atlantic (Fig. 4.15). Similar upwelling areas are well known off the coast of Chile and Peru where the Humboldt and Peru Current turns westward, and off the coast of California where surface waters move away from the coast (cf. Chapt. XIII). It is now known that although such upwelling is of great biological significance in that deeper water is brought towards the surface, the actual depth from which such upwelled water is normally drawn is not of very great magnitude. Depths of the order

FIG. 4.15 Surface currents in the Atlantic Ocean. Arrows joined to open circles indicate upwelling. Arrows ending in solid circles indicate converging and sinking water masses (from Harvey, 1955).

of 100 m or in extreme cases of perhaps 300 m appear to be the limits for such upwelling currents. Contrasting with the upwelling areas, waters which are piled up against the coast by surface currents moving onshore cause a sinking of surface water. Similarly where surface currents meet each other, there may also be areas where sinking of surface water occurs (cf. Fig. 4.14 and 4.15).

Although we have so far spoken of these currents as surface currents, their effect can extend to considerable depths. In equatorial currents the depths may not be more than 100–200 m, but in the case of the Gulf Stream some effect of the current can certainly be experienced at 1000 m depth. It must be remembered that less dense, warmer water layers generally lie on the surface in the seas and colder layers below, and although the changes in density are continuous, it is useful to think of a series of layers of increasing density. But the effect

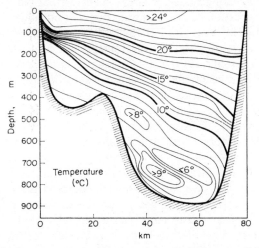

FIG. 4.16 Temperature profile across the Gulf Stream off Miami (from Sverdrup *et al.*, 1946).

of the earth's rotation is to tilt these density layers in an ocean current in the northern hemisphere to the right. Thus the lighter, warmer water is deeper on the right side of a current in the northern hemisphere. For example, the 15 °C isotherm in the Gulf Stream is only at *ca.* 100 m depth south of Miami, but reaches nearly 500 m depth on the eastern side of the current near the Bahama Bank (Fig. 4.16). One effect of this piling up of water on one side of a current is that water is picked up from other sources as the current flows along.

The quantity of water which such great ocean currents transport is enormous. Wust computed the flow of the Florida Current in a section across the Florida Straits, and calculated that 26 million m³ of water were transported per second. The Antilles Current was responsible for an additional 12 million m³/sec; the total flow would therefore amount to approximately 38 million m³/sec. As the Gulf Stream proceeds along its path, however, it drags in water from other areas, particularly from the waters bordering the Sargasso Sea and from the continental shelf water. Thus Stommel (1958) states that one estimate for the total transport of the Gulf Stream off Chesapeake Bay, assuming a 2000 m reference level, was 82 million m³/sec. However, he emphasizes the great differences obtained in computing transport volumes when the assumed depth of no motion is varied. Moreover there may be counter flows along the sides of the main current which will reduce the net transport of water. Thus one computation suggests a transport of 74 million m³/sec, which is reduced by a south-westerly counter flow of slope water, to give a net transport of *ca.* 55 million m³/sec. Stommel also points out that a deep counter current may exist beneath the Gulf Stream which may reduce the transport to something nearer 35 million m³/sec. In any event, a considerable admixture of water masses must occur as the Gulf Stream proceeds, especially with contributions levied from the more coastal waters and from the Sargasso Sea. More recent investigations, particularly by American oceanographers, have shown that the Gulf Stream is a current of extraordinary complexity. Narrow streams of water subdivide and change course and give rise to complex eddies in the general stream as a whole. Moreover, it appears that the intricate pattern changes with time, perhaps seasonally (cf. Stommel, 1958). Nevertheless the current as a whole turns more and more eastwards south of Newfoundland where some admixture of very cold water from the Labrador Current occurs. However, with such very large volumes of water of the original Gulf Stream being transported, the specific characteristics of temperature and salinity can still be discerned in the North Atlantic even after the current has proceeded for thousands of miles, and has reached sub-Arctic and even Arctic areas.

Although surface ocean currents will then contribute greatly to mixing even down to a considerable depth, it is clear that the deepest waters of the oceans must presumably be circulated by currents other than those we have so far envisaged. The cooling of warm but saline water in high latitudes leads to deep mass sinking of water. In the North Atlantic Ocean deep currents are set up mainly proceeding southwards from the Arctic and sub-Arctic regions as the North Atlantic Intermediate Water (Fig. 4.17). In the Atlantic Ocean a further contributor to this intermediate circulation, which reaches very considerable depths, comes from the Mediterranean Sea. In the

Mediterranean, owing to the high temperatures and relatively little run-off from the land, there is an excess of evaporation and highly saline water exists there (cf. Fig. 4.17.1). In winter, with the cooling of the land masses round the relatively enclosed Mediterranean Sea, this very saline surface water becomes cooled and acquires such a very high density that it sinks to the bottom. A bottom current of high salinity water thus passes out through the Straits of Gibraltar at considerable depths, and this contributes to the general deeper circulation of the North Atlantic (Figs. 4.17 and 4.18). There is in

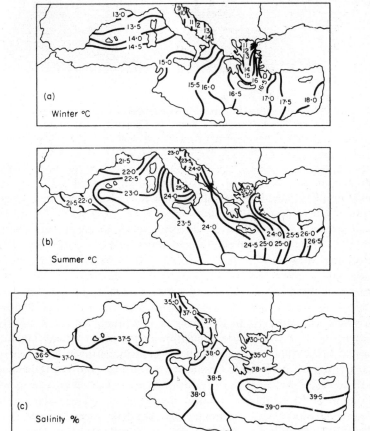

FIG. 4.17.1 Surface temperatures in winter (a) and in summer (b) and surface salinities (c) in Mediterranean Sea (from Bruns, 1958).

general, therefore, a very deep and slow current in the North Atlantic, the water being of mixed origin; most of this water tends to drift slowly south, across the equator and into the South Atlantic Ocean.

In the Antarctic there is an enormous ice barrier where the water is of somewhat reduced salinity. A very cold layer of water stretches out towards the north turning east with the prevailing wind from the Antarctic barrier (Fig. 4.13). The water, although cold, remains

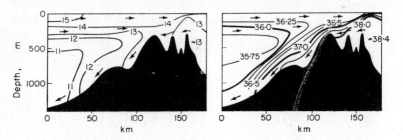

FIG. 4.18 Deep outflowing current from the Mediterranean into the Atlantic Ocean through the Straits of Gibraltar. Left—temperature; right—salinity. Note: Outflow of high salinity water (from Sverdrup *et al.*, 1946).

on the surface because of its reduced salinity (*ca.* $34^0/_{00}$). With the melting of the ice, however, deeper water is also cooled and a very slow but very deep current slides down from the Antarctic continent and proceeds as a northwardly directed current at the greatest depths of the ocean. This current is sometimes known as the Antarctic Bottom Current or Drift (Fig. 4.19). The occurrence of a surface drift and a slower bottom drift north from the Antarctic must lead to a compensating movement of water. Slightly warmer water from very considerable depths thus rises towards the surface and flows towards the Antarctic in the form of upwelling, but on a gigantic scale (Fig. 4.19). A massive circulation of the ocean waters therefore occurs in the Antarctic area, which also contributes towards the general circulation of the Atlantic Ocean. As the surface cold but rather low salinity layer proceeds north eastwards it meets, somewhere in the latitude of 50° S, relatively warm though more saline water of the South Atlantic Ocean. Although the Antarctic surface water is of lower salinity, it is so cold that its density exceeds the more temperate South Atlantic water. The Antarctic water thus sinks beneath the warmer layer, the meeting of the two water masses being a fairly well defined area known as the Antarctic Convergence (Figs. 4.20; 4.21). The Antarctic surface water, now at intermediate though relatively shallow depths, mixes to some extent with bordering water layers but proceeds northwards as a well defined water mass known as the Antarctic Intermediate Current (cf. Fig. 4.19). In Fig. 4.20 the 5 °C isotherm at 1000 m indicates this water mass. This current

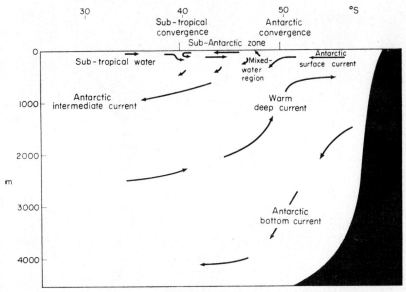

FIG. 4.19 Diagram of the main water movements in the Antarctic showing the Antarctic Intermediate and Bottom Currents and the up-welling warmer water mass (from Deacon, 1937).

proceeds in the South Atlantic Ocean towards the north, and can be recognized even north of the equator. In this manner it contributes to the general circulation at intermediate depths, and although the water is to some extent of mixed origin, its characteristics persist so that it can be recognized as Antarctic Intermediate Water even many thousands of miles from its point of origin.

In summary, it will be seen that owing largely to the sinking of high density water and to the effects of freezing and thawing of sea-ice at the Poles, there is a very slow but deep circulation of water throughout the whole of the oceans. Broadly speaking, deep water has originated as shallow water of high latitudes. In the Atlantic at

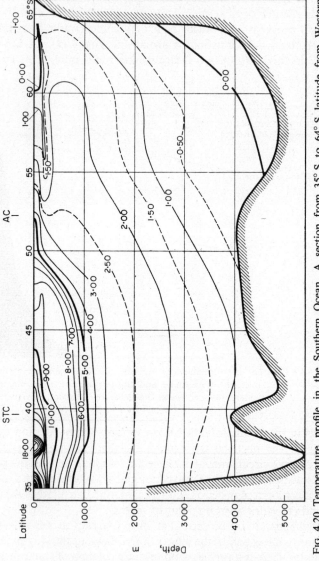

FIG. 4.20 Temperature profile in the Southern Ocean. A section from 35° S to 64° S latitude from Western Australia to the ice-edge in 130° E longitude (from Deacon, 1937).

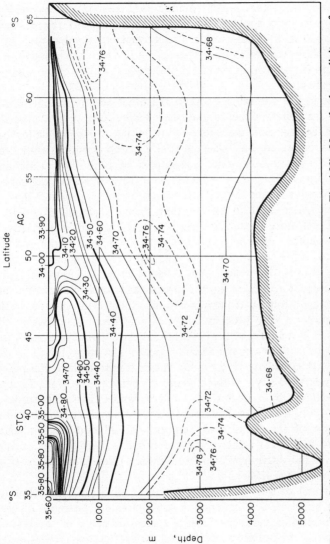

FIG. 4.21 Salinity profile in the Southern Ocean (same section as Fig. 4.20). Note the low salinity surface water at high latitudes descending at the Antarctic Convergence (AC) to give the Antarctic Intermediate Water moving to the north as a layer of somewhat lowered salinity (from Deacon, 1937).

somewhat shallower intermediate depths there is a current proceeding from the Antarctic and South Atlantic towards the equator; at greater depths is the North Atlantic Intermediate water which is mainly proceeding southwards. Finally in the deepest regions there is the bottom Antarctic water also proceeding northwards. As a result of these and the more surface currents which are usually much better known, a general circulation of the whole waters of the Atlantic region exists.

Although the current systems in the other oceans are not so well studied, the general effect is somewhat similar, and in particular the effect of the Antarctic currents in contributing to the circulation has been demonstrated (cf. Deacon, 1937). Deep bottom water and Antarctic intermediate water are known in both the Pacific and Indian Oceans (Fig. 4.17). The Pacific shows several marked differences as compared with the Atlantic, however. There is a greater flow of sub-arctic water south in the Northern Pacific at depths of less than 2500 m, and more Arctic Intermediate water is formed at relatively shallow depths, especially off Japan (Fig. 4.17). But the greatest difference lies in the much more sluggish circulation in the Pacific at great depths. Whereas North Atlantic Deep and Bottom Water cross the equator into the South Atlantic, and Antarctic Intermediate Water and Bottom Drift move north into the North Atlantic, in the Pacific there is very little exchange of any deep water across the equator. It is doubtful also whether the Antarctic Intermediate Water reaches the equator in the Pacific Ocean. The importance of this Antarctic Intermediate Water in the Pacific is nevertheless undisputed. A recent detailed study of the circulation of the waters of the Tasman and Coral Seas by Rochford (1960) demonstrates its significant role. Thus in the South and in the North Pacific Oceans there is the essential circulation of the great ocean currents at all depths. The maps (Fig. 4.14 and 4.17) representing the broad pattern of the current systems in the Atlantic, Pacific and Indian Oceans are taken from Sewell's summary (1948).

As a result of this general circulation in all oceans, the whole of the vast water mass is undergoing some mixing. The speed of deep ocean currents is very low however. Measurements of the periods necessary for the replacement of ocean waters, including more recent estimates based on the carbon isotopes in seawater, suggest that the age of ocean water should be reckoned in hundreds or even in thousands of years. This would in turn suggest a very sluggish oceanic circulation, with the deeper ocean currents flowing at rates not exceeding 5 miles per year. However, calculations such as those of Deacon (1933) on the changes in oxygen and salinity would suggest a rate of flow for the Antarctic Intermediate Water of about 1.3 to 2.5 miles per day. Observations on other deep ocean currents also indicate that rates approaching 5 miles per day may occasionally be experienced. These speeds are at least three hundred times those suggested from replacement time data. In the North Atlantic also there is a suggestion that replacement may be more rapid. Worthington (1954) shows that the oxygen content of the North Atlantic Deep Water appears to have been reduced over the last twenty years. Much of this water must be derived by the excessive cooling of water at high latitudes and this may indicate that a considerable bulk was formed in the remarkably cold period of 1810–1820. The discrepancy may to some extent be explained by the occurrence of a considerable amount of recirculation and mixing of the deeper ocean currents (cf. Cooper, 1956). The determination of the age of North Atlantic water is indeed a complex problem. Cold, highly saline water, sunk in the deeper layers of the Norwegian Sea, has been envisaged as spilling over the ridge between Greenland and the Faroes as a series of boluses into the deep Atlantic (Cooper, 1961). Each bolus represents comparatively young water, which, as it spreads out between the deeper layers, mixes with much older Atlantic water. Age determinations on samples may, therefore, be variable.

Some recent direct measurements on the speeds of currents indicate that at very great depths, rates even exceeding 5 miles per day may be found, but that the speeds are apparently very variable both temporally, and from one area of a current to another (cf. p. 30). Whatever the rates of the deeper currents, since all the waters of the oceans are maintained in circulation, oxygen and nutrients, as well as heat, are able to be transmitted, not only horizontally from one water mass to another, but also vertically. Despite warming and cooling effects being confined to the surface of the oceans, therefore, some transference of heat occurs vertically through the water layers. Similarly, we have now an explanation of the fact that no parts of the oceans (except for seas such as the Black Sea cut off from the general circulation) become stagnant and de-oxygenated; oxygen can be transported by means of the total mixing processes to all depths of the ocean. The outstanding biological significance is that no part of the oceans is uninhabited by some species of animal. Furthermore the circulation of the waters, albeit slow, provides transport of food particles to sedentary and sessile, filter feeding animals of the ocean floor. Moreover, the current system allows gametes to be circulated, assisting in fertilization, and also helps in the distribution of the young stages of marine animals.

6. *Mixing processes off the continental shelf*

In relatively shallow water in the region of the continental shelf, it has already been demonstrated that some mixing processes, for example, wave action and mass sinking, are of much greater signi-

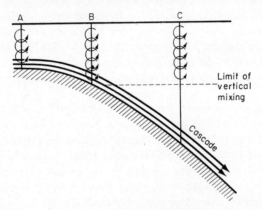

Fig. 4.22 Diagram to indicate cascading of water (from Cooper and Vaux, 1949).

ficance than in the deeper strata of the open ocean. Special considerations have been shown to apply to continental shelves and slopes. Cooper and Vaux (1949) investigated a phenomenon which they speak of as "cascading" off the continental slope of the south west British Isles. It is believed that in exceptionally cold winters the marked winter cooling of the sea surface may lead to such mass sinking that a flow of dense water occurs near the bottom down the edge of the continental slope (Fig. 4.22). Off the south west coast of Britain where the submarine valleys tend to run in a fairly specific direction, the flow of such deep cascading water, mainly along the submarine valleys, might have an effect on the deeper currents. If, on the other hand, the main cascading current ran at an angle to the submarine valleys turbulence would be increased.

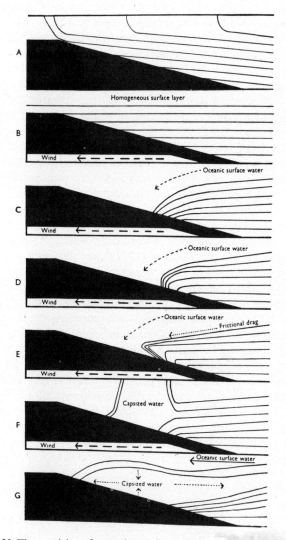

FIG. 4.23 The capsizing of water layers due to steady strong winds blowing against a continental slope (from Cooper, 1952).

As a result of such cascading, compensation water must flow from other areas. In the area south west of the British Isles it seems unlikely that simultaneous upwelling occurs; more probably warmer, less dense surface water is drawn from the Atlantic or less saline water from neighbouring coastal areas. In any case the inflowing of such surface water will not lead to any enrichment of nutrients. In the spring and summer, when no cascading can occur, the growth of plankton will produce detritus which will fall towards the bottom. If cascading should occur again during winter there will tend to be a general slight enrichment of the deeper continental slope areas, and with this, an impoverishment of the more shore-ward regions. Cascading appears to be true in certain winters in the British Isles area; how far it is true of other seas is not known, but Boden and Kampa (1953) have described it as occurring at Bermuda. Cooled surface water sinks during winter months to the lagoon floor and then down the sides of this oceanic island.

In contrast to the process of cascading which tends to deplete coastal areas of nutrients, Cooper (1952a) has shown that an enrichment of waters bordering on continental slopes may occur. Let us suppose that steady strong winds blow against the continental slope so causing the water layers of different density to lie at an angle (Fig. 4.23). If very strong onshore winds continue to blow, an unstable situation may result sufficient to cause "capsizing" of the waters. In capsizing, the surface water is turned below, but to compensate, denser originally deeper water is brought to the surface, and the whole water mass soon becomes homogeneously mixed. Such capsizing could lead to considerable enrichment of the water by deeper water masses. Cooper has also raised the interesting point that if such capsizing occurs against a continental slope it could lead to oscillations of the water mass, which might contribute to the formation of oceanic internal waves.

CHAPTER V

THE PHYTOPLANKTON

THE SEAS support a vast population of organisms which either swim or float in the various water layers and are independent of the bottom. Included in these pelagic organisms as they a e termed, are plants and animals, mostly of rather small size, which float and drift in the water layers. Although these organisms may have scme powers of independent movement, they cannot perform any effective horizontal migrations against the set of tides and currents. These floating animals and plants comprise the well-known community of the plankton. Part of this plankton consists of an array of plant species, all of which contain chlorophyll and are thus able to perform photosynthesis. Such autotrophic organisms constitute the phytoplankton.

By far the most obvious and often the most numerous of the phytoplankton forms are the diatoms. These are uni-cellular plants with a characteristic skeleton or capsule composed of two valves, the hypotheca and epitheca, each composed of pectin with a considerable amount of silica. The valves have flanges with extensions which overlap and may show some structural modifications forming the so-called girdle (Fig. 5.1). In one group of diatoms referred to as the pennate forms, many species have a slit along the valve (the raphe) through which the protoplasm may be in contact with the water (Fig. 5.2). Most marine species belong to the centric group of diatoms which have no raphe, but the valves usually have pores of varied pattern. Mucilage is very commonly exuded from the cells. Inside

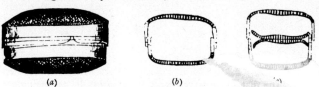

(a)　　　　　　(b)

FIG. 5.1 (a) Cell-wall of a diatom *Coscinodiscus* (b) showing hypotheca and epitheca (c) section showing cell division
(from Gran, 1912, in Murray and Hjort).

the valves the cytoplasm forms a relatively thin lining surrounding a large vacuole filled with cell sap; the nucleus is more or less central in position with cytoplasmic strands extending across the vacuole. Numerous chromatophores occur throughout the cell, but with intense light they may arrange themselves parallel to the end faces (valve) of the cells (cf. Fig. 5.3). These chromatophores contain

FIG. 5.2 *Navicula*—a pennate diatom, 95 μ long. Raphe seen in right picture (after Lebour, 1930).

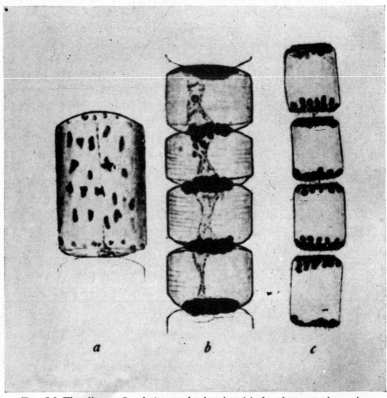

FIG. 5.3 The diatom *Lauderia annula* showing (a) the chromatophores in normal position, (b) aggregated at the end faces of the cells. (c) Aggregation of chromatophores in *Detonula schroederi* (from Gran, 1912, in Murray and Hjort).

a mixture of chlorophylls *a* and *c* together with several carotenoids, mainly β-carotene and α-xanthophyll which is similar if not identical to fucoxanthin (cf. Fogg, 1953); and the diatoms therefore appear brown in colour. Diatoms normally store oil or fatty acids as the end product of photosynthetic activity. Grøntved (1952) has described

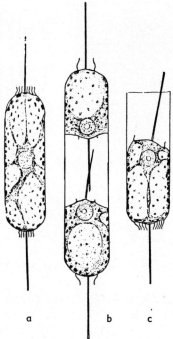

a   b   c

FIG. 5.4 *Ditylum* (a) a normal vegetative cell, (b) cell in process of division, (c) a recent daughter cell from such a division (from Gross, 1937).

an exceptional condition where a particularly rich patch of *Coscinodiscus* in the North Sea produced so much oil that an oily patch or slick of several square miles was evident. Diatoms are uni-cellular and usually occur singly, e.g. *Ditylum* (Fig. 5.4), *Coscinodiscus* (Fig. 5.5), *Nitzschia* (Fig. 5.6), but some species form chains, as in *Chaetoceros* (Fig. 5.7), *Thalassiosira* (Fig. 5.8) or *Lauderia* (Fig. 5.9). The cells are held together by protoplasmic threads or strands of mucilage, or, as in *Chaetoceros*, spiny or hair-like projections of the individual cells may lock together. Sometimes the pattern made by the cells may be complex; *Asterionella* (Fig. 5.10) forms a stellate grouping and other diatoms show spirally twisted patterns. Mucilage secretion may be so abundant as to form a slimy colony (Fig. 5.11).

Some diatom cells are relatively large: e.g., *Ditylum* can approach 100 μ in diameter and may exceed 150 μ in length. Species of *Coscinodiscus* and *Rhizosolenia* (Figs. 5.12 and 5.13) can also be of relatively

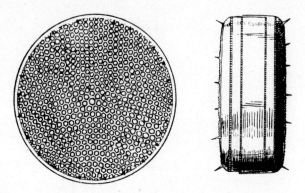

FIG. 5.5 *Coscinodiscus excentricus* 70 μ across (from Lebour, 1930).

FIG. 5.6 *Nitzschia closterium* (from Lebour, 1930).

large size — the largest approach 1 mm. At the other extreme many species of diatoms are less than 10 μ so that, as Harvey (1950) has shown, the volume of different species of diatoms can vary enormously, approximately from 2×10^{-2} mm^3 to 2×10^{-8} mm^3. Moreover, the variation in size does not apply to species alone. Individuals of the same species can vary greatly in volume, so that *Ditylum brightwelli*, for example, may show a thirtyfold increase in size within the same species. Part of this size variation is due to the type of reproduction. At each cell division of a diatom, the valves separate, one passing to each daughter cell in each of which one new valve is formed. The hypotheca of the original diatom thus now forms the epitheca for one of the daughter cells (Fig. 5.1). In this way a continuously dividing population of diatoms must decrease in average cell size as division continues. The investigations of Wimpenny (1936a, 1946) and of Lucas and Stubbings (1948) show that a gradual decline in cell size may be followed in natural populations of the diatom

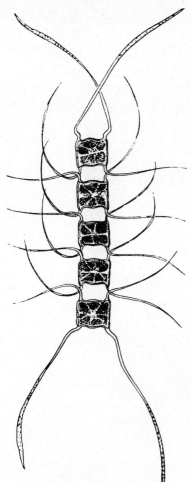

FIG. 5.7 *Chaetoceros laciniosus*
25 μ across
(from Lebour, 1930).

FIG. 5.8 *Thalassiosira gravida.*
A chain of cells (from Gran,
1912, in Murray and Hjort).

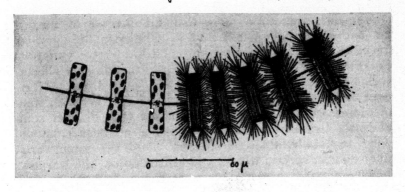

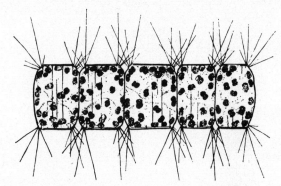

FIG. 5.9 *Lauderia borealis* 38 μ across (from Lebour. 1930).

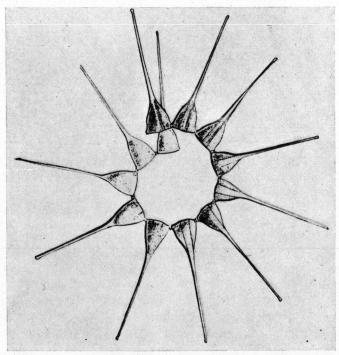

FIG. 5.10 *Asterionella japonica* 58 μ broad (from Lebour, 1930).

Rhizosolenia styliformis; the decline is succeeded by a sudden rise in cell diameter consequent upon auxospore formation (*vide infra*). The history of a population of the diatom may thus be followed by the changes in cell size. These investigations have demonstrated, however, that different stocks of the diatom exist in the North Sea,

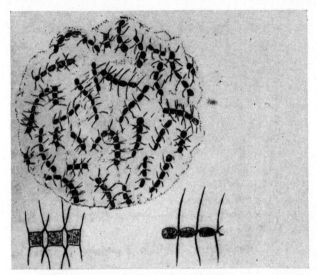

FIG. 5.11 *Chaetoceros socialis* 15 μ across. Chains embedded in a slimy colony (from Lebour, 1930).

these stocks being distinguished by size differences. Environmental factors such as temperature and salinity may possibly be associated with the mean size of the various stocks. Cushing (1953) has further used the decline in mean size of a diatom population as an indication of the division rate.

Diatoms multiply very rapidly. Under culture conditions where the external factors may approach optimal value, Gran for example has shown rates of division for various diatom species considerably faster than one division a day. Harvey *et al.*, (1935) also consider that some species can divide once in 18–36 hr. In the sea, where growth conditions are hardly ever as favourable as in culture, a division rate of once every one or two days is probably nearer the maximum. But the rates of division vary from species to species, and even more, will depend on the environmental conditions and

FIG. 5.12 *Rhizosolenia alata* 12 μ across (from Lebour, 1930).   FIG. 5.13 *Rhizosolenia hebetata* 10 μ across (from Lebour, 1930).

also on the previous history of the diatoms themselves. Thus Harvey (1955) has shown that the temperature and the light intensity which prevailed during a previous period of growth will affect the subsequent growth rate in *Biddulphia mobiliensis* (Fig. 5.14). *B. mobiliensis* grown previously in dim light, grew best at intensities of about 4000 lux, whilst cells grown at relatively high light intensities showed maximum growth rate at about 18000 lux. Similarly, cells which had been ac-

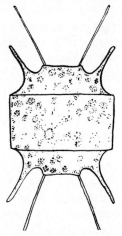

FIG. 5.14 *Biddulphia mobiliensis* 50 μ across (from Lebour, 1930).

climatized to grow at relatively low temperatures grew better when later exposed to those temperatures than to higher ranges. Internal differences between stocks of diatoms, including differences due to previous growth conditions, can be generally spoken of as "the physiological state of the cells". Apart, however, from the physiological state, such obvious factors as concentration of nutrients, the occurrence of accessory growth factors, light intensity, temperature and pH all affect the division rate of diatoms. How far external metabolites produced by phytoplankton and by other organisms in the water, especially in dense plankton bloomings, may affect the reproduction of diatoms is one of the more fascinating of the other factors affecting division rate. Lucas, (1938, 1947, 1955 and 1961) has especially discussed the effect of such substances and we know definitely that antibiotic substances are produced by algae, as also there is some evidence for the existence of growth promoting substances in the sea (cf. Jones, 1959; Sieburth and Burkholder, 1959; Johnston, 1959).

The range in division rate of diatoms is truly remarkable. Spencer (1954) has shown a maximum rate for *Phaeodactylum* (*Nitzschia*) of 1 division in 10–12 hr. Raymont and Adams (1958) have shown that in large scale culture a division rate of once in just under 24 hr may be obtained, whereas at the other extreme one division in as much as 18 or more days may occur, though the culture may still appear healthy.

It is clear that with a prolonged period of reproductive activity the average size of the diatom cell will decrease rapidly. The restoration of the maximum size of the diatoms may be achieved by the formation of auxospores where the protoplast, consisting of cytoplasm, nucleus and chromatophores, throws off the old valves and increases considerably in size. A membrane consisting largely of pectic substances with a little silica is formed around the auxospores and new valves of larger size in conformity with the enlarged protoplast are then developed. The maximum size of the diatom cell is thus restored. Auxospores of several species of diatoms (*Ditylum, Thalassiosira, Melosira*) are shown in Figs. 5.15, 5.16 and 5.17. While continued division leading to a diminution in size would appear to be the important factor in auxospore formation, environmental factors undoubtedly play some part. Gross (1937) concludes that once a minimal size of diatom cell has been reached, then external factors, especially density of culture which would presumably involve reduction in nutrients, as well as release of metabolites, and possibly also reduced light intensity, may influence auxospore formation. Apparently auxospores do not act as resting stages; resting spores are, however, known in some diatoms, more especially in neritic forms, where they appear to tide the diatoms over an unfavourable period. In their formation, there appears to be a considerable loss of cell-sap and a relatively dense protoplast rounds itself off inside the cell. Such denser cells tend to sink into deeper layers but with the return of favourable conditions they will germinate (Fig. 5.18). Turbulence presumably will bring these denser cells into the uppermost layers. Overcrowding in culture appears to promote spore formation; in the sea the main factors are probably low light intensity, poor nutrient conditions and low temperature. Microspores of somewhat uncertain function are also produced by some diatoms (e.g. *Biddulphia mobiliensis, Rhizosolenia styliformis, Chaetoceros* spp.).

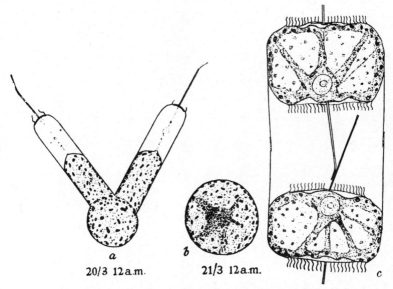

20/3 12a.m.   21/3 12a.m.

FIG. 5.15 *Ditylum* (a) auxospore formation; (b) the completed auxospore;
(c) a broad cell developed from an auxospore in process of
division (from Gross, 1937).

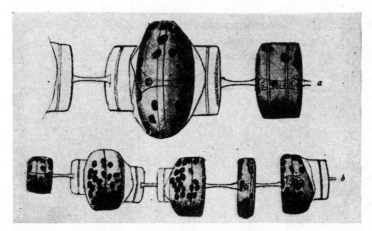

FIG. 5.16 *Thalassiosira gravida* showing in (a) a recently formed auxospore.
In (b) a new chain of relatively large cells is developing by division of an auxospore; the small cell on the extreme left has not
yet, however, undergone auxospore formation (from Gran,
1912, in Murray and Hjort).

Fig. 5.17 A newly formed auxospore in *Melosira borreri*
(from Gross, 1937).

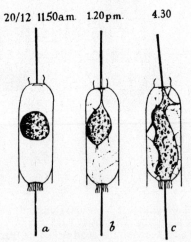

Fig. 5.18 (a) Resting spore of *Ditylum*. (b) and (c) Stages in germination
(from Gross, 1937).

In some species the spores are reported to be flagellated swarmers, but in others they are non-motile (cf. Fig. 5.19). Gross (1937) held that such swarmers probably did not act as gametes, but both Braarud (1939) and Wimpenny (1946) believed that microspores were concerned in sexual reproduction. According to Chadefaud and Emberger (1960), auxospore formation in diatoms may be preceded by sexual reproduction. In centric diatoms an oosphere,

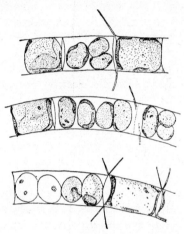

FIG. 5.19 Microspore-like bodies inside some cells in a chain of *Chaetoceros pseudocrinitus* (from Gross, 1937).

formed from a vegetative cell, may be fertilized by a flagellated spermatozoid. Thus in *Biddulphia mobiliensis*, a cell may undergo meiotic division to produce two oospheres, each of which is retained in one half of the original cell wall. By division of another diatom cell, numerous small flagellated spermatozoids are formed with the haploid number of chromosomes. These swarmers, liberated into the water, effect fertilization of the oospheres, and the resulting zygotes develop into auxospores. Similar flagellated swarmers have been described for other species of centric diatoms. It has been suggested that in certain forms a kind of autogamous sexual reproduction may precede auxospore formation. In *Chaetoceros borealis*, for example, the cell nucleus has been described as undergoing meiotic division to form four nuclei, two of which degenerate. The remaining nuclei fuse to form the zygotic nucleus, and the cell then develops into an auxospore.

In pennate diatoms a type of sexual reproduction by conjugation may occur, and auxospores are thereafter developed. After association of the two cells, meiotic division effects the production of a haploid nucleus in each cell. The two cells then fuse to form the zygote, which afterwards develops into an auxospore. Some pennate species, however, show autogamous reproduction, whereby in one and the same cell, haploid gametic nuclei are produced, which by fusion form a zygote nucleus. For further details concerning the structure and reproduction of diatoms the reader is referred to Fritsch (1948), and to Chadefaud and Emberger (1960).

All diatoms are characterized by the siliceous valves which have pores and striae in patterns typical of the species. Recently, detailed studies have been made with the electron microscope on the submicroscopic structure of the valves (cf. Hendey, 1959). The remarkable complexity of the siliceous structure has been emphasised by these investigations. The electron microscope studies have indicated, however, that species belonging to totally unrelated groups may show similar submicroscopic structure, and also that species of a clearly recognized genus may exhibit widely different microstructure. It is unlikely that any immediate and far reaching revision of the taxonomy of diatoms will be undertaken as a result of these researches, though relatively minor changes such as the separation of varieties may be made.

Whereas most marine planktonic diatoms are non-motile, the next major constituent of the phytoplankton, the dinoflagellates, possess the power of movement. Included in the dinoflagellates are purely holozoic forms (e.g. *Noctiluca*), species which are probably partly holozoic and partly saprophytic, and some which appear to be photosynthetic under certain conditions of nutrition but which can live by absorbing organic substances when photosynthesis is depressed. It is possible that some diatoms may also be capable of heterotrophy (cf. Lewin and Lewin, 1959). We are here, however, restricting our considerations to the truly photosynthetic dinoflagellates. In a typical dinoflagellate cell there are usually numerous chromatophores. These contain a mixture of chlorophylls *a* and *c* as well as several carotenoids including peridinin, but fucoxanthin does not appear to be important (cf. Fogg, 1953). The chromatophores may be brown or even red in colour. All dinoflagellates are characterized by possessing two flagella and therefore they are capable of some degree of movement in the water. In the great majority of marine species one flagellum ("longitudinal") lies partly in a shallow groove ("sulcus") but trails in the water, whereas the second or "transverse" flagellum is situated in a conspicuous transversely running groove ("girdle"), which divides the cell into an anterior epicone and a posterior hypocone (Figs. 5.20, 5.21, 5.22). In a very few species, however (*Exuviella, Prorocentrum*), there is no transverse groove and the two flagella are situated together (Fig. 5.23). The great

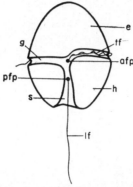

FIG. 5.20 Diagram to show structure of a naked dinoflagellate. e = epicone; h = hypocone; g = girdle; s = sulcus; tf = transverse flagellum; lf = longitudinal flagellum; afp = anterior flagellar pore; pfp = posterior flagellar pore (from Lebour, 1925).

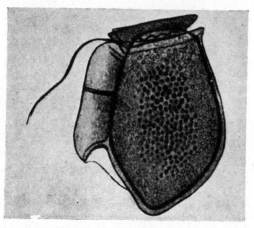

FIG. 5.21 *Dinophysis*—The two flagella are visible, the transverse flagellum is lying in the girdle (after Gran, 1912, in Murray and Hjort).

majority of dinoflagellates which possess the transverse groove are also characterized by the epicone and hypocone being covered by an armour of cellulose plates. There are never fewer than three of these plates and often they are further subdivided. The pattern of the plates

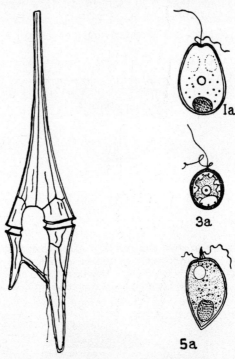

FIG. 5.22 *Ceratium furca* 150 μ long; the girdle and longitudinal flagellum are clearly seen (from Lebour, 1925).

FIG. 5.23 1a—*Exuviella marina* 36 μ long; 3a—*E. perforata* 22 μ long and 5a—*Prorocentrum micans* 37 μ long (from Lebour, 1925).

is typical for the species. The plates are typically sculptured by lines and by pores. Such armoured dinoflagellates are known as thecate forms and they include such common genera as *Ceratium* (Figs. 5.22 and 5.24), *Peridinium* (Fig. 5.25) and *Goniaulax* (Fig. 5.26). A very few species, however, lack the armour of plates and are called naked forms (e.g. *Gymnodinium*) (Fig. 5.27).

The typical method of reproduction for dinoflagellates is by fission (Fig. 5.28); the plane of division is only approximately longitudinal being inclined at an oblique angle. Fission may occur during active movement, at least in some species. There have been various reports of a type of sexual reproduction in some dinoflagellates but further confirmation is needed. The rate of reproduction may be

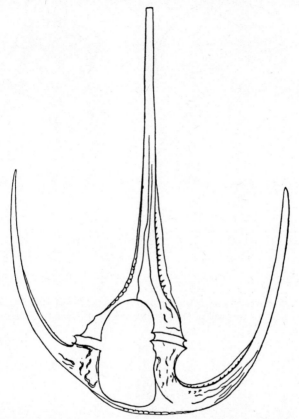

FIG. 5.24 *Ceratium tripos* 270 μ long (from Lebour, 1925).

high and similar factors appear to affect the division rates of dino-flagellates as affect diatoms. The "physiological state" of the cell may again be significant. Some species of dinoflagellates can on occasion surround themselves with a gelatinous coat – presumably this is a type of resting stage. Species of *Goniaulax, Ceratium* and *Peridinium* are among those which are believed to produce resting spores (Smayda, 1958).

Phytoplankton occurs in all seas, but it is often possible to classify species as arctic, antarctic, temperate and tropical (cf. Gran, 1912, Lebour, 1930). Some species again are typical of more coastal con-

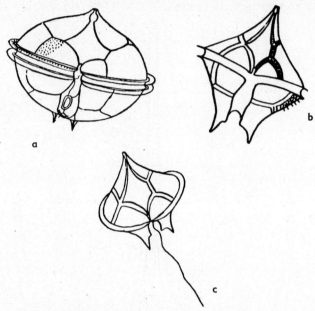

FIG. 5:25 *Peridinium* (a) *P. oratum* 64 μ across (b) *P. divergens* 56 μ across (c) a living cell of the same species (from Lebour, 1925).

FIG. 5.26 *Goniaulax polyedra* 42 μ long. (from Lebour, 1925).

ditions and may be classed as neritic (e.g. *Asterionella*) though often these may occur at some considerable distance offshore. A particular sea area, especially near shore, may show some mixture of oceanic and neritic species drawn from different biogeographical regions. Gran and Braarud (1935) have listed the majority of the phytoplankton species taken in the Gulf of Maine according to their probable biogeographical relationships. Some eurythermal and euryhaline species, however, may show very wide distributions; *Biddulphia sinensis* is a well-known example of a diatom which,

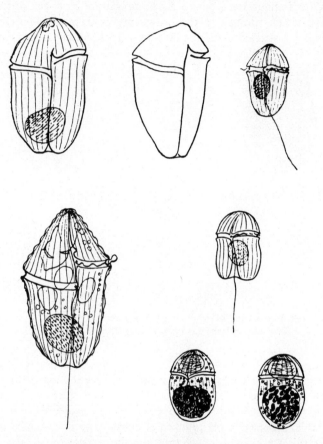

FIG. 5.27 Various species of *Gymnodinium* ranging in length from 39 to 84 μ. In some the longitudinal and transverse flagella are visible but all species are unarmoured (from Lebour, 1925).

typically distributed in Indo-Pacific seas, has colonized the waters of north west Europe, during the last fifty years. Smayda (1958) quotes the diatoms *Thalassionema nitzschioides* and *Skeletonema costatum*, amongst others, and some dinoflagellates (e.g. *Exuviella baltica, Procentrum micans*) as cosmopolitan species with marked eurythermal and euryhaline characteristics. These species are mainly coastal, though they can survive oceanic conditions. By contrast, *Thalassiosira antarctica* is a stenothermal and stenohaline diatom confined to the cold circumpolar antarctic waters, while *Planktoniella sol* is a circumtropical species, which, though it can withstand an appreciable degree of cooling, is restricted in its distribution to high salinity waters. Species

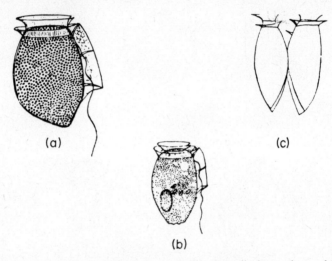

(a)

(b)

(c)

FIG. 5.28 *Dinophysis*, 44–54 μ long. In (b) the cell shows the nucleus and chloroplasts; (c) cell dividing (from Lebour, 1925).

of diatoms and other phytoplankton may thus be characteristic of a particular area of sea, though Smayda criticizes the use of the terms neritic and oceanic for phytoplankton, unless further subdivison into more precise ecological groupings is also made. He points out that while a considerable number of coastal species produce resting spores, this is not true for such typical inshore species as *Skeletonema, Asterionella* and *Thalassionema nitzschioides:* Neritic conditions are also sufficiently diverse to warrant further subdivision.

From the most abundant species of phytoplankton characteristic of an area it is possible to describe phytoplankton communities as relatively permanent associations of plants (cf. Lucas, 1941, 1942). It is even possible to use some species of phytoplankton as indicators of water movement [e.g. *Planktoniella sol*], though in general zooplankton indicators are probably more convenient (cf. Chapter XIII).

For a fairly recent study of the phytoplankton communities of the North Sea the paper by Braarud, Gaarder and Grøntved (1953) should be consulted.

Although both diatoms and dinoflagellates occur in all seas it is undoubtedly true that at high latitudes especially in polar regions, the diatoms are overwhelmingly important (cf. Gran, 1929a, Kreps et al., 1930; Hart, 1934 and 1942; Bigelow, 1926). Here they may contribute to a diatom ooze on the ocean floor. It is significant that in the Southern Ocean the northern limit of the diatom ooze deposit almost parallels the Antarctic Convergence. By contrast, in more tropical waters the number of diatoms tends to decrease and dinoflagellates become a much more important constituent of the phytoplankton (cf. Lohmann, 1911). Marshall (1933) suggests in open oceanic waters the diatoms may decline from > 60% of the phytoplankton in temperate areas to < 5% in the tropics, and the dinoflagellates and coccolithophores (*vide infra*) on the other hand may make up as much as 50% of the tropical phytoplankton. On the Great Barrier Reef, however, diatoms were usually dominant over most of the year. Riley (1957) has also shown in the North Sargasso that diatoms are still an important constituent of the phytoplankton.

In the tropics certain blue-green algae, especially *Trichodesmium*, may become very important, but Cyanophyceae are rather rare outside the tropics; some are recorded in inshore areas such as the oyster polls of Norwegian fjords, and Steemann Nielsen (1940) found a few in Baltic waters. Other algae which contribute to the phytoplankton include the coccolithophores which are very small plant cells, about 5–40 μ in diameter, protected by tiny plates of calcium carbonate (Fig. 5. 29). They are biflagellate forms and may become very common in tropical seas though their actual bulk may be small. A few species may also be very common in colder waters, e.g. *Pontosphaera huxleyi* and *Syracosphaera* spp. (cf. Gran, 1929a; Steemann Nielsen, 1935; Braarud, Gaarder and Grøntved, 1953; Lillick, 1940). Silico-flagellates (Fig. 5.30) are small flagellate forms which have siliceous shells, and occur more in colder seas, though they usually do not contribute greatly in mass as compared with other phytoplankton (cf. Lillick, 1940; Conover, 1956). In some waters, especially in more neritic areas, *Phaeocystis* may occur in vast numbers. This is a brown coloured flagellated plant cell which forms large gelatinous colonies even large enough to become visible to the naked eye (Fig. 5.31). *Phaeocystis* may become so plentiful on occasions

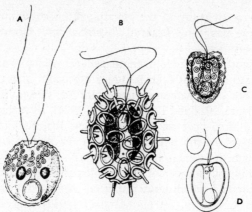

FIG. 5.29 Coccolithophores. A = *Syracosphaera carterae* (only some of calcareous plates are shown); B = *S. subsalsa*; C, D = *Hymenomonas roseola* (from Grassé, 1952).

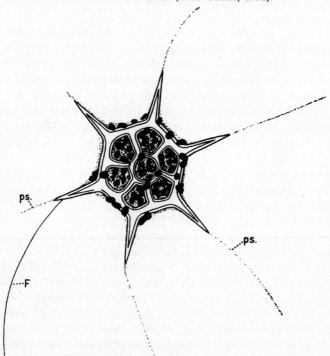

FIG. 5.30 A silicoflagellate, *Distephanus speculum*, F = flagellum; ps = pseudopodia (from Marshall, 1934).

as to clog collecting nets. Kornmann (1955) has shown that the colonial stage may be regarded as a palmelloid phase in the life history. If the vegetative cells are separated from the colony, they are rapidly transformed into "swarmer" cells; these have two flagella and a shorter non-motile one. After coming to rest, these swarmers produce new colonies by cell division. In ageing cultures Kornmann also observed the formation of microzoospores. These are smaller than the "swarmer" cells but also have two flagella and a short supplementary flagellum. These microzoospores can reproduce by

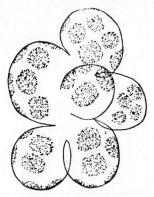

FIG. 5.31 *Phaeocystis* (from Gran, 1912, in Murray and Hjort).

fission and may continue free swimming, but they can settle and give rise to new colonies. The life cycle includes therefore a palmelloid colonial phase and a motile phase, and both can reproduce vegetatively. Kornmann suggests that *Phaeocystis* represents a particular family of the group Chrysophyceae. *Halosphaera* is another phytoplankton species which can become extremely common on occasions. It is very widely distributed, occurring in temperate and warmer seas, and also at times being very abundant in the Antarctic. It is a uni-cellular green alga reproducing by zoospores.

Many diatoms and dinoflagellates are of extremely small size; some are less than 10 μ. These small species with the coccolithophores and silicoflagellates, which have already been mentioned, and various naked, green flagellate or non-motile cells of very small size have been termed collectively the nannoplankton. Some workers include bacteria and even very small Protozoa, but it is preferable to restrict the term nannoplankton to truly photosynthetic plant organisms. The nannoplankton might be defined as those minute plant cells which are not normally retained by the finest silk plankton nets. This is obviously a very poor and incomplete definition. The finest silk nets (200 meshes to the inch) will vary in porosity; Harvey (1950) quotes the aperture size for a wet net as approximating to $40\,\mu$ by $50\,\mu$; Sverdrup *et al.* (1946) give the aperture size of the finest nets as approximately $60\,\mu$. But apart from variations in mesh size due to type of manufacture, to degree of wetting and to strain, the nets will clog to varying degrees, depending on the waters in which they are used so that very minute organisms can be retained to some extent. Nevertheless a very large number of species and individuals of minute photosynthetic organisms normally pass through the finest nets.

Lohmann first discovered the nannoplankton algae on the "houses" of appendicularians. During the past twenty years there has been a considerable increase in our knowledge of the commoner species. But the quantitative estimation of nannoplankton is still extremely difficult. Some investigators have used the centrifuge but it appears that not all species are brought down quantitatively by normal centrifuging. Some workers have suggested employing a haemocytometer for direct counts of unconcentrated seawater samples, but this may give misleading results if nannoplankton organisms are few. One of the commonest methods today is to filter seawater samples through membrane or similar special filters of very fine and standard porosity. Attempts have been made to count the nannoplankton organisms retained on the filter, but the most usual method is to extract the chlorophyll from the algal cells and thus to estimate the nannoplankton as chlorophyll (Richards and Thompson, 1952). Even then the selection of the porosity of the filter is a difficulty in the method, as it is necessary to choose a filter which is not so fine that the filtration rate is unnecessarily low. There is the further difficulty of distinguishing between chlorophyll-containing, minute organisms on the filter mat, which may be regarded as autotrophic, and excessively small particulate matter which may yield pigment on extraction (cf. Krey, 1958 a).

The nannoplankton organisms vary greatly in size; many of them are of the order of $5\,\mu$ in diameter or less, but they may exceed a diameter of $20\,\mu$. They belong to a variety of plant groups, Chrysophyceae, Chlorophyceae and Cryptophyceae, and appear green, brown, red or golden in colour. In the two former groups the pig-

mentation is due to the mixture of carotenoids with chlorophyll
which occurs in the chromatophores. (Figs. 5.32, 5.33 and 5.34.) In
the Cryptophyceae phycobilins are present masking the chlorophyll.
Early studies on these organisms were made by Gross (1937)
but investigations of the detailed structure of different nannoplankton
species, including electron microscopic studies, are especially due

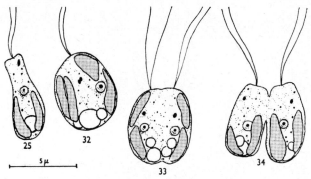

FIG. 5.32 *Isochrysis galbana*, 25 = Young motile stage; 32–34 = stages in
fission (from Parke, 1949).

to Parke (1949) and to Parke, Manton and Clarke (e.g. 1955, 1956,
1959). Now that unialgal cultures have been maintained for some
nannoplankton organisms it is possible to investigate some of the
problems connected with their growth and reproduction. We know
that the rate of reproduction of some nannoplankton species may be
very high. Parke (1949), for example, states that one flagellate can
undergo fission more frequently than once every 5 hr under optimal
conditions. Although binary fission is the usual method of reproduction for nannoplankton, we require details of the life histories
of different species. An illustration of the complexity of the problem
may be drawn from the coccolithophores which may apparently
include motile and non-motile species. Bernard (1948) suggested
that *Coccolithus fragilis* might form spores and could pass into a
type of encysted stage. He also drew attention to the existence of
two forms of the species. Parke and Adams (1960) recently
investigated a species known as *Crystallolithus hyalinus*. This is a
motile biflagellate coccolithophore, 8–18 μ in diameter, which reproduces by binary fission, but can pass into a non-motile stage when
the cell increases in size. This stage is apparently identical with the
non-motile coccolithophore, *Coccolithus pelagicus*, a cell some 25

to 40 μ in diameter. Reproduction of this cell involves the formation of four daughter cells which can then develop into the motile stage (*Crystallolithus hyalinus*).

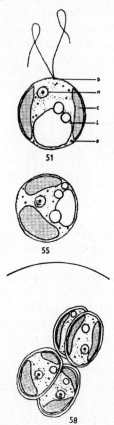

FIG. 5.33 *Dicrateria inornata*, 51 = Motile cell *ca.* 5 μ diameter; 55 and 58 = stages in reproduction in palmelloid phase; b = basal granule; c = chromatophore; l = leucosin; n = nucleus; o = oil globule (from Parke, 1949).

The high rate of reproduction of most nannoplankton permits the establishment of dense cultures in a comparatively short time. In the sea their actual numbers may be very high at times, even outweighing the more obvious diatoms and dino-flagellates normally retained on silk nets. Harvey (1950) has used various filters to estimate the total crop of phytoplankton, and he has shown that at times estimates of phytoplankton density as derived from net hauls may be entirely misleading. This has also been stressed by Steemann

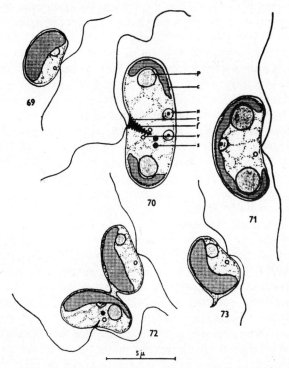

FIG. 5.34 *Hemiselmis rufescens*, 69 = Young motile cell; 71 = older motile individual; 70, 72 = stages in fission; 73 = daughter-cell just after fission; c = chromatophore; f = furrow; p = pyrenoid; s = stigma; t = trichocysts; v = contractile vacuole
(from Parke, 1949).

Nielsen (1958). The nannoplankton organisms are perhaps more abundant and of greater importance in inshore waters (cf. Gross *et al.*, 1947, 1950). At Laboe, Lohmann (1908, 1911) found that although diatoms (chiefly *Skeletonema* and *Chaetoceros*) dominated the phytoplankton by volume over most of the year, nannoplankton could become important numerically at certain times. *Exuviella* and *Prorocentrum* were common; both chrysomonads and crypto-monads assumed greater importance over winter; *Rhodomonas* was abundant all through the year. Coccolithophores were present in significant numbers at Laboe only in August. In warm seas such as the Mediterranean, however, coccolithophores contributed to a much greater extent to the phytoplankton. Lohmann suggested a rich stratum from 20–80 m depth. In the equatorial Pacific Hasle (1959) has shown that coccolithophores were more abundant than diatoms or dino-flagellates. (Naked nannoplankton species were not included in this investigation.) The main zone of phytoplankton abundance was limited to the upper 50 or 100 m and the number of photosynthetic cells below 150 m was unimportant. Bernard (1953) has also recently stressed the importance of the coccolithophores in warmer seas. He suggests, however, that reduced populations may be found even at considerable depths. Some of the cells are un-doubtedly spore stages, probably in process of sinking from the photosynthetic zone above. But flagellated cells are also present and these must presumably live heterotrophically. Nannoplankton organisms generally appear to occur frequently in relatively high numbers in tropical and sub-tropical seas; Riley (1957) for example, has demonstrated that the nannoplankton is the most important constituent of the phytoplankton in the North Sargasso Sea area. Bsharah (1957) emphasizes its importance in waters of the Florida Current. Bernard (1953), however, has indicated that coccolithophores, which may form such an important part of the nannoplankton, may show a comparatively low reproductive rate when compared with typical boreal diatoms. He suggests that in warm-temperate seas coccolithophores divide approximately once in six days; but periods of rest intervene which may reduce the division rate still further. Bernard's data indicate that densities of the order of 3000 coccolithophores per c.c. may occasionally be experienced, but usually the densities amount to some hundreds of cells per c.c. Bain-bridge (1957) has summarized our recent knowledge of phytoplankton concentrations. For diatoms, excessively rich concentrations have occasionally been found; 5.6 cell/mm^3 (i.e. 5600 cells/c.c.) were noted in Deception Island harbour, and isolated instances of even higher densities (25–40 cells/mm^3) have been recorded. Even in the exceedingly rich open waters of the Antarctic, however, maximum diatom concentrations did not exceed 1 cell/mm^3. On the other hand, for nannoplankton flagellates, omitting such remarkable densities as 2400/mm^3 for unfertilized waters of Loch Sween, numbers may reach 50 cells/mm^3 in red tide outbreaks. Bainbridge suggests, however, that maximal densities for phytoplankton are more usually of the order of 0.5 cells/mm³ for diatoms, and 2.5 cells/mm³ for flagellates. Where concentrated patches occur, approximately twenty times these densities of both diatoms and nannoplankton may be experienced. Our knowledge of the density of nannoplankton in different seas is, however, extremely limited. The discovery of nannoplankton is comparatively recent and few quantitative investigations have been attempted. Steemann Nielsen (1935) noted considerable numbers of flagellates in the seas round Iceland and the Faroes. He also showed (1951) that relatively large numbers of flagellates may occur in the phytoplankton of Baltic waters. Lillick (1938, 1940) mentions occasional large numbers of flagellates of small size in waters off the north-east coast of the United States (cf. also Braarud, Gaarder and Grøntved, 1953, for the North Sea).

Yentsch and Ryther (1959) have compared the quantities of net phytoplankton and nannoplankton for the waters of Vineyard Sound, near Woods Hole. Estimates of chlorophyll and of cell densities revealed a much larger amount as nannoplankton; the average net plankton over the period of investigation was only 8% of the total chlorophyll and 9% of the total cell density (Fig. 5.34.1). The cell count for nannoplankton revealed no obvious seasonal trend, although the net phytoplankton was clearly most abundant in March, April and May. Flagellates formed only a very small fraction of this nannoplankton, however; the bulk consisted mainly of small diatoms. Yentsch and Ryther believe that in open seas, where the smaller phytoplankton becomes of importance, the major part is made up of small diatoms rather than micro-flagellates.

Although our knowledge of the density of nannoplankton organisms is slight, there is no doubt that in bulk the nannoplankton is greatly outweighed by diatoms, especially in temperate and high latitudes. The nannoplankton may nevertheless be of very great importance in providing basic food material, especially in tropical areas. It provides a food supply of very small sized particles, which may be all important in the nutrition of small larvae such as veligers.

Flotation in phytoplankton

Several observers, such as Moore and Hart, who have examined bottom deposits suggest that the great majority of the siliceous skeletons of diatoms on the bottom are broken, and appear to have been eaten during their descent to the bottom. On the other hand some phytoplankton cells sink and pass out of the optimum lighted zone. Although normally most phytoplankton cells are eaten and relatively few descend uneaten to the bottom deposit, there are a few records of a diatom maximum being encountered at considerable

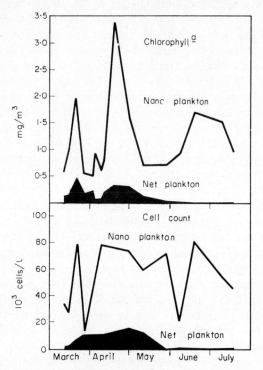

FIG. 5.34.1 Comparison of nanoplankton and net plankton (from Yentsch and Ryther, 1959).

depths, where obviously the cells could not be photosynthesizing; such a population was probably in process of sinking.

Since protoplasm is usually slightly denser than water, and since diatoms have heavy frustules composed partly of silica, the cells would appear to have a higher specific gravity than the water. Many workers, such as Apstein, have therefore regarded diatoms as a surface drifting population which is nevertheless sinking very very slowly into deeper water. Among other factors, the rate of sinking would be dependent on the ratio: surplus weight/friction. Any increased frictional resistance which diatoms and other plankton cells can maintain against the water would presumably slow down the sinking rate. A large surface to volume ratio will be of value in this connexion and undoubtedly the generally very small size of phytoplankton organisms is in part an adaptation to the floating existence. Reduction of specific gravity is useful and generally, for example, pelagic diatoms have thinner cell walls than typical bottom species.

Adaptations to flotation would certainly appear to be significant. Gran in Murray and Hjort (1912) has followed suggestions made by

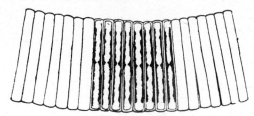

FIG. 5.35 *Fragilaria* 55 μ broad (from Lebour, 1930).

other workers in grouping diatoms into various types according to their methods of flotation. The "bladder type" is characterized by having a fairly large cell but the cell wall is a relatively very thin membrane surrounding a large inner vacuole, thus reducing the specific gravity. An example is *Coscinodiscus*; related species, *Eth-modiscus rex* and *E. gazellae*, though relatively large, can occur in warmer waters of the Pacific, and *E. gazellae*, in the Atlantic Ocean (cf. Wiseman and Hendey, 1953; McHugh, 1954). In the "ribbon type", the cell is flattened along one plane so as to enlarge the surface, as well as being sometimes twisted. The cells may be associated in ribbon-shaped colonies e.g. *Fragilaria* (Fig. 5.35) and *Eucampia zoodiacus* (Fig. 5.36). The cell walls of these species are again very thin. In the "hair type" the cell is greatly elongated along one axis to give a typically hair-shaped cell, e.g. *Rhizosolenia*. When a cell such as *Rhizosolenia* is suspended horizontally in the water, there is a great deal of friction and the sinking rate is reduced. The cell would however sink comparatively rapidly if it happened to be in a perpendicular position. But apparently when sinking in such a position, it tends to be brought back approximately to the horizontal position during the movement, owing to a slight twist along the axis of the cell. The diatom would in fact sink in the water in a long spiral path. The "branching type" of cell is drawn out into hairs and spines; usually such cells are associated in long chains. There are numerous examples, of which *Chaetoceros* and *Bacteriastrum* are most characteristic. Other species of diatoms may exhibit more complicated

FIG. 5.36 *Eucampia zoodiacus* 25 μ across (from Lebour, 1930).

patterns in the way in which the individual cells associate to form colonies (e.g. *Asterionella*). Adaptations to flotation are not confined to the shape of the cell. Since oils have low specific gravities, the production of oils or fatty acids by diatoms as the end product of metabolism may be useful in assisting flotation. A very few pelagic diatoms also display very limited powers of independent movement (e.g. *Bacillaria paradoxa*) though the way by which the movement is achieved is not quite clear.

Since both salinity and temperature affect the specific gravity of seawater these two factors will presumably play a part in the sinking rates of the phytoplankton. The viscosity of sea water will also have a very strong effect, and viscosity decreases markedly with increasing temperature. It might be expected, therefore, that the colder seas would have phytoplankton populations with possibly fewer marked adaptations to resist sinking than those of warmer waters. In fact the

development of special types of cells and hairs and spines is frequently
observed in diatoms from both warm and cold oceans. Nevertheless,
to some extent a few species of diatoms can adapt their floating abilities to the demands made on them. Where there is a marked difference between summer and winter temperatures, there may sometimes appear different forms of the same diatom species which are
adapted to the difference in viscosity of the water. So-called summer

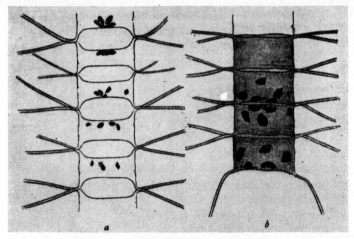

FIG. 5.37 *Chaetoceros decipiens* (a) summer (b) winter varieties (from
Gran, 1912, in Murray and Hjort).

varieties are frequently thinner shelled, and may have a more slender
structure. Gran quotes as an example *Chaetoceros decipiens* which
occurs in the northern Atlantic. In summer the cells of this species,
which are combined into a chain, have four long setae each, and the
end faces of the cells have relatively large-sized openings between
them. In winter and spring, on the other hand, when the water is
colder, this same species has cells with thicker cell walls and stouter
setae, and the interstices between the cells are much smaller (Fig. 5.37).
Another well-known example found in several seas is *Rhizosolenia
hebetata* (Fig. 5.13). At one time two species were considered to
exist, *R. hebetata* and *R. semispina*. *R. semispina* has thinner walls,
is much longer, and has a hair-like point at the end of the cell. The
heavier, thicker-walled *Rhizosolenia hebetata* is typically cold water
in distribution, but it now appears that the two are varieties of one
and the same species. There appears to be no rule for diatoms how-

ever that the larger species occur in colder waters. Species of the large diatom *Ethmodiscus* are present in warm tropical seas, and Wimpenny (1936a) has noted many genera in which the smallest species occur in cold areas. For *Rhizosolenia styliformis* in fact, Wimpenny suggested a direct correlation between cell diameter and water temperature.

Dinoflagellates being furnished with flagella, can to some extent maintain themselves by their own movements in the lighted upper layers

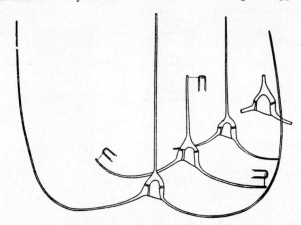

FIG. 5.38 *Ceratium trichoceros* showing adaptation in length of horns
(from Gran, 1912, in Murray and Hjort).

of the sea. Nevertheless, there are adaptations rather similar to those of diatoms which suggest that flotation is still a problem. Species such as *Ceratium* are furnished with three long horns which presumably increase frictional resistance in the same way as the spines and setae of diatoms. *Ceratium trichoceros* can apparently regulate the length of the horns in relation to the temperature, and thus the viscosity and specific gravity of the water in which the population is living (Fig. 5.38). The thickness of the cellulose plates also seems to vary with the temperature of the water. *Ceratium platycorne* shows differences in the shape of its horns, the much flatter form being typical of the variety living in warmer sub-tropical waters and the less flattened horns being characteristic of the form found in colder seas (Fig. 5.39). Other dinoflagellate species may have different projections of the body, presumably again as adaptations to the floating life. For example, the membranes of *Dinophysis*, the parachute-like extensions of *Ornithocercus* (Fig. 5.40), the bladder-like shape of *Pyrocystis* and perhaps the slimy, bladder-like colonies of *Phaeocystis* are probably adaptations to the planktonic habit.

More recent work has suggested that although such adaptations in diatoms and dinoflagellates are probably of significance in slowing the sinking of phytoplankton cells, it is likely that at least some

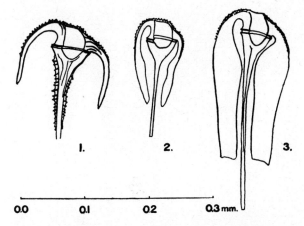

FIG. 5.39 *Ceratium platycorne*—variation in the degree of flattening of horns (from Gran, 1912, in Murray and Hjort).

phytoplankton species are not truly sinking provided that they are in healthy physiological condition. It is common experience in actively growing uni-algal cultures of phytoplankton that the cells remain suspended. Any factor, however, which interferes with the healthy physiological condition of the cells causes them to sink, often extremely rapidly, although they are still alive. This type of behaviour may be associated with the senescence which Riley has described in phytoplankton. In examining this sinking, Gross (1940) found a peculiar osmotic relationship in the large diatom cell *Ditylum*. He suggested that *Ditylum* cells are truly floating and when healthy they are permanently suspended, but any interference with the normal physiological state causes osmotic unbalance and therefore sinking. In more recent work Gross and Zeuthen (1948) have shown that in *Ditylum* and probably in other diatoms, the buoyancy is due to a low concentration of the bivalent ions in the cell sap (sulphate, calcium and magnesium), though as a whole the sap is isotonic with seawater. This must be an active ionic regulation. How far this is true of phytoplankton generally is unknown, but it is likely that some species of phytoplankton may have real buoyancy to some extent, and that some of the adaptations which we have already discussed, though significant, may be of secondary importance in planktonic life.

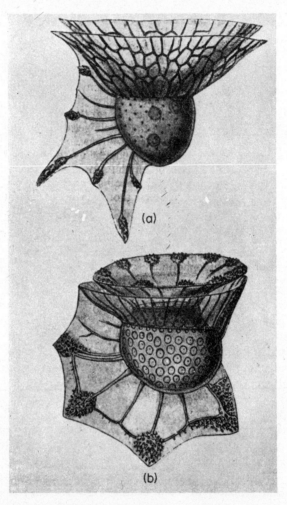

FIG. 5.40 *Ornithocercus* (a) *O. splendidus* (b) *O. steinii*. Note the parachute-like extensions (from Gran, 1912, in Murray and Hjort).

CHAPTER VI

PRODUCTION—PLANT PLANKTON AND SEAWEEDS

THE OUTSTANDING importance of the phytoplankton organisms, whatever the species, is that this population represents the first link in the primary food chain from inorganic to organic substances, i.e. these are the real or primary producers in the sea. The relatively high rate of reproduction for diatoms, dinoflagellates and for other phytoplankton cells of diverse kinds means that relatively high populations of vegetative cells can be built up in a short time. As many workers, notably Clarke (1939, 1946) have pointed out, it is the rate of production of organic (plant) material rather than the numerical crop of plant cells present in any area at a given time which determines ultimately the real productivity of the area. Nevertheless, by and large the areas which show the larger standing crops of phytoplankton also tend to have high productivity. We therefore look to the large and rapidly increasing phytoplankton populations, since to them the primary production in the seas is due.

The chemical composition of phytoplankton is highly suitable as a basic food supply. Ketchum and Redfield (1949), analysing six different species of unicellular algae, showed that the organic dry weight is composed of some 40–55% of protein, some 20–40% of carbohydrate, and some 20–25% of lipid. The amount of protein and of lipid is high as compared with land plants. These analyses were carried out mostly on freshwater species, but they included the marine diatom *Nitzschia* which gave similar proportions of protein, lipid and carbohydrate.

There have been few analyses made on natural phytoplankton populations. The difficulty is that in all these there must be some mixture of zooplankton and detritus; thus Moberg (1926) showed that the proportion of protein in his analyses varied considerably as between inshore and offshore hauls. Even so, the proportion of protein to total organic matter would appear to be high. Moberg's figures

129

suggest a range of from 25% for hauls nearest the shore, to more than 60% for offshore plankton. Brandt (1898) analysed some plankton hauls in which diatoms and peridinians predominated, and in general his figures suggest a rather lower content, the average for diatoms being about 30%. There is little doubt, however, from the few analyses of natural phytoplankton populations which have been carried out, that the results suggest a much higher protein content than for land plants, and that usually quite an appreciable proportion of fatty material is present.

It has also been shown, largely on freshwater species (cf. Burlew, 1953; Fogg, 1953) that the conditions under which a species grows may modify considerably its chemical composition. This is almost certainly true for marine forms also; Barker (1935a), for example, suggests that any factor retarding cell division in diatoms (e.g. nitrogen deficiency) may cause an increase in the cell fat content. Low light intensity probably has a similar effect.

It may seem surprising that while the role of the phytoplankton, the individual cells of which are of such very small size, has been emphasized so far, the part played by much larger seaweeds has been neglected. It is true that around many rocky coasts, particularly in the intertidal areas in temperate latitudes such as our own, extensive growths of seaweed occur. The big seaweeds, especially the laminarias, also continue to grow below low tide level. Submarine surveys such as those of Walker (1947, 1954) and Walker and Richardson (1957) show that extensive forests of such species as *Laminaria hyperborea* (= *cloustoni*) and *L. saccharina* extend to many metres (exceeding 15 m) below extreme low water. Even more remarkable in size are the giant kelps which are found on the west coast of North America. Such seaweeds are, of course, confined to rocky shores, but on the more muddy sandy areas occur a few flowering plants, especially *Zostera* and *Ruppia*. Nor must bottom living diatoms be forgotten in that as photosynthetic organisms they will make a considerable contribution to production (cf. Mare, 1942; Aleem, 1950).

All plant organisms, however, whatever their kind, must be limited to the lighted zone for effective production, and, as we have seen in an earlier chapter, radiation of all kinds, including visible radiation, is relatively rapidly absorbed in seawater. It is very difficult to quote average figures for light penetration for different regions of the world. But in temperate regions in the open seas, effective light penetration (i.e. light of sufficient intensity for photo-synthesis) probably does not go much below 50 m in summer, and with the greater obliquity of the rays, is probably limited to 10–15 m in winter. An added difficulty is that as one approaches the shore the greater turbidity and the increased amount of detritus present in coastal waters may cut down penetration of light to a much greater

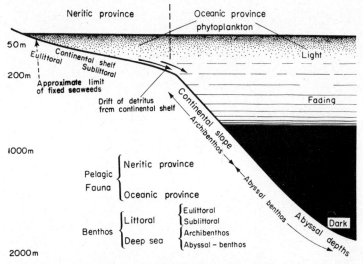

FIG. 6.1 Diagrammatic representation of an ocean showing the major divisions of the marine environment.

degree (cf. Chapter VIII). It is not surprising then that fixed plants are limited in depth in the open sea. Approximate figures are about 20 m for the Baltic, which, being a relatively enclosed area, has considerably greater turbidity. On the other hand, off Iceland the limit may approach 50 m, and in the clear waters of the Mediterranean fixed algae can be taken in depths well exceeding 100 m. If, for temperate seas, we take 30 m as a rough average for the depth limit of fixed algae, it is abundantly clear that the area capable of pro-ducing seaweeds is going to be absurdly small as compared with the vast depths of the oceans (Fig. 6.1).

In extensive shallow areas, particularly in the Danish fjords, growth of bottom algae will make an important contribution to production. Petersen (1918), for example, considered the role of phytoplankton to be small in the Danish fjords, and he attempted to draw up a scheme of production based on *Zostera*, which was the most abundant plant organism in those relatively shallow areas (Fig. 6.2). The importance of *Zostera* in such shallow seas is undoubtedly real, though more recent work has suggested that Petersen perhaps under-estimated the part contributed by the phytoplankton. Steemann Nielsen (1951) in an investigation of the Isefjord showed that bottom

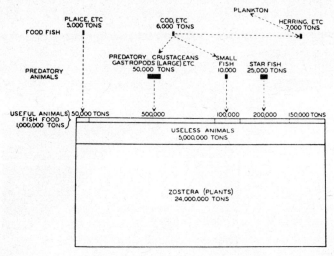

FIG. 6.2 Food chains dependent on *Zostera* as the primary producer (from Petersen, 1918).

algae, both macro- and micro-species, and phytoplankton, all play their parts in production. Marshall and Orr (1948) have shown that in a very shallow marine pond *Zostera* and other fixed weeds may compete with the phytoplankton for available nutrients. In a very different type of environment Kohn and Helfrich (1957) have shown that in coral reefs off Hawaii the very high rate of production is probably mainly to be attributed to the benthic algae which are richly distributed over the reef. Very high rates of primary production have been found by Odum (1957) over very shallow tidal beds due to the marine grass *Thallassia*.

Mare (1942) demonstrated that bottom living diatoms and other photosynthetic organisms can contribute significantly to the organic production of shallow waters, and Smyth (1955) has investigated the abundance of some bottom diatoms off the west coast of Scotland. There is some suggestion that bottom diatoms may have rather lower light requirements than the ordinary pelagic diatom species. Grøntved (1956), working in the Baltic, claims that the micro-vegetation of the benthos is probably the more important, but the considerable crop of such macro-vegetation as *Zostera* and *Ruppia* is demonstrated by his later investigations (Grøntved, 1958). In shallower areas, especially inter-tidal zones, diatoms may occur on mud (Aleem, 1950), on rock surfaces, or on the thalli of seaweeds. Aleem showed that those on the mud surfaces occurred all through the year though they were less abundant in winter. Bottom diatoms may thus contribute to the organic production. Nevertheless, it is abundantly clear that although some of these bottom forms may be able to photosynthesize at rather lower light intensities than pelagic species, all these plant producers must be limited to a very narrow strip of coast of very small depth. According to Aleem the reduction in light intensity produced by heavy cloud, or by the stirring of the mud at high tide, caused the littoral diatoms to disappear from the surface. This accentuates the great reduction of light close inshore, and reduces the level of effective plant growth. Over the vast oceans of the world it is the phytoplankton alone which is effective as a primary producer. Shallow coastal zones will of course be much richer in general in primary productivity, owing to the contribution by fixed seaweeds and bottom micro-vegetation as well as by the pelagic phytoplankton. In offshore regions the detritus resulting from the total activity of all these plant organisms will also contribute to the food of organisms. But even in offshore neritic areas the production usually attributable to fixed seaweeds makes only a very minor contribution as compared with the production by phytoplankton (Fig. 6.1).

Even with phytoplankton, light of course will be a limiting factor. But the zone which can support plant life extends now right across the whole vast areas of the oceans (Fig. 6.1). The depth of this photosynthetic or euphotic zone will vary with latitude, season, degree of turbidity, etc. Thus the photosynthetic zone in tropical areas, with clear water, and with the light rays approaching the vertical over a considerable part of the day, may extend well over 100 m in depth, whereas in temperate regions the depth may be considerably less than 50 m in summer, and may be a few metres only in winter. The closer and closer the shore is approached, the shallower becomes the productive layer, owing to the turbidity, until in really turbid harbour areas only a matter of a metre or two of the topmost water can be productive.

Clearly production will vary very greatly between summer and winter in the higher latitudes, until the extreme condition is reached in the Antarctic and Arctic zones where high production in the continuous light of the summer will alternate with zero primary production during the long continuous dark of winter. In tropical areas, by contrast, the production will continue throughout the year at a more or less steady level.

However thick the photosynthetic layer may be, it is obvious that phytoplankton cells can be carried or can passively sink to greater depths where the light will fade to such an extent that they will not be able to grow nor reproduce. Thus arises the concept of the compensation depth, i.e. that depth at which the rate of photosynthesis equals the rate of respiration. Below the compensation depth, plants lose more by respiration than they gain by their photosynthetic activity, and therefore, no production can be evident.

One of the chief methods for estimating the primary productivity by phytoplankton, by which is meant the amount of carbon "fixed" per m^2 or per m^3 in a unit of time is by means of the measurement of the oxygen produced during the photosynthetic process. This is a method successfully used by Gaarder and Gran (1927), but since that time it has been taken up by many workers (e.g. Marshall and Orr, Clarke, Steemann Nielsen, Riley) and it is still being used very successfully. A brief discussion of other methods of estimating primary productivity and of the difference between production and standing crop is included in Chapter X.

In the oxygen bottle type of experiment as it may be termed, sealed bottles containing phytoplankton populations are lowered to varying depths in the sea, the oxygen content of the water in the bottles being first determined. The phytoplankton is then allowed to photosynthesize in the bottles for a known period of time, and the oxygen content of each bottle then redetermined. In the upper few metres of the lighted zone there will be a distinct increase in oxygen owing to photosynthetic activity. At a certain depth, however, there will be no change; that is, the oxygen produced by photosynthesis exactly balances the amount absorbed by respiration (Table 6.1). This therefore represents the compensation depth, and the light intensity at this depth is the compensation intensity. It should be noted that this does not represent the lowest depth at which any photosynthesis can occur, i.e. plants can photosynthesize to some extent below the compensation depth, but there will not be effective production below that limit.

Oster and Clarke (1935) showed that in the Gulf of Maine during
the summer the compensation depth lay at about 25–30 m, but some
degree of photosynthesis could go on as deep as 40 m. Even at the
compensation depth the intensity of the light is too low for any
increase in the crop of plant cells; the phytoplankton only maintains
itself at that depth. Experiments on oxygen production can also
give estimates of rates of primary productivity by phytoplankton.
A series of duplicate bottles similar to those used in compensation
depth experiments is prepared, but these "dark" bottles are first
covered with black material, and they are then placed at the same
depths as the normal "light" bottles. The change in the amount
of oxygen is determined in these "dark" bottles also, the amount
of oxygen consumed being due to the respiration of the plant cells
as well as to bacteria. This amount due to respiration can then be
added to the changed oxygen value in the "light" bottles to give the
gross primary production. Errors can arise particularly if oxygen
bubbles form in near-surface bottles, and also if zooplankton is included in the plankton or if bacteria multiply excessively. Thus
the use of extended oxygen bottle experiments, particularly with
very low rates of primary productivity, has been criticized, especially
by Steemann Nielsen (1952, 1954). It is generally agreed, however,
that the oxygen-bottle technique is extremely useful in more inshore
waters with higher rates of production (cf. Ryther and Vaccaro, 1954),
and that good agreement can be obtained between this and other
methods.

Some of the earlier compensation depth determinations using
oxygen bottles were carried out with natural mixed phytoplankton
populations. But species may differ in their light requirements.
Gaarder and Gran (1927) obtained a compensation depth for experiments in March for a mixed phytoplankton, in which the diatoms
Lauderia, *Thalassiosira gravida* and *T. nordenskioldii* were dominant,
of about 10 m. The rapid multiplication of *Lauderia* and of *T. gravida*
was chiefly in the upper 2 m extending down to more than 5 m.
T. gravida possibly showed the best growth right at the surface. On
the other hand, *T. nordenskioldii* showed the best growth at 2 and 5 m,
and even at 10 m depth, cell multiplication was higher than at the
surface (Table 6.1). This suggests that *T. nordenskioldii* has a lower
light optimum than *T. gravida* and *Lauderia*, and this would agree
with Conover's observation (Conover, 1956) that *T. nordenskioldii*
is a winter-spring diatom which tends to be succeeded in late spring

by *T. gravida*. Later work attempting to determine the compensation intensity for a particular species was possible when uni-algal cultures of diatoms or flagellates were employed. Marshall and Orr (1928, 1930) worked on the single species of diatom *Coscinosira polychorda*. They found the compensation point to lie at about 20–30 m in

TABLE 6.1.

Culture experiment 22–25 March, 1916. Average increase in 24 hr (from Gaarder and Gran, 1927)

Depth, m	Oxygen, c.c./l.	% Increase in Cell Numbers		
		Lauderia glacialis	*Thalassiosira gravida*	*Thalassiosira nordenskioldii*
0	+ 0.20	77	59	10
2	+ 0.19	79	58	73
5	+ 0.13	70	55	67
10	0	28	34	23
20	− 0.03	0	0	0
30	− 0.05	0	0	0
40	− 0.07	0	0	0

summer, whereas it was much higher in winter with the reduced light intensity. They obtained similar results for a species of *Chaetoceros*, but during summer in bright sunlight optimum growth occurred a little beneath the surface i.e. growth right at the surface was inhibited at the highest light intensities. Jenkin (1937), working in the English Channel on the diatom *Coscinodiscus excentricus*, obtained a compensation depth at about 45 m; she also showed that the optimum occurred somewhat below the surface, and there was some inhibition in bright sunshine right at the surface (Fig. 6.3). Jenkin was able to estimate production in *Coscinodiscus* and relate this to the light energy values. She found that the compensation point was equivalent to about 0.55 joules/cm²/hr (approximately 0.13 gm cal/cm²/hr). Between this value and an energy flux of approximately 7.5 joules/cm² per hr the oxygen production, which is a measure of the photosynthetic activity, increased practically linearly with the light energy. Above this value of 7.5 joules/cm²/hr, oxygen production continued to rise with increased light, but at a somewhat reduced rate, indicating that some inhibition was operating (cf. Fig. 6.4). Maximal photosynthesis was observed when the light energy approximated to

30 joules/cm²/hr, but Jenkin states that the results at these higher intensities were less consistent. At much higher energy fluxes exceeding 40 joules/cm²/hr, re-arrangement of the chloroplasts (systrophe) frequently occurred. Using unialgal cultures of another species of diatom (*Chaetoceros affinis*), Talling (1960) has obtained

August 9–10th 1934

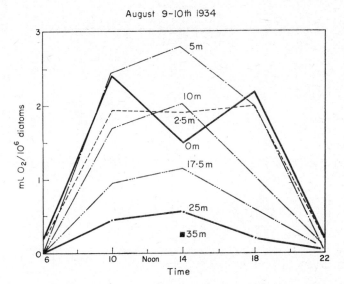

FIG. 6.3 Variation of oxygen production with depth by the diatom *Coscinodiscus excentricus* in the English Channel (after Jenkin, 1937).

general agreement with Jenkin's results by both laboratory and field trials in Californian waters. Talling also found a steady rise in oxygen production with increasing light intensity at relatively low intensities, but at a mean value of *ca.* 5000 lux (7.5 joules/cm² per hr) photosynthetic rate began to level off, and light saturation appeared to be satisfied at intensities of 24,000–27,000 lux (36–40.5 joules/cm² per hr). Some inhibition occurred in field experiments at high light intensities experienced close to the surface of the sea.

There is no doubt, however, that different species of phytoplankton which have been investigated show differences in their light requirements. Both the compensation intensities and saturation intensities vary between species of algae and depend also on the physiological state of the algal cells. *Coscinodiscus* and *Biddulphia*, for example, became light saturated at about 1200 ft c. whereas *Goniaulax* may be saturated at only 800 ft c. Again, inhibition according to Steemann Nielsen, occurs for natural boreal plankton at about 2150 ft c., but on the other hand tropical plankton species may show only saturation at intensities exceeding 3000 ft c.

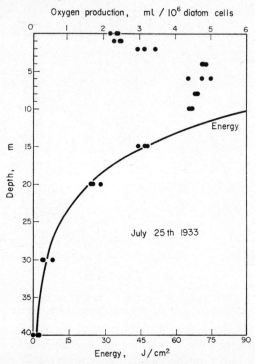

FIG. 6.4 Photosynthesis as a measure of available light energy. Note some inhibition of photosynthesis near the surface (after Jenkin, 1937).

Ryther (1956), investigating a considerable number of species of various groups of phytoplankton, summarizes his results by stating that Chlorophyta, including *Dunaliella*, *Stichococcus*, *Platymonas* and *Nannochloris*, were saturated at 500–750 ft c. and dinoflagellates, including *Gymnodinium*, *Exuviella* and *Amphidinium*, at much higher intensities of about 2500–3000 ft c. Diatoms such as *Nitzschia*, *Navicula* and *Skeletonema* became light saturated at intensities intermediate between the values for the green algae and the dinoflagellates (Fig. 6.5). For all phytoplankton species investigated inhibition was apparent at about 1000 ft c. above the saturation value. At intensities of 8000–10,000 ft c., which was equal to about full noon sunshine, photosynthesis in green algae and diatoms was only 5%–10% of that at saturation intensity, whilst in dinoflagellates it amounted to 20–30%.

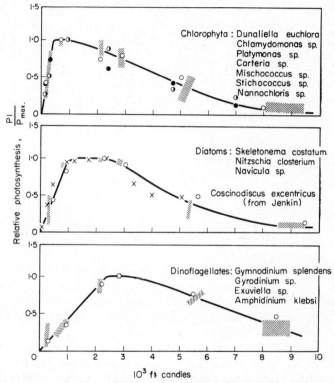

FIG. 6.5 The relation between photosynthesis and light intensity for some marine phytoplankton (after Ryther, 1956).

Steemann Nielsen and Hansen (1959) have especially commented on adaptations to light intensity shown by phytoplankton species from different oceanic habitats. For example, they have shown that the rate of photosynthesis per unit of chlorophyll increases with light intensity, at first at approximately the same rate for a variety of marine phytoplankton. However, light saturation occurs at very different light intensities for shade species, arctic surface-living species, and tropical surface species, respectively. Also the rates of photosynthesis per unit of chlorophyll at light saturation intensities differ greatly in the several groups of phytoplankton (Fig. 6.6).

While recognizing these important differences, it is possible to say that for many phytoplankton species there is rough agreement that the compensation point is at a light intensity of about 350–500 lux,

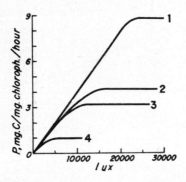

FIG. 6.6 Light intensity and the rate of gross photosynthesis for marine phytoplankton from different habitats (from Steemann Nielsen, 1959). (cf. also Steemann Nielsen and Hansen, 1959.)

which according to Clarke (1939a) corresponds to about 0.3% of noon sunlight. Clearly, the compensation depth is going to vary enormously with factors like latitude and season, with the transparency of water, the size of the phytoplankton population, and with all weather factors, particularly cloudiness and wave action, which together affect light penetration. Thus Jenkin comments that silt stirred up by wave action may greatly reduce light penetration; the intensity at 20 m in the already neritic English Channel is still twice that of the shallow inshore waters of Whitsand Bay near Plymouth. Clarke (1936) found in Woods Hole Harbour, where conditions are markedly turbid, that the compensation depth lay at about 7 m. On the other hand, in the Gulf of Maine, at approximately the same latitude but in less turbid water, the compensation depth was at 25 m. Similarly, Rustad (1946) using a culture of *Skeletonema* found a compensation depth ranging from $2\frac{1}{2}$–12 m for the Oslo Fjord, a rather turbid area. The variations in depth were apparently associated with differing degrees of turbidity. Thus near Oslo the compensation depth was least, and the transparency of the water as shown by Secchi disc readings was lower than at points further down the Fjord. On the other hand, in the Sargasso Sea, which is one of the most transparent areas of seawater in the world, some degree of inhibition of photosynthesis could be detected in the upper layers, and Clarke estimated the compensation depth as distinctly more than 100 m. More recent work by Steemann Nielsen in the same

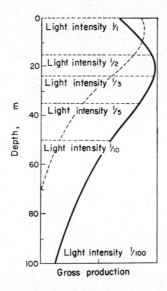

Fig. 6.7 Inhibition of photosynthesis in the upper layers of tropical oceans. Reduction of incident light [e.g. due to cloudiness] causes a rise towards the surface of a given level of production (hatched curve) (modified from Steemann Nielsen, 1952).

area would suggest a compensation depth of about 120 m, or according to Riley (1939), of 150 m. The effect of latitude and of turbidity then is clearly seen from these figures. The investigations of Steemann Nielsen (1952, 1954) show that in tropical waters there is generally some inhibition of photosynthesis in the uppermost layers. The depth for maximum photosynthesis is *ca.* 10–20 m below the surface, after which production falls off (Fig. 6.7). When the incident light is obscured by cloud a general rise towards the surface of the depth of any given level of production in the sea occurs, as shown in the diagram. Similarly Riley (1939) finds 10–15 m depth for maximum photosynthesis in the region of Tortugas. Currie (1958) has also shown that the total carbon assimilation per day in areas off the Portuguese coast is greater at a depth of 10–20 m than at the surface, presumably indicating an inhibitory effect of intense surface illumination. The rate of photosynthesis was very much greater at the inshore station than in more oceanic water but on the other hand, effective light penetration was far deeper in ocean water (cf. Fig. 6.8 a, b).

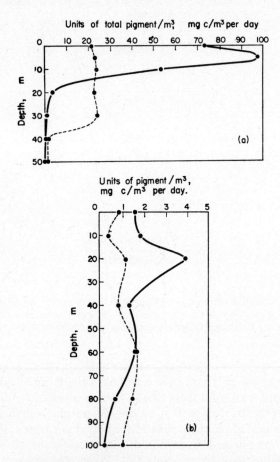

FIG. 6.8 The rate of photosynthesis in relation to depth at an inshore station (a) and an oceanic station (b) off the coast of Portugal. Hatched lines indicate the density of phytoplankton expressed as pigment units (after Currie, 1958).

Many of the experiments on compensation depth have been conducted for comparatively short periods. From the all-important point of view of net production, however, a 24 hr period should be considered. Jenkin (1937) also emphasized the difference between the level at which photosynthesis and respiration balance over the period of an experiment (the light intensity at this level she has termed the "compensation intensity"), and the level at which a balance occurs reckoned over a 24 hr period (this intensity has been designated as the "compensation point"). Clearly the illumination at the compensation point must be considerably greater than the illumination at the compensation intensity, yet it is still by definition too low to permit any crop increase. Some of Marshall and Orr's determinations for *Coscinosira* were reckoned over a 24 hr period; the compensation depth varied from 30 m in summer to only 2 m or so in winter. It is not surprising, therefore, that during winter in temperate latitudes there is usually no effective production, although short-lived bursts of phytoplankton have been recorded from the open sea by many workers. Obviously the over-riding consideration is the changing light intensity between summer and winter in temperate and high latitudes. Harvey (1955) gives the intensity at noon on a sunny summer's day as approximately 130,000 lux, and he shows this could be halved if the sun is temporarily obscured. On a winter's day at noon in bright sunshine there may be *ca.* 25,000 lux, but with a markedly cloudy condition this may be greatly reduced. Steemann Nielsen (1937a) gives some even more striking figures from the Baltic. A comparison of the brightest days with the darkest days in any month shows that in both January and June the darkest days can have an intensity only 10% of that of the brightest day. Even so, in June the light intensity on those days with the worst light conditions permits active photosynthesis, and to this must be added the much greater length of day. Photosynthesis can go on, for example, for 10 hr or more in June, whereas in January the much greater reduction of intensity is combined with an extreme shortness of day. Taking the two factors together, Harvey reckons that about one ninth of the total light falls daily on the sea surface during winter as compared with summer. This is, of course, an average figure, and whereas a cloudy day in mid-summer will cause the optimum zone for photosynthesis to rise only slightly in the water, in winter a very cloudy day may stop photosynthesis altogether. In any event, during winter, only at the surface is photosynthesis effective in temperate latitudes. Undoubtedly the somewhat lower light requirements of some species of phytoplankton will be of help here (cf. Steemann Nielsen and Hansen, 1959). It has been found, for example, that in the Arctic diatoms will grow sometimes under the ice, even in March when the light intensity must be very low indeed. Some species of flagellates (cf. Barker, 1935a, b) appear to have different light requirements from diatoms. However, for all phytoplankton the winter intensities are usually too low.

It is not surprising then that just as there must be a limit in depth to fixed algae, so there must be a limit for phytoplankton. Clearly the zone of abundance will vary with latitude and other conditions. Off California the maximum zone of abundance varies from about 25–50 m, whereas in most areas of northern Europe it is nearer 10–30 m. On the other hand in tropical areas Riley has found the maximum to be at about 100 m, and that some phytoplankton is still occurring and apparently healthy at depths exceeding 300 m (Fig. 6.9). Whatever the latitude, as one comes close inshore the marked increase in turbidity with reduction in light intensity rapidly reduces the depth at which the phytoplankton can live (Fig. 6.9).

So far, only light has been considered in reviewing compensation depth. Temperature does have an indirect effect and this will be discussed more fully later. But temperature is of little *direct* importance in photosynthesis in the sea. Photosynthesis may occur at maximum efficiency in the Antarctic where temperatures may be permanently below 0 °C; equally well it takes place at temperatures approaching 30 °C in tropical regions. An effect of lowered temperature on photosynthesis can be noted but this is largely offset by the fact that lowered temperature also reduces the respiratory needs of the plant cells. Higher temperatures increase respiratory requirements and the beneficial effect of higher temperature on photosynthesis is negligible unless high light intensities are available. Experimentally it is known that at high light intensities increased temperature can cause an increase in photosynthesis. Such intensities are not normally experienced in the sea and this factor has not been investigated very fully on phytoplankton organisms. One recent experiment on the effect of temperature on photosynthetic rate, given a standard and high illumination, is that of Wimpenny (1958). He investigated the carbon uptake of *Rhizosolenia* at three temperatures, 5°, 10° and 15 °C, using a standard illumination of 16,000 lux. The percentage daily increase was 55% at 5 °C, 122% at 10 °C and a more modest increase to 168% at 15 °C. Thus given a high light intensity, there is a marked effect of temperature on photosynthetic rate. Wimpenny's results also suggested that a high rate of photosynthesis occurred during the autumn flowering of diatoms in the area of the North Sea

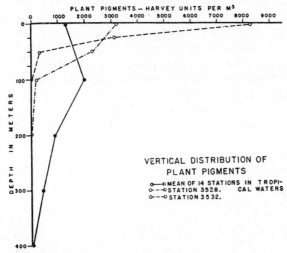

FIG. 6.9 Vertical distribution of phytoplankton, expressed as plant pigment units, in northern and tropical Atlantic waters.
Stat. 3532—south east of Long Island—N. Atlantic slope water.
Stat. 3528—deeper water, transitional between slope and tropical water.
Tropical stations—Sargasso Sea, Cuba and Florida Straits
(from Riley, 1939).

which he was investigating. By contrast, the production in February appeared to be about minimal, and this is undoubtedly associated with the very poor light penetration during February, 1% of the surface green light occurring at only 3 m during that month as compared with 1% at a depth of 15–20 m during October. It is abundantly clear therefore that the over-riding influence generally in determining the depth for effective photosynthesis is light intensity.

The penetration of visible light into seawater will be discussed more fully later, but it may be said here that a considerable change in the quality of the light occurs. The red and infra red rays are absorbed very rapidly and most of the light will, therefore, be in the blue/green/yellow range. Considerable work has now been done to show that maximum absorption by chlorophyll lies in the red and in the blue end of the spectrum. However, the presence of fucoxanthin and other carotenoids means that a considerable absorption of all wavelengths occurs, and although the precise method of functioning of carotenoids is still debatable, it appears that phytoplankton in general can use all wavelengths effectively. Although, therefore, there is a considerable change in the quality of the light, it is the total energy penetrating into the depths that is the real factor in productivity (cf. Stanbury, 1931). Indeed, Tanada suggests that between 400 and 700 mμ, diatoms use light with almost equal quantum efficiency. Fogg (1953) points out that although light absorbed by fucoxanthin is utilized in photosynthesis with about the same efficiency as that absorbed by chlorophyll, this does not hold apparently for other carotenoids. However, accessory carotenoids are obviously of great importance. Adaptations by marine algae to lower intensities appear to follow two paths, increased chlorophyll content, and the possession of active accessory carotenoids. This further emphasizes the great significance of the generally low light intensities which prevail in the marine environment.

CHAPTER VII

FACTORS AFFECTING PRIMARY PRODUCTION–I NUTRIENTS

WHILE the concentrations in the sea of some of the inorganic nutrients which are known to be essential for growth of plants (e.g. sulphate, magnesium, potassium) are quite high, some other essential elements, like nitrogen and phosphorus, as well as iron, are present only in extremely minute amounts. With only very small quantities amounting to a few milligrams of phosphorus as phosphate per cubic metre and usually a somewhat larger amount (about eight times by weight) of nitrate nitrogen, however, growth of phytoplankton can go on reasonably. Ketchum (1939) showed in culture that growth of the diatom *Nitzschia* was unaffected as long as about 17 mg P as phosphate/m^3 were present, but that growth also continued at concentrations considerably below that figure at reduced rates. Experiments on some flagellates (e.g. Barker, 1935b) have shown that other phytoplankton species can grow effectively at greater dilutions even than this, though Kain and Fogg's result (1958) for *Isochrysis*, using cell crop and phosphate requirements per cell, suggest higher phosphate needs. The remarkable growth of marine phytoplankton as compared with the growth of land plants at such great dilution is partly explained by the microscopic size of the phytoplanton cells, which makes for better diffusion of nutrients and also confers a vastly greater surface to volume ratio which promotes absorption. Nevertheless, the very small amounts of nitrate and phosphate and of some other nutrients in seawater, as compared with the relatively large amounts of potassium, sulphate, magnesium and other essential ions means that these minor constituents may become limiting both in space and in time. One of the more complete pictures of the cycles of these nutrients is available for the south-west English Channel area and is due mainly to the work of Atkins, Harvey and Cooper.

Phosphate

In the English Channel there appears to be a regular seasonal cycle in phosphate. The maximum occurs during the winter when at the surface some 14–22 mg phosphate P/m^3 may be present. The upper layers may suffer total depletion during the summer, but normally, even then, in deeper water some 5 mg PO_4-P/m^3 or so may remain (Fig. 7.1) (cf. Atkins, 1926; Harvey, 1928, 1945). The marked reduction

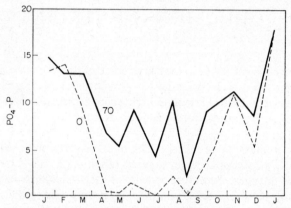

FIG. 7.1 Seasonal changes during 1925 in phosphate concentration at Station E1 in the English Channel at surface and bottom (70 m). To correct for salt error P values should be multiplied by 1.35 (Redrawn from Atkins, 1926).

in phosphate occurs during the early spring and has been associated with the outburst of phytoplankton growth which occurs at that time. This is difficult to follow precisely, but Marshall and Orr (1927, 1930) have been able to show for a comparatively enclosed area like Loch Striven that a marked rise in diatom numbers and a corresponding fall in phosphate has occurred, at least in some years. They have even been able to follow these changes beginning at the surface and then progressing down to 5 and 10 m depth. These concomitant changes in phosphate and diatom density often cannot be followed in the open sea since mixing processes obliterate the relationship.

In general throughout the summer phosphate values tend to remain low, though there may be some fluctuations; then, during the autumn, there is a rise until winter maximum values are re-established.

The North Sea shows rather similar changes to the English Channel (cf. Barnes, 1957). In spring and summer the surface phosphate may be reduced almost to zero, and in shallower regions this depletion may extend to the lower water layers. In the more northern areas, especially over deeper water, however, although the surface may be very low in phosphate concentration, the deeper layers may have an appreciable store of nutrients which at some points is brought to the surface with turbulence.

In an area such as Friday Harbour, Washington State, the winter maximum is at a much higher level (ca. 55 mg $PO_4 - P/m^3$) than in the English Channel, though there is the same trend in the seasonal cycle of phosphate, with the lowest concentration (some 35–40 mg $PO_4 - P/m^3$) occurring in early summer. This minimum is much higher than the maximum winter concentration for the English Channel, however, and clearly depletion never takes place, so that phosphate never limits phytoplankton production. The large quantities of phosphate in the Friday Harbour area are due to marked turbulence constantly replenishing the surface layers from the phosphate-rich deeper water.

Even in the absence of constant turbulence, however, some temperate regions may be richer in phosphate than the English Channel. The Gulf of Maine, for example, is definitely richer in phosphate; Bigelow, Lillick and Sears (1940) showed that the winter maximum concentration amounted to 30–35 mg $PO_4 - P/m^3$, and that even during summer nearly 10 mg P/m^3 remained in the surface layers over most of the Gulf, though local impoverishment might occur. Indeed it appeared likely that the very sharp fall in nitrate concentration during summer over the Gulf of Maine acted as the main limiting factor to phytoplankton growth rather than phosphate reduction. Redfield, Smith and Ketchum's results (1937) confirm rich phosphate in the Gulf of Maine; the upper 60 m gives an average concentration of 18 mg $PO_4 - P/m^3$ even in May and the deep water below 180 m changes little with the seasons from ca. 50–38 mg P/m^3.

Apart from the special conditions prevailing in Friday Harbour it is often true that inshore regions may show greater quantities of nutrients. Thus in Long Island Sound Riley and Conover (1956) showed that the concentration of phosphate may reach a winter maximum exceeding 60 mg $PO_4 - P/m^3$, and despite a drop to ca. 15 mg/m^3 after the spring flowering, there were still appreciable quantities over spring and early summer (Fig. 7.2). While there was some increase in nutrient concentration from surface to bottom during spring and summer, Riley and Conover's results suggest little difference in phosphate with depth at other times of the year. They believe that the inflow of richer water at deeper levels into Long Island Sound is mainly responsible for the high phosphate.

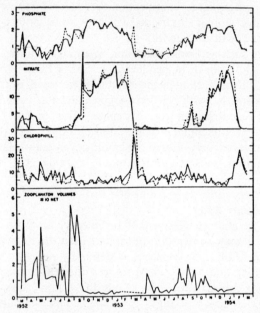

Fig. 7.2 Weekly averages of observations on phosphate, nitrate, chlorophyll and zooplankton at inshore stations in Long Island Sound. Solid line shows surface; dotted line, bottom. Phosphate and nitrate as μg-at./l.; chlorophyll as μg/l.; zooplankton as displacement volume in ml/l. in haul from bottom to surface (from Riley and Conover, 1956).

Kalle (1953) reports high phosphate in coastal regions of the North Sea near the outflow of the River Thames which he attributes mainly to freshwater drainage. This would agree with unpublished findings by Raymont and Carrie for Southampton Water, where high winter phosphate concentrations (50–60 mg $PO_4 - P/m^3$) are found higher up the estuary in the fresher upper layers, with lower concentrations of some 25 mg P/m^3 to seaward (Fig. 7.3 A and B). These values may be compared with the normal winter maximum of 15–20 mg $PO_4 - P/m^3$ in the English Channel.

In the Arctic the deeper water layers show distinctly high concentrations of phosphate (35–40 mg P/m^3) and in some regions fairly high surface values occur. However, in other areas complete exhaustion of phosphate may take place at the surface over summer, owing to

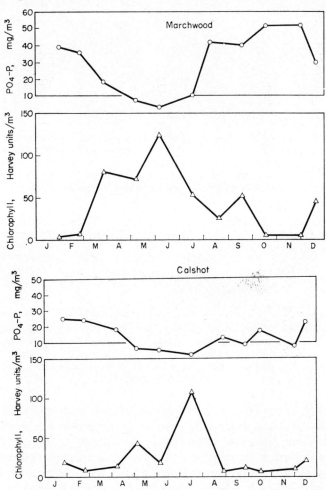

FIG. 7.3 Seasonal variations in the concentration of phosphate and the density of phytoplankton expressed as plant pigment units (A) at Marchwood, Test Estuary, Southampton, (B) at Calshot, 7 miles to seaward in Southampton Water. All values relate to surface samplings.

the intense phytoplankton growth and turbulence being insufficient
to replenish phosphate from the deeper levels.

Kreps and Verjbinskaya (1930, 1932) quote surface values for the
Barents Sea in winter ranging from < 18 mg $PO_4 - P/m^3$ in the coastal

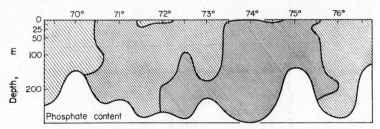

FIG. 7.4 The concentration of phosphate in Arctic waters (Kola-meridian,
33° 30′ E) from latitude 69–79 °N during March. Shading denotes
phosphate concentration ranging from <18 mgP/m^3 (light)
to 22 mg P/m^3 (darkest shading). Depth to bottom *ca.* 200 m
(slightly modified from Kreps and Verjbinskaya, 1930).

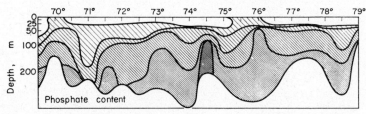

FIG. 7.5 The concentration of phosphate in Arctic waters along the
Kola-meridian during September. Shading denotes increasing
phosphate concentration ranging from 0–8 mg P/m^3 at surface, to
20 to >25 mg P/m^3 in deepest layers (slightly modified from Kreps
and Verjbinskaya, 1930).

regions to 20 mg P/m^3 in the inflowing Atlantic water and to 22 mg
P/m^3 in the Arctic waters (Fig. 7.4). With the growth of the phytoplankton the phosphate concentration is reduced to < 5 mg P/m^3
or even to zero in the uppermost layer in summer, but rich phosphate
is still present in deeper waters (Fig. 7.5). Regeneration is particularly
active about October/November and uniformly rich phosphate is
re-established during winter.

In some Arctic regions there may be sufficient vertical mixing to
give fairly high phosphate concentrations at the surface, even during
the summer. Kreps and Verjbinskaya noted this effect where submarine

plateaux occurred. Kalle (1957) found high P values at intermediate depths in the Irminger Sea, amounting to nearly 40 mg PO_4-P/m^3, and at the surface in summer (June) about half that quantity was still present in the Irminger Sea water proper, with 10 mg P/m^3 in the adjoining Gulf Stream water. Gillbricht (1959) also obtained similar surface phosphate values (15 mg P/m^3) in June in the Irminger Sea, and he showed fair agreement between phosphate concentration and turbidity measurements as an index of phytoplankton crop. A similar earlier study was made by Steemann Nielsen (1935) on the variations in the crop of phytoplankton in the areas of the North Atlantic region from the Faroes to Greenland; he has shown how

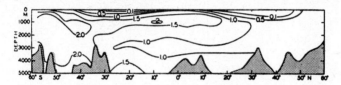

FIG. 7.6 Distribution of phosphate in a longitudinal section in the central Atlantic Ocean. Units μg-at. P/l. (from Sverdrup *et al.*, 1946).

the quantities of phytoplankton may be related to the concentrations of nutrients available, consequent on vertical mixing. It is well known that in regions where submarine barriers may deflect currents, a much greater degree of vertical mixing may occur. Atkins found in the region of the submarine ridge running between Scotland and Iceland phosphate values, even at the surface during the summer, of 14 mg PO_4-P/m^3 owing to the deeper water being forced up towards the surface.

In general, however, over the temperate North Atlantic the surface waters are low in phosphate and show the same seasonal cycle as in such inshore waters as the English Channel. Total depletion may occur in summer or a few mg PO_4-P/m^3 only may remain. These low P values may extend to 100 m or more in depth, the depleted layer being generally thicker in middle latitudes. Below this layer the phosphate content rises fairly rapidly and tends to reach a maximum value of *ca.* 40–50 mg PO_4-P/m^3 at about 500–1000 m. Below this depth again the value falls slightly to 30–40 mg P/m^3 (Fig. 7.6). The maximum layer may not, however, be clearly marked (cf. Table 7.1).

The maximum layer is much better defined in the tropical areas of the Atlantic, and here the amount of P is also much higher (cf. Fig. 7.7). The surface layers in tropical regions have extremely little phosphate at any time (Fig. 7.8). The only exceptions appear in the

TABLE 7.1. Discovery Station 2659 (47° 24′ N, 07° 52′ W) May, 1950. (modified from Discovery Reports, 1957).

Depth	Phosphate (mg P/m³)
0	12
50	16
100	16
200	19
300	25
400	25
600	31
900	37
1000	37
1500	40
2000	40
2500	43
3400	47
3800	50

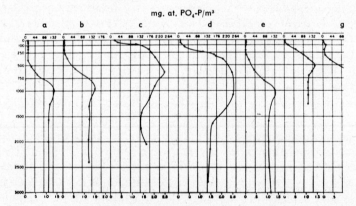

FIG. 7.7 Vertical distribution of phosphate in the northwestern Atlantic (a) Northern Sargasso Sea (b) 40th meridian north of 27 °N (c) the same about 8 °N (d) the same at Equator (e) and (f) along a line from Bermuda to Chesapeake Bay (g) between Nova Scotia and Bermuda (from Barnes, 1957, after Seiwell, 1935).

upwelling regions, as off the coast of South West Africa, where high phosphate occurs (Fig. 7.9). As in temperate areas, the amount of phosphate increases with depth below the euphotic zone, but in the tropical regions a maximum of 70 or even *ca.* 80 mg $PO_4 - P/m^3$ at roughly 1000 m depth may occur (cf. Clowes, 1938). This maximum

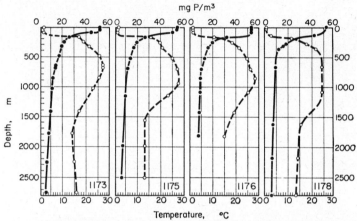

FIG. 7.8 The vertical distribution of phosphate (P), open circles, and of temperature (T), solid circles, at four "Atlantis" Stations in the tropical north Atlantic Ocean ranging in latitude from 10 °N (1173) to 2 °N (1178); longitude *ca.* 40 °W (after Seiwell, 1935).

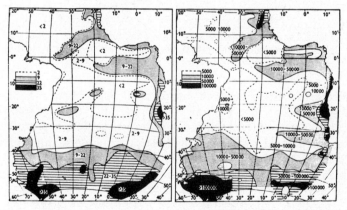

FIG. 7.9 Distribution of phosphate (left) in mgP/m³ and the density of plankton organisms (number per litre) (right) in the upper 50 m layer in the South Atlantic (after Hentschel and Wattenberg, 1930; Harvey, 1955).

of phosphate seems to coincide with the zone of lowered oxygen below the thermocline which has been already referred to, and below this depth the amount of phosphate declines somewhat to about 45–50 mg/m^3. The depletion of phosphate will tend to go deeper in tropical and sub-tropical seas. Thus Riley (1939) shows that from the

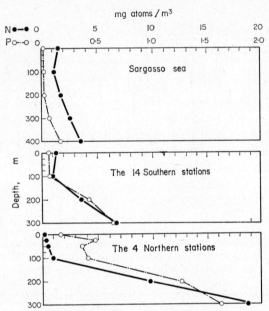

FIG. 7.10 The vertical distribution of nitrate and phosphate at various sub-tropical and temperate stations in the western North Atlantic Ocean (units mg-at./m^3) (from Riley, 1939).

surface to *ca.* 100 m depth in the Sargasso Sea < 1 mg $PO_4 - P/m^3$ was present, and that even at 300 m, < 5 mg P/m^3 was recorded (Fig. 7.10). On the other hand, at more northern stations in the Atlantic there was a rapid increase in phosphate from 3–5 mg P/m^3 at the surface, to > 10 mg P/m^3 at 100 m and to nearly 50 mg P/m^3 at a depth of 300 m (Fig. 7.10).

As one passes south into the South Atlantic Ocean, in general the phosphate content of the deeper water tends to increase some-what. South of the Rio Grande Ridge (*ca.* 35° S latitude) in deep water as much as 80–90 mg $PO_4 - P/m^3$ may occur, especially in the intermediate water layers (Fig. 7.6). Clowes' (1938) analyses suggest rather richer concentrations in the western sector. This richer water in the temperate and tropical regions may be partly due to organisms from high latitudes, where plankton production is so intense, having slowly drifted into somewhat deeper water at lower latitudes. Undoubtedly it is also due to the general contribution of deep currents rich in nutrients.

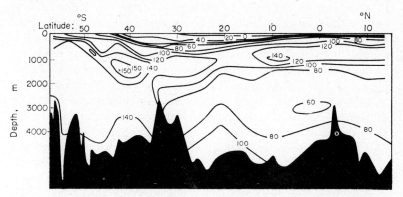

Fig. 7.11 Distribution of phosphate in the South Atlantic April/May 1931 (units mg P_2O_5/m^3) (from Deacon, 1933).

Far south, at high latitudes, the Antarctic region has remarkably high phosphorus contents even in the surface water (Fig. 7.11). Deacon (1933) shows an average content even during the southern spring, when presumably owing to the phytoplankton outburst phosphate will be reduced, corresponding to about 35 mg P/m^3 for the open sea. He states that phosphate never fell below 30 mg P/m^3 (i.e. a much higher value than occurs even at the winter maximum in our British waters). In the southern winter a high value of some 60 mg $PO_4 - P/m^3$ occurs at the surface, with even higher values near the ice edge. The deep water will contain > 80 mg P/m^3. There is, therefore, a cycle of phosphate in the Antarctic region with the massive demands on phosphate made by the production of phytoplankton, but phosphate is clearly never limiting in that area. The results of Clowes' investigations also show that phosphate is not limiting in the Sub-Antarctic.

The abundance of phosphate in the surface layers is due to the hydrographic conditions in the Antarctic region. It will be remembered that surface currents leave the Antarctic continent and are replaced by upwelling of deep water on a very large scale (cf. Fig. 4.19, Chapter IV). The surface water will carry organisms and detritus away from the Antarctic, but since this water sinks at the Convergence, much of this material decomposes and the phosphate is regenerated and mixes with the deeper water flowing back towards the Antarctic continent. As this enriched water upwells it will cause high surface concentrations of phosphate of the order of 60 mg P/m^3 over the Antarctic. The limit of this very rich surface layer is approximately the Antarctic Convergence (roughly 50° S) where, it will be remembered, the low salinity but very cold waters of the Antarctic region pass below the warmer waters of the South Atlantic and reach intermediate depths. North of the Convergence the value of surface phosphate drops to perhaps 35–25 mg P/m^3 in summer, with higher concentrations in winter, but this comparatively rich zone extends right to the sub-tropical convergence at a latitude of approximately 40° S. Throughout this vast sea area, phosphate is never seriously depleted, rarely reaching a value lower than about 20 mg $PO_4 - P/m^3$. Immediately the sub-tropical water is reached, however, the surface phosphate content drops remarkably to only a few mg P/m^3, and in the tropics there is virtually no phosphate detectable, i.e. it is used up as soon as it is regenerated from the bodies and excreta of the plankton organisms.

It is true, however, that at the Equator and at about 10° N latitude, the meeting of the Equatorial and Counter Equatorial Currents cause divergence of water masses leading to vertical circulation above the thermocline. The nutrient-poor layer is, therefore, thinner here and the constant mixing of the upper layers does assist in providing nutrients to the euphotic zone. A remarkable correspondence between the density of plankton and the distribution of phosphate in the surface waters of the Central and South Atlantic has been demonstrated from the work of Hentschel and Wattenberg (Fig. 7.9).

It must be appreciated that although details have been given for the Atlantic Ocean which is perhaps best known, the depths in any ocean represent a great store of phosphate. In the tropical and sub-tropical areas of the Pacific and Indian Oceans it appears that the amount of phosphate in the deeper layers is somewhat greater than in the Atlantic (Sverdrup et al., 1946), reaching a maximum of ca. 90 mg P/m^3. There is the same relatively rapid rise in phosphate concentration from the surface to a depth of the order of 1000 m, but the slight reduction in phosphate seen in the Atlantic in still deeper layers is not so obvious in the Pacific and Indian Oceans (Fig. 7.12). To some extent, however, this may be a result o: our lesser knowledge of the phosphate concentrations. Clowes (1938) quotes values for the Indian Ocean of up to 90 mg P/m³ just north of the equator at about 1000 m depth, and at intermediate depths near the Ant-

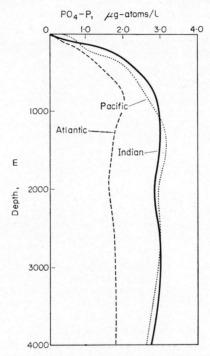

FIG. 7.12 Vertical distribution of phosphate in the three Oceans. Based on data obtained mainly from tropical and subtropical stations (from Sverdrup *et al.*, 1946).

arctic Convergence similar concentrations were found. The greater richness of phosphate in the Pacific and Indian Oceans, as compared with the Atlantic, has been confirmed by more recent investigations, summarized by Redfield (1958). He shows, as a result of about 1600 measurements of phosphate at a depth of *ca.* 2000 m, that a minimal value (< 40 mg P/m³) occurs in the North Atlantic, and maximal concentrations (> 90 mg P/m³) are present in the Indian and North Pacific Oceans.

At the surface in all oceans the amount of phosphate is extraordinarily low in tropical and sub-tropical areas, rising somewhat in temperate regions. In the North Pacific, at higher latitudes, the surface waters have high phosphate values owing apparently to relatively rich water spreading south from the Bering Sea. However, in the Pacific Ocean phosphate concentration does not increase on passing south of the Equator. The highest phosphate is found at intermediate

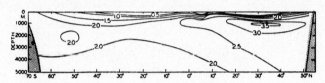

FIG. 7.13 Distribution of phosphate in a longitudinal section of the Pacific Ocean (units µg-at. P/l.) (from Sverdrup *et al.*, 1946).

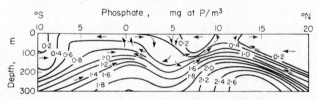

FIG. 7.14 Section across equatorial region in the Pacific Ocean showing regions of convergence and divergence and the effect on phosphate distribution (from Barnes, 1957).

depths in the North Pacific where it amounts to > 100 mg P/m³ (Fig. 7.13). The difference between the Atlantic and Pacific is due to the marked southerly flow of deeper waters past the Equator in the Atlantic Ocean, and to the lack of such an exchange of deep water on any scale in the Pacific. The Antarctic waters of all three oceans are generally similar in that high concentrations of phosphate occur from the surface downwards.

Considerable upwelling in the tropical Pacific very close to the Equator is now known from the work of Cromwell (1953) and others. Higher phosphate values occur there (Fig. 7.14) and plankton production appears to be greater than in surrounding tropical areas where the movement of deeper water to the surface is not taking place. (The deep water below 400 m may have very high phosphate exceeding 90 mg P/m³, cf. Fig. 7.13.)

Inorganic combined nitrogen

The combined inorganic nitrogen which is available for plant growth in the sea is present in several different forms: nitrate, nitrite and ammonium. To a very small extent other nitrogenous compounds such as urea, uric acid and amino-acids are also detectable in seawater, being produced largely by the excretion of animals. Some of these organic nitrogen compounds can be directly utilized by phyto-plankton, but they are also fairly rapidly converted to ammonium so that discussion for the present may be limited to nitrate, nitrite and ammonium. Of these, nitrate is almost always the most abundant.

The detection of nitrate is difficult and involves delicate colori-metric methods, the earlier work in the formulation of these methods being largely due to Atkins, Harvey and Cooper. But the methods for nitrate determination are not as accurate and straight-forward as those for detecting phosphate, and on the whole, therefore, fewer accurate figures are available for nutrient nitrogen compounds in seawater; this applies particularly to deeper waters. Very often, at any rate in earlier work, values for nitrate have included nitrite.

On the whole the variations in nitrate parallel those of phosphate. Thus in temperate zones, and indeed in parts of the Arctic, the surface waters may be largely depleted of nitrate with the diatom outburst. Nitrate nitrogen however is much more abundant than phosphate in the sea. By weight it can vary between 4 and 13 times as much as phosphorus, though the more usual figure is about 7 or 8 times. The normal ratio on the basis of atoms is 15 nitrogen to 1 phos-phorus atom. In the English Channel, the maximum winter amount of nitrate corresponds to about 100 mg N/m^3 on the surface, though this is depleted to almost zero value with the diatom outburst (Har-vey, 1928). Just as for phosphate, the depletion is not so great in the deeper waters, and usually a small amount, perhaps some 10 mg N/m^3, will remain in the deeper layers of the English Channel even during the summer period (Fig. 7.15) (Cooper, 1933). On the other hand, off the New South Wales coast, Dakin and Colefax (1935) found that although the surface could rapidly recover its phosphate after depletion, the concentration of nitrate tended to be generally lower than for the English Channel. The maximum at the surface was only about 40 mg N/m^3. During diatom outbursts nitrate was depleted to trace values, and although a fair amount was present in the deeper waters, there was a sufficient barrier to mixing during

the summer to prevent nitrate reaching the surface in any quantity.
It appears, therefore, that off the New South Wales coast it was the
nitrate concentration which particularly tended to regulate the diatom
outbursts.

In the Gulf of Maine, Bigelow, Lillick and Sears (1940) found
nitrate contents of > 100 mg N/m³ (in some areas > 150 mg N/m³)

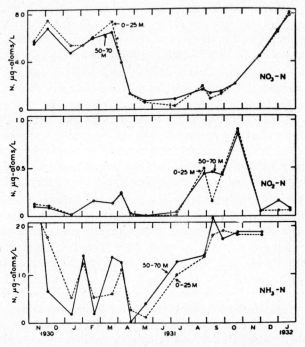

FIG. 7.15 Seasonal variations in nitrate, nitrite and ammonia in the surface
layer (0–25 m) and in the bottom layer (50–70 m) in the English
Channel (from Sverdrup *et al.*, 1946, after Cooper).

in winter, but after the vernal outburst of phytoplankton there was
in many areas < 5 mg N/m³ at the surface, and even total exhaustion
in summer. Rakestraw (1936) similarly found 140–200 mg N/m³ in
the surface waters of the Gulf of Maine during the winter maximum,
with a sharp reduction during the spring and summer (Fig. 7.16). In
deep waters, however (below 100 m), there was a relatively large
amount of nitrate all through the year, exceeding 140 mg $NO_3 - N/m^3$,

and at depths of more than 150 m even larger amounts, > 200 mg N/m³, were present (Fig. 7.16).

In Friday Harbour upwelling and turbulence cause high levels of nitrate, just as the phosphate content is increased. Although an annual cycle of nitrate occurs, the winter maximum exceeds 300 mg $NO_3 - N/m^3$ and this falls only to *ca.* 200 mg N/m³ during the summer.

Close inshore nitrate concentrations may tend to increase, and this may be partly a result of land drainage. Riley and Conover (1956) found winter nitrate maxima exceeding 250 mg N/m³ in Long Island Sound, though with the intense early spring flowering of diatoms the nitrate was exhausted, and remained depleted both at the surface and at deeper levels until about the end of August, after which there was a gradual build up in concentration to the winter maximum (Fig. 7.2). The high winter values are believed to be partly a result of transport of deeper, richer water from outside and partly a result of freshwater drainage. Harris (1959) has confirmed the very marked depletion of nitrate in Long Island Sound during spring and summer.

In general over the temperate North Atlantic it appears that only very low concentrations of a few milligrams of nitrate per cubic metre remain at the surface over summer, but deeper ocean layers show a marked rise in nitrate so that, as for phosphate, the deep oceans represent a great store of nutrients (Harvey, 1926). For the Bay of Biscay, Harvey (1926) showed that 150–200 mg $NO_3 - N/m^3$ were present at depths of about 500 m. A little further south off Portugal, similar concentrations occurred at the same depth, but at 1000–3000 m values of over 250 mg N/m³ as nitrate were recorded. This agrees with determinations by Rakestraw (1936) for other areas of the North Atlantic where deep water layers have > 250 mg N/m³ (Table 7.2). In the Arctic, Kreps and Verjbinskaya (1930, 1932) have shown that the mixture of relatively rich Arctic and Atlantic water can cause high surface values of nitrate in the Barents Sea. In coastal regions approximately 140 mg N/m³ may be present in winter, but in latitudes about 70–73 °N, corresponding to the more open Atlantic water, 150–200 mg N/m³, and in the Arctic water, 200–250 mg N/m³ may be present from the surface down to > 200 m (Fig. 7.17). Despite these high values, there is marked depletion and even total exhaustion of nitrate in summer in the uppermost layer, the coastal and Arctic waters showing more rapid depletion and earlier phytoplankton growth. Much nitrate is still present in deep

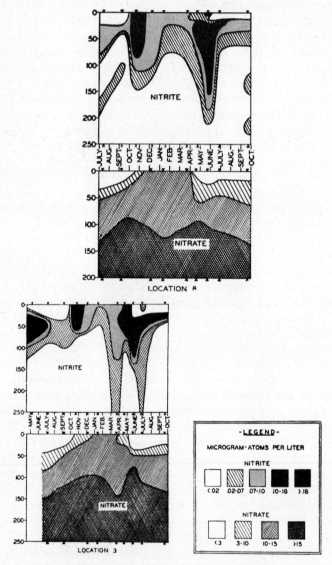

FIG. 7.16 Seasonal variations in nitrate and nitrite at two stations in the Gulf of Maine (slightly modified from Rakestraw, 1936).

waters (Fig. 7.18). Maxima up to 300 mg N/m^3 have been recorded for other Arctic areas.

In the tropics and middle latitudes in the Atlantic Ocean, while the surface is generally very low in nitrate, there is a rapid increase

TABLE 7.2. Station 1734 (July, 1933) in Western N. Atlantic Ocean to east of Cape Hatteras. Relation of nitrite to ammonia and nitrate. Concentrations in $\mu g/l$. (Modified from Rakestraw, 1936.)

Depth in metres	Nitrite	Ammonia	Nitrate
0	0	—	—
77	0.01	0.4	1.1
100	0.05	—	—
340	0	0.3	4.6
855	0	0.3	19.5
2650	(0)	0.6	20
3280	(0)	0.4	—
3725	(0)	0.3	20.5
4180	(0)	0.6	23

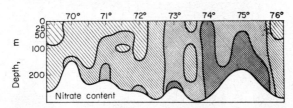

FIG. 7.17 The concentration of nitrate along the Kola-meridian (33° 30′ E) from latitude 69–76 °N during December. Shading denotes nitrate concentration ranging from <150 mg N/m^3 (light) to >300 mg N/m^3 (darkest shading). Depth to bottom *ca.* 200 m (from Kreps and Verjbinskaya, 1930).

with depth, and apparently a maximum nitrate concentration appears at intermediate depths of from 500–1000 m, which seems to correspond roughly with the minimum oxygen zone. It will be remembered that a similar maximum at intermediate depths occurred with phosphate. Rakestraw and Carritt (1948) have suggested from observations in Pacific oceanic waters that the depths of the nitrate and phosphate maximum change during the year in association with variations in the thermocline. In the Atlantic below the maximum layer the amount of nitrate decreases slightly to an average value of *ca.* 250 mg N/m³ which changes little with depth (Fig. 7.20).

As for phosphate, there is often in low latitudes a considerably thicker zone which shows reduction in nitrate concentration owing

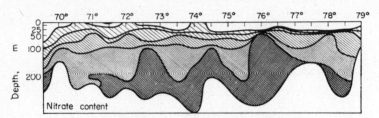

FIG. 7.18 The concentration of nitrate along the Kola-meridian during September. Shading denotes nitrate concentration ranging from 0–50 mg N/m³ (lightest) to >250 mg N/m³ (darkest shading) (from Kreps and Verjbinskaya, 1930).

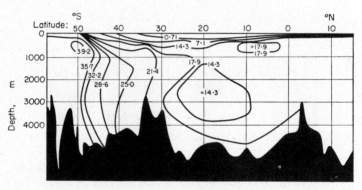

FIG. 7.19 The distribution of nitrate in the South Atlantic April/May 1931 (units μg-at. N/l.) (from Deacon, 1933, modified by Barnes, 1957).

to the greater depth of the photosynthetic layer than in temperate and high latitudes. Riley (1939) found a very rapid increase in nitrate with depth at more northerly stations in the North Atlantic, ranging from only just detectable values at the surface to > 250 mg N/m³ at a depth of 300 m. On the other hand, in the Sargasso Sea, minimal nitrate concentrations (*ca.* 14 mg N/m³) extended to 100 m, and even at 400 m only 50 mg N/m³ was present (Fig. 7.10).

In general the picture of nitrate distribution in the other oceans of the world is similar in that the surface tends to be low and there is a rapid increase in nitrate to a maximum at intermediate depths. In the Pacific and Indian Oceans, however, the amounts of nitrate in deeper water appear to be greater than in the Atlantic, considerably exceeding 400 mg $NO_3 - N/m^3$ (cf. Sverdrup *et al.*, 1946), and there is little change in concentration in really deep water (Fig. 7.20).

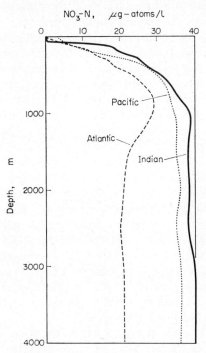

FIG. 7.20 Vertical distribution of nitrate in the three Oceans from data obtained mainly from tropical and subtropical stations (from Sverdrup *et al.*, 1946).

We have already seen that, in the case of phosphate, extremely high values are found in the Antarctic even at the surface, owing to the rising of very deep water continuously on a grand scale. Deacon (1933) has given fairly full data for the nitrate content of Antarctic waters (Fig. 7.19). The amounts are surprisingly high. For example, at its maximum which occurs about October and November, the surface water in the Antarctic has some 550 mg $NO_3 - N/m^3$. There is the usual effect of the great diatom outburst in the Antarctic in that the surface nitrate is reduced in the Antarctic summer, but even so, the amount in the surface water is only reduced to a little under 300 mg $NO_3 - N/m^3$. In the seas north of the Antarctic Convergence (sub-antarctic waters) the values for nitrate at the surface are lower, but they are still comparatively very high and amount to something approaching 150–200 mg $NO_3 - N/m^3$. As with phosphate, however, the nitrate content drops very rapidly at the surface on passing north of the sub-tropical convergence, and in the tropics proper the usual condition obtains of extremely low nutrients amounting to only 5 mg $NO_3 - N/m^3$. Indeed Deacon says that thunderstorms are important in that the relatively small amount of nitrate produced to some extent replenishes the nitrogen in the surface layer of the tropics. Nitrate can usually be detected in surface tropical waters though in extremely small amounts, but phosphate may be totally depleted.

There is no doubt that in the Atlantic Ocean, although the deep water generally is rich in nitrate, the South Atlantic waters are richer then the North. This parallels the condition for phosphate but again probably does not hold for the Pacific Ocean where the North Pacific is generally richer in nutrients. Thus in the South Atlantic from about latitude 30° S the amount of nitrate rises (Fig. 7.19). At about 40° S, for example, the surface has *ca.* 200 mg $NO_3 - N/m^3$ and double that concentration occurs at 1000 m. At 50° S the amount of nitrate approaches 500 mg $NO_3 - N/m^3$ at a depth of only 500 m, and in even higher latitudes, concentrations of nitrate exceeding 500 mg N/m^3 pass right up from the deep water to the surface (Fig. 7.19). This increase in nitrate as one passes south in the Atlantic can be seen in Table 7.3 (Harvey, 1955).

In dealing with the nitrogen compounds which are available as plant nutrients in the sea we must also consider ammonium and nitrite. These, though they are of importance, never reach concentrations as high as nitrate. However, ammonium can be present in considerable amounts at certain times of the year. Redfield and Keys (1938) found a maximum concentration occurred in the Gulf of Maine at about 50–100 m depth, with 60 mg $NH_4 - N/m^3$. Amounts of the same order have been found in the upper layers of the Norwegian Sea, but for the English Channel Cooper found a maximum of only approximately 30 mg $NH_4 - N/m^3$. On the whole it appears that it is the upper strata of water (*ca.* 50 m depth) which contain most of the ammonium, though the extreme surface layer may show

TABLE 7.3. Nitrate and nitrite-nitrogen in mg N/m³ in the water at positions along the 30° W meridian of longitude during April–May, 1931 (after HARVEY, 1955).

Depth (m)	57° 36' S	53° 33' S	46° 43' S	38° 10' S	21° 13' S	3° N	9° N	14° 27' N
0	510	–	210	60	2	2	2	3
20	500	–	210	36	0	1	2	1
40	490	490	210	42	0	1	2	1
60	500	490	230	30	0	2	0	1
80	510	490	240	42	1	29	27	1
100	530	500	250	89	1	63	47	28
150	530	510	310	101	7	170	200	170
200	530	530	380	131	100	220	210	200
400	530	540	450	260	240	230	220	210
800	530	540	480	310	170	220	250	240
1500	510	540	450	360	180	220	210	210
2500	510	530	420	330	–	220	210	210
3200	500	–	–	–	–	–	–	–
3500	–	510	450	320	170	–	210	210
4500	–	–	440	–	–	–	210	210
4900	–	–	–	–	280	–	–	–
5300	–	–	–	–	–	–	–	210

very little. On the other hand in shallower inshore seas bottom water can show some quantities of ammonium (cf. Cooper, 1937). Close to land higher values for ammonium may be found; for example, Cooper found up to 200 mg $NH_4 - N/m^3$ in the English Channel close inshore, and probably part of this ammonium is derived from land drainage. Over the sea surface generally, thunderstorms and rain may contribute to a small extent to the ammonium content.

In the Baltic, values for ammonium range from 7–40 mg $NH_4 - N/m^3$; and in the Arctic approximately the same concentrations have been found in sub-surface waters as have been found in north temperate regions, with maxima of from 30–50 mg $NH_4 - N/m^3$. Somewhat higher values are given by Robinson and Wirth (1934a) for the relatively enclosed inshore waters of Puget Sound with concentrations of up to 80 mg N/m^3 as ammonium, and even occasional higher values but these were mainly in the upper 50 m. The general level was less than 20 mg N/m^3 and the few high concentrations may have been due to land drainage. Only small quantities of ammonium were present in the deeper water close inshore in the Puget Sound area. The same authors (Robinson and Wirth, 1934b) point out that over deep oceanic water off the Washington coast, ammonium rarely exceeded 30 mg N/m^3. The majority of the ammonium again occurred in the upper 100 m layer where the average concentration was *ca.* 20 mg N/m^3; in deep layers (1500 m) the average concentration was only 2 mg N/m^3 (Fig. 7.21). The only figures published by Rakestraw (1936) for ammonium in a deep oceanic station suggest uniformly very low values (cf. Table 7.2). That ammonium is present in lower concentrations in offshore waters is also confirmed by the results of Redfield and Keys (1938) for waters of the North West Atlantic. At a station in continental slope water they showed that although some 10 mg $NH_4 - N/m^3$ was present in the upper 60 m, from a depth of 100–2000 m no ammonium was detectable.

Comparatively few seasonal surveys have been made as regards ammonium content, but Cooper (1933, 1937) for the English Channel, shows that on the whole the lowest ammonium values occur in spring. The amount tends to rise in late summer but most of the ammonium is present during autumn/winter (Fig. 7.15). This is confirmed by the observations of Redfield and Keys (1938) for the Gulf of Maine, where although data are available for only two months (May and September), the ammonium content was shown to have increased somewhat by the latter month. Further, whereas in May ammonium was minimal at the surface and the maximum concentrations occurred in a definite layer between 30 and 60 m (Fig. 7.22), in September the concentration was more uniform. Ammonium was virtually absent from deeper water in spring. Barnes (1957) also

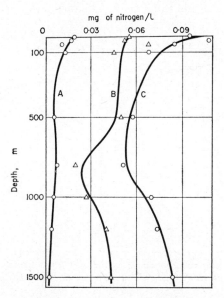

FIG. 7.21 Average distribution with depth of free ammonia (A), albuminoid N (B) and organic N (C) in the Pacific Ocean off Washington State and Vancouver Island (from Robinson and Wirth, 1934).

suggests that in general ammonium is more abundant during the winter months when it presumably arises largely from the bacterial decomposition of the organic material produced over the summer. At the same time it must be remembered that small quantities of ammonium will be released during the summer, especially in the uppermost layers with the excretion of the planktonic organisms, though this ammonium may be used immediately.

The concentration of nitrite in seawater can be estimated accurately, and results in general confirm that in almost all parts of the world the amount of nitrite tends to be small; very much smaller than nitrate and usually considerably smaller than ammonium. For the Friday Harbour area, for example, where high values of nitrate exceeding 300 mg NO_3-N/m^3 are attained by constant turbulence, the amount of nitrite, though it shows seasonal variation, is of a very different order and amounts at its maximum to only 6 mg NO_2-N/m^3. In contrast to the nitrate cycle, this maximum of nitrite appeared in the late summer; the minimum concentration, which was only of the order of a milligram or so per cubic metre,

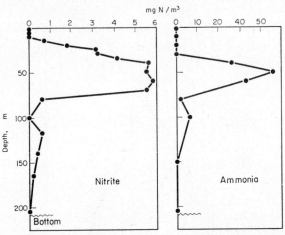

FIG. 7.22 Vertical distribution of nitrite and ammonia in the Gulf of Maine (May 1934). Units mg N as NO_2^- and NH_3/m^3 (from Redfield and Keys, 1938).

occurred about January/February, when nitrate was at its maximum. These very small amounts of nitrite appear to be confirmed elsewhere. Rakestraw (1936) working in the Gulf of Maine and Western Atlantic region rarely obtained as much as 2–3 mg NO_2-N/m^3. The maximum quantity was present in the upper layers and only in very shallow inshore waters were higher concentrations found. Nitrite was very low in January and February and virtually disappeared with growth of phytoplankton during spring, though some still remained just below the photosynthetic zone. The maximum for nitrite occurred in summer from June to September, and for the Gulf of Maine this maximum was experienced at a depth of 50–100 m; in deeper layers nitrite was virtually absent, despite large amounts of nitrate (Fig. 7.16). Similarly in more oceanic stations, the nitrite maximum occurred at about 100 m with recognisable amounts down to even 200 m, but below this depth nitrite was negligible (Table 7.2). Redfield and Keys (1938) found a maximum concentration of nitrite in May at about 50 m depth in the Gulf of Maine (Fig. 7.22). The amount was about 7 mg $NO_2 - N/m^3$; at the bottom, at approximately 200 m, no nitrite was detectable. Very low concentrations of nitrite with usually less than 1 mg $NO_2 - N/m^3$ were also recorded by Braarud and Klem (1931) from Norwegian waters; slightly higher values were found just below the photosynthetic zone. In the Barents Sea, the maximum for nitrite was similarly found to be immediately below the euphotic zone. Verjbinskaya (1932) found that the yearly maximum occurred about August and rarely amounted to 10 mg $NO_2 - N/m^3$. Over winter, nitrite practically disappeared and the mean value for the upper 100 m layer was about one hundredth of the nitrate concentration.

It seems, however, that nitrite regeneration can occur near the bottom also, at least in shallow inshore waters. Cooper (1937) found in the relatively shallow English Channel that amounts of nitrite equal to sub-surface amounts were obtained near the bottom, the concentration increasing in August and reaching a maximum of *ca.* 10 mg $NO_2 - N/m^3$ in October. By January there was virtually no nitrite in upper or lower layers (Fig. 7.15). For the open sea, however, it would appear that maximum nitrite is just below the photosynthetic zone. In the south Atlantic, Deacon found 30 mg $NO_2 - N/m^3$ in the tropical region below the photosynthetic zone, and in the Indian Ocean, Thompson and Gilson found relatively high concentrations at a depth of about 100 m. In both these cases the amount of nitrite in the deeper water was very small indeed. It is particularly significant that in Antarctic waters with very high nitrate concentrations, Deacon (1933) recorded only up to 8 mg $NO_2 - N/m^3$ and this was in the upper layers; no nitrite whatsoever was found in the deeper waters below 150 m. There is no doubt, therefore, that in the deeper waters of the open oceans the combined inorganic nitrogen exists almost entirely as nitrate and that large amounts of nitrite are very rarely found anywhere in the seas. Some recent figures published in the station lists of Discovery Reports (1957) for stations in the Indian Ocean for May 1950, suggest very high concentrations of nitrate may exist in deep water but the nitrite content is still very low and is confined to about the upper 100 m. On the other hand, Brandhorst (1959) working in the Eastern Pacific Ocean has found high nitrite concentrations in certain tropical areas. Values up to *ca.* 15 mg N/m^3 are found in the upper 100 m layer associated with a marked thermocline (Fig. 7.23). Brandhorst attributes this maximum to nitrification processes associated with the remineralization of decomposing plankton. But he also finds an extensive area with very low oxygen concentration (*ca.* 0.10 c.c. O_2/l.) at depths varying from 150 to 1000 m. In association with this markedly reduced oxygen layer he finds just below the thermocline a second nitrite maximum with

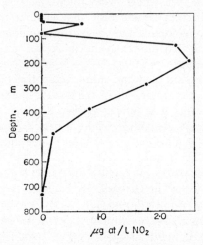

FIG. 7.23 Vertical distribution of nitrite in the tropical Eastern Pacific at a station off Mexico (latitude approximately 20 °N). Note the nitrite maximum at 200 m depth in a zone of greatly reduced oxygen content (slightly modified from Brandhorst, 1959).

values up to 35 mg NO_2-N/m^3 (Fig. 7.23). Brandhorst regards this nitrite as resulting from denitrification activities of anaerobic bacteria (cf. Chapter XVI) and he quotes even higher nitrite values from Thompson and Gilson's work in the Indian Ocean which are also believed to arise from denitrification. Another possible source of nitrite in the seas is discussed in Chapter XVI.

In reviewing the amounts of nitrate, nitrite and ammonium present in seawater it should be remembered that all three forms of nitrogen can be utilized by phytoplankton directly, and indeed Harvey has shown that ammonium seems to be preferred to nitrate by some phytoplankton species. Generally, during the spring outburst of diatoms in temperate seas and at high latitudes, it is the nitrate, present in large amounts, which the phytoplankton draws upon heavily, but the reduction in ammonium and nitrite seen later in the uppermost layers is doubtless partly a result of utilization by plants.

Other essential elements

The number of other constituents essential for the growth of phytoplankton is not fully known, though we do know that quite a number of elements are required by plants at extremely low concentrations. For example, copper occurs in seawater in very small amounts, the solubility of cupric copper being very low in seawater. Atkins quoted a mean figure of some 10 mg Cu/m^3 but in a later paper (1953) he includes data from workers from various regions of the Atlantic suggesting a range of 6–25 mg Cu/m^3. Chow and Thompson (1952) quote analyses from different sea areas which show a very wide range in concentrations, the minimum is < 1 mg Cu/m^3. Some of the relatively very high values may be misleading owing to metallic contamination but where true high concentrations have been recorded these are associated with coastal drainage. For example, Riley (1937) gives a maximum of 15 mg Cu/m^3 for waters in the Gulf of Mexico near the Mississippi mouth (Fig. 7.24), but even higher values are given for the Baltic. In some recent determinations from inshore English Channel waters using an all-plastic sampling device we have, however, not yet recorded copper concentrations exceeding 4 mg Cu/m^3.

Many invertebrates possess the copper compound haemocyanin in the blood, and copper is also an essential constituent of certain enzymes concerned in oxidative metabolism. Some animals, including sponges and oysters, concentrate copper to a considerable extent and this is true even more of some seaweeds. Goldberg (1957) gives an enrichment factor of × 7500. 'Since copper enters into the composition of both plants and animals, very small amounts would appear to be essential. In this connexion Atkins (1953) has been able to demonstrate a seasonal variation in copper from 1–25 mg Cu/m^3 for the English Channel. Gallium, zinc, molybdenum, cobalt and other elements have also been claimed as essential for the growth of marine organisms from experiments on the culture of marine algal species. Recent investigations by Nicholls, Curl and Bowen (1959) have indicated wide differences in the content of a large number of trace elements in different species of zooplankton. Each of the elements also appears to be concentrated, at least by some of the species. Thus copper is concentrated by a number of zooplankton forms including *Calanus*; nickel by *Calanus* and especially *Sagitta*; lead by *Centropages*; and cobalt by *Sagitta* and *Limacina*. How far this variety of trace elements is essential to phytoplankton and zooplankton is still, however, uncertain. But, of the better known trace elements, three may be discussed more fully.

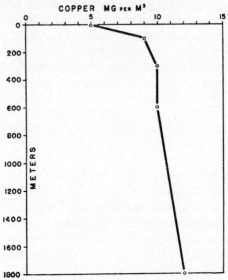

Fig. 7.24 Vertical distribution of copper in the Gulf of Mexico south of Mississippi delta (from Riley, 1937).

Iron

Iron is known to be an essential constituent of plants and animals. It is a part of the cytochrome system and in plant cells it occurs as part of the chlorophyll molecule. In the sea, iron is present in minute traces, of the order of less than 1 mg Fe/m^3 to a maximum of 50 mg Fe/m^3. The iron occurs almost entirely as ferric hydroxide and this is highly insoluble in seawater. Small quantities of ferric phosphate may occur also. Cooper has shown that the amount of true ionic ferric iron present in seawater is an extremely minute quantity, and most of the small amounts of iron which do occur in the sea are present as either very small particles or as colloidal matter. One of the difficulties in estimating the amount of iron in seawater is to separate the coarser particulate iron from what might be termed the colloidal fraction (cf. Fox *et al.*, 1952).

For the English Channel, Cooper (1935a) suggested that the amount of total iron varied from *ca.* 4–25 mg Fe/m³. In Norwegian waters Braarud and Klem (1931) found similar variations with the higher concentrations at the surface near to land. More recently Armstrong (1957), using a different analytical method, has found higher values for total iron. Near Plymouth the surface waters may contain even as much as 200 mg Fe/m³; further offshore, although the surface concentration may reach 100 mg Fe/m³, the average for the water column rarely exceeded 70 mg Fe/m³. Minimum concentrations might fall below 5 mg Fe/m³. Armstrong, therefore,

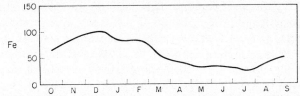

Fig. 7.25 Seasonal variations in iron content of seawater at Friday Harbour, Washington, plotted as monthly means. Units mg Fe/m³ (Redrawn from data from Thompson and Bremner, 1935).

confirms Cooper's finding of a marked seasonal variation in iron. The reduction in quantity appears to take place, as might be expected, after the main spring growth of diatoms, but the values tend to be less regular than with other nutrients. In the open oceans only a milligram or two of iron per cubic metre may be detectable in the uppermost layers. Seiwell (1935a), working in the Gulf of Maine down to a depth of 300 m, found a range of 5–40 mg/m³ in the deeper layers; the upper 40 or 50 m showed a rather similar range but in one area during August the concentration of iron was zero in the first 40 m. It is possible, as Harvey suggests, that larger aggregations of colloidal particles in the open oceans may sediment to some extent in the absence of turbulence so denuding the uppermost layers of iron. Inshore waters may show larger amounts of iron. Thus Thompson and Bremner (1935) found a maximum of nearly 100 mg Fe/m³ (total iron) in Friday Harbour, but there was an obvious fall in March to 26 mg Fe/m³ and fairly low concentrations persisted till about September (Fig. 7.25). Even in the deep water off the continental shelf the same authors found rather higher total iron (12 to > 50 mg/m³) than in the English Channel and there was a suggestion of a slight increase in deeper water. Cooper (1948) gives a mean value for the upper waters of the English Channel (down to

50 m depth) of 14 mg Fe/m^3 during mid-winter, almost the whole of this iron being particulate; but he shows that the water near the bottom was much richer in iron, the amount also being more variable. This is probably partly due to a more coarsely particulate fraction, which to a small extent may be carried into the upper layers. It appears from the work of Harvey (1937a), who tested the effect of very minute amounts of colloidal ferric hydroxide on the growth of diatoms, that only a very small amount of iron is necessary for healthy plant growth. It is still possible, however, that on certain occasions the amount of iron in the upper layers of open oceans may temporarily become limiting. This lack of iron would appear to depend chiefly on the aggregation of particles. Aggregation, however, is prevented to a considerable extent by the minute amount of organic substances in seawater, especially those released during defaecation by the zooplankton. Thus the feeding activity may be of significance in preventing sedimentation. Furthermore, since the colloidal particles may be readily adsorbed on plankton, the iron present in the upper layers may pass fairly rapidly through several cycles of uptake by plants and return to the water by zooplankton.*

Phytoplankton cells have been shown by Harvey to make use of these colloidal particles or larger aggregates of ferric hydroxide which adhere to the surfaces of the cells, presumably by adsorption. Thus an analysis of phytoplankton tends to show much higher quantities of iron than could possibly be obtained by the plants from iron in true solution; indeed the amount of iron recovered from diatoms exceeds the amount of phosphate. The mechanism by which this particulate iron enters the protoplasm of the plant cells is debatable. It is possible that the particles are actually engulfed or ingested by the protoplasm, but where the cells have a complete layer of cellulose or other material without interstices, it is believed that a very slow solution of the adherent particles must take place at the surface, possibly at a lower pH. This amount is sufficient to satisfy the requirements of the plant cells (Harvey, 1955). A recent observation by Goldberg shows that one marine diatom, *Asterionella japonica*, can use only particulate or colloidal iron as a growth nutrient. Ionically-complexed ferric iron is not available for growth. Goldberg has also

* This might explain the lack of a seasonal cycle in total iron recently demonstrated by Menzel and Spaeth (1962 a) for the Sargasso. They found also little variation with depth (Maximum 5 mg Fe/m^3).

shown that titanium may be adsorbed with iron, so that the amount of titanium sometimes recovered from phytoplankton appears unusually large as compared with the extraordinarily low concentrations in the sea-water. In shallow waters turbulence extending to the bottom deposit may be of importance in returning iron into circulation. Cooper (1948) suggests that iron may be partly immobilized on the bottom and that it is probably essential for part of such iron to pass through the guts of bottom feeding animals. It then occurs largely in the form of faecal pellets and in such a modified condition can be more readily converted by bacterial action and returned by stirring to the upper layers as assimilable particles.

Manganese

Harvey (1947, 1949) has also demonstrated the beneficial effect of very small amounts of manganese in cultures of various phytoplankton species. It appears that concentrations of only a milligram or so in a cubic metre are essential for healthy growth, and even fractions of a milligram per cubic metre added to deficient cultures can show some degree of stimulation.

Harvey (1955) gives a range of 1–10 mg Mn/m^3 for the sea, studies in Pacific waters showing the same order of concentration; Goldberg's (1957) average figure of 2 mg/m^3 is similar. In the English Channel Harvey found a maximum of 1.0 mg/m^3; a few determinations which we have made further up the Channel confirm concentrations usually below 2 mg Mn/m^3. However, some water samples from the Irish Sea gave slightly higher manganese values, and results on the growth of some green flagellates suggest that perhaps differences of this order in manganese concentration may be of significance in affecting the crop at least of some phytoplankton species in the sea. It appears also that there is little or no data on manganese from the open oceans. McAllister, Parsons and Strickland (1960) quote low values ranging from 0.9–0.3 mg/m^3 for open waters of the northeast Pacific, but these analyses refer to samples collected only over a few weeks. Undoubtedly some of the manganese in seawater is present as particulate matter as oxides; manganese, like iron, can be adsorbed on the surface of particles in the sea, particularly on detritus and presumably on plankton. Since manganese is essential for healthy plant growth it is possible in some localities, particularly in sea areas far from land, that it may at least temporarily occur in such low concentrations as to affect the growth of phytoplankton. The possibility of sedimentation of particles in open oceans in the absence of turbulence must be reckoned with, as with iron.

Silica

Silicon occurs in the sea as silica and probably in true solution as silicate ion. The amounts in the oceans are very variable and the pattern of distribution cannot be summarized as easily as, for example,

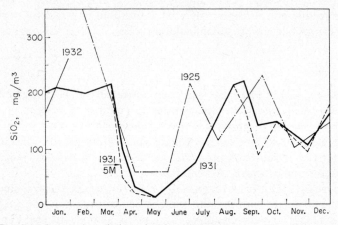

FIG. 7.26 Seasonal variations in the silicate content of surface water at Station El (English Channel) in different years (from Cooper, 1933).

for phosphate. Atkins, and also Cooper (1933), and later Armstrong (1954) have followed the seasonal changes in the English Channel: the distribution is somewhat irregular, though there is a minimum of silicate in the spring about April, May and June, with a concentration of 10–20 mg Si/m³ (Fig. 7.26). This reduction is of course due to the rapid utilization of silica by diatoms in the formation of the frustules. The amount of silica tends to reach its maximum during the winter period when concentrations exceeding 100 mg Si/m³ may occur — in some years > 150 mg/m³. Figure 7.26 shows the changes in several years from the results of both Atkins and Cooper. Rather irregular increases in silica can occur both in the surface and in deep water. Cooper records a marked regeneration in some years in August (Fig. 7.26). It is almost certain that silica is more rapidly regenerated than other nutrients, so that several cycles may be passed through, the dead diatom valves dissolving, and the silica being used again during the course of a year. Re-solution of silica can occur in the upper layers, but will also take place near the bottom from diatom frustules which settle there. Near land the amount of silica may be much higher as the amount brought down by rivers can out-weigh to a marked extent the quantities normally present in sea-water.

The amount of silica in some parts of the oceans can be very high and in general deep water shows very large amounts. It appears, however, that there is no maximum concentration of silicate at intermediate depths but that the amount of silica tends to increase with depth. Where turbulence occurs and deeper water is brought to the surface, very high silicate values may occur in the upper waters. For example, in Friday Harbour, U.S.A., just as the nitrate and phos-phate values are very high owing to turbulence, so the amount of silica is extremely high varying from about 1500 mg Si/m^3 to a lower value of just over 1000 mg Si/m^3. The minimum again occurs during the diatom increase over spring and early summer.

The silica content of the upper layers of the North Atlantic Ocean varies from *ca.* 20 near the surface to > 100 mg Si/m^3 at about 400 m depth (Cooper, 1952b). At 2000 m the concentration is > 550 mg Si/m^3 and this amount continues to increase with depth, being doubled at 4000 m. As one proceeds into the South Atlantic Ocean the amount of silicate rises, especially south of the sub-tropical convergence, and concentrations of the order of 1400 mg Si/m^3 occur in the deepest layers (Clowes, 1938) (Fig. 7.27). The highest value found by Clowes for the Antarctic was 3700 mg Si/m^3. More usually the maximum which occurred in deep water at about 4000 m averaged 3000 mg Si/m^3 (Fig. 7.27). The surface water in the Antarctic contains 1000–1500 mg Si/m^3 during winter, but with the growth of diatoms this is reduced to 250–450 mg/m^3 near the ice edge, and to lower values in more northern regions, where even total depletion may occur. In sub-antarctic waters, also, while some 100–300 mg Si/m^3 may be present in winter, low summer concentrations have been recorded with temporary total depletion in some areas. While the silica content of the surface waters in sub-tropical regions is not much less than sub-antarctic regions there is less obvious utilization, pre-sumably owing to the smaller numbers of diatoms. Hart (1942) also considers that the extraordinarily rich outburst of diatoms in the Antarctic causes a remarkable depletion of silicon in the upper layers.

The occurrence of thin shelled specimens of diatoms, in contrast to the usual normal shelled forms, he believes, suggests that silicon may be temporarily reduced to such a degree as to slow down diatom growth. There is little doubt, however, that silicon may be very rapidly regenerated and cannot be thought of as normally limiting

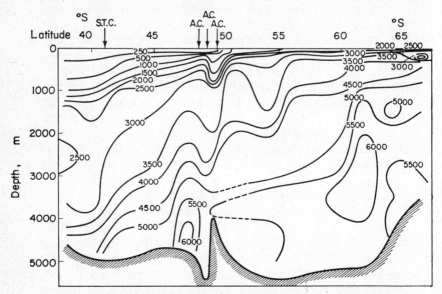

FIG. 7.27 Distribution of silicate in Southern Ocean along a section from Cape Town to the ice-edge in $66\frac{1}{2}°$ S, $42\frac{1}{2}°$ E. Feb/March 1935. Units SiO_2 mg/m^3 (not corrected for salt error) Note: The Antarctic Convergence (AC) has been crossed several times in the section (from Clowes, 1938).

growth for any extended period of time. Clowes points out that apart from silica regenerated directly from diatoms, much of the silica in phytoplankton consumed by zooplankton is fairly rapidly excreted and so returned to the water where it is utilized again. Hart also emphasizes the rapid return of silica in regeneration. However, Cooper (1952b) points out that some species of diatoms possess silica skeletons which when intact are remarkably resistant to solution. But in broken skeletons the fractured silica surface appears to be much more soluble. Thus diatom shells broken during the feeding of herbivores probably contribute considerably to restoring the concentration of silicate in seawater. However, solution of silicate from dispersed clays, derived from land drainage, must also play a large part in the silicate cycle.

Sverdrup *et al.* (1946) give vertical distributions for silicate at some stations which would suggest somewhat higher concentrations in deeper water in the Indian Ocean as compared with the Atlantic (Fig. 7.28). In the North Pacific, however, the deep water is very much richer (cf. Barnes, 1957) with concentrations exceeding 4500 mg Si/m³, i.e. even greater than the Antarctic regions (Fig. 7.28).

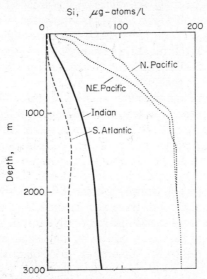

FIG. 7.28 Vertical distribution of silicate at individual localities in the North Pacific, South Atlantic and Indian Oceans (from Sverdrup *et al.*, 1946).

Effects of land drainage on nutrients

Mention has been made from time to time of the effect of river drainage from the land, e.g. in carrying silica into the sea. Some workers (e.g. Bigelow, Gran 1927) have suggested that melting of snow with the consequent run off from land into sea areas might carry sufficient nutrients to stimulate phytoplankton increase earlier inshore than in the offshore regions. It must be appreciated that rivers carry considerable quantities of nitrate and phosphate and these presumably assist in the maintenance of relatively high levels in inshore waters. Harvey (1945) points out that rivers rarely carry more than 5–10 mg of phosphate phosphorus/m³, unless markedly polluted. He suggests that these nutrients, however, are greatly reduced in summer, being rapidly utilized by the plant life of the estuary, and even in winter, when the plant life is greatly diminished, the beneficial effect of these nutrients in the sea is probably limited to a comparatively few miles close to shore. There is no doubt that estuaries can show considerably larger quantities of phosphate. For example, in waters around Southampton observations over the last year or two have shown values of the order of 40–50 mg phosphate phosphorus/m³ (Fig. 7.3A) as compared with the normal 15–20 mg which occur in the English Channel. High values are also given by Rees (1939) for the Bristol Channel. It must also be remembered that though the beneficial effect of these nutrients being poured into the sea may be limited to a small distance offshore, nevertheless the addition of these nutrients is partly responsible for the increased production in inshore waters. The results of Riley's investigation of Long Island Sound show the marked beneficial effect of increased nutrients, and in Southampton Water, frequent large outbursts of phytoplankton occur, presumably in response to the abundant nutrients which are being carried down. Kalle (1953) similarly calls attention to the strong fertilizing effect of land drainage, especially that due to the outflow of the River Thames, on the coastal waters in the area. This is believed to be responsible for the high chlorophyll and the relatively greater productivity of the area. Aurich (1949) also claims that the higher standing crops of diatoms and of nanno-plankton (especially *Rhodomonas*) near shore off the North Friesian coast are partly a result of higher nutrient due to intense mixing and, to some extent, land drainage. The effect of land drainage, however, may be masked to some extent if strong currents set along the shore line, thus carrying away extra nitrate and phosphate.

At the outfall of really large rivers the effect of the extra nitrate and phosphate may be distributed further into the seas. Riley (1937) has examined the effect of the river water outflowing at the mouth of the Mississippi. He showed that the great majority of phosphorus which is carried in the river water is in soluble form and, therefore, directly utilizable by plants, and he has also demonstrated that the phosphate is not exhausted where the river water reaches its mouth. He estimated that approximately 50,000 kilos of phosphate phosphorus are poured into the Gulf of Mexico daily. This would be sufficient to contribute 1 mg phosphate phosphorus/m³ every day to a layer of water some 50 m deep over an area of 1000 square kilometres (about 400 square miles). The contribution in combined nitrogen is also considerable. The Mississippi water contains on an average about 200 mg $NO_3 - N/m^3$ and even larger quantities of albuminoid nitrogen and some ammonium. The surface water of the mouth of the Mississippi thus has a higher nutrient content than generally in the Gulf of Mexico, and the phytoplankton is definitely more dense within approximately 80 miles radius of the mouth. The effect of this river can thus be regarded as of distinct importance as regards productivity, though even for this very great river system the beneficial effect is limited to a comparatively small area near its mouth. While the effect of land drainage, therefore, cannot be neglected in coastal areas, it cannot to any extent be an important factor in the fertility of really deep oceanic waters.

On the other hand, rain, and snow in higher latitudes, makes a small contribution to the combined nitrogen in the upper layers of all seas in the form of ammonium and nitric nitrogen. It has been held that this enrichment may be of greater significance in the tropics where the general level of nutrients is very low.

A rather special condition appears to hold for the Mediterranean (Bernard, 1939). Phosphate is low in deep water as water is constantly lost to the Atlantic and the inflowing Atlantic surface layer is low in nutrients. But the surface waters of the Mediterranean, though very low in phosphate are relatively rich in nitrate, and this, Bernard believes, is due mainly to enrichment by rain.

We have, therefore, now reviewed in some detail the more important of the minor constituents which are concerned with plant growth in marine waters. Some such as iron and manganese are fairly obviously concerned in healthy plant growth. Others such as copper, zinc, molybdenum, gallium, etc., have been shown to have a beneficial effect on certain algae in culture but whether they are even limiting in the sea is unknown. Two compounds, phosphate and nitrate, (together with nitrite and ammonium to some extent) are clearly of extreme importance to marine plant growth. In general it may be said that the values of both these essential nutrients in the upper photosynthetic zone, which is the only one directly concerned in basic productivity, are very low and fairly constant in sub-tropical and tropical areas. It would appear, therefore, that only a rather low production is possible in the tropics and sub-tropics and that production proceeds at a fairly steady level. The overall production considered on a yearly basis may be considerably greater than would appear at first sight, since the nutrients are probably more rapidly regenerated at the higher sea temperatures of the tropical regions and thus pass through several cycles during the course of a year. Nevertheless it appears true that over the tropical seas of the world the phytoplankton crop tends to be low at any one time, but as Riley (1939) has pointed out, the thickness of the productive photosynthetic zone may be considerably greater in tropical seas, so increasing the total crop.

On the other hand, in temperate zones, and to a considerable extent in the Arctic regions, there is a strong seasonal fluctuation in nitrate and phosphate with little more than trace values occurring during the late spring and summer. A summary of the changes in three of the important nutrients, nitrate, phosphate and silicate over a year in the surface and bottom waters of the English Channel is shown in Fig. 7.29. Only in the Antarctic is the quantity of nutrients relatively so large that much remains during the Antarctic summer despite the heavy demands made by the huge diatom crop. Liebig's idea of the law of a minimum has been applied to the production of phytoplankton in temperate latitudes, and to some extent in the Arctic, by Brandt, who suggested that the crop was limited by the quantity of nitrate and phosphate, whichever was in shortest supply. Phytoplankton production is not necessarily stopped by low nitrate and phosphate values, but low concentrations of these nutrients greatly decrease the rate of multiplication of the algal cells. For example, we have already quoted the results of Ketchum for *Nitzschia* that phosphate concentrations above *ca.* 17 mg P/m^3 do not affect the rate of growth. But below this value the growth rate decreases, and at concentrations less than 10 mg P/m^3, and even more strongly below 5 mg P/m^3, the rate of division falls off very greatly.

Steemann Nielsen (1954) and Steemann Nielsen and Aabye Jensen (1957) have roughly divided the oceans of the world into broad categories depending on the daily organic production, and this largely follows the amounts of nutrients available in the upper waters. Inshore temperate seas, which are fairly rich in nutrients, and also rich upwelling areas anywhere, can show a production of 0.5–3.0 g carbon/m^2/day. These regions have a very considerable admixture of nutrient-rich water, originating from medium depths, in the photo-synthetic zone. Those regions which have only a fairly steady admixture of such water as, for example, in the neighbourhood of divergences caused by Equatorial Counter-Currents, show a lesser production of about 0.2–0.5 g carbon/m²/day. As compared with this, the majority of the open oceans, especially in tropical and subtropical regions, show a production of only 0.1–0.2 g carbon/m²/day,

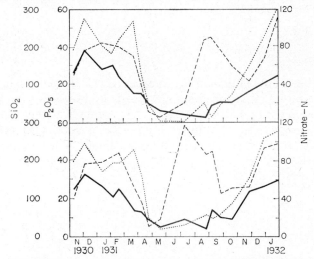

FIG. 7.29 Phosphate silicate and nitrate at Station E1 (English Channel) during 1931. Phosphate (full line) as P_2O_5 mg/m³; silicate (pecked) as SiO_2 mg/m³; nitrate and nitrite (dotted) as N mg/m³. Lower graphs—changes at bottom. Upper graphs—changes at surface, except that on April 7 and 22 phosphate values at 5 m depth (from Cooper, 1933).

and in special areas, where the upper water layers depleted in nutrients extend to greater depths (e.g. the Sargasso Sea), the production may be even lower..

Note to Chapter VII

The concentration of dissolved orthophosphate in seawater is usually reckoned in terms of the amount of P present as phosphate. This may be expressed as phosphate-P ($PO_4 - P$). Some early results expressed quantities as P_2O_5. Concentrations quoted by earlier workers were usually not corrected for "salt error". Thus some of the values listed in Chapter VII are too low. The corrected P values are approximately 1.3 times greater.

The amount of phosphate–P is today reckoned as mg–atoms P/m^3, or as μg–at. P/l. However, much of the extensive earlier literature quoted mg P/m^3 as a unit. Most of the values listed in Chapter VII have therefore been converted to mg P/m^3, though a few of the tables and figures quote the original units. Some indication of the equivalence of the various units is given below.

mg P/m^3	2	10	15	20	30	60
mg–at. $P/m^3 = \mu g$–at. P/l.	0.06	0.32	0.48	0.64	0.97	1.94
mg P_2O_5/m^3	5	23	34	46	69	137

The quantities of each of the three inorganic nitrogen compounds, nitrate, nitrite and ammonium are usually expressed as the amount of nitrogen, i.e. nitrate-N $(NO_3 - N)$; nitrite-N $(NO_2 - N)$ and ammonium-N $(NH_4 - N)$. In modern practice quantities are reckoned as mg–at. N/m^3 (or μg–at./l.). Most older literature, however, employed the unit mg N/m^3, and this unit has been normally adopted in Chapter VII.

CHAPTER VIII

FACTORS AFFECTING PRIMARY PRODUCTION–II LIGHT AND TEMPERATURE

IN TEMPERATE and high latitudes the main phytoplankton outburst consisting largely of diatoms occurs during the spring; the crop of phytoplankton cells soon reaches a peak density but then usually falls off rapidly. At about the same time the nutrient concentrations (nitrate and phosphate) drop very greatly (cf. Fig. 7.29, Chapter VII), as has been shown by Marshall and Orr (1927, 1928) for the enclosed waters of Loch Striven, and also by Harvey *et al.* (1935), Gran (1931), Bigelow, Sears and Lillick (1940), Riley (1939, 1941), Riley and Conover (1956) and many other workers for a variety of seas. In coastal waters and over banks, the great richness of the diatom crop seen in spring is often spoken of as a "bloom", but even in the more open seas, in temperate and high latitudes the spring increase in phytoplankton reaches remarkable densities. In northern temperate zones (e.g. Great Britain), following the spring peak which occurs about March, the crop in the summer tends to be fairly low, though varying in amount from month to month so that small peak densities may occur. Often the autumn sees a small increase again, but even when this occurs the phytoplankton, after this temporary rise, soon shows a decline in density, and in the approaching winter months reaches the very low values which are usually maintained over the whole winter (Fig. 8.1). In high northern latitudes the spring increase so called, may occur much later, e.g. in May or June as recorded by Gran (1931), Steemann Nielsen (1935), Kreps and Verjbinskaya (1930) and Gillbricht (1959) in Arctic waters. Digby (1953) found that the spring outburst off East Greenland did not commence till May, the main growth occurred in June and July with the peak density in that month. After a fall in crop at the beginning of August there was some recovery, but by September the remarkably low winter

189

levels were reached (Fig. 8.2). Thus not only does the outburst become later at high latitudes but apparently there may be only one major burst of diatom growth of very great density which lasts only a comparatively short summer period of some three months. Corlett (1953) has also shown differences in timing of the spring diatom outburst

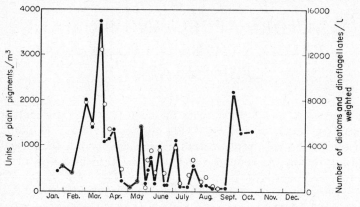

FIG. 8.1 Seasonal change in the density of phytoplankton off Plymouth, reckoned as units of plant pigment per m³ (solid circles and curve) and as total number of diatoms and dinoflagellates per m³ (open circles). Values apply to water column from 0–45 m (from Harvey *et al.*, 1935).

with latitude in oceanic areas of the North Atlantic, but rather further south. At approximately 60° N the increase began in late April or May; at a point some 370 miles south, the flowering was a month or even two months earlier in different years. At both stations, however, Corlett recorded an autumn increase in phytoplankton (Fig. 8.3). Comparable observations have been put forward by Hart (1934, 1942) from his work on the phytoplankton of the Antarctic. Hart shows that the timing of the spring increase definitely tends to become later as one proceeds south at relatively high southern latitudes in a similar way to passing north towards the Arctic, but due allowance must be made for the more severe conditions at comparable latitudes in the southern hemisphere (Fig. 8.4). At the highest southern latitudes Hart states that there is a continuous burst of phytoplankton production which occurs only after the midsummer period. This implies that at these latitudes there is no second autumn maximum — there is one burst of (mainly diatom) growth of great intensity which

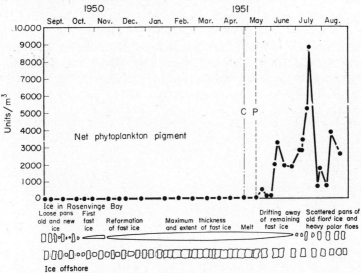

FIG. 8.2 Seasonal changes in growth of phytoplankton and in ice conditions in Scoresby Sound, Greenland.

C = date of onset of phytoplankton growth as seen by cell counts.
P = date by which phytoplankton growth was indicated by net pigment (after Digby, 1953).

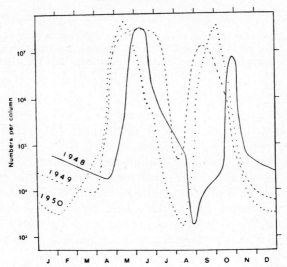

FIG. 8.3 Seasonal cycles of diatoms over 3 years from samplings from Ocean Weather Ship at Station "I" (from Corlett, 1953).

lasts over the short summer season (cf. Digby). At the latitude of South Georgia, however, Hart found the increase typically occurring in the southern spring with the maximum in November and rather lesser densities in December/January. By March the populations were distinctly lower but there was a slight increase in May indicative of a small autumn rise; populations then fell to the very low winter densities (Fig. 8.5).

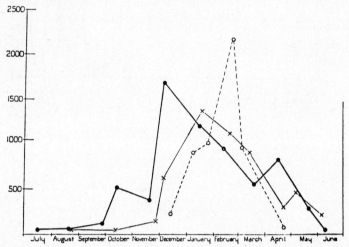

FIG. 8.4 Seasonal variation in phytoplankton, expressed as plant pigments per m³, in three Antarctic oceanic regions. Thick line = Northern Region; thin line = Intermediate Region; pecked line = Southern Region (after Hart, 1942).

The much stronger polar influence in the southern hemisphere is seen in the date of the spring increase off South Georgia. The latitude is comparable to north Britain in the northern hemisphere, yet the spring increase in South Georgia is in November which would correspond to the month of May in the north. But in Britain the outburst occurs in March, some two months earlier (Fig. 8.5). Corlett's comparisons also emphasise the more severe conditions at similar latitudes in the southern hemisphere. On the whole, Hart believes that the phytoplankton production at the highest latitudes in the Antarctic is less than slightly further north in Antarctic waters but the crop is also less variable from year to year.

In the northern hemisphere even earlier phytoplankton flowerings than March may take place at lower latitudes. Fish (1925) found that the increase was apparent as early as December at Woods Hole, and Conover (1956) working in Long Island Sound, records a 'late winter' increase, certainly as early as February. Here, however, complications arise due to nearness to land, and even partial enclosure of waters. Many authorities, as we shall see, have pointed out that spring

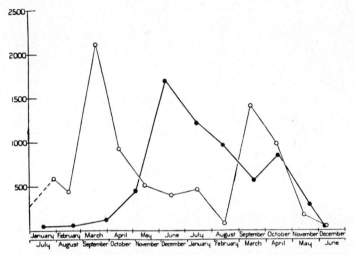

FIG. 8.5 A comparison of the seasonal changes in plant pigment per m³ in the Northern Antarctic Region (thick line) and in the English Channel (thin line) (after Hart, 1942).

flowerings often take place earlier close to land than offshore in comparable latitudes. Certainly latitude is not the only factor in the timing of the spring outburst of phytoplankton. A good example of the discrepancies which may occur is the observation by Riley (1957) that in the North Sargasso Sea at a latitude of about 35° N a small diatom increase, apparently analogous to the typical spring burst of more northern latitudes, was recorded, but during the month of April, whereas, for example, off Plymouth the vernal increase is usually early in March, as off the Norwegian coast.

The typical flowering in spring in temperate latitudes coincides with the increase in daylight. There may also be some change in sea temperature (*vide infra*). Nutrients, represented essentially by nitrates and phosphates, are at maximal concentrations which have persisted throughout the winter. It has, therefore, been considered that the rapid diatom bloom in the spring is a result of the increasing daylight, combined with an abundant nutrient supply. The rapid burst of diatom growth depletes the nutrients in the upper layers, and despite the favourable light conditions over the summer, the lack of nutrients, particularly with the establishment of a thermocline which restricts the supply of nutrients to the surface from the richer waters below,

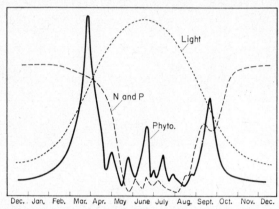

FIG. 8.6 Diagrammatic representation of the seasonal cycles in light, nitrate and phosphate, and phytoplankton in a typical northern temperate sea.

causes the amount of phytoplankton to be severely limited. With the coming of autumn, the cooling of the surface water and the occurrence of storms break up the thermocline and lead to mixing. A supply of nutrients, therefore becomes available again in the upper layers, and provided sufficient light is still available, a burst of phytoplankton growth can occur leading to the so-called autumn maximum. However, this growth is short-lived owing to the declining light intensities, and with the returning wintry days, the phytoplankton virtually ceases growth; although nitrate and phosphate are now building up to their maximum winter values with the processes of regeneration, the phytoplankton declines to its winter minimum (Fig. 8.6).

It seems at first sight that in such a cycle in temperate seas the beneficial effect of the returning spring could be partly due to light and partly to temperature conditions. Although different phytoplankton species have different temperature optima (cf. Chapter XI), it has been already shown that the effect of temperature on photosynthesis is largely masked by its effect on respiration. It has also been demonstrated that any increase of photosynthesis due to higher temperature can occur only in the presence of relatively high light intensities which are not usually experienced below the surface in the sea. Phytoplankton can occur in all the seas of the world, and it has long been known that some limited growth of diatoms may even occur under an ice layer—a point confirmed by Digby's observations. In any event, many investigations in the Arctic have shown that a marked outburst of diatom growth commences as soon as the ice begins to melt. Braarud (1935), for example, emphasized that a rapid production of diatoms occurred about June in the extremely cold waters of the Denmark Strait, off Greenland, as soon as the ice melted. Light was insufficient for phytoplankton growth while the ice was present, but the outburst of growth was independent of temperature. Hart (1934, 1942), has called attention to the same happening in Antarctic regions. There indeed the vast richness of phytoplankton growth over enormous areas of ocean takes place at temperatures ranging from about 2 °C to less than − 1 °C. It seems unlikely then that temperature has a direct effect on phytoplankton growth, though changing temperatures in the spring might still initiate the phytoplankton outburst. However, the seasons are delayed in the sea so that at the time of the spring outburst there is frequently little or no rise in temperature, and indeed temperature may be minimal then. Moreover, Marshall and Orr (1930) have studied the time of the spring outburst over several years in Loch Striven, and although they found some small variation in the time of the beginning of phytoplankton growth, these variations did not seem to be correlated with any precise sea temperature being reached. In most years the diatom *Skeletonema* is responsible for the spring increase in Loch Striven, and it appears somewhat unlikely that temperature initiates this outburst as this species flourishes in other seas from *ca.* 2–9 °C, i.e. at temperatures both below and above that found by Marshall and Orr for Scottish waters (*ca.* 6 °C).

There are also too many discrepancies between the time of initiation of the spring outburst in different seas and the temperature conditions prevailing to support the theory that it is temperature which controls the outburst. Thus in British waters the diatom bloom occurs about March/April with temperatures about 6–7 °C, whereas it commences at the same time in the Gulf of Maine where the waters may be only 2–3 °C, and off the Norwegian Coast at the same time at a temperature of 4–5 °C. Moreover, Kreps and Verjbinskaya (1930) observed a diatom outburst beginning in May at a latitude of 73° N in Arctic waters where the water temperature was − 1 °C, whereas further south at latitude 70° N, in water of Atlantic origin with a temperature considerably higher (2.5 °C) the outburst had not yet begun (Table 8.1). Bigelow, working in the Gulf of Maine, various investigators such as Gran in Norwegian waters and Steemann Nielsen for waters off Iceland, have all observed discrepancies in the time of the spring outburst which cannot be explained on a basis of temperature differences. Although as will be demonstrated later, temperature can be of very great significance *indirectly* in relation to phytoplankton growth, it appears that it does not have a direct effect in initiating the diatom outburst in the spring.

The importance of light as a factor in primary productivity hardly needs emphasis. Earlier discussions on compensation depth (Chapter VI) have drawn attention not only to the variation in incident light falling on the sea surface but also to the relatively rapid absorption of light in the ocean. We must first look at differences in the incident light. Kimball has computed values for the total solar radiation reckoned as gramme calories falling on a horizontal surface one square centimetre in area for different parts of the world. At sea level the average solar radiation for the whole earth is approximately 1.5 g cal/cm²/min, but the amount varies greatly with latitude, and a very strong seasonal effect is experienced, particularly at high latitudes. Thus in polar regions there is virtually no solar radiation for three or four winter months, whereas light is continuous day and night near midsummer. Factors other than latitude, especially cloudiness, however, affect incident light. Table 8.2 taken from Sverdrup *et al.* (1946) shows the average amounts of radiation from the sun and sky for each month of the year for various latitudes, taking into consideration both latitude and cloudiness and also other smaller factors. In March, when the sun is overhead at the equator, the intensity of sunlight at 50 °N latitude is only about one half that at the equator. Harvey (1955) gives another form of comparison: he has calculated that approximately 600 kilolux hours falls each day as a surface illumination on tropical regions throughout the year, whereas it is only during the height of the summer, about May/June, that such illumination is experienced at 50 °N latitude. In mid-winter at 50 °N the incident illumination is only just over a tenth of this value.

These differences between the incident light at different latitudes and also between summer and winter intensities at higher latitudes

TABLE 8.1. Chlorophyll content in the upper 25 m and of nutrient salts in the upper 10m, Kola meridian (long. 33° 30' E) May, 1929 (from KREPS and VERJBINSKAYA, 1930).

Position	69° 30' N	70° N	70° 30' N	71° N	71° 30' N	72° N	72° 30' N	73° N	73° 30' N
P_2O_5 mg/m³	12	36	36	44	38	21	21	21	17
Nitrate N_2 mg/m³	27	90	65	81	74	54	53	17	16
Chlorophyll mg/m³	12×10^{-2}	0	0	0	0	6.5×10^{-2}	8.2×10^{-2}	1.8×10^{-2}	4.1×10^{-2}

are, however, greatly accentuated when one also takes into consideration the relatively poor penetration of light into the oceans. There
is first of all the question of loss of light falling on the surface of the
sea due to reflection. This surface loss has been shown to depend
very greatly on the altitude of the sun. The nearer the sun approaches
to being directly overhead, the smaller is the amount lost by reflection.
At altitudes down to about 30° the loss is still small; taking the reflection from the sun directly and also that from the sky both into

TABLE 8.2. Average amounts of radiation from sun and sky,
expressed in gm. cal/cm²/min, which reaches the sea surface in the
stated localities (after Kimball) (from Sverdrup et al., 1946).

Locality		Month					
Lat.	Long.	Febr.	Apr.	June	Aug.	Oct.	Dec.
60° N	7° E−56° W	0.053	0.207	0.292	0.212	0.074	0
52° N	10° W	0.089	0.219	0.267	0.211	0.104	0.041
42° N	66−70° W	0.138	0.272	0.329	0.267	0.174	0.086
30° N	65−77° W	0.165	0.285	0.310	0.282	0.188	0.142
10° N	61−69° W	0.276	0.305	0.276	0.292	0.269	0.239
0°	48° W and 170° E	0.265	0.297	0.300	0.340	0.362	0.278
10° S	72−171° E	0.308	0.289	0.253	0.306	0.313	0.303
30° S	110° W	0.330	0.209	0.130	0.176	0.321	0.390
52° S	58° W	0.237	0.112	0.039	0.097	0.222	0.302
60° S	45° W	0.171	0.056	0	0.054	0.156	0.221

account, it amounts to not more than about 6%. Below an altitude
of 30°, however, the amount reflected increases very much, so that,
for example, at an altitude of 10° as much as a quarter of the total
incident light may be reflected from the surface of the sea. It is clear
that this surface loss will be very considerable even at moderate latitudes during the early morning and in the evening when the sun is
near rising or near setting, and also during the very short days of
winter at high latitudes. Surface reflection does vary slightly apart
from altitude; for instance, it is increased somewhat by the
presence of waves. The amount of light which can penetrate the sea
may therefore be considerably reduced, particularly at high latitudes,
but now the problem arises of how much reaches deeper water.
    It will be remembered that of the total solar radiation reaching
the surface of the sea, a considerable amount, almost 50%, is in the
infra-red, and this region of the spectrum is extremely rapidly ab-

sorbed in seawater so that only a small fraction remains after the first metre or so (Chapter I). Ultra-violet rays are also rapidly absorbed so that it is the visible region of the spectrum which penetrates best into the oceans. Nevertheless *all* wavelengths of the spectrum including the visible are *relatively* rapidly absorbed, so that for the clearest oceanic water it has been computed that nearly 60% of the total incoming energy is absorbed in the first metre, and about 80% in the first 10 m (Fig. 1.2, Table 8.3).

TABLE 8.3. Percentage amounts of total incident solar energy at various depths for different types of seawater (modified from Jerlov, 1951).

Depth (metres)	Oceanic Water		Coastal Waters		
	Type I	Type II	Type 1	Type 3	Type 9
0	100	100	100	100	100
1	44.5	42.0	36.9	33.0	17.6
5	30.2	23.4	14.2	9.3	1.0
10	22.2	14.2	5.9	2.7	0.05
50	5.3	0.70	0.02	0.0006	—
100	0.53	0.02	—	—	—

Type I = clearest ocean water.
Type II = relatively turbid oceanic water (e.g. Red Sea).
Types 1, 3, 9 = coastal waters of increasing turbidity.

We may now, however, restrict consideration to the visible part of the spectrum which roughly may be thought of as consisting of those wavelengths from red (about 750 mμ) to violet (about 350 mμ). Approximately almost one half of the total emission from the sun is in this visible region. Absorption even in pure water is relatively rapid: about half the total visible light remains at a depth of only 10 m in pure water. In the sea there tends to be a greater loss than this, even in oceanic waters. The rapid loss of light is due both to absorption, and to scattering of the light by water molecules and by particles suspended in the water. Thus the rate of absorption is greatly accelerated as the turbidity of the water increases (Fig. 8.7).

The method most generally used now for measuring the absorption of light in water is to suspend a photometer enclosed in a watertight casing to various depths in the sea. The photocell is mounted behind a clear glass window with a diffusing disc on the outside. The photocell is suspended by an electrical cable so that the current generated at various depths can be read on a sensitive micro-ammeter. One difficulty is that the incident light intensity can vary greatly, especially with clouds temporarily obscuring the sun. Therefore a matched photocell in a similar housing is mounted on the deck of the ship which is attempting to measure submarine light intensities, so that

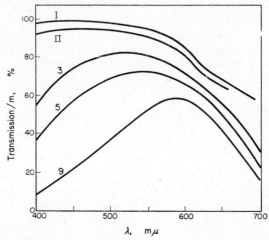

FIG. 8.7 Light penetration for 2 types of ocean water (I and II), and 3 types of coastal waters (3, 5 and 9) of increasing turbidity. Transmission per cent per metre (redrawn from Jerlov, 1951).

the incident solar radiation can be measured simultaneously with the sub-surface intensity. Care must be taken in siting the photometer on the deck of the ship to avoid shadow. The rate at which the visible radiation decreases with depth is usually expressed as the extinction coefficient (k). This extinction coefficient may be defined as follows:

$$k = 2.3 \frac{(\log I_1 - \log I_2)}{d_2 - d_1}.$$

where I_1 is the intensity at depth (d_1) measured in metres, and I_2 is the intensity at a greater depth (d_2).

Before the development of the submarine photometer by such workers as Atkins, Poole, Clarke and Jerlov, the use of the Secchi Disc was prevalent. This is a white disc of standard size which can be lowered from the research vessel; the depth is noted at which it just disappears from sight. Clearly such a method is open to error owing to differences in personal observation and to many other factors. Nevertheless it is a useful method for obtaining a rough estimate of the transparency of the water, and it has been shown by Harvey that an approximate value for the extinction coefficient can be calculated from Secchi Disc observations, provided these have been obtained by a well trained observer. The formula is as follows:

$$k = \frac{1.7}{d},$$ where $k =$ the extinction coefficient and $d =$ depth at

which the Disc just disappears from sight.

The extreme uppermost layers of the sea often appear to be somewhat less transparent to light rays than lower layers, and, quite apart from the amount of light which is reflected from the surface, there often appears to be a very rapid absorption in the first metre. This has sometimes been included with the surface loss due to reflection. Powell and Clarke (1936), by suspending an inverted submarine photometer just beneath the surface of the sea, were able to investigate this loss, and they found that it increased considerably during rough weather. It appears that the 'loss' is not a true reflection but is largely an absorption of light due to foam and air bubbles occurring in the uppermost stratum, a metre or less in depth. Apart from this immediate reduction in light, there is often a relatively sudden decrease in transparency of seawater where there is a fairly sharp density change with depth, i.e. especially in the region of the thermocline. It is probable that this rapid loss in transparency is due to the absorption and scattering of light, due to the presence of rather larger amounts of detritus, which tend to accumulate about the level of the thermocline.

As light passes down in the sea it is not only absorbed and scattered; its spectral composition changes with depth; that is to say, seawater and indeed freshwater and pure water display different degrees of transparency to the various wavelengths of visible light. Strictly speaking, therefore, in quoting an extinction coefficient for any mass of seawater, it is necessary to specify the particular wavelength.

Distilled water is most transparent in the blue region of the spectrum, and violet and green wave-bands are somewhat more rapidly absorbed. The longer wavelengths corresponding to the red region, are, by contrast, extremely rapidly absorbed in pure water. Investigations, especially by Clarke (1936), Jerlov (1951) and others, have demonstrated that the clearest tropical oceanic water such as occurs in the Sargasso Sea, or in mid-Pacific, is practically speaking as transparent as distilled water and shows maximum transparency at the blue end of the spectrum (Figs. 8.8, 8.9). Even so, for the purest ocean water light rays are still very rapidly absorbed (Fig. 8.10). In the clearest tropical waters, of the blue rays which penetrate best, only approx-

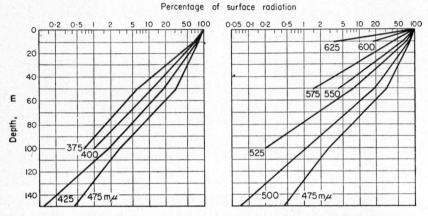

FIG. 8.8 Penetration of daylight in oceanic waters off Bermuda. The penetration expressed as percentage of surface radiation is shown for various wavelengths (after Jerlov, 1951).

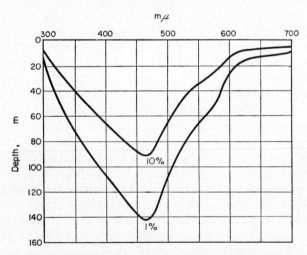

FIG. 8.9 Depths at which the percentage of the surface radiation reaches 10% and 1% respectively for various wavelengths in the clearest ocean waters (after Jerlov, 1951).

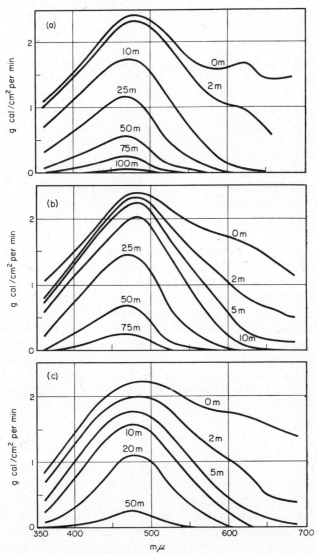

FIG. 8.10 The amounts of light of different wavelengths reaching various
depths for 3 tropical oceanic regions:
(a) = Indian Ocean, 11°25' S, 102°08' E (Stat. 192),
(b) = E. Mediterranean, 33°54' N, 28°17' E (Stat. 277),
(c) = Caribbean Sea, 14°54' N, 63°55' W (Stat. 28).
(from Jerlov, 1951)

imately 1% of the surface intensity remains at a depth of about 140 m. For green light in the purest ocean waters, 1% of the surf :e intensity occurs at a depth of about 100 m, whereas for red light, which is so rapidly absorbed, 1% remains at a depth of only 5–10 m (Figs. 8.8, 8.9).

As one approaches more coastal waters, light absorption is very much more rapid, but there is also a change in the relative penetration of different wave lengths. It is not the blue rays which penetrate farthest but the green (Fig. 8.7). Thus in off-shore waters such as the Gulf of Maine and in the English Channel the green rays penetrate best. But the general marked reduction in transparency of the water is such that in the Gulf of Maine 1% of the surface light intensity even for the best penetrating rays, i.e. the green band, is reached at a depth of only about 40 m. In very turbid waters, close inshore, the reduction in light penetration is really remarkable so that, for example, in Woods Hole Harbour Clarke (1936) has observed only 1% of the incident light remaining at a depth of approximately 16 m for the yellow/green rays which penetrate best. This progressive shift to the yellow/green for maximal penetration in very turbid waters has been noted by many other workers. The rapid absorption of light in coastal waters is largely due to the suspended fine particles which scatter and absorb the light rays. The quantity of such particles increases very considerably with nearness to shore and, of course, with increased turbulence. Strong wave action, which stirs up the materials in inshore coastal waters, will markedly reduce the light intensity so that in shallow waters the light penetration may vary considerably even from one day to another, depending on weather conditions. It must also be remembered that the plankton itself will cause reduction in the penetration of light.

Apart, however, from the suspended and filterable matter in sea-water, which certainly reduces light penetration, it was shown by Kalle that there is present in seawater a soluble yellow pigment which to some extent is responsible for the rapid extinction of light. Jerlov (1951) has investigated the effects of this pigment material on light penetration, and it seems fairly clear that a large part of the difference between the transparency of oceanic and of coastal waters is due to the different amounts of the yellow substance which are present. It is believed that the substance may arise from carbohydrate-like material derived from plants, especially phytoplankton, but it appears to be brought down to the sea, to a considerable extent, by rivers.

In general, tropical rivers such as the Nile, carry small amounts; on the other hand, Scandinavian rivers according to Jerlov, appear to carry relatively large quantities, and there therefore tends to be a fair amount of the pigment in Baltic waters. There appears to be a fluorescent substance associated with the yellow pigment, but this has apparently little effect on transparency. Generally, the yellow substance occurs in relatively high concentration where particles are also present in quantity; thus in the very rich upwelling areas off West Africa and off the west coasts of South America, selective absorption due to the yellow substance is relatively high and this effect can be detected at considerable distances out into the ocean with the westward spread of the currents. A particularly interesting observation by Jerlov was the distinctly lower transparency in the Red Sea where, for a wavelength of 465 mμ (normally about the maximum wavelength penetration for clear oceanic waters), the illumination was reduced to 1% at only 70 m depth. This lowered transparency was not associated with an abundance of suspended particles but was probably a marked colour effect, possibly associated with the decomposition of an alga such as the well-known *Trichodesmium*, so abundant at times in the Red Sea. Coastal waters generally have relatively large quantities of yellow substance, and waters at higher latitudes tend to have larger amounts than oceanic tropical waters. Whatever the origin of the substance, as a result of its occurrence and of the presence of suspended material, tropical ocean waters are generally very much more transparent to light rays than are the waters of more northern and especially of coastal seas. The yellow substance is also at least partly responsible for the shift in maximum penetration towards the green in coastal waters. The extremely low transparency of turbid coastal seas to ultra-violet wavelengths is largely due to the pigment. Jerlov has demonstrated that while U.V. light is relatively very rapidly absorbed by all waters, clear oceanic water, low in yellow substance, is distinctly more transparent to U.V. radiation than coastal waters.

In the determination of extinction coefficients, only the vertical component of light is considered. The actual maximum intensity below the surface is in the direction of the refracted sun's rays. It must be remembered, however, that light is scattered in all directions during its transmission through the water, and considerably more light is scattered horizontally than vertically. Atkins and Poole (1940) found that the ratio horizontal light/vertical light was of the order of 73–84%, and that there was no obvious change in the ratio with depth. This has been confirmed by Jerlov (1951) who obtained a mean figure of 68% for Baltic waters, and again by Atkins and Poole (1958), though the ratio varied between 58% and 85%. Apparently as light penetrates into deeper water, a balance is struck between absorption and scattering preserving the obliquity of the rays. It appears then that the directional character of solar radiation below the surface of the sea is lost only very slowly. Murray and Hjort (1912) state that even at a depth of 500 m in tropical waters the vertical radiation is considerably more intense than the horizontal.

The penetration of light into seawater was discussed mainly in order to amplify the point that the light intensity anywhere beneath the sea surface is rapidly reduced. The rapid absorption of light by seawater is in fact responsible for the very low utilization of the incident light energy in the marine environment. Steemann Nielsen and Aabye Jensen (1957), for example, calculate that only 0.02% of the total incident energy is utilized in tropical and subtropical seas in organic production, although algae are able to utilize low light intensities quite effectively. Throughout the year, even in the tropics, therefore, the productive zone is shallow. But in temperate and high latitudes, during the winter, not only is the radiation reaching the surface of the sea greatly reduced, but also, owing to surface reflection and to the extraordinarily rapid absorption of all wavelengths, penetration is ineffective. Thus, if we consider the integrated radiation in the marine environment, especially at really high latitudes, it is clear that the difference in the total radiation over a day in summer and in winter is infinitely more marked in the sea than it is on land, and it is perhaps not surprising that winter in the sea in temperate and high latitudes is a period of little production. However, phytoplankton can grow well in winter both in the laboratory in cultures and in the sea. Small outbursts of phytoplankton growth have been observed by many workers in widely different sea areas, but such bursts of growth usually appear to be extremely short-lived (cf. Bigelow et al., 1940). The explanation is that the rate of growth of diatoms or other algal cells, is markedly reduced by the shorter day and the very much reduced light beneath the surface in winter. It will be remembered that observations on the compensation depth in temperate and high latitudes have shown how near to the surface this depth rises during the winter season. In fact observations from our own waters and from many other middle and high latitudes have shown fairly conclusively that only a mere surface skin can be productive over the winter. The phytoplankton cells, owing to turbulence, will easily be carried out of this surface layer, and with wave action will pass down into deeper layers where the light is no longer effective. They will, therefore, lose more by respiration than they gain by photosynthesis, and in this way production over winter is virtually

TABLE 8.4. Average energy in g cal/cm²/day in Lat. 52° N,
January to June, reaching the surface and reduced by the energy extinction
coefficient of coastal water (Type 1 of Jerlov, 1951) (after Cushing, 1959).

	Jan.	Febr.	March	Apr.	May	June
Surface	18.98	44.91	92.09	164.25	219.20	242.06
1 m	7.00	16.57	33.98	60.61	80.88	89.32
5 m	2.70	6.38	13.08	23.32	31.13	34.37
10 m	1.12	2.65	5.43	9.69	12.93	14.28
20 m			1.20	2.14	2.85	3.15
30 m					0.66	0.73

zero. An indication of the steadily increasing amount of light energy reaching various depths in the sea from January to June is given in Table 8.4. During the spring, therefore, the effective photosynthetic zone gradually becomes thicker in depth, and thus the phytoplankton cells are less likely to be carried out of this lighted zone (Fig. 8.11).

The initiation of the phytoplankton spring increase in temperate and high latitudes is thus held to be the result of the increasing light intensity. In Loch Striven, Marshall and Orr have shown that the initiation date is fairly constant over many years. There was, however, no exact correspondence between this date and the quantity of winter and early spring sunshine, and these workers have considered that it is the *total* light (i.e. the length of day and brightness) which is the responsible factor. This would also agree with the work of other investigators that any wavelength in the visible spectrum can be utilised by phytoplankton, and it is generally now conceded that the initiation of growth is a result of increasing light intensity and length of day.

It must be admitted, however, as we have previously indicated, that there are often anomalies in the time of the start of the spring increase. For example, in Norway the diatom bloom begins earlier inside the sheltered fjords than it does in the outside waters (Gran, 1931); in the Gulf of Maine different areas show variations in the timing of the spring increase (Bigelow, Lillick and Sears, 1940). A very important factor which must be reckoned with is the effect of turbulence, an effect stressed by Riley (1946), among other workers. Riley has shown that at the beginning of the spring increase the rate of phytoplankton population increase is roughly proportional to the

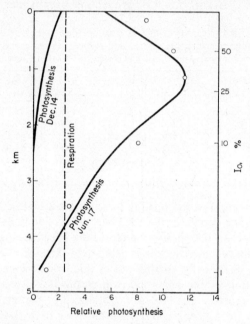

FIG. 8.11 Integrated daily relative photosynthesis from surface to depth of penetration of 1% of surface light for two dates, 14th December and 17th June, 1952. Dotted line represents respiration (after Ryther, 1956).

reciprocal of the depth of turbulence (Fig. 8.12); in other words, there is direct correlation between the phytoplankton rate of increase and the stability of the water column. While this relationship holds during the earlier weeks of the diatom blooming, later on, as the nutrients are exhausted in the upper layers, the increasing stability of the water column has an adverse rather than a beneficial effect on phytoplankton production in that it hinders the carrying up of nutrients from the deeper layers. Nevertheless, in the early stages of diatom increase turbulence can be inimical to the rapid development of the cells.

An explanation of the somewhat earlier diatom bloom in the Norwegian fjords is that the waters inside the coasts are sheltered and therefore rather more stable (cf. Braarud and Klem 1931), especially as there may be a reduction of salinity at the surface. Steemann Nielsen (1935, 1940) has also shown that in parts of the Baltic the reduced salinity of the uppermost layers throughout the year

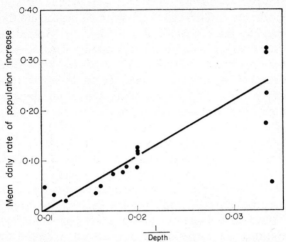

FIG. 8.12 Estimated mean daily rate of phytoplankton increase during March–April in relation to the reciprocal of depth of the zone of vertical turbulence (after Riley, 1942).

produces stability such that effective diatom production can go on even during the winter months in a very shallow uppermost layer (Fig. 8.19). Similar conditions have been found by Gross, Marshall Orr and Raymont (1947) and Marshall and Orr (1948) in Loch Craiglin, a shallow, enclosed sea loch with a water layer of lowered salinity on the surface. Marked phytoplankton production was possible throughout the winter months in such conditions. At the opposite extreme, Gran and Braarud (1935) have shown that the Bay of Fundy is an area where constant and very marked turbulence occurs. This region is, therefore, constantly rich in nutrients owing to stirring mixing the deeper layers, but, on the other hand, the lack of stabilization of the water prevents the diatoms being kept in an illuminated zone, and the stirring up of detritus by the turbulence of the water also reduces the light penetration. As a result the crop of diatoms in the Bay of Fundy never approaches the value which would be expected from the rich nutrients available. Curl (1960) has also found high rates of primary production in northern coastal waters off South America in the region of the Gulf of Cariaco. But off Margarita Island, where upwelling was strong, the high turbidity similarly prevented marked photosynthetic production, despite comparatively high levels of nutrients.

It would seem probable then that some degree of stratification is necessary in the euphotic zone for effective phytoplankton production, at least in the early spring, and that the start of the spring increase is delayed if some degree of stability does not occur. This was early emphasized by Riley (1942, 1946) and more recently has been investigated by Sverdrup (1953). He has re-introduced the term 'critical depth'; this may be defined as that depth above which the total photosynthesis is equivalent to total respiration per unit of surface. The significance of critical depth is that it can be related to both the depth of light penetration and the thickness of the mixed water layers. Sverdrup assumes that in the throughly mixed upper water layers the plankton will be almost evenly distributed. Production will thus decrease logarithmically with depth, since light decreases logarithmically, but respiration will be approximately constant. Since for population increase, total production must exceed total respiration, for a phytoplankton bloom to occur there must be a critical depth which must exceed the thickness of the mixed layer. Above the critical depth phytoplankton will increase, but if the mixed layer is so thick that turbulence sweeps the algal cells to greater depths, total photosynthesis in the column will not exceed total algal respiration and there can be no crop increase. Sverdrup was indeed able to show from data from the Norwegian Sea that during March the mixed layer varied from *ca.* 100–400 m whereas the critical depth was always less than 100 m and no phytoplankton increase occurred. In early April a great bloom was experienced; this coincided with the period when there was increased stability so that the mixed layer varied between only 50 and 100 m, whereas the critical depth with increasing daylight had deepened to > 100 m. Another similar observation is that of Marshall (1958) in relation to the earlier initiation of the spring diatom increase in the Arctic waters of the Bear Island area than in the adjoining deeper Atlantic waters. Marshall, by calculating the amount of incident radiation on the sea surface near Bear Island and the rate of absorption of light, first obtained a theoretical rate of reproduction for the algae in the euphotic zone. From this the theoretical production of carbon per day by the algae was estimated and this was checked against some actual measurements of production: production it thus appeared should begin in the Arctic waters in March/April. This may

TABLE 8.5. Comparison of critical depth of the mixed layer in Arctic and Atlantic water near Bear Island (after Marshall, 1958).

	Nov./Feb.	March/April	May	June	July/Oct.
Critical depth	0.5 m	30–140 m	140–190 m	190–240 m	240–300 m
Depth of Mixed Layer					
Arctic water stations	75 m	50 m	25 m	25 m	30–60 m
Atlantic water stations	200 m	200 m	150 m	25–75 m	40–80 m

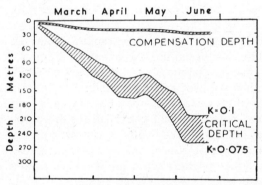

FIG. 8.13 Change in the critical depth off Bear Island from March to June (after Marshall, 1958).

be surprising at first sight as production did not begin in the Atlantic water near this same area until May/June. A comparison of the thickness of the mixed upper water layer showed, however, that whereas the Arctic waters off Bear Island showed the mixed layer less than the critical depth in March/April (when production of phytoplankton began), in the warmer Atlantic water the mixed layer only became less than the critical depth about May/June (Table 8.5, Fig. 8.13). Marshall believes that the shallowness of the mixed layer in Arctic waters is due partly to the intrinsic shallowness of the area but largely to the melting of sea ice promoting stability near the surface. For this reason the phytoplankton outburst follows the ice-edge north as it retreats with the late spring and early summer thaw.

The stability of a water column must depend to a large degree on the temperature conditions, i.e. slight warming of the surface layers will cause them to become less dense, restricting mixing with the underlying layers and thus causing stability of the column. Temperature can, therefore, be shown to have a positive effect on phytoplankton production, especially during the early flowering in the spring; a similar relationship in fact to the correlation already established with stabilization (cf. Riley, 1942, 1946). It will be remembered that temperature was shown to have little or no *direct* effect on phytoplankton production, but in causing stabilization of the water column, temperature may have the most important indirect effects. Slight change in salinity may also play a part in stabilization as we have already seen from Marshall's results. Certainly in the Antarctic the major diatom increase does not appear to begin immediately with the return of sufficient daylight but, as Hart and others have noted, it appears to follow rapidly upon the melting of ice. Probably this again implies some stabilization of the water column so that the diatoms are not repeatedly carried by turbulence out of the photosynthetic zone. The relation of the critical depth to the thickness of the mixed layer would clearly be of interest. Possibly such concepts might also help to explain the differences in the date of the vernal outburst already noted in the work of Kreps and Verjbinskaya — namely that coastal and Arctic areas in the Barents Sea showed an earlier phytoplankton growth than regions of warmer Atlantic water lying between (Table 8.1).

It would appear that lessened salinity at the surface plays a part generally in assisting stability in coastal waters. Thus Iselin (1939) considers that the slight lowering of salinity due to land drainage in the upper waters off the North American coast increases the stability of the water in that area. Nearshore areas generally must show greater stability, but the force and persistence of winds must also play a part in resisting stabilization and thus delaying spring blooming of diatoms. Corlett believes that some of the differences observed by him in the initiation of the vernal increase may be partly due to wind. Nearshore and especially partly enclosed areas may perhaps be protected, as well as benefiting from slightly reduced surface salinity and higher surface temperatures. Perhaps such factors together explain the early increase in Long Island Sound (Conover, 1956) and the even earlier flowerings at Woods Hole (Fish, 1925). Earlier suggestions considered whether nearshore areas benefited from extra micro-nutrients brought down by land drainage (e.g. Gran), and with our increasing knowledge of the particular requirements especially of organic substances by some plant organisms, this effect cannot be entirely excluded. Hart also noted the effects of land influence on diatom growth. Gran (1931), in discussing the variations in plankton production both regionally and in time, suggested that the supply of overwintering resting spores of diatoms may be more favourable in inshore shallow areas, the flowerings tending to spread out from the coast. Many other workers have considered the supply of phytoplankton cells necessary to begin the spring growth. A particular case is that of the ice-edges in polar regions. There is no doubt that the sea ice acts as a pseudo-neritic area, and both in the Arctic and Antarctic the characteristic diatoms found near the edge differ from the species typical of open oceans. Hart (1934) for example, quotes clearly neritic species such as *Fragilaria antarctica*, *Thalassiothrix antarctica* and *Nitzschia seriata* as abundant. It is possible that resting spores of such neritic forms are carried in the ice and thus early growth is promoted.

Several factors may probably, therefore, influence the start of the vernal increase of phytoplankton and certainly the variations in date cannot always be readily explained. Bigelow *et al.* (1940) discussed variations in date of commencement of the spring outburst in the Gulf of Maine and differences in the time of attainment of maximal phytoplankton concentrations. They showed that the western coastal sectors and western parts of Georges Bank were normally earlier (mid to late March) than the northern sectors and main central regions of the Gulf (late April), and that the difference in time could amount to as much as six weeks. They pointed out that neither temperature nor incident light could explain the differences completely.

Following the spring outburst there is no doubt that during the summer the setting up of a fairly strong thermocline with continued rise in temperature causes the upper layers to be partially cut off from the deeper waters. The lack of nutrients in the upper layers consequent on the flowering of diatoms then acts as a brake on the rate of phytoplankton production. (Fig. 8.14). Marshall and Orr in Loch Striven found that in certain years the stabilization of the water column came rather later in the season, so that the phosphate was not reduced so rapidly. As soon as marked stabilization occurs in any water, however, the phytoplankton crop tends to decrease. Off Plymouth, Harvey *et al.* (1935) suggested that stabilization set

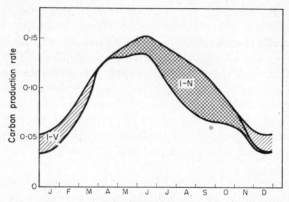

FIG. 8.14 Estimated rate of photosynthesis over a year in relation to light intensity, turbulence and nutrient depletion. Uppermost curve represents rate in relation to light.
1−V = effect of vertical turbulence,
1−N = effect of nutrient depletion
(after Riley, 1946).

in about May, and throughout the summer the crop tended to be small (Fig. 8.1). Bigelow *et al.* (1940) similarly showed that generally over the Gulf of Maine lack of turbulence during the summer limited the phytoplankton crop. On the other hand, it has been long appreciated that in areas where special conditions obtain so that considerable vertical mixing can occur in the summer, a marked continued production of phytoplankton may take place. Thus in the Gulf of Maine, the tidal currents impinging on the special shallow area of Georges Bank cause constant mixing; a fairly rich diatom crop exists, therefore, right throughout the spring and summer with the relatively more abundant nutrients. Friday Harbour has already been mentioned as an area where tidal flow causes marked turbulence; high nutrients are maintained throughout the summer with rich phytoplankton. At the same time turbulence at some seasons of the year may cause a marked reduction in light intensity, and the two factors, supply of nutrients and light penetration, to some extent must be balanced. In the Bay of Fundy, for example, the light penetration is relatively poor so that the crop is markedly reduced [cf. p. 209]. The compensation depth is much nearer the surface than in the adjoining Gulf of Maine, and only locally, where owing to run-off and temperature change a moderate degree of stratification obtains, does a modest surface production occur (cf. Gran and Braarud, 1935).

In certain areas the disposition of prevailing currents and winds, sometimes with the configuration of the bottom leads to deeper water being constantly brought to the surface. Where such upwelling occurs on a grand scale, a very obviously increased production of phytoplankton is experienced. In major upwelling areas, relatively deep water from perhaps 100–200 m is brought up to the surface and a constant supply of nutrients is carried into the upper lighted zones. One of the best known regions of upwelling is off the coast of Chile and Peru. The Humboldt Current and the Peru Coastal Current both have a fairly high nutrient concentration, but as the Current turns in a more westerly direction offshore, considerable upwelling areas occur. Gunther (1936) states that the average depth of the upwelling water is little more than 100 m, though this varies from place to place. The phosphate values correspond extremely well in that where upwelling is very active, high values even exceeding 35 mg $PO_4 - P/m^3$ occur, whereas lower values (less than 20 mg $PO_4 - P/m^3$) were found over the general Peruvian Current area. The total plankton is very rich in these upwelling regions. This applies both to the phytoplankton density and to the zooplankton. Though the intense upwelling areas tend to carry a somewhat heavier crop, the whole region is one of extremely high productivity and the mass of plankton is consistently large. With this rich plankton is associated enormous shoals of fish, particularly anchovies, and in turn, these shoals are responsible for a tremendous richness in bird life which is the basis of the well-known guano industry of the country.

The west coast of Africa is another well-known region of marked upwelling and high productivity (Fig. 8.15) (cf. Steemann Nielsen, 1954). The phosphate value is very high as compared with the general south Atlantic tropical and sub-tropical areas, and the plankton is markedly more abundant on the west coast in correlation with the rich supply of nutrients (cf. Chapter VII; Fig. 7.9). Another area where upwelling has been well studied is off the coast of California. Sverdrup and Allen (1939) have shown that a south-easterly flowing current is responsible for causing upwelling of deeper water over a considerable area. In general there was good correspondence between phytoplankton density and upwelling. Thus water at the surface which on its characteristics of temperature and salinity appeared to have existed as surface water for a considerable period of time, always had relatively few diatoms, presumably owing to the depletion

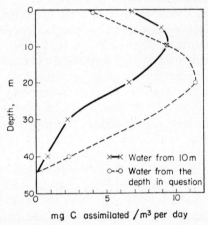

FIG. 8.15 Photosynthetic production with depth in Benguela Current, off Loanda, West Africa (from Steemann Nielsen, 1952).

of nutrients. On the other hand, water, which on its physical characteristics appeared to have only recently upwelled, generally had a much richer diatom crop. The persistent upwelling at very high southern latitudes bringing relatively very high concentrations of nitrate and phosphate continually towards the surface layers (cf. Figs. 4.19; 7.11) leads in a similar way to the remarkably dense crops of phytoplankton in Antarctic seas. As we have seen, the absence of light over winter months stops production completely, and at the highest latitudes the phytoplankton outburst of incredible richness is compressed into a period of three or four months. But despite the very heavy utilization of nutrients at this time, nitrate and phosphate never become limiting in Antarctic waters. Areas of divergence may also cause nutrient-rich water to reach the surface. The now well-known divergence close to the equator in the Pacific Ocean (p. 160) thus has surface enriched water, and Austin and Brock (1959) call attention to the high rate of productivity and the large crops of phytoplankton and zooplankton in this area which contrast markedly with the nutrient-poor tropical and subtropical waters to north and south. Bogorov (1959) similarly notes the high nutrient level and large crop of phytoplankton in equatorial Pacific regions of up-welling.

Outside rich upwelling areas the density of phytoplankton is the resultant of a number of different factors including, light, temperature and nutrient concentration. Moreover, the intensity of these factors

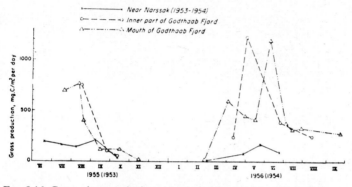

FIG. 8.16 Gross photosynthetic production at 3 coastal localities off Greenland
(a) = continuous line – Narssak.
(b and c) = broken curves; two areas of Godthaab Fjord (after
Steemann Nielsen, 1958).

changes with time. A good example is temperature with its effect on stabilization of the water column. Although early in the season temperature increase has a strong positive effect on production, later on, further rise in temperature has a marked negative influence. Similarly, reduced surface salinity may act as a barrier to upward passage of salts and tend to lower production later in a season. Thus off Greenland, Steemann Nielsen (1958b) has shown that various coastal areas give very different values for gross production over the year; very poor production is associated with cold but light surface water (e.g. at Narssak, Fig. 8.16a), which prevents the nutrient-rich warmer oceanic water coming to the surface. On the other hand, where there is mixing as in Godthaab Fjord (Fig. 8.16b and c), a very high production occurs. More generally in the waters round Greenland a high rate of production obtains where eddies are found bringing nutrient-rich water to the surface (Fig. 8.17). Somewhat comparable conditions are found in the North Sea; some areas show a more weakly developed thermocline over the summer and the increased supply of nitrate and phosphate can then give greater production. Gran, as early as 1931,

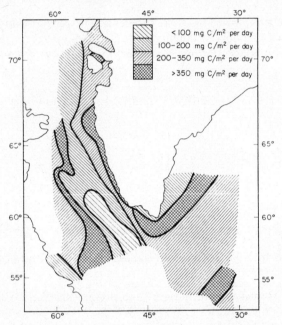

FIG. 8.17 Regions in the waters round Greenland showing marked differences in primary production (after Steemann Nielsen, 1958).

dealing with the regional and seasonal variations in plankton production, drew attention to the importance of nitrate and phosphate supply as well as light and temperature, and he pointed to the significance of turbulence, convection currents, and of current boundaries in renewing nutrients, apart from the grander process of upwelling. Holmes (1958), working in the North-Eastern Pacific, shows a fair agreement between standing crop and rate of production of phytoplankton and the concentration of phosphate in the euphotic zone. Indeed, other things being equal, the productivity was closely related to the rate of replenishment of nutrients to the upper layers. Thus while high values were typical of the waters near the Aleutian Islands (especially in the Bering Sea), off the South Californian coast and off no.thern South America, on the other hand, the tropical and subtropical north-eastern oceanic Pacific gave low production. Bogorov (1958 a) similarly compares the more boreal plankton just south of the Kurile Islands in the Pacific, with that in the typically tropical waters of the Kuroshio Current. The boreal area shows a high biomass of plankton (> 500 mg/m³) and a high rate of producti-

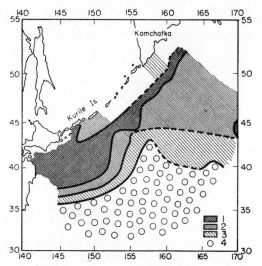

FIG. 8.18 Zones indicating different levels of primary production in the
region S.W. of the Kurile Islands, Pacific Ocean
(after Bogorov, 1958).

vity, whereas in the warm Kuroshio waters the biomass was < 100 mg/m³, and often below 20 mg/m³, and the productivity was about one-tenth that of the boreal waters. Bogorov states that on both biomass and productivity the boreal area is some tenfold richer than the tropical waters and he attributes this largely to the greater amount of nutrient available owing to vertical mixing. He emphasizes also that the mass of plankton for the whole water column from surface to bottom is much greater in the boreal regions (Fig. 8.18).

The supply of nutrient salts depends not only on the amount present in the layers and their replenishment, but to some extent on the rate of regeneration (cf. Chapter VII). Thus Steemann Nielsen (1958b) has noted that in the Danish waters of the Great Belt the maximum production, based on an average of four years, occurred in summer (August), and though there was a spring maximum in March, this was not so great as the summer peak. There was even a small production in winter, owing probably to the water layers being stabilized during the winter period (Fig. 8.19). Steemann Nielsen believes that the high rate of production of the summer is probably due to the higher summer temperatures determining the rate of regeneration of nutrient salts.

The significance of nutrient supply in phytoplankton production was of course early recognized by Brandt. As a broad generalization

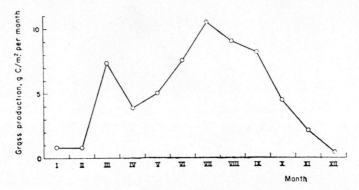

FIG. 8.19 Seasonal cycle in production in Great Belt waters (Baltic).
Mean monthly values are indicated
(from Steemann Nielsen, 1958).

it was suggested that the usually low level of nutrient salts in tropical and subtropical seas, omitting areas of upwelling, was associated with generally poor phytoplankton growth. This condition was contrasted with the generally rich nutrient waters of high latitudes which were characterized by high densities of phytoplankton. Though we may have to modify this view somewhat in the light of modern research, and though we must examine rates of production as well as biomass, the recent surveys of Bogorov and of Holmes generally support the original concept. The data in Table 8.6 taken from Hart's researches (1934) also suggest the vastly greater richness of high latitudes in the southern seas as compared with the tropics. The contrast is even more striking than the data suggest, as Hart points out that the phytoplankton productive season was largely past at the extreme southern stations, and the populations there were not nearly so rich as in the proper season of growth. Hart's results also illustrate another well-known general principle, that diatoms tend to predominate in polar or subpolar plankton whereas dinoflagellates, coccolithophores and other members of the phytoplankton make up a large proportion of the populations in warm seas. (Coccolitho-

TABLE 8.6

Stat. No.	Latitude	Diatomales		Dinoflagellata		Schizophyceae	
		Total	%	Total	%	Total	%
661	57° 36′ S	11,046,400	99.88	12,800	0.12	–	–
663	53° 34½′ S	6,249,200	100.00	–	–	–	–
666	49° 58¾′ S	354,600	98.42	5,700	1.58	–	–
670	44° 52′ S	14,700	89.09	1,800	10.91	–	–
671	43° 08′ S	52,200	76.99	15,600	23.01	–	–
673	38° 10½′ S	1,200	26.67	2,400	53.33	900	20.00
675	34° 08′ S	–	–	1,800	100.00	–	–
677	31° 16¼′ S	4,200	35.00	7,800	65.00	–	–
679	26° 06½′ S	22,500	81.53	5,100	18.47	–	–
681	21° 13′ S	2,000	20.83	7,600	79.17	–	–
684	15° 37′ S	400	8.69	3,600	78.26	600	13.05
687	09° 47′ S	2,600	26.00	7,400	74.00	–	–
690	03° 17¾′ S	800	2.98	6,000	22.39	20,000+	74.63
693	02° 59′ N	5,400	7.11	4,600	6.05	66,000+	86.84
699	14° 27¼′ N	1,600	12.31	9,000	69.23	2,400	18.46

(from Hart, 1934.)

phore numbers are not given in Table 8.6 as they were not quantitatively sampled.) With the high proportion of diatoms in cold seas goes a relatively small number of really abundant species. Thus in the Antarctic, though many species of diatoms can be collected, only some six or eight – *Chaetoceros* spp., *Thalassiosira antarctica*, *Nitzschia seriata*, *Corethron valdiviae*, *Rhizosolenia*, *Fragilaria*, etc. – are markedly dominant. In tropical waters a greater variety is usual.

The effects of more regular replenishment of nutrient salts to the euphotic layer is almost certainly one of the main factors responsible for the general observation that, at a given latitude, production of phytoplankton in inshore waters is usually considerably greater than in oceanic areas. Currie's recent data (1958) for near-shore and oceanic seas off Portugal suggest that both the rate of production and the biomass at the oceanic station is a mere fraction of that inshore (cf. Chapter VI, Fig. 6.8). It is difficult to avoid consideration of the biomass of zooplankton as well as phytoplankton in these discussions. Investigations such as those of Bigelow and Sears (1939) and Clarke (1940) indicate the richness of inshore waters as against oceanic regions and point again to the importance of nutrient salt supply. It is indeed most significant that the majority of the great fishery areas, omitting pelagic fisheries, lie mainly in relatively shallow seas, especially over banks and plateaux, where production of plankton is generally high. Almost all investigations—the North Sea, Gulf of Maine, off the Faroes, Iceland, etc.,—suggest the much greater productivity in general associated with near-shore regions, and this must surely depend ultimately on the greater primary productivity of the phytoplankton. A rather special type of comparison of the richness of phytoplankton in oceanic and neritic areas comes from the work of Hart (1942) in the Antarctic. The northern, intermediate and southern regions of the Antarctic Ocean develop similar standing crops which are only about one-tenth that of the area around South Georgia (Fig. 8.20). It must be appreciated that this neritic area, as it is called, extends for a very great distance from the shore. There is a suggestion that in this case the increased crop is not due to nitrate and phosphate primarily, but rather to such micro-nutrients as iron or manganese, which may become temporarily limiting with the excessive diatom growth (cf. Chapter VII), and which are enriched in broad zones in the neighbourhood of islands. However, the richness of even the oceanic Antarctic areas is outstanding in that the biomass is approximately equal to that of a neritic area—the English Channel (Fig. 8.20).

Riley, Stommel and Bumpus (1949) suggest that in offshore waters of the Western North Atlantic at lower latitudes, the crop of phytoplankton reckoned as the number of cells under a square metre may not be on an average, very much smaller than that of a typically rich boreal area such as the Gulf of Maine, provided that the short vernal flowering period of boreal waters is excluded. The average concentrations per cubic metre were less in the oceanic waters, but the depth of the productive column was greater. As an indication of the difference in surface concentrations, Riley et al. quote a seasonal range of 2500–45,000 for Georges Bank, 1000–23,000 for the "slope" water to the south, and 140–1900 in the Sargasso Sea, all being plant pigment (Harvey) units/m^3. Total phytoplankton crops beneath a square metre of sea surface at various times of the year are given in Table 8.7 (Riley *et al.*), though the peak spring densities in the Gulf of Maine have been missed. Riley suggests from the data that the total population for the year is about the same in the "slope"

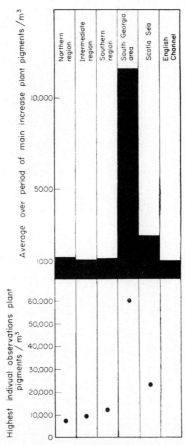

Fig. 8.20 Comparisons of the crop of phytoplankton, expressed as plant pigments per m³, over the period of the main increase in different areas (from Hart, 1942).

water as on Georges Bank; once again, despite the smaller concentration in the "slope" water, the vertical range is greater. With the Sargasso Sea water, however, there seems little doubt that the total population is distinctly less than in temperate waters, despite the greater vertical range (Table 8.7). The little data available on

TABLE 8.7. Summary of all available plant pigment analyses (Thousands of Harvey units per m² of sea surface) in the Western North Atlantic. Figures in parentheses show the number of observations on which the average is based (from RILEY et al., 1949).

Area	Year	Jan.	March	Apr.	May	June	Aug.	Sept.	Dec.
Gulf of Maine	1939	—	—	—	—	—	—	560(2)	—
	1940	85(1)	310(1)	620(1)	—	490(2)	—	—	—
	1941	—	820(1)	690(1)	1230(2)	—	—	—	—
Georges Bank	1939	—	—	—	—	—	—	560(22)	—
	1940	110(8)	1040(13)	2250(15)	860(20)	500(28)	—	—	—
	1941	—	350(29)	1390(31)	1280(29)	330(29)	—	—	—
Coastal Water Cape Cod – Montauk Point	1939	—	—	—	90(2)	—	—	—	—
	1947	—	460(3)	—	—	—	—	—	200(3)
Slope Water	1939	—	—	—	—	—	—	380(2)	—
	1940	250(2)	470(1)	3800(1)	220(2)	250(2)	—	—	—
	1941	—	890(1)	3540(2)	1180(1)	340(1)	—	—	—
	1947	—	370(1)	—	270(2)	—	—	—	300(1)
Sargasso Sea — N.W. of Bermuda	1939	—	—	—	310(5)	—	—	—	—
	1947	—	—	—	—	—	—	—	410(2)
Sargasso Sea — Bermuda to Azores	1947	—	—	—	—	100(3)	50(5)	—	—
	1948	—	—	—	—	—	—	—	420(7)
Gulf Stream System — Florida Straits	{1937 1939	—	—	—	480(5)	—	100(1)	—	—
Carolinas	1939	—	—	—	370(2)	—	—	—	—
Off Montauk Pt.	1939	—	—	—	300(1)	—	—	—	—

other waters at low latitudes confirm our earlier suggestion that the standing crop of phytoplankton in tropical and sub-tropical waters is distinctly lower than that of higher latitudes. Investigations such as these of Riley (1939) and later discussions (1953, 1957) suggest, however, that the rate of primary productivity in oceanic waters at low latitudes can on occasions be quite high. Ryther and Yentsch

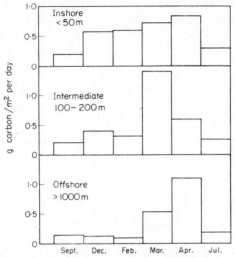

Fig. 8.21 Comparisons of the daily primary production for certain months at shallow inshore, intermediate, and deep off-shore stations (from Ryther and Yentsch, 1958).

(1958) have compared the production in inshore waters, "slope" waters and oceanic areas and have shown that the range of daily primary production beneath a square metre of surface is of the same order of magnitude (Fig. 8.21), provided various months of the year are included in the study. The range of gross production agrees well with Riley's estimate (1957). Ryther and Yentsch, however, point out that the total production over a year is not comparable, the inshore waters showing a considerably higher value than "slope" or oceanic stations. Offshore waters, it is believed, can occasionally show enrichment of nutrients which, with the considerable depth of the euphotic zone, will give a relatively high carbon production. But the constant and regular enrichment of inshore waters, together with the longer and usually greater spring increase, gives a total annual production which is of far greater magnitude.

226 PLANKTON AND PRODUCTIVITY IN THE OCEANS

The changes in temperature, and the effects of the subsequent setting up of a thermocline on production have been followed by Steele (1956), for the Fladen Ground in the northern North Sea. A typical spring increase with the establishment of a thermocline was observed, and production is then limited by the amount of nutrients in the euphotic layer. The tremendous importance of vertical mixing in supplying nutrients to the upper layers is clear in this study. A limited amount of phosphate passes vertically during the summer until the destruction of the thermocline in autumn. Steele associates differences in production for the area as a whole from year to year,

TABLE 8.8. Comparison of Northern North Sea, English Channel and Georges Bank (from Steele, 1956).

	Winter phosphate (g at/l.)	Yearly production (g C/m²)	Maximum plant population, mg chlorophyll/m²	Maximum zooplankton (g C/m²)
Fladen	0.7	54–82	100	5
Inshore	0.6	104–127	175	5
English Channel	0.35	55–91	210	5
Georges Bank	1.1	120–300	660	30

as well as differences between one area and another, chiefly to variations in mixing which act as a brake on production; he further correlates the extent of mixing mainly with wind. Inshore stations are richer (cf. Table 8.8) largely due to tidal mixing reinforcing wind effects. Steele does not include regeneration of phosphate in his estimates but he says this may be important to the extent of increasing annual production by some 25–30%. Ketchum, Ryther, Yentsch and Corwin (1958) have also emphasized the great importance of vertical mixing and of regeneration in supplying nutrients for plant production, while accepting the significance of light intensity, temperature and possible other factors. They have raised the very interesting suggestion that typically nutrient-impoverished oceanic tropical waters show especially low rates of *net* photosynthesis. It appears that if nitrate and phosphate are very low, these nutrients limit photosynthesis in the sense that most of the synthetic production is used again in respiration, so that there can be very little net production. Limiting values for phosphate definitely lower the ratio: net photosynthesis/gross photosynthesis. This may help to explain the general poverty of tropical oceanic waters, despite the fact that relatively high gross photosynthetic rates may be recorded. Ketchum *et al.* compare the gross and net photosynthesis in inshore and offshore stations. Apart from a far greater gross productivity inshore on occasions (range 0.6–13.3 mg C/m³/hr as compared with 0.6–1.7 mg C/m³/hr offshore), the net photosynthesis/gross photosynthesis ratio ranged from 0.4–0.9 at inshore

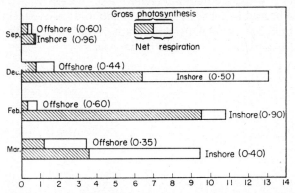

FIG. 8.22 A comparison of the gross and net photosynthetic production for inshore and offshore stations (after Ketchum *et al.*, 1958).

stations whereas it was only 0.35–0.6 throughout the year offshore (Fig. 8.22). The authors suggest that this may indicate that the phytoplankton in more oceanic areas is less healthy, perhaps on account of the generally low nutrient level. This might affect the levels of chlorophyll and of carotenoids in the cells. A further interesting suggestion on factors limiting production in the subtropical oceanic waters of the Sargasso Sea comes from recent experiments by Menzel and Ryther (1961). Using the rate of C^{14} assimilation as an estimate of production (*vide* Chapter X), they have shown that enrichment with phosphate, nitrate and vitamins did not increase the photosynthetic rate, but that of the minor inorganic nutrients, the addition of iron caused a rise in the rate of carbon assimilation. Iron thus appears to be the limiting factor, although with the very low concentrations of nitrate and phosphate, these nutrients also rapidly become limiting in more prolonged experiments.

In the next chapter we shall examine the suggestion that certain organic materials present in seawater in extreme dilution may influence the growth rate and density of the phytoplankton. Whether variations in the rate of multiplication of diatoms and flagellates can occur due to internal changes in physiological state ("senescence") as distinct from the effects of these varied external factors is not known for certain. In any event, variations in light, temperature, nutrients such as nitrate and phosphate, as well as possibly substances like iron and manganese, may all affect the multiplication rate of phytoplankton in a very complex manner. But changes in the rate of cell division lead to changes in the population density which in turn can be modified by sinking and death of the phytoplankton cells and by consumption of the algae by animals.

CHAPTER IX

FACTORS AFFECTING PRIMARY PRODUCTION— III ORGANIC MICRO-NUTRIENTS AND INHIBITORS

EARLY WORK on the laboratory culture of marine algae, especially that of Allen and Nelson (1910), suggested that even if all the known inorganic nutrients were available in sufficient quantities the cultures would not flourish. The addition of a small quantity of natural seawater was often sufficient for good growth in the laboratory. Evidence slowly accumulated for belief in the existence of substances in seawater in great dilution, possibly both organic and inorganic, which were essential for the healthy culture of marine algae (cf. Gran, 1931). The use of soil extract in "erdschreiber" medium (cf. Gross, 1937b) was a further example of the need for these accessory growth substances. We already have discussed the need for certain inorganic ions in trace amounts. Harvey and others demonstrated, however, that while such extracts as "erdschreiber" contained inorganic materials such as iron, even when these were added to a culture medium, the growth was not as great as with the complete soil extract. Later work of Harvey and others demonstrated fairly clearly that this was due to organic vitamin-like substances; the presence of thiamin and biotin as well as other substances in soil extract has now been recognized. A review of the development of media for the culture of marine algae is given by Provasoli, McLaughlin and Droop (1957). Clear evidence is provided for the need of both organic and inorganic micro-nutrients. While, therefore, vitamin-like substances or accessory growth factors must be present in sea water in small amounts for the healthy growth of many marine algae, some algal species appear to be able to grow in the absence of these substances. In other words they are presumably able to synthesize the necessary substances from simple components. *Phaeodactylum* is apparently such an alga which is able to grow successfully in the absence of several growth promoting factors which have been shown to be necessary for other species. It is improbable that we can list all the vitamin-like substances required by many algae. Thus Harvey suggested that substances like cystine were favourable to the growth of some diatoms, though it is not quite clear how far these are required; probably divalent sulphur is essential (cf. Provasoli *et al.*, 1957). However, vitamins of the B-complex are obviously commonly needed. For example, the more recent work of Provasoli and his colleagues (e.g. Provasoli, 1958) and of Lewin, Droop and others have shown that vitamin B_{12} or cobalamine is essential for the growth of a number of dinoflagellates, μ-flagellates and some diatoms, for example the planktonic species *Skeletonema costatum*. Droop (1957) points out that some algae such as *Rhodomonas, Dunaliella, Nannochloris* and *Phaeodactylum* do not require vitamin B_{12}; they presumably synthesize it from relatively simple substances. Other species, however, requiring B_{12} show considerable differences in their ability to grow successfully with various analogues of B_{12}. Thus of a total of fourteen species tested, only three responded to all the analogues presented to them. About half the species required B_{12} itself or closely similar substances. (See Table 9.1.)

If a factor such as this vitamin is essential for the growth of some phytoplankton it seems likely that vitamin B_{12} should be present in seawater. Preliminary observations by Droop suggested that considerable amounts, sufficient for the needs of the algae, were present in inshore waters (5–10 mμg/l), but investigations in more offshore areas such as the Northern North Sea and Norwegian Deeps by Cowey (1956) showed that, while in winter relatively high values of *ca.* 2 mμg/l might be present, in summer the concentration fell to about one tenth of this value (Fig. 9.1). The results obtained by Daisley and Fisher (1958) on the vertical distribution of vitamin B_{12} in the Bay of Biscay down to considerable depths are also of great interest. The euphotic zone and the greatest depths showed lower concentrations (mean 0.6 mμg/l) while intermediate depths varying from 200–2000 m gave higher values (mean 2.3 mμg/l).*

More information on the differences in vitamin B_{12} content of seawater from different regions and with the seasons is urgently

* Menzel and Spaeth (1962b) find up to 0.1 mμg/l vitamin B_{12} in the upper layers of the Sargasso Sea and the occurrence of a seasonal cycle. Below 200 m the concentration (*ca.* 0.2 mμg/l) was relatively constant.

TABLE 9.1. Specificity towards vitamin B_{12}-like factors (from Droop, 1957). Factor.

	B_{12} (5,6-dimethyl-benziminazole)	5,6-dichlorobenzi-minazole analogue	Benziminazole analogue	B_{12} III (Factor I)	Factor A (2-methyladenine)	Factor H (2-methyl-hypoxanthine)	Pseudo-B_{12} (adenine)	Factor B (No nucleotide)
Prymnesium parvum	+	+	+	+	0	0	0	0
Microglena arenicola	+	+	+	+	0	0	0	0
Syracosphaera elongata	+	+	+	+	0	0	0	0
Isochrysis galbana	+	+	+	+	0	0	0	0
Hemiselmis virescens	+	+	+	+	0	0	0	0
Gyrodinium californicum	+	+	+	+	0	0	0	0
Gyrodinium sp.	+	+	+	+	0	0	0	0
Amphidinium klebsii	+	+	+	+	+	+	0	0
A. rhyncocephalum	+	+	+	+	+	+	0	0
Monochrysis lutheri	+	+	+	+	+	+	+	0
Amphora perpusilla	+	+	+	+	+	+	+	+
Skeletonema costatum				+	+		+	+
Phormidium persicinum	+	+	+	+	+	+	+	+

+ = Activity 25% or more; 0 = Activity less than 1%; as compared with vitamin B_{12}

required. How far the vitamin content may influence production is
unknown, but with the different requirements of various algal species
the vitamin content could be of profound ecological significance
in determining which alga may bloom at a particular time, and thus
the distribution of vitamin B-like substances might play a very great
part in the spatial distribution as well as the temporal succession
of phytoplankton.

The arguments that have been advanced for the significance of
vitamin B_{12} may be put forward also for other vitamins. Droop (1958)

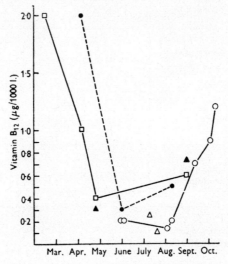

Fig. 9.1 Vitamin B_{12} content of filtered preserved sea-water samples
collected during 1955. □, Butt of Lewis; ●, Norwegian Deeps;
○, Northern North Sea; ▲, Faroe Channel; △, North Atlantic
(after Cowey, 1956).

investigated the thiamin requirements of several marine algae, some
littoral, and some truly planktonic. For several of the species investigated thiamin was essential for growth, but *Phaeodactylum* and
Nannochloris, (which do not require vitamin B_{12}) could also grow
successfully without thiamin. On the other hand, for the planktonic
diatom *Skeletonema* which requires B_{12}, thiamin was not essential.
Droop points out that whereas species such as *Hemiselmis* and
Oxyrrhis need the thiazol portion of the thiamin, other species such
as *Prymnesium* and *Syracosphaera* need the pyrimidin portion.

While vitamins such as thiamin, cobalamine and biotin are now often, therefore, used in culture media, we must recognize that a very much greater variety of substances may be present naturally in seawater. Some of these are growth promoting and some inhibiting. Perhaps the most widely known group of substances are those usually of an inhibitory nature, sometimes severely toxic, which are produced during mass blooms of algae. But we may also obtain evidence of extra-cellular metabolites liberated in soluble form into the water from experiments on uni-algal, preferably bacterial-free, cultures. From the results of some of these culture experiments it would appear very likely that carbohydrate-like substances and amino-acids, as well as carotenoids, fatty materials and other substances, occur in the sea. Johnson (1955) has given some account of the various chemical fractions which he has isolated from natural sea waters. One extract adsorbed on carbon showed marked growth-promoting properties on several species of phytoplankton cultures; other fractions would exhibit growth-promoting or inhibiting characteristics. In a series of papers Lucas (1947, 1955, 1961) has called attention to the importance of external metabolites in the sea. The production of extra-cellular substances imposes a biological history on the water and thus Lucas emphasizes that as well as various species of phytoplankton and zooplankton exhibiting species succession, the complex relationship between phytoplankton and zooplankton may not be one of the predator-prey type only.

The effects of extra-cellular metabolites produced during phytoplankton blooms may be so dramatic that perhaps these should be discussed further. Noxious marine plankton flowerings are usually due to organisms which tend to be red, yellow or brown in colour, and the term "red tide" is, therefore, usually applied to them. Minor bloomings often occur without markedly toxic effects, but some red tide outbreaks cause mass mortality of fish, crustaceans, bivalves and other bottom fauna, even of catastrophic proportions. Many of the earlier blooms cannot be positively identified as to the causative organism, but it is known that blue-green, and occasionally green algae can be responsible, but especially dinoflagellates. Of these, *Gymnodinium* spp. and *Goniaulax* spp. are probably the most important, but *Glenodinium* and *Prorocentrum* and sometimes other species have been identified. Apart from phytoplankton, ciliates and other organisms may also cause mortality in the sea with mass bloomings. One of the most strikingly toxic organisms is *Gymnodinium breve* (cf. Gunter, Williams, Davis and Walton-Smith, 1948), and more recently, Ballentine isolated the toxic species *G. veneficum* which has been shown (Abbott and Ballentine, 1957) to be extremely poisonous to a whole variety of animals: coelenterates, annelids, echinoderms, crustaceans (including zooplanktonic species), molluscs and fishes, as well as to non-marine vertebrates. A summary of red tide outbreaks is given by Brongersma Sanders (1957). It must be recognized that mass mortalities associated with red tide phenomena are not always directly due to toxins formed by the plant plankton but may be associated with depleted oxygen, organic debris and high bacterial populations.

It is of interest that *Gymnodinium* concentrations, among the few toxic flagellates tested by Bainbridge (1953), were apparently "avoided" by zooplankton. Concentrations of diatoms of several species and of some flagellates were entered readily by plankton animals, and mixtures of phytoplankton did not discourage migrations by zooplankton. Hardy, in Hardy and Gunther (1936), suggested that very dense patches of phytoplankton might be avoided by zooplankton or at least might limit their vertical migrations, and the release of extra-cellular metabolites by phytoplankton would suggest itself as a suitable antagonistic influence. Although Bainbridge's results suggest this is rather unlikely, except with readily recognized toxic phytoplankton species, less obvious effects depressing migrations are still possible. The avoidance by *Calanus* and herring of patches of *Phaeocystis* and *Rhizosolenia* in the North Sea is still a possible instance, though the harmful effects of the phytoplankton in this case may not be due to toxic substances. Beklemishev (1957) indeed doubts whether any clear instance exists of avoidance of planktonic algal patches by zooplankton owing to adverse chemical effects.

There seems little doubt that species of phytoplankton may prove antagonistic to each other. A study by Proctor (1957) on freshwater species of algae shows that of five common species, all grew better in unialgal culture, but two (*Chlamydomonas* and *Haematococcus*) definitely inhibited each other, with *Chlamydomonas* eventually becoming dominant. On the other hand, the flowering of some algae produces metabolites which are favourable to a later development of another species (cf. Chapter V).

There appears to be little doubt then that both growth inhibiting and growth promoting substances occur in seawater, some produced by phytoplankton and some by bacteria (cf. Chapter XVI) and possibly by other organisms. Thus Belser (1959) using a bio-assay method on a marine bacterium, demonstrated that of ten growth-promoting substances for which tests were made, three (biotin, uracil and isoleucine) appeared frequently in seawater samples. Other substances (glycine, threonine and tryptophane) were occasionally recognized. The concentrations of at least uracil and isoleucine showed considerable variations with time.

Again, Jorgénsen and Steemann Nielsen (1959) have obtained evidence of substances produced by unicellular algae which have both growth-promoting and growth-inhibiting effects on *Staphylococcus aureus*. It seems probable that only a minor part of the inhibitory substances were allowed to pass into the seawater; most was retained in the cell walls of the algae. Jones (1959) investigated growth promoting and inhibiting organic matter in seawater using bacteria for bioassay. Most obvious inhibition was obtained from an ether-extract of seawater containing a "blooming" of *Goniaulax polyhedra*. With some seawater samples, depending on the concentration of the extracts, a stimulatory effect on marine bacteria was shown. Bentley (1960) also claims that extracts of phytoplankton (mostly diatom species) gave evidence of biological activity of a plant hormone (auxin) type. Zooplankton, chiefly copepod, extracts and samples of seawater also showed some hormone-like activity.

In Proctor's study a fatty-like extra-cellular material was found which appears to be the inhibiting agent—probably a long-chain fatty acid. Collier (1953) had earlier reported the presence of a carbohydrate-like substance, apparently produced by algae, in seawater which affected the filtration rate of oysters. The effect appeared to be quantitative, and evidence suggested a threshold level of concentration for the substance. Collier pointed out that different types of carbohydrate-like substances existed in seawater though only a rhamnoside was identified. Other protein-like materials and also traces of ascorbic acid were reported by Collier, and he believed that these might have stimulatory or inhibitory effects on the growth and activities of marine animals. Wangersky (1952) had confirmed the presence of ascorbic acid as well as carbohydrates in seawater. Later studies by Collier, Ray and Wilson (1956) suggested that the ascorbic acid, as well as nicotinamide, which is probably also present in seawater, may have marked effects on some marine species. Such studies focus attention on the importance and nature of organic substances in seawater. Guillard and Wangersky (1958) have demonstrated the production of a soluble extra-cellular carbohydrate by a variety of flagellates (*Isochrysis, Monochrysis, Dunaliella, Chlamydomonas, Pyraminomonas*), the amount released being highest in stationary or declining cultures rather than in those in a state of rapid growth. The significance of this in algal blooms is clear. In Long Island Sound, Wangersky (1959) obtained only low values for carbohydrate and the distribution was patchy. No carbohydrate was detected during the spring diatom bloom, and appreciable quantities were found only after a summer peak of mixed diatoms and dino-flagellates. Probably this indicates that the amount of carbohydrate released varies with the species of phytoplankton as well as with the stage of growth. Carbohydrate even in these small quantities may be of considerable significance, being utilized as fast as it is formed. Collier (1958) has also shown the production of carbohydrate-like substances by *Prorocentrum* and to a lesser extent by *Gymnodinium breve*. He finds the amounts of carbohydrate and of protein (tyrosine) as dissolved organic matter in seawater and in estuaries is variable and patchy in distribution, which may imply the release of variable quantities of these substances during phytoplankton blooms. Collier finds *Gymnodinium breve* bursts are associated with multiplication of a marine bacterium and he suggests that the extra-cellular meta-bolites from *Gymnodinium* promote the growth of the bacterium which in turn can form vitamin B_{12}, thus conditioning the water for further phytoplankton growth.

Guillard and Wangersky's results stress the importance of the stage of growth of algae in relation to the production of extra-cellular metabolites. This had been shown earlier for freshwater algae; *Chlorella* produces a substance chlorellin, which may be secreted into the water in different amounts at various stages of growth. Ryther (1954a) showed that the feeding and survival of the freshwater species *Daphnia* was affected by the stage of growth of the phytoplankton cultures on which it fed. Anyone who has fed marine copepods on algal cultures in the laboratory is also familiar with the fact that at times they appear to feed very little, although apparently healthy, and it is suspected that at least one factor involved is the age of the phytoplankton cultures used.

The effect of different "types" of seawater may be mediated by the agency of the bacterial flora, metabolites encouraging or dis-couraging the growth of the bacteria. Thus Walne (1958) has suggested that the density of bacteria may influence the survival of oyster larvae, and that the concentration of metabolites in the various types of seawater may encourage different bacterial floras and thus affect the chances of growth and settlement of oysters. In a study by Raymont and Adams (1958) on mass culture of *Phaeodactylum*, the cultures were found to be nearly always infected with a flagellate *Monas* sp. This organism, however, was in very low concentration provided the *Phaeodactylum* was in the logarithmic growth phase, but as soon as growth slowed *Monas* increased very greatly. More recent work by Adams (unpublished) has suggested that the effect is due to a rapid multiplication of bacteria as *Phaeodactylum* slows in growth, probably due to the liberation of metabolites, the bacteria in turn encouraging the growth of *Monas*. It is important to recognize, however, that bacteria can be of tremendous value in conditioning seawater by producing vitamins and similar growth promoting substances. This is discussed in more detail in Chapter XVI.

A further aspect of the study of external metabolites is that connected with the different qualities of seawater which may limit the successful breeding and perhaps distribution of species. The work of Wilson at Plymouth on the culture and growth of larvae, especially of polychaetes and of echinoderms, has shown that different water masses appear to have very different potentialities as regards survival and growth of the larvae. Although satisfactory food cultures were fed to the larvae, some of the types of seawater employed would not give good growth or survival. Recent results by Wilson and Armstrong (1958) suggest that even water from near the bottom and from the surface of the sea in the same locality may have very different effects upon survival of larvae (*Echinus*). Moreover, their results indicate that bacteria do not always necessarily exert a harmful effect on larvae, but on the other hand soil extracts of various kinds and extracts of phytoplankton do not always supply the larvae with the essential requirements. It might be concluded from this type of investigation that an innate quality of the seawater is the real factor affecting survival. This innate factor may of course be the concentration of growth promoting organic constituents which may be supplied by phytoplankton, bacteria, detritus, animals, or in other ways.

It is possible that the different qualities of seawater — those minute differences which are not generally perceptible except by bioassay — may be also responsible for the different populations of animals and of plants which characterize different areas of the seas. Certain species of plankton appear to be fairly sharply confined to distinct areas; there are neritic and oceanic forms, but even in neritic and oceanic zones, distinct communities may exist. Some planktonic species are sufficiently characteristic of a particular water mass to be used as indications of water movements (cf. Chapter XII). Although temperature and salinity play a part in delimiting plankton communities, these factors alone cannot account for many of the differences in communities and it is likely that minute variations in the quality of the water masses are of significance.

Biological conditioning of seawater is clearly one of the fascinating and challenging fields for future study. There seems little doubt that extra-cellular metabolites of various kinds may be of great significance in the succession of both phytoplankton and zooplankton species, so characteristic of plankton communities, and of the interrelationships between phytoplankton and zooplankton. They may influence the successful breeding, settlement and distribution of organisms. Finally, while the productivity of different bodies of seawater is so clearly very largely determined by the concentration of nitrates, phosphates and other inorganic substances, it is likely that productivity may be to some extent affected by the minute traces of organic substances such as vitamins.

CHAPTER X

FACTORS
AFFECTING PRIMARY PRODUCTION—
IV GRAZING

THE very sharp fall in the vernal flowering of diatoms often does
not correspond exactly in time with the decline in nitrate and phosphate. Thus Marshall and Orr, working in Loch Striven, in one
year found that *Skeletonema* disappeared before all the phosphate
was used up. Investigators, therefore, have looked for factors other
than depletion of nutrients which might be responsible for the loss of
phytoplankton. In some years Marshall and Orr observed that an
appreciable number of the diatom frustules were found on the bottom.
Moore was able to collect dead diatoms in trays set out in the mud.
However, faecal pellets were also recovered in considerable numbers
from the mud and from collecting trays, and on certain occasions the
diatoms disappeared without a large number of cells being found
in the bottom deposit. On one occasion such an apparent disappearance
of phytoplankton coincided with an abundance of zooplankton
(polychaete larvae).

Harvey *et al.* (1935) also observed the sudden drop in diatom
numbers off Plymouth during the vernal outburst and showed that
the drop was accompanied on some occasions by a rapid increase
in the larger copepods. These workers observed a great number of
green faecal pellets in the water at the time of the spring burst of
diatoms (Fig. 10.1). The conclusion appears inevitable that the
diatoms are reduced during the spring growth by the grazing activity
of the zooplankton. But the grazing of the phytoplankton crop
continues through summer. Indeed in the observations made by
Harvey *et al.* off Plymouth, over a number of months during the
spring and summer, a reciprocal relation appeared to hold between
zooplankton and phytoplankton. When the copepods and other
members of the zooplankton were reaching high densities the phytoplankton tended to be reduced, but as the crop of zooplankton

declined so the plant population tended to rise again. Thus over the productive months of the year the periods of rich zooplankton and phytoplankton more or less alternated with each other (Fig. 10.2). Clarke (1939b) has summarized the position by saying, "copepods in fact regulate the plant population". This grazing activity of the zooplankton has been confirmed by many other workers, for example,

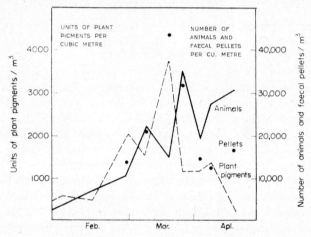

FIG. 10.1 The effect of changes in abundance of zooplankton (full-line curve) on density of phytoplankton expressed as plant pigment (dotted curve). Black circles show number of faecal pellets per m³ (from Harvey *et al.*, 1935).

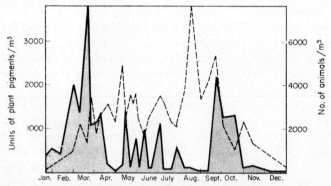

FIG. 10.2 Reciprocal relationship between the density of phytoplankton and zooplankton (continuous line—units of plant pigments per m³; dotted line—density of zooplankton) (from Harvey *et al.*, 1935).

by Bigelow, Lillick and Sears (1940) for the Gulf of Maine area, and by Wimpenny (1936b, 1938) in the North Sea. Hart (1942) also considers grazing of the greatest importance in the Antarctic where, despite the tremendous production of phytoplankton during the short summer, the crop is extensively grazed down by the massive zooplankton population. The diatom frustules appearing in huge numbers on the sea bed in the Antarctic are, according to Hart, mainly broken, suggesting that the diatoms have been eaten before being voided as faecal pellets and descending to the ocean floor. We know from field studies such as those of Lebour (1922) that phytoplankton forms a major part of the diet of many zooplankton species, especially copepods. It is known also from experimental work in the laboratory that many members of the zooplankton eat phytoplankton cells extensively; moreover, though precise grazing rates are difficult to determine, there is some suggestion that copepods and probably other herbivores will eat far more than their needs if the phytoplankton is rich. Not only copepods, but other zooplankton groups such as euphausids, shelled pteropods and appendicularians, as well as the larval forms of many different classes and orders of both bottom living and pelagic marine animals appear to be herbivorous on the phytoplankton. A fuller treatment of the specific food requirements, both qualitative and quantitative, of different members of the zooplankton, will be left to a later chapter (Chapter XVII). It is sufficient to emphasize now that since a very large number of plankton animals graze on the phytoplankton, the size of animal crop will affect considerably the density of the phytoplankton. On the other hand, the crop of phytoplankton must determine to a large extent the successful breeding of the zooplankton.

The rapidity with which zooplankton grazers can reduce a phytoplankton crop is truly remarkable. Fleming (1939) has given an illustration for a diatom population with an initial concentration of one million cells/l. in which the diatoms are dividing at an average rate of one division per day. At this division rate the animal grazing population is assumed to be removing the crop which is produced per day so that the phytoplankton remains at the same concentration of one million cells/l. Fleming shows what would happen if the diatoms maintain their reproductive rate but the zooplankton doubles in density. In two days, for example, the phytoplankton is reduced to about 237,000 cells/l., and in five days the density is only 27,000 cells/l. (Table 10.1). An even more remarkable reduction is obtained if the zooplankton grazers increase five fold, while the diatoms maintain their steady rate of reproduction. Thus after three days Fleming shows that the density of the diatoms has been reduced to only 240 cells/l., and in five days less than one cell/l. remains (Table 10.1). The decrease in a diatom population from an established peak will result from sinking and death of the diatom cells, as well as

TABLE 10.1. The rapid changes in population when the phytoplankton is dividing at constant rate but grazing intensity is increased (from Fleming, 1939).

Time in days	Population (cells per litre)	
	Grazing intensity doubled	Grazing intensity increased 5-fold
0	1,000,000	1,000,000
1	487,000	62,000
2	237,000	3,900
3	106,000	240
4	56,000	15
5	27,000	< 1

from grazing by zooplankton animals. But Harvey was one of the first to emphasize that of these factors grazing is usually by far the most important. The population density or standing crop of phytoplankton can, therefore, give a very misleading impression of the primary productivity. In Chapter VI, brief reference was made to the difference between standing crop and productivity, but we must now examine some of the methods used to determine both these characteristics of a phytoplankton population.

For the estimation of standing crop the original method was to collect phytoplankton, using the finest silk nets (200 mesh/in.), and to measure the volume of water filtered either by employing standard vertical hauls or by using a flow meter of some type in the net mouth. Apart from errors in volume filtered, there were many difficulties in variation of mesh size when a net was used. But even if reasonably standardized conditions were achieved, it is now widely recognized that much of the phytoplankton is of such a small size that it passes through the nets employed, and this applies even more strongly when much of the crop consists of small naked flagellates, small dinoflagellates, coccolithophores and other small phytoplankton forms which together make up the nannoplankton. Comparisons of standing crop, using first the net method and then employing the filtration of water through either filter paper or membrane filters (e.g. Harvey, 1950), have clearly demonstrated the errors inherent in the use of net collections for quantitative estimates of phytoplankton. It is accepted, however, that where the phytoplankton is mainly composed of the larger diatoms, net hauls may give a fair approximation.

Attempts have been made to collect phytoplankton quantitatively on paper or on membrane filters for counting, but the recovery and identification of the plant cells is then difficult. We have already referred in Chapter V, dealing specifically with the nannoplankton, to the use of centrifuging as a method for estimating algal crop. Some algae, however, are not easily brought down, even by prolonged centrifugation, and others, especially naked flagellates, may be destroyed during the process. Undoubtedly one of the most useful quantitative methods is to fix a sample of seawater and allow the algal cells to sediment. The phytoplankton may then be counted, preferably using a reversed microscope, or as an alternative, the settled volume of phytoplankton may be determined. Again, some of the more delicate cells are destroyed during the fixation process, and determinations of volume may be more erroneous, especially owing to different degrees of packing of the settled cells.

A most valuable alternative method for estimating standing crop is by the measurement of the density of chlorophyll pigment extracted from algal cells. A known volume of water is centrifuged or, more preferably, is filtered through a hardened paper or membrane filter of standard porosity; the pigment is extracted usually with acetone, and is then either estimated as chlorophyll (Richards and Thompson, 1952; Creitz and Richards, 1955), or as plant pigment units (Harvey, 1934). This chlorophyll method, however, is best confined to periods when phytoplankton conditions are uniform and stable. There are difficulties when different types of water are compared, or if the crop of phytoplankton is estimated at different seasons. The amount of chlorophyll in relation to the carbon content of the cell, or to the cell volume, can vary, particularly with nutrient conditions, light intensity and the physiological state of the cell, and it is also well known that the amount of chlorophyll varies with different species of plankton. Krey (1958a) indicates the large variations which may occur betweeen different species (Table 10.2). Chlorophyll content may show a diurnal periodicity even in one and the same species (cf. Doty and

Oguri, 1957). Yentsch and Scagel (1958) found that in a natural phytoplankton population there was a marked variation in the chlorophyll content, the shallowest-living phytoplankton showing the highest amount of chlorophyll about midnight. Carotenoids did not show marked fluctuations. There is still considerable argument as to how far chlorophyll, which has been recently released from growing cells, may be included in the evaluation of quantities of phytoplankton in the sea. In other words, it is difficult, to say the least, to distinguish between 'living' and 'recently dead' chlorophyll. Nonetheless, chloro-

TABLE 10.2. 1 mg chlorophyll is contained in

50 mm^3	*Chlorella*
86 mm^3	*Chaetoceros gracilis*
560 mm^3	*Thalassiosira gravida*
59 mm^3	*Nitzschia closterium*
97 mm^3	*Gymnodium sp.*
260 mm^3	*Hemiselmis rufescens*
181 mm^3	mixed phytoplankton (Gillbricht)
279 mm^3	dinoflagellates (Gillbricht)
139 mm^3	diatoms (Gillbricht)
47 mm^3	phytoplankton (Ri¹ey)

(from Krey, 1958)

phyll measurement is one of the most valuable and convenient methods for estimating phytoplankton crop, and as we shall see, even production also, but the method must be used with due caution.

In view of the differences in sizes and volumes of various species of algae and even of size variations in the same species, and remembering also the variations which may be encountered in the amount of ash to dry organic weight, undoubtedly the most accurate measurement of algal crop would be by chemical methods, such as the determination of the amount of carbon, of phosphorus or of nitrogen in phytoplankton samples. These methods, however, are rather slow and laborious and on the whole have not been widely used. Thus sedimentation estimates and the extraction of chlorophyll are most generally employed, and considerable efforts have now been made to try to relate the amount of chlorophyll to the amount of carbon or to the dry organic weight of the phytoplankton. Cushing (1958) has estimated that 1 μg chlorophyll is equal approximately to 35 μg of dry organic matter, or to 17.3 μg of carbon. On an approximate basis, the amount of algae as settled volume may be related also to the amount of carbon or dry organic matter present in the phytoplankton. Whatever the method, it is most useful if the standing crop of phytoplankton can be finally expressed as the weight of carbon per m² or m³.

So far we have discussed methods for estimating the standing crop of phytoplankton. We have already defined primary productivity as the amount of carbon fixed per m² or per m³ in a unit of time. In Chapter VI we described the oxygen bottle technique as one of the earliest methods which is still widely used for determining primary productivity by the phytoplankton. Other methods, however, should be considered. The total productivity over a period of time, such as the duration of the main spring outburst of phytoplankton, may be assessed by the changes in the amount of a nutrient such as phosphate or nitrate, which is essential for the growth of phytoplankton. In a similar way, changes in pH which reflect CO_2 uptake, or the changes in the amount of oxygen during the period of phytoplankton growth can be employed to assess production. Many problems arise in the use of these methods. A particular difficulty with fall in nutrient level as an index of production is that the extent of regeneration is usually unknown, and the production value thus tends to be minimal. Another problem is concerned with water movements through the area being studied. Any large-scale lateral exchange of water can clearly vitiate the results. These errors were recognized in the earlier work of Atkins, Harvey and Cooper for the English Channel. Nonetheless, Cooper (1934) was able to make a useful summary for minimal production of phytoplankton from about February to July, and there was very fair agreement for estimates based on CO_2, O_2, phosphate and nitrate changes. On the other hand, calculations made on fall in silica were widely different, presumably due to the relatively rapid use and regeneration of silica (Table 10.3). Hart (1942) has employed similar methods for assessing production in the Antarctic, and among others, Seiwell (1935b) used oxygen and phosphate levels in an attempt to measure productivity in tropical waters. More recently Steele (1956, 1958) has used phosphate changes to calculate production of phytoplankton in an area of the North Sea where very little lateral transport of water occurs. On the assumption that the changes in phosphate were due to utilization and vertical transport, Steele has integrated the phosphate uptake for the euphotic column, and by studying nutrient changes over relatively short periods, he has been able to calculate monthly production from April to October (Fig. 10.3). Very valuable results may be obtained from such an analysis; some complicating factors still remain, however, such as rates of carbon assimilation when phosphate is very low and also the extent of phosphate regeneration.

Provided fairly accurate data are available for the density of chlorophyll in a water column and that light intensities at various depths in the euphotic zone are also known, a useful approximation

TABLE 10.3. The theoretical minimal production of phytoplankton in the English Channel calculated on the basis of chemical changes in the water (the period of production is from January/February to July) (from Cooper, 1933).

Basis	Minimum production of phyto-plankton wet weight metric tons per sq. km
CO_2	1600
O_2	1000
Phosphate	1400
Nitrate	1500
Silicate	110

for primary productivity may be obtained from a relationship suggested by Ryther and Yentsch (1957). At light saturation, they claim that marine phytoplankton has a mean assimilation rate of 3.7 g carbon/hr/g chlorophyll.

The relationship:

$$P = \frac{R}{k} \times C \times 3.7$$

gives an indication of the method of calculating production for a homogeneously distributed phytoplankton column where

P = photosynthesis of the population in $gC/m^2/day$
R = relative photosynthetic rate dependent on the surface light intensity
C = g chlorophyll/m^3 in the column.

Undoubtedly, however, the most widely used and accurate method of estimating primary productivity, apart from the oxygen bottle technique, is the ^{14}C technique described in detail by Steemann Nielsen and Aabye Jensen (1957). A briefer account by Steemann

Nielsen (1958c) may be summarized as follows: A definite amount of $^{14}CO_2$ is added to a bottle of seawater the productivity of which is to be measured, the total content of CO_2 in the water being known. Assuming that all the $^{14}CO_2$ is assimilated by the algae, the total carbon assimilated may be calculated by determining the ^{14}C present in the plankton when the experiment has ended. The amount of ^{14}C is measured by the β-radiation from the phytoplankton, retained on a filter. It is necessary to know only the ratio between the total CO_2 and the $^{14}CO_2$ in the water at the beginning of the experiment, assuming of course that $^{14}CO_2$ is used in photosynthesis at the same rate as $^{12}CO_2$. It is probable that estimates of this type give a measure near to net photosynthesis for the duration of the experiment, though Steemann Nielsen suggests that if an adjustment for the amount of $^{14}CO_2$ lost by respiration during the period of the experiment is made, then estimates by the ^{14}C method can give a measure of the gross photosynthetic rate. He believes that a reasonable estimate for tropical and sub-tropical waters is that net production is some 60% of gross production (Steemann Nielsen, 1958c). At higher latitudes, the net production will be much more variable depending on the time of the year. Thus during the summer, at high latitudes, with the longer period of daylight, the net production may be far greater than 60%, but during the winter it would be, of course, extremely low. A series of papers by Steemann Nielsen and his colleagues, and by Ryther, Riley and others have dealt with the difficulties of equating the oxygen bottle and ^{14}C method for estimating primary productivity. The main difficulty appears to concern tropical waters, where long-term experiments with the oxygen bottle method on the whole gave considerably higher rates of production than the ^{14}C technique. However, more recent papers (e.g. Steemann Nielsen, 1958c) suggest that the discrepancy between the two kinds of experimental result may be less than was previously thought; some of the difficulties undoubtedly concern the difference between gross and net production (cf. Menzel and Ryther, 1960). Another suggestion is that with oligotrophic ocean waters, determinations by the oxygen bottle technique may be affected in that anti-biotic substances are released in the light bottles which reduce the bacterial population to a greater extent than in the dark bottles. In any event, there seems to be little doubt that at moderate rates of photosynthesis, the ^{14}C method and the oxygen bottle method can give comparable results. Steele has also compared the production of phytoplankton by the phosphate method and by the ^{14}C method, and has shown a considerable measure of agreement between the results (Fig. 10.3).

Perhaps sufficient has been said of some of the chief methods for estimating productivity (for details see Plankton Symposium-Rapp. et Procès Verb.–1958), and we may now return to consider the effect of herbivores grazing on a phytoplankton population. While we

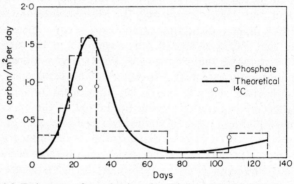

Fig. 10.3 Estimates of production for Fladen (North Sea) based on phosphate, ^{14}C, and theoretical model (from Steele, 1958).

may define productivity as the weight of carbon or number of algal cells (or pigment units) formed in a unit volume per unit of time, we may consider *total production* as that productivity integrated over a period of time. Following Fleming (1939) we can define the difference between an initial population of diatom cells and the population at some future time as the "increment". Clearly the total production can be equivalent to the increment only if no death of cells or removal by grazing of the zooplankton occurs. Even if no deaths occur, an animal population may remove a considerable proportion of the phytoplankton and thus the density of plant cells at a given instant may be a mere fraction of the total production. Fleming has proposed the term "yield" for the difference between the total production and the increment, assuming that the difference is due to the removal of the algae by grazers only.

The rate of change of a phytoplankton population [P] may be expressed by the equation: $\dfrac{dP}{dt} = P\{a - (b + ct)\}$, where $a =$ the rate of division of the phytoplankton cell, $b =$ the initial grazing rate, $c =$ the rate of increase in grazing intensity. When a peak is reached in a period of phytoplankton growth, then $\dfrac{dP}{dt} = 0$, that is the rate of increase of the phytoplankton population is exactly balanced by the rate of consumption by the grazers. If we assume that the grazing rate is constant (i.e. $c = 0$) and if $a - b$ is positive, that is to say, if the rate of division of the diatoms exceeds the constant grazing rate, then the phytoplankton population must continue to increase. However, the rate of increase in density of the cells appears to be slower than the true rate of division of the algae owing to the constant grazing effect. The actual population increase of the phytoplankton may indeed be very slow if the fraction removed per day is only slightly smaller than the division rate of the diatoms, although in point of fact many diatom cells are being formed each day. If the grazing rate exceeds the rate of division of the diatoms, then the phytoplankton density must fall although many diatom cells may be produced daily. Using his equation for the rate of change of a diatom population, Fleming has computed a population curve for the spring diatom increase in the English Channel fitting Harvey's initial and maximal populations to the curve. The agreement between the theoretical and actual population changes (Fig. 10.4) is striking, but such a curve gives no indication of the relation between the standing crop of phytoplankton and its reproductive potential. Harvey himself commented on the abundance of green faecal pellets produced presumably by herbivorous zooplankton during this spring burst (Fig. 10.1). Fleming (1939) compared the total production during this same vernal increase with the population, accepting Harvey's estimate that the diatoms were dividing once in 36 hours and assuming that the division rate was constant over the time. The peak in the phytoplankton was achieved in 37 days; during that time Fleming shows that the zooplankton increased the fraction which they removed per day ("diurnal grazing fraction") by 25%. But more remarkable, as the phytoplankton apparently declined to a very small population after a further period of 37 days, the total production increased enormously, and the yield, that is the amount removed by the zooplankton, was correspondingly very great (Fig. 10.5). The population or standing crop of diatom cells was, therefore, a mere fraction of the total production. Harvey had earlier calculated the theoretical phytoplankton density from the decrease in phosphate; for 1933 the density should have been about 85,000 plant pigment units/m³; the actual value of the standing crop was only 2500 units/m³, some

3% of the production. In 1934 about 2% of the theoretical production was found. Harvey attributed the vast reduction of the phytoplankton to grazing.

Many other workers (Riley, 1946; Gauld, 1950; Cushing, 1959a) have experienced the relatively small standing crop of phytoplankton obtaining when zooplankton is in high density, and have attributed

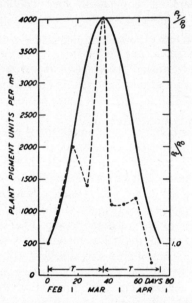

FIG. 10.4 Computed population curve for spring diatom increase observed by Harvey *et al.* in English Channel (continuous line). Dotted line joins observed densities (from Fleming, 1939).

the difference to the large grazing fraction removed. Sverdrup (1953) has drawn attention to the densities of phytoplankton and zooplankton in the Norwegian Sea. He shows that in April and early May the phytoplankton was dense, with few copepods being present, but at the end of May when conditions seemed to favour a very heavy phytoplankton crop, the density was reduced owing to a large outburst of copepod grazers. Hart (1942) also points out that the drop in phytoplankton in the Antarctic after the spring outburst cannot be attributed to lack of nitrate and phosphate, and in view of the tremendous number of faecal pellets accompanying the lowered phytoplankton populations, considers grazing as the most important

factor. Following Harvey, he has calculated the minimum population
from the reduction in nitrate and phosphate, and shows once more
that there is an enormous discrepancy between the calculated production and the observed standing crop. For the South Georgia
neritic area, the grazing factor is about of the same order as in the
English Channel, i.e. the standing crop is some 2% of the calculated

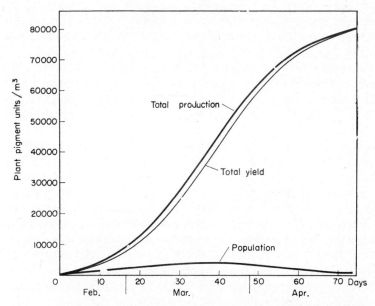

FIG. 10.5 Calculated total production, total yield, and population based
on observations of Harvey *et al.* Total yield represents total
amount removed by grazing (assumed rate of division once
in 36 hours) (from Fleming, 1939).

production. For oceanic areas in the northern Antarctic region,
however, the grazing is almost three times as intense so that the standing crop is only approximately 0.5% of the calculated production.
Mare (1940) similarly found an inverse relationship existing usually
between copepods as the chief herbivores and the phytoplankton.

In any large sea area dense patches of phytoplankton often more
or less alternate with rich zooplankton patches. The grazing theory
is one of the chief explanations which has been put forward to account
for this alternation (cf. Harvey *et al.*, 1935). Due attention must be
paid to the time relations. Zooplankton can graze down a plant crop

in a matter of a few days, whereas the animals grow and reproduce much more slowly. Therefore, the beneficial effect of a phytoplankton crop on the growth of a population of zooplankton animals is due to a food supply which has occurred many weeks previously, at the time when the zooplankton was occurring mainly as young and immature stages. The importance of this time factor in phyto-plankton/zooplankton relationships has been well emphasized by both Steemann Nielsen (1937b) and Clarke (1939b). Let us, for example, consider an area characterized by rich phytoplankton but having only a small brood of zooplankton. After some weeks the zooplankton may be assumed to have spawned, and the growth of the new brood will then give rise to a comparatively rich zooplankton patch. During the growth of this zooplankton brood, however, the phytoplankton has been extensively grazed down and will occur in very low densities. Another patch of phytoplankton which may not have happened to carry grazers will of course remain as a dense area. But Steemann Nielsen (1956) has recently emphasized that rich phytoplankton and zooplankton often co-exist and it is erroneous to believe that dense phytoplankton and zooplankton must always alternate with each other. This view has also been stressed by Beklemishev (1957), who agrees that when a clear inverse relationship does occur this is a result of zooplankton grazing. Beklemishev points out that more complex phytoplankton/zooplankton relationships may exist, in particular, situations where zooplankton is in denser con-centrations around the edges of rich algal patches. He attributes these variations in distribution mainly to seasonal differences in the development of both phytoplankton and zooplankton populations, in addition to the grazing effect.

In analysing phytoplankton zooplankton relationships, there have undoubtedly been many instances where the biomass of phytoplankton or of zooplankton has been badly underestimated. The use of fine plankton nets for measuring phytoplankton crop may be misleading if nannoplankton organisms form a considerable proportion of the crop, and in estimating the density of zooplankton, if coarse nets be used, a distorted picture will result if smaller copepods, nauplii and other small zooplankton animals form an appreciable part of the population.

As we have seen, however, assuming correct sampling of the plankton, rich patches of phytoplankton and of zooplankton may on some occasions co-exist, but they may at other times clearly alternate.

In temperate and higher latitudes a spring outburst of phytoplankton is usually evident and the rise in zooplankton tends to follow this outburst but more slowly. Beginning, therefore, in winter with minimal values for both phyto- and zooplankton, a positive correlation may be shown between the horizontal distributions of the two communities in the spring. Riley and Bumpus (1946) show a typical phytoplankton curve for Georges Bank rising from a winter minimum to a spring maximum. The zooplankton is also rising slowly in the spring and a positive correlation exists between the two populations throughout January, February, March and April. A little later, however, the zooplankton which has been rising slowly, shows an accelerated increase, and with this the diatoms decline so that a marked negative correlation is observed during May (Fig. 10.6). This change from a positive to a negative correlation may be applied to several different groups of zooplankton animals (*Calanus, Metridia, Limacina*, cyclopoid copepods, etc.). All these animals showed similar changes; a slow rate of population increase early in the year when phytoplankton was also increasing, so that a positive correlation existed between the two. Later on, there was a sharp change to a negative correlation with the phytoplankton, at a time depending on the month when the particular zooplankton species reached its seasonal peak (Fig. 10.7). Riley and Bumpus show by the use of partial correlations that whilst the early positive correlation between phytoplankton and zooplankton might be partly due to some factor such as increasing temperature, the sharp change to an inverse relationship in May can be safely ascribed to grazing. Some impression of the intensity of the grazing may be gained from Table 10.4 which shows the large fraction of phytoplankton removed in May. To some extent turbulence, especially in an area such as Georges Bank, will tend to distribute plankton populations and reduce the patchiness effected by grazing, but zooplankton is probably less liable to dispersal owing to the animals migrating to the deeper layers by day.

The intensity of grazing must vary from area to area, as well as with time, and the variations in intensity of other factors such as transparency, stability and nutrient supply, all will combine to influence the size of the phytoplankton crop. Even in areas at similar latitudes, differences may appear in plankton population. We have already referred to the variations in the timing of the spring outburst in the areas round the Gulf of Maine but the size of crop is variable also. Riley (1947a) has compared Georges Bank with the waters off

Woods Hole from all the data available. The earlier (late winter) flowering at Woods Hole (Fig. 10.8) is probably associated with land drainage increasing the stability of the water. As on Georges Bank, however, a strong grazing effect is discernible and this is responsible

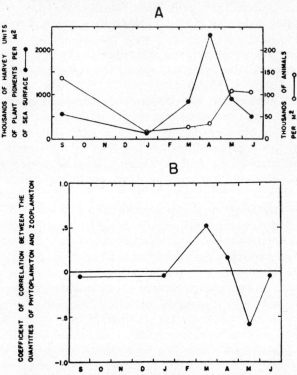

FIG. 10.6 Seasonal changes in the populations of phytoplankton and zooplankton on Georges Bank (A), and the correlation between the abundance of phytoplankton and zooplankton (B) (from Riley and Bumpus, 1946).

for reduction of the spring flowering, though it occurs earlier in time than on Georges Bank. The differences in extent and timing of grazing are seen in Fig. 10.9E. Following this reduction of the phytoplankton crop, nutrient depletion reduces any further outburst of growth. The overall differences in the phytoplankton populations at Woods Hole and on Georges Bank, Riley attributes to the greater availability of nutrients over deeper water; but, on the other hand, regeneration over summer in the shallower area allows small quantities of nutrients to reach the euphotic zone off Woods Hole at irregular times over summer, during the more general depletion, yielding small bursts of phytoplankton (cf. Figs. 10.8, 10.9). In Long Island Sound, Conover (1956) concludes that nutrient (nitrate) depletion is the main controlling factor after the spring flowering, although grazing probably had some effect on the size of the summer phytoplankton populations. An analysis by Riley (1955) suggests that while the standing crop of phytoplankton is much greater than, for instance,

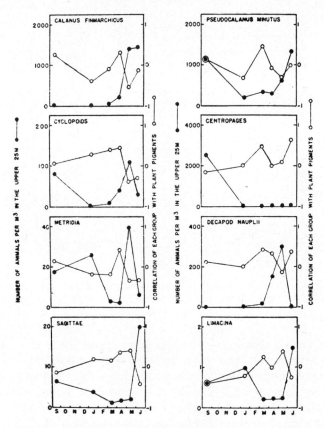

FIG. 10.7 Seasonal changes in the densities of various zooplankton animals on Georges Bank, and the correlation between their abundance and the phytoplankton expressed as plant pigments
(from Riley and Bumpus, 1946).

TABLE 10.4. Quantitative comparisons of phytoplankton and zooplankton with estimates of grazing, on Georges Bank (modified from Riley and Bumpus, 1946).

Month	Mean plant pigments 10^3 Harvey units/m^2	Dry weight of phyto-plankton g/m^2	Mean no. of animals/m^2	Estimated total con-sumption 10^3 Harvey units/m^2	% of phyto-plankton crop consumed	Food require-ments, % of zooplankton weight
Sept.	560	19.6	135,000	35	6	13
Jan.	120	4.2	14,000	−7	−5	−7
March	830	29.0	24,000	15	2	3
Apr.	2300	80.5	32,000	170	7	30
May	870	30.4	106,000	371	43	34
June	480	16.8	103,000	56	12	13

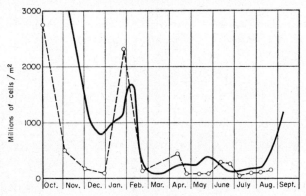

FIG. 10.8 Calculated (solid line) and observed (dotted line) seasonal changes in the density of phytoplankton off Woods Hole (from Riley, 1947a).

in the English Channel, the zooplankton population is only slightly larger. Presumably grazing is less intense or at least less efficient. In heavily fertilized areas such as Moriches Bay (Ryther, 1954b), the vast crop of small flagellates is dependent mainly upon the high nitrogen level, and grazing would appear to have little effect on the size of crop, probably due to the brackish conditions and rather restricted zooplankton population. Deevey (1948) investigating the phytoplankton/zooplankton relationships in Tisbury Great Pond, another brackish body of water with fluctuating environmental

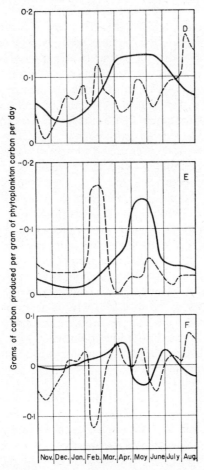

Fig. 10.9 Comparison of phytoplankton growth processes and environmental factors for Georges Bank (solid line) and Woods Hole
(dotted line).

D = Photosynthetic rate based on solar radiation, turbulence,
transparency and nutrient depletion.

E = Estimated grazing rate.

F = Estimated rate of change of phytoplankton population
(Phytoplankton growth as g. C produced/g. phytoplankton
C/per day) (from Riley, 1947a).

conditions, found that the changes in phytoplankton crop did not appear to be related to zooplankton numbers and grazing intensity.

We must, therefore, allow that the effect of grazing on the phytoplankton crop may vary from the most extreme gorging witnessed during the massive diatom outbursts at high latitudes to the steady but very inconspicuous consumption by herbivores of the small crop of algae in tropical areas. In any area the intensity of grazing may vary enormously with season, especially at high latitudes. In other words, we must recognize that grazing, like all other parameters of phytoplankton density, is variable both spatially and temporally. Several attempts have been made to assess the changing values of these different parameters, and to correlate these with the overall effect on algal production. One of the best known of these mathematical models of production is that of Riley (1946), further developed by Riley, Stommel and Bumpus (1949). It is essential to know the effects of various environmental factors on the physiology of the plankton. Secondly, in the area to be studied, the seasonal variations in the different physico-chemical factors must be known, and as a first approximation, these seasonal changes are expressed as smoothed curves based on the means of the field observations. A brief summary of the approach may be included here, taken from Riley's analysis for Georges Bank, but for details the original papers should be consulted. The theoretical study commences with a basic equation for the rate of change of a phytoplankton population, which is similar to that of Fleming (p. 248)

$$\frac{dP}{dt} = P(Ph - R - G)$$

which indicates that the rate of change of the population P is determined by the photosynthetic rate per unit of population (Ph), less the respiratory rate of the phytoplankton (R) and the rate of reduction by grazing (G). In the absence of restriction in photosynthetic rate due to nutrient depletion, the rate is proportional to the light intensity, and thus is equal to the average daily solar radiation multiplied by a constant which is the weight in grams of carbon produced per gram of surface algal carbon per day. Knowing the extinction coefficient and assuming the productive euphotic zone to be limited to a depth where the light intensity is equal to $0.0015\,g\ cal/cm^2/min$ (an average compensation depth and intensity), a mean photosynthetic rate for the whole euphotic zone may be calculated. Corrections may now be applied for nutrient depletion. Riley assumed a reduction in photosynthetic rate when phosphate concentration fell below 0.55 mg atom P/m³ (= *ca.* 16 mg P/m³) and obviously a similar correction could equally be applied for nitrogen lack. Since turbulence will carry diatoms out of the photosynthetic zone, a factor is also

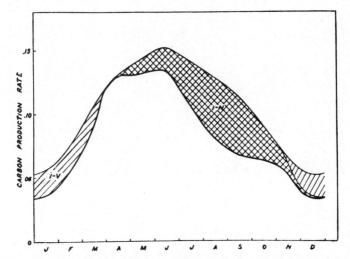

FIG. 10.10 Estimated mean photosynthetic rate. Upper curve is the maximum possible rate according to incident radiation and transparency. Lower curve represents estimate after correcting for vertical turbulence (V) and nutrient depletion (N) (from Riley, 1946).

applied for the depth of the homogeneously mixed water layer, if this is greater than the euphotic zone. From the mean variations over the year in the various factors so far considered for Georges Bank, Riley thus estimates the changes in photosynthetic rate over that area (Fig. 10.10).

The respiration of the phytoplankton itself of course reduces the production. Hence a correction is applied to the photosynthetic rate depending on the respiratory rate and the effect of temperature on algal respiration. Finally, the grazing rate is subtracted from the production rate from a knowledge of the seasonal changes in the density of zooplankton on Georges Bank. The final estimated rate of change of the phytoplankton is shown in Fig. 10.11. Thus from a knowledge of such factors as temperature, transparency of the water, solar radiation, nutrients, depth of the mixed layer and zooplankton density, an equation can be derived for the rate of change of the phytoplankton. By integration it is possible, therefore, to calculate the seasonal variations in production of phytoplankton, and this curve may then be compared with the data obtained from the field

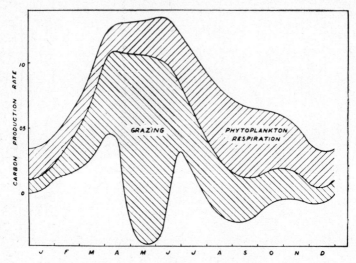

Fig. 10.11 Estimated rates of production and consumption of carbon by plankton. Top curve is photosynthetic rate. By subtracting the respiratory rate, the lower curve is obtained representing phytoplankton production rate. By subtracting the zooplankton grazing rate, the lowest curve is reached—the estimated rate of change of the phytoplankton (from Riley, 1946).

for the actual crop of algae through the year on Georges Bank. The good measure of agreement seen in Fig. 10.12, indicates the great value of the use of such a theoretical model. The analysis may be carried further; for example, with an assessment of eddy diffusion and the concentration of deep water phosphate, the phosphate distribution in the upper layers may be computed (cf. Riley *et al.*, 1949). Modifications may be introduced also for loss of crop due to sinking and death apart from grazing. The models due to Steele (1956, 1958) and the considerable measure of agreement found by him for estimates of production for the Fladen ground based on phosphate changes and ^{14}C measurements on the one hand and on the theoretical calculations on the other (Fig. 10.3) demonstrate again the remarkable usefulness of the mathematical approach. A mathematical basis for the study of marine algal populations would thus appear to be well founded. But in a recent review, Steele (1959) has emphasized the difficulty of applying such methods to fisheries problems, especially in view of our poor quantitative knowledge of factors affecting the higher trophic levels in the sea. All workers have emphasized the

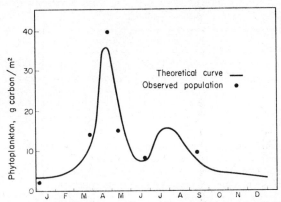

FIG. 10.12 The seasonal cycle of phytoplankton calculated by approximate integration of the equation for the rate of change of the population. For comparison, observed quantities of phytoplankton are shown as dots (from Riley, 1946).

need for much more precise knowledge of the physiology of both phytoplankton and zooplankton if models are to be used successfully in plankton research. The effect of reduced nutrients on algal growth, the inter-relationships of light and temperature on photosynthesis and respiration, the variations in grazing rates of zooplankton, and the effect of several environmental factors, especially temperature on metabolism, changes in the percentage of carbon in plankton, and differences in the physiological characters of dominant species— these are but some of the factors that must affect very considerably the operation of mathematical concepts. Nonetheless, models are now proving to be most useful tools for obtaining broad comparative data and for crystallizing research programmes, and with more accurate physiological knowledge and field data, it should be possible to operate them even more successfully in the future.

Cushing (1959 a) has developed a particular model for an area of the North Sea, which differs, however, from the studies so far described in that for a period of about six months covering the spring outburst, no very significant nutrient depletion is believed to have occurred. Thus the rate of increase of the diatom population is calculated from observations on the division rates at the various light intensities (Table 10.5) together with data on light penetration,

TABLE 10.5. Derivation of the theoretical division rates for the algae (from Cushing, 1959).

	Jan.	Feb.	March	April	May	June
D_c at midday	11.9	17.0	19.5	22.0	23.2	23.3
D_m	55.4	57.0	40.2	37.2	29.8	30.2
D_c/D_m	0.151	0.201	0.321	0.394	0.521	0.505
R_p	0.65	0.73	0.88	0.98	0.97	0.97
$R_p \times D_c/D_m = R$	0.098	0.147	0.282	0.386	0.505	0.490

D_c = the compensation depth, in metres.
D_m = the depth of frictional resistance, in metres.
R_p = the estimated division rates in the euphotic zone.
R = the estimated division rates for the whole water column.

compensation depth and thickness of the mixed layer, much as before; but a theoretical curve for the seasonal changes in phytoplankton crop is then obtained from a knowledge of the initial population of herbivorous copepods and the rate of change of that population depending on egg production and mortality rates (cf. Chapter XVII — Fig. 17.18). From the agreement between the calculated algal and copepod crops and the few field observations available, Cushing concludes that the emphasis which he places on grazing is justified. He believes that practically the whole of the production is grazed over the spring burst, so that the final standing crop is very small (Fig. 10.13). We may, therefore, envisage at the one extreme, a population size determined almost entirely by grazing intensity (e.g. areas of constant upwelling) and at the other, an area where nutrient level is all important, assuming in both cases sufficient light is available.

Part of the interest in the productivity of tropical areas is that, with the high illumination and the considerable depth of the photosynthetic zone, a high rate of photosynthesis is possible, though this is undoubtedly in most cases markedly limited in oligotrophic areas by the relatively low amount of nutrients available in the seawater.

In certain very special instances the limiting factors in the tropical areas may not always be nutrient lack. Thus Bernard (1958) suggests that the southern Mediterranean has very few diatoms, and by far the great majority of the phytoplankton are coccolithophores. These appear to have a very much slower multiplication rate than diatoms,

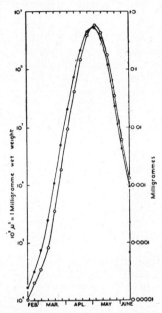

FIG. 10.13 The theoretical curve of algal production (●——●) with the quantity of algae eaten (o——o) (from Cushing, 1959).

a division rate of approximately one-fifth that of the typical diatoms of northern waters. He suggests that the relatively poor fertility of the Mediterranean is due to this slow rate of growth of the predominant phytoplankton rather than to any lack of nutrient salts. Riley *et al.* (1949) also suggest that while a comparison of inshore and offshore plankton shows the typical nearshore richness, with a mean ratio for coastal, slope and tropical waters of approximately 10 : 4 : 1 (cf. Table 10.6), the shallowness of the nearshore waters implies that the total organic production reckoned per square metre of surface is comparable. However, offshore plankton appears to have a much lower organic content and the density of near surface plankton is very much lower and less liable to seasonal fluctuations (cf. Table 10.7);

the classic view of the low standing crop of phytoplankton in tropical areas is therefore generally confirmed. The suggestion has been repeatedly put forward, however, that an accelerated rate of turnover in warmer waters may give a reasonably high overall production for the year, although the generally low populations of the tropical oceans maintain a greater constancy in density than at

TABLE 10.6. Volume of zooplankton in cc per 30 minute haul. Average of all stations. Numbers in parentheses are recomputed averages omitting a series of stations on July 9–17, 1938, when salps were unusually abundant (from Riley, Stommel and Bumpus, 1949).

	Depth (metres)	Total Zooplankton	Crustacean Plankton
Coastal Area	25–0	118 (120)	41
	Bottom–25	220 (119)	50
	Mean	194 (120)	50
Slope Water	25 or 50–0	77	18
	275–25 or 50	50	18
	Mean	52	18
Sargasso Sea	50–0	29	17
	100–50	27	17
	500–100	8	5
	900–500	5	3
	Mean	12	7

higher latitudes. Many workers (e.g. Marshall, 1933) have commented that the number of phytoplankton organisms in warm seas is usually rather low but tends to be more constant. Cushing (1959a, b) has recently re-examined this problem and has pointed out that the results of Riley et al. (1949) and Bernard (1939) for warm seas such as the Sargasso and the Mediterranean, suggest a slight seasonal fluctuation in phytoplankton crop, with the more productive season in mid-winter. Nearer the equator, the productive season is perhaps even earlier, but the amplitude of change of phytoplankton density with the seasons is far less; Cushing suggests an amplitude of five times for the Sargasso Sea as against possibly fifty times for seas in higher latitudes. Studies by Menzel and Ryther (1960) and Ryther and Menzel (1960) confirm that a distinct seasonal cycle of primary production is true of the semi-tropical area of the North-western Sargasso Sea off Bermuda, although the magnitude of the cycle is

TABLE 10.7. Summary of Regional Plankton Comparisons (from Riley, Stommel and Bumpus, 1949).

	Coastal water	Georges Bank		Slope water	Gulf Stream	Sargasso Sea
		May	June			
Herbivores, 10^{-9} g C/cc	15.5	72.0	150.0	17.2	5.2	2.9
Carnivores, 10^{-9} g C/cc	1.1	12.6	3.7	2.8	0.4	0.1
Both, 10^{9} g C/cc	16.6	84.6	153.7	20.0	5.6	3.0
Depth Range, metres	0–50	0–50	0–50	0–200	0–400	0–400
Zooplankton, g C/m^2	0.83	4.2	7.7	4.0	2.2	1.2
Carbon, % of wet wt	5	5	5	2.4	2.4	2.4
Zooplankton (g wet wt/m^2)						
Calculated	17	85	154	167	92	50
Observed	21	72	81	122	85(?)	45
Plant Pigment Units: Surface (per m^3)						
Calculated	1650	6760	5250	1340	1650	1050
Observed	2500	4490	8660	1840	800	860
Total (per m^2)						
Calculated	163,600	501,250	239,000	444,200	272,400	330,000
Observed	122,400	458,800	315,900	267,300	295,000	310,000

much less than in boreal and temperate waters. Production was high during winter and early spring, when the upper water layers were mixed almost to the depth of the permanent thermocline (*ca.* 400 m). Enrichment from the thermocline was negligible, and production was apparently dependant on the rapid re-cycling of nutrients, present in very low concentrations in the upper layers. Phytoplankton, as determined by chlorophyll densities, also showed relatively high values in winter, with a peak in April. During summer and early autumn, when the upper layers were thermally stratified, production was at a minimum, and chlorophyll densities were low. The enrichment of the upper layers above the thermocline with winter mixing, together with the intense solar radiation over winter and the high transparency of the water would therefore appear to be responsible for the higher winter production.

By contrast, to the south of Bermuda, in tropical waters, the upper water layers are virtually permanently stratified owing to the lack of winter cooling. Ryther and Menzel suggest that the level of primary production is much lower than in the semi-tropical waters to the north, and that the low level is maintained with relatively little change throughout the year. These observations, therefore, generally support the idea of a gradual reduction in amplitude of the seasonal cycle of primary production as one approaches the equator.

In temperate latitudes not only does an annual peak come in the spring, with a second peak usually in the autumn, but the peak is far greater in magnitude. This is partly attributable to the delay involved in the reproduction of the herbivores before they can graze upon the algae to a significant extent. This delay, Cushing suggests, is partly due to the necessity of the zooplankton receiving sufficient food for effective egg production (*vide infra*), and partly to the time required for the moulting of the copepodites. The seasonal peak in phytoplankton is even more striking at high latitudes where, as we have already seen, the season begins very late, and is compressed into a matter of about three months (cf. Heinrich, 1962; p. 391).

Considering temperate seas in general, Cushing agrees that nutrient depletion may effect a slowing down of production during the peak of the crop of phytoplankton, but then grazing makes more nutrients available, since grazing capacity is so large that a considerable amount of nutrients are regenerated directly. The decline in nutrients is, therefore, largely a balance between the uptake by the reproduction of algae and regeneration due to grazing. It is thus claimed that production is never halted by nutrient lack. One must remember, however, even if this idea be accepted, that abnormally low nitrate and phosphate levels can affect net photosynthesis and general algal physiology so greatly that there may be no real production. The concept of a balance is perhaps more applicable to tropical seas, though McAllister, Parsons and Strickland (1960) have recently suggested that in the north-east Pacific Ocean, where considerable rates of primary production can be achieved mainly from the nannoplankton, the crop is maintained at a comparatively low level. This check does not appear to be due to lack of light or of nutrients but is due to excessive grazing. This is in contrast to coastal areas in the same latitude where a marked bloom of phytoplankton is followed by a reduction. More generally, however, the low level of crop would probably apply to tropical oceans, where Cushing suggests that, in view of the more rapid utilization and regeneration of nutrients, the system of plankton production may be more efficient, even though gross production is lower than at higher latitudes. Any delay between the increase in phytoplankton and the consequent egg production by the herbivores, leading to a rise in zooplankton, is comparatively short. Grazing does not tend to be excessive, and in Cushing's words the phytoplankton/zooplankton relationship approaches a "steady state", i.e. there is an approximate balance between the reproductive rate of the algae and the grazing rate of the herbivorous zooplankton. The herbivores are maintained at a fairly low and steady level and the small standing stock of phytoplankton changes relatively little. Similarly, the nutrients with constant and continuous regeneration remain at about the same level, which is always very low, since they are absorbed continually as they are regenerated. This is usually in contrast to the highest latitudes, where an enormous burst of phytoplankton is succeeded by very heavy grazing, but where a marked time lag occurs between the rise in phytoplankton and in herbivores. Only when the standing stock has been reduced to some extent does nutrient regeneration begin to take place. Each level of organism in the food chain experiences a rise in density and then a decline and is succeeded by the next level. Tropical areas with low nutrient levels are not necessarily unproductive therefore, but it does appear that in general, greater densities of zooplankton are carried by larger standing phytoplankton crops (Table 10.7). How far the observation by Marshall and Orr that rich phytoplankton stimulates egg production of *Calanus* should be applied to zooplankton generally is not known, but it may well be a significant factor in size of animal crop. Marshall (1949) suggests that in Loch Striven the presence of abundant diatoms increased the production of eggs, nauplii and younger stages over the year as a whole. Gauld (1950) has also demonstrated that in a fertilized area (Kyle Scotnish) the continued reproduction of phytoplankton permitted the establishment and maintenance of an increased crop of zooplankton. The areas of upwelling with high nutrient level and massive phytoplankton growth, as well as plateaux and banks, where owing to turbulence a heavy phytoplankton crop exists throughout a part of the year, are the regions which experience large crops of zooplankton. In general, inshore waters with their heavier phytoplankton crops also show larger populations of animals, even though in nearly all these cases there may be great fluctuations in the animal crop. For the open oceans Steemann Nielsen and Aabye Jensen (1957) suggest that the direct dependence of zooplankton crop on the production of algae is the rule. Their results for the distribution of rates of organic production over the South Atlantic are in striking agreement with the distribution of phytoplankton and of zooplankton organisms over the same ocean, as determined by Hentschel and Wattenberg.

Of the very few experiments which have been carried out using high concentrations of nitrate and phosphate to stimulate plankton growth in isolated tanks, Gross and Clarke (1949, unpublished) obtained populations of several hundred copepods per litre in the presence of very rich phytoplankton crops as compared with 50 per litre as a maximum in the sea. Raymont and Miller (1962) have similarly obtained several hundred calanoids per litre in fertilized tanks at Woods Hole with very large phytoplankton densities. The few attempts to increase production by the addition of nitrates and phosphates to small, enclosed bodies of seawater (Gross, Orr, Marshall and Raymont, 1947; Gross, Nutman, Gauld and Raymont, 1950) also show this relation between relatively high nutrient and rich though fluctuating bursts of plant and animal growth. In these experiments, the increase in crop applied not only to the plankton but to the bottom fauna density and to some extent to fish growth. This would agree with the greater density of the benthos and of bottom feeding fish in shallower areas over banks and continental shelves; this is associated with the establishment of commercial trawling fisheries in such areas. It appears that the heavy grazing of the zooplankton on a changing but, at times, rich phytoplankton crop is undoubtedly less efficient, but the gorging of the zooplankton releases food materials for a rich bottom fauna. Some degree of "wastefulness" and inefficiency as regards plankton feeding may, therefore, be essential for a rich benthic fishery.

In conclusion we return to our view of the cycle of phytoplankton in temperate and high latitudes with its marked seasonal changes as resulting from the inter-action of many factors. Amongst these, light is clearly important as are nutrients, especially nitrate and phosphate, but possibly other accessory nutrient factors including organic substances. Turbulence and thermal stability are of considerable significance, especially early in the year, and grazing is a most potent factor, but the relative importance of each of these factors varies from one area to another, and even more, changes in any one area with time. It would seem more realistic to summarize the factors controlling algal populations in such terms than to take extreme views (which may be applicable to particular areas at certain times) that one factor such as nutrient level is insignificant or all-important.

CHAPTER XI

THE SEASONAL SUCCESSION IN PHYTOPLANKTON

IT HAS been long appreciated that whatever the density of phytoplankton during the various seasons of the year in temperate latitudes, there are also changes in species composition. Usually only one or more species of diatom or dinoflagellate is markedly abundant at one time, and the dominant species change during the course of the year. There is thus what may be termed a species succession, and although the dominant forms can vary to some extent from one year to another, the pattern is often reasonably clear and constant. To a large degree temperature is important in determining the species composition of the phytoplankton; there are characteristic cold-water species as well as warm-water species and in more temperate regions there will tend to be a variation in the species composition depending on the change in temperature of the water during the year. Sverdrup *et al.* (1946) quote a series of species for certain months in the Gulf of Maine:

April, 3 °C	*Thalassiosira nordenskioldii*
	Porosira glacialis
	Chaetoceros diadema
May, 6 °C	*Chaetoceros debilis*
June, 9 °C	*Chaetoceros compressus*
August, 12 °C	*Chaetoceros constrictus*
	Chaetocero cinctus
	Skeletonen 2 costatum.

They suggest that the surface temperature is to some extent responsible for the change in composition of the phytoplankton.

Species of phytoplankton differ according to whether they are somewhat eurythermal or extremely stenothermal, and there are also differences between neritic as opposed to oceanic species. Different species of plankton are also known to have different light optima (cf. Chapter VI) so that the changing intensity of light through the seasons is probably a minor factor in species composition, and perhaps nutrient levels may play a part in the abundance of particular species. By and large, however, it would seem that temperature is a major factor affecting the succession of species.

It is necessary to study the composition of the phytoplankton over several years to gain a clear idea of the succession of species. An example which has been well worked out is that given by Johnstone, Scott and Chadwick (1924) after several years of study in the Irish Sea area. The authors suggest that during the winter period, when of course the density of phytoplankton is low, the plants are dominated largely by species of *Coscinodiscus*, and also, somewhat later in the winter, by *Biddulphia mobiliensis*. The spring burst of diatoms is largely characterized by species of *Chaetoceros* together with *Thalassiosira* and *Lauderia*. During the summer *Guinardia* becomes abundant and species of *Rhizosolenia* are also present. As we have seen, there is frequently an autumn maximum, even though this is not so large as the spring peak; in the Irish Sea area this is mainly due to species of *Chaetoceros* again, together with the diatom *Rhizosolenia setigera*. Apart from the diatoms, Johnstone, Scott and Chadwick suggest that peridinians are plentiful mainly during the summer period; thus *Peridinium* itself is abundant in May to July only. Of the other dinoflagellates *Ceratium* has its main abundance in the months June to August, but it may occur in smaller numbers later in the autumn and winter and indeed may occur to some extent throughout the year. In a succession such as this it might be claimed that temperature was the chief factor; for example, the peridinians probably prefer rather higher temperatures than the spring diatoms. This view is also expressed by Gran (1929b) in dealing with the succession of phytoplankton species in Norwegian waters. However, recent experimental data reveal discrepancies between laboratory temperature optima for certain diatoms and their seasonal field distribution, though for several dinoflagellates the temperature optima are relatively high and approach the summer sea temperatures when they are most abundant (cf. Braarud, 1961). Often also, whilst the spring burst, so typical of temperate regions, is characterized by a marked abundance of one or two species of diatoms, soon after the peak has been reached there is a sharp decline in these particular species, followed shortly after by a new peak of a third or fourth species. It seems doubtful whether the succession is in such a case due to a change in temperature alone. Often indeed there is no marked change in temperature; often also a species which has been abundant in the colder early half of the year may show a secondary peak later on although the temperature conditions are markedly different. Neither can the change in abundance of a particular species be attributed to nutrient level; often the decline in algal numbers precedes any obvious nutrient fall. Admittedly it seems likely that some peridinians are able to flourish at rather lower nutrient levels than diatoms. Barker (1935b) states that the nitrogen and probably phosphorus requirements of some species of dinoflagellates are exceedingly low. Peridinians, therefore, may become more abundant than diatom species in temperate regions later on in the season. Gran and Braarud (1935) also suggest that not only higher temperature but lower nutrient levels may be responsible for the growth of *Ceratium, Pontosphaera* and the diatom *Rhizosolenia alata* during late summer in the Gulf of Maine. Ryther, however, has demonstrated that low nutrient requirement is certainly not typical of all dinoflagellates; probably a range of nutrient levels is true for various species in different algal groups. The investigations of Ryther (1954b) suggest for instance that the green algae *Nannochloris* and *Stichococcus* flourish at relatively high nitrogen concentrations where a considerable proportion of the nutrient is in forms other than nitrate.

Recent results (Braarud, 1961) suggest that some species of dinoflagellates (*Ceratium* spp., *Peridinium* spp., *Prorocentrum micans*) reproduce more actively at lowered salinities. In inshore areas changing salinity might thus influence species composition. It is clear, however, that the marked succession seen particularly in diatoms is partly dependent, at least on many occasions, on factors other than temperature, salinity, or nutrient level. It has been suggested that the conditioning of the water by the flowering of one species of diatom may itself give rise to conditions leading to the decline of that species and the subsequent rise of another. The biological history of a body of seawater is almost certainly a most important factor in ecological succession and the occurrence of metabolites in the sea, both those promoting growth and those tending to inhibit growth, are probably of the greatest importance in determining the successive flowering of different species of plankton (cf. Chapter IX). This point has been emphasized by Lucas (e.g. Lucas, 1947, 1955, 1961), and has also been taken up by Johnston (1955). Recent work such as that of Rice (1954) and Proctor (1957) has shown the antagonisms, at least under culture conditions, which can exist between freshwater algal species. Talling (1957), however, failed to obtain evidence from cultures of the freshwater planktonic diatoms, *Asterionella formosa* and *Fragilaria crotonensis*, for any production of extra-cellular substances which could modify the growth of either species (cf. Chapter IX).

Margalef (1958) has attempted a summary of the general pattern of phytoplankton succession. He believes that a burst of growth commences with mainly small-celled diatoms capable of rapid division, and that these are succeeded by medium-sized species, and finally by an increasing proportion of motile phytoplankton forms (mostly dinoflagellates) with a lower rate of increase. The decline in nutrient concentration is held to be one of the major factors in this succession, but Margalef draws attention to the importance of external metabolites; the third phase in the succession tends to be marked by the prevalence of organisms with metabolites of high toxicity. He suggests that these phytoplankton species have a relatively high immunity to the toxic substances.

The observations of Lillick (1940) on the phytoplankton in the Gulf of Maine provide another example of species succession. Lillick shows that, speaking generally for the Gulf of Maine as a whole, the winter flora is usually dominated by *Coscinodiscus* together with peridinians, particularly *Ceratium* (Figs. 11.1, 11.2). The spring outburst of diatoms is mainly due to *Thalassiosira*, but once this diatom has reached its peak it declines very sharply to be succeeded by an equally abrupt peak of *Chaetoceros* spp. (Fig. 11.2). Over the summer a mixture of diatoms may occur, but to a considerable extent the phytoplankton consists of peridinians, especially *Ceratium*, together with coccolithophores (Figs. 11.1, 11.2). During the late summer, another flowering of diatoms frequently occurs, the major species being *Rhizosolenia*, *Guinardia* and often *Skeletonema*, but peridinians and coccolithophores continue to be reasonably abundant. Finally, a considerable mixture of species over the autumn gives way to the very much reduced winter flora of peridinians and *Coscinodiscus* (Fig. 11.2). This picture is, however, only a broad one and Lillick's observations show that in the different areas of the Gulf of Maine there may be considerable variations in the species succession. Even the two areas illustrated in Figs. 11.1 and 11.2 show some remarkable differences in flora. Some idea of the differences between areas and the complexity of the whole succession may be gained from

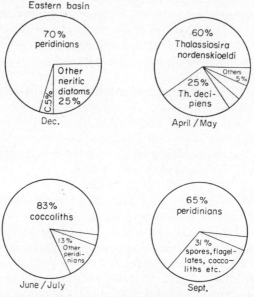

Eastern basin

70% peridinians

Other neritic diatoms 25%

C. 5%

Dec.

60% Thalassiosira nordenskioeldi

Others 5%

25% Th. deci-piens

April / May

83% coccoliths

13% Other peridi-nians

June / July

65% peridinians

31% spores, flagel-lates, cocco-liths etc.

Sept.

FIG. 11.1 Percentage composition of the phytoplankton in the Eastern Basin, Gulf of Maine, over different months (modified from Lillick, 1940).

Fig. 11.3 which is taken from Lillick's paper. To some extent the succession may again be tied to temperature changes; for example the earlier flowering of *Thalassiosira* and the take-over by *Chaetoceros* may partly depend upon the lower temperature requirements of the first species. But Lillick shows how abruptly one species is succeeded by another; the change is almost certainly not dependent upon temperature alone. The differences in succession between the shallower waters and off-shore areas also suggest more subtle influences.

Conover (1956) has described a rather similar study farther south in Long Island Sound. The early spring flowering was dominated by *Thalassiosira nordenskioldii* and *Skeletonema costatum*, and there was some indication that *Thalassiosira* was more abundant at the rather lower light intensities and somewhat lower temperature in the earliest part of the season. A slight rise in temperature tended to favour *Skeletonema*. Other species, including *Chaetoceros* spp.,

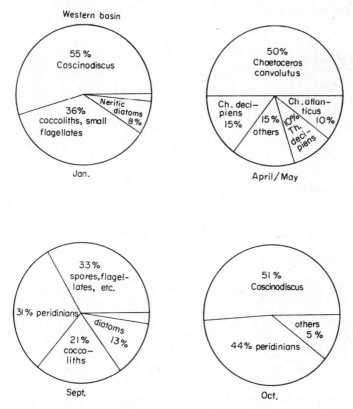

FIG. 11.2 Percentage composition of the phytoplankton in the Western Basin, Gulf of Maine, over different months (modified from Lillick, 1940).

Leptocylindricus danicus, Peridinium trochoideum, Asterionella japonica, Lauderia, and *Schroederella delicatula* appeared a little later after the main spring flowering. Conover, like other workers, suggests that the conditioning of the water is an important aspect of this succession. In particular she suggests that *Schroederella* is perhaps favoured by the product of the earlier flowering. *Thalassiosira gravida* replaced *T. nordenskioldii* in the later spring months, and in May the important species included *Guinardia* and *Rhizosolenia fragillissima*. Over the summer months, dinoflagellates, and probably small flagellates, were more abundant than diatoms, but in the early part of the autumn *Chatoceros* again became abundant together with other

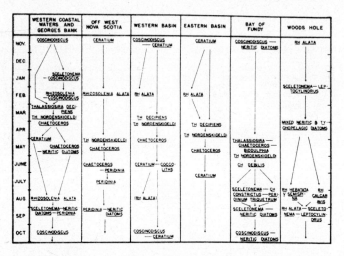

FIG. 11.3 Seasonal succession of dominant phytoplankton species in representative parts of the Gulf of Maine (from Lillick, 1940).

diatoms. Conover emphasizes that a succession of species was one of the most marked features of the phytoplankton over the year, even though the precise succession could vary from one year to another.

Succession of species is not by any means true only of temperate regions. Various investigations in high latitudes have suggested that a marked ecological succession is also true of very cold waters. Investigations by Digby (1953) in Scoresby Sound off East Greenland indicated an autumn and winter plankton, which was of course greatly reduced in density, consisting mainly of a mixture of species of *Chaetoceros* with a few peridinians. The rise in phytoplankton numbers in April/May was due mainly to *Nitzschia*, *Amphiprora*, *Fragilaria*, *Navicula* and *Thalassiosira*. On the other hand, in July and August, species of *Chaetoceros* were common, together with *Ceratium* and other peridinians. *Phaeocystis* could occur commonly throughout the summer apparently independent of any succession. Digby summarizes the researches of various other investigators such as Braarud, Steemann Nielsen and Shirsov, which suggest that the spring burst of *Nitzschia* and *Fragilaria*, and later *Thalassiosira*, followed by a summer population of *Chaetoceros* and *Ceratium* would appear to be typical of far northern waters. In the Antarctic, Hart (1934) also concludes that there is a species succession with forms like *Thalassiosira antarctica* being typical of spring, *Corethron valdiviae* lasting through spring and summer, *Fragilaria antarctica* having both spring and autumn maxima, but a species such as *Dactyliosolen antarcticus* being typical only of late summer and autumn.

As regards warmer waters, Riley (1957) reports on the seasonal changes in the phytoplankton in an area of the north-central Sargasso Sea (latitude 35 °N). Again there was a change in species composition through the year. Riley was able to classify his diatoms as winter, spring flowering and summer autumn species, although some species showed bursts of abundance at different seasons of the year, so that presumably too much emphasis should not be placed on temperature as the only factor in succession. Thus the spring flowering consisted of species of *Chaetoceros* and *Rhizosolenia stolterfothii*, whereas a diatom such as *Dactyliosolen mediterraneus* was present through the year, though it was denser during the winter time. Riley noticed that in the summer autumn period the density of diatoms was much lower as compared with dinoflagellates. Nannoplankton flagellates also showed alterations in density during the year, though the following of a succession in species of nannoplankton has yet to be accomplished. A succession in the phytoplankton has been confirmed by Hulburt, Ryther and Guillard (1960) for the warm oceanic waters off Bermuda, though the order of occurrence of the different communities probably varies. Coccolithophores dominate the phytoplankton over most of the year, with *Coccolithus huxleyi* being clearly dominant over winter. A short spring flowering of diatoms follows in April, but during the summer the phytoplankton is sparse, with a few coccolithophores, diatoms and dinoflagellates. Finally, the observations of Marshall (1933) on the Great Barrier Reef demonstrated that under what might be called sub-tropical neritic conditions, diatoms were dominant except for bursts of *Trichodesmium*. The species of diatoms varied considerably, however, through the year with rather irregular small bursts. Species of *Chaetoceros* and *Rhizo-*

solenia were more important from March to July or August. On the other hand, the coccolithophores were much more abundant during the period August to November.

Species succession would appear to be a very widespread phenomenon among phytoplankton. Although temperature, and to a lesser extent light intensity, and perhaps nutrient concentration may play a part in the changes, more subtle differences, particularly the biological history of the water, have an important role.

CHAPTER XII

ZOOPLANKTON–
I GENERAL ACCOUNT–
THE NERITIC PLANKTON

IN DISCUSSING the phytoplankton, especially as regards the changes in density of the plant plankton, we have had occasion to speak of the floating animal population – the zooplankton. It is now essential to examine this great community in some detail. In the first place it differs appreciably from the phytoplankton in that this vast collection of floating animals is drawn from a very wide variety of animal phyla. Moreover, although a very large number of zooplankton animals remain planktonic throughout their existence (e.g. copepods, sagittae, siphonophores) a large array of animals occur in the plankton during only a part of their lives. These are known as meroplanktonic animals in contrast to those holoplanktonic forms which remain in the plankton for the whole of their existence. The meroplankton will include the larvae of bottom invertebrates such as trochophores, veligers, the nauplii of cirripedes, zoea larvae (Fig. 12.1) and the larvae of echinoderms, as well as medusae of the hydromedusan type (cf. Fig. 12.20). Also included in the meroplankton are the eggs and larval stages of most fishes which when adult become part of the nekton.

In speaking of both phyto- and zooplankton we have previously referred to the coastal plankton over continental shelves. This coastal plankton may be roughly delimited as occurring in depths not exceeding 200 m, for this marks approximately the extent of the continental shelf, and from about this point the sea bottom falls away more rapidly down the continental slope before plunging to the abyssal depths. The animals which occur in this relatively shallow zone roughly delimited by the 200 m bottom contour may be classed as neritic forms. It is possible, therefore, to speak of a neritic zooplankton community as opposed to the oceanic zooplankton which occurs over great ocean depths. Although these two communities

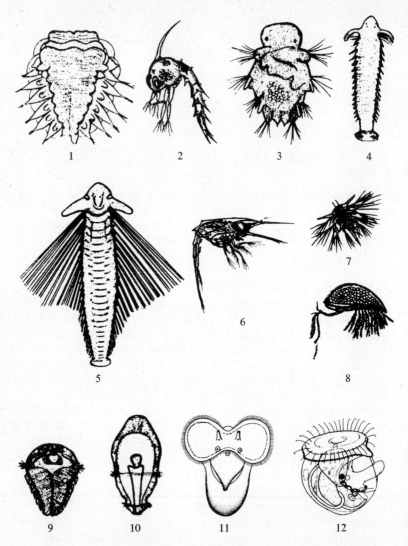

FIG. 12.1 Meroplanktonic larvae. 1 = polynoid post larva; 2 = zoea of
Inachus leptocheirus; 3 = *Pelagobia longicirrata*; 4 and 5 = spio-
nid post larvae; 6 = *Eupagurus bernhardus*; 7 = nauplius of
Balanus improvisus; 8 = cyprid of *Balanus improvisus*; 9 = polynoid post larva; 10 = trochophore; 11 = veliger of *Rissoa
parva*; 12 = *Ostrea edulis* larva; (after various authors – Johnstone
Scott and Chadwick, 1924; Graham, 1956; Kunne, 1950).

are not sharply separated they show differences. For example, the neritic plankton tends to have a far higher proportion of meroplanktonic forms. Oceanic zooplankton, though it may include a few larvae such as phyllosomas which can be long lived, in general has mostly holoplanktonic members.

Among the variety of animals which are found in the zooplankton as a whole, the Crustacea easily predominate, both in numbers and

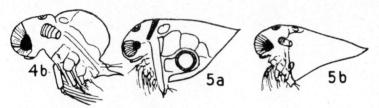

FIG. 12.2 Cladocera. 4b = *Podon leuckarti* ♂; 5a = *Evadne nordmanni* ♀; 5b = *Evadne nordmanni* ♂ (from Rammner 1939).

in species. Of the groups occurring, the Cladocera are represented only by very few genera e.g., *Podon*, *Evadne* and *Penilia* (Figs. 12.2, 12.3). One or two families of ostracods are well represented in the plankton, some being bathypelagic like the relatively large *Gigantocypris* (Fig. 12.4). A few mysids and cumaceans (Fig. 12.5) are truly planktonic, though many that are found in the plankton rise into the water near the sea bottom for only a part of the 24 hr, especially towards night-fall. They are bottom living animals that make only a brief appearance in the plankton. Some amphipods similarly live in the bottom mud and sand, but come into the plankton for a short time, mainly at night. On the other hand, some amphipods, particularly the Hyperiidae, are truly planktonic throughout their existence. Genera such as *Euthemisto* and *Hyperia* are known almost throughout the world and at times can be important members of the zooplankton community (Figs. 12.5.1, 12.6).

The euphausids are mainly a planktonic crustacean group and some of them are exceedingly abundant, more particularly in higher latitudes or in the deeper water layers. Species of *Thysanoessa* are very well known; two or three being common in British waters (cf. Fig. 12.7). But the euphausid which perhaps contributes the greatest mass to the zooplankton is *Euphausia superba* (Fig. 12.7.1) which in quantity, although not in numbers, is the most important member of the zooplankton in Antarctic regions.

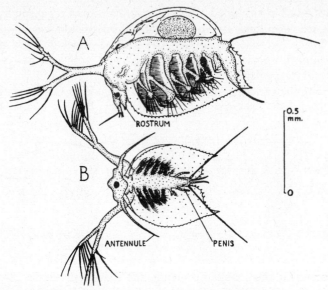

FIG. 12.3 *Penilia avirostris*. A = mature ♀ with resting egg in brood sac;
B = male (from Lochhead, 1954).

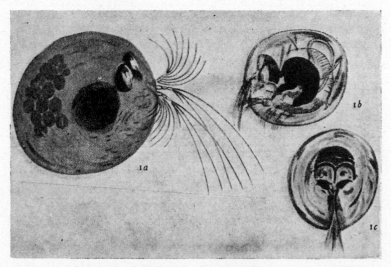

FIG. 12.4 *Gigantocypris mulleri*. 1 a = adult with **eggs**; 1 b and 1 c = younger
specimens (from Hardy, 1956).

Fig. 12.5 *Diastylis rathkei* (from Sars, 1900).

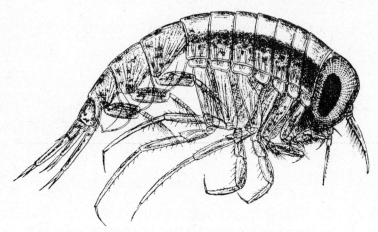

FIG. 12.5.1 *Parathemisto oblivia* [= *gracilipes*] (♀) (from Sars, 1895).

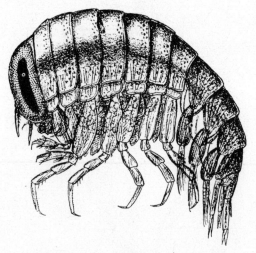

FIG. 12.6 *Hyperia galba* (♀) (from Sars, 1895)

FIG. 12.7 Crustacean zooplankton. 3 = phyllosoma of *Palinurus vulgaris*;
4 = *Thysanoessa longicaudata*; 7 = *Temora longicornis* (♀);
8 = *Candacia armata* (♂) (from Graham, 1956).

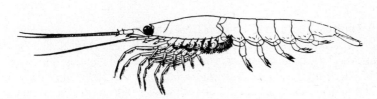

FIG. 12.7.1 *Euphausia superba* (from Mackintosh and Wheeler, 1929).

It is however, the copepods which represent the major group of Crustacea in the zooplankton, most of the species of copepods belonging to the Calanoida. *Calanus finmarchicus*, for example, is

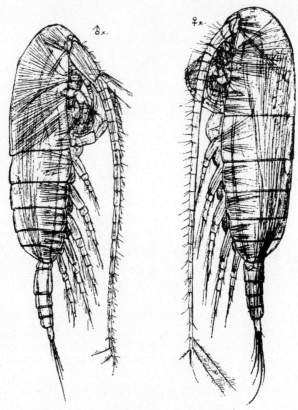

FIG. 12.8 *Calanus finmarchicus* (♂) and (♀) (from Sars, 1903)

perhaps the best known of all marine copepods, and occurs in count-less numbers in temperate as well as Arctic seas (Fig. 12.8). There are very great numbers of planktonic calanoid species, but a few Harpacticoida, such as *Euterpina acutifrons* (Fig. 12.9), also occur in the plankton and can have a very wide distribution. Some cyclopoid copepods are planktonic in the oceans, (e.g. *Corycaeus anglicus* in British waters (Fig. 12.10)), but the majority of cyclopoid species are found in tropical and sub-tropical areas. The composition of the zooplankton varies greatly in different parts of the world and also with the seasons. Nevertheless, it is possible to generalize to some degree, and in the oceans of the world as a whole the calanoid copepods usually contribute the largest part.

The juvenile stages of the various groups of Crustacea which have already been noted as holoplanktonic will, of course, contribute to

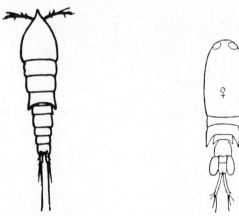

FIG. 12.9   *Euterpina acutifrons* (♀)   FIG. 12.10   *Corycaeus anglicus* (♀)
(from Klie, 1943).   (from Rose, 1933).

the total numbers of Crustacea. Thus in temperate latitudes, in spring the nauplii of copepods may form by far the greatest portion numerically of the zooplankton, (cf. Bigelow, 1926; Nicholls, 1933a). But to this juvenile population must be added the larvae of bottom living Crustacea which undergo their early development as planktonic animals. Here the nauplii of cirripedes are extremely important, (cf. Pyefinch, 1948; Raymont and Carrie, 1959), at times dominating inshore neritic zooplankton. Other meroplanktonic crustacean larvae include the zoeas and megalopas of crabs and the larvae of other decapods.

The Chordata have zooplankton representatives. Apart from the contribution made by the eggs and larvae of fishes to the meroplankton there are, among the chordates, the salps, doliolids and *Pyrosoma*, which occur sometimes in considerable numbers (Figs. 12.11, 12.12). More particularly in tropical seas salps have been observed in countless numbers to the partial exclusion of other species (cf. Russell and Colman, 1935; Wickstead, 1958). Rich hauls of salps are sometimes taken in warm currents at higher latitudes (cf. Hansen, 1959). Of the appendicularians, species of *Oikopleura* (Fig. 12.13) and *Fritillaria* are very well known in almost all waters of the world.

Molluscs occur in the plankton as young veliger larvae, but a few groups of Mollusca are pelagic even as adults. The Heteropoda are entirely planktonic Mollusca, though they are restricted to the

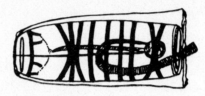

FIG. 12.11 *Salpa fusiformis* (solitary form) (from Fraser, 1947).

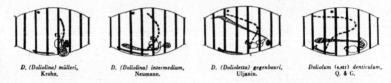

D. (Doliolina) mülleri, D. (Doliolina) intermedium, D. (Dolioletta) gegenbauri, Doliolum (s.str) denticulum,
Krohn.   Neumann.   Uljanin.   Q. & G.

FIG. 12.12 Gonozoids of four species of *Doliolum* (from Fraser, 1947).

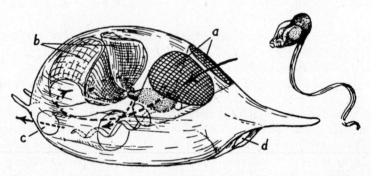

FIG. 12.13 *Oikopleura. Left*, in its "house"; *right*, swimming freely.
a = protective grids over water entrances; b = very fine filters;
c = water outlet; d = emergency exit (from Hardy, 1956).

warmer seas. They include such highly modified forms as *Carinaria* (Fig. 12.14) and *Pterotrachea* (Fig. 12.14.1).The Pteropoda are also well adapted to planktonic existence. Some few species occur in colder water, such as the shelled form *Limacina* (Fig. 12.15) which in the northern hemisphere contributes to some extent to the food of whales. The shelled pteropods are largely herbivorous on the phytoplankton, but there are also unshelled naked pteropods such as *Clione* (Fig. 12.16) which are carnivorous plankton feeders. Though

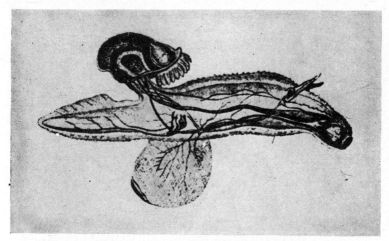

FIG. 12.14 *Carinaria lamarcki* (from Murray and Hjort, 1912).

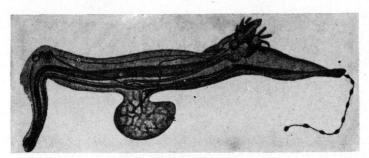

FIG. 12.14.1 *Pterotrachea coronata* (from Murray and Hjort, 1912).

species such as *Limacina helicina* and *L. balea* are abundant in cold seas, most of the pteropod species are found in warmer waters.

Annelids contribute rather little to the zooplankton apart from the large number of trochophores and post-trochophores which occur at times, especially in neritic areas. There is one well-known holoplanktonic family (the Alciopidae) mainly in warmer seas. Another small family includes the genus *Tomopteris*, with several species, known in almost all the seas of the world (cf. Fig. 12.18). Of minor zoological groups the rotifers may sometimes be abundant in neritic areas.

Some pelagic nemertines are known (cf. Fig. 12.17). They are mostly deep water forms; several new species have been described from the work of the Bermuda Oceanographic and Discovery Expeditions

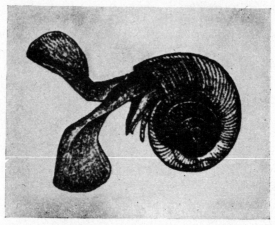

FIG. 12.15 *Limacina retroversa* (from Murray and Hjort, 1912).

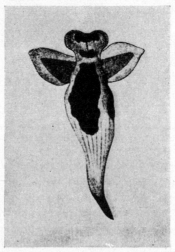

FIG. 12.16 *Clione limacina* (from Murray and Hjort, 1912).

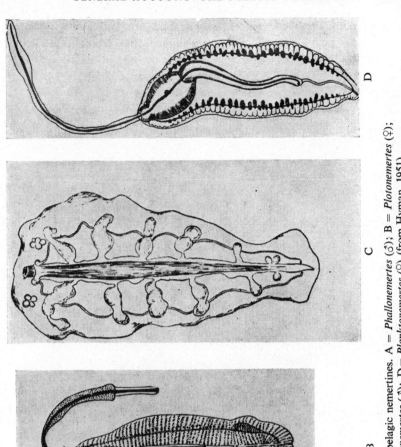

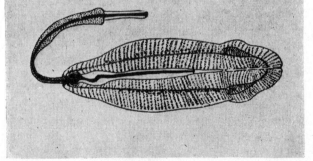

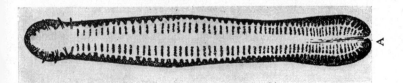

Fig. 12.17 Bathypelagic nemertines. A = *Phallonemertes* (♂); B = *Plotonemertes* (♀); C = *Pelagonemertes* (♂); D = *Planktonemertes* (♀) (from Hyman, 1951).

(e.g. Wheeler, 1934; Coe, 1935). Although the Chaetognatha is a very small zoological group containing only four or five genera, it makes a very significant contribution to the plankton. The largest genus is *Sagitta* (cf. Fig. 12.18). Almost all the chaetognaths are holoplanktonic, and they can be extremely abundant. They are voracious carnivores, feeding on copepods and the like. Other holoplanktonic carnivorous types include the Ctenophora, such as *Pleurobrachia* and *Beroe* (Fig. 12.19), which feed so voraciously that they can affect the composition and richness of a zooplankton population. Ctenophores are found in almost all seas from the coldest Arctic waters to the tropics. The coelenterates also include carnivorous members since many medusae occur in the zooplankton. Some like *Aglantha* (Fig. 12.20) and other Trachylina are holoplanktonic forms and this is also true

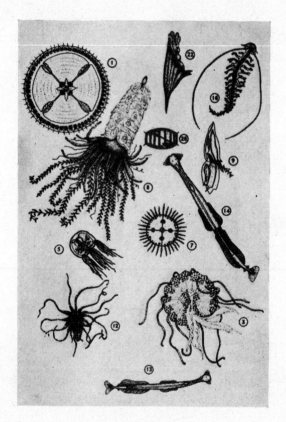

FIG. 12.18

FIG. 12.18 General non-crustacean zooplankton 1. *Cosmetira megalotis*; 2. *Laodicea undulata*; 3. *Pelagia perla*; 4. *Hybocodon prolifer*; 5. *Bougainvillia superciliaris*; 6. *Aglantha digitale*; 7. Medusa of *Obelia*; 8. *Physophora hydrostatica*; 9. *Chelophyes appendiculata*; 10. *Muggiaea atlantica*; 11. *Pleurobrachia pileus*; 12. "Arachnactis" larva; 13. *Sagitta setosa*; 14. *Sagitta elegans*; 15. *Sagitta serratodentata*; 16. *Eukrohnia hamata*; 17. Larva of *Polydora*; 18. *Tomopteris helgolandica*; 19. Young stage of *Spisula*; 20. *Limacina retroversa*; 21. *Clione limacina*; 22. *Clio pyramidata*; 23. *Clio cuspidata*; 24. Pluteus larva of *Ophiothrix*; 25. Metamorphosing larva of *Luidia*; 26. *Oikopleura dioica*; 27. *Salpa fusiformis*; 28. *Dolioletta gegenbauri*
(from Graham 1956).

of the Siphonophora which are mostly found in tropical waters (cf. Fig. 12.18). Members of the Scyphozoa such as *Aurelia aurita*, *Cyanea* and *Chrysaora* (cf. Fig. 12.21) are very widely distributed in coastal waters. In boreal waters *Aurelia* and *Cyanea* may become exceedingly abundant for short periods, and in more oceanic boreal seas the trachyline medusa, *Aglantha*, may sometimes be very plentiful.

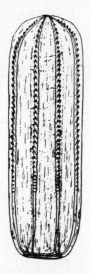 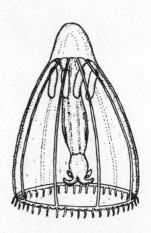

FIG. 12.19 *Beroe gracilis* (from   FIG. 12.20 *Aglantha digitalis* (from
Kunne, 1950).   Kunne, 1950).

Ctenophores may also show peaks of abundance in colder seas. The typical hydromedusae (Fig. 12.21.1) are liberated from hydroid forms and spend only a portion of their lives as planktonic members but they feed readily on other zooplankton. In the region of coral reefs planulae larvae may occur as temporary members of the zooplankton.

The Protozoa include several groups which can be very abundant as zooplankton species. Among the dinoflagellates we have already discussed the chlorophyll-containing members as part of the phytoplankton. But there are also non-green species such as *Noctiluca* which feed on diatoms and other members of the plankton community. The Foraminifera include large numbers of planktonic members as well as bottom living forms. Some of the planktonic species, such as

Globigerina, are so common in tropical and sub-tropical seas, that their calcareous shells, falling to the bottom, form an ooze over many square miles of the sea floor. The Radiolaria similarly have

FIG. 12.21 Scyphozoa.   1 = *Cyanea   lamarcki*;   2 = *Pelagia   noctiluca*;
3 = *Chrysaora hysoscella*; 4 = *Rhizostoma octopus*
(from Hardy, 1956).

zooplankton members, and these may be found in the colder regions of the world (Fig. 12.22). The siliceous skeletons derived from Radiolaria of the plankton, when they fall to the bottom, can contribute to the formation of Radiolarian ooze. Other forms of Protozoa such as Tintinnids, which are minute shelled ciliated forms, occur sometimes in considerable numbers. We have rather little knowledge of

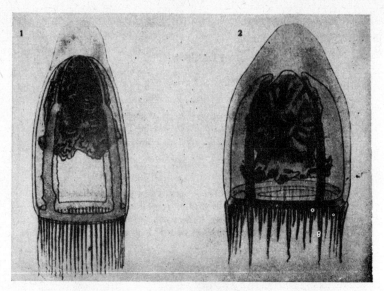

FIG. 12.21.1 *Neoturris pileata* (1) and *Leuckartiara breviconis* (2) (from Russell, 1953).

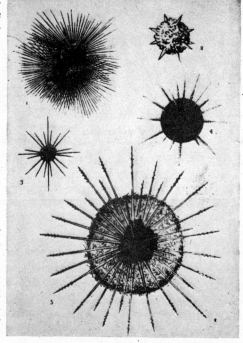

FIG. 12.22 Planktonic Protozoa. 1 = a foraminiferan (*Globigerina bulloides*). 2–5 radiolarians: 2 = *Acanthosphaera* sp.; 3 = *Acanthometron bifidum*; 4 = *Acanthonia mulleri*; 5 = *Aulacantha scolymantha* (from Hardy, 1956).

the other types of flagellates, ciliates and amoebae which apparently may occur in large numbers though they are not taken normally in net hauls because of their small size. An examination of the contribution made by some of these lesser known Protozoa is given from the work of Bigelow, Lillick and Sears (1940).

Practically every phylum, therefore, makes some contribution to the zooplankton, though some may occur almost solely as larvae as, for example, small animal groups such as the Polyzoa and the Phoronidea. The Echinodermata appear in the plankton as larvae, such as bipinnariae, auriculariae and plutei, but even among the echinoderms one or two adult forms are pelagic, (e.g. *Pelagothuria* and *Planktothuria*).

The variety of the zooplankton thus appears to be very great, but it is true that in temperate and more especially in polar plankton hauls, a very considerable monotony is often apparent. One species, such as *Calanus finmarchicus* in northern waters or *Euphausia superba* in the Antarctic, can dominate the plankton to such an extraordinary degree that at first sight it would appear that no other species is present. The majority of the main animal groups have a large number of species in the warm tropical waters and generally rather few representatives in waters from high latitudes. A list of the number of species in warm and cold waters as given by Russell (1935) is shown in Table 12.1.

Despite the fact that the zooplankton is drawn from such different groups of animals, the members of the community very broadly resemble each other in certain characteristics. Thus, while some plankton animals from deep water may be red, purple or black in colour, (e.g. *Acanthephyra* [Fig. 12.23], *Atolla*, [Fig. 12.24] *Eucopia*) the vast majority of the zooplankton tends to be transparent. Even more characteristic is the small size of planktonic animals. There are a few exceptions; for example some medusae may be a foot or more across and some Siphonophora measure several inches. But in general the great majority of zooplankton animals are less than a centimetre in length and many of them do not exceed two or three millimetres. There is little doubt that this marked restriction on size is partly attributable to the necessity for permanent floating life which planktonic existence demands. In this regard, in contrast to most phytoplankton organisms, almost all members of the animal plankton have an advantage in possessing some means of movement. They are provided with limbs or some form of swimming appendages,

TABLE 12.1. Numbers of species of holoplanktonic animals, and meroplanktonic coelenterates (modified from Russell, 1935).

	Arctic	Arctic-Boreal and Boreal	Antarctic	Sub-Antarctic	Bipolar-Epiplanktonic	Cosmo-politan	Warm	Deep Sea	Total	Distribution of warm water species in 3 Oceans
COELENTERATA										
Antho-, Lepto-, and Scyphomedusae	20	100	10	15	—	—	370	20	535	11
Trachy-, and Narco-medusae	4	10	3	6	—	—	90	21	134	15
Siphonophora										
Calycophorae	—	—	2	—	1	—	64	5	72	24
Physophorae	—	?1	2	—	—	—	29	2	34	10
Ctenophora	1	2	2	1	—	2	69?	3	80	2
NEMERTEA	—	—	—	—	—	—	—	34	34	—
POLYCHAETA										
Tomopteridae	—	?1	?4	—	1	—	38	?	44	3
CHAETOGNATHA	—	2	2	—	2	—	18	6	30	9
CRUSTACEA										
Copepoda	7	10	32	5	1(5)	10	489	195	754	146
Amphipoda Hyperiidea	2	—	10	—	—	2	250	28	292	54
Euphausiacea	—	6	2	7	(1)	—	46	23	85	14
MOLLUSCA										
Pteropoda										
Thecosomata	—	—	2	—	1(1)?	—	44	3	51	24
Gymnosomata	—	1	2	—	(1)?	—	37	?	41	5
Heteropoda	—	—	—	—	—	—	90	—	90	8
TUNICATA										
Appendicularia	2	1	6	—	—	1	48	3	61	9
Thaliacea	—	—	2?	—	—	—	43	—	45	24

or have other forms of muscular movement (e.g. nectocalyces). Some members of the zooplankton move by means of cilia or flagella. Even so, the expenditure of energy in maintaining level, especially over great oceanic depths, must be very considerable. Gardiner (1933)

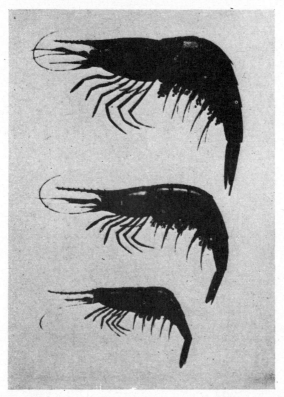

FIG. 12.23 Bathypelagic decapods. (Top) = *Acanthephyra multispina*; (Centre) = *A. purpurea*; (Bottom) = *Systellaspis debilis* (from Murray and Hjort, 1912).

showed that *Calanus* would sink at a very appreciable rate if the animal was anaesthetized, and it is obvious from watching living plankton that the animals are constantly swimming upwards to maintain their level in the water. As seawater can vary considerably in density and in viscosity, according to salinity and temperature, there is no doubt that such changes will affect flotation and thus will have an influence on the size and form of planktonic animals. Very broadly

speaking plankton from brackish areas tends to be rather small in size.
Sewell (1948) has demonstrated for certain species of copepods (*Acartia*,
Acrocalanus, *Labidocera*, *Centropages*, etc.) that where the species is
capable of existence over a very wide range of salinity, it is nearly

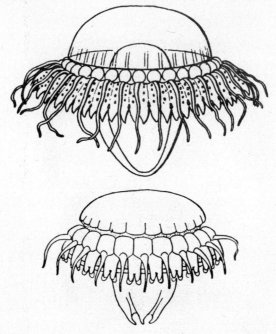

FIG. 12.24 *Atolla chuni* (upper) and *A. wyvillei* (lower) (from Mayer, 1910).

always true that those races living in brackish waters tend to be smaller
than those members of the species living in normal seawater. There
appears to be a very definite tendency also for greater size of zooplankton to be associated with waters of lower temperature. It is
not suggested that this is a direct effect of the greater viscosity of
seawater at lower temperatures which will assist the flotation of
animals; nevertheless, it is true that animals in warmer waters will
experience more difficulty in maintaining their level if they are of
relatively large size. Sewell, following earlier workers, has demonstrated for a large number of copepod species a general tendency for
increasing size with decreasing temperature.

It has been recognized for some time where several broods of an
animal, such as a sagitta or a copepod, are passed through during a

year, that in temperate regions with considerable differences in temperature throughout the year, the brood showing the maximal mean size tends to occur during the coldest months. The smallest individuals usually develop in waters at the highest temperature (cf. Russell, 1935; Jespersen, 1939; Marshall and Orr, 1955). It is much less easy to discuss the size of pelagic organisms in relation to different species or different genera. Nevertheless, although there are many exceptions, it may be said that larger forms in any zooplankton group tend to inhabit the higher latitudes, or alternatively, live at considerable depths where the water is cold. Relatively large zooplankton animals may occur in tropical seas, but those living in the upper less dense layers often tend to have a jelly-like watery consistency of lower specific gravity, while the denser larger species such as euphausids appear to inhabit deeper and therefore colder layers. Tropical surface-loving copepods are believed to have a lower specific gravity than typical Arctic or Antarctic species. Some measurements of specific gravity would be of interest. As examples of the relationship between water density and size we may instance the Challengeridae which are rather larger in size among radiolarians and which tend to be deep water forms. Similarly the bathypelagic genus *Gigantocypris* among the ostracods is a very large form. It is, however, more fair to compare closely allied species, or even forms or sub-species of a single zooplankton species. Sewell compares several varieties of the species *Pleuromamma gracilis*, and shows that the smallest form lives in the upper levels of tropical and sub-tropical regions, while the larger forms inhabit the deeper and colder waters. Similarly he shows that in the genus *Rhincalanus*, *R. cornutus*, which is the smallest species, inhabits the surface layer in the tropics, *R. nasutus* (Fig. 12.25) which is rather larger, occurs at intermediate depths, and finally the largest, *R. gigas*, lives at the deepest levels and also occurs in the colder waters of the Antarctic. A similar comparison may possibly be made for the genus *Calanus*; *Calanus hyperboreus*, which is a high polar form, is considerably larger than the much more widely distributed *Calanus finmarchicus*.

A tendency to reduction in size is by no means the only adaptation to planktonic life, however. Some zooplankton animals have gas bladders, (e.g. some Siphonophora), which may reduce the specific gravity of the body so much as to allow them to float on the surface, as in the case of *Physalia* (Fig. 12.26). Other members of the zooplankton have oil globules which can also serve as hydrostatic organs.

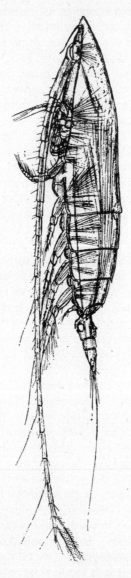

FIG. 12.25 *Rhincalanus nasutus* (♀) (from Sars, 1903).

Among the Crustacea, especially, the development of spines and hairs is particularly marked and it appears that these are of value in increasing the frictional resistance to the water and so delaying sinking. Very broadly, the most marked development of spines and plumose

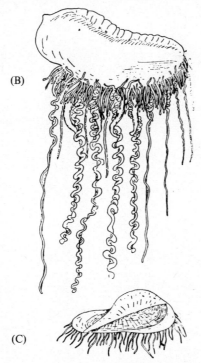

(B)

(C)

FIG. 12.26 *Physalia physalis* (B) and *Velella velella* (C) (from Hyman, 1940).

appendages occurs in tropical forms. The warm water copepod *Calocalanus plumulosus*, for example, (Fig. 12.27) has the most wonderful array of spines, particularly on the caudal furca. Of the few Harpacticoida which are planktonic, the tropical *Macrosetella* (Fig. 12.28) has a very large pair of posterior spines. Marked flattening of the body is found in a few zooplanktonic forms such as *Sapphirina* (Fig. 12.29), and in phyllosoma larvae (Fig. 12.7), and this would also appear to be an adaptation to reduce the sinking rate. The shells and skeletons of pelagic species (e.g. molluscs) are usually very thin and the chitinous exoskeletons of many planktonic crustaceans weigh comparatively little.

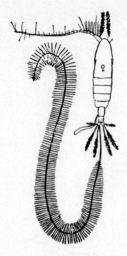

FIG. 12.27 *Calocalanus plumulosus*
(♀) (from Rose, 1933).

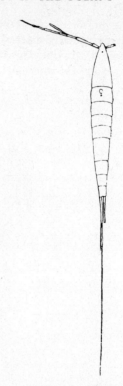

FIG. 12.28 *Macrosetella gracilis* (♀)
(from Rose, 1933).

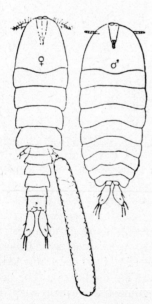

FIG. 12.29 *Sapphirina iris* (♀ and ♂)
(from Rose, 1933).

It is possible that physiological as well as morphological adaptations may occur as a response to the need for flotation. It has been claimed that *Noctiluca* has an intracellular fluid which, although isotonic with seawater, possesses a considerable concentration of ammonium ions, thus reducing the specific gravity. Whether such a mechanism exists in other plankton animals is not known. Hardy and Gunther (1936) have suggested that the vertical migration of some copepods in Antarctic waters over a 24 hour period is of such an extent that some change in specific gravity might occur to assist the move to the surface. It is clear that flotation is of vast importance to plankton animals and recently the problem has attracted a good deal of attention. Denton and Shaw (1962), for example, have studied gelatinous animals including, medusae, ctenophores, tunicates, heteropod and pteropod molluscs. They find that these animals are close to neutral buoyancy (i.e. they have the same density as that of seawater); some even float upwards in still water. Lift is obtained from their body fluids, which, although isotonic with sea water, have dense sulphate ions replaced by chloride ions. In any event, any adaptations which can reduce the sinking rate will be of real value to planktonic animals in that they effect a saving of the energy requirements.

Although a different community of zooplankton animals exists near coasts, as Ekman (1953) emphasized, it is difficult to delimit sharply the neritic from the oceanic plankton. The distance to which this neritic zooplankton extends from the shore is very variable, depending on the topography of the coast and the depth of water as well as on the local water currents. The English Channel may be regarded as a neritic area almost throughout, and this is true to a large extent of the North Sea. On the other hand, in relatively isolated oceanic islands, the oceanic zooplankton approaches very close to the shore. Neritic plankton, on the whole, appears to include many species which are somewhat more eurythermal than oceanic forms, and indeed zooplankton animals in coastal areas appear to prefer slightly warmer conditions for their development than their oceanic relatives. The water in which neritic plankton exists also tends to have slightly reduced salinity, and on the whole neritic animals are somewhat more euryhaline. Oceanic animals may to some degree, therefore, be prevented from colonizing coastal waters owing to the somewhat more variable temperature and salinity conditions inshore.

It is somewhat more difficult to suggest why neritic zooplankton species cannot spread out over the high oceans, and indeed some species, like *Pleurobrachia*, can occur equally well in neritic and oceanic water over very wide areas of the ocean. Meroplanktonic forms are obviously restricted to waters fairly near the coast in order to complete their life history. But holoplankton neritic animals appear to be able to withstand considerable changes in temperature and salinity and, therefore, it is not immediately apparent why they should not spread out much further from the coast. Conversely, it is not really clear why oceanic forms cannot proceed further in towards the coast than they usually do. The few experiments which have been done on offshore plankton suggest that often these animals can tolerate, at least under experimental conditions, a degree of variation both in temperature and salinity which is probably greater than they would experience in drifting closer to coasts. Marshall and Orr (1955) have questioned why *Calanus finmarchicus* cannot spread more widely than it does, even though it is a very broadly distributed species. Its tolerance of temperature and salinity changes under experimental conditions seems to be high enough for it to colonize more widely. The problem is somewhat more complex in that apart from oceanic and neritic areas, various types of water appear to exist, each with its own characteristic species. As Fraser (1939, 1952) has remarked, the limitation of different species of zooplankton animals to particular bodies of water cannot be explained only on the assumption that the restriction is due to a variation of one or two parts per thousand in salinity or to a change of a degree or so in temperature. A partial explanation may be that the younger stages of zooplankton animals are often more susceptible to environmental change than the adults. But the problem of restriction of species, including neritic and oceanic forms, introduces the whole question of minute biological differences between different types of sea water. Studies, especially such as those of Wilson, on the survival of polychaete and echinoderm larvae have shown that sea waters of apparently identical chemical composition and with the same physical characters can differ in their suitability for growth of larvae. Such waters must differ presumably in minute traces of organic (or possibly inorganic) constituents which are either inimical to or essential for healthy development. We are here again dealing with the biological conditioning of sea water; with the production of vitamins, antibiotics and of other organic materials in trace quantities formed as metabolites, probably by bacteria and by plant and animal populations, and then liberated into the water. Lucas (1955) particularly, has called attention to this conditioning of seawater (cf. Chapter IX). Only further studies can show whether this is partially responsible for the restriction of neritic and of oceanic species to their particular environment.

Meroplanktonic animals are obviously numerically important in neritic zooplankton, and in temperate areas such as British waters, a strong seasonal effect is evident in the abundance of meroplanktonic forms. Generally speaking it is in the early spring and summer that the greatest numbers of most bottom invertebrate larvae, as well as considerable numbers of fish eggs and larvae, occur in the plankton. Some species (e.g. the ascidians *Dendrodoa* and *Ciona*) can spawn over an extended period but with peak spawning in different months. However, apart from these species, the bottom animals which produce planktonic larvae vary somewhat in their spawning times throughout the year, so that although the greatest abundance of juveniles is normally in early spring and summer, there is almost no time of the year when a few species of larvae are not represented in the plankton. Orton (1920) has investigated some of the different spawning times of animals represented in the meroplankton of British waters. He emphasizes temperature as the main controlling factor. On the whole, those species of benthic animals which are near the limit of their southern distribution in Britain tend to produce their larvae at the coldest time of the year (e.g. *Balanus balanoides*). On the other hand, warm water species occur in British seas; these then tend to spawn in late summer when the waters are much warmer. The European oyster will not spawn below 16–17 °C—almost the yearly maximum. This variation in the spawning times is by no means restricted to British waters. A similar pattern has been demonstrated for the spawning times of echinoderms in Norway, (Table 12.2). Barnes (1957b) discusses the variations in spawning times with latitude especially for barnacles. He suggests synchronization of spawning with the main phytoplankton outburst so that the timing is only indirectly related to temperature. It is striking that at Woods Hole, where the phytoplankton outburst is as early as December, the spawning of *Balanus balanoides* is some 2–3 months earlier than in Britain (Barnes and Barnes, 1958).

Even in British waters some differences are observable in the spawning times of particular species of animals according to whether northern or southern regions are investigated, but it is possible from

TABLE 12.2. Spawning periods of some Arctic-Boreal, Boreal and Mediterranean-Boreal Animals at Bergen, Norway. Lat. 60° 25′ N (after Sverdrup et al., 1946).

Fauna	Animal	Jan.	Feb.	March	Apr.	May	June	July	Aug.	Sept.	Oct.	Nov.	Dec.
Arctic-boreal	Strongylocentrotus drobachiensis		+	+	+								
	Cucumaria frondosa	+	+	+									
	Dentronotus frondosus	+	+										
Boreal	Pleuronectes platessa			+	+	+							
	Mytilus edulis			+	+	+	+	+					
	Echinus esculentus			+	+	+	+						
	Asterias rubens			+	+	+	+						
Mediterranean-boreal	Psammechinus miliaris					+	+	+	+	+			
	Echinocyamus pusillus					+	+	+	+	+			
	Echinocardium flavescens						+	+	+	+			
	Echinocardium cordatum						+	+	+				
	Ciona intestinalis					+	+	+	+		+		

the investigations of Johnstone, Scott and Chadwick (1924), Harvey *et al.* (1935) and of Mare (1940) to generalize as regards the main times of appearance of meroplanktonic larvae in British waters. Some gasteropod and lamellibranch larvae occur almost all the year round, though the period of maximum abundance is usually about February/ March and again in late autumn. Polychaete larvae usually are more frequent in the early months of the year, and in local studies in Southampton Water there is normally a peak about May/June. Echinoderm larvae seem to be fairly sharply divided; most appear early in the year, about March, but a smaller second maximum may occur about September. In most British areas zoeas may begin to be abundant in March, with megalopa larvae appearing about a month later, but both stages, with the spawning of different species of crabs, may spread over practically the whole of the spring and summer in inshore waters. However, individual species may have a more restricted period. In the local waters round Southampton the larvae of *Porcellana*, for example, appear in large numbers *only* during June and July. Cirripede larvae are among the clearest examples of a restricted spawning period. Not only work in British seas, but investigations such as those of Bigelow (1926) and Deevey (1952, 1956) for American waters suggest that early spring is the time of maximal abundance of cirripede larvae.

At the same time, data on cirripedes show that broad generalizations on whole groups of bottom animals can be misleading. Investigations by Pyefinch (1948) have indicated that different species of barnacles spawn at different times; a strict study of the annual cycle for each species of barnacle is necessary. Pyefinch finds that *Balanus balanoides* shows a very sharp burst of larvae from about the last week of February through the first two or three weeks of March. The cyprids appear at the beginning of April. Thereafter no *Balanus balanoides* normally appear in the plankton. *Balanus crenatus* shows a similar main outburst in March and early April, but this species also continues to liberate larvae at intervals throughout the summer months. *Verruca stroemia* shows a main outburst of larvae from mid-February and through March and early April, but very much smaller numbers of larvae may be liberated apparently almost throughout the whole year. Studies made by Soares (1957) in Southampton Water have confirmed the sharp timing of the liberation of larvae of *Balanus balanoides* in the area. *Balanus crenatus* is also restricted mainly to the coldest months of the year, but some larvae occur later in the summer. In Southampton Water the immigrant New Zealand barnacle *Elminius modestus* occurs, and the larvae appear in great numbers about May and often dominate the plankton populations throughout the summer until September. Small numbers of this barnacle can appear in any month, however, throughout the year. Studies such as these on the larvae of cirripedes emphasize the dangers of broad generalizations, and focus attention on the need for studies on individual species of planktonic larvae. The fact that some species such as *Elminius* may spawn over a considerable part of the year makes the problem even more complex. Moreover, it seems likely that with extended spawning times there can be much variation. For example, it is known that *Mytilus* can spawn almost at any time beginning in the spring and continuing to about July or August. The more precise timing probably depends to some extent on the special conditions obtaining during the year, and also on local factors. Many authors have suggested that the exact time of spawning may depend on the attainment of a critical temperature and thus there can be variation from year to year. Kandler (1950) claims that the time of spawning of some food fishes is directly related to prevailing temperatures, so that cold winters may cause a delay of 1–2 months. Cod and plaice which may spawn as early as February in a mild winter, for example, may not spawn until March or April in an abnormally cold year.

One of the most complete studies on the periods of abundance of different species of planktonic larvae has been made by Russell in a series of papers in the 1930's on the distribution of fish larvae off Plymouth. Russell has shown that flat fish such as plaice, flounder and the sole, *Solea vulgaris*, as well as fish like cod, haddock, whiting and pollack, produce very abundant eggs about March or April with the larvae appearing in the plankton a few weeks afterwards. On the other hand, herring eggs which are, of course, demersal are laid through the winter period and the larvae appear about January and February. *Callionymus* apparently spawns off Plymouth slightly later than the bulk of species in spring, with the post larvae appearing in May and June. A group of fishes including the soles, *Solea lutea* and *S. lascaris*, *Trachinus*, *Caranx*, various gobies and *Mullus* appear to be summer spawners, so that the post larvae, according to Russell's investigations, appear in the plankton in July and August. Species of *Arnoglossus* are even slightly later, the post larvae being found during September. To take examples from two other groups of plankton animals, Kandler (1950) has given the following as the times of maximal abundance of certain medusae: *Sarsia tubulosa* (Fig. 12.30) – mainly April–June; *Rathkea octopunctata* – April or May; *Hybocodon prolifer* (Fig. 12.18) – April; *Phialidium hemisphericum* (Fig. 12.31) and *Euphysia aurata*

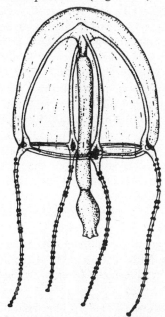

FIG. 12.30 *Sarsia tubulosa* (from Kunne, 1950).

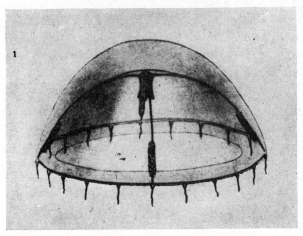

FIG. 12.31 *Phialidium hemisphericum* (from Russell, 1953).

mainly August–November; ephyrae of *Aurelia* and *Cyanea* – February–April. The following times are quoted for some decapod crustacean larvae: *Carcinus maenas* – July–October; *Portunus* – September–November. The two species *Eupagurus bernhardus* and *Crangon vulgaris* may have larvae almost at any time of the year in the plankton except, during December, January and February, but the time for maximal abundance is during the summer from June to September. Russell (1935c) and Qasim (1956) have discussed the differences in spawning times of some of the fishes in British waters and have correlated the times with the division of the species into boreal or more southern forms (Table 12.3).

Obviously many meroplanktonic larvae are produced very close to the shore, or even between tide marks, e.g. *Balanus*, *Mytilus*, *Cardium* and some polychaete larvae. Thus great local swarms of meroplanktonic forms may arise and may contribute to the patchy distribution of neritic plankton. These patches will be dispersed, but the time necessary for this dispersal depends on the set of the currents and tides. Dispersal is also influenced by the extent of the neritic zone which varies greatly in different parts of the world. Bigelow (1938), for example, finds that only 3% of the medusae off Bermuda are of neritic type at a distance of only 10 miles from the islands; the majority of the species of Scyphozoa are also oceanic, holoplanktonic forms. The oceanic water must approach Bermuda very closely. Sometimes species which are generally regarded as neritic may be found at great distances from the coast, even over oceanic depths. Wiborg (1954, 1955) has called attention to the finding of medusae of neritic type as well as the cladoceran *Evadne* in the Norwegian Sea far away from coastal areas. He has also shown that in *Pseudocalanus* the form regarded as *Pseudocalanus elongatus* (Fig. 12.32) appears to be restricted to coastal areas, whereas *Pseudocalanus minutus* stretches out into oceanic regions.

The meroplankton does not always form a conspicuous part of neritic zooplankton communities. In high latitudes, both in the Arctic and especially in the Antarctic, there is a strong tendency for benthic animals to develop directly or to have at the best only a very brief planktonic larval stage (cf. Thorson, 1950). In the Antarctic plankton Hardy and Gunther (1936) showed that, despite the richness of the benthic echinoderm fauna, only one echinoderm larva (*Auricularia antarctica*) (Fig. 13.29) appeared in their hauls. In high latitudes, therefore, the neritic plankton will tend to have a high proportion

TABLE 12.3
(from Qasim, 1956)

Fauna	Species	Time and duration of spawning in British waters											
		Dec.	Jan.	Feb.	March	Apr.	May	Jun.	July	Aug.	Sep.	Oct.	Nov.
Northern species (arctic-boreal)	*Centronotus gunnellus* (Gunnel)		+	+	+								
	Clupea harengus (Herring)	+	+	+									
	Cottus scorpius (Sea scorpion)	+	+	+	+								
	Gadus aeglefinus (Haddock)		+	+	+	+							
	Gadus callarias (Cod)			+	+	+							
	Pleuronectes platessa (Plaice)	+	+	+	+								
Southern species (mediterranean-boreal)	*Blennius pholis* (Shanny)				+	+	+	+	+	+			
	Clupea pilchardus (Pilchard)				+	+	+	+	+	+	+		
	Clupea sprattus (Sprat)				+	+	+	+	+	+			
	Gadus merlangus (Whiting)			+		+	+	+					
	Merluccius merluccius (Hake)					+	+	+	+	+			
	Scomber scombrus (Mackerel)				+	+	+	+	+				

11   PPO

of holoplanktonic forms. Even in more temperate latitudes, however, the neritic plankton is by no means dominated throughout by larvae of benthic animals. Certain species of copepods appear to occur only in the neritic plankton and do not stretch far out into oceanic areas.

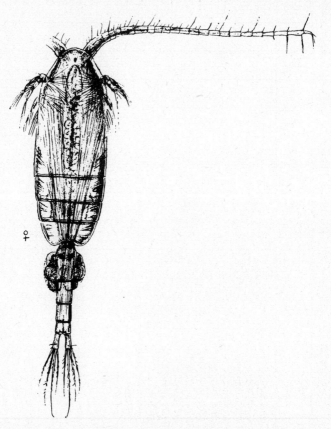

FIG. 12.32 *Pseudocalanus elongatus* (♀) (from Sars, 1903).

Various species of *Eurytemora*, as well as *Temora longicornis* (Fig. 12.7), *Labidocera wollastoni* and *Anomalocera patersoni* (Fig. 12.33) appear to be such neritic species. Many species of *Acartia*, particularly *Acartia tonsa* (Fig. 12.34) in North American, and *Acartia discaudata* (Fig. 12.35) in British waters, are also neritic. In North America the genus *Tortanus* appears to be restricted to the coast, and in both

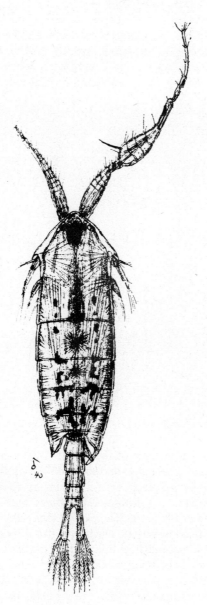

FIG. 12.33 *Anomalocera patersoni* (♂) (from Sars, 1903).

European and North American waters the species *Centropages hamatus* appears to be a neritic form. *Sagitta setosa* is a neritic holoplanktonic species and the cladocerans *Podon* and *Evadne* are neritic, though *Evadne* may on occasions spread far out over the deep seas. It is of interest that some coast-loving species appear under neritic conditions over a considerable range of latitude. Johnson(1958)

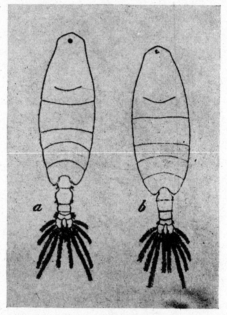

FIG. 12.34 *Acartia tonsa* (a) ♂; (b) ♀ (from Wilson, 1932).

has recently shown that some of the neritic American copepods such as *Eurytemora* and *Tortanus* are found off Point Barrow, Alaska. Ponomareva (1957) lists such neritic species as *Temora longicornis*, *Centropages hamatus*, *Eurytemora hirundoides* and *Acartia bifilosa* in the cold waters of the Kara Sea, though these copepods also range much further south along coasts. The harpacticoid *Euterpina acutifrons* appears to have a wide distribution in temperate and warm coastal seas. The finding of the small calanoid, *Paracalanus crassirostris*, on the coast of north-east America perhaps indicates that this warmer-water copepod is also more widely distributed, but further studies on the geographical limits of many neritic species are clearly necessary.

FIG. 12.35 *Acartia discaudata* (♀) (from Sars, 1903).

CHAPTER XIII

ZOOPLANKTON–
II OCEANIC ZOOPLANKTON–
GEOGRAPHICAL DISTRIBUTION

THE OCEANIC plankton occurs typically far from the coasts over great depths, and over such oceanic depths different species of zooplankton are present apparently in all layers of the ocean. The plankton is mainly composed of holoplanktonic members, though a few ex-

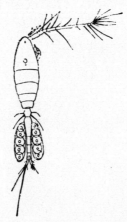

FIG. 13.1 *Oithona similis* (♀) (from Rose, 1933).

ceptions occur, such as the leptocephali of eels and phyllosoma larvae (cf. Fig. 12.7) which appear to be fairly long lived. It is not surprising that such oceanic plankton has usually an extraordinarily wide distribution. Some species, for instance, occur in all oceans of the world; such cosmopolitan species include *Beroe cucumis*, *Pleurobrachia pileus* (cf. Fig. 12.18), *Oithona similis* (Fig. 13.1) and *Scolecithricella minor* (Fig. 13.2), the polychaete *Tomopteris ligulata* and probably the siphonophore *Lensia conoidea*. Though some of these may avoid the coldest waters they are sufficiently widely distributed to be called cosmopolitan. By contrast, many species of oceanic zooplankton are restricted to certain water masses and it appears that the main factor in the distribution is temperature

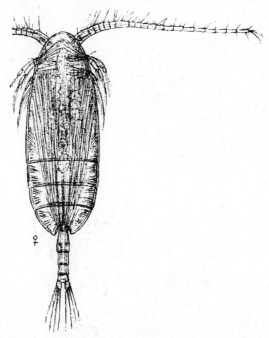

FIG. 13.2 *Scolecithricella minor* (♀) (from Sars, 1903).

(cf. Russell, 1935). Thus a geographical distribution of copepods, based mainly on temperature, has been attempted by Steuer, Sewell and others.

Ekman (1953), discussing the geographical distribution of zooplankton more generally, points out that one of the difficulties is that ocean currents may carry the zooplankton in the water far from its normal centre of distribution. Since the temperature of such water masses changes fairly slowly, the zooplankton may be carried many hundreds, or even thousands, of miles and the animals may still remain alive, though they may not reproduce successfully. Finally, of course, the temperature of the water mass will change to such an extent that zooplankton of foreign origin will be killed.

Ekman speaks of an "expatriation area" to denote this carrying of zooplankton to areas far from where they are normally spawned. Thus Bigelow (1926) has shown that *Sagitta serratodentata* (Fig. 13.3), a warm water species, is carried into the cooler waters of the Gulf

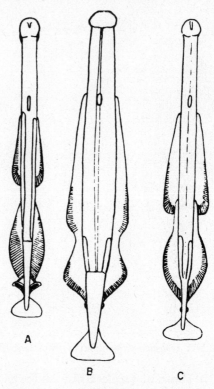

FIG. 13.3 (A) *Sagitta serratodentata*, (B) *S. maxima* and (C) *S. lyra* (from Russell, 1939).

of Maine, and lives there for some time growing to large size although it cannot reproduce. Similarly, warm water salps are sometimes carried round the north of Scotland into the North Sea; they may continue to live for some time but cannot normally reproduce in the colder waters.

Despite the carrying of animals far afield by ocean currents, it is possible to characterize the zooplankton of warm tropical seas. Salps, *Pyrosoma* and *Doliolum* are characteristic of warm water plankton, although one species of salp and one of *Doliolum* occur in Antarctic water; none, however, are found in high northern latitudes. The Heteropoda are all warm water species and the great

FIG. 13.4 *Creseis acicula* (from Murray and Hjort, 1912).

majority of the pteropods, including *Limacina inflata*, *Creseis virgula* and *Creseis acicula* (Fig. 13.4), *Clio pyramidata* (Fig. 13.5) and the whole genus *Cavolinia*, inhabit the warmer oceans. Among the chaetognaths *Sagitta hexaptera* and *S. enflata* are some of the most typical tropical forms (Fig. 13.6). The various species of the amphipod genus *Phronima* (Fig. 13.7) are characteristic of warm water, and there

are also a number of copepods which characterize the warm holoplankton. Almost all species of *Copilia* (Fig. 13.8) and *Sapphirina*
as well as the great majority of *Corycaeus* are tropical, though

FIG. 13.5 *Clio pyramidata* (from
Murray and Hjort, 1912).

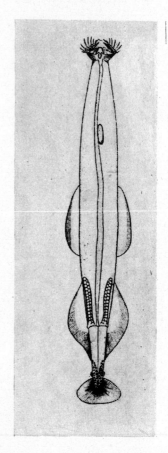

FIG. 13.6 *Sagitta enflata* (from
Dakin and Colefax, 1940).

C. anglicus does occur in British waters (cf. Chapter XII). *Eucalanus
elongatus* and *Pleuromamma abdominalis* (Fig. 13.9) are warm water
copepods, as are *Rhincalanus cornutus* and, to a slightly lesser extent,
Rhincalanus nasutus (cf. Fig. 12.25).

It is essential to realize there are no sharp lines to be drawn between
warm water and more temperate plankton. For example, *Sagitta
lyra* (Fig. 13.3) is somewhat less strictly tropical than *S.enflata*, and
Sagitta serratodentata, though a generally warm water species, can

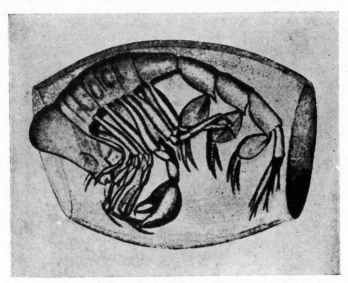

FIG. 13.7 *Phronima* sp. (from Murray and Hjort, 1912).

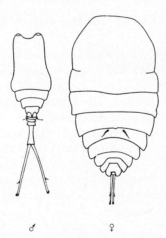

♂   ♀

FIG. 13.8 *Copilia mirabilis* (♀ = 3.7 mm; ♂ = 5 mm) (from Dakin and Colefax, 1940)

withstand considerable cooling. Of copepods, Bigelow (1926) suggested that *Euchirella rostrata* is somewhat more eurythermal than other tropical species. However, as a very rough generalization it may be said that the surface 15 °C isotherm marks off the main limits of distribution for tropical plankton, although isolated records

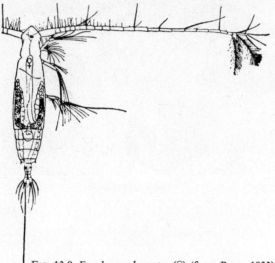

FIG. 13.9 *Eucalanus elongatus* (♀) (from Rose, 1933).

may exist for many truly tropical forms outside this area. Above all, it must always be remembered that warm currents such as the Gulf Stream will carry tropical species far outside their normal area of distribution.

Other groups of animals also show typically tropical species. Among the siphonophores, for example, *Velella* and *Porpita* (Fig. 12.26) and *Diphyes dispar* are tropical, and other species such as *Agalma elegans* and *Physophora hydrostatica* (Fig. 13.10), though they may be distributed a little farther from the tropics, are still fundamentally warm-water forms. Frequently with tropical oceanic animals, the same species or closely related species of the same genus may be found in all three tropical oceans (cf. Table 12.1). Ekman mentions that of forty-eight species of euphausids which occur in tropical seas, at least 34 are to be found in all three oceans.

The variety of species is an outstanding and delightful characteristic of tropical zooplankton. As we have mentioned in a previous chapter, in practically every major holoplanktonic group, the greatest

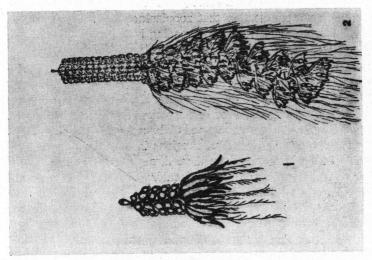

FIG. 13.10 Siphonophores, (1) *Physophora hydrostatica*, (2) *Forskalia edwardsi* and (3) *Againa* sp. (from Hyman, 1940).

number of species occur in tropical warm waters and only comparatively few species spread to the cold regions of the world (cf. Table 12.1).
There is a strong indication that zooplankton has evolved mainly
in warm surface waters, species spreading both to the deeper cold
waters as well as on the surface to the cold north and south.

Apart from the typically warm water oceanic plankton, there are
a few species which are very widely distributed in the world, though
they apparently avoid the warmest water. Ekman suggests the term
"cold-water cosmopolites" for such species. Perhaps the most obvious of all is the well known copepod *Calanus finmarchicus* (Fig. 12.8).
This species occurs in high Arctic regions in both the Atlantic and
Pacific sectors and spreads from there through the temperate waters
of the North Atlantic and North Pacific.* *C. finmarchicus* occurs,
however, in sub-tropical and tropical waters. For example, in the
Atlantic region it has been taken off the Azores and in the Mediterranean, including the Adriatic Sea and the Black Sea, and it occurs
in the South Atlantic as far as the Cape of Good Hope. In the Pacific
the same copepod is known on the Californian Coast and on the west
coast of South America, and there are some records from as far
afield as the Fiji Islands, the Malay Archipelago and the south-east
of Australia. It is claimed that *C. finmarchicus* has occasionally been
found in the Indian Ocean, but then apparently in the deeper waters.
This is true in general of its appearance in sub-tropical and tropical
areas, and it is suggested that the copepod occurs only in the deeper
layers in order to avoid the warm surface waters. The precise limits
of distribution of *Calanus* are difficult to establish, however, since
two closely similar forms, *Calanus finmarchicus* and *Calanus helgolandicus* are known to occur, the latter apparently having a more
temperate distribution (Rees, 1949). It may be that in the Pacific
a further variety is really present. Recent surveys by Brodsky (1959)
and similar work by Bary (1959) suggest that there may be several
closely allied species or possibly varieties in the various oceanic
areas. Nevertheless, it is clear that *Calanus finmarchicus* is an extremely widely distributed species, though it seems to avoid the
warmer waters. It must be emphasized, however, that to judge from
the regions of real abundance *Calanus* is clearly a cold-water form.
It occurs in vast numbers in high latitudes where it is usually the

---

* Grainger (1961), however, claims that *C. Finmarchicus* is replaced at the
highest latitudes by *Calanus glacialis*, with which it has been confused.

dominant copepod, and, though present in warmer waters, it is far less common there.

Other species with a somewhat similar distribution may be cited. One of the best known is the chaetognath *Eukrohnia hamata* (Fig. 13.11), which occurs at high latitudes in the Atlantic, but is also common in more temperate waters. It is known from tropical areas, but it is present there probably only in the deeper water layers. The siphonophore *Dimophyes arctica* (Fig. 13.29) has a distribution from the High Arctic

FIG. 13.11 *Eukrohnia hamata* (from Russell, 1939).

regions to the Antarctic Ocean, including the deep waters of the warmer intermediate region, and a similar distribution is known for *Tomopteris septentrionalis*, and the amphipods, *Hyperia galba* and *Parathemisto gaudichaudi* (Fig. 13.31). More species with a similar distribution may be discovered when investigations of waters, other than those of the North Atlantic Ocean, have become more extensive. As an indication of the wide temperature and salinity range which a typical cold water cosmopolite such as *Calanus* can include, Marshall and Orr (1955) quote its temperature range as between -2 and $22\,^\circ$C and its salinity limits as $29\text{–}35\,^\circ/_{00}$.

A few species of oceanic plankton appear to be fairly strictly confined to the very coldest water. Among truly Arctic species may

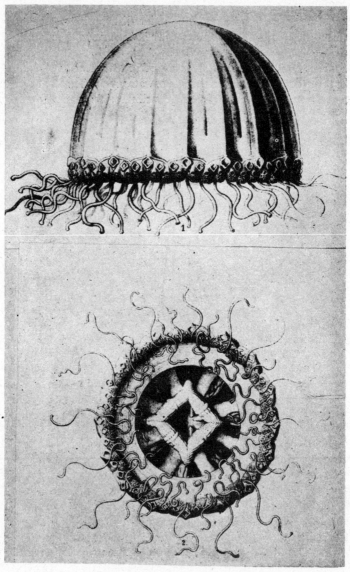

FIG. 13.12 *Ptychogastria polaris* (from Haeckel, 1881).

be mentioned the ctenophore, *Mertensia ovum*, and the medusae, *Ptychogastria polaris* (Fig. 13.12) and *Crossota norvegica*. Two copepods, *Pareuchaeta glacialis* (Fig. 13.13) and *Chiridius acutifrons*,

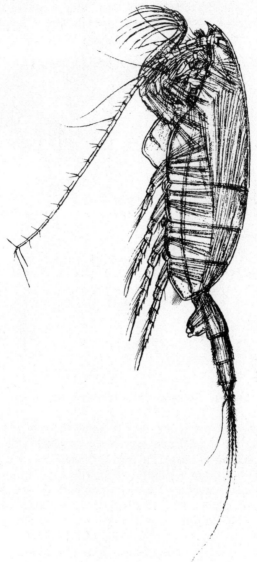

FIG. 13.13 *Pareuchaeta glacialis* (♀) (from Sars, 1903).

also appear to be confined to the High Arctic, as is the amphiphod, *Euthemisto libellula* (Fig. 13.14). The precise limits of such Arctic forms are very difficult to determine, since the animals may occur in deeper water layers outside the Arctic Circle, thus avoiding the slightly warmer surface waters. Among other typically very cold-water species, which are normally found in the highest latitudes but which may

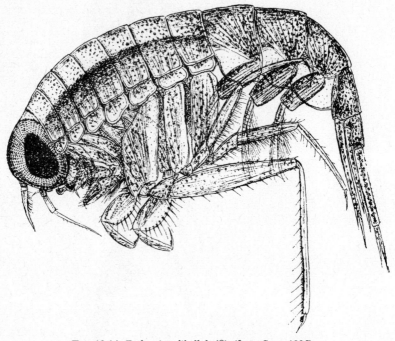

FIG. 13.14 *Euthemisto libellula* (♀) (from Sars, 1895).

drift somewhat further south, may be listed the copepods, *Metridia longa* (Fig. 13.15) and *Calanus hyperboreus*, together with such other forms as *Limacina helicina* (Fig. 13.16), *Clione limacina* and *Oikopleura labradoriensis* (cf. Kielhorn, 1952). This latter species can occur as far south as the southern North Sea and here also can be included a list of many sub-Arctic, typically cold-water forms, which nevertheless can survive in somewhat more temperate conditions. *Aglantha digitalis*, *Meganyctiphanes norvegica* (Fig.13.17), and other euphausids, *Thysanoessa raschii*, *T. longicaudata* and *T. inermis* (Fig. 13.18), together with the copepod, *Euchaeta norvegica* (Fig. 13.19) and perhaps the chaetognath, *Sagitta maxima* (Fig. 13.3), are examples of these essentially cold-water planktonic species which can exist under slightly warmer conditions. It is nevertheless typical of such forms as *Aglantha*, *Thysanoessa* spp. and *Euchaeta*, that they are far more abundant in Arctic and sub-Arctic waters. It is clear, therefore, that no absolute hard-and-fast lines can be drawn between cold water and temperate species, or between temperate and tropical species, especially in view of the spread due to ocean currents and the possible colonization of the deeper water layers so that unfavourable temperature strata may be avoided.

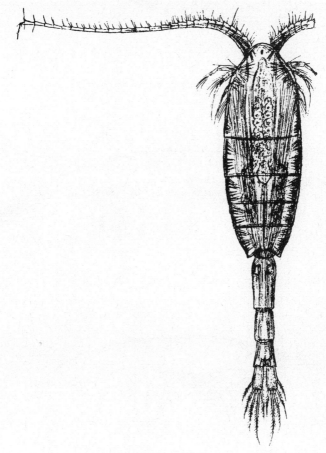

FIG. 13.15 *Metridia longa* (♀) (from Sars, 1903).

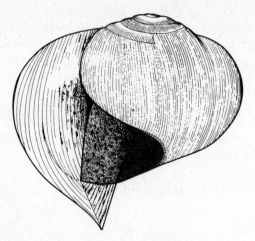

FIG. 13.16 *Limacina helicina* (from Tesch, 1947).

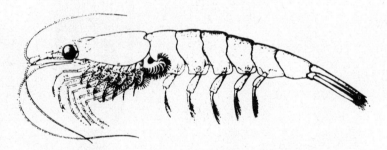

FIG. 13.17 *Meganyctiphanes norvegica* (from Einarsson, 1945).

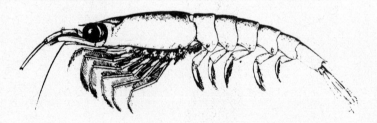

FIG. 13.18 *Thysanoessa inermis* (from Einarsson, 1945).

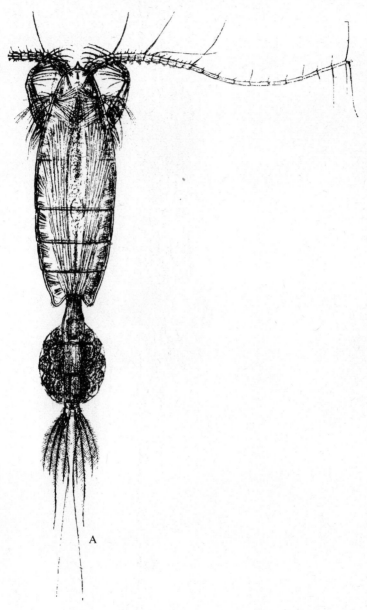

Fig. 13.19 A *Euchaeta norvegica* (♀) (from Sars, 1903).

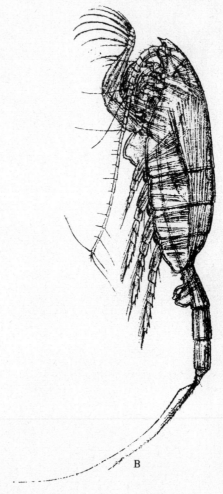

FIG. 13.19 B *Euchaeta norvegica* (♀) (from Sars, 1903).

FIG. 13.20 *Calanus hyperboreus* (♀) (from Sars, 1903).

Since there are comparatively few of the colder loving zooplankton species, as we have already said, the plankton of high latitudes is often dominated by a few species. One of the commonest plankton communities, very typical of the colder parts of the North Atlantic, is the *Calanus* community (Bigelow, 1926). This is dominated by the species, *Calanus finmarchicus*, with, in more northern latitudes, *Calanus hyperboreus* (Fig. 13.20) entering in considerable numbers. In the more boreal waters *Calanus finmarchicus* is accompanied by *Metridia*, *Euchaeta*, *Pseudocalanus*, *Euthemisto* and *Thysanoessa* spp. and, under slightly less oceanic conditions, by the two species *Mega-*

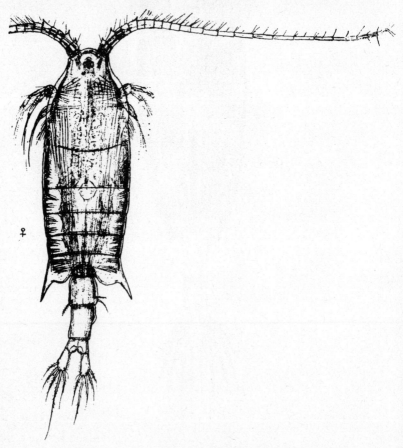

Fig. 13.21 *Centropages typicus* (♀) (from Sars, 1903).

nyctiphanes norvegica and *Sagitta elegans. Centropages typicus* may also occur commonly at times (Fig. 13.21). Bigelow (1926) finds such a community typical of the more open waters of the Gulf of Maine and of the waters of the North Atlantic, but as more coastal areas of the Gulf are approached the numbers of more neritic species increase. This community, dominated by *Calanus*, is limited on the American side of the Atlantic to the south by the warmer, higher salinity, water of the Gulf Stream (cf. Bigelow and Sears, 1939; Clarke, 1940), but to the north and east it spreads across the Atlantic over such regions as Iceland and the south of Greenland to Norway and Britain. The work of Jespersen (1940, 1944) in the region of the Faroes and

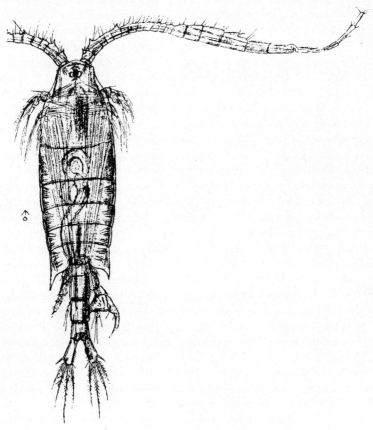

FIG. 13.21 *Centropages typicus* (♂) (from Sars, 1903).

Iceland has shown this community to be present there, and Wiborg (1954, 1955) finds it similarly in Norwegian waters. Rae and Fraser (1941) and Rae and Rees (1947) have shown a similar zooplankton to exist in the North Sea, though as the coasts and banks are approached, just as in American waters, the number of neritic species becomes greater. This type of zooplankton community is recorded in the Barents and Kara Seas by Ponomareva (1957). *Calanus finmarchicus* was usually dominant in the biomass of plankton of the Kara Sea, though *Pseudocalanus* was more abundant in some areas. Other important species were *Oithona similis, Sagitta elegans, Metridia,* appendicularians, *Thysanoessa* and *Aglantha*. Other coelenterates and further neritic zooplankton species became more plentiful in coastal areas. Grainger (1959), working in a coastal section of the Canadian Arctic, also found medusae, ctenophore fragments and sagittae abundantly represented in the shallow water plankton, as well as the more oceanic sub-Arctic/boreal species such as *Calanus finmarchicus, C. hyperboreus, Pseudocalanus, Oithona* and *Aglantha*. In general over the North Atlantic, the density of *Calanus finmarchicus* becomes greater at higher latitudes, but the proportion of the extremely cold-loving species such as *Calanus hyperboreus, Metridia longa* and *Aglantha* tends to increase (cf. Jespersen, 1939, 1940).

To an observer at the entrance to the English Channel it would appear likely that water entering from the Atlantic Ocean should have a great mixture of oceanic planktonic species, some of which, such as *Thysanoessa, Aglantha, Meganyctiphanes* and *Clione limacina* would be of boreal origin, whereas others, such as *Agalma elegans* and *Sagitta serratodentata* would be typical of warmer Gulf Stream water. The occurrence of both groups of species would indicate that water from the Atlantic reaching the English Channel was thus of mixed origin. Russell's work (Russell 1934, 1935b, 1936, 1939) on the zooplankton appearing off Plymouth has shown that such a mixture may indeed occur. But the meroplanktonic medusa, *Cosmetira pilosella* (Fig. 13.22), may also appear in the Channel. This medusa breeds off south-west Ireland and not in the English Channel itself, but it can enter the Channel with Atlantic water which has already circulated off the Irish coast. *Sagitta elegans* appears in great numbers in this incoming Atlantic water which is mixed with some water of more coastal origin.

At times, salps and *Doliolum* may appear at the mouth of the English Channel, and since no species of salp or of *Doliolum* is boreal or Arctic in distribution, but all North Atlantic forms are sub-tropical or tropical their presence indicates a flow of warmer Atlantic origin. Russell called this water of warm origin bringing salps and *Doliolum* off Plymouth "south-western water". Accompanying these forms are *Muggiaea* spp. (Fig. 13.23), *Physophora borealis, Arachnactis* larvae (cf. Fig. 12.18) and *Lepas fascicularis*, sometimes with such warmer-water copepods as *Euchaeta hebes, Rhincalanus*, etc.

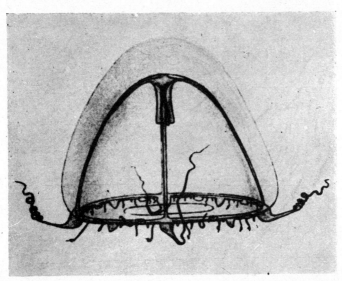

Fig. 13.22 *Cosmetira pilosella*, very young stage (from Russell, 1953).

We have previously seen that there are some species of plankton which are typically brackish forms (*Eurytemora affinis*) while others, though not quite so brackish in distribution, such as *Acartia bifilosa* and *Oithona nana*, are confined normally to rather low salinity water; *Centropages hamatus* is a typically neritic species. Although the majority of meroplanktonic forms tend to be most plentiful under coastal conditions, there are some holoplanktonic species, apart from the copepods listed, (e.g. *Sagitta setosa*), which appear to be confined to certain neritic waters. It is thus obvious that the appearance of some zooplankton species, normally found offshore, in the essentially neritic English Channel can be indicative of waters of more distant origin flowing into the Channel. These species may be regarded as plankton indicators, that is, plankton organisms which may be of value in indicating the movements of particular masses of water. Many species are too widespread to be useful as indicators, and cosmopolites, such as *Pleurobrachia* and *Calanus finmarchicus*, are obvious examples. Russell (1935b) has pointed out that plankton indicators may be selected from any zoological group, but often it

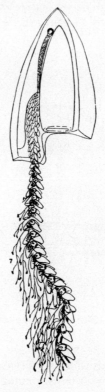

FIG. 13.23 *Muggiaea* sp. (from Hyman, 1940).

will be the association of several species from different groups which will indicate the flow of a particular mass of seawater. He has emphasized that an indicator must be practical, that is, it must be of reasonable size and fairly easily recognized if it is going to be of value.

Sometimes individuals of species outside their normal area of distribution occur as secondary constituents of the plankton, together with indigenous species which are much more numerous, and the water may then be regarded as of mixed origin, as in the North Sea. Local conditions, however, need full study before any indicator can be accepted. In other words, a species which is a true indicator of water movements in one region may not be effective in another sea area. Few indicators may be regarded as universal, though forms such as *Cyanea* and *Aurelia* are typical of coastal conditions. Some other indicators are of very wide use; for example, the Arctic species *Limacina helicina* (Fig. 13.16), if it appears off the New England Coast, off the south of Iceland or off the coasts of North-west Europe, may be regarded as indicating a flow of Arctic water. *Calanus hyperboreus* would similarly appear to be a fairly good indicator of Arctic water to the north of the British Isles. On the other hand, Bigelow (1926) has demonstrated that off the north-east coast of America, although most *Calanus hyperboreus* is brought in by an Arctic current flowing south in the spring, the copepod apparently has a small centre of local reproduction in the waters north of Cape Cod. Similarly, in some of the Norwegian fjords *Calanus hyperboreus* occurs in the deeper layers. This copepod is therefore useless as an Arctic indicator off Norway and off the north-east American coasts. The distribution of *Metridia longa*, another Arctic form, in the Gulf of Maine appears to be similar. *Clione limacina* is normally thought of as an Arctic form, but it appears to be able to live fairly successfully perhaps as a slightly different variety in the more temperate parts of the North Atlantic. Thus, when it appears in the English Channel where no Arctic water is possible, it can be of use as an indicator of Atlantic water, but it cannot be regarded as demonstrating a flow of Arctic water.

The use of some indicators in determining the movements of particular water masses will now be followed in more detail, the first example being from the work of Russell on water movements in the western English Channel area off Plymouth. Russell showed that there are three types of water: (1) the warm south-west Channel or Biscay water, in which the characteristic indicators are salps, *Doliolum*, *Muggiaea* spp., and the medusa *Liriope exigua*, which probably is included in this water as it sweeps round the French coast. From time to time other warm water species such as *Rhincalanus* may appear with this flow of more southern water. (2) Western water which occurs flowing past the south of Ireland. (3) True Channel water. The elucidation of the last two bodies of water was based mainly on an analysis of *Sagitta* populations off the Plymouth coast (Fig. 13.24). Russell showed that *Sagitta elegans* dominated the catches off Plymouth to the exclusion of *Sagitta setosa* up to the autumn of 1930, but thereafter *Sagitta setosa* occurred and very few *S. elegans* were taken. It was possible that both species lived in competition off Plymouth, but it was observed by Russell that the medusa *Cosmetira pilosella*, a species which typically occurs in

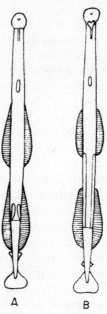

A   B

FIG. 13.24 (A) *Sagitta setosa* and (B) *S. elegans* (from Russell, 1939).

deeper waters off the south-west coast of Ireland, was always associated with large populations of *Sagitta elegans*, whereas it did not occur with *Sagitta setosa*. The waters to the south of Ireland are also rich in *Sagitta elegans* but *Sagitta setosa* does not occur there. It would appear, therefore, that when western or Atlantic water, having such boreal species as *Aglantha*, *Clione limacina*, *Meganyctiphanes* and *Thysanoessa*, as well as the medusa *Cosmetira* flowed past Plymouth, there was an incursion of *Sagitta elegans*. When, on the other hand, only small populations of *S. elegans* were found off Plymouth, the boreal Atlantic species occurred only in small numbers. The boreal species together indicate a strong flow of mixed Atlantic water, of which *S. elegans* is so characteristic that Russell has applied the term "elegans water" to such a water mass. Occasionally the oceanic and somewhat warmer water species, *Sagitta serratodentata*, occurs off Plymouth at the same time as *Sagitta elegans*, probably indicating a flow of water from rather farther out in the Atlantic Ocean.

Russell linked these changes with the cyclonic circulation in the Celtic Sea, and suggested that the water increases in nutrient content with upwelling off the Atlantic slope. In this mixing of true oceanic Atlantic water with more coastal seawater, *Sagitta elegans* really flourishes. The production of zooplankton is very high in this mixed ("elegans") water and, apart from the species which have already been mentioned, there are a number of other boreal forms, such as *Metridia lucens* and *Themisto*, which may appear. But there are also very high densities of such typical copepods as *Calanus*, *Centropages typicus*, *Paracalanus* and *Pseudocalanus* when the flow of Atlantic western water into the Channel is strong. These four calanoids are normally present in the Channel in considerable numbers, and therefore they cannot be used as indicators. Nevertheless, the abundance of these species is obvious, and this agrees with the general high nutrient content of the inflowing mixed "elegans" water. Apart from the increase in nitrate and phosphate, the mixing of water masses frequently appears to have a beneficial effect upon production. It is likely that the supply of organic growth-promoting substances such as vitamins is increased by the mixing of waters of different origin.

By contrast, when *Sagitta setosa* is dominant off Plymouth, the water is generally low in phosphate as well as being of somewhat lower salinity, typical of Channel water. The term "Channel" or "setosa" water has been used by Russell for this type of water, and in general it shows a marked poverty of zooplankton. *Sagitta setosa* occurs in the English Channel and in the southern North Sea, as well as in the Skagerrak and Kattegat. It is found also in the inshore waters of Liverpool Bay and the Bristol Channel, although the major part of the Irish Sea appears to be characterized by *S. elegans*. When "setosa" water occurs off Plymouth there are present such typically widely distributed copepods as *Calanus*, *Pseudocalanus*, *Oithona*, *Centropages*, *Paracalanus*, *Temora* and *Acartia*, as well as the cladocerans, *Podon* and *Evadne*. Meroplanktonic forms may also be observed sometimes in fair numbers, but the density of the whole zooplankton tends to be low. Russell (1939) later suggested that the medusa *Turritopsis* (Fig. 13.25) is another indicator of Channel water.

Biscay water is also characterized by having very little zooplankton, but at the time of Russell's investigation there was considerable green flocculent matter present so that it was possible to
distinguish the three types of water even without detailed microscopic
examination. At times the south-western water from Biscay, while

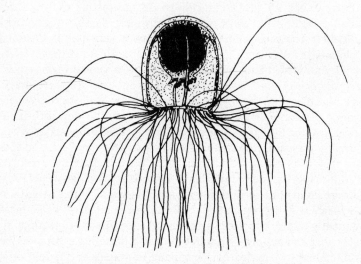

FIG. 13.25 *Turritopsis nutricula* (from Russell, 1953).

mainly oceanic, can vary in its flow, and be replaced by rather more
coastal water of lower salinity entering round Ushant.

Russell has correlated the occurrence of "elegans" or "setosa"
water off Plymouth with the strength of flow of water from the
English Channel into the North Sea as measured by current meters
in the Dover Straits area. He suggests that when the circulation off
south-west Ireland results in a fairly strong inflow of mixed Atlantic
"elegans" water, an increased easterly flow of water occurs through
the Dover Straits. To some extent a strong flow of Atlantic water
round the north of Scotland may be accompanied by a lessened
current through Dover Straits, causing Channel water dominated
by *Sagitta setosa* to occur off Plymouth. At times, also, when the flow
through the Straits is weak, southwest Biscay water may creep past
Plymouth (cf. Fig. 13.28).

While the study of these water masses off Plymouth is in itself of great fundamental interest, the results are not without practical significance. Russell (1930–1947) has shown that on the whole the nutrient-rich water typical of *S. elegans* off Plymouth, was accompanied by relatively large numbers of young fish, excluding clupeids, in the area. Presumably the high phosphate levels which were demonstrated over the same years from the work of Atkins, Harvey

FIG. 13.26 Deviation from the mean winter maximum of phosphate (black columns), and from the mean number of summer-spawned fish (white columns), for years 1924 to 1937. (Means calculated for the 12-year-period) (from Harvey, 1945.)

and Cooper, had the effect of increasing phytoplankton and zooplankton production, and thus abundant food was provided for young fish. Relatively high phosphates of the order of 20 mg $PO_4 - P/m^3$ (winter maximum) were demonstrated up to about 1930, but following that year the winter maximum of phosphate fell to about 14 mg $PO_4 - P/m^3$, and the numbers of young fish also fell very considerably (cf. Cooper, 1938). A relationship can thus be established between the numbers of young fish which survive in any year, and the winter maximum of phosphate of the previous year (cf. Russell, 1930–1947; Harvey, 1945; Fig. 13.26). Our knowledge of the distribution of indicator organisms in the western Channel area has been increased recently by Southward (1961; 1962), who has defined more clearly the annual cycle of events. Dealing with the macroplankton, Southward suggests that there are north-westerly species (e.g. *Aglantha*, *Sagitta elegans*), which are approximately equivalent to the forms previously named as western species. Many of these are northerly species verging on their southern limits of distribution. They tend, however, to extend their distribution across the entrance to the English Channel from May to July. By contrast, what may be described as southwesterly forms (e.g. *Euchaeta hebes*) are mostly warm water species near their northerly limits of distribution. While restricted in their area of abundance to the south-west of Ushant, they tend to extend across the Channel entrance from July to January. These movements appear to be correlated with the anti-clockwise swirl off the entrance to the Channel, south-westerly forms becoming dominant as water moves from the south-west as the swirl contracts, and north-westerly species becoming more abundant as lower salinity water moves south with the expansion of the swirl. The appearance of particular indicator species off Plymouth will be further complicated by the changing pattern of the surface currents in the western Channel as between summer and winter. Southward's analysis suggests that the observed biological changes in the Channel approaches observed in earlier years may be partly a result of generally rising surface temperature in the area, and thus a shift in the boundaries of distribution of some indicator species.

A study of plankton indicators rather similar to that of Russell has been made by Fraser (1939) off the Scottish coast. Fraser shows that *Sagitta elegans* is absent from truly oceanic water entering the Scottish area. It is not found in the Faroe Channel and is rare to the west of Scotland, but is commoner in the sea lochs of the west coast and in the channel between the islands and the mainland. It is really abundant, however, in the northern North Sea off the east coast of Scotland. This distribution suggests that *Sagitta elegans* is a species which flourishes in a mixture of oceanic and coastal water, as Russell showed off Plymouth, where the Atlantic water mixed with the more coastal water off Ireland. Fraser finds that this mixed water includes species such as *Thysanoessa*, *Themisto* and *Aglantha*, which are Atlantic forms, as well as *Calanus finmarchicus* and *Limacina retroversa*. There are also fair numbers of medusae like *Cosmetira* and *Laodicea* from deeper offshore areas, as well as other species such as *Neoturris* and *Bougainvillia* (Fig. 13.26.1) derived from more coastal regions of north Scotland. This mixed water seems to favour the breeding of Crustacea, so important as fish food, and indeed the whole zooplankton tends to be rich. Fraser believes that the mixing of water on the edge of the continental shelf causes a considerable enrichment of nutrients. This is responsible for rich phytoplankton growth, and this in turn promotes production of zooplankton. In other words, this rich mixed water off northern Scotland would correspond to the rich "elegans" water found by Russell off the south-west coast of Britain.

Fraser finds that there are various types of water flowing round the north of Scotland. The oceanic water flowing in from the Atlantic contains a number of species, some of which can be recognized as typically cold, and others as typically warm, oceanic species. *Sagitta arctica*, *Calanus hyperboreus* and *Metridia longa* may well be regarded

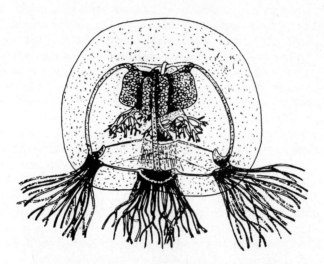

FIG. 13.26.1 *Bougainvillia principis* (from Russell, 1953).

as very cold water forms, indicating even subarctic inflow, and Fraser has shown how north of the Shetlands there is a greater proportion of these cold water forms. *Pleuromamma robusta* is an Atlantic form, and *Sagitta maxima* is another Atlantic, but deeper living species. On the other hand, warm water species such as *Sagitta hexaptera* and the more warm-temperate *Sagitta serratodentata* can occur, together with such typical warm water indicators as salps, doliolids, *Rhincalanus*, *Euchirella* and *Physophora*. The incoming Atlantic oceanic water thus contains a mixture of cold and warmer water zooplankton. Further studies by Fraser (1952, 1955) have demonstrated that the Atlantic zooplankton, especially some of the warmer water forms, include species derived from the comparatively deep warm outflow from the Mediterranean Sea (cf. page 83, Chapter IV). Part of this outflow, after leaving the Mediterranean, at a depth of *ca*. 1250 m, proceeds northwards as a current at *ca*. 950 m depth through the Bay of Biscay. Thence it appears to pass even further north at somewhat shallower depths to the west of Ireland, though the extent of the flow probably varies from year to year. The fauna, modified by the addition of plankton from the deeper waters between the Azores and the Bay of Biscay, has been designated by Fraser as the "Lusitanian fauna". It includes *Pelagia noctiluca*, *Sagitta lyra*, doliolids, *Vibilia* spp. *Lensia* spp., *Chuniphyes multi-tentaculata*, *Vogtia* spp., *Sapphirina* spp., *Praya cymbiformis* and *Rosacea plicata*. West of Scotland this deep warm flow may emerge on the surface to some extent by upwelling against the continental slope. "Lusitanian" species, may, therefore, appear in the incoming Atlantic water round the north of Scotland. The "Lusitanian" flow tends to keep to the more southern parts of the Faroe Channel according to Fraser; the North Atlantic Drift water is more northerly. As the strength of flow of the "Lusitanian" water varies considerably from year to year, in some years it may reach little farther than the west of Ireland, whereas in years of strong flow, it may stream between the Shetland and Orkney Islands and so reach the North Sea (Fig. 13.27). Even in years of strong flow, however, "Lusitanian" water does not appear to pass north of the Shetlands. By contrast, the western North Atlantic water enters the North Sea to an appreciable extent by this route. This water is much richer in *Calanus* and other crustaceans, and is marked by the presence of other species such as *Clione limacina*, *Dimophyes arctica*, *Agalma elegans*, *Laodicea* and *Eukrohnia*. There are several zooplankton species, however, which are common to both the "Lusitanian" and Atlantic water — *Aglantha*, *Clio*, *Rhincalanus*, *Eucalanus*, *Thysanoessa longicaudata*, *Sagitta planctonis*, and to some extent, *S. lyra* and *S. maxima*. As the islands and mainland of the Scottish coast are reached, the Atlantic water, including any "Lusitanian" flow when this is strong, grades into the mixed "elegans" water. Another body of water which may be regarded as of North Sea origin is characterized by *Sagitta setosa*. As with the "setosa" water of the English Channel, the zooplankton population is relatively poor, and there is a reasonably clear demarcation between the rich "elegans" and the poor "setosa" water (Fig. 13.28). The farther the Atlantic water flows round the north of Scotland into the North Sea, the more the exotic species typical of the warm Atlantic and "Lusitanian" waters tend to die out. More cold water inflows containing zooplankton may be added between the Faroes anu Shetlands, but as the water moves farther southwards into the North Sea proper, these cold water forms are also killed, and more and more neritic zooplankton species are added from the Scottish coast. The fauna will therefore change relatively rapidly with the flow into the North Sea, though under exceptional conditions, with a greater degree of inflow, a few of the original Atlantic

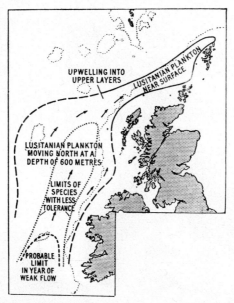

FIG. 13.27 The movement of "Lusitanian" plankton off British coasts (from Hardy, 1956).

species may survive and may even breed for a short time before being killed off (e.g. asexual breeding of salps).

To a considerable extent plankton production over the Dogger Bank, particularly in the region of the swirl which occurs in the area, is largely a result of the strength of Atlantic inflow around the north of Scotland. Rivers such as the Thames draining into the North Sea and carrying nutrients make some slight contribution to the general productivity of the area, but the main productive capacity depends on the inflow of water from the north. In a year of strong Atlantic inflow the relatively high nutrient content of the water leads to a rich production of plankton. In the Dogger Bank area *Ceratium longipes* and *Ceratium tripos* tend to be present in considerable numbers, and with high phosphate and nitrate concentrations, there may occur the typical intense bloomings of *Rhizosolenia* and *Phaeocystis*, as has been noted by Hardy, Savage, Wimpenny and others (cf. Fig. 13.28).

FIG. 13.28 Generalized picture of the distribution of plankton around the British Isles in an autumn when the influx of Atlantic water into the North Sea from the North was strong. SET & SETOSA = *Sagitta setosa*; EL & ELEGANS = *S. elegans*; SER = *S. serratodentata* (from Russell, 1939).

Patches of these particular species of phytoplankton may become so dense in some years that the herring shoals will avoid them. The productivity must depend in the long run on the quantity of upwelled water, rich in nutrients, from the continental shelf present in the inflow from the north. However, such a rich plankton will ultimately die down, and to some extent nitrate and phosphate will be regenerated, to rise above the thermocline in a succeeding year, so that the effect of a strong inflow of nutrient-rich water may last over several seasons.

Our study of plankton indicators arose mainly from the consideration of temperature as a factor controlling the distribution and survival of zooplankton. Nevertheless, the existence or the non-occurrence of certain species of zooplankton often cannot be explained so simply. As Fraser has pointed out in his work on the chaetognaths, a species such as *S. elegans* appears to be limited to a particular type of water, though it could certainly live under the very slight differences of temperature and salinity which hold for an adjoining water mass. Similarly, Glover (1961), from results obtained with the Plankton Recorder, has drawn attention to the abundance of *Sagitta elegans* in mixed oceanic and coastal shelf water round Britain; although the chaetognath appeared to be uncommon in oceanic water, it could occur in mixed waters over a wide range of temperature. By contrast, both *Calanus minor* and *Pleuromamma robusta* were restricted to oceanic water; *Calanus* to the warmer and *Pleuromamma* to the colder water. Thus temperature and salinity characteristics, while convenient for marking the various water masses, are probably not the major factors limiting such distributions of planktonic species. Presumably more subtle characteristics in the "quality" of the sea water are responsible. Fraser (1961) has shown that although water masses derived from a mixture of oceanic and coastal ("elegans") water gave better survival of fish larvae in the northern North Sea, the number of fish eggs produced in "elegans" water was no higher than in coastal ("setosa") water. Fraser attributes the better survival of fish larvae only in part to increased food supply; he suggests that the quality of "elegans" water may be superior for the survival of the larvae. Biological qualities of different water masses have also been considered to be associated with the migrations of some fishes (cf. Rae, 1958). To some extent these subtle differences may be influential also in the distribution of species and varieties of phytoplankton. In the North Sea phytoplankton has sometimes been used as an indication of water movements. A species may exist as distinct varieties (e.g. *Rhizosolenia styliformis*) and these may be characteristic of various water masses (cf. Wimpenny, 1946). The distribution of varieties may sometimes be correlated with temperature and salinity characteristics of the water, but it is likely that the "quality" of the sea water must also be included. Even when readily accepted morphological varieties of a species are not present, different populations may be useful. Lucas and Stubbings (1948) showed that stocks of the diatom *Biddulphia sinensis*, marked by clear size differences, existed in parts of the North Sea; possibly such stocks might be employed in following the history of water movements.

Although our examples of detailed investigations on plankton indicators and of the effects of mixture of water masses on production have been drawn from the North Atlantic, some brief reference will be made to studies elsewhere on plankton communities and to the effect of water masses on fisheries.

In the remarkably productive Chilean and Peruvian Current region (cf. Chapter VII), Gunther (1936) has distinguished the northerly flowing Peru Coastal Current from the Peru Oceanic Current further offshore, which is characterized by rather higher temperature and by the flow being mainly westerly. Gunther noted that the offshore current was marked by the presence of more oceanic species as compared with the many neritic forms in the coastal current. For the phytoplankton, for example, Gunther showed that a comparatively cosmopolitan genus such as *Chaetoceros* was generally common everywhere; however, the oceanic genera *Rhizosolenia* and *Planktoniella* were more abundant in offshore waters. *Thalassiosira* and *Coscinodiscus* were commoner on the more northerly coastal waters, and *Corethron* occurred more to the south. The coastal current, reinforced by marked upwelling, was rich in nutrients and in plankton. Associated with this was an abundance of anchovies and a wealth of marine mammal and bird life. The whole zone was not uniformly fertile, but areas of mixture of water masses were especially productive, as has been suggested for other regions. By contrast, the oceanic offshore current had a much lower nutrient content and was generally poorer in plankton.

To the north, the Peru Coastal Current is limited by the warm, less saline, tropical waters of the Equatorial Counter-current. This sharp biological boundary is well known; the warming of the Peruvian coastal flow by a southern extension of the less saline, warmer, northern waters ("El Niño") may lead to widespread death of the rich cold-loving plankton, and a consequent mass mortality of other marine life. Although the warming of the Peruvian current waters may possibly be attributed to other factors (cf. Sears, 1954), the normal limitation of plankton communities to particular water masses is well exemplified in this area.

Off South Africa, studies of water masses, especially of the rich productive Benguela Current, have also been made. Off the west coast of South Africa this Current is responsible for the remarkable plankton production and the wealth of marine life in this area (cf. Chapter VII). Offshore, to the west of the Benguela Current, lie oceanic subtropical waters which are characterized by relatively high temperature and salinity, but low nutrient content. According to Clowes (1950, 1954) upwelling is most obvious in a comparatively narrow belt of colder, low salinity water close to the West African coast. The very rich St. Helena Bay region, for example, which is the centre of the commercial pilchard fishery, is an area of high nutrient content, the enrichment being due to upwelled water derived ultimately from the mixed Antarctic Intermediate Water in the deeper strata, and to a minor extent to local coastal regeneration. In the St. Helena Bay area as a whole, Clowes states that the mean annual phosphate content at the surface is *ca.* 19 mg P/m³. Only slight variations in nutrient occur from year to year, but at individual stations much larger variations may appear. Clowes believes that these may ultimately influence the feeding and breeding of the pilchard, especially since this fish feeds almost exclusively on diatoms.

To the south-east of South Africa is the warm, strongly flowing Agulhas Current. This consists of surface and subsurface subtropical water from the Indian Ocean, contrasting sharply in temperature, salinity and nutrient content with the cold but nutrient-rich Benguela Current. The Agulhas Current is deflected eastwards off the south of the Union of South Africa and most of the water is returned to the Indian Ocean. Clowes believes that only some water of mixed subtropical and deeper Antarctic Intermediate origin actually penetrates the South Atlantic. In any event, the area to the south of Cape Town is marked by a mixing of Atlantic and Indian Ocean water and swirls occur in this region. Recent investigations (e.g. Buys, 1959) suggest that the meeting of the Agulhas Current and the colder coastal waters may have a marked influence on the distribution of the important pilchard and maasbanker fish shoals.

Later investigations on the Benguela Current (Currie, 1953; Hart, 1953; Hart and Currie, 1960) have yielded results very similar to those obtained for the Peruvian Current. Close to the African coast, cooler and less saline water is fairly sharply delimited from warmer oceanic water further offshore. The cooler coastal water receives very considerable contributions from upwelling, the water rising from depths of 200–300 m. These upwelling waters of the Benguela Current are exceedingly rich in phosphate; concentrations of the order of 60 mg PO_4-P/m^3 are found. By contrast, the poor oceanic waters have almost zero phosphate content. The upwelled coastal water is also low in oxygen. As in the Peruvian Current, upwelling does not seem to be equally strong at all points in the Benguela Current; regions of very strong upwelling are marked by very high productivity (e.g. near Luderitz Bay, where the richest concentrations of phytoplankton were found). Dense diatom concentrations are found in the coastal water, though as in the upwelling regions off California, time must be allowed for the flowering of diatoms to occur in the high nutrient water. The dense phytoplankton of the coastal waters is in sharp contrast to the very scanty phytoplankton offshore; the difference between the coastal and oceanic phytoplankton may amount to three orders of magnitude. Hart shows that certain diatoms are typical of the offshore oceanic waters, particularly *Planktoniella sol* and *Thalassiothrix longissima*. *Planktoniella* would seem to be a particularly good indicator of oceanic water, since where tongues of this water reach further towards the coast, this diatom is found more frequently. In inshore waters, species of *Chaetoceros* are particularly abundant; on occasions, the different species amounting to 60–90% of the total phytoplankton. Other neritic diatoms such as *Eucampia zoodiacus* and *Asterionella* may also be abundant in the upwelled coastal waters.

The very high productivity of the coastal Benguela Current is also reflected in the exceedingly rich zooplankton as compared with the poorer oceanic offshore waters. Euphausids were commonest in the region of rich phytoplankton and very large numbers of pteropods were also found there. Some zooplankton such as the cladocerans are found only near the coast. With the rich abundance of plankton in the inshore waters may be associated the very large numbers of pelagic fish, especially *Sardinops*, and the abundance of other marine life. The biology of the Benguela Current is thus very similar to that of the Peruvian Current and the Californian Current—other regions of marked upwelling.

We return, however, from this discussion of the effects of mixing of water masses to our main consideration that temperature acts frequently in limiting the distribution of species of zooplankton. Generally in the seas, spatial changes in temperature are very gradual. An exception is the region off Cape Cod, Massachusetts, where, as we have seen, the cold Labrador current and the warm Gulf Stream approach each other closely. This region thus forms a comparatively sharp faunistic boundary. A similar boundary occurs between the warm Kuroshio and cold Oyashio currents off Japan and south of the Kurile Islands, where a sharp demarcation exists between two different plankton populations. Bogorov (1958b) has summarized the results of investigations by stating that arctic, boreal and tropical zooplankton communities may be recognized in the North-West Pacific. The boreal and tropical waters meet along a more or less narrow front approximating to 40–42 °N latitude. In the boreal waters, which may range in surface temperature as much as from 3–15 °C, the characteristic species are clearly marked off from the tropical forms. Thus of the copepods, some two dozen, including such common species as *Eucalanus bungii*, *Calanus cristatus* and *Calanus plumchrus*, are found in the upper layers of the boreal waters but not in the tropical regions. In the tropical surface waters, which range from 18–27 °C, more than 70 species of copepod have been found which do not occur in the cold boreal waters. The species of phytoplankton show a similar division into the two biogeographical regions, with a great abundance of species including dinoflagellates in the warm waters. The "zone of mixing" at the boundary of the Kuroshio and Oyashio Currents is comparatively narrow but shows many plankton species typical of both geographical regions.

Further observations on the distribution of zooplankton and the major water masses in the North Pacific arise from investigations on the euphausid populations. According to Boden, Johnson and Brinton (1955) and Boden and Brinton (1957), if we omit from consideration such coastal species as *Nyctiphanes simplex* and *Thysanoessa spinifera*, certain euphausid species typically inhabit the cold "sub-arctic" waters including regions stretching southwards from the far north to about 45 °N. These species include *Thysanoessa inermis*, *Th. longipes*, and *Euphausia pacifica*. Further south, in the more central North Pacific and extending to about 20 °N, are such species as *Thysanoessa gregaria* and *Thysanopoda acutifrons*, this latter form extending perhaps a little further north. Other forms *Euphausia recurva*, *Nematoscelis difficilis* and *Nem. atlantica* also occur in this central region. A large number of species including *Nematoscelis gracilis*, *Thysanopoda tricuspidata*, *Euphausia eximia*, *E. paragibba*, *E. tenera*, *E. lamelligera* and *E. diomedeae*, all inhabit the tropical belt north and south of the equator, and other species, though essentially tropical and subtropical, spread out from the warm waters to the somewhat cooler waters of the Pacific (e.g. *Thysanopoda aequalis*).

An example of a relatively sharp marine faunistic boundary occurs in the Antarctic and is known largely from the work of Mackintosh (1934). Mackintosh points out that at the Antarctic Convergence there is a relatively rapid change in surface sea temperature, certainly far more rapid than is usually experienced in the ocean. In the areas around South Georgia, and the South Shetlands, the mean surface temperature during summer changes from less than $-1\,°C$ to more than $+5\,°C$ over only a few degrees of latitude. This zone is found to mark the southern limit of many warmer sub-Antarctic, or what are often referred to as antiboreal, forms, and conversely the northern limit of many cold-loving, typically Antarctic, species. Some of the commoner Antarctic planktonic animals are shown in Fig. 13.29, 13.30, 13.31. A particularly clear example of geographical distribution correlated with the temperature characteristics of this area appears from the work of John (1936) on the euphausids. He shows that *Euphausia crystallorophias* is confined to the coldest water and as a neritic species is mainly near the Antarctic coast line, whereas *Euphausia superba* is more widely distributed among the ice, though it is still a very cold-loving species. *E. frigida*, however, approaches and even reaches the Antarctic Convergence, as does *E. triacantha*. On the other hand, *Euphausia vallentini* is really found only in the sub-Antarctic (anti-boreal) region north of the Antarctic Convergence, and finally, species such as *E. lucens* and *E. similis* are typical of the warmer waters of the southern hemisphere (cf. Fig. 13.32), *E. similis* having a very wide distribution. This study has been extended by Boden (1954) who has investigated the geographical range of species of *Euphausia* off South Africa. While a large number of species are tropical and sub-tropical, *E. similis* spreads from the sub-tropics to the sub-Antarctic zone. Three forms (*E. vallentini*, *E. lucens*, *E. longirostris*) are essentially sub-Antarctic, however.

Apart from the euphausids, Mackintosh suggests that species such as *Calanus simillimus*, *Candacia* sp., *Eucalanus* sp., *Pleuromamma robusta*, *Eukrohnia*, *Parathemisto gaudichaudi* and *Limacina balea* are typical of the somewhat warmer Antarctic waters and seldom occur in the colder areas (cf. Fig. 13.33). By contrast, *Vanadis antarctica*, *Diphyes antarctica*, *Sibogita borchgrevinki*, *Eusirus antarcticus* and especially *Haloptilus ocellatus* are species typical of the coldest regions and rarely approach the Antarctic Convergence, while other species such as *Metridia gerlachei, Cleodora sulcata, Tomopteris* and *Limacina helicina,* while fairly restricted to cold water, may occur as far north as the Convergence (cf. Fig. 13.33). There

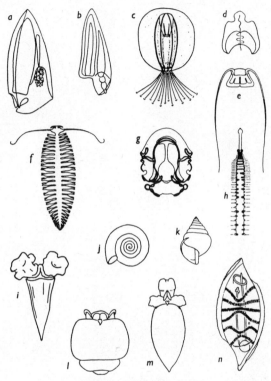

Fig. 13.29 Species of Antarctic macroplankton.
a = *Diphyes antarctica*; b = *Dimophyes arctica*; c = *Sibogita borchgrevinki*; d = *Pyrostephos vanhoffeni*; e = *Solmundella* sp.; f = *Tomopteris carpenteri*; g = *Auricularia antarctica*; h = *Vanadis antarctica*; i = *Cleodora sulcata*; j = *Limacina helicina*; k = *Limacina balea*; l = *Spongiobranchaea australis*; m = *Clione antarctica*; n = *Salpa fusiformis* f. *aspera* (from Mackintosh, 1934).

are also widespread species in the Antarctic, including the amphipods, *Primno* and *Vibilia* and the two commonest copepods, *Calanus acutus* and *Rhincalanus gigas.* These species would appear more eurythermal than those so far listed, although *Calanus acutus* apparently has a slight preference for colder waters, whereas *Rhincalanus gigas* occurs more generally in warmer Antarctic areas. More precise limits in the distribution of the Antarctic zooplankton are difficult

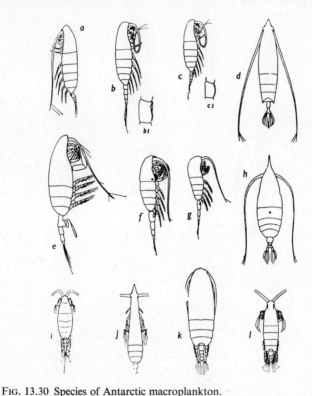

FIG. 13.30 Species of Antarctic macroplankton.
a = *Calanus acutus*; b = *Calanus propinquus*; c = *Calanus simillimus*; d = *Rhincalanus gigas*; e = *Pareuchaeta antarctica*; f = *Pleuromamma robusta*; g = *Metridia gerlachei*; h = *Haloptilus ocellatus*; i = *Heterorhabdus* sp.; j = *Eucalanus* sp.; k = *Euchirella* sp.; l = *Candacia* sp. (from Mackintosh, 1934).

to determine, especially as the zooplankton tends to be very patchy at times. Mackintosh, and also Hardy and Gunther, have commented particularly on the patchiness of *Euphausia superba*. Although it is only the third commonest zooplankton species, its relatively large size and tendency to form dense shoals make it especially conspicuous so that it may mask the distribution patterns of other species.

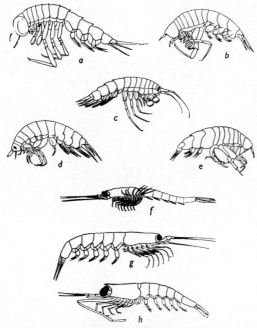

FIG. 13.31 Species of Antarctic macroplankton.
a = *Parathemisto gaudichaudi*; b = *Cyllopus* sp,; c = *Eusirus antarcticus*; d = *Vibilia antarctica*; e = *Primno macropa*; f = *Antarctomysis maxima*; g = *Euphausia superba*; h = *Thysanoessa macrura* (from Mackintosh, 1934).

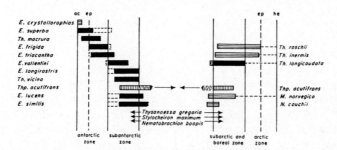

FIG. 13.32 Diagrammatic comparison of the euphausid faunas of Arctic and Antarctic (Atlantic) waters. hc = high Arctic coast line; ac = Antarctic coast line; vertical shading = deep water species; black = surface species; horizontal shading = coastal species (from Einarsson, 1945).

In considering the geographical distribution of zooplankton, Russell (1935a) has pointed out that, apart from the fact that in practically every zoological group there are far more warm water than cold water species, there is also a preponderance of cold

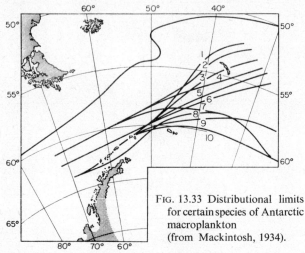

FIG. 13.33 Distributional limits for certain species of Antarctic macroplankton (from Mackintosh, 1934).

1. Northern limit of *Diphyes ant arctica* and normal northern limit of *Euphausia superba*.
2. Northern limit of *Sibogita borchgrevinki*.
3. Northern limit of pelagic *Eusirus antarcticus*.
4. Southern limit of *Euphausia vallentini*.
5. Northern limit of *Auricularia antarctica*.

6. Southern limit of *Euphausia triacantha*.
7. Southern limit of *Candacia* sp.
8. Southern limit of *Limacina balea*.
9. Southern limit of *Calanus simillimus*.
10. Southern limit of *Pleuromamma robusta* and northern limit of *Haloptilus ocellatus*.

water species living in Antarctic as compared with Arctic areas (cf. Table 12.3, Chapter XII). This comparison appears to have been made for the Atlantic Ocean only. The occurrence of certain species living in the surface waters of Arctic regions and in the upper layers of the Antarctic seas has already been referred to, and in those cases where such species occur in tropical and sub-tropical latitudes, they are present probably only in the deeper water layers (cf. Fig. 13.34). The term "epiplanktonic-bipolar" species has been applied to such forms, and it has been suggested by Russell that their occurrence in the Atlantic Ocean and the preponderance of Antarctic over Arctic species might be explained on the distribution of deep currents in the Atlantic. Except for the northward flow of Atlantic bottom water from the Antarctic, the general main flow of the deep layers of the Atlantic Ocean is in a north/south direction. Russell suggests, on the assumption that most species of plankton organisms have evolved in the surface layers of tropical regions, that those which have become adapted to cooler conditions will spread out both to north and south on the surface. But some species will spread into deep water, and in this case they will tend to be carried south in the Atlantic by the deep flowing currents. Even those species

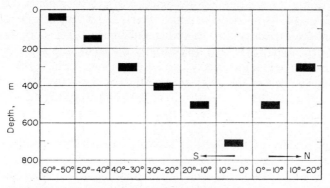

FIG. 13.34 The greatest frequency of *Eukrohnia hamata* in the Atlantic in relation to depth (from Ekman, 1953).

which have eventually colonized the surface layers of the Arctic may tend to be carried towards the south if they sink in the water. There tends, therefore, to be a drift of species towards the Antarctic in the Atlantic Ocean and Russell believes that this is responsible for the preponderance of cold water species in Antarctic regions.

The problem of the effect of drift on the maintenance of a planktonic community in the area where it is normally actively reproducing, is one which is by no means easy to elucidate. We have already seen that a zooplankton population will tend to be carried out of its normal endemic region to expatriation areas. But drifting currents could carry such a large proportion of the plankton stock so far away that the question arises, how are sufficient animals left in the normal area of reproduction to maintain the stock?

This problem was considered by Damas (1905) with particular reference to the chief copepods in the Norwegian Sea area. Damas envisaged a very large anti-clockwise circulation of water which carried some of the copepods from the Norwegian coast westwards in a great circle till they approached the coasts of Iceland, finally returning a portion of the stock to the Norwegian coast, where they commenced reproduction again.

It appears, however, that the maintenance of plankton communities in a given region is often, though not inevitably, correlated with changes in depth distribution of the zooplankton. Sømme (1934) showed that the maintenance of a stock of *Calanus* in Norwegian coastal waters is at least in part connected with their vertical depth migrations. Over winter the *Calanus* mostly descended into deep water, but in the spring they rose into the upper layers, and a very prolific reproduction occurred over the late spring and summer. The stock drifted mainly in a northerly or north-easterly direction, and some of the zooplankton was undoubtedly carried into more Arctic waters. But towards the end of the summer a portion of the actively spawning stock migrated into the deeper layers (200–300 m) of the Norwegian fjords, and there the copepods over-wintered, rising again to maintain the stock in the following year.

The problem of the possible loss of the very rich zooplankton from the Antarctic with the prevailing currents has been examined by Mackintosh (1937). It would appear that the actively reproducing zooplankton in the upper 200 m layer of Antarctic waters must tend to drift northwards towards the Antarctic Convergence with the main surface current. At the Antarctic Convergence this surface water moves deeper and continues northwards into the Atlantic as the Antarctic Intermediate Current. The rich zooplankton population contained in the upper layers would tend to disappear beneath the surface at the Antarctic Convergence and would continue to be carried north, eventually dying off. There would thus be a continual loss of zooplankton from Antarctic waters. Mackintosh suggested that some mechanism must exist which would be responsible for returning at least a large proportion of the stock of zooplankton to the south.

In the area of the Antarctic which Mackintosh was investigating, three species of zooplankton were dominant in the catches—the copepods *Rhincalanus gigas*, *Calanus acutus* and the chaetognath *Eukrohnia hamata*. Each of these three species was present in the upper layers during the Antarctic summer, when active reproduction occurred. By an analysis of divided plankton hauls taken down to a depth of at least 1500 m throughout a large part of the year, Mackintosh was able to show that, with the onset of winter, the plankton migrated vertically into the deeper layers. For example, late in the

Antarctic winter (September), although the total quantity of zoo-plankton was greatly reduced, it was also spread out in depth to a great extent, with the majority of the animals between 500 and 750 m; the surface layers had least of all (Fig. 13.35). Both *Rhincalanus* and *Eukrohnia* showed a maximum in winter at about 500 m, with a reasonable concentration below 1000 m, but *Calanus acutus* had an even more remarkable distribution, being completely absent from the surface during the winter period and being most abundant from 750 to more than 1000 m. At such depths beneath the upper 200 m or so, all this plankton will be living in the rather warmer waters which are drifting southwards towards the Antarctic continent.

In early spring (October), Mackintosh observed that the plankton was generally higher in the water, mostly lying at a depth between 300 and 100 m, and with the advance of spring there was a progressive rise, though the surface was still poor in numbers (Fig. 13.35). By December most of the zooplankton was near the surface, and during the following two or three months the great burst of reproduction of the zooplankton occurred in the surface waters (Fig. 13.35). Thus, from about December to March the zooplankton will mainly be in the surface waters drifting northwards, whereas over the winter, the zooplankton though reduced in numbers, will be chiefly in the deeper water layers drifting south towards the Antarctic again. This is indeed a very large-scale circulation, amounting in depth to at least 500 m, and horizontally to some hundreds of miles.

The phenomenon of diurnal vertical migration will be considered in some detail in a later chapter, but it may be said here that the three species which dominated the zooplankton in Mackintosh's catches appeared to show no obvious daily vertical migrations. On the other hand, certain zooplankton species which appeared in Mackintosh's collections in smaller numbers, did not seem to show the marked changes in seasonal depth distribution which would have returned them to the Antarctic continent as we have postulated. Such species included the copepod, *Pleuromamma robusta*, and euphausids such as *Euphausia triacantha* and *E. frigida*. However, other studies on these three zooplankton species have shown that they, as well as many others, display a pronounced diurnal vertical migration. *Pleuromamma robusta*, for example, lives in comparatively deep water at a depth of about 500–700 m by day, but it performs a diurnal vertical migration on an enormous scale, passing at night to the upper 50

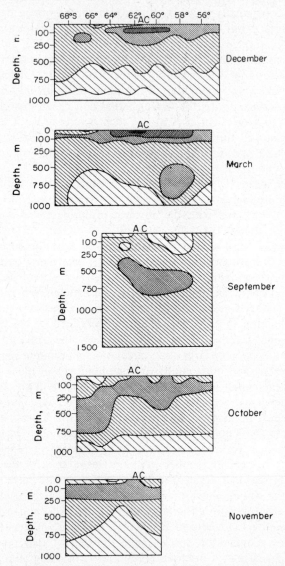

FIG. 13.35 Changes in the vertical distribution of the zooplankton throughout the year in the Antarctic. (Heaviest shading denotes
largest density) (from Mackintosh, 1937.)

or 100 m (cf. Hardy and Gunther, 1936). The euphausids also migrate daily through at least 200 m. It appears likely, therefore, that these species, instead of compensating for surface drift by a seasonal change in depth, are alternately drifting a little north in the surface layers during the night-time, and drifting southwards in the warmer deeper layers during their day-time distribution. In the case of some species there is admittedly insufficient knowledge of diurnal or seasonal

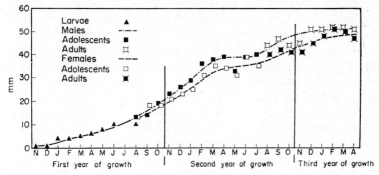

Fig. 13.36 A diagram of the life history of *Euphausia superba* (from Bargmann, 1945).

depth distributions to suggest how they are maintained as a stock in their area of normal reproduction. But at least one further pattern is noteworthy, as exemplified by that most abundant Antarctic species, *Euphausia superba*. The life history of *Euphausia superba* is known mainly from the work of F. C. Fraser (1936) and Bargmann (1945). It appears that the life cycle takes just under two years. Of this about nine months is occupied by the larval life, which includes the nauplius, calyptopis and furcilia stages (cf. Chapter XIV), and a further year is necessary for the growth of the post-larvae into adolescents and for the attainment of maturity (Fig. 13.36). Spawning occurs over a fairly extended period of perhaps as much as four or five months, so that the populations tend to be very heterogeneous. The most important matter, though, from the point of view of the maintenance of the community, is that spawning starts about November or December, when the adults are fairly far north approaching the Antarctic Convergence. The eggs are laid in fairly deep water (*ca.* 200 m), and as they sink further they are caught in the southerly-flowing Antarctic deep water. During the nine months of larval development, the broods of *Euphausia superba* are, therefore, being returned mainly towards the Antarctic continent in the deeper water layers. Fraser showed, however, that the calyptopis and the earlier furcilia stages exhibit a pronounced diurnal vertical migration, reaching the surface layers during darkness (Fig. 15.25). During the dark hours they must, therefore, drift northwards to some extent, the amount depending on the time they spend at the surface. It appears that on balance they spend more time in the deeper layers and so drift slowly southwards. The late furcilia stages show a lessened vertical migration (cf. Fig. 15.25) so that the latest larval stages gradually drift further south towards the ice-edge. About September of the following year they begin to come up towards the surface layers as post-larval stages. In the succeeding 12 months they are drifting north in the surface waters as post-larvae, or adolescents, growing up to maturity, and they show little or no evidence of vertical migration. In this way, with the younger stages of *Euphausia superba* drifting mainly south in deeper water and the adolescents drifting northwards in the surface layers, the stock is largely maintained in Antarctic waters.

The problem of the maintenance of a zooplankton community is accentuated under estuarine conditions, and it has been shown, for example by Barlow (1955), that copepods such as *Acartia tonsa* in an estuary are partly retained by migrating between the water layers of different salinities flowing in and out of the estuary. Banse (1957) demonstrated the existence of concentrations of plankton animals at different depths in shallow waters exhibiting thermal or saline stratification. For meroplanktonic larvae and for copepods, the zones of abundance could be very sharply defined. Banse observed, however, that the day and night depth distribution of the zooplankton was almost unchanged; he believes that the massing of the plankton into layers is not conditioned by temperature or salinity preferences, and is not much influenced by diurnal vertical migration, but is largely determined by the prevailing movements of the stratified water layers. In an earlier study, Banse (1956) demonstrated that echinoderm and polychaete larvae occurring off Kiel were closely bound to particular water layers, and that the origin and fate of this meroplankton is largely determined by hydrographic events. In estuaries, undoubtedly, constant reproduction of the zooplankton is essential to maintain any stock, since a large proportion of the population is continuously being carried out to sea.

The whole question of the reproduction of populations of zooplankton is intimately bound up with the problem of immigration and emigration. Redfield (1939) has shown that *Limacina retroversa* enters the Gulf of Maine where it is widely transported by the prevailing, mainly anti-clockwise, circulation. Immigration would appear to be mainly responsible for the *Limacina retroversa* populations in the Gulf. Thus in one year, Redfield showed that a population entered about December and was transported round the Gulf growing up successfully during the following six months, until most of the individuals disappeared by the following June. However, two months before, in April, a second incursion of *Limacina* occurred in the eastern sectors of the Gulf: again these spread round throughout the summer, though growing faster than the earlier immigrants. There was almost certainly some local reproduction in the Gulf from these immigrant populations, but despite this local reproduction over the summer months, *Limacina* does not seem to be able to maintain its numbers without constant incursions from offshore waters. The real centre for production of *Limacina* is presumably eastward of the Gulf of Maine, and the population at any time inside the Gulf is the difference between immigration and any local reproduction on the one hand, and mortality and drift on the other.

Redfield (1941) has also shown that the general great anti-clockwise eddy, which is typical of the water movements of the Gulf of Maine, with a time period of approximately three months, is largely responsible for the changes in distribution and abundance of the calanoid population of the area (cf. Fig. 13.37). He shows that the *Calanus* community of the upper water layers has its maximum abundance in the autumn period in the northern parts of the Gulf of Maine off the Mount Desert area, but as the winter approaches there is a shift in maximal population south to the coast of Massachusetts, and thence in the spring and early summer months, the maximum area of abundance of calanoids changes to just north of Georges Bank, east of Cape Cod. The late summer and early autumn populations reach their peak again in the more northern areas of the Gulf of Maine to give the distribution seen in the previous year. Redfield interprets these results on the grounds that in the late spring and summer the inflow through the eastern channel of waters off the Nova Scotia area into the Gulf of Maine is lessened, and a fairly rich zooplankton is established in the northern areas of the Gulf. Later in the year, with the general anti-clockwise circulation, this zooplankton tends to be carried south towards the Massachusetts coast, and this movement is reinforced by new water flowing in round the coast of Nova Scotia. This main inflow is maximal over the winter period, but it tends to carry a poor zooplankton population, so that over the winter only low densities of zooplankton are experienced in the northern sectors of the Gulf. The general flow of the older water, which has already been for some time circulating in the Gulf of Maine, and which has continued to support a fair zooplankton population,

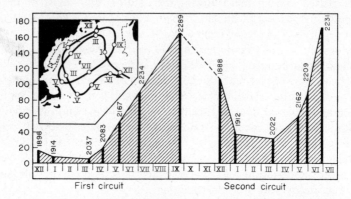

FIG. 13.37 The circulation of the calanoid community in the Gulf of Maine. The growth of the population in a mass of water assumed to move along a course indicated in inset. Zooplankton as volumes cc/m². Black bars indicate the volumes caught at selected stations (from Redfield, 1941).

is towards the southern regions of the Gulf near the Georges Bank area. With the strong flow of new water into the Gulf during winter, a considerable loss of plankton-rich water must occur, and this is expelled mainly off Georges Bank, and is passed to the waters of the Atlantic. In the late spring and summer, however, with the considerable lessening of inflow into the Gulf of Maine, a part of this water circulating as a great eddy can turn north again instead of being driven out of the Gulf. This water, rich in zooplankton, thus adds to the relatively dense populations of zooplankton which accumulate about September in the more northerly regions (cf. Fig. 13.37). To a small extent there may be some reinforcement also at this time by some zooplankton drifting from the Nova Scotia banks, but the general over-all circulation is mainly responsible for maintaining a rich calanoid population in the Gulf, with the sharpest seasonal effects occurring in the more northern areas.

The maintenance of a population of zooplankton in any area is complicated not only by immigration but by the extent to which the immigrants can breed. There is every gradation from a completely successful breeding population on the one hand, through those species which can undergo a very slight degree of breeding, to those forms which can live for a long time in their expatriation area but cannot reproduce at all. On the other hand, there are those immigrants that are killed almost immediately as soon as they enter a new area. The Gulf of Maine again provides an interesting example of an area where the different species of chaetognaths in particular show varying degrees of ability to survive as immigrants. The elucidation of the problem is largely due to the work of Bigelow (1926) and to the investigations of Redfield and Beale (1940). The results suggest that, of the chaetognaths, only *Sagitta elegans* reproduces really successfully in the waters of the Gulf of Maine. This species is not abundant in the waters offshore outside the Gulf, and therefore relatively few are brought in with incoming water. However, the flow of water through the Gulf is of great significance as in some sectors *Sagitta elegans* is liable to be swept out and the population lost, causing this species to fluctuate greatly in numbers. Over Georges Bank, however, a subsidiary separate anticyclonic eddy maintains populations of *S. elegans* almost continuously through the year; there is very successful breeding so that large numbers can be taken at most seasons.

By contrast, *Sagitta serratodentata* is an immigrant species which flows in with the surface waters mainly via the eastern channel approach to the Gulf of Maine. As we have already seen in other parts of the Atlantic, *Sagitta serratodentata*, though a warmer water chaetognath, can survive quite extensive cooling. It comes in as a surface immigrant in summer only, since water of a rather warmer character seems to enter at this time of the year. The appearances of *Sagitta serratodentata* are therefore highly seasonal, and it does not reproduce at all in the colder conditions of the Gulf of Maine. It may be classed as a "terminal immigrant". Not unreasonably, this chaetognath is found rather more commonly near the area of main inflow into the Gulf, though it does spread out to some extent more widely before dying off. Three other chaetognaths, *Eukrohnia hamata*, *Sagitta maxima* and *Sagitta lyra*, are found in the Gulf waters, but these all enter via the deeper inflow, whereas *Sagitta serratodentata* is brought in mainly in the superficial water layers. *Eukrohnia* is reasonably abundant but *Sagitta maxima* and *Sagitta lyra* are both very scarce indeed. All three species appear to be terminal immigrants in that although they come in with the inflowing water there is no evidence of any breeding in the Gulf. They persist for a time, but in the case of *Sagitta lyra* and *Sagitta maxima*, Redfield and Beale have shown fairly clearly that their numbers diminish rapidly the further one goes from their main point of entry. On the other hand, *Eukrohnia hamata* appears in more or less the same density in the deeper layers all over the Gulf of Maine area. Undoubtedly far greater numbers of *Eukrohnia* are brought in from outside waters, but this chaetognath also appears to persist longer. Probably it withstands the lowered temperatures of the Gulf waters better, and the individuals have a longer life expectancy.

There are also some very occasional immigrants to the Gulf of Maine which have an exceedingly short life, as they are rapidly killed by the change in hydrographic conditions. These immigrants fall mainly into two classes: firstly, the tropical or sub-tropical planktonic forms which occur in the warmer waters off the continental slope to the south of Cape Cod, such as tropical pteropods, siphonophores, salps, the copepods *Rhincalanus* and *Sapphirina*, and the chaetognath *Sagitta enflata*. In contrast to the other chaetognaths we have discussed, *S. enflata*, therefore, makes only a very occasional and short-lived appearance in the Gulf of Maine, being rapidly killed by the fall in temperature. In the second class are occasional visitors brought in by the ice-cold surface waters of the Nova Scotia current flowing from the north, and carrying Arctic immigrants, especially in spring. These include such Arctic forms as *Mertensia ovum*, *Limacina helicina*, and *Oikopleura vanhoffeni*. These also occur only rarely in the Gulf of Maine, and they persist for a very limited time as they cannot withstand the slightly warmeᐟ waters of the Gulf.

CHAPTER XIV

SEASONAL CHANGES AND BREEDING OF THE ZOOPLANKTON

THE bursts of larvae of bottom animals which appear in the plankton of coastal areas in temperate and high latitudes cause very considerable changes in the seasonal abundance of the total zooplankton. But over oceanic areas also, in temperate and polar regions, there is a marked seasonal fluctuation in zooplankton densities, with the late spring or early summer and sometimes also autumn being periods of abundance. Even with coastal or neritic plankton it is not the meroplanktonic species which cause the main seasonal fluctuations. The holoplanktonic members are also subject to seasonal breeding, which, together with changes due to inflow of immigrants in some areas, cause marked fluctuations in density.

For the Gulf of Maine, Bigelow (1926) has suggested that the total zooplankton was minimal about late February or March, but in April there was a very marked increase which consisted almost entirely of the young stages of the copepod, *Calanus finmarchicus*. By June, although the proportion of the young stages of *Calanus* had decreased, the zooplankton as a whole was at its maximum density and was very monotonous with the dominant species, *Calanus finmarchicus*, evident everywhere. However, other copepods and holo-planktonic forms such as euphausids, hyperiid amphipods, sagittae and *Limacina*, reproduced over the later spring and summer months. There was a much greater variety in the zooplankton, therefore, during the summer months, but during July and August the total quantity of plankton was less than in early June. Other species including the copepods *Centropages typicus* and *Temora longicornis* became more important as the year advanced, and with continued reproduction of other holoplanktonic species a second augmentation occurred in September and October. Following this increase, however, the total density of zooplankton began to fall, and a rapid decrease followed in the first months of the year to its late winter minimum.

371

Although in the more coastal neritic areas Bigelow noted that cirripede nauplii became abundant about March or April, echinoderm and polychaete larvae and fish eggs slightly later in spring, and medusae increased about May, nevertheless the overall zooplankton changes were clearly the result of the breeding of holoplankton, especially calanoids. The observations of Fish and Johnson (1937) in the Gulf of Maine have confirmed these conclusions (cf. Fig. 14.1).

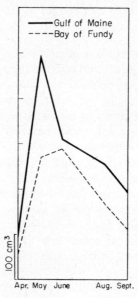

Fig. 14.1 Changes in the mean volume of zooplankton in the Gulf of Maine and Bay of Fundy (from Fish & Johnson, 1937).

The greatest changes in the total plankton are due to *Calanus finmarchicus*, though *Pseudocalanus minutus* and euphausids are also important. The maximum quantity of zooplankton occurs in May or June and the later summer sees a fall in the population with a second rise in autumn.

At Kiel, Lohmann found that the zooplankton, of which copepods were the chief constituent, was fairly low and at a steady value in the winter months from January to early spring. A very sharp rise occurred in the late spring (May), and very high densities of zooplankton were reached, though this was followed by relatively low values over the summer. The late summer and autumn saw another large increase, leading to a maximum which was as late as October, but thereafter there was a rapid fall to the winter minimum. Rotifers and bivalve larvae made some significant contribution to the summer populations, but the major increases were attributable to the two copepods *Acartia*, mainly in spring, and *Oithona*, in the autumn

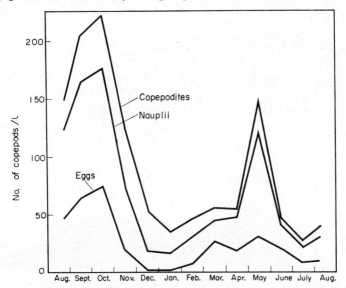

FIG. 14.2 Seasonal variation in the abundance of copepods at Laboe (after Lohmann, 1908, redrawn).

(Fig. 14.2). Harvey *et al.* (1935) have also demonstrated marked zooplankton changes with the seasons for the English Channel. The minimum occurred about January, but in the early spring there was a large augmentation of zooplankton so that during April/May the volume of zooplankton was maximal for the year. Over the summer the numbers though high, showed marked fluctuations, but a second maximum occurred about August/September (Fig. 14.3). This later maximum was actually the greatest for the year, if total number of animals be considered, though in volume the zooplankton was slightly less than the spring peak. Harvey's results suggested that changes due to meroplankton were small, apart from a fair contribution by cirripede larvae at the usual time, about March. As regards the holoplankton, almost the whole of the changes were due to the fluctuations in numbers of copepods, although there were small increases in summer of appendicularians and *Limacina* (Fig 14.3). The copepods, however, truly dominated the entire zooplankton. Thus from about the beginning of April to autumn there were great numbers of copepod nauplii, with copepodite stages becoming more important towards the late summer. The changes were due largely

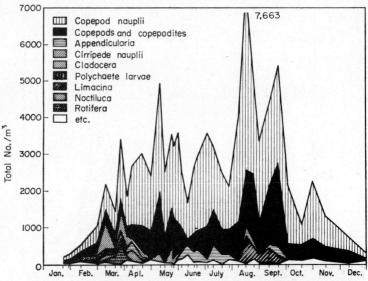

FIG. 14.3 The total number and composition of the zooplankton caught per cubic metre at a station in the English Channel off Plymouth during 1934. Depth: surface to 45 m (from Harvey *et al.*, 1935).

to *Oithona*, *Pseudocalanus*, and other small copepods, with a rather large number of *Temora* occurring in the first peak in May (Fig. 14.4). This pattern of zooplankton changes throughout the year off Plymouth has been confirmed by the work of Mare (1940), who showed a very low zooplankton minimum in January/February, a sharp rise in April and May due to the reproduction of copepods, and a decline in summer followed by a second maximum in the late summer. The results of the investigations of Deevey (1956) on the zooplankton of the inshore areas of Long Island Sound and Block Island Sound show marked seasonal fluctuations in zooplankton densities with maximum numbers appearing in the summer. The main changes were due to copepod reproduction, especially to the species *Acartia tonsa*, *A. clausi*, *Oithona* sp., *Temora longicornis*, and *Paracalanus crassirostris* (Fig. 14.5). Wiborg (1954) found that the contribution

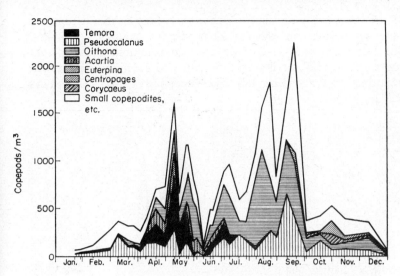

FIG. 14.4 The numbers of copepods caught off Plymouth during 1934
(from Harvey *et al.*, 1935).

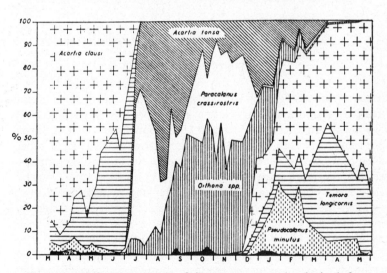

FIG. 14.5 Relative percentages of important copepods obtained from
March 1952 to June 1953 in Long Island Sound
(from Deevey, 1956).

of meroplankton in coastal Norwegian waters was small; the copepods were responsible for the overall population changes contributing generally some 80%–90% of the total zooplankton. Of other holo-plankton, appendicularians, cladocerans and euphausid larvae were important at times (Fig. 14.6). The copepods *Calanus finmarchicus,*

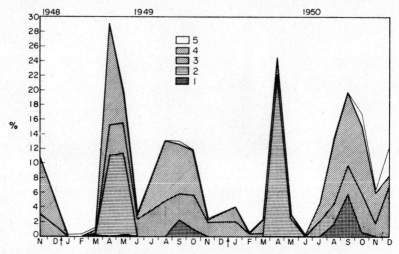

FIG. 14.6 The relative importance of "non-copepod zooplankton" at Eggum, Norway. 1 = Cladocera; 2 = euphausid eggs and larvae; 3 = Appendicularia; 4 = bottom invertebrate larvae; 5 = other organisms (from Wiborg, 1954).

Pseudocalanus elongatus, Microcalanus pusillus and *Oithona similis* were most significant numerically over the year as a whole (Fig. 14.7). Two peaks occurred in the zooplankton population, the first during spring and early summer, and the second between August and October. These peaks would appear to reflect chiefly the seasonal reproductive cycle of the more important copepods.

We shall examine in some detail later the remarkable changes in abundance of *Calanus finmarchicus* in some parts of the Clyde Sea Area, such as Loch Striven (cf. Nicholls, 1933a). But apart from *Calanus*, Marshall (1949) has shown that the smaller copepods in Loch Striven have marked seasonal breeding. It appears that the maximum numbers of all the species except *Temora* occurred in July or August, though the precise date varied from one species to another. This summer maximum was true for all stages – nauplii as well as copepodites. There was usually a secondary, smaller, and variable maximum in the spring about April or May, but in the case of *Temora* this peak was somewhat larger than the late summer density.

In higher latitudes the period of abundance of the zooplankton is usually even more obvious than in temperate areas and it tends to be compressed into a rather shorter summer period. The work of

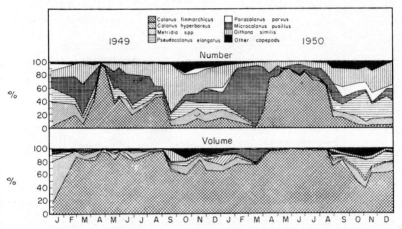

Fig. 14.7 Variations in the percentage composition of the copepods at Eggum, Norway (from Wiborg, 1954).

Steemann Nielsen suggests that in northern waters the augmentation of the plankton may be as late as June or July and that numbers are declining again from September onwards. Digby (1953), analyzed the changes in biomass of the zooplankton in East Greenland waters and found that the maximum occurred in July and August and the minimum towards the end of March. The late summer biomass was almost twenty times that of the winter minimum. Medusae and ctenophores occurred all the year round, and during late summer a great quantity of gelatinous material occurred, which was apparently derived largely from ctenophores. Appendicularians were also fairly abundant in late summer. Other organisms contributed very little to the total zooplankton apart from copepods, which were once again undoubtedly responsible for the major changes in zooplankton abundance (cf. Fig. 14.8). Other workers have noted that relatively large increases in zooplankton may be due to bursts of medusae and ctenophores in Arctic waters, and in the rather warmer waters, to an abundance of salps. There is general agreement, however, that the major fluctuations in zooplankton abundance are due to copepods. Thus Fish (1954) noticed that the very marked augmentation of the zooplankton in oceanic waters off Labrador was most obviously associated with the rapid increase in calanoids, especially *Calanus finmarchicus*, over the same period. This copepod dominated the whole of the changes in the total zooplankton, except for a short time

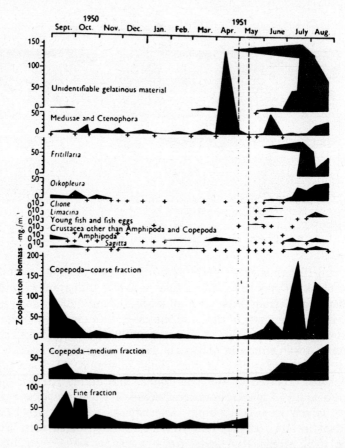

FIG. 14.8 Biomass of zooplankton organisms in the upper 50 m at Scoresby Sound, Greenland. Vertical hatched lines represent the onset of spring phytoplankton production as shown by the appearance of diatoms and by plant pigment analyses (after Digby, 1953, slightly modified).

over the winter minimum, and contributed about 80% of the population during the main periods of abundance. The peak density occurred in July and August (cf. Fig. 14.35). The major species appeared to have a single brood during the relatively short summer. Kielhorn (1952) had earlier drawn attention to the outstanding importance of *Calanus finmarchicus* in the total zooplankton of the central Labrador Sea. The copepod appeared to have one main annual reproductive cycle and the main augmentation in numbers took place in late July. However, two copepods, *Oithona atlantica*, which was numerically fairly abundant, and *Metridia longa*, bred in mid-winter. For Antarctic waters, Mackintosh suggests that a rapid increase in zooplankton occurs in November or December (the southern spring) and that zooplankton is extremely abundant over the summer with a peak value about February. But by April the population is declining again to reach low values over the winter period.

The marked changes in zooplankton density, therefore, focus attention on the breeding cycles of holoplanktonic animals especially copepods. Comparatively few species have been extensively studied, the best known being *Calanus finmarchicus*. It is perhaps necessary to emphasize that as far as is known all calanoid copepods show a similar pattern of development, passing through six naupliar stages and six copepodite stages, of which the last, Stage VI, is the adult (cf. Oberg, Kraefft, Lebour, M. W. Johnson, etc.).

The most extensive study of the reproduction of *Calanus finmarchicus* is that of Marshall, Nicholls and Orr (1933–35) for copepods of the Clyde Sea Area. They showed that in autumn the number of copepods was falling to reach a minimum density about February/ March. The autumn and early winter was passed chiefly as the Stage V copepodite, but about the end of December, those copepodites which had survived the early winter commenced their final moult to the adult condition. Thus by February, although the actual numbers of *Calanus* were very low indeed, the percentage of adults found in the catches was at its maximum for the year, and these adults included a considerable proportion of males which are normally scarce (cf. Fig. 14.9, 14.10). This stock which had persisted through autumn and part of the winter now spawned, so that the eggs comprised a large percentage of the catch towards the end of February and beginning of March. Although the percentage of *Calanus* ova was high, the number of eggs obtained from the small breeding population

(Fig. 14.9) was not very large. The eggs developed during March, the percentage of nauplii being very large towards the beginning of the month, but gradually declining as the development of the brood proceeded. It was possible to follow a succession of naupliar and copepodite stages. This first brood attained maturity by about the

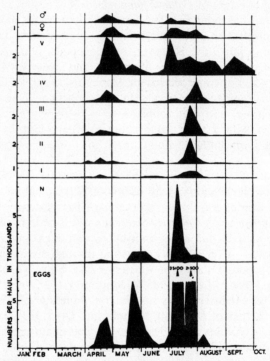

FIG. 14.9 Numbers of each stage of *Calanus* in Loch Striven, Scotland, in 1933 (from Marshall & Orr, 1955).

beginning of April, and a second spawning occurred about April/May when the usual high proportion of eggs and nauplii was evident. The actual number of this generation was overwhelmingly greater at certain of the stations sampled, so that a very sudden rise in the overall population of *Calanus* was experienced in these areas at this time. This second brood in turn grew up and became adult, and a third spawning of ova occurred about June/July. This third generation passed through the various successive naupliar and copepodite stages as had the earlier broods of the year, and it is possible that a few of them passed through the final moult to attain the adult condition. But the main proportion of the third generation ceased moulting at the Stage V copepodite stage. As a result there tended to be an accumu-

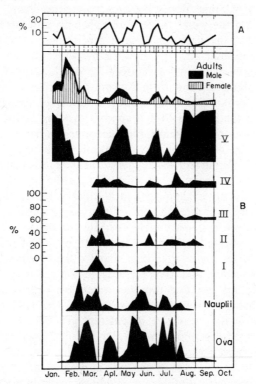

FIG. 14.10 Percentage composition of hauls of *Calanus* in Loch Striven, Scotland, in 1933. A = percentage of ♀♀ bearing spermatophores; B = succession of developmental stages through each breeding period (from Marshall & Orr, 1955).

lation of Stage V copepodites over the late summer (August/September) (Fig. 14.10).

Nicholls and his fellow workers noticed on some occasions small numbers of eggs and nauplii during the August/September period, and this suggested that there may have been some small-scale, irregular breeding after the third main generation of June/July (Fig. 14.10). This implied that a few of the ova from the June/July spawning developed to Stage V, but instead of persisting in this stage, moulted to give adult *Calanus* which bred to give rise to a very small number of ova. In any event, the offspring of these irregular small-scale spawnings grew up only to the Stage V copepodite condition and added to the general stock of Stage V which are overwintering forms. It appears, therefore, from the work of Marshall, Nicholls and Orr that in the Clyde Sea Area there are three major generations: February/March, April/May and June/July. Later work by Marshall and Orr (1955) suggests that in such temperate areas the development from egg to adult takes about one month in *Calanus finmarchicus*, and a further period of approximately one month is necessary for the ripening of the ova in the females. But it appears that egg laying can go on for at least two or three weeks, the release of ova being considerably affected by the density of phytoplankton available as food. The total life span for a female *C. finmarchicus* of the main spring or summer stocks is, therefore, at least of the order of two and a half months. On the other hand, the stock which is spawned about June or July persists until after the end of the year. Approximately seven months therefore is a reasonable estimate for the life span of that particular overwintering brood. The length of life of male *Calanus* seems to be distinctly shorter than that for the females. It was suggested by Raymont and Gross (1942) that males not only had a shorter adult life, but that they fed much less extensively, a point which has been confirmed by Marshall and Orr (1955).

Variations in the mean size of different generations of copepods have been noted for some time. Adler and Jespersen (1920) found the size of *Temora*, *Pseudocalanus* and *Calanus*, including copepodites and adults, to be minimal in summer and maximal in spring. They suggested that temperature was probably the most important factor, but differences existed even between North Sea and Kattegat populations. Marshall, Nicholls and Orr (1933–35) found that there was a considerable size variation in the broods of *Calanus* which they studied; the maximum size and weight normally was typical of the first brood that matured about the end of March, i.e. those copepods which were developing in the coldest water. By contrast, the smallest size occurred in the summer/autumn brood, among those copepods, that is, which developed in the warmest water. Nicholls also claimed that for any brood there was a decrease in mean size towards the end of the breeding period. Though temperature has a marked effect on size, other factors must certainly play some part. Wiborg (1955) holds that the availability of food as between one brood and another is responsible for considerable size differences, an opinion which is also shared by Ussing (1938) and Grainger (1959).

For British waters it would appear from the work of Russell (1935a) and Bogorov (1934) in the Plymouth area, and from the work of Wimpenny (1936b) in the North Sea, that the three main breeding periods suggested by Nicholls for the Clyde Sea Area for *Calanus*

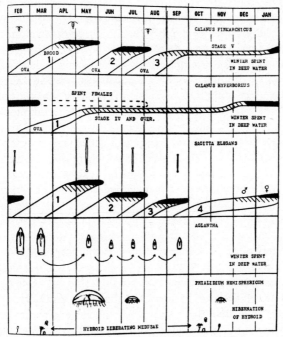

FIG. 14.11 Diagrammatic representation of life histories of five zooplankton animals under boreal conditions. An indication of the different sizes of the various broods of the species is included (from Russell, 1935).

finmarchicus hold generally, the first brood occurring about March. Results from the various investigations have also established that the overwintering Stage V pass into the deeper water layers and remain there during the late autumn/winter, during which time they appear to be more or less irresponsive to light and show no diurnal vertical migration. After attaining maturity the adults rise towards the surface and spawn (Fig. 14.11). It is suggested that the overwintering copepods may be living economically, largely on their fat reserves during this period when food is relatively scarce. It would be of interest to know if a lowered metabolic rate is true of these overwintering Stage V, as Marshall and Orr have recently shown (1958) that variations in metabolic rate occur with the seasons.

The reproduction of *Calanus finmarchicus* has fortunately been studied in several other areas, and it appears that the rapidity of development, the number of generations per year and the date of beginning of reproduction may vary considerably with the area. In general it would seem that reproduction in colder waters is slower and begins later, and that there tend to be fewer broods produced during the year. For example, Fish (1936a) concluded that in the Gulf of Maine the first brood of *Calanus* occurred in March/April, and a second spawning in June/July. It is possible that a third smaller breeding took place in September. The over-wintering stock was of Stage V copepodites, and these copepods were derived partly from the June spawning and partly from the smaller later brood when this occurred. Some of the copepodites must, therefore, have lived from June until April or May of the following year, a period of 10 or 11 months, most of the time existing as Stage V. Clarke (1940) confirmed that off the north east coast of North America there were two major generations of *Calanus*.

Off the coast of Norway the work of Ruud (1929) suggested that only two spawnings of *Calanus* occurred: the first in March and the second about June. But Wiborg (1954) has pointed out that Ruud's observations did not continue beyond July, and his own analysis of the breeding of *Calanus* at least for the more southern regions of Norway suggests that there were four breeding periods: February/March, May/June, July/August and September/October. However, Wiborg's observations support the general contention advanced by Marshall and Orr that in more northern waters generations tend to be reduced, for in the Lofoten area of Norway Wiborg found only three: April/May, June and July/September.

In even colder areas Poulsen (1904) has recorded one main brood of *Calanus* which was extended, lasting from approximately March to June, with a possible second breeding period later in Icelandic waters. The observations of Fish also suggest one major brood for the Labrador area. Perhaps the most extreme case for the slowing of reproduction in *Calanus* at high latitudes comes from the work of Digby (1954) off Greenland. Most of the *Calanus finmarchicus* took one year for development, the nauplii occurring as a single brood spread out from May to October but mainly during the months of June, July and August. Development proceeded as far as the copepodite stages by the early autumn, but in those polar regions overwintering could occur apparently in any of the copepodite stages, Stage III–V. It had earlier been observed that even in more northern Norwegian waters Stages IV and V both occurred as overwintering stages. Digby found that at high latitudes moulting to the adult condition could take place about the beginning of the year in January, but the single brood did not appear until June or July. But Digby's results suggested that for some individuals of *Calanus* in the polar regions development was even more prolonged. Some of the yearly brood did not proceed nearly as rapidly with their development and thus were only very early copepodites by the beginning of autumn. These overwintered as Stage I or II copepodites and had only reached the typical Stage V overwintering stage by the following autumn. Thus they lived for almost two years before they spawned.

The closely related *Calanus hyperboreus* appears from the work of Sømme (1934) and of Wiborg (1954) to have a clear single breeding period in the waters of the Norwegian Sea where it is endemic. *Calanus hyperboreus* overwinters much as *C. finmarchicus* as a reduced stock mostly in the Stage V condition, and it occurs very deep in the Norwegian fjords. It moults about January to the adult condition and a single spawning takes place about February or March. The eggs pass through their earliest development in deep water, but by April the young stages reach the surface layers and continue their development to reach the Stage V copepodite during the summer months. They then descend to deep water to complete the annual cycle (Fig. 14.11). Beklemishev (1954), summarizing the work of other investigators, suggests that the reproductive cycle of the Pacific copepods, *Calanus tonsus* and *C. cristatus*, is similar. There is a single annual brood, the females spawning in deep water. He believes that the females do not feed but produce eggs at the expense of the fat reserves stored by the Stage V copepodites.

For the species *Rhincalanus gigas*, the common copepod of Antarctic waters, Ommaney (1936) showed that there are two breeding periods during a year. The first spawning occurs in the Antarctic summer, beginning about mid-December and continuing throughout January, the somewhat warmer waters being the first to show the spawning. Most *Rhincalanus* spawn only in Antarctic waters ranging between about +1 to +4 °C. With such an extended spawning period there will be a mixture of copepodite stages persisting throughout the Antarctic summer. But about April this summer stock descends into deeper water and is mostly present then as adults. These adults spawn in deeper water about May/June, the second spawning for the year, and the offspring from this second spawning persist as a deep-living, overwintering stock, mainly as copepodites III, IV and V. By about October, which corresponds to early spring in the Antarctic, these copepodites begin to rise towards the surface, mainly as Stages IV and V, and they mature late in November to produce the first spawning of the new year. Ommaney suggests that the overwintering stage appears to depend to some extent on the temperature: in the warmer sub-Antarctic waters the overwintering stages are predominantly copepodites IV and V, but in colder regions there may be a considerable mixture of Stage III copepodites. There is some similarity in the breeding of this copepod to the breeding of *Calanus finmarchicus* in the more northern Norwegian and Icelandic waters, but a marked difference is that the second spawning is due to a deep-living summer stock, and the early development is in deep water.

There appears to be considerable evidence for the view that what might be termed the smaller calanoid copepods, *Pseudocalanus*, *Acartia, Microcalanus, Temora*, etc., as well as the cyclopoid *Oithona*, tend to have rather more generations during a year than *Calanus finmarchicus* from the same area. The breeding time also appears to be shorter for the smaller species. Fish (1936b) who obtained two main broods of *Calanus* in the Gulf of Maine, found for instance that *Pseudocalanus minutus* has at least three broods, March/April, May/June and July/August, with a possible further brood in September, and that *Oithona similis* had four broods. According to Fish (1936c) the life cycle of *Oithona* is shorter in the summer when the main weight of reproduction occurs, and at this time a brood may be passed through in approximately four or five weeks. This has been to some extent confirmed by the work of Deevey who suggests a period of four to six weeks for summer broods of *Paracalanus crassirostris, Oithona* and other copepods. *Acartia tonsa* has been investigated by Conover (1956) and he claims a period of approximately one month for a summer brood to develop, a suggestion which is supported by tank experiments on breeding of copepods by Raymont and Miller (1962).

Marshall (1949) has also investigated the breeding of smaller copepods in Loch Striven, the same area in which the spawning of

Calanus finmarchicus was studied. In general, Marshall found that the smaller copepods began to breed about March/April, approximately the time of the spring diatom increase, and that a succession of broods, usually three or four, was produced throughout the summer. But later in the year, especially about September and October, broods were not so clearly distinguished and a more or less continuous breeding occurred, at least to October and perhaps

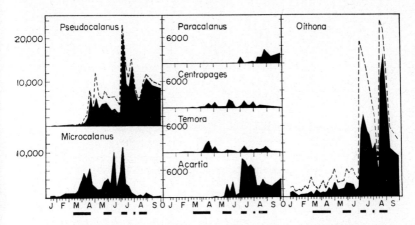

Fig. 14.12 Total numbers of seven species of copepods throughout the year in Loch Striven, Scotland, all on the same scale. Black = nauplii and copepodites; dotted line (*Pseudocalanus* and *Oithona*) = total including eggs. The dark lines beneath the figure mark the periods of main diatom outbursts (from Marshall, 1949).

further into the year (Fig. 14.12). *Microcalanus* was somewhat exceptional in that the broods were more distinctly separated, as for *Calanus*, and some weeks were apparently necessary for adult *Microcalanus* to mature before they were ready to deposit eggs. *Microcalanus* also tended to commence breeding earlier in the year (Fig. 14.13).

Marshall found for *Pseudocalanus minutus* and *Paracalanus parvus* that a considerable stock of Stage IV and V copepodites was built up about October, presumably the overwintering condition, and that breeding was probably ending about that time for the year (Fig. 14.14). Wiborg's investigations suggested a spawning certainly as late as October, but his data also indicate an accumulation of Stage IV and V copepodites from November onwards. On the other hand,

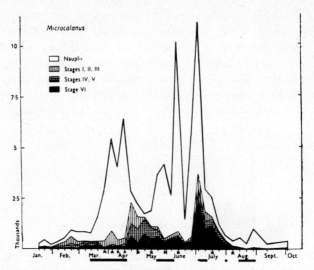

FIG. 14.13 Total numbers per haul of *Microcalanus pygmaeus* in Loch
Striven throughout the year (from Marshall, 1949).

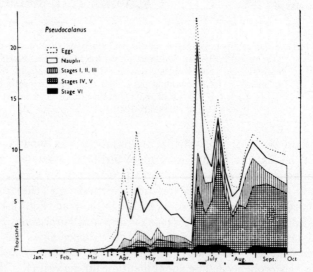

FIG. 14.14 Total numbers per haul of *Pseudocalanus minutus* in Loch
Striven throughout the year (from Marshall, 1949).
(In FIGS. 14.13 to 14.15 the dark lines below mark diatom
outbursts).

in the case of *Microcalanus*, *Centropages*, *Temora longicornis* and to some extent, of *Acartia clausi* and *Oithona similis*, we cannot be sure whether a true overwintering stage exists. Marshall found that a

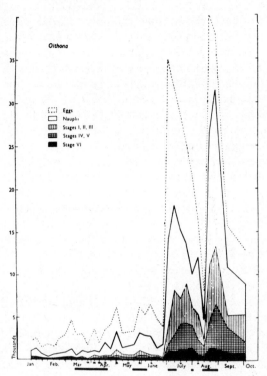

FIG. 14.15 Total numbers per haul of *Oithona similis* in Loch Striven throughout the year (from Marshall, 1949).

considerable percentage of eggs and nauplii of these species was still present in October when her investigations ended (Fig. 14.15). The work of Digby (1950) on small copepods in Plymouth waters also indicated breeding stocks which persisted to some extent throughout the year, though of course numbers were greatly reduced over the winter period. Digby suggests that the various copepod species produced five broods during the year. There was great similarity in the breeding of the different species in that the generations kept more or less in step. He believes that this may well reflect the dependence of copepod broods on phytoplankton crop. Digby found that most species showed a considerable percentage of nauplii even during the winter, although with *Pseudocalanus* there was a suggestion of an increase in the proportion of late copepodites during autumn. Quantitative zooplankton investigations in Southampton Water by Raymont and Carrie (1959) have shown that certainly *Acartia discaudata* and perhaps other calanoids such as *Centropages hamatus* and *Temora longicornis* continue breeding throughout the whole of the year, though numbers, particularly over the period January/February, are small. Lohmann's investigations at Laboe showed that although very few copepod eggs and nauplii occurred during January and February, some were present, especially *Oithona*, all through the year (cf. Fig. 14.2). Wiborg's results for *Oithona* similarly suggested that though there might be marked differences in abundance of the copepod during the year, propagation could occur in any month. We must recognize that in temperate latitudes at least, a limited amount of reproduction of some species of smaller copepods can go on even during the winter. Even with the medium-sized copepod, *Metridia lucens*, Wiborg pointed out that there were probably three main generations in Norwegian waters during the year, agreeing with the results of Rae (1950) who suggested three distinct generations in the North Sea. Nevertheless a considerable number of nauplii of *Metridia* appeared in Wiborg's hauls even in December and January. There is evidence that in the cold waters of high latitudes the number of broods of the smaller copepods is reduced, as we found for *Calanus finmarchicus*. Digby (1953) suggests a single main brood for several species off Greenland (Fig. 14.16), and Fish believes that most of the zooplankton off Labrador breeds only once a year. *Oithona*, however, appears to be able to continue breeding over a large part of the year (Fig. 14.16). Grainger's (1959) investigations in the Canadian Arctic also led him to the conclusion that there was one major breeding period for the typically herbivorous copepods, with a peak density of nauplii in June and a second larger peak in August. *Pseudocalanus* appeared to have at least one brood annually; *Calanus finmarchicus*, although it showed one brood per year, had an extended life cycle at these high latitudes, as Digby suggested, so that some individuals survived a second winter and were two years old when adult. Grainger makes the interesting observation that while the herbivorous zooplankton reproduced close to the time of the phytoplankton maximum, the carnivorous plankton (medusae, ctenophores, sagittae, amphipods and *Clione*) showed relatively little numerical change over the year, and many of the carnivorous species reproduced over the winter.

Heinrich (1962) has suggested that at higher latitudes the type of life history of the dominant species of herbivorous copepod may

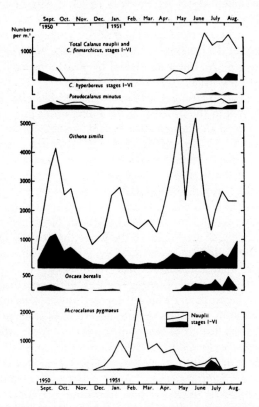

FIG. 14.16 The abundance of the commoner copepods in Scoresby Sound, Greenland, as nauplii and as copepodite stages I–VI, all drawn to the same scale (from Digby, 1954).

play a significant part in the occurrence of the successive maxima of phytoplankton and zooplankton. He distinguishes three main types of life history: In species such as *Calanus finmarchicus*, *C. acutus*, and *C. propinquus* breeding begins only with the vernal outburst of phytoplankton and the copepod maximum occurs later. However, *Calanus cristatus* and *C. plumchrus* in the N. Pacific reproduce in winter before the vernal growth of phytoplankton has begun, and the adult females do not feed. *C. hyperboreus*, and possibly *Microcalanus pygmaeus*, in waters off Greenland have a similar life history, though here the adult females feed actively. In the third type of life history, represented especially by the smaller copepods, the species may breed almost at any time in the year, but the size of a brood is greatly affected by food supply, and after the main vernal outburst of phytoplankton the generations of copepod become more numerous and may overlap. At lower latitudes, tropical copepods appear to have life histories usually of this latter type.

As for *Calanus*, there are usually considerable size differences in any area between the different generations of a particular species of copepod. Marshall showed considerable differences in the small copepods from Loch Striven (cf. Fig. 14.17a and b), and Wiborg and Digby obtained similar results from Norwegian waters and the English Channel respectively. In general, there appears to be a minimum size in the autumn period, and size tends to be maximal during the late spring. There is also a change in depth distribution with the different generations. In the Clyde Area during April and May most of the small copepods are higher in the water than earlier in the year, but during the following months of late spring and summer the copepods tend to go somewhat deeper.

Although the breeding of copepods has perhaps attracted most attention from investigators who are concerned with seasonal changes and reproduction of the zooplankton, nevertheless some information is available on the broods of other holoplanktonic forms. Redfield has shown that *Limacina* goes through two main generations with a possible third in the Gulf of Maine region. Russell (1932, 1933) has investigated the breeding of *Sagitta elegans* in the waters off Plymouth. This chaetognath appears to have four spawning periods in Channel waters: February, May, June/July and September. The life history of this species is particularly instructive as the offspring of the last September spawning apparently do not continue their development up to complete maturity during the autumn period. Russell found that the stock grew up but overwintered in an immature stage. Moreover there were indications that they descended to somewhat deeper levels during this overwintering period—a marked similarity to the behaviour of *Calanus*. By about December this overwintering chaetognath stock began to mature, the testes developing first, followed by the ovaries in the following month. The adults arising

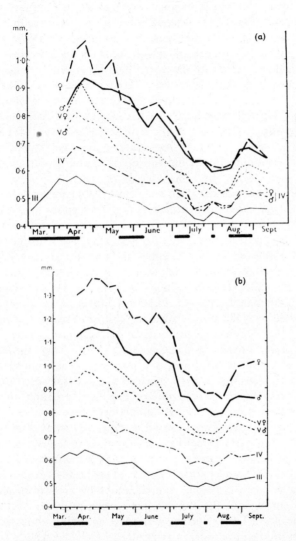

FIG. 14.17 Median size of copepodite Stages III–VI throughout the year
in Loch Striven. Dark lines beneath the figures indicate periods
of main diatom outbursts.
(a) = *Temora longicornis*; (b) = *Centropages hamatus*; (from
Marshall, 1949).

from the overwintering stock then spawned about February to give the first brood (Fig. 14.11). Russell's results suggest that adult length is highest about May so that these would appear to be the animals that arise from the February spawning and would be developing over the coldest period of the year. The mean length tends to fall during June, July and September. Temperature would thus again appear to be an important factor affecting size. In the North Sea, Wimpenny (1936a) concluded that *Sagitta elegans* had only three main generations. However, in the Irish Sea, Pierce (1941) found that although *S. elegans* began to reproduce in February, breeding was apparently continuous until the end of May, and no further broods then followed during the remainder of the year.

In the Gulf of Maine, Redfield and Beale (1940) believed that *Sagitta elegans* had an extended breeding period over spring and summer. Clarke, Pierce and Bumpus (1943), however, found that over Georges Bank the chief breeding time was April or May, and a distinct second generation followed in late summer or autumn. In any event, it would appear that in the colder waters of the Gulf of Maine area, the breeding of *S. elegans* exhibits a reduction in the number of broods as compared with the English Channel. This may perhaps be associated with the somewhat lower temperature. It is of interest, therefore, that Dunbar (1940) believes that *Sagitta elegans arctica* has even fewer broods in the Canadian Arctic. Two distinct age-groups are present at any time, and one brood has completed only approxinately half its growth when the other spawns. Although the time of spawning is not quite certain, it is probable that only a single spawning occurs during autumn, and therefore these *Sagitta* in the Arctic take two years to reach maturity. Russell (1935) believes that a breeding cycle somewhat similar to *Sagitta* may be true of the trachymedusan *Aglantha*, a typical high latitude boreal species. He considers that an overwintering stock of medusae spawns in March, producing a fairly large size brood, and then smaller broods are produced throughout the summer amounting probably to three in all for the year. The offspring of the last spawning about August/September produce the overwintering stock.which may tend to descend into deeper water (Fig. 14.11). Russell considers that it is quite likely that typical boreal species such as *Aglantha* will show the same characteristics which have been suggested for *Calanus*, namely that while having several generations in more temperate seas, they will tend to show a reduction in the number of broods and a rather slower development in the colder seas of higher latitudes. Dunbar (1946) has investigated the life cycle of the amphipod *Themisto libellula* in Canadian Arctic waters. This very important species appears to commence breeding about March but the period is extended and continues probably till July. During the summer Dunbar found two distinct size groups of *Themisto*; both the smaller "juveniles" and the larger "adolescents" are sexually immature. The "juveniles" appear to be the products of the spring/summer breeding; the "adolescents" possibly become mature and breed in autumn. It is likely, however, that they delay breeding until the following spring, in which case the total life-cycle occupies two years instead of one. In either event, Dunbar points out that two distinct age-groups, which are not offspring and parent, exist at the same time; when newly spawned individuals are present, there are three distinct age-groups. This type of breeding cycle Dunbar has found with other planktonic animals such as *Sagitta elegans* (*vide supra*) and *Thysanoessa* spp.

It must be recognized, however, that even in boreal waters, although some calanoid copepods and non-crustacean species such as *Sagitta elegans* may have two or three generations in a year, there is a tendency for other species to be annual. Fish and Johnson (1937) suggest that for the Gulf of Maine most of the larger crustaceans and probably many non-crustacean zooplankton breed only once a year. Of the larger Crustacea the euphausids represent one of the most important plankton groups. The life cycle includes nauplius, metanauplius, three calyptopis and several furcilia stages (cf. Fig. 14.17.1). In the Gulf of Maine Fish and Johnson found that *Thysanoessa inermis* and *Meganyctiphanes norvegica* bred during the late spring. The young stages survived the winter and reached maturity in the following spring to give rise to the new brood. While *Thysanoessa* appeared to be strictly annual, *Meganyctiphanes* probably had another breeding about August. Possibly some *Meganyctiphanes* also survived for a second year. The observations of Whiteley (1948) confirmed the suggestion that most of the larger Crustacea are annual in boreal waters; possibly some large decapod crustaceans may live even longer.

For euphausids there is additional information on the number of broods for several species in the North Atlantic. In the waters of the English Channel, Lebour (1924) showed that the temperate and coastal species, *Nyctiphanes couchi* (Fig. 14.18), reproduced mainly during the spring, with a peak of spawning about May. However, Lebour reported that some spawning appeared to occur all the year round so that possibly there is more than one brood during the year, at least in temperate waters, for this species. Einarsson (1945) believes that some North Atlantic species of euphausids are annual, whereas others take two years or even more to complete the life cycle. Moreover for some euphausids a lowering of temperature tends to delay maturity and slow development, an effect similar to that seen in many

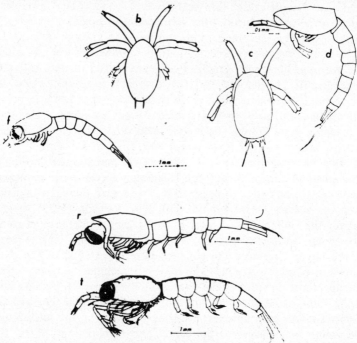

FIG. 14.17.1 Life history of *Thysanoessa inermis* b = Nauplius II c = Meta-nauplius d = Calyptopis III f = Furcilia I r = Furcilia IV t = Furcilia VII (from Einarsson, 1945).

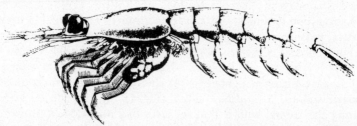

FIG. 14.18 *Nyctiphanes couchi* (ovigerous ♀) (from Einarsson, 1945).

calanoid copepods. The deep water euphausid *Thysanopoda acutifrons*, throughout its range in the North Atlantic, appears to take two years to mature. Spawning occurs about May, and the animals grow to a size of about 30 mm by the end of their second summer. They mature during the following winter and spawn at an average

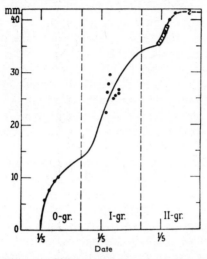

FIG. 14.19 The life cycle of *Thysanopoda acutifrons*. The double contoured part of the curve denotes the first spawning (from Einarsson, 1945).

length of some 40 mm, after which the majority of the 2 yr-old stock dies off (cf. Fig. 14.19). The effect of temperature variation on breeding is not seen in this species, probably owing to its living in deep water where conditions are more uniform than in the upper layers. According to Einarsson, *Meganyctiphanes norvegica* reaches maturity in one year in Atlantic waters. However, in the more southern part of its range, spawning occurs from about February to April and most of the animals die at the age of one year. In more northern waters the spawning is somewhat later (March to July), and although *Meganyctiphanes* becomes mature in one year, a considerable portion of the stock appears to persist for a further year and spawns a second time (cf. Whiteley, 1948). This history of the breeding cycle is confirmed by the investigations of Mauchline (1959) for the Clyde. Spawning of *Meganyctiphanes* extended over spring and summer with peaks in April and at the end of June. Development to the adolescent stage, when the animals averaged 25 mm length, occupied 2–3 months. Sexual maturity was attained only in late winter, transference of spermatophores occurring in January to February. Many of the males died at this time; the females spawned in spring, and a heavy mortality followed after spawning. However, a number of females persisted through the summer (when they exceeded 35 mm in length) and they survived for a second winter, spawning again in the following spring. Mauchline believes that a very small percentage of these females may persist even after the second year and might spawn for a third time. According to Einarsson (1945) the life history of *Thysanoessa longicaudata* in cold northern (Greenland) waters appears to be somewhat similar, in that the euphausid matures in one year, but a portion of the stock persists for a longer time. However, in the more southern areas the whole stock, after growing to maturity in a year, dies off.

A marked effect of temperature on reproduction occurs with two species of *Thysanoessa*, *T. inermis* and *T. raschii*. Both spawn during the spring, and they may become sexually mature in one year, when they are comparatively small, measuring only about 14–17 mm. In the more temperate areas these euphausids persist into a second year and reproduce again in the subsequent spring. By this time the animals have grown in length to exceed 20 mm. In sub-Arctic waters, however (e.g. north of Iceland), these two species of euphausid do not breed in the first year. Sexual maturity is delayed until the second spring, when they spawn at a length rather similar to those euphausids of two years old in the more southern regions (Fig. 14.20). It appears that in the extremely cold Arctic waters of west Greenland, *Thysanoessa inermis* and *Thysanoessa raschii* survive at least for a third year and spawn again (Fig. 14.20). In general, the body size of euphausids occurring in the very cold waters exceeds that of the same species in more temperate parts of the N. Atlantic (cf. copepods). The life cycle of some euphausids from high southern latitudes would also appear to occupy two years. The Antarctic species *Euphausia superba* is biennial (cf. Chapter XIII), and Baker (1959) has shown that the somewhat warmer species *E. triacantha* also has a 2-year cycle. It has been suggested (Chapter XIII) that *E. superba* spawns in deeper waters and that the eggs and earliest stages live deeper than the adolescents and adults. This does not appear to hold for northern euphausids. For *Thysanopoda acutifrons*, for example, Einarsson has shown that the young larvae are found mainly in the uppermost hundred metres; the adolescents mostly below 200 m, but the adults live at depths exceeding 2000 m. *Meganyctiphanes* is by contrast a fairly shallow living species in the North Atlantic; nevertheless the larvae again live at shallower levels than the adults.

Although temperature exerts a considerable influence on the breeding cycles of zooplankton, other factors such as food may play

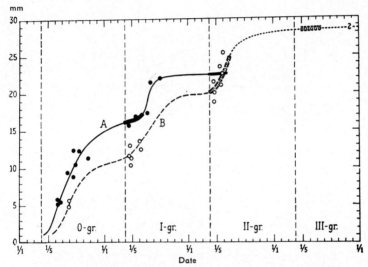

FIG. 14.20 The life cycle of *Thysanoessa inermis*. A: in southern localities of the North Atlantic; thickened parts of the curve denote first and second spawnings. B: growth in north and east Icelandic waters (stippled curve), and further growth of the species in West Greenland (dotted curve). Spawning indicated by double contoured curve (from Einarsson, 1945).

a part. The rate of growth may be strongly influenced by food supply. In the Antarctic the euphausids appear to grow rapidly during the periods of phytoplankton abundance. Temperature has been claimed to be a significant factor in the breeding of marine Cladocera. For *Evadne nordmanni* it was suggested that the reproductive capacity was greater in waters of higher temperatures. The matter is complex, however, in that these cladocerans reproduce mainly by parthenogenesis, and the number of young per brood produced in the parthenogenetic generations appears to vary considerably. Moreover, according to Bainbridge (1958), although there is an intense period of sexual reproduction in October, some sexual individuals can occur over most of the year. For the parthenogenetic individuals, Cheng (1947), working in the Clyde Area, suggested that larger sized female *Evadne* generally had greater numbers of embryos than smaller females, but Bainbridge, sampling the same area, showed that embryos may be resorbed

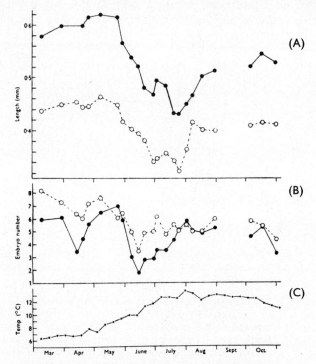

FIG. 14.21 Fluctuations in the mean length (A), and mean embryo number (B), of primiparae with early-stage embryos (0–0), and females with late-stage embryos (●—●) of *Evadne nordmanni*. C represents the changes in surface temperature at Keppel Pier, Millport (from Bainbridge, 1958).

during development. On the whole Bainbridge found that the number of young in a first brood appeared to be lower than in subsequent broods. Moreover, the mean size of individuals and the number of embryos produced showed considerable fluctuations with the seasons. Over the spring months, March to May, both size and embryo number tended to be at a maximum, and this might to some extent be correlated with lower sea temperatures (Fig. 14.21). But although a fall in both size and embryo number occurred in June/July, this was succeeded by a rise in August when temperatures are about maximal (Fig. 14.21). Bainbridge considers, therefore, that although temperature may have some influence on reproductive capacity of *Evadne*, food supply is equally important, and internal physiological factors probably play some part.

The marked seasonal fluctuations in the zooplankton of temperate and high latitudes is widely recognized. In tropical waters seasonal effects are slight; differences in the crop of zooplankton in various months are usually small. The reproductive cycles of members of the tropical zooplankton have been relatively little studied. The lack of a strong seasonal effect, therefore, led some workers to assume that tropical species reproduced almost continuously throughout the year. It is doubtful, however, whether many species breed in this manner. As Prasad (1954) has shown for Indian waters, species may have a protracted breeding period extending over several months, but the breeding is still discontinuous. A marked characteristic of tropical zooplankton, however, is that different species breed at different periods throughout the whole year, so that any intensification of breeding at a particular time tends to be only slight as compared with colder waters. Prasad, for example, found two relatively small maxima for the year during March and April, and again from August to October. But the fluctuations between the two maxima and the minimum were far less than at higher latitudes.

The investigations of Russell and Colman (1934, 1935) on the zooplankton of the Great Barrier Reef give considerable information on the fluctuations in abundance, seasonal cycles and relative importance of different species of tropical zooplankton. However, in considering these results it must be remembered that the area is neritic, and seasonal changes may be different in oceanic tropical regions. Despite the variety of the zooplankton so characteristic of tropical waters, Russell and Colman found a great preponderance of copepods on the Barrier Reef. Indeed this dominance of copepods appears to hold for the zooplankton of all seas. On the Barrier Reef copepods usually formed about 70% of the population. Other important holoplankton animals included tunicates, chaetognaths, pteropods, heteropods and siphonophores (Fig. 14.22). Despite the neritic character of the Reef, the temporary plankton amounted to only 11% of the whole zooplankton. The copepods themselves showed considerable variety: Farran (1949) lists 28 species as fairly common.

But there were distinct seasonal differences in the relative abundance of the various copepods, implying that seasonal breeding was probably true for these tropical forms. Precise breeding cycles are not known; the younger copepodite stages were not estimated except for a few species such as *Calanus pauper* (Fig. 14.23). Nevertheless,

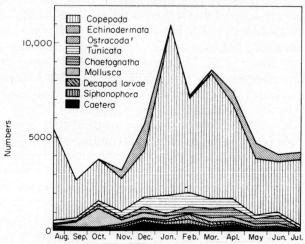

FIG. 14.22 The composition of the average catches of zooplankton for each month in vertical hauls with a coarse silk net near Low Isles, Great Barrier Reef lagoon, 1928/29 (from Russell & Colman, 1934).

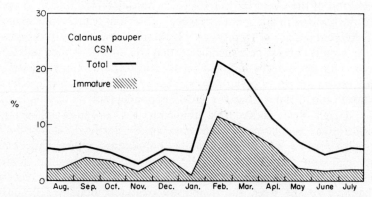

FIG. 14.23 Average catches of the copepod, *Calanus pauper* near Low Isles, Great Barrier Reef. CSN = coarse silk net (from Farran, 1949).

the variations in abundance of different species suggested that certain copepods bred only over particular periods of the year. Many species, however, showed immature stages almost throughout the year (e.g. *Calanus pauper, Paracalanus aculeatus*). Even with these species there were changes in density. *C. pauper*, for example, showed a burst of breeding about February (Fig. 14.23); for *P. aculeatus* numbers fell from September to January. Probably therefore a succession of broods

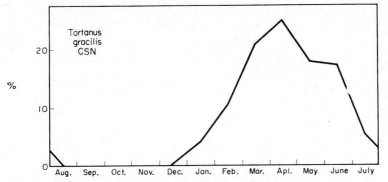

FIG. 14.24 Average catches of the copepod, *Tortanus gracilis* near Low Isles, Great Barrier Reef. CSN = coarse silk net (from Farran, 1949).

occurred during the year, with some intensification of breeding at particular periods. On the other hand, some species became abundant only over a restricted period of the year, e.g. *Calanopia aurivilli* occurred from January to April; *Centropages orsinii* from December to March; *Tortanus gracilis* showed a clear maximum about March/ April (Fig. 14.24); and *Clausocalanus furcatus* was abundant only in September and October (Fig. 14.25). Some of these copepods were entirely absent from the catches for several months of the year. To some extent in a neritic area, changes in population will be caused by incursions of zooplankton from outside waters, but the major fluctuations appear to depend on local breeding. In the species *Labidocera acuta*, though the copepod was present only from December to July, rather sharp increases in population occurred at intervals—December, February, April and June (Fig. 14.26). Even where fairly clear breeding periods exist, it is noticeable that the different species of copepods, unlike those of boreal waters, tend to breed in different months.

The extended breeding periods and the tendency for species to show an intensified breeding at various months throughout the year appear to hold for other zooplankton groups in the Great Barrier Reef waters. For appendicularians, Russell and Colman found considerable variations in abundance throughout the year with a maxi-

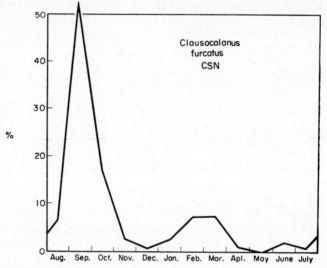

FIG. 14.25 Average catches of the copepod, *Clausocalanus furcatus* ne Low Isles, Great Barrier Reef. CSN = coarse silk net
(from Farran, 1949).

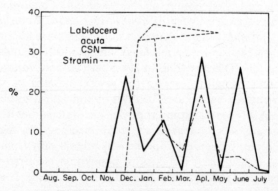

FIG. 14.26 Average catches of the copepod, *Labidocera acuta* near Low Isles, Great Barrier Reef. CSN = coarse silk net; dotted curve = hauls with stramin net (from Farran, 1949).

mum about January or February. But the annual fluctuation was not nearly as great as that experienced in colder waters. With doliolids there were considerable fluctuations but there was a long period of relative abundance lasting from December till June, and a reasonable number of individuals occurred during other months. Marked changes in density of salps were seen, though these were more probably associated with swarms of individuals brought into the area. There were two periods of abundance during the year apart from the more

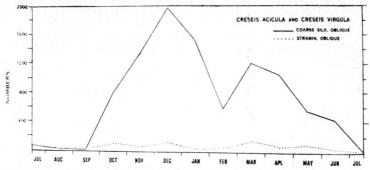

FIG. 14.27 The average catch of *Creseis acicula* and *Creseis virgula* combined for each month near Low Isles, Great Barrier Reef. (Coarse silk and stramin hauls are shown) (from Russell & Colman, 1935).

violent fluctuations in density. Russell and Colman suggest that the periods of greatest reproduction may be associated with temperature changes, reproduction being most marked when the temperature ranged between 24 and 28 °C. Of the pelagic pteropods, two species of *Creseis*, *C. virgula* and *C. acicula* were by far the most abundant. There were clear indications of seasonal variation in abundance (Fig. 14.27). At the same time over a large period of the year these pteropods were relatively abundant, which would indicate that reproduction was not so strictly limited as in colder waters. A considerable number of species of siphonophores were obtained by Russell and Colman. Variations in reproductive intensity occurred during the year, but the times of maximal reproduction again varied from species to species. For instance, *Diphyes chamissonis* had its maximum abundance about July or August, and numbers were decreasing from about January (Fig. 14.28 A). On the other hand, *Lensia subtiloides* (Fig. 14.28 B) showed a very clear maximum of abundance about December or January.

The work of Moore (1947) on the zooplankton of the warm Bermuda waters suggests that in these more oceanic conditions, the ᴧbundance of the plankton, estimated as volumes, showed little seasonal change (Fig. 14.29). Moore attributes the slight seasonal fluctuations to changes in wind producing variations in the local currents and so bringing richer areas of plankton to the sampling point. At the same time scme species of the zooplankton showed

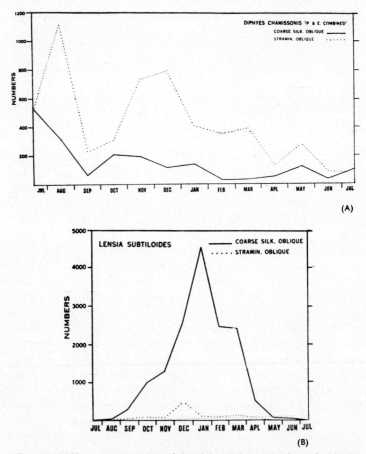

FIG. 14.28 The average catches of the siphonophores, *Diphyes chamissonis* (A), and *Lensia subtiloides* (B) for each month near Low Isles, Great Barrier Reef (Coarse silk and stramin hauls are shown) (from Russell & Colman, 1935).

fairly clear breeding periods, though these occurred at different times of the year. The surface dwelling medusa *Liriope tetraphyllum* showed a peak density in May (Fig. 14.30). The copepod *Lucicutia* had a winter maximum and *Calanus minor* a spring maximum, while species such as *Clausocalanus* and *Mecynocera clausi* appeared

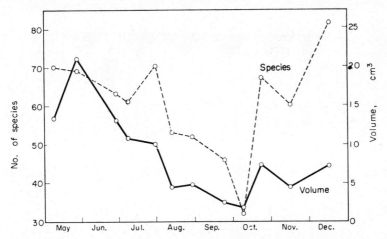

FIG. 14.29 Changes in the total volume of zooplankton and in the number of species in waters at one station off Bermuda (from Moore, 1949).

to show no obvious period of abundance. Some pteropods (*Limacina inflata* and *Creseis acicula*) exhibited a fairly clear winter or early spring maximum (Fig. 14.31). Siphonophores showed differences in times of abundance; for *Lensia fowleri* the maximum was in summer, while *Eudoxoides spiralis* showed maxima in winter or spring and again in the autumn. Moore was able to demonstrate three broods during the year in this last species. For the related *E. mitra* and for the siphonophore *Bassia*, he believes that five broods occurred in a year. Another holoplanktonic animal that was very abundant and which showed a distinct winter maximum was the salp, *Salpa (Thalia) democratica*. This species completed three life cycles during a year. Although the life spans of the tropical holoplankton are poorly known, Moore's results suggest that distinct broods are probably characteristic of many tropical species, but that numbers of broods occur, spread out over the entire year. According to Bsharah (1957) the maximal volumes of zooplankton obtained by Moore in May or June were about

twice the minimal volumes found in October. Bsharah's own investigations of the Florida current plankton suggest a small seasonal
fluctuation, with the larger quantities, found in March to June,
averaging twice or three times that for the remainder of the year.
Counts of the copepod population confirmed the presence of a
spring peak, with a density × 2 to × 3 that of the other months.

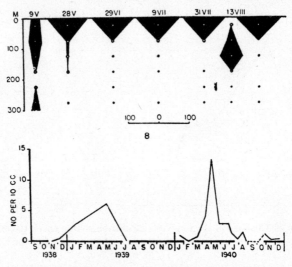

FIG. 14.30 Changes in the abundance of *Liriope tetraphyllum* in Bermuda
waters. The upper figure shows the depth distribution (from
Moore, 1949).

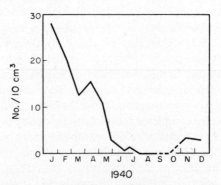

FIG. 14.31 Changes in the abundance of *Limacina inflata* in Bermuda
waters (from Moore, 1949).

Wickstead (1958) demonstrated that there are constant fluctuations in the zooplankton in the Singapore Straits with changes simulating a "spring" and "autumn" peak. If fluctuations due to sudden intensive swarmings of thaliaceans, mainly *Salpa democratica*, be omitted, the total zooplankton shows a maximum change in density of about five times. Although the periods of maximal abundance appear to be correlated with changes in salinity and temperature, Wickstead suggests that the real causative factor is the occurrence of the monsoon. During the change in the monsoon, which takes place twice per year, a fresh body of water, rich in nutrients and plankton, is brought into the area of the Singapore Straits, which leads to a burst in zooplankton production. On the other hand, in a coastal area (Chicken Key, South Florida), Woodmansee (1958) found no spring maximum and plankton volumes were minimal over the summer when the temperature averaged ca. 30 °C. The zooplankton reached its maximum during October though this may have resulted from local weather conditions influencing run-off from the land and hence nutrient supply. Woodmansee agrees with other investigators working in tropical and subtropical areas that various species of zooplankton have their maximal periods of abundance at different times of the year; and that there may be several broods of any one species. He suggests for instance that *Acartia tonsa*, the dominant copepod, in Chicken Key may have passed through about 11 generations in a year. Menzel and Ryther (1961) found a comparatively small spring maximum of zooplankton in the Sargasso Sea; over the year as a whole the standing crop of zooplankton was low and fairly constant. The small zooplankton maximum approximated closely in time to the phytoplankton increase. In general the animal plankton maintains itself at a level where almost all the plant production is utilized, so that there is little food surplus or wastage (cf. Cushing, Chapter X).

Investigations in tropical neritic waters off the coasts of India suggest some seasonal variation in the total amount of plankton. Although the extent of the fluctuation is doubtful on present data, it is clear that different members of the zooplankton become abundant at different periods as Russell and Colman found for the Great Barrier Reef. Thus George (1953) finds siphonophores most plentiful from September to April, and ctenophores during March and April, *Pleurobrachia* itself showing a peak from February to May. Chaetognaths occurred in large numbers from November to January. As usual, the copepods formed an important part of the zooplankton being dominant from November to May. Two cladocerans showed a fairly clear seasonal abundance, *Evadne* occurring from May to September, with a peak in August, and *Penilia* very slightly later, sometimes lasting until November. The importance of different holoplanktonic species having an intensified breeding period is obvious; the breeding may however be spread over a considerable period as with the zooplankton of other tropical regions.

Menon (1945), dealing with the zooplankton of the Trivandrum coast of India, suggests that copepods become abundant in October, and a regular succession of maxima occur from December to March for *Oithona*, *Acartia* and *Paracalanus*. *Temora*, however, is rare from December to February but becomes the dominant copepod from April to May. The harpacticoid *Euterpina* reaches its maximum somewhat later in July.

The factors responsible for the fluctuations in total plankton and for the seasonal breeding of plankton species in tropical waters are difficult to elucidate. Indian investigators, working in inshore waters, emphasize the correlations which may be noted with the seasonal monsoons (cf. Subrahmanyan, 1959). Changes in temperature and salinity must play a part, and this would appear to be true also of the Great Barrier Reef neritic area. But generally under oceanic conditions changes in salinity are negligible. Even temperature fluctuations are small, and other factors such as food supply and lunar periodicity probably all contribute to a complex pattern of factors modifying the reproduction of the plankton.

Comparisons of the amplitude of the seasonal change in zooplankton from tropical regions and at high latitudes are few. In part this may be attributed to the different methods employed in the investigations. Nets of various mesh sizes have been used; some workers have sampled only surface or subsurface levels while others have taken plankton from a considerable depth of water. Some investigators have used the number of zooplankton as an index of the crop while others have measured the volume of the plankton. Thus direct comparisons of the standing crop of zooplankton in tropical seas and in colder waters may be open to criticism. There is general agreement, however, that the standing crop in warmer seas is usually smaller, and that the seasonal changes are much less extensive. Jespersen (1924) has shown that there may be considerable variations in crop apart from latitude. In the subtropical and tropical North Atlantic the volume of zooplankton, mainly macroplankton, appears to fall sharply from areas off the American coast towards Bermuda. Considerably greater quantities were found north of the Azores and again towards the Spanish coast, where the volume was some eight

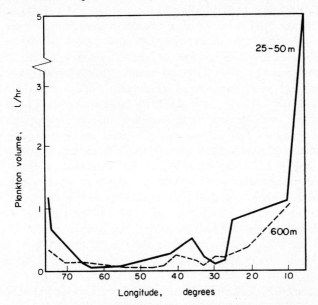

Fig. 14.32 Variations in the abundance of zooplankton with longitude in the North Atlantic at two depths. The line of stations runs from off Norfolk (U.S.A), eastwards towards Bermuda and the Azores; then northwards towards the mouth of the English Channel (redrawn from Jespersen, 1924/25).

times that found near Bermuda. There was a sharp fall in the amount of zooplankton in the Mediterranean, especially from western to eastern regions. However, Jespersen emphasizes the very much greater standing crop of macroplankton found in typically boreal waters. As compared with volumes ranging from 200–2000 ml/hr found in different tropical and subtropical regions, very much greater volumes were typical towards the mouth of the English Channel (Fig. 14.32). West of Ireland volumes approached 7–8 l/hr and in the colder seas round the Shetlands and the Faroes relatively huge volumes of 18–19 l/hr were obtained. In later investigations Jespersen (1935) has confirmed the poverty of macroplankton in the Sargasso

Sea as compared with the temperate North Atlantic. He suggests that by volume the temperate areas may be some seven times richer. However, in the vicinity of the Cape Verde Islands and off the African mainland in waters of greater nutrient content, rich hauls of zooplankton were obtained. In the Pacific Ocean, Jespersen similarly found that whereas high densities of zooplankton were found off the Galapagos Islands in the nutrient-rich waters of the Peru Current, in the central southern Pacific, especially near Samoa and Fiji, the zooplankton was very poor. In the warm waters of the Indian Ocean, large quantities of zooplankton were occasionally taken at certain stations, but these were always associated with large concentrations of salps. Jespersen's investigations have confirmed that in the tropical waters of the Sulu Sea and Celebes Sea a distinct seasonal change in the abundance of zooplankton occurs; there is an appreciable increase from spring to summer. Nevertheless it is clear that the quantities of macroplankton generally present at any time in tropical waters do not approximate to the rich hauls obtained by Jespersen in the North Atlantic. He states that the results of the German Plankton Expedition suggest that for open oceans the average crop of zooplankton in the cold northern waters is about eight times that of tropical seas. He attributes this largely to the greater crop of phytoplankton typically found in more northern waters (Table 14.1).

Foxton (1956) has analysed the crop of zooplankton in the Southern Ocean. He shows that the amount of plankton rises as the temperature of the water decreases with latitude. The maximum volume of plankton occurs in the Antarctic region with a summer temperature of

TABLE 14.1. Data taken from Lohmann's centrifuge plankton for North Atlantic (modified from Jespersen, 1924/25).

Depth	North Latitude			
	50–40°	40–30°	20–10°	10–0°
0 m	20,000	7000	2000	3000
50 m	20,000	5000	1500	2000
100 m	3000	2000	700	400
200 m	3000	200	80	100
400 m	2500	100	5	60
Average: 0–400 m	6000	2000	500	600

The numbers indicate the mean number of centrifuge organisms per litre.

between 4 and 1.5 °C; in winter the temperature range is between 1.5 and 0 °C. Generally the greatest volumes were found at latitudes of about 50–55 °S. At higher latitudes, somewhat lesser amounts were taken, but Foxton points out that large concentrations of *Euphausia superba* occurring at high latitudes were not properly sampled. It is possible, therefore, that the real standing crop at the

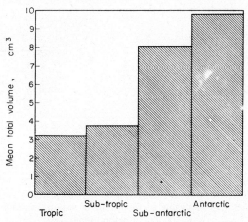

Fig. 14.33 Comparison of the mean total volume of zooplankton 1000–0 m) in the Antarctic, sub-Antarctic, sub-tropic and tropic zones of the Southern Ocean (from Foxton, 1956).

higher latitudes should be considerably greater. With sampling to 1000 m depth, Foxton shows that seasonal variations in volume of plankton in Antarctic regions are small. It is abundantly clear, however, that the crop of plankton increases from tropical to subtropical regions, and again from the subtropics to the Sub-Antarctic. The Antarctic is in turn marked by a higher standing crop than sub-Antarctic areas (Fig. 14.33). Foxton's very conservative estimate suggests that the standing crop in the Antarctic is four times that of tropical southern areas. The results of other plankton investigations in the open oceans confirm the greater value of the standing crop of zooplankton at high northern and southern latitudes (Fig. 14.34). Fish (1954) has compared the zooplankton of the central parts of the Labrador Sea with a subtropical area of the Sargasso. He has shown that considerable variations in abundance occurred in the Sargasso during late winter, spring and summer with a peak population in June. Copepods were important, comprising nearly half the total zooplankton. On the other hand, the boreo-arctic waters off Labrador showed a very much greater seasonal change with a very pronounced summer breeding, and copepods were relatively much more important. Fish concludes that on a numerical basis the average annual crop of zooplankton was about three times richer in the colder seas (Fig. 14.35). Marked regional differences in the standing

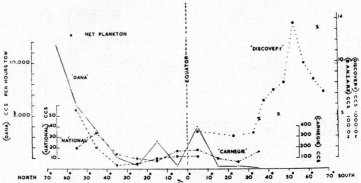

FIG. 14.34 The volumes of "zooplankton" ("net plankton") at various latitudes according to the results of various expeditions (from Foxton, 1956).

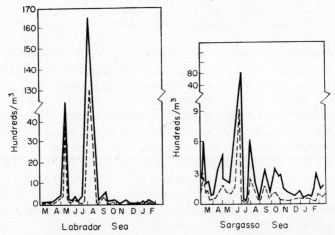

FIG. 14.35 A comparison of the annual cycle of zooplankton at an oceanic station in the Labrador Sea, and at an oceanic station in the Sargasso. Full line = total zooplankton. Hatched line for Labrador Sea = *Calanus finmarchicus*. Hatched line for Sargasso Sea = all copepods (redrawn from Fish, 1954).

crop in tropical seas must still be recognized, however. King and Demond (1953) and King and Hida (1957) have shown that although in the Central Pacific seasonal changes in zooplankton abundance are relatively slight, greater concentrations of zooplankton are found at the Equator in the region of upwelling and divergence. The effect of the convergent zone in this area also tends towards a concentration of the plankton. This increased fertility of the equatorial Pacific is borne out by the recent investigations of Hasle (1959) on the standing crop of phytoplankton. Algal counts were approximately equal to the maximal counts recorded for tropical areas of the Atlantic Ocean, and were much higher than the values suggested by Lohmann and by Hentschel.

At any latitude, neritic plankton tends to be richer and also to suffer greater fluctuations than that of offshore areas (cf. Jespersen). These differences between the crop of plankton in coastal and oceanic regions have been noted in the investigations of Clarke (1940). The inshore waters south-east of New York were found to be far richer than an area in the Sargasso Sea in latitude about 35 °N. Clarke emphasizes the marked variations which can appear between hauls taken comparatively close together in any area. However, a marked seasonal difference was obvious in coastal waters; the plankton was at a minimum in winter but in July or August was from 20–40 times as rich. In the "slope" water, which is an area of mixing between the continental slope and the Gulf Stream, fluctuations were more irregular. Moreover the richest hauls obtained in May and October were only some 10 times greater than the winter minimal hauls. The crustacean plankton in the coastal region was characterized by an abundance of *Calanus finmarchicus* and *Centropagus typicus*, and showed the same large seasonal fluctuations as the total zooplankton. In offshore waters these copepods were far less abundant and the variations in seasonal abundance were smaller. The average volume of zooplankton was about four times greater in the coastal area than in the "slope" water. The average volume of hauls from the Sargasso Sea was some four times less than that of the "slope" stations. Moreover, although some irregular fluctuations occurred in the Sargasso area, Clarke could not detect any clear seasonal change. Various estimates have been made of a 10–20 fold increase in zooplankton from the winter minimum to the late summer maximum for cold northern waters. Clarke's figure for the fluctuation in coastal waters is much greater. This, however, agrees with the observations of Russell and Colman (1934) who summarized the findings on seasonal fluctuations for several northern, but inshore, seas (Table 14.2). In some of these essentially neritic areas the increase at the summer peak is far beyond Clarke's 40-fold increase. Russell compared these changes with that in a neritic but tropical region—the Great Barrier Reef. The seasonal change from the minimum population occurring in September to the maximum in January amounts to a 4-fold increase (Table 14.2). This is larger than in oceanic tropical

TABLE 14.2 (after Russell and Colman, 1934).

Locality	Average catch for year—total animals	Ratio largest monthly average catch/smallest monthly average catch
Anholt Knob	⎰2737 ⎱2243	⎰10.6 ⎱ 6.9
Smith's Knoll	1131	61.3
Borkumriff	8238	18.1
Varne	618	218.5
Sevenstones	1924	47.2
Great Barrier Reef Lagoon	5684	4.1

areas, but is still far below that of neritic colder seas. Even in inshore tropical waters, therefore, the tendency to spread periods of abundance of different zooplankton species throughout the year markedly reduces the overall seasonal changes (cf. George, Menon). The extraordinary richness of the plankton of inshore colder seas during a short summer period must be viewed, however, against the total crop over the year. Table 14.2, taken from Russell, shows that the Great Barrier Reef Lagoon produces a very rich average crop for the year as compared with many northern waters. Russell also compared the neritic zooplankton off Plymouth with that of the Great Barrier Reef Lagoon. In July and August when the maximum population occurs off Plymouth, the density is at least twice as rich as on the Great Barrier Reef. When, however, it is remembered that very low densities of zooplankton are encountered in the English Channel during the colder months of the year, the annual crop of plankton at Plymouth would not appear to be so rich as the annual crop in the neritic tropical waters. The view is supported by the recent observations of Subrahmanyan (1959) on plankton changes over several years in shallow waters off the west coast of India. In comparison with boreal waters, the standing crop of zooplankton appears to be remarkably high. Some fluctuations in density over the year are seen, with a small peak following shortly after the peak in phytoplankton abundance; but different zooplankton groups become plentiful at different periods, and the overall yearly fluctuation is comparatively small. The *total* plankton, reckoned as dry weight, showed little change throughout the year. Further comparisons of inshore tropical and boreal waters are clearly necessary before the average richness of the crops can be compared. In occanic areas, however, there would appear to be fairly general agreement that higher latitudes show a greater annual crop. Most authorities would correlate this with the generally larger amounts of phytoplankton available at higher latitudes. As against this must be reckoned the higher rate of turnover at low latitudes. Rates of production must not be confused with standing crop. Just as, with the higher temperatures of tropical waters, cycles of primary production by the phytoplankton may be accelerated, so the number of broods of zooplankton may be increased. A rapid production of zooplankton with a low level of crop may be typical of tropical seas. Increased temperature will lead, however, to a higher rate of metabolism in the plankton, increasing the food demands. While comparatively rich zooplankton areas in tropical seas support pelagic fisheries such as tuna (cf. King *et al.*), it would appear to be no accident that the major fisheries and whaling regions of the world are in the seas of higher latitudes.

CHAPTER XV

VERTICAL DISTRIBUTION
AND MIGRATION OF ZOOPLANKTON

IN FAIRLY shallow water near the coasts, although some species of zooplankton such as the copepods *Anomalocera*, *Centropages* and *Acartia* appear to favour the surface, in general both the numbers of species and of individuals tend to increase towards intermediate depths. The younger stages of many plankton animals are often nearer the surface. The vertical distribution of plankton in shallow water, however, changes greatly between day and night through vertical migration, and also is modified by seasonal variations in level (cf. Nicholls, Russell, Bogorov, Marshall).

In oceanic areas planktonic animals are known down to the greatest depths (cf. Marshall, 1954). Deep living planktonic animals have been observed from the bathysphere (cf. Beebe, 1935). The later dives of the bathyscaphe off Toulon and Villefranche have confirmed the presence of zooplankton to depths exceeding 2000 m. Bernard observed siphonophores, medusae, radiolarians and other zooplankton in the deeper layers, but by far the majority were copepods. He estimated the density of this bathypelagic plankton as varying from 0 to more than 100 animals per m^3—more usually $3-10/m^3$. These observations agree with the results of deep tow-net samplings, although, because of the difficulty of carrying out really deep hauls, it is often impossible to state the exact levels of distribution of bathypelagic species. Nevertheless, certain members of the families Challengeridae (e.g. *Pharyngella*) and Tuscaroridae among the radiolarians, the medusae *Atolla*, *Periphylla* (Fig. 15.1) and *Nausithoe*, some pelagic nemertines and ostracods, as well as many species of copepods, euphausids and decapods, are bathypelagic. The very few hauls that have been made in hadal depths (i.e. exceeding 6000—7000 m) by Russian scientists have demonstrated that a planktonic fauna, apparently mainly composed of copepods, amphipods and ostracods, exists even in such excessive depths of the ocean (cf. Wolff, 1960).

The results of hauls from deep water suggest that at really great depths, of the order of 2000 m or more, the density of plankton decreases and the number of species declines (cf. Leavitt, 1935; Bogorov, 1958 b). It must not, however, be assumed that the maximum

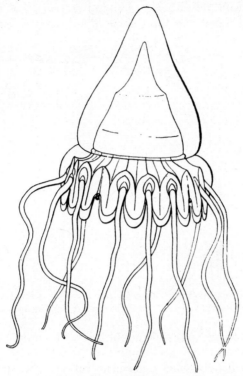

FIG. 15.1 *Periphylla periphylla* (from Mayer, 1910).

is at the surface, and indeed the results of the Challenger Expedition suggested that at depths of a few hundred metres there was probably a greater density of plankton than at the surface. The results of later expeditions have given more definite information on depth distribution of zooplankton and the pattern appears to change in different oceanic areas. Jespersen (1935), for example, showed that marked differences existed in the depth distribution of macroplankton on the two sides of the Isthmus of Panama. In the Pacific (Gulf of Panama) the volumes of plankton were much greater in the deeper layers (500–1500 m) than at the surface, whereas in the Atlantic (Caribbean

Sea) the plankton volumes were greatest near the surface. Observations by Leavitt (1938) in the Sargasso Sea and the temperate western Atlantic suggested that the total volume of zooplankton was greatest in the upper 800 m, though the precise depth varied, presumably with vertical migration and the extent of the euphotic zone. Leavitt found that the volume of zooplankton fell to a mini-

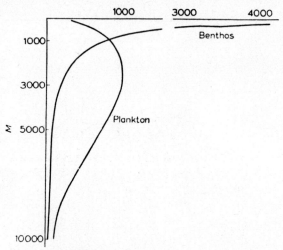

FIG. 15.1.1 The abundance of zooplankton and of benthos with depth in Pacific waters (from Zenkevitch & Birstein, 1956).

mum at a depth of 1200–1800 m but below that level, at some 1500 to 2500 m, somewhat greater quantities of plankton were encountered. There was generally good agreement between the vertical distribution of the total plankton and that of the major groups – decapods, euphausids, copepods, chaetognaths and coelenterates.

Sewell (1948) has summarized our ideas with relation to the vertical distribution of the planktonic copepods. He states that in North Atlantic areas there is a strong suggestion that copepods prefer a level distinctly beneath the surface at a depth which may vary from 200–1000 m. However, the distribution both in number of species and in individuals is by no means constant. For example, Farran's work indicated that the maximum number of species occurred at a depth of approximately 1000–1500 m, although the greatest number of individuals appeared at shallower depths, two maxima being present, one at 100–300 m, and the other at 250–450 m. Other investigations have suggested that there are frequently two maxima in the numbers of species of copepods: one at a depth around 750 m and another at 1000 m or more. Most results agree in indicating that below a depth of 2000 m the numbers of species and of individuals tend to drop off sharply. Zenkevitch and Birstein (1956) summarize results for northern Pacific waters by pointing out that the biomass of zooplankton decreases from the surface downwards. The reduction is marked at a depth of 500–1000 m, and at very great depths exceedingly little plankton is present. The number of species, however, reaches a maximum at intermediate depths, even as deep as 2000–3000 m. This appears to hold for such groups as copepods, chaetognaths, coelenterates, planktonic gammarids, mysids and prawns. In really great depths the number of species is sharply reduced (cf. Fig. 15.1.1).

The results quoted by Sewell himself for the John Murray Expedition in the Indian Ocean show that in density of individuals and in number of species there is a maximum in the surface layer extending to approximately 100 m, and a second maximum at about 600 m or more. Sewell found a marked falling off in numbers below 1500 m depth. In the South Georgia region of the Antarctic, Hardy and Gunther (1936) obtained a steady increase in the number of species from the surface downwards, with a maximum at about 600–700 m (Fig. 15.2). In the Antarctic the surface definitely has fewer species than deeper layers, but it should be remembered that the surface layer in that region is a particularly cold water mass.

Sewell suggests that it is possible to divide the planktonic copepods in many oceanic areas, especially the tropical and sub-tropical seas, into two main groups: those which inhabit the uppermost 100 m where they live in a comparatively warm upper layer, and those which inhabit the colder deeper water with a maximum which varies from one ocean to another, but falls within the range 500 to 1200 m. It must be recognized that there is no sharp boundary between these two groups. It seems clear, however, that the maximum number of deep-sea copepods are found at about 500–1200 m, and Sewell proposes that this may be associated with the minimum oxygen layer which occurs at about the same depth (Fig. 15.3).

In the rather warmer seas of the world it is thus possible to divide the waters roughly into a warm troposphere and a colder stratosphere (Fig. 15.3), and Bruun (1957) has suggested that the most useful boundary between these two regions is that marked by the 10 °C isotherm. The actual depth of the discontinuity layer between these two zones varies greatly according to the area of sea studied. Below the troposphere the animals which inhabit the water layers may be referred to approximately as bathypelagic species, but it is very difficult to determine their precise depth distribution. We know,

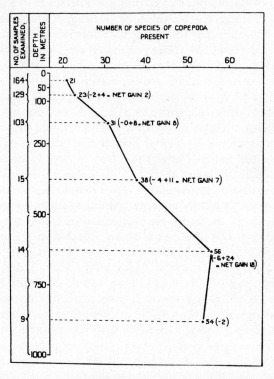

FIG. 15.2 Distribution of species of Copepoda with depth in the Antarctic (from Hardy & Gunther, 1936).

for example, that some calanoids including species of *Bathycalanus* (Fig. 15.3.1), *Bradycalanus*, *Spinocalanus*, *Valdiviella* (Fig. 15.4), *Megacalanus* (Fig. 15.5), *Pseudeuchaeta* and *Gaetanus* (Fig. 15.6, 15.7) are hardly ever taken in the uppermost layers, and may be regarded as true bathypelagic forms; but many others such as *Eucalanus elongatus* and species of *Euchirella* (Fig. 15.8), *Gaidius* (Fig. 15.9) and *Pleuromamma* (Fig. 15.10) while fairly deep living, may appear near the surface at times at least in some oceans. Among the

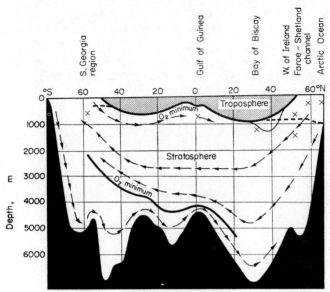

FIG. 15.3 Section of the Atlantic Ocean showing the depth of the oxygen minimum layer and the greatest abundance of species (indicated by X) (from Sewell, 1948).

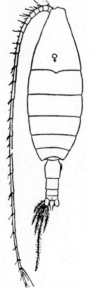

FIG. 15.3.1 *Bathycalanus richardi*(♀) (from Rose, 1933).

arrowworms, *Eukrohnia fowleri, Sagitta macrocephala, S. zetesios* and *S. planctonis* would appear to be bathypelagic species (cf. Fraser, 1952; David, 1958). Some amphipods are deep living, but it is perhaps among the prawn-like crustaceans that some of the most characteristic bathypelagic species are to be found. Mysids such as *Eucopia*,

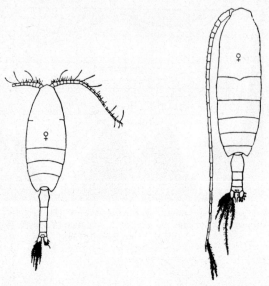

FIG. 15.4 *Valdiviella brevicornis* (♀)   FIG. 15.5 *Megacalanus princeps* (♀)
(from Rose, 1933).   (from Rose, 1933).

FIG. 15.6 *Gaetanus kruppi* (♀) (from Rose, 1933).

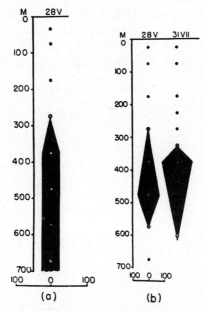

FIG. 15.7 Day depth distribution of (a) *Gaetanus miles* and (b) *G. minor* off Bermuda (from Moore, 1949).

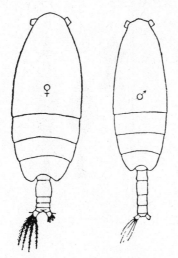

FIG. 15.8 *Euchirella rostrata* (♀ and ♂) (from Rose, 1933).

Gnathophausia (Fig. 15.11, 15.12) and *Nebaliopsis* are typically deep sea genera; so, among the decapods, are species of *Acanthephyra*, *Systellapsis* and *Sergestes*, as well as *Hymenodora glacialis* (Fig. 15.13) and *Parapasiphae sulcatifrons*. Two euphausids, *Nematoscelis megalops* and *Thysanopoda acutifrons* (Fig. 15.14) are recorded as bathy-

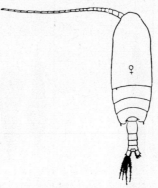

FIG. 15.9 *Gaidius brevispinus* (♀) (from Rose, 1933).

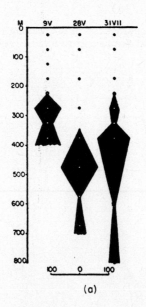

(a)

FIG. 15.10 (a)

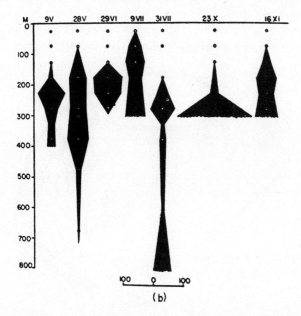

FIG. 15.10 Depth   distribution (day) of *Pleuromamma abdominalis* (a)
and *Pl. gracilis* and *Pl. piseki* (b) off Bermuda
(from Moore, 1949).

pelagic forms by Waterman *et al.* (1939). These workers demonstrated
that many of these prawns were living at a depth of 1000–600 m
during the day. Einarsson's (1945) results indicate that *Thysanopoda*
is a very deep living euphausid. Many other species of euphausids
live at more moderate depths in the oceans (cf. Fig. 15.15, 13.32).

It is easier, in discussing the vertical distribution of animals, to
consider rather shallower water. Bigelow (1926) in his investigations
of the Gulf of Maine pointed out that although the immediate surface
in summer tended to be rather barren as compared with the lower
layers, there was what might be termed a surface community down
to a depth of 20 or 25 m. This was characterized by certain copepods
like *Acartia, Temora, Centropages* and *Anomalocera*; by the medusae,
Aurelia, Cyanea and *Phialidium*; by appendicularians and cladocerans; and by the eggs and larvae of fishes. He also observed that
the juvenile stages of the majority of zooplanktonic forms, including
the eggs and nauplii of copepods, the young stages of hyperiid

amphipods and euphausids, young sagittae, as well as meroplanktonic
larvae such as cirripede nauplii, tended to inhabit the upper layers.
The mid-depths down to approximately 100 m were occupied by the

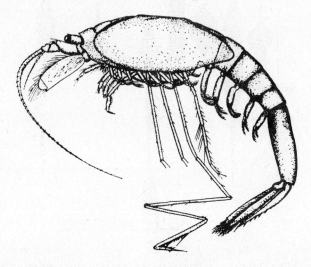

FIG. 15.11 *Eucopia unguiculata* (from Tattersall and Tattersall, 1951).

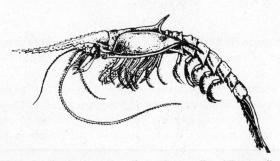

FIG. 15.12 *Gnathophausia gigas* (from Tattersall and Tattersall, 1951).

typical boreal *Calanus* community, dominated by *Calanus finmarchicus*, and including such typical representatives as *Metridia, Sagitta
elegans, Pseudocalanus, Euthemisto, Thysanoessa* and *Limacina*.
There were differences, however, in precise depth distribution; for
example, the calanoids appeared to be somewhat shallower than
Sagitta and *Thysanoessa*. Bigelow states that in the deepest water

layers, below 100 m and stretching down to more than 150 m, there occurred a "Euchaeta community", in which *Euchaeta norvegica* and *Eukrohnia hamata*, usually with *Meganyctiphanes norvegica*, were

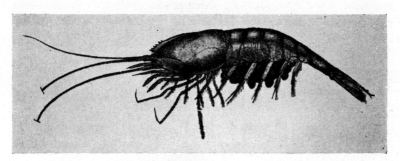

FIG. 15.13 *Hymenodora glacialis* (from Murray and Hjort, 1912).

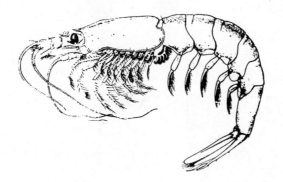

FIG. 15.14 *Thysanopoda acutifrons* (from Einarsson, 1945).

the main species. He points out, however, that the typical *Calanus* community could spread down into the deeper layers, though in reduced numbers, and that there were no clear barriers to distribution between the three main strata. It is of interest that Damas (1905), working in the deeper oceanic regions of the Norwegian Sea, had earlier pointed out that the *Calanus* community occurred in the shallower waters with the younger stages especially in the upper 50 m, whereas a bathypelagic community existed, mainly below the *Calanus* zone, dominated by *Euchaeta* spp. and including *Chiridius* and *Heterorhabdus*.

In discussing the vertical distribution of zooplankton it is impossible not to consider at the same time the migration between day and night which is so characteristic of this drifting population of animals. Even the roughest comparisons between surface tow-nettings taken during the day and at night show that far greater numbers of animals occur in the uppermost layers during the dark

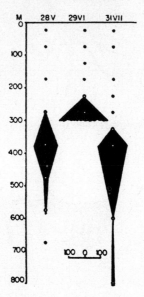

FIG. 15.15 Day depth distribution of *Euphausia brevis* off Bermuda (from Moore, 1949).

hours. The migration of zooplankton from at least 200 m depth towards the surface at night was known from the results of the Challenger Expedition, and since that time the widespread nature of this diurnal vertical migration has been recognized as one of the most striking and characteristic aspects of the behaviour of marine zooplankton. Hardly a single major group of animals represented in the marine zooplankton does not show at least some species displaying diurnal vertical migration. Among the Protozoa, for example, it is known in some dinoflagellates; it has been observed in many medusae, siphonophores (cf. Fig. 15.16) and ctenophores, in sagittae and in pteropods (Fig. 15.17), as well as in fish larvae, salps and appendicularians. But perhaps it has been most extensively studied in the various groups of Crustacea: euphausids, amphipods, copepods, ostracods and decapods, as well as in meroplanktonic larval species.

As early as 1912 Esterly showed that off the Californian coast *Calanus* would migrate from as great a depth as 400 m as its daytime level of concentration to near the surface at night. *Metridia lucens*

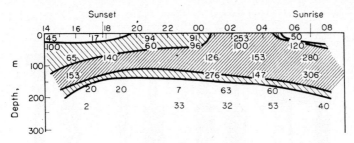

FIG. 15.16 Diurnal vertical migration in *Eudoxoides spiralis* off Bermuda (Numbers represent animals per haul) (from Moore, 1949).

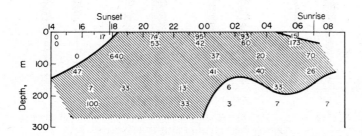

FIG. 15.17 Diurnal vertical migration in *Limacina inflata* off Bermuda (Numbers represent animals per haul) (from Moore, 1949).

migrated similarly from a daytime depth of about 300 m, approaching the surface at night, and other less abundant species of copepod also exhibited migration to the surface with the onset of darkness. Some six species, however, including *Euchirella galeata* and *Gaetanus unicornis*, were deep living during the day, mostly below 400 m, and though there was clear evidence of a rise during the night to depths of less than 200 m, these species were never taken at the surface. The question of how far truly bathypelagic plankton was involved in diurnal migrations was a difficult one, though the work of Murray and Hjort (1912) demonstrated that plankton down to 800 m would migrate towards the surface. Hardy and Gunther (1936) also showed that certain fairly deep-living copepods such as *Metridia* spp., *Scolecithricella minor* and especially *Pleuromamma robusta* in Antarctic waters, might migrate a distance of 400–500 m every day, moving towards the surface during the hours of fading daylight (Fig. 15.18). Later work by Waterman *et al.* (1939) demonstrated a

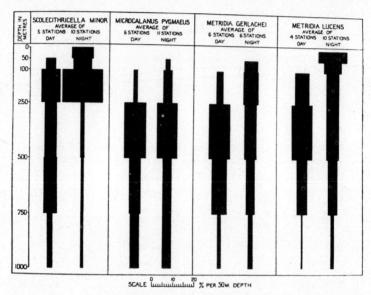

FIG. 15.18 Diurnal vertical migration in four deep-living species of copepod in Antarctic waters (from Hardy and Gunther, 1936).

diurnal vertical migration by various decapods, mysids, euphausids and amphipods living at depths down to at least 1000 m; it appeared that the range of movement for the different species exceeded 200 m and might amount to as much as 600 m (Fig. 15.18.1). The work of Moore also suggests that various planktonic crustaceans including copepods (e.g. *Pleuromamma* spp. Fig. 15.19) and euphausids (e.g. *Euphausia brevis* Fig. 15.20; *E. tenera* and *E. hemigibba*) live by day at considerable depths; they move up towards the surface at night and down again the following day (*vide infra*).

In considering very extensive vertical migrations of this type the speed of swimming is an important problem. Hardy and Gunther considered that in the migration of Antarctic species such as *Euphausia triacantha* and *Euphausia frigida*, which appeared to climb some 200 m

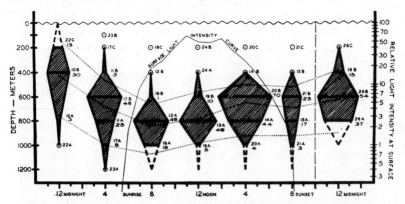

FIG. 15.18.1 Changes in the vertical distribution at different times of the day of adults of the bathypelagic species *Gennadas elegans*. The light intensity curve is an average from measurements on four days (from Waterman, Nunnemacher, Chace and Clarke, 1939).

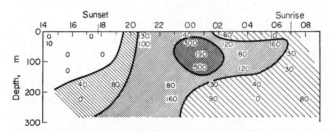

FIG. 15.19 Diurnal vertical migration in *Pleuromamma abdominalis* off Bermuda (Numbers represent animals per haul) (from Moore, 1949).

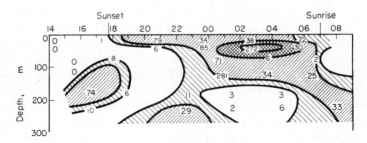

FIG. 15.20 Diurnal vertical migration in *Euphausia brevis* off Bermuda (Numbers represent animals per haul). (from Moore, 1949).

in a matter of a couple of hours or so, possibly some change in density
assisted the movement towards the surface. The difficulties involved
in determining the speed of movement of zooplankton animals under
natural conditions are very considerable. Experiments such as watching
their swimming movements in restricted tubes of seawater are often
vitiated by the fact that the animals behave unnaturally or move
against the side. The work of Hardy and Bainbridge (1954) is perhaps
the most illuminating on this subject. They employed a very ingenious
"plankton wheel" such that the zooplankton swam continuously
as it were in an endless tube. The speed of movement of some zooplankton animals suggested by Hardy and Bainbridge's results are
indeed remarkable: *Calanus* can move upwards at a rate of some
15 m an hour, *Centropages* at nearly double this speed; even the small
copepod *Acartia* manages 9 m in an hour, while the euphausid
Meganyctiphanes norvegica can swim upwards at over 90 m an hour.
These speeds can be maintained for one hour. They have also shown that
for short bursts, the speed, both upwards and downwards can be far
higher. Thus, over a period of two minutes *Calanus* swam downwards
at over 100 m/hr, *Euchaeta* at 135 m/hr, and *Meganyctiphanes* and
the pelagic polychaete *Tomopteris* achieved speeds of more than
200 m/hr. In most of the plankton animals tested the movement
under a strong light stimulus was a steady swimming, although species
like *Acartia clausi* performed rapid zigzag movements. It appears,
therefore, that previously we have underestimated the speed of swimming of plankton animals when they are stimulated to migrate, and
Hardy and Bainbridge believe that the speed achieved by zooplankton
and the duration of swimming are such that the extensive vertical
migrations observed are perfectly possible.

One of the most fascinating problems has been the investigation
of the factors responsible for the diurnal vertical migration. It should
be emphasized here that the factors involved in "triggering off"
this behaviour in individual plankton animals are by no means
necessarily the same as those which are responsible for the preservation
of this migration pattern in the life of species. What might be termed
the survival value of diurnal vertical migration will be discussed
later on. Changes in pH and in oxygen tension of the uppermost
layers where, owing to photosynthesis by the phytoplankton, differences between day and night might be expected, were early put forward as possible factors influencing the diurnal vertical migration,
but in general the magnitude of changes in such factors are so small

that any directional influence on the movement of animals would appear to be well nigh impossible. Temperature and salinity differences have also been quoted, but a marked salinity gradient is difficult to envisage, except under very particular conditions such as estuaries (cf. Chapter III). Light was suggested to be one of the most important factors responsible for vertical migration, even in the earliest investigations. For example, Michael (1911) showed that off California *Sagitta bipunctata* migrated from near the surface during early morning to reach a depth exceeding 50 metres by about noon. He noted that by late afternoon the *Sagitta* were rising, to reach the surface in maximal numbers about 1 hr after sunset. During the hours of darkness the number of *Sagitta* at the surface declined, but a second surface concentration occurred shortly after sunrise. Michael suggested that the light conditions below 40–50 m were optimal for *Sagitta* during the daytime; the vertical movements of the animals were due mainly to the changing light conditions, so that they moved towards the surface at dusk and down again at dawn. It was possible for temperature and perhaps salinity, to modify the vertical migration. Thus the sagittae tended to avoid the surface during twilight and darkness if the surface temperature exceeded about 17.5 °C. Temperature was considered by other workers to be of considerable importance, though a year later Esterly (1912), reviewing the vertical migrations of copepods, pointed out that of sixteen species which were performing marked diurnal vertical migrations, the bulk of the *Calanus* population moved from a zone in the day with a temperature of approximately 9 °C to near surface at night where the temperature was about 17 °C. He therefore believed that temperature was unimportant and quoted light as the most likely controlling factor in vertical migration. Much later Clarke (1933), however, suggested that *Metridia* would not move across the thermocline in the Gulf of Maine in their day and night movements (cf. Fig. 15.13), and Farran (1947) believed that higher surface temperature modified the vertical movement of the same copepod in the seas to the south of Ireland. Nikitin also showed that in the Black Sea *Centropages* did not migrate beyond a certain depth which marked the discontinuity layer. It has, however, become increasingly apparent that light with its regular rhythmical changes between day and night is undoubtedly the most important factor controlling the vertical movement of plankton populations (cf. Cushing, 1951).

Although we have fascinating results from some investigations on the migration of bathypelagic plankton, the main bulk of work has been on shallower water species. The extensive work of Russell, published in a series of papers from 1925–1934, on the vertical distribution and migration of zooplankton off Plymouth is outstanding. Russell gives a daytime distribution for some of the species in the Plymouth plankton which may be approximately summarized in the following manner: *Anomalocera* and larvae of *Corystes*—at the surface; *Calanus*—abundant below 10 m; *Leuckartiara*—a little

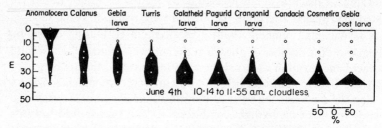

FIG. 15.21 Vertical distribution of ten species of zooplankton on the same day off Plymouth. Depth in metres (after Russell, 1927).

deeper, below 15 m; Galatheid larvae—at about 20 m; *Sagitta*—at 25 m, followed by *Cosmetira*; and deeper still, probably mainly below 40 m, the post-larvae of *Upogebia* (Fig. 15.21). Russell points out that some species were more or less irregularly distributed at all depths; such include *Pleurobrachia*, *Phialidium* and *Obelia*. A strict check on the depth distribution of a particular species of the zooplankton showed that the precise depth varied from day to day, and it appeared that this was correlated with different surface light intensities. For example, many of the species were somewhat higher in the water on cloudy days and particularly during foggy weather, whereas in bright sunshine they tended to be deeper. Russell observed that there was a marked tendency for various species to move upwards towards the surface at night; some species such as *Calanus*, *Sagitta* and *Leuckartiara* would move right to the surface, whereas others, particularly those that lived near the bottom during the day, would move only into the intermediate layers. A study of the night swimming plankton by other workers has suggested that some animals which live essentially in the bottom sand and mud during the day leave the bottom for water immediately above, or even reach the intermediate layers, and swim in the plankton during the night

Colman and Segrove (1955) found that mysids, cumaceans, and some amphipods such as *Nototropis* and *Apherusa* were the most typical animals which entered the night plankton over intertidal areas. Some amphipods common in the sands, such as *Bathyporeia*, appeared only to enter the plankton for a very short time. Most investigators list mysids, cumaceans and amphipods as most typical, but some workers include some isopods (e.g. *Idothea*) as leaving the bottom at night. Bossanyi (1957) found considerable numbers of *Bathyporeia* in shallow waters. He points out that the mixed assemblages of animals which leave the bottom deposit at night, swim close to the bottom and displace the typical planktonic copepods in dominating the bottom plankton during night-time. There is a suggestion that light is the most likely factor which prevents bottom living species from entering the water layers during normal daylight hours. At the same time it is possible that some of the animals are not so completely restricted in their habits. Stubbings (personal communication) has observed on many occasions considerable numbers of the isopod, *Idothea linearis*, swimming near the surface in inshore waters during the day in bright sunlight. This species has also been found on drifting weed.

In a series of investigations on the vertical distribution of zooplankton, Russell (1925–1934) correlated the depth distribution of a species during days of different light conditions with the submarine light intensity, bearing in mind the transparency. He suggested further that the movement of a species to and from the surface was predominantly an effect of light. Following the work of Rose (1925), Russell assumed that the many species of zooplankton exhibiting vertical migration might each be considered to have an optimum light intensity; with this optimum there will also be a range of intensities over which the particular species can live successfully. On this basis Russell (1927) constructed theoretical distribution patterns for different zooplankton species. He demonstrated that since light is absorbed logarithmically in the sea, a species with a relatively large range would have a distribution pattern such as is shown in (a) in the accompanying figure (Fig. 15.22), whereas a species which had a very narrow range would have a theoretical distribution more similar to (b). He then proceeded to show that *Calanus finmarchicus* had a daytime distribution which was very similar to the theoretical pattern (a), and that *Cosmetira pilosella*, which lives deeper at about 30 m off Plymouth, had a daytime distribution which was very similar to (b). Although certain discrepancies can occur, Russell claimed that the daytime distributions and the diurnal vertical migration patterns of many species of zooplankton were best explained on the assumption that each species was concentrated round a light optimum during the day, and that as the optimum light intensity moved towards the surface with the fading light of late afternoon and evening, the animals would follow t.....

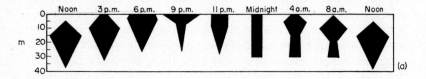

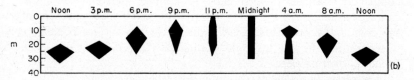

FIG. 15.22 Hypothetical vertical distributions at different times over 24 hours for *Calanus finmarchicus* (a) and *Cosmetira pilosella* (b) off Plymouth; based on observations (from Russell, 1927). Note: The diagrammatic representation for the daytime distribution of *Cosmetira* should be somewhat more kite-shaped, since light intensity decreases logarithmically in the sea (Russell, personal communication).

optima into the upper layers. At night, assuming that moonlight was absent or ineffective, the stimulus for upward migration was removed, and the animals would move more or less at random. Many of Russell's results show a remarkable tendency for the animals to sink somewhat and to be more regularly distributed during the dark hours. At dawn, with the coming of the light stimulus, the animals would take up their distribution patterns again, and as the light increased they followed their optimum intensity moving down to the lower water layers. The diurnal vertical migration might be summed up in fact by saying that the intensity of light varying regularly between day and night caused the vertical movements, since each species followed its optimum.

We shall return later to consider more precisely the factors responsible for diurnal vertical migration, but if we accept for the moment the theory that change in submarine illumination is the most important reason for the vertical movement, we can see some remarkable agreements between the results of field studies made on diurnal migration and the theoretical patterns constructed by Russell. Thus, beginning with a daytime distribution pattern for *Calanus* in the English Channel, Russell (1927) constructed a pattern for its diurnal vertical migrations. Nicholls (1933b) studied these vertical movements for female *Calanus finmarchicus* in the Clyde Sea Area.

The depth of water in the Clyde Area was considerably greater than the English Channel and the copepods were nearly all below 50 m by day, extending down to more than 100 m, instead of some 15–20 m for the Channel. Nevertheless, the pattern of behaviour in the Clyde conformed to an extraordinary degree to Russell's suggestions for the copepods. They rose during the late afternoon and approached the surface itself, though during the hours of darkness there was a marked ꞌtendency for a more even distribution from the surface downwards. From dawn, they followed the increasing light, and had taken up their normal daytime distribution below 50 m by about midday (Fig. 15.23).

Russell (1931) correlated the migrations of *Sagitta* with *calculated* diurnal changes in submarine illumination, but in the work of Clarke (1933, 1934) on the vertical migration of *Metridia* and *Calanus*, the movements of the copepods were correlated with actual measurements of the changing light intensities during the day. The migrations of *Metridia lucens* agreed very well with the changes in submarine illumination over the 24-hour period, excluding of course the dark hours (Fig. 15.23). There was a relatively rapid migration upwards at dusk and a downward movement at dawn. A similar result was also obtained at certain sampling stations for *Calanus finmarchicus* (Fig. 15.24).

While, therefore, several examples can be quoted of marked agreement in the migration of a zooplankton species over a 24-hour period and changing illumination, it has been recognized for a long time that the behaviour of the same species of plankton animal can vary considerably both seasonally and in relation to generation. Moreover, almost every worker on vertical distribution of plankton has observed that frequently the various developmental stages of one species show different distribution patterns. In general, the youngest stages tend to be nearer the surface and, according to Russell's hypothesis, would therefore be living at a higher light optimum. These differences may apply even to meroplanktonic forms; Russell found that the younger larval stages of pagurid and galatheid larvae inhabited a shallower layer

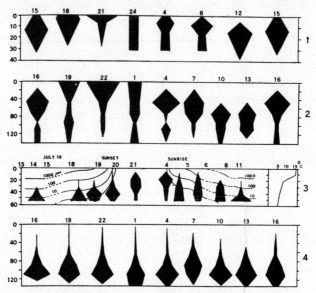

FIG. 15.23 Vertical distribution of plankton animals.
1 = Hypothetical distribution over 24 hours of *Calanus fin-marchicus*. 2 = Vertical distribution of female *Calanus* in the Clyde Area from Nicholls' (1933) observations. 3 = Diurnal vertical migration of female *Metridia lucens* in the Gulf of Maine from Clarke's (1933) observations. Changes in illumination are indicated; also the temperature/depth curve to show the thermocline. 4 = Vertical distribution of St. V *Calanus* in the Clyde Area from Nicholls' (1933) observations
(from Russell, 1935).

than the later post-larvae. Similarly, the distribution of the naupliar and the cyprid stages of the same species of *Balanus* are stated by Pyefinch to occur at different levels. As regards the holoplankton, we have already noted that F. C. Fraser (1936) observed that, whereas the larval stages of *Euphausia superba* lived at about 200 m and performed vertical migrations, the adolescent stages were living nearer the surface and showed no tendency to make diurnal migrations (cf. Fig. 15.25 A, B). The younger stages of some of the bathypelagic

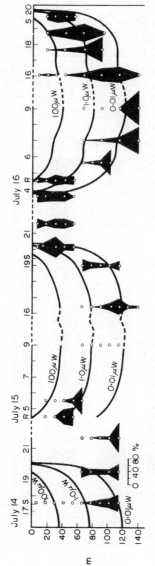

FIG. 15.24 The diurnal migration of female *Calanus finmarchicus* at the deep station in the Gulf of Maine. Changes in submarine illumination, as the intensity of the blue component of daylight in μW/cm^2, are represented. S = sunset; R = sunrise. Broken lines indicate a shortening of the time scale; observations were not discontinued during these periods (from Clarke, 1934).

prawns appear to live at shallower depths than the adults, and Sewell (1948) records the same type of behaviour for deep-living copepods. In earlier work on the depth distribution of chaetognaths the younger stages were noted as living nearer the surface. For *Sagitta elegans*, Farran (1947) observed that the largest individuals were near the bottom by day and moved into the upper 30 m at night, with a tendency to spread down during darkness. Younger *Sagitta* were distributed nearer the surface by day and appeared to move right to the surface at nightfall (Fig. 15.26). It is, however, with the copepods that we have the fullest investigations of the varied migration

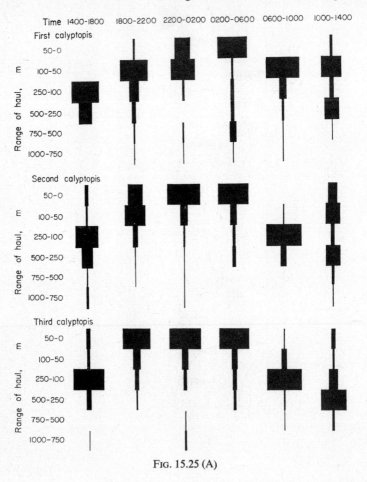

FIG. 15.25 (A)

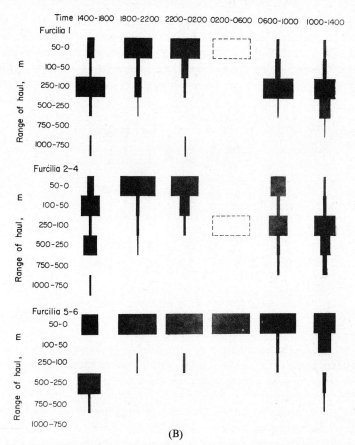

FIG. 15.25 The diurnal vertical migration in *Euphausia superba*: A = ca-
lytopis; B = furcilia stages. Areas enclosed by broken lines
indicate results obtained from inadequate data
(from Fraser, 1936).

patterns for different developmental stages. The work of Nicholls
for *Calanus* in the Clyde Area is again important. The eggs and nauplii
of *Calanus* were nearly always in the upper 30 m and there was little
change in the distribution of the nauplii between day and night.
Copepodite Stages I, II and III were abundant down to 45 m or so,
and they showed a slight tendency to rise towards the uppermost
layers during the hours of darkness. Nicholls suggests that it was
Stage III which showed the main movement. The next stage (Cop. IV)

exhibited a very definite diurnal vertical migration, most of the individuals being very deep (*ca.* 100 m) during the day, and moving right to the surface by nightfall (Fig. 15.27). On the other hand, Stage V copepodites seemed very unresponsive as regards vertical migration. Cop. V was a deep-living stage, occurring mostly from

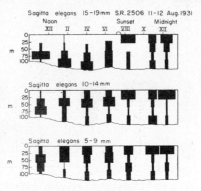

FIG. 15.26 Vertical distribution of *Sagitta elegans* at a station south
of Ireland (50° 40′ N; 9° 05′ W) in August 1931. Three size
groups of *Sagitta* are distinguished (from Farran, 1947).

80–100 m depth, and there was little change between day and night. Nicholls found that male *Calanus*, which were mostly deep-living, were also largely unresponsive as regards vertical migration and contrasted sharply in this respect with females (cf. Fig. 15.27). Farran (1947) also observed marked differences in behaviour of the various copepodite stages of *Calanus*. Females showed the clearest diurnal migration with Stages V and IV being rather unresponsive (Fig. 15.28). Young copepodites were mainly in the upper layers by day. On the other hand, for *Metridia lucens*, Stages I–IV were mainly below 50 m, and females and Stage V, though deep-living by day, moved into intermediate layers at night.

Superimposed on differences in behaviour of the various stages there would also appear to be marked differences between the vertical distribution of generations. Many workers have noted daytime surface swarming of copepods, particularly *Calanus*, including adults and Stage V copepodites. This massing close to the surface seems often of a local and rather temporary nature. Russell has suggested that this behaviour, which is so different from the usual day depth distribution, may be due to physiological differences between generations.

Off Plymouth, he showed that not only was there surface swarming, but that the distribution of adults followed definite changes with the season (Russell 1928, 1934c). In April, for example, the maximum for *Calanus* was at about 10 m depth, but the maximum sank gradually to about 20 m by June. This might be explained as an increase in depth with the gradually increasing penetration of light from spring to mid-summer. But about July, August and September there was

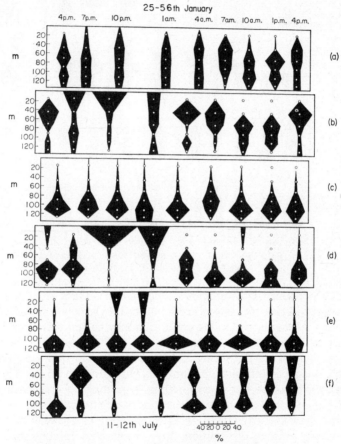

FIG. 15.27 Diurnal vertical migration at different times of the year and for different stages of *Calanus finmarchicus* in the Clyde Area. a = males, January; b = females, January; c = St. V, January; d = females, July; e = St. V, July; f = St. IV, July; (from Marshall and Orr,1955).

a sharp rise towards the surface which clearly cannot be correlated with a light change. The individuals swarming in the late summer were exceptionally small, and Russell believes that this generation produced late in the year, had different physiological requirements including

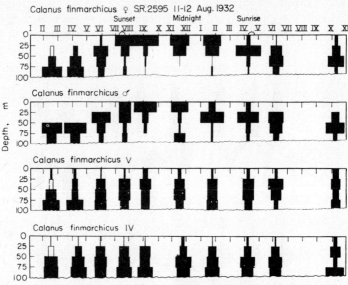

FIG. 15.28 Vertical distribution of *Calanus finmarchicus*, female, male, St. V and St. IV, at a station south of Ireland (51° 10′ N; 8° 00′ W) in August 1932 (from Farran, 1947).

a much higher light optimum. Stage V copepodites also vary considerably in their behaviour according to the particular brood. Thus, Stage V of the overwintering generation may be very unresponsive to light changes and show little or no vertical migration. On the other hand, Stage V of the spring and early summer broods can perform more distinct vertical migrations (cf. Nicholls, Fig. 15.27) The unresponsiveness of the overwintering stage may be associated with the conservation of energy when food is relatively scarce.

Marshall and Orr (1955), in their summary of the vertical migrations and vertical distribution, have emphasized the complexity of the behaviour of *Calanus*. For example, in the Clyde Sea Area, female *Calanus* are deep living by day during late winter and early spring, though marked migrations occur at night. About April/May, however, there is a sudden rise in the water, and surface swarming occurs, after which the later brood tends to descend towards deeper levels. In other words, the times of the year at which the generations approach the surface vary even between the Clyde and Plymouth. In other areas the changes in depth pattern may be different from what have been observed in British waters. In polar waters Bogorov

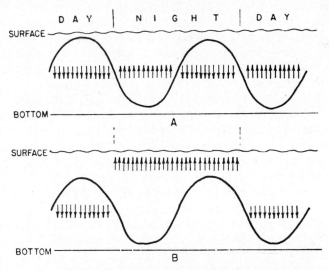

FIG. 15.29 Diagram of patterns of diurnal vertical migration under polar conditions, (A) in summer with 24 hours of daylight, (B) in autumn with alternating days and nights (from Bogorov, 1946).

(1946) has observed *Calanus* swarming at the surface during the summer months of continuous light. Not only *Calanus* but all the dominant zooplankton species appeared to maintain themselves in the uppermost layers and to show no daily vertical movement to deeper water. In autumn, however, with alternating light and darkness, all the major copepods, including *Calanus*, *Pseudocalanus*, *Microcalanus* and *Metridia*, performed pronounced diurnal vertical migrations, even from as deep as 100–200 m to near the surface (Fig. 15.29). Only *Oithona* appeared unaffected. During the continuous darkness of winter the copepods maintained their level constant in deep water.

These results furnish yet another example of different behaviour patterns even in polar waters, for whereas Bogorov claims that *Metridia* spp. and *Microcalanus* were at the surface in summer,

Ussing (1938), working off East Greenland, found that *Metridia longa* (and probably *Microcalanus*) occurred in the upper layers in winter, but in deep water during continuous summer. He agrees that *Metridia* make extensive vertical migrations during late summer/ autumn. Ussing's results would indeed imply that *Calanus* on the one hand, and *Metridia* (and *Microcalanus*) on the other, represent two distinct types of behaviour. Digby (1954), however, suggests that a limited amount of vertical migration occurs with *Calanus* even during winter; both *Metridia* and *Calanus* exhibit migration, but the apparent difference in behaviour pattern arises from the fact that *Metridia* lives at a deeper level over the summer.

One of the most remarkable observations on differences in the vertical movements of a single species was that of Clarke (1934) in the Gulf of Maine. Clarke observed that *Calanus* and *Metridia* migrated from considerable depths of over 120 m towards the surface at night, the migration for *Calanus* including adults, Stage IV and Stage V copepodites. This pronounced movement occurred at a comparatively deep station in the Gulf where the depth of the bottom was of the order of 200 m, whereas at the same time over the shallow Georges Bank, Clarke found that *Calanus* was confined to approximately the upper 30 m and showed very little movement (Fig. 15.30). *Metridia*, however, continued to perform well marked vertical migrations. He attributed the difference in behaviour of *Calanus* to different generations occurring over the Georges Bank area and in the deeper part of the Gulf. With the remarkable circulation of the calanoid population in the Gulf of Maine which Redfield (1941) has investigated, it is quite possible that different broods could occur in the two regions. The variable nature of diurnal vertical migration is also borne out by the observations made by many workers (cf. Farran, Nicholls) that even with one and the same population of zooplankton, individuals belonging to the same species, sex and stage may exhibit different vertical migration patterns. It is likely that differences in physiological state due to such factors as ripening gonads and food, are partly responsible for such variations in behaviour. Marshall and Orr (1960) have recently demonstrated the variability of diurnal vertical migration from year to year. The ripeness of the gonad is certainly a factor in migration, ripe females migrating more actively.

Although changes in the vertical distribution with brood and season are best known for *Calanus finmarchicus*, some data are also available for other smaller copepods. We have already referred to the results of Bogorov and Ussing on *Microcalanus*. Marshall (1949), investigating the depth distribution of the same species in Loch Striven (Clyde Area), found, as Ussing had, that all stages of the calanoid

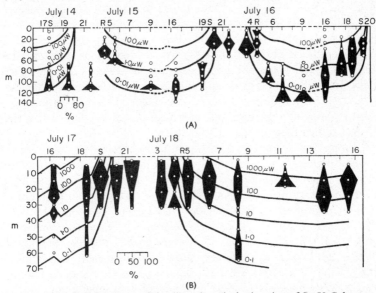

(A)

(B)

FIG. 15.30 A comparison of the diurnal vertical migration of St. V *Calanus* at two stations, (A) deep station, (B) Bank station, in the Gulf of Maine. Changes in intensity of the blue component of daylight are also represented in μW/cm². S = sunset; R = sunrise. Broken lines indicate a shortening of the time scale; observations were not discontinued during these periods (from Clarke, 1934).

were absent from the surface during spring and summer, though it possibly approached the upper layers during winter. The other small copepods in Loch Striven all showed a similar depth distribution —from April till June they were in the upper layers, but they descended to a deeper level during July and August. *Pseudocalanus* and *Acartia* exhibited this change in level most clearly; in *Centropages* and *Temora* the descent was slightly less marked, and in *Oithona* less still. As with *Calanus*, the younger stages of all species tended to be nearer the surface.

It is interesting to find that change in depth distribution somewhat similar to that for copepods is seen for other zooplankton. Russell (1931), for example, investigated the distribution of *Sagitta*. He suggests that for both *Sagitta elegans* and *Sagitta setosa* there is a tendency for the animals in daytime to move somewhat deeper from about April to June, from a depth of some 15–20 m to well below 25 m. This may perhaps again be explained as a reaction to the increasing light intensities from spring to summer. In July/September, however, the sagittae rose considerably, entering intensities which they avoided before, and it may be that this is again a reflection of a difference in physiological state (cf. Fig. 14.11). As for copepods, whatever the generation, the younger sagittae appeared to live considerably nearer the surface than the adults, and they migrated first towards the surface at dusk (cf. Farran, 1947). All stages showed a pronounced diurnal vertical migration, but the older stages left the surface first to descend to their greater daytime depth.

Among the Antarctic zooplankton some species, notably *Calanus acutus, Rhincalanus gigas* and *Eukrohnia* apparently do not perform diurnal vertical migrations, but show a clear seasonal change in depth distribution. Other Antarctic species take part in pronounced diurnal migrations; these include *Pleuromamma robusta, Metridia, Pareuchaeta antarctica, Scolecithricella minor, Euphausia triacantha* (Fig. 15.31) and *E. frigida. Salpa fusiformis* and the amphipod, *Vibilia antarctica*, by contrast, show some evidence of migration, though the vertical movement is slower and occurs later in the day. Again, *Drepanopus pectinatus* migrates very rapidly to the surface at night from a depth of at least 200 m, and another copepod, *Calanus simillimus*, though not showing such extensive migrations, moves from a daytime depth of some 150–100 m right to the surface at night, regularly and rapidly (Fig. 15.32). The amphipod *Parathemisto* also appears to migrate from about 80 or 100 m to the surface, though the migration is somewhat slower (Hardy and Gunther, 1936). There appear to be all grades of migration in the Antarctic, similar to those observed in other areas, but during the long period of darkness over the Antarctic winter we do not know how the behavioural patterns are modified.

It is necessary now to consider more precisely the mechanisms which may be responsible for diurnal vertical migration. Although it is generally conceded that light is probably the most important factor, the precise way in which the light exerts its effect and how far other factors may be concerned, has not yet been decided. One of the earlier suggestions was that of Loeb, who postulated that for nauplii of *Balanus* there was a movement towards light of low intensities, but a reversal of phototactic sign with increasing light intensity occurred, so that the nauplii moved away from intense light. He thus explained vertical migration as a phototaxis with a reversal of phototactic sign. Later Loeb considered that geotaxis might be important,

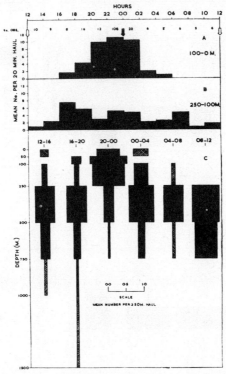

FIG. 15.31 Vertical distribution of adolescent and adult *Euphausia triacantha* over 24-hour period (Cross hatching denotes means based on single specimen only.) (from Baker, 1959).

the animals being negatively geotactic in weak light or in darkness so that they would tend to move surfacewards at dusk and at night. Parker (1902), working on *Labidocera*, also considered that geotactic reactions were important. He held that the female copepods were negatively geotactic and also positively phototactic in weak light, but light of high intensity produced a strong negative phototaxis which over-rode all other behaviour patterns. Parker found a marked difference between the behaviour of the two sexes. The males appeared to be more or less unresponsive to light changes, but followed the females in their migrations, and he suggested that a chemotaxis might be involved. Many workers in considering the sinking rates

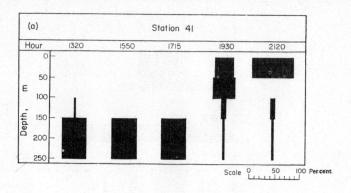

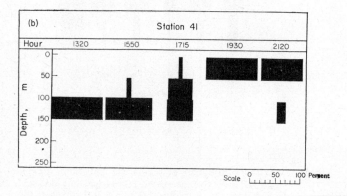

FIG. 15.32 Diurnal vertical migration of two copepods in Antarctic seas (a) *Drepanopus pectinatus* (b) *Calanus simillimus* (from Hardy and Gunther, 1936).

of planktonic animals have suggested that these may play a part in the migratory movements. Ostwald and also Eyden (1923) maintained that, following temperature changes between day and night, a change in the viscosity of the water might take place, and this could be responsible for the animals sinking further in the day. It is almost certain from our knowledge of the very slight depth of diurnal temperature change in the sea that viscosity changes would be too slight. Eyden attempted to explain vertical movements in the freshwater cladoceran, *Daphnia pulex*, partly on the assumption that the animals fed on the phytoplankton in the upper layers during the night, and that the excess weight due to feeding caused their density to increase, so that they dropped into deeper levels by day.

In watching plankton swimming vertically in a column of water it is relatively easy to see how the animals sink as soon as the swimming movements cease, and it must be remembered that constant upward swimming is necessary for the animals to maintain themselves at their selected depth. As a development of this observation, Ewald (1912), working on *Balanus* larvae, suggested that the vertical migration could be explained on the grounds that in weak diffuse light the larvae swam steadily upwards, but that in intense light swimming movements were inhibited and the animals sank to a greater depth. Thus, by constantly swimming up and then passively sinking, the animals were maintained roughly at a constant depth during the day, but rose towards the surface in the evening. Ewald believed that such vertical movements might be applied fairly widely to crustacean plankton. This type of behaviour is a particular case of the well known kineses, behavioural patterns in which variations in the intensity of a non-directional stimulus cause variations in speed of movement. Ewald, in fact, observed that small increases in light intensity temporarily increased swimming speed. Many workers, therefore, have attempted to explain the movements of plankton on the grounds that the movements are rapid at low light intensities so that the animals will tend to swim upwards. Ussing (1938), for example, suggests that copepods such as *Calanus* need the constant photokinetic stimulus of low light intensities. Cushing (1951) quotes several cases of a positive kinetic effect of light on zooplankton, though high intensities may cause inhibition as may *rapid* increases in intensity. He also suggests from a later study (Cushing, 1955) on the behaviour of *Temora* and *Pseudocalanus* allowed to aggregate in tubes, that the results are more consistent with photokinesis being an important factor in migration. At the "optimum zone" the copepods apparently move most slowly: above and below this light intensity, movement increases. Although kinetic effects may play a part in vertical migration, as Cushing admits, other reactions are also involved. Even though some of the directed orientated movements observed in laboratory experiments on zooplankton may prove to be artefacts, the movements including even downward swimming observed, for example, by Hardy and Bainbridge, would appear to be natural directed migrations.

To these various behavioural mechanisms some workers, notably Esterly (1917, 1919) have added the possibility of internal rhythms of behaviour which maintain the vertical migration. These could continue to some extent even under constant conditions, such as darkness. Esterly obtained evidence for such rhythms in *Acartia tonsa* and *A. clausi*, and in *Calanus*. However, with *Calanus*, only some individuals appeared to display the rhythmic behaviour. Esterly emphasizes the differences in behavioural patterns exhibited by species of zooplankton and even by individuals of the same species. Thus, in *Acartia tonsa*, surface and deep living specimens were found with differing reactions to light and gravity. Despite such differences, for the majority of zooplankton species investigated, responses to both light and gravity appeared to play a significant part in the daily vertical movements. Schallek (1942, 1943) also believed that geotactic responses were concerned in the migration of *Acartia* but he did not obtain evidence for the continuation of rhythmic responses under constant conditions.

There seems little doubt that true phototactic movements occur in some zooplankton. Rose considered that most zooplankton were negatively phototactic to high daylight intensities which they would encounter near the surface, but they became positively phototactic to lowered intensities deeper down. One might thus think of a plankton animal as being more or less indifferent to light at its optimum intensity. If such an animal wandered upwards, encountering increasing intensities, it would become negatively phototactic, whereas if it descended into the deeper layers, it would become photopositive and would move under the influence of phototaxis towards its normal depth layer. Workers such as Ewald (1912) and Rose (1925) believed that many other factors, particularly temperature, oxygen and pH, might modify the phototaxis, but in the sea the extent of changes in these factors is so slight, apart from temperature, that it is very doubtful whether they would have any effect (cf. Kikuchi, 1930). As regards temperature, there was evidence that high temperatures tend to induce or increase negative phototaxis; low temperatures, on the other hand, cause the animals to become positively phototactic. Rose considered that temperatures exceeding 20 °C were of great importance in causing negative phototaxis. Despite the fact that there are clear cases of vertical migration right through a thermo-cline (cf. Esterly, 1912), there are examples such as Nikitin described where a temperature barrier may apparently affect the vertical distri-bution of plankton. Farran (1947) also suggested that the upward migration of *Metridia* in the sea off the south of Ireland was limited in one year by the higher temperatures prevailing in the upper layers. Hansen (1951), working in the Oslo Fjord during the summer, noted a marked discontinuity layer at about 10 m depth with a fall in tem-perature approaching 10 °C and a considerable rise in salinity. While some copepods (e.g. *Calanus* females, *Centropages hamatus*) were mostly between the discontinuity layer and the surface by day and rose towards the surface at night, others (*Calanus* males, *Temora longicornis*) appeared to remain in or near the discontinuity layer throughout the 24 hr. Yet other species (*Pseudocalanus* females, *Sagitta*, *Meganyctiphanes*) were mainly below the discontinuity layer during daytime, and although they moved upwards to the layer at night, they did not pass beyond it; presumably their upward movement was limited by the relatively high surface temperature. On the other hand, Banse (1957) observed only very weak vertical movements for the copepods, *Temora longicornis* and *Centropages hamatus*, in the stratified shallow waters near Kiel. For these and for other copepods (*Pseudocalanus*, *Oithona*) there was an obvious massing of the populations into narrow depth zones (cf. Chapter XIII), but there was no clear migration in relation to the movement of isolumes; day and night distributions were similar. Banse believes that movements of the water layers were mainly responsible for the changes in distri-bution of the zooplankton.

The laboratory experiments of Harder (e.g. Harder, 1952, 1957), however, suggest that some zooplankton animals such as cladocerans and copepods actively seek discontinuity layers, both thermal and haline, when illuminated from above or when left in darkness. These animals are probably reacting to the density of the medium. Although polychaete larvae, mysids and chaetognaths were found to distribute themselves without reference to discontinuity layers, and forms such as fish eggs and medusae might be massed at a boundary layer entirely passively on account of their body density, Harder claims that several copepod species (*Acartia*, *Pseudocalanus*, *Centropages*, *Temora*) migrate to a discontinuity layer. They could be sufficiently sensitive to react to layers differing by as little as 0.2°/00.

In more offshore waters such salinity gradients are unlikely to occur, but temperature changes may be sufficiently marked to modify diurnal vertical migration. Bogorov (1958c), for example, suggests from results of Vinogradov that in Far Eastern waters the presence of a cold intermediate layer affected diurnal migration. Most of the zooplankton moved vertically only in the superficial layers between depths of about 25–50 m. *Metridia pacifica*, however, was not limited by the cold sub-surface stratum, and migrated through the layer to reach a day depth of some 500 m. It may be as Moore (1950, 1952) and Moore and Corwin (1956) have suggested, that while many zooplankton species appear to be little affected by temperature, for some forms both temperature and light may be important. This is perhaps borne out by the earlier results of Clarke (1934) on the migrations of two copepods in the Gulf of Maine. *Calanus* migrated from deep water right to the surface and in doing so crossed a marked thermocline, whereas *Metridia*, though showing a pronounced vertical migration, did not seem to rise higher than the discontinuity layer (cf. Fig. 15.23).

Moore has discussed the diurnal vertical movements of the deep scattering layers of the oceans. He suggested that the shallower scattering layer was probably associated with shoals of euphausids, whereas the deepest layer which might be at a depth of the order of 1000 m was more likely to be due to deep-living prawns. Both layers, however, showed extensive vertical movements and Moore points out that in sub-tropical oceanic areas a movement from a depth of over 700 m to near the surface might involve a temperature change of 10 or even 15 °C. Downward movement in the day in response mainly to illumination changes might therefore be stopped by the occurrence of too cold a layer of water, and Moore quotes some examples (*Nematoscelis megalops* and *Euphausia kronii*), where it would appear that a lower temperature limit did in fact restrict the downward migration during the day hours. In a somewhat comparable way, it is possible that species which approach the surface from really deep water, where the light intensity is very greatly reduced, may be stopped partly by the higher temperature of the upper layers, but to a considerable extent also by bright moonlight which may be sufficiently intense to limit the upward migration of such particularly light sensitive species. In general, the work of Moore brings out two factors, temperature and illumination, which together determine the vertical distribution of the plankton; shallower living species are perhaps more sensitive to light changes and deeper ones to temperature changes.

Although Moore obtained fairly good agreement between movements of isotherms and movements of lines of equal illumination on the one hand, and the changes in the depth distribution of many of the zooplankton species on the other, he encountered many discrepancies which he believes may be explained on the grounds of a third factor, which varies directly with depth. This third factor may perhaps be equated to pressure. The three factors, temperature, light and pressure, therefore, determine the distribution of the overall zooplankton population and of the individual species. For each species, and indeed probably for the different members of one species, there is a value for each of the three factors where the animal is not stimulated to perform any movement. As the three environmental factors change from this "nul" value, so the animal is stimulated to move and its distribution is a resultant of the operation of the three factors. Hardy and Bainbridge, and also Knight-Jones and Qasim (1955), have considered pressure as a factor of importance in the movements of certain plankton animals. Decapod larvae, particularly, seem to be affected by pressure changes.

Although, undoubtedly, factors such as temperature changes and perhaps pressure, as well as other modifying influences may play a part in the diurnal vertical movements of plankton animals, it is conceded by all workers that light is the dominant factor (cf. Cushing, 1951; Kikuchi, 1930). The precise way in which the light stimulus acts on the animals is, however, very difficult to ascertain. We have already seen that photokinetic effects may play some part, but orientated phototactic movements appear to be true of many zooplankton species. One of the simplest explanations of animals aggregating in an optimum zone is the reversal of phototactic sign with change of light intensity (*vide supra*). But such a reversal of phototactic sign, though it has been shown for *Balanus* nauplii, is by no means easy to demonstrate for the majority of plankton animals. Spooner (1933) observed that various species of the zooplankton moved in the direction of the light rays either positively or negatively, but this was true irrespective of any accompanying changes in intensity. Clarke considered that it was the rate of change of light intensity rather than the absolute magnitude of illumination which was the factor in inducing migration. Any reduction in intensity tended to render the animals photopositive. In this connection

Johnson (1938) found that *Acartia clausi* was normally negatively phototactic, and that under constant light intensity or during increasing light intensity the negativity was maintained; with a reduction in light intensity the animal became temporarily photopositive. This, however, contrasted with later results, obtained by Johnson and Raymont (1939) on *Centropages*, where no migration of *Centropages* away from a light source could be produced either with increasing the light or with constant but relatively high light intensities. Many workers (Esterly, Clarke) have suggested that the real response is geotactic; that the changing light intensities effect geotactic

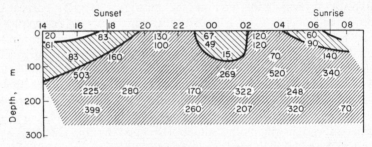

FIG. 15.33 Diurnal vertical migration in *Sagitta bipunctata* off Bermuda. Note the "midnight scattering" (Numbers represent animals per haul) (from Moore, 1949).

responses of the animals rather than causing phototactic reactions. Negatively geotactic movements are induced by fading light intensities, whereas strong illumination or increasing light causes a positively geotactic movement, so inducing downward migration.

A negative geotaxis in darkness would, of course, be a useful mechanism for retaining zooplankton in the uppermost layers during the night. Many investigators have obtained results on diurnal vertical migrations which apparently show a departure of the zooplankton from the surface during darkness (cf. Fig. 15.33). This "midnight sinking", as it has been termed, has been explained by Russell as due to the random wanderings of the animals in the absence of any light stimulus. Cushing also believes that midnight sinking is common; on a photokinesis theory, movement is negligible and the animals may sink. Where sinking occurs and the plankton appears to become more or less evenly distributed during the night, a rise towards the surface may follow at, or just before, dawn. This "dawn rise" has been regarded as a light reaction by the animals to the very low dawn light intensity — "the plankton takes up its optimum". Many examples from plankton investigations seem to show midnight sinking and dawn rise (cf. Kikuchi, 1930). To some extent a fall in level at night may be due to an active downward migration. If animals migrate to the surface from great depths where the light intensity is extra-ordinarily low, the intensity at the surface in bright moonlight may be too high and they may go deeper over the time of most intense moonlight. At the same time, some species appear to remain truly aggregated at the surface during the dark, and there is no tendency to spread downwards. It is difficult to envisage any stimulus, other than a negative geotaxis, which is responsible for such a sharp distribution. With the coming of light, of course, the geotaxis is reversed or over-riden by a negative reaction to light.

Numerous workers have attempted to elucidate the behaviour of zooplankton by means of laboratory experiment. One of the troubles is that the results of such experiments are always complicated (some-times almost vitiated) by the difficulty of maintaining zooplankton animals in good physiological condition in the laboratory. As well as the intrinsic factors of age and brood, which appear to cause marked variations in behaviour, animals brought into the laboratory probably do not show their normal reactions. A zooplankton species may show its main centre of vertical distribution at a certain depth but with a number of individuals scattered at other levels; thus the depth at which the animals are captured for experiment may modify the results. Another complicating factor is that zooplankton species probably exhibit adaptation to light intensity. Field experiments by Russell indicated that older specimens of *Sagitta* were more sensitive to light in the early morning after a prolonged period of darkness; during the day they became adapted to higher light intensities. *Calanus* also appeared to show increasing adaptation throughout the hours of daylight. In laboratory experiments, therefore, the state of adaptation must be considered (cf. Clarke, 1930; Johnson, 1938). Often too the light intensities employed in the laboratory are excessively high and out-side the animals' normal range; frequently plankton animals are harmed by crowding in experimental vessels. Thus the results of laboratory investigations must be accepted with caution. The in-genious experiments of Hardy and Paton (1947) in which cope-pods were allowed to swim in closing chambers operated in the sea, and the further experiments by Hardy and Bainbridge (1954) with the continuous wheel, point the way to new types of experiments which may be more properly related to natural conditions. As an example of the differences seen in behaviour in the laboratory and in the field, Schallek (1942, 1943) stated that *Acartia tonsa* in diffuse light exhibited movement towards the surface at sunset or in darkness, probably as the result of a geotactic response; with diffuse illumination of higher intensity they ceased swimming and tended to descend. However, in the laboratory, with highly directional light, *Acartia* was very strongly positively phototactic and swam constantly towards a light source. One of the many problems involved in experiments is to maintain the zooplankton feeding under more or less natural conditions. It seems very likely that the reactions of zooplankton to environmental factors such as light will be strongly conditioned by the amount and perhaps even by the type of food which they have taken.

It is extremely improbable that any one complete explanation of the diurnal vertical migration of plankton can be given which would be true for all the many species and the numerous classes of animals which are involved. Light would appear to be the most important factor for the vast majority of species, though this may act through a geotactic mechanism. The attempt by Moore to include light, temperature and a pressure factor is also significant, particularly if one accepts his idea that the relative importance of the three factors varies from species to species and even from individual to individual. But it is almost certain that the precise triggering mechanism which sets off diurnal vertical migration will differ from one species to another; will perhaps change even among populations of the same species occurring in different areas, and probably varies with the generation, stage of development and state of maturity.

Most of the work on diurnal vertical migration has concerned the more shallow living zooplankton but our reference to the investigations of Waterman *et al.* and of Moore indicates that there is considerable evidence for vertical migrations among deeper living plankton. The more recent work has particularly been concerned with movements of the deep scattering layers of the oceans, and evidence has accumulated for the view that at least some of the deep scattering layers are made up largely of planktonic animals, especially larger crustaceans such as euphausids. If we include light, temperature and possibly pressure as factors affecting diurnal migration, we must now consider how far light intensities can change in deep ocean water. In an earlier chapter we showed that, even in the clearest tropical waters, light is ineffective for photosynthetic activity below a maximum depth of about 150 m. But light can penetrate much further into the sea and may, therefore, be of great importance in relation to vision and to the photic reactions of animals generally, quite apart from photosynthesis.

Some earlier observations using photographic plates suggested that an appreciable quantity of light was present at depths exceeding 500 m. For instance, Murray and Hjort showed that photographic plates would show some degree of blackening even at depths of 1000 m in oceanic waters, though they failed to detect any effect on plates exposed at depths of 1700 m. Observations from diving bells also showed that very small amounts of light could be detected at several hundred metres depth. Beebe (1935) found that complete darkness to the human eye was reached in Bermuda waters at a depth between 500 and 600 m. How far light produced by luminescence from marine animals could affect the general distribution and amount of light in the depths of the ocean was largely unknown. Jerlov and Koczy (1951) obtained some measurements of light penetration into water down to about 300 m which suggested that the extinction coefficient in the deeper layers was fairly constant. They confirmed the view that appreciable amounts of light must still be present at depths of several hundred metres.

Recent observations by Clarke and Wertheim (1956) and Clarke and Backus (1956) have given us more information on the penetration of light into deeper waters and on the role of luminescent light. These observations were made possible by the development by Clarke and his collaborators of an ingenious bathyphotometer which combines a depth meter with a photomultiplier capable of detecting illumination at an intensity of about 10^{-12} that of full sunlight. With this apparatus, it was possible to measure light penetration in ocean water to depths of about 600 m. The results so far available suggest that the deeper ocean water between depths of 100 and 600 m has a relatively uniform and fairly high transparency (cf. Fig. 15.34). Some idea of the relatively great attenuation of light in the depths may be gained from Fig. 15.34 which indicates that at depths of about 600 m the light was of the order of 10^{-11} that of the surface intensity during the day, whereas at night at the surface the light was about 10^{-7} that of the incident day intensity.

Clarke and his co-workers found that below a depth of about 200 to 300 m the amount of light registered by the bathyphotometer was subject to relatively sharp fluctuations. These are believed to have been due to flashes of luminescent light emitted by marine animals. At greater depths the amount of bioluminescent light appears to have been greater than that due to the penetration of daylight. Further observations showed that this background of light in deep water could be resolved to some extent into individual flashes of relatively high intensity. Figure 15.35 taken from the paper by Clarke and Backus (1956) shows that these flashes may be obtained in relatively shallow water, but also at greater depths, down to at least 400 m.

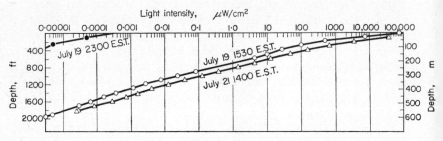

FIG. 15.34 The relation between depth and light intensity (Log scale) at stations 200 miles S.E. of New York (from Clarke and Wertheim, 1956).

The record, obtained during daylight hours, shows a maximum at about 70 m depth in the euphotic zone, and the intensity of the flashes at shallow depths is actually much higher than at deeper levels owing to the fact that these light intensities must be reckoned against the ordinary illumination due to daylight. There is a clear smaller maximum at a depth approaching 300 m and this is presumably due to organisms of the deep scattering layer which occurred about this depth during the daytime. Earlier observations from diving work suggested that bioluminescence could occur at all depths, but the work of Clarke and his collaborators indicates that variations in intensity of bioluminescence may occur with depth and with different types of water. Later work by Clarke and Hubbard (1959) has revealed that, apart from a relatively shallow zone exhibiting maximal bioluminescent flashing, another maximum zone occurred at a depth of about 900 m. This is of especial interest as this depth approximates to a zone of maximum zooplankton abundance found by Leavitt in the same oceanic area. Clarke and Hubbard found that flashing tended to diminish in greater depths, but they were able to obtain records of bioluminescent flashes even down to depths of 3750 m. Working in shallower waters off San Diego, Kampa and Boden (1956) were able to demonstrate that the frequency of bioluminescent flashing varied apparently with the diurnal vertical migration of the deep scattering layer. The euphausid, *Euphausia*

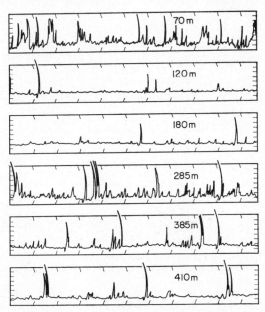

FIG. 15.35 Sections of a record showing luminescent flashes at the indicated depths at 1945–2130 EST, 8 Sept. 1955; Position: 39° 23′ N; 70° 16′ W (from Clarke and Backus, 1956).

pacifica, may be one of the more important species associated with the flashing.

The migrations of deeper living plankton in relation to light intensity have also been examined by Clarke *et al.* (1956). Fig. 15.36 shows lines of equal light intensity ("isolumes") calculated from the surface light using the extinction coefficients which were found for the water column. Observations were made on the movement of these isolumes with the changing incident daylight over a considerable portion of the day, and at the same time the pattern of the vertical migration of a deep scattering layer was also determined. The animals forming the deep scattering layer appeared to move with the changing light intensities during the day but resolved themselves into two different populations. During the afternoon these populations appeared to move upwards faster than the changing light intensities and in fact reached illuminations in one case more than a hundred times brighter than what they had experienced previously at mid-day.

These observations then would suggest that while changing light intensities are of significance in migration, an optimum zone of

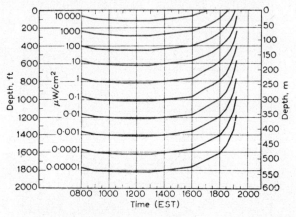

FIG. 15.36 Isolumes for 21 July calculated from surface light using the extinction coefficient measured for the water column at stations about 200 miles S.E. of New York
(from Clarke and Backus, 1956).

light intensity is not the only factor determining the vertical movement of deep water animals of the scattering layer. Either the animals must adapt during the day to considerably different light intensities, or the rate of change of light intensity may trigger off other behavioural patterns which cause the animals to move into higher light intensities during the latter part of the day. Further work is clearly necessary, but these observations are significant in attempting correlations between movements of deep living pelagic animal populations and changing physical factors such as light intensities. It is also worth noting that this and other work on the deep scattering layer suggests that the animals may move vertically at a rate of the order of 5 m per minute. This is considerably higher than the rates which have been recorded for copepods and other planktonic animals (*vide supra*), and Clarke therefore suggests that the movements of such deep scattering animals are probably those of strong swimmers — fishes or large crustaceans such as euphausids and acanthephyrids.

Although an explanation of the precise mechanisms controlling diurnal vertical migration may still be wanting, we must now examine the problem of whether the migration is of value to the species and to the individual. It must be remembered that a very considerable output of energy is necessary, especially in those animals we have just been considering which may perform very extensive migrations of several hundred metres every day. We have already seen the relatively high climbing speeds recorded by Hardy and Bainbridge, and the even greater rates amounting to some hundreds of metres per hour seen during short bursts of swimming. Moore (1950) has claimed a rate of some 2 m/min for the copepod *Pleuromamma abdominalis* which performs extensive vertical migrations, and Clarke's rates for larger zooplankton are even higher. Since the energy expenditure in these relatively rapid daily movements must be very great, one is tempted to think of the migration as of considerable survival value. Harris (1953), however, believes that diurnal vertical migration may be no more than a concomitant of a behavioural pattern by which a plankton species navigates at a particular depth. As a result of work on the freshwater cladoceran *Daphnia*, Harris suggests that in weak light the animals move upwards owing to a negative geotaxis, but at higher light intensities a dorsal light reflex is invoked. The animals swim along a horizontal path maintaining a more or less constant level by keeping a particular portion of the eye constantly illuminated. Light and gravity are the stimuli involved in an orientating depth mechanism; the diurnal vertical migration is an incidental and inevitable pattern of behaviour forced on the animals, as it were, by the regularly changing light intensities over the 24-hour period.

On the other hand, earlier suggestions stressed the value of diurnal vertical migration. Zooplankton animals are well known to be adversely affected by high light intensities, and presumably they are unable normally to remain near the surface during daylight hours. But a movement towards the surface to the zone most thickly populated by the phytoplankton would be of survival value in that the animals could feed extensively in the uppermost layers during the night. They would have to move away during the day owing to the inimical influence of light. Whether factors other than light in the uppermost layers could play a part is uncertain. Hardy suggested from work in the Antarctic and in the North Sea that very dense patches of phytoplankton are unfavourable to zooplankton so that the animals cannot stay in the vicinity of such very rich phytoplankton for long. Perhaps active photosynthesis causes the production of harmful metabolites, though Bainbridge's results, as far as they go, hardly support this. More recently, Hardy (1956) has advanced a more general theory for the value of the diurnal vertical migration. He points out that in almost all seas the uppermost layers are moving at higher speeds, and often even in different directions, from the lower layers. The regular movement of plankton between the layers therefore allows the animals to be carried over greater distances when moving at night in the uppermost layers than during the day. The plankton population can be distributed over a much greater area of the ocean than if it continually moved with one body of water. By fortuitously drifting with water masses moving at different speeds, the zooplankton is able, as it were, to sample a much wider area of ocean. We have observed that among the same species at particular times of the year certain individuals or stages show little or no diurnal vertical migration. In some cases it is possible to suggest conservation of energy in overwintering stages, but this explanation cannot always hold. David (1961) has suggested that marine planktonic species may tend to become divided into relatively small, separate populations if they drift continually in one stratum, since they would not normally encounter any directional stimuli to horizontal migration. If such a hypothesis is true, a main function of diurnal vertical migration is to encourage interchange of zooplankton populations. Species migrating at slightly different times to various depths would be mixed by the varied current speeds of the different water layers. This would promote gene flow throughout the populations. At this stage no conclusive answer can be given to the question as to the value of diurnal vertical migration, but the tremendously wide occurrence of this phenomenon in the seas is one of the most challenging aspects of marine plankton study.

CHAPTER XVI

BACTERIA OF THE SEA
AND REGENERATION PROCESSES

THE FEEDING of zooplankton on phytoplankton results in a large production of faecal pellets which break up in the sea and contribute
to detritus. More important as a source of detritus, both phytoplankton and zooplankton die and the decomposition of the bodies
of these plants and animals contributes to particulate matter in the
seawater. Feeding by fishes and such large animals as whales and
seals also produces faecal detrital matter, but, even more important,
the death of these larger animals will yield particulate matter as their
bodies decompose. Most of the particulate matter from the bodies
of the larger nektonic animals and from the bodies of the array of
bottom living invertebrates comprising the benthos will accumulate
on the sea floor. But a considerable amount of particulate material
must be generally distributed in seawater, and although, as Bruun
(1957) has suggested, over great depths this rain of particles, mainly
derived from the plankton, will be rapidly consumed by the animals
below, there must be a considerable amount of detritus which can
always be detected in seawater especially nearer coasts. In the vicinity
of coasts, drainage from the land contributes a large portion of
detrital material which is both organic and inorganic in nature.
Organic material of terrestrial origin can no doubt play a considerable
part in the nutrition of bottom feeders, especially shallower water
species. But we shall largely confine our attention to the detritus
which comes from the marine environment.

The formation of detritus by the gradual breaking up of the
bodies of plants and animals is of course dependent on bacterial
decomposition. This brings to our attention the bacteria of the sea.
Zobell (1946) in particular has investigated the density and types
of bacteria present in seawater. The population density of bacteria does increase in inshore waters but even so the bacteria occurring
in the sea are particularly adapted to life in the marine environment.

The majority of freshwater bacteria survive for only a very limited period in seawater, and, fortunately, pathogenic bacteria and the great numbers of coliform bacteria which are discharged in sewage die fairly soon after entering the sea. Ketchum *et al.* (1949, 1952) have investigated the death of coliform bacteria in seawater. They point out that whereas in estuaries and harbours, densities of many thousands of bacteria per c.c., including coliform types, can occur, coliform bacteria are never found in unpolluted open sea conditions. When natural seawater was stored, the usual large increase in the population of marine bacteria followed. When, however, such cultures were inoculated with *Escherichia coli*, the numbers of these coliform bacteria were very rapidly reduced, indicating a marked bactericidal action of the seawater. This bactericidal effect was greatly impaired by autoclaving the seawater. Further studies suggested that dilution and possible predation were together responsible for only a small part of the reduction in numbers of coliform bacteria during their passage down an estuary. Natural seawater appeared to possess substances, possibly produced by its own flora, which tend to kill off foreign bacteria entering the sea from freshwater sources. The investigations of Guelin (1954) would also suggest that coliform bacteria, which may survive for a short period in estuarine inshore polluted waters, do not become acclimatized to living in the intestines of marine fishes. Guelin was able to infect the marine teleost, *Ctenolabrus rupestris*, with *Escherichia coli*, but the intestines of these fishes were completely cleared of the bacteria in one week. Fish occurring naturally even in inshore and somewhat polluted waters also showed no trace of *E. coli* in the gut.

If we now consider truly marine bacteria, species are known which bring about the decomposition of animal and plant matter including cellulose and such resistant materials as chitin and lignin. It therefore appears inevitable that following the production of detritus in the sea from the bodies of plants and animals, there will be a further breakdown which will lead ultimately to the production of dissolved organic matter present in the seawater. Part of this dissolved matter arises from the excretory products of animals, but by far the vast majority are relatively stable compounds arising from the decomposition of animals and plants.

The quantity of such dissolved organic matter present in the sea varies considerably from one place to another. In particular, it tends to be low in deep sea areas and is high in shallow water near the coasts.

However, for open-sea areas Krogh (1934), from a single series of observations in the oceanic waters off Bermuda, suggested that the concentration of dissolved organic matter amounted to some 2.4 g carbon/m^3. Moreover, samples at approximately every 1000 m from the surface to 4750 m seemed to show the same concentration at all depths. Krogh pointed out that such a quantity would correspond to a little more than 5 g of organic matter per m^3, and that this represented an extraordinarily low concentration (5 p.p.m.) of organic matter. As a result of later work by Keys, Christensen and Krogh (1935) it was believed that, broadly speaking, the sea generally contained dissolved organic matter of the order of 1.2–2 g of carbon/m^3; this would correspond to some 2 or 3 g of dissolved organic matter/m^3. Krogh suggested that this amount did not vary very greatly either temporally or with depth. It is likely, however, that the quantity of dissolved organic matter is somewhat more variable than Krogh's results indicated. Plunkett and Rakestraw (1955) found a variation with depth off California; the concentration of dissolved organic carbon varied between 2.8 and 1.4 g C/m^3 with the intermediate depths showing the smallest quantities. In the northwest Pacific, working to even greater depths, they again showed variations with depth; the intermediate layers tended to have the least concentrations, but the general level of organic carbon was lower, with an extreme minimal value of 0.6 g C/m^3. Richards (1957a) quotes Datyko as finding from 2.0–2.6 g C/m^3 as dissolved organic matter in the waters off Greenland and in the White Sea.

Whatever the precise level of concentration, it is clear that the quantity of dissolved organic matter in seawater is very low, amounting to only a few parts per million. Even so, it is a vastly greater quantity of organic matter than the particulate organic fraction (plankton and detritus). Thus a very conservative estimate by Krogh suggested that the dry weight of living organic matter was only 1/300 of the dissolved organic matter. Putter (1909, 1925) believed that very much larger quantities of dissolved organic matter were present in seawater, and he held that much of it was leached out from phytoplankton during their active metabolism. It is almost certain that Putter was incorrect in the quantities which he suggested. But, more important, he claimed that the dissolved organic matter was a major constituent of the diet of marine animals. This idea has been challenged by many workers, the most notable review being that of Krogh (1931), from which it would appear that metazoan

:narine animals do not use dissolved organic matter to any signi-ficant degree. Indeed, from the work of Fuller and Clarke (1936), it appears unlikely that animals such as copepods can make very much use of even particulate matter of the dimensions of bacteria, a point which Ussing (1938) has also emphasized. It should be mentioned, however, that marine organisms such as bacteria, fungi and probably many Protozoa, can make extensive use of dissolved organic matter, and that especially at the surface of the deep sea oozes, this supply of nutriment may represent one of the main sources of nutrition.

There is also evidence that perhaps some photosynthetic organisms may make use of dissolved organic matter in the absence of light energy, and some recent studies have suggested that some metazoan marine animals can utilize amino-acids in solution. Although it is unlikely that dissolved organic substances contribute much as food for plankton, Putter's suggestions should not be entirely forgotten. As Bruun (1957) has recently emphasized, the extraordinarily small amount of detrital material which can arrive at the bottom of the great oceans makes it all the more probable that one of the main food chains in oceanic depths begins with the utilization of dissolved organic matter by bacteria and other micro-organisms. These in their turn may form the food of the very small benthic animals (meio-benthos, cf. Chapter XVIII), though they probably are also consumed by larger mud-feeding benthic species.

The border line between dissolved organic matter and the most minute particulate organic detritus is by no means easy to draw. The work of Fox and his collaborators (cf. Fox *et al.*, 1952; Gold-berg *et al.*, 1952; Fox, 1957) has brought into prominence the oc-currence of leptopel which consists of the finest particulate organic and inorganic material (cf. Chapter III). Fox suggests that the con-centration of the organic leptopel, which contains protein, lipid and polysaccharide fractions, can vary greatly, especially in neritic waters. Above all, the material can be adsorbed on fine silt, muds and oozes so that the actual concentration on these particles may be many, many times higher than that suspended in the seawater. Fox believes that this organic leptopel may make a very significant contribution to the feeding of certain animals, particularly bottom feeders in fairly shallow waters.

Although it is difficult to determine the precise limits between dissolved organic matter and suspended particulate matter, especially owing to the presence of colloidal micellae, it is important to compare the two fractions in seawater. We have already referred to the suggestion by Krogh that although only a few parts per million of dissolved organic matter occur in the seas, the amount is usually far greater than the particulate organic matter. Later investigations have generally confirmed this idea. Von Brand, for example, points out that usually 100–200 mg of nitrogen/m³ are present in seawater as dissolved

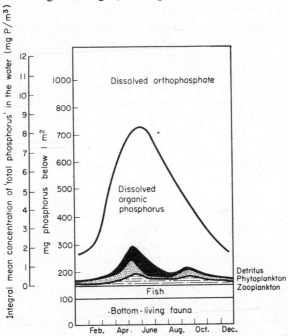

FIG. 16.1 The distribution of the total phosphorus in a water column from surface to bottom off Plymouth. The amounts of phosphorus present as phosphate and as dissolved organic matter in the water are shown, together with the particulate phosphorus present as plankton, nekton, benthos, etc. (from Harvey, 1955).

organic nitrogen, whereas the amount of particulate nitrogen is very much smaller, amounting to a mere few mg N/m³. Similarly, if the comparison is made for phosphorus, it has been shown by Redfield, Smith and Ketchum (1937) that the amount of dissolved organic phosphorus is considerably greater than the amount of particulate phosphorus. Harvey (1955) gives in the accompanying diagram a particularly clear representation of the inorganic phosphate, the dissolved organic phosphorus, and the particulate phosphorus represented by plankton and detritus in the waters of the English Channel (Fig. 16.1). With the vast volume of the oceans, even a minute amount of dissolved organic matter present in every cubic metre of water will represent a tremendous quantity of organic matter locked up in the oceans, and not utilized directly as food except by bacteria and Protozoa. Furthermore this dissolved material represents a very considerable fraction of the organic matter built up originally by the synthetic activities of plants. This synthesis depends among other things upon a constant supply of nutrients such as nitrogen and phosphorus which, as we have already seen, are in relatively short supply in the oceans. It is, therefore, not surprising that in the whole inorganic/organic cycle of life in the sea the dissolved organic matter is finally converted into inorganic compounds or, as many research workers say, the organic matter is "mineralized". Among other products of this mineralization are nitrates and phosphates. This further breakdown of relatively stable molecules of dissolved organic material is again the work of marine bacteria. A constant cycle therefore exists in the sea, as on land: the upbuilding of plant material and animal material forms particulate matter; this is decomposed to produce first detritus and then dissolved organic material; then follow the mineralization processes regenerating inorganic compounds such as nitrate and phosphate, which can again with the help of sunlight be utilized by plants in photosynthesis (Fig. 16.2). Much of the nitrate and phosphate is temporarily lost to the deep water where it cannot be utilized, but by means of deep currents and upwelling it is to some extent returned to the upper layers. Thus the regeneration of nitrate and phosphate plays as important a part in the life cycle of the oceans as photosynthesis by phytoplankton. Over great depths the regenerated inorganic nutrients do not tend to reach the surface layers near where they sank as decomposing detritus. Slow ocean currents carry the nutrients away so that they may reach the surface again only after being transported hundreds or thousands of miles. In shallow seas, on the other hand, at least a portion of the regenerated nutrients may pass to the upper layers near where it was remineralized. Despite upwelling and other mixing processes, there is a slow gradual loss of nutrients to the deepest layers in oceanic areas, but clearly much must be returned, however slowly, or life in the oceans would cease. Another loss of nutrients arises from the fact that apparently not all detritus is completely decomposed; a small resistant fraction may pass to the bottom as "humus" (cf. Waksman, 1933).

If we consider the regeneration of phosphorus compounds, first of all there is little evidence that phytoplankton generally utilizes phosphorus-containing compounds other than ortho-phosphate. Results from certain culture experiments suggest that a few algae can grow with organic phosphorus-containing compounds, but it is pos-

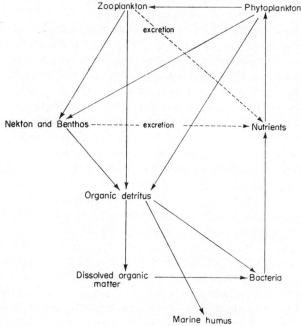

FIG. 16.2 A diagrammatic representation of the cycle of life in the sea. Note the importance of bacteria in regenerating nutrients from organic detritus.

sible even then that phosphatases on the surfaces of the cells release phosphate ions which are absorbed. In any case, in the sea it appears that phosphate is the only phosphorus containing substance normally utilized. The regeneration of phosphorus has been admirably summarized by Harvey (1945, 1955). One may first distinguish the "direct" regeneration of phosphate, which is a relatively rapid process in which phosphate is released either in the euphotic zone or immediately below, and can be rapidly utilized by the phytoplankton again (Fig. 16.2). Animals excrete phosphates during their metabolism. Gardiner (1937) observed also that during the feeding of zooplankton, phosphate increased in the water. It appears that in the green faecal pellets which herbivorous plankton produce, some of the organic phosphorus is in a labile state and phosphatases can produce phosphate rapidly and directly. Cushing (1959) claimed that much greater quantities of phosphate are liberated by zooplankton during excessive grazing. Harris (1959) has called attention to the release of significant quantities of phosphate by zooplankton. Marshall and Orr's (1961) experiments also indicate a rapid excretion of labelled phosphorus; even starved copepods may excrete a large fraction of their total phosphorus. These same authors point out that zooplankton tends to liberate both inorganic and organic phosphorus rapidly on death; the majority of the phosphorus is released in a matter of days, mainly by autolysis. The excretion and the rapid liberation of phosphate is probably of the greatest importance, especially during summer, in making this essential nutrient available to the phytoplankton above the thermocline. In the death of diatoms also, part of the organic phosphorus is relatively rapidly converted into phosphate, probably by phosphatases released by the cells. Hoffman (1956) claimed that with the death of diatom cells, autolysis is responsible for the release of up to 25% of the total phosphorus as inorganic phosphate. Equally important however, is the release, immediately on death, of approximately one third of the total phosphorus as dissolved organic compounds. About 70% of the remaining phosphorus is remineralized in a matter of two days. Hoffman has confirmed the rapid release of phosphorus compounds on the death of copepod zooplankton. Although less phosphate is produced immediately, about a third of the total phosphorus is released to the water in dissolved organic form, and the remaining particulate phosphorus is rapidly remineralized. Hoffman also emphasizes the significant contribution made to the turn-over of phosphorus by plankton in the upper water layers. At the same time, the majority of the organic matter of plants and animals in the whole water column is in the form of relatively stable compounds, and only a slower decomposition will finally release this fraction of the phosphorus. This "indirect regeneration" is due to bacterial action and occurs chiefly in deeper water below the euphotic zone. Much of the regeneration goes on during the late autumn and winter, and this will lead to the maximum concentration of inorganic phosphate which is seen in relatively shallow waters during late winter. The various stages in the conversion of organic into inorganic phosphorus compounds are not known, but considerable work has been done in studying the fractions of phosphorus in seawater, first by determining the total phosphorus, then the particulate and inorganic phosphorus and, by difference, the dissolved organic phosphorus.

Redfield, Smith and Ketchum (1937) showed for the Gulf of Maine that most of the dissolved organic phosphorus was present during summer and autumn. There was a marked increase in summer when up to 16 mg P/m^3 occurred as dissolved organic matter, whereas during winter there was a marked decline, presumably due to mineralization, i.e. the formation of phosphate. About 90% of the total phosphorus was present as phosphate over the winter period. Ketchum (1947), also working in the Gulf of Maine, showed that in May there was comparatively little dissolved organic phosphorus; this was almost entirely confined to the upper 60 m with a concentration of ca. 30 mg P/m^3. The same upper layer also had more particulate phosphorus (i.e. plankton and detritus) though this amounted to only ca. 20 mg P/m^3 (Fig. 16.3). By autumn (November) the particulate phosphorus concentration had the same low value but was more or less evenly distributed to the bottom indicating the sinking into deeper water layers of detrital material. There was, however, a great increase in dissolved phosphorus at this time, presumably due to the decomposition of plankton and detritus which was produced mainly over the summer period. This decomposition might proceed at any depth and, therefore, in November the dissolved phosphorus was more or less evenly distributed with depth (Fig. 16.3). The progressive increase in the inorganic phosphate fraction with the advance of winter was clear, and later on its utilization with the phytoplankton outburst in spring was also obvious. The greatest changes in the three phosphorus fractions were at the surface. A summary of the results for the uppermost metre is shown in Fig. 16.4.

Changes in the three phosphorus fractions may also be followed experimentally with tank cultures. In certain recent experiments (Crowley, Shackley and Raymont, unpublished) we have grown unialgal cultures of *Phaeodactylum* in tanks of 1000 l. capacity, and have followed the utilization of inorganic phosphate and the rise in particulate phosphorus with the growth of the culture. Then, following the decline of the culture and the decomposition of the algal cells, we have been able to observe the rise in the dissolved organic phosphorus fraction, and finally the beginning of the regeneration of inorganic phosphate (cf. Fig. 16.5).

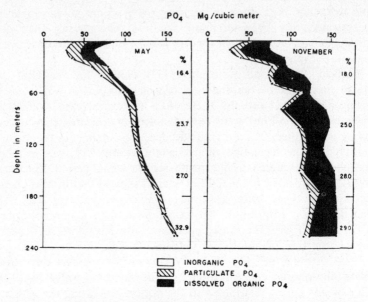

FIG. 16.3 Changes in the dissolved inorganic phosphorus, dissolved
organic phosphorus and particulate phosphorus in a water
column (Gulf of Maine) (from Ketchum, 1947).

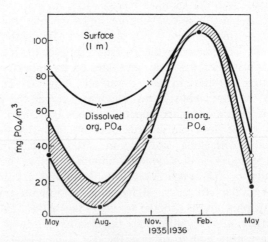

FIG. 16.4 Seasonal changes in dissolved inorganic phosphorus, dissolved
organic phosphorus and particulate phosphorus in surface waters
(Particulate P as hatched shading). (from Ketchum, 1947).

The work of Harvey and of Armstrong has added greatly to our knowledge of the three fractions of phosphorus-containing materials present in the seas off Plymouth. Their results in general confirm those of Redfield *et al.*, in that in winter the greater part of the phosphorus, amounting to 80–90% of the total, is present as inorganic phosphate, whereas in early summer the phosphate is reduced to as little as 40% of the total and the amount of dissolved organic phos-

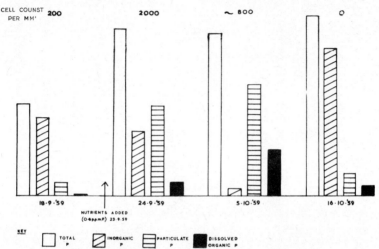

FIG. 16.5 Changes in the three phosphorus fractions (dissolved inorganic; dissolved organic; particulate P) in a 1000 litre tank culture of *Phaeodactylum*. Note the rise in particulate and dissolved organic P during the middle period of the experiment and the regeneration of inorganic phosphate P at the end as the culture declined. Cell counts shown above (from Crowley, Shackley and Raymont, unpublished).

phorus and particulate phosphorus rises (Fig. 16.6). The amount of particulate matter, however, is again very low. It is not surprising that in deep water well away from the coast, practically the whole of the phosphorus is present apparently throughout the year as phosphate (Fig. 16.7). In the equatorial Atlantic, Ketchum, Corwin and Keen (1955) have found that while the upper layers are very low in phosphate, an appreciable fraction of phosphorus may be present in dissolved organic form. All deep water samples, certainly exceeding 1000 m, however, while showing far greater quantities of phosphate, gave very little organic dissolved phosphorus.

Whereas the upper euphotic zone is the layer which sees the conversion of inorganic phosphorus into particulate matter, by the sinking of detritus and the passing down of herbivorous plankton into

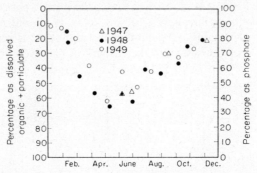

FIG. 16.6 Seasonal changes in the percentage of phosphate-P and of dissolved organic + particulate-P off Plymouth
(from Harvey, 1955).

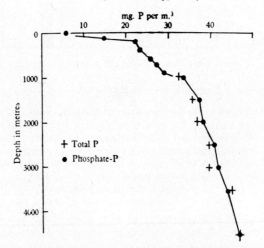

FIG. 16.7 The relation between phosphate-P and total phosphorus in deep oceanic waters (from Harvey, 1955).

the deeper layers, particulate matter will descend to the deeper waters. The conversion of particulate into dissolved organic phosphorus can go on at all levels, and the total amount of phosphorus in the whole column of water should remain the same unless there is a horizontal exchange of water. Ketchum has shown that over

Georges Bank, during the main period of photosynthetic activity from April to September, some 14 mg of phosphorus were removed every day from each square metre of water. He believes that about 25% of this phosphorus came from the upper euphotic zone by decomposition and regenerative changes, whereas the remaining 75% came by vertical transport from the deeper layers. It is clear that direct regeneration is of considerable importance in keeping the euphotic layer supplied with phosphorus during the spring and summer, when, with the establishment of a thermocline, the amount passing from the deep layers into the lighted upper zone is reduced to a low value. However, the major process of indirect regeneration will go on particularly through the autumn and winter months. In regions where the depth of water is considerable, it appears that regeneration takes place mainly in the water mass and there is little or no loss of material to the bottom and no absorption of phosphorus in the bottom mud. In shallower areas, however, much of the organic matter may reach the bottom and a considerable part of the regeneration process must occur at the mud/water interface. It seems likely that some of the phosphorus is absorbed at the mud surface. Marshall and Orr (1948) suggested from their work on the fertilization of a sea loch with large quantities of phosphate, that the rapid disappearance of phosphorus was partially due to absorption at the mud-water interface. Moore (1930) analysed the phosphate content of muds in coastal waters and found that there were relatively large amounts particularly near the surface of the bottom deposit. Stephenson (1949) also obtained relatively large quantities of phosphate on shaking marine mud with seawater. On the other hand, it should be noted that Harvey (1955), working in the English Channel, found that the layer of water immediately over the sandy bottom did not appear to be notably richer in total phosphorus. Cooper's (1951) results suggest that muddy bottom deposits possess higher quantities of phosphorus than sandy areas, and that regeneration of phosphate is favoured in regions of finer sediments of higher organic content. Pomeroy and Bush (1959) have raised the interesting point that direct return of phosphate due to the excretory products of animals, apart from regeneration by micro-organisms, need not be confined to the zooplankton. Especially in shallow inshore waters, the bottom fauna as well as nekton such as fish and aquatic mammals may, according to the results of these investigators, play a significant part in returning phosphate direct to the organic cycle (cf. Kuenzler, 1961).

It is clear that the speed of regeneration of phosphate may be a very significant factor in the rate of turn-over of organic material. Pratt (1949, 1950) suggested that the rate of regeneration of phosphate in tank fertilization experiments was lower than the rate of assimilation and, therefore, that regeneration limited the velocity of the organic cycle. It has also been suggested that with the higher temperatures in the surface waters of tropical and sub-tropical regions, the total annual production may be high owing to the rapid turn-over of phosphorus and other nutrients, even though the standing crop appears usually to be so much lower than at high latitudes.

During the spring and summer in temperate and high latitudes we have seen that those nitrogen compounds which can be utilized by phytoplankton are usually so greatly reduced that they can limit production. The rate of regeneration of nitrogenous compounds is therefore of the greatest importance in maintaining production in the upper layers. As with the phosphorus cycle, a proportion of the nitrogen is returned to the upper layers by "direct regeneration". Animals excrete a variety of nitrogenous products, especially ammonia, as well as urea, uric acid and to some extent amino-acids. In the case of teleost fishes, trimethylamine oxide, $(CH_3)_3NO$, is excreted. The work of Harvey has demonstrated clearly that phytoplankton can utilize ammonium with the greatest ease; in fact often in preference to nitrate. It appears also that many phytoplankton species can utilize urea and uric acid, and that some species can make use of amino-acids, though a bacterial flora associated with the phytoplankton is often necessary to deaminate the amino-acids first with the liberation of ammonia (cf. Chapter VII). The only significant product among the excretions of animals which, it appears, cannot be used directly by phytoplankton is trimethylamine oxide. Harris (1959) has drawn attention to the importance of the zooplankton in maintaining nitrogen supplies to the algae in the photosynthetic zone. By direct experiment, Harris showed that the zooplankton excretes significant amounts of ammonium. One of his results suggests that during summer > 70% of the total available nitrogen was derived from ammonium. Indeed, in the late spring and summer, Harris's calculations suggest that for Long Island Sound, algal photosynthesis in the upper water layers is kept running by the ammonium made available by the zooplankton. The slower, mainly bacterial, decomposition of organic matter, leading to the formation of nitrate, becomes an important source of nitrogen for the water layers only during autumn and winter.

The ammonium released by the zooplankton, is directly and immediately utilized by the phytoplankton, thus maintaining carbon assimilation over the summer. Harris has calculated the average daily nitrogen requirements of the algae in Long Island Sound during the period of phytoplankton growth. Approximately 50% arises from zooplankton excretion; up to 40% from bacterial activity and transport of nitrogen into the area from outside; and possibly some 10% from the excretions of benthic animals. The importance of the zooplankton, at least over part of the year in Long Island Sound, in providing nitrogen to the algae is thus clear.

The bulk of dissolved organic matter, or rather its nitrogenous fraction in seawater, is not, however, derived from excretory substances but from the breaking down of organic detritus, both plant and animal, by bacterial action. There have been rather few determinations of the organic nitrogen in seawater. Krogh (1934) suggested that the amount of nitrogen present as dissolved organic matter for waters off Bermuda was 244 mg N/m^3 and that the concentration did not change with depth. However, Robinson and Wirth (1934a, b) found lower amounts of organic dissolved nitrogen for Pacific waters off the coast of Washington. The highest concentrations were at the surface and were a little more than 100 mg/m^3; but there was a rapid fall with depth to a minimum at about 800−1000 m of only 40−50 mg/m^3, after which a rise occurred in the deeper layers to values of *ca.* 90 mg N/m^3. In the inshore waters of Puget Sound, however, the same authors obtained much higher dissolved organic nitrogen concentrations. There was again a marked decline with depth, but near-surface layers had concentrations even exceeding 300 mg N/m^3. They associated this maximum with the previous growth of phytoplankton in the upper layers. Von Brand and Rakestraw (1941) also found that whereas inshore water had only some 110–170 mg N/m^3 as dissolved organic matter, when diatoms were added and the water then stored in darkness, the dissolved nitrogen rose to 370 mg N/m^3 in a few days, declining somewhat to below 300 mg N/m^3 afterwards. In offshore Atlantic water they found deeper water samples had a richer organic nitrogen content (average 214 mg N/m^3) than surface samples (147 mg N/m^3), but since the water had been stored for a considerable time, the difference might have been due to storage. The data available suggest that dissolved organic nitrogen may vary considerably with depth, but that the maximum probably will not exceed 250 mg N/m^3 in ocean waters; somewhat higher values (even exceeding 300 mg N/m^3)

may occur in inshore waters. The seasonal variation in the amount of dissolved organic nitrogen does not appear to have been much studied, but it is probable that a considerable increase occurs particularly in the upper layers during late spring and summer. Harris (1959) has demonstrated in Long Island Sound that as the inorganic dissolved nitrogen, represented during winter mainly by nitrate, is sharply reduced with the early spring diatom flowering, the particulate nitrogen, including plankton, bacteria and detritus, rises markedly. The changes in the dissolved organic nitrogen fraction are unfortunately not so clear; during early spring the quantities appear to be low, and at least at some stations in the Sound an increase occurs in late spring or summer. This suggests some secretion of organic matter by the phytoplankton, or more probably some decomposition of the algae. Some stations, however, showed fairly high concentrations of dissolved organic nitrogen during autumn; mineralization had presumably not yet proceeded very far. In any event, this mineralization of dissolved organic nitrogen (i.e. its conversion into inorganic nitrogen compounds) is again a slow process, depending on bacterial action, and occurring mainly in the waters below the photosynthetic zone, especially during the autumn/winter period. There is some evidence that the organic nitrogenous substances are rather more stable than the phosphorus substances and that indirect regeneration is slower. In any case there appears to be some permanent loss of nitrogeneous as well as of phosphorus-containing materials to the sea floor (cf. Rittenberg, Emery and Orr, 1955). The majority, however, is mineralized by bacterial action. It is possible that by the direct action of enzymes in seawater, and, at the very surface, even by direct oxidation, nitrogen compounds may be converted to nitrate, as Cooper has suggested, but all workers are agreed that such a process, if it occurs, is an extremely minor one.

In the case of the regeneration of nitrogenous compounds it appears clear that one of the commonest breakdown paths results in the formation of ammonium. Ammonium is in turn oxidized to nitrite with, according to Cooper, hyponitrite as an intermediate short-lived stage, and finally nitrite is oxidized to nitrate — generally the major fraction of inorganic nitrogen in the sea. It should be remembered, however, that all three nitrogeneous substances, ammonium, nitrite and nitrate, are utilized by the phytoplankton. It would appear likely that nitrifying bacteria, similar to those which occur on land, must be present in the sea carrying out the oxidation of ammonium to nitrite and of nitrite to nitrate, and it has indeed proved possible to demonstrate the occurrence of such nitrifying bacteria, mainly in the bottom deposits, but to some extent also in the upper layers of coastal water. But the main body of seawater in ocean depths away from the land is very largely inactive in conversion of nitrogenous compounds, and it must be admitted that nitrifying bacteria generally are not readily identified in the sea. Carey (1938) showed that whereas material on the bottom exhibited nitrification, water just above gave some nitrite production but no nitrate. Nitrifying bacteria were presumably fewer. Moreover, water away from land influence and far from the bottom deposit showed no nitrification, though with the addition of inshore plankton, a little nitrite was produced. Thus, if nitrifying bacteria are present in the seas apart from the bottom mud or plankton, they must be so very sparsely distributed that any nitrification is an extremely slow and long term process. Zobell (1946) has summarized our knowledge by pointing out that while bottom muds usually have active populations of nitrifying bacteria, this is not invariably the case, and mud from great depths produces nitrite only slowly. Surface waters, on the other hand, unless near shore, appear to have no nitrifying bacteria or only very few. However, stored plankton does show nitrification of ammonium even though nitrifying bacteria cannot be identified (cf. von Brand *et al.*, 1937). It is also curious that *Nitrosomonas*, although it has been identified in the sea does not appear to have specific marine types. Similarly, *Nitrobacter*-like forms have been demonstrated in the sea, but although these nitrate-forming bacteria have been shown to occur in some shallow-sea muds, they are generally not common and are especially rare in the open sea. There is no doubt that there is a considerable gap in our knowledge of the micro-organisms responsible for nitrification, and Zobell believes that there must be types of nitrifying bacteria other than the soil-like species which have so far eluded us.

In shallow depths the water just above the bottom is an active nitrification centre. Cooper (1933), for example, found regeneration of nitrate at the bottom during the autumn in the English Channel. On the other hand, ammonium is normally hardly detectable except in the upper layers (cf. Cooper, 1933; Redfield and Keys, 1938; Rakestraw and Carritt, 1948). Robinson and Wirth (1934b), for open Pacific waters, found ammonium practically restricted to the upper layers; and in the Gulf of Maine, Rakestraw found that nitrite was practically confined to the first hundred metres of water (cf. Chapter VII).

It would appear that the depth of water is important in determining the active centre of nitrification, and that whereas in really shallow water nitrification may go on at the bottom as well as near the surface, in deeper water it occurs only in the water column itself. Certainly in the great depths of the ocean the really deep water layers away from the land have all the inorganic nitrogen present as nitrate in unchanging concentration (cf. Chapter VII).

We have already referred to the occurrence of bacteria in seawater which are responsible for the decomposition of animals and plants. There are also bacteria concerned with the oxidation of ammonium to nitrite, from nitrite to nitrate, as well as bacteria which are concerned in phosphorus regeneration. Denitrifying bacteria are also known from the sea which can reduce nitrate to nitrite or even to nitrogen gas. Bacteria are concerned in the cycle of sulphur in the sea. Almost the whole of the sulphur compounds in plants and animals yield hydrogen sulphide as a result of bacterial break-down. Zobell (1946) quotes as many as 10^4–10^6 bacteria per gram of mud deposit as producing hydrogen sulphide. But other bacteria are known which, in the absence of oxygen and in the presence of sufficient quantities of organic matter, will reduce sulphate to hydrogen sulphide or to sulphur. The reverse process of the oxidation of sulphur compounds to sulphate in the marine environment is also due to bacterial activity. A considerable number of different species of bacteria can oxidize hydrogen sulphide and sulphur to sulphate thus maintaining the cycle of sulphur in the sea. Some are autotrophic forms obtaining their energy under aerobic conditions from the chemosynthesis. Others, occurring in the lighted zones of the seas can utilize the energy of sunlight for the oxidation, while there are numerous saprophytic sulphur bacteria which can live under anaerobic conditions. By producing hydrogen sulphide, bacteria involved in the sulphur cycle can influence the precipitation of iron and may affect the pH of seawater.

Most of the bacteria occurring in bottom deposits tend to create reducing conditions, lowering the redox potential. Zobell (1957) refers to bacteria which destroy organic compounds of calcium and, by producing carbon dioxide in their metabolism, may affect the precipitation or solution of calcium carbonate. Other bacteria may bring about changes in iron, manganese, hydrogen and other elements in the sea. Bacteria thus play a significant role in the submarine deposition of minerals, the redox potential of the deposit being one of the important factors. There are also bacteria which produce and act upon hydrocarbons and which may, therefore, have some responsibility in the production of oil. It is clear from the work of Zobell and his colleagues, who have done so much to amplify our knowledge of marine micro-organisms, that despite the importance of bacteria in marine organic cycles, we are only at the beginning of understanding the many processes for which bacteria are responsible.

Wood (1952) has especially stressed the wide range of types of bacteria. Apart from the autotrophic sulphur and iron bacteria and the sulphur reducing forms, there are numerous heterotrophic species, many of these being apparently facultative anaerobes. Proteolytic species were especially common, but carbohydrate fermenting and amino-acid decomposing types are also numerous; bacteria attacking cellulose were not apparently very common except in estuarine muds, but some forms are known decomposing agar and alginates. Species reducing nitrate to nitrite were well represented but those reducing nitrite further were few. Urea-attacking species were also identified. Zobell has shown that lipolytic bacteria are widely distributed in the sea and that chitin-decomposing bacteria also occur, though the breakdown of chitin is slow. Hock (1941) has also isolated a number of types of bacteria capable of decomposing chitin from seawater and from marine sands and muds. Waksman *et al.* (1933) found numbers of bacteria capable of attacking cellulose and some other polysaccharides. It is obvious, therefore, that a wealth of bacterial types exists in the sea capable of decomposing plant and animal remains and excreta of all kinds.

But Wood emphasizes the versatility of marine bacteria. This can apply even to morphological form but the adaptability is especially true of function. A wide range of variants and strains with variable physiological characters exist, and this causes the identification of marine bacteria, and indeed the whole study of bacterial systematics, to be exceedingly complex. Owing to their versatility, however, bacteria appear to be adaptable to almost any marine environment and to be able to catalyse reactions of nearly every kind involving organic as well as many inorganic compounds.

It is perhaps rather surprising therefore to find that although bacteria are of such tremendous significance in the sea, their numbers over most oceanic waters are extremely small when compared with the terrestrial environment. The density of bacteria in the immediate surface of the sea is usually low. It is suggested that the strong sunlight has a bactericidal action but the effect very rapidly wears off with depth, probably owing to the rapid absorption of the markedly bactericidal ultra-violet rays. The abundance of bacteria increases rapidly from the surface downwards and it is in the upper 50 m or so in the open oceans, corresponding more or less to the euphotic zone, that a maximum density is reached. Below this depth the numbers

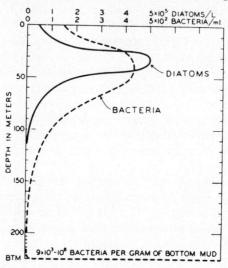

FIG. 16.8 The distribution of bacteria in relation to depth in a sea area (from Sverdrup *et al.*, 1946).

decline very sharply so that in open oceans in the deeper layers less than 10 bacteria/c.c. may be commonly found (Fig. 16.8). The maximum in the euphotic zone usually amounts to some hundreds of bacteria/c.c. belonging to some 25–35 species. Zobell (1957) however, comments on the fact that laboratory plating procedures usually detect only a small percentage of the viable cells and that some hundreds of thousands per c.c. may occur. This point is also made by Kriss and Rukina (1952 – seen in summary only) who suggest that in the upper water layers the concentrations of bacteria are not infrequently of the order of thousands per c.c. The recent work of Kriss and his collaborators (e.g. Kriss, Mitzkevich, Mishustina and Abyzov, 1961) suggests that differences in the vertical distribution of marine micro-organisms may be closely related to the type of water, with larger microbial densities occurring at current boundaries. Kriss *et al.* have demonstrated that heterotrophic bacteria are relatively much more plentiful in warm waters, especially in the tropical equatorial zones of all three oceans, whereas in Arctic and Antarctic waters few heterotrophs are present. Their occurrence may be related to a greater concentration of relatively easily assimilable organic matter. The density of heterotrophic bacteria may thus be helpful in recognizing different water masses; the occurrence of rich microbial populations in subtropical, sub-Antarctic or sub-Arctic areas of the Indian, Pacific and Atlantic Oceans has been taken as evidence for the presence of water of tropical origin.

The special conditions of deoxygenation in the deeper layers of the Black Sea are responsible for an abnormal depth distribution of marine bacteria. In the central areas of the Sea the numbers and biomass of micro-organisms are at a minimum at a depth of about 150 m which corresponds to the upper hydrogen sulphide limit. The number of bacteria increases rapidly below this depth to a relatively high density of some 10^8 micro-organisms per m^3, and this density continues to a depth of 2000 m (Fig. 16.9). All workers appear to agree, however, that in the open oceans very greatly reduced numbers of bacteria occur in deep water, and that the upper maximum of bacteria is associated with the phytoplankton zone. Kriss and Rukina suggest that a second maximum may occur at a depth of just below 100 m which corresponds to an abundant zone of zooplankton, but in the area which they investigated, the really deep water was extraordinarily sparsely populated by bacteria. It is only when one approaches the mud-water interface at the bottom of the sea that a tremendous sudden rise in bacterial populations occurs. This is undoubtedly associated with the mud particles at the ocean bottom. Concentrations of the order of 10^4–10^9 bacteria per gram of mud are quoted by Sverdrup et al. (1946) (cf. Fig. 16.8). Zobell (1957) states that there may be enough to give 0.3–2 mg of living bacteria per gram of mud, reckoned on a dry weight basis.

For the open seawater above the bottom, however, Wood (1953) also confirms the low density of bacteria in waters off the S.E. Australian coast. The average was 100 bacteria per c.c. with a range of 4–500 per c.c. for the upper water layers to a depth of 50 m. Only on a few occasions in the vicinity of Botany Bay were counts exceeding 1000 per c.c. recorded, and these relatively high densities were associated with heavy rainfall. Wood believes that plating procedures give a fair representation of the density of bacteria in the open sea, but they may be misleading if applied to muds where direct counts give much higher values. He also stresses the greater densities associated with muds, and indicates that maximum adsorption effects and high bacterial populations are correlated with silts of fine particle size (especially 2–5 μ). On settling plates, however, Wood (1950)

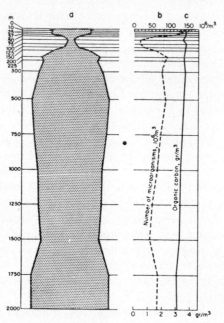

FIG. 16.9 (a) The distribution of micro-organisms with depth in the Black Sea. The number (b) and organic weight (c) of micro-organisms is also shown (from Caspers, 1957).

found considerably lower numbers of bacteria than Zobell; algal spores, diatoms, etc. outweighed the bulk of bacteria.

There is no doubt, however, that a very sharp contrast may be made between the bacterial densities at the mud surface on the sea floor and the water layers above. As Zobell states, there may be several millions of bacteria per c.c. at the mud-water interface as compared with the few hundreds per c.c. which occur at the maximum layer of the euphotic zone. Even in this zone, in the open oceans where plankton may be very sparse, very low numbers of bacteria are occasionally found.

The investigations of Waksman *et al.* (1933), Zobell and almost all workers on marine bacteriology suggest that the limitation in numbers of bacteria at intermediate depths is largely concerned with the lack of surface for attachment. Marine bacteria seem to occur particularly on the surfaces of phytoplankton and probably of zooplankton organisms; they may also attach to inorganic particles. They thus are particularly abundant on the fine particles at the mud surface at the sea bottom. The investigations of Waksman and Vartiovaara (1938) and Wood (1953) suggest that the bacteria may be adsorbed on fine mud particles, but that though temporarily inactivated, they do not suffer any injurious effects on growth and metabolism (cf. Armstrong, 1958). Zobell has shown that in diminished numbers they occur quite deep in ocean cores. There appears little doubt that few bacteria occur free in seawater. This may be a reflection of the relatively very small quantity of organic substances dissolved in seawater. For a flourishing bacterial population the nutrient supply is extraordinarily low. It is probable that the organic substances are concentrated from the very dilute solution by adsorption on surfaces: in this way bacteria attached to a surface can have a greater concentration on which to live. Undoubtedly there seems to be some natural brake on the growth of bacteria in the open sea; lack of surface and an extremely dilute nutrient concentration would appear to be among the major factors.

The surface effect can be well shown by storing seawater in glass bottles when great numbers of bacteria can be seen to develop on the glass surface. In one experiment by Zobell, within 24 hr, more than twice as many bacteria were attached to the surface of the glass as were suspended in the water. Zobell and Anderson (1936) have also shown that the numbers of bacteria developed in volumes of seawater stored in glass stoppered bottles of different capacities increased greatly according to the area of glass surface per unit volume. For example, in bottles of 14 c.c. capacity the density of bacteria per c.c. was more than three times the density in bottles of 1225 c.c. capacity. Experiments by these and other investigators have also demonstrated that the filling of a bottle of seawater with small glass beads or sterile sand greatly increases the bacterial count, presumably owing to the increased surface. If, however, a sufficient quantity of nutriment such as peptone or other organic matter is added to the water in such experiments, a high bacterial density is achieved in both bottles, regardless of the surface effect. It would seem that the effect of surface appears only when the bacteria are developing in seawater containing food materials at very great dilution – the normal condition. This suggests again that one of the advantages of attachment to marine bacteria may be a greater concentration of the food substances, and that exo-enzymes secreted by the bacteria may be retained until digested foods can be absorbed by the cells.

In the presence of sufficient food and other suitable conditions, marine bacteria divide rapidly so that a heavy population is soon built up. If the organic matter used as food contains more phosphorus and nitrogen than is required by the bacteria, a part of the excess is converted into phosphate and a nitrogenous compound, usually ammonium, and released to the seawater. The respiration of the bacterial cell is extraordinarily rapid. Harvey (1955) quotes a calculation that 1 g of actively growing marine bacteria consumes about 30 c.c. of oxygen per hour. If the organic matter used as food has insufficient nitrogen or phosphorus, some marine bacteria can draw on phosphate or inorganic nitrogenous compounds present in the seawater. The addition of such compounds can therefore increase the rate of growth of certain bacterial populations. As the supply of dissolved organic matter becomes limiting, however, the large bacterial population which has been built up and which has been synthesizing cell tissue from this material, begins to die off. The bacterial cells are very rapidly decomposed and with their relatively high nitrogen and phosphorus content a very rapid release of material to the seawater occurs. Practically all the phosphorus is released as phosphate, and the nitrogen apparently as ammonium. Harvey suggests from experiments on storing seawater that, once the food supply for the bacteria has run out, almost all the phosphorus in the bacterial cells is returned as phosphate to the seawater within a week.

Since the organic food supply generally appears to be a markedly limiting factor on marine bacteria, it is not surprising that the addition even of non-nitrogen containing foods, such as sugars, to seawater can bring about an increase in the growth of bacteria. The oxygen consumption will rise with the growth of the bacterial population, the bacteria using the nitrogen present in the water with the carbohydrate which has been added. Waksman and Carey (1935), for example, show that with inshore water the addition of 2.5 mg/l. of glucose doubled the oxygen consumption of the seawater, but further additions of glucose were not followed by increased oxygen uptake, suggesting no further bacterial growth, unless extra nitrogen was supplied. If nitrogen such as ammonium sulphate were added to the seawater, however, a further increase in oxygen consumption was evident, and direct counts also showed a marked rise in bacterial density (cf. Fig. 16.10). The rate of glucose utilization is thus a function of the liberation of nitrogen. Waksman and Renn (1936) also demonstrated a rapid increase in oxygen consumption by seawater

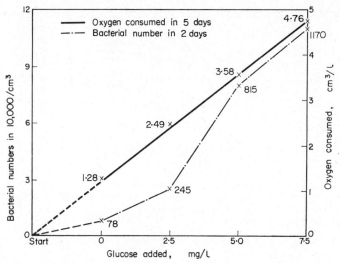

FIG. 16.10 Changes in the population density of marine bacteria with the addition of glucose (from Waksman and Carey, 1935).

to which amino-acids were added, owing to the decomposition and oxidation of these organic nitrogenous substances by bacteria. The investigations suggest that of the average amount of organic matter present in seawater (about 5 gm/m³) at least 25% is rapidly decomposed, with a corresponding return of mineral nutrients to the seawater. The bacteria themselves can also serve as food (cf. Chapter XVIII) so that their importance is clear. Zobell (1946) indeed states that given sufficient time and favourable conditions, bacteria can utilize organic matter almost quantitatively in the sea, mineralizing roughly two-thirds as against one-third converted into cell substance or some intermediate products.

The storage of raw seawater containing detritus as well as small organisms may lead, therefore, to a fairly rapid increase in bacterial population and a considerable proportion of organic matter in seawater, both dissolved and particulate, can be fairly rapidly decomposed. Temperature affects the rate and extent of decomposition. Thus Waksman and Renn (1936) demonstrated that in the first five days, with seawater stored at just over 20 °C, a rapid increase in bacteria was obvious; a slower multiplication of bacteria occurred in water stored at 4 °C. With the rise in the bacterial population

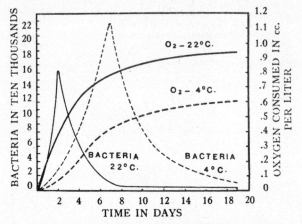

FIG. 16.11 Changes in bacterial population and the consumption of oxygen with temperature (from Waksman and Renn, 1936).

a rise in oxygen consumption occurred which was very rapid at first but then slowed off very considerably (Fig. 16.11). In general, water from offshore consumes less oxygen, reflecting a smaller increase in bacterial population than inshore waters. This is probably in part due to the smaller amounts of dissolved organic matter and partly to the smaller numbers of plankton in offshore waters leading to a smaller bacterial flora.

While a marine bacterial population develops more rapidly and presumably metabolic activities also increase with temperature, Zobell has emphasized that there is no suggestion that low temperature limits the distribution of marine bacteria. Indeed the optimum temperature for multiplication of most marine micro-organisms is relatively low, below 20 °C, probably reflecting the generally moderate temperature of the marine environment. Of particular interest are the observations by Zobell who has obtained bacteria from some of the deepest trenches of the ocean. He has shown that these micro-organisms are in no way limited by the prevailing low temperatures in the deeps and their optimum temperature appears to be distinctly low. Furthermore, Zobell and Johnson (1949) have shown that hydrostatic pressure is an important environmental factor for deep sea bacteria. Species from the surface of the sea do not flourish with high hydrostatic pressure, whereas those which have been taken from the depths of the ocean grow preferentially or even exclusively at the high pressures which occur in their natural habitat. There are very few observations on the changes in abundance of marine bacteria with seasonal temperature fluctuations in any one area. On the whole there is some suggestion that the populations are rather stable in density.

Zobell and Anderson (1936) found that there was a progressive reduction in the number of species of marine bacteria with time of incubation. In general, as the density of the micro-organisms increases, the number of species declines. This suggests that some antagonism exists between species. To some extent this may be competition for available food, or rather, that below a certain level of nutrients some species cannot flourish. There is strong evidence, however, that micro-organisms produce specific substances which, when released into the water may prove toxic to other species. A thermolabile substance has been found in seawater which is toxic to bacteria and which can be precipitated or adsorbed on active charcoal, etc. How far bacteriophages for certain bacterial species occur in the sea is not fully known; they appear to be present at least in polluted waters. Guelin (1954, 1955) has identified bacteriophages of both the coli and the typhoid group from seawater. Although most of the positive water samples originated from polluted estuaries, coli-phage was identified at a distance of 3000 m to seaward from Plymouth, and in Mediterranean waters, phages have been identified in waters 100 m from the coast. Guelin noted a marked seasonal variation in abundance of one type of bacteriophage; it was plentiful during December, January and February, but declined during spring and summer. The bacteriophage was shown by Guelin to be photosensitive, and he attributed its decline in summer to the effect of sunlight on the surface waters. The wider study of the distribution of bacteriophages and the degree to which they limit marine bacteria is of the greatest interest. Waksman and Hotchkiss (1937) discuss various other factors which reduce bacterial populations in the sea and include toxic substances liberated in the water as well as the consumption of bacteria by Protozoa and other organisms.

It is necessary to add that bacteria by their activities may not produce metabolites which are necessarily harmful to other species. Certainly some micro-organisms may be of enormous importance in producing as metabolites vitamins and other growth-promoting factors (cf. Chapter IX). Thus Burkholder and Burkholder (1956) and Burkholder (1959) have shown that different strains of marine bacteria can produce vitamins of the B-complex including B_{12}, thiamine, biotin and nicotinic acid. Mixed populations of micro-organisms in the shallow seas and marine muds also appear to produce B-vitamins in quantities of ecological significance. In near-shore waters, some of these substances are produced by terrestrial micro-organisms and are carried into the sea. Starr, Jones, and Martinez (1957) also found that a considerable number of strains of marine bacteria produced vitamin B_{12} or similar compounds. A portion of the vitamin-like activity was present in the supernatant water though a greater amount was present in the cell residues. The source of supply and production of vitamins of the B-complex in deep waters and sediments is doubtful. However, micro-organisms appear to be the most likely source generally in the seas. In inshore waters some sea-weeds, especially red weeds, have relatively large amounts of vitamin B_{12}; it is possible that these weeds synthesize the vitamin but more probably they tend to accumulate it from the seawater. Provasoli (1958) has suggested that the high fertility of inshore waters may be partly associated with high vitamin content, derived from bacteria, from decomposing seaweeds, and to some extent, from run-off from the land.

The course of the decomposition of plankton added to seawater and the production of nitrogenous compounds and phosphate have been followed by several workers. Waksman, Carey and Reuszer (1933) observed that more than half of the nitrogen from dead zooplankton added to seawater was liberated as ammonium in just under three weeks. There was a rapid breakdown during the first few days which was probably largely a decomposition of protein. Results suggested that material comparatively low in nitrogen decomposed more slowly, and that bacteria from the mud surface were more active than those in the sea-water. Destruction of seaweeds also occurred, but very little ammonium was produced and apparently some nitrogen source was necessary for the decomposition of seaweeds low in nitrogen such as *Fucus*. Waksman and Renn (1936) also suggest that the high amount of nitrogen in zooplankton promotes rapid destruction.

Cooper (1935) showed that phosphate was liberated fairly rapidly from dead zooplankton, an amount of phosphate approximately equivalent to that added as plankton being released in about 6 days. Cooper's results suggested, however, that following this rapid regeneration there was a slower production which reached its peak in about six to eight weeks. The total amount of phosphate liberated was considerably greater than the quantity present originally as added zooplankton, which suggests that the bacterial flora which developed also produced phosphate from the dissolved organic matter present in seawater. Decomposition of phytoplankton samples, on the other hand, showed a brief time lag and although in about one month a maximum of phosphate was reached, this represented only a part of that added as plant plankton. We have already pointed out that offshore water does not normally regenerate much nutrient and only a very limited bacterial population will develop unless the water is contaminated with bottom deposit. When plankton is added to such offshore water, nitrite and eventually nitrate is regenerated, but this regeneration occurs only slowly. This suggests that in the relatively plankton-free offshore water very few bacteria are present or that they are largely inactive.

The failure to obtain oxidation of ammonium to nitrite Spencer (1956) believes may be largely due to unsuitable nutrient conditions for a flourishing bacterial flora rather than to absence of the bacteria. In particular, there may be insufficient iron to allow the bacterial flora to develop and this could well be true of open ocean waters, while inshore waters generally have more than sufficient.

The most full investigation of the breakdown of organic matter, especially phytoplankton, and the regeneration of nitrogenous compounds in seawater has been undertaken by von Brand and his colleagues (1937–1947). The decomposition of mixed plankton occurred with a very rapid appearance of ammonium. This could continue for even about one month, but as ammonia production ceased, a production of nitrite occurred, bacteria of the *Nitrosomonas* group apparently being active here. Nitrate appears as the final stage as nitrite production slows down and the total four-stage cycle: particulate matter $\rightarrow NH_4^+ \rightarrow NO_2^- \rightarrow NO_3^-$, could take 45–65 days. Nitrate formation appears to be somewhat slower than the other stages, bacteria of the *Nitrobacter* type being concerned (Fig. 16.12).

The decomposition of phytoplankton would seem to be somewhat slower than mixed plankton. Using cultures of *Nitzschia*, von Brand showed, however, that the same step by step process occurred following the death of the diatom cells. Thus on storage, the particulate matter began to break down and the first, relatively rapid stage was the production of ammonia. This occupied altogether of the order of one month and was succeeded in the second month by the formation of nitrite. Nitrate was slower to form, indicating perhaps that the

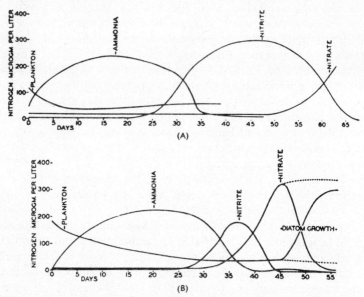

Fig. 16.12 The successive formation of ammonia, nitrite and nitrate with the decomposition of plankton. In (B) after 45 days, nitrate consumption is shown consequent upon a fresh growth of diatoms (from von Brand, Rakestraw and Renn, 1937).

growth of the bacterial flora effecting the final oxidation is slower and more difficult. Nitrate only appeared when nitrite was disappearing in the culture. Von Brand points out that the sequence of events seemed to be the same in all the experiments, though the duration of the various stages could vary considerably, nitrite being particularly irregular. Spencer (1956) suggests that *Nitrosomonas* may be inhibited by the presence of organic matter so that oxidation of ammonia may be delayed. At least in some experiments there was a time lag before ammonia was produced, suggesting perhaps that the breakdown of the particulate material might involve a stage as dissolved organic substances. When an experiment was conducted under anaerobic conditions the production of ammonium occurred but there was no oxidation to nitrite or nitrate. In one series of experiments diatoms were stored in darkness until decomposition and nitrification to form nitrate had occurred, when a fresh diaton inoculation was made and the culture placed in the light. A new growth of diatoms resulted with a rapid utilization of the nitrate. In this way three cycles were studied of progressive regeneration of nitrogen compounds and their subsequent utilization by fresh growths of diatoms. It was shown, however, that not all the nitrogen material was consumed in the regeneration process. A small amount of presumably more resistant material remained as residual organic matter and this increased by the time the third cycle had occurred (Fig. 16.13). The various stages in the nitrification cycle are surely associated with the successive development of different bacterial floras dealing with the different substrates. But in the sea presumably the floras will be mixed. Von Brand showed that, although the steps in the cycle always occurred in the same order, the process could be speeded by adding dead diatoms or other inorganic matter to a culture where a bacterial flora had already been built up. Thus if nitrite production is already occurring, addition of further particulate matter does not stop the process, but only a small amount of ammonia is formed as it is rapidly oxidized by the existing flora to nitrite. Again, addition of materials to a culture where a nitrate flora has already been built up results in both ammonia and nitrite appearing rapidly and only in relatively small quantities; nitrate is built up in a considerably shorter period. The length of the decomposition and regeneration cycle depends on the source of the seawater used, as well as on the type of organic matter. Thus as well as providing bacteria for multiplication, there may be factors in the water promoting bacterial growth. All stages of the cycle can go on simultaneously, though the bacteria may react differently to environmental factors. For example, the nitrite-forming flora appears to be inhibited or at least retarded by low temperature. It appears also that whereas NO_2^- and NO_3^- formation is due to fairly specific bacterial types, as judged from their similar reactions to poisons, the bacteria producing ammonia are nonspecific.

To sum up, bacteria occur in the sea which oxidize the ammonium liberated in the decomposition of animals and plants by other bacteria to produce nitrate. These bacteria are present particularly in shallow water immediately above the bottom and to some extent in the upper layers. In deep oceanic waters they are probably mainly in the water layers below the photosynthetic zone and to a lesser extent in the sediments of the abyssal depths.

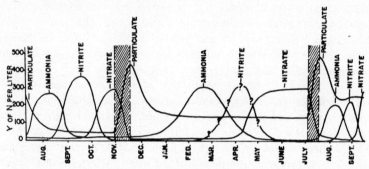

FIG. 16.13 Successive cycles of regeneration of nitrate with decomposition of phytoplankton in darkness, and of utilization of nitrate with growth of phytoplankton in the light (from von Brand, Rakestraw and Renn, 1939).

Two species of nitrogen-fixing bacteria, the aerobic *Azotobacter* and the anaerobic form, *Clostridium*, have been isolated in seawater, *Azotobacter* occurring attached to organisms and in bottom deposits and also free in the water (cf. Waksman, Reuszer, Carey, Hotchkiss and Renn, 1933). *Clostridium* presumably is more restricted to the bottom deposits. There is no doubt that these organisms can fix atmospheric nitrogen. They could thus increase the supply of nitrogen compounds, but they require a relatively high amount of organic matter to multiply abundantly and it is doubtful whether they contribute appreciably to the quantities of nitrogenous compounds in the sea. On the other hand, denitrifying bacteria are also known from the oceans, capable under culture conditions of reducing nitrate to nitrite and, even further, nitrite to gaseous nitrogen. However, it is doubtful whether the production of nitrogen from nitrogenous compounds goes on to any extent in the seas under normal conditions, as these denitrifying bacteria require a relatively high concentration of food materials which is probably rarely found. In exceptional areas such as the anaerobic Cariaco Trench, Richards and Benson (1961) have suggested that some free nitrogen may be formed from the decomposition of organic matter. It would appear that nitrate is first produced during the decomposition cycle, but that some denitrification of nitrate to nitrogen may follow. Apart from such probably very rare cases, there is still a considerable likelihood that some reduction of nitrate to nitrite goes on in the oceans. Waksman et al. (1933) considered that this occurred in the upper water layers, though reduction to nitrogen did not occur. In the oxygen minimum zone of the oceans nitrite is sometimes found in relatively large amounts (cf. Chapter VII). It is difficult to tell in the present state of our knowledge whether this nitrite is in process of being oxidized to nitrate or whether it is in course of reduction. Thompson and Gilson (1937) considered that the presence of a nitrite-rich layer below the euphotic zone in the Indian Ocean was probably due to reduction of nitrate. More recently, Brandhorst (1959) has considered that the nitrite occurring in association with the very low oxygen concentrations encountered off the east coast of South America was due to reducing bacteria (cf. Chapter VII). Even though bacterial reduction of nitrate is true of certain areas of the oceans it certainly would not appear to be widespread. Vaccaro and Ryther (1960) have suggested, however, another method by which nitrite may be produced in the oceans. They point out that laboratory cultures of nitrate-deficient phytoplankton, when supplied again with abundant nitrate, absorb this very rapidly. In the reduction of nitrate, however, significant amounts of nitrite may be liberated by the cells into the medium. Low light intensity appears to favour the production of nitrite. Thus, in the seas phytoplankton might itself effect a reduction of nitrate to nitrite. This would presumably occur only under particular conditions such as might be found in shallow temperate waters in early winter with abundant nitrate but where light was not sufficient to allow a real outburst of phytoplankton. Under tropical oceanic seas, a production of nitrite might similarly go on below the compensation depth near the limit of the euphotic zone. An increase of nitrite has been observed in such a layer by the authors. Even though nitrite is produced in observable quantities by both bacteria and phytoplankton, it can be utilized by the algal cells directly.

The return of phosphate and nitrate as well as of some other compounds to the waters of the ocean from the bodies of animals and plants, primarily by bacterial action, is thus of the utmost significance in allowing further photosynthetic cycles and upbuilding of tissue to occur. However, it is the speed of the regeneration process as much as its extent which is significant in terms of annual production. The importance of bacteria in the marine environment is therefore clear. They are responsible for the return of all the chemical constituents, locked up in plant and animal tissues, to the seawater in mineralized form; they provide much of the growth promoting, vitamin-like substances; moreover, by absorbing dissolved organic matter from the seawater, and converting it into the particulate organic material of their own bodies, they provide food for protozoans in particular, but also for many bottom feeding, and perhaps for some planktonic animals.

CHAPTER XVII

FEEDING AND RESPIRATION
OF THE ZOOPLANKTON

COPEPODS and other herbivores among the zooplankton are remarkably efficient in grazing upon the phytoplankton (cf. Chapter X). Lohmann (1908) and many later workers pointed out that in most temperate seas during the spring the standing crop of phytoplankton appeared to be large enough to be in excess of the nutritional demands of the zooplankton. On the other hand, during winter the paucity of phytoplankton suggested a lack of food for the zooplankton. Putter's theory (1909, 1925) of the use of dissolved organic substances as food by zooplankton partly stemmed from the lack of particulate food over the lean months of the year. Putter had also obtained high values for the respiratory rates of zooplankton which led him to postulate very large food requirements for pelagic animals. Although there is little direct evidence for Putter's theory, there is considerable support from the work of Ussing, Riley, Digby and others that little algal food is available to the zooplankton during winter. It is necessary, therefore, to review critically the food requirements of plankton animals. Nutritional needs must be examined both quantitatively and qualitatively, and not only must each class of animals be considered but the specific food requirements of particular species must be investigated.

The zooplankton includes herbivores and carnivores. Many species are omnivorous and the animals probably change their diet to a considerable extent depending on the availability of food (cf. Lebour, 1922). Detritus may also be used as food, at least to supplement nutritional demands. Riley (1959) has recently drawn attention to the large fraction of the total particulate matter present as detritus in Long Island Sound during late spring and summer. He has questioned whether heavy zooplankton grazers such as *Acartia*, which appear to require nearly 30% of their body weight daily as food, do not

utilize detritus over summer. The importance of detritus in the eco-
nomy of the sea has been emphasized by Krey (1961). Quoting the
results of Hagmeier for Icelandic waters, Krey shows that detritus
can account for 44– > 95% of the total organic suspended matter,
even in the surface layers where the contribution from living plankton
might be expected to be maximal. Although the actual quantity
of organic matter was lower, as would be expected, in the deeper
layers, the proportion of detritus might reach almost 100%. For
the North Sea, some areas such as the Dogger Bank did not show
such a very high proportion of detritus, though even when the spring
phytoplankton blooming was taking place, detritus still accounted
for 50% of the total organic suspended matter. And some areas
(e.g. English coastal waters of the southern North Sea) gave relatively
high weights of detritus (4.6 mg/l.), equivalent to more than 90%
of the total organic suspended matter. Banse also found for the
German Bight some 96% as detritus, compared with only 4% as
plankton, in the organic particulate matter of the water. In the more
open Baltic, the surface showed the lowest percentage of detritus,
but in the discontinuity layer and the bottom stratum, 80–90% of
the organic particulate matter was detritus. Off Kiel, Gillbricht
obtained very high percentages of detritus, but a recent analysis
of the weight of organic matter showed once again lower values
at the surface (even as low as 21%), with, however, as much as 96%
of the particulate organic matter as detritus in the bottom waters.
Clearly, in the few areas so far investigated, detritus occurs in very
significant amounts as compared with living particulate matter.
But we know too little of its distribution, especially in deeper oceanic
regions, and little is known regarding its digestibility. Nevertheless,
the importance of detritus as a source of food for plankton (and
for benthos) must not be overlooked.

The determination of specific food requirements for a particular
species of zooplankton is no simple matter. Examination of gut
contents of specimens taken in the field may prove helpful but a
large percentage of the plankton population usually shows the gut to
be devoid of food. One reason for this is that feeding processes in
zooplankton appear to be rapid. Harvey (1942) quotes *Calanus* as
discharging a green faecal pellet every twenty minutes. Gauld (1953)
states that the gut of a copepod will fill within an hour of placing
the animal in a feeding medium. The gut will similarly empty itself
an hour from transferring the copepod to a dish without food.

Another method of assessing specific food requirements is by controlled laboratory experiments using pure food cultures. One difficulty in interpreting the results of experiments is that many herbivorous zooplankton species will readily ingest food, but much of the material may be subsequently defaecated without a significant amount having been assimilated.

In spite of these and many other difficulties certain major groups of zooplankton may be generally classified as herbivores or carnivores, largely as a result of field examinations. Medusae, ctenophores, sagittae, the gymnosomatous pteropods, tomopterids and alciopids, as well as the vast majority of fish larvae are carnivorous, preying on the other members of the zooplankton. Most decapod larvae also feed on other plankton animals. The specific food organisms for these various carnivores are virtually unknown. Sagittae and medusae prey largely on copepods but this may be mainly a reflection of the relative abundance of these crustaceans. Ctenophores as well as medusae and sagittae will feed voraciously on young fish larvae (Lebour, 1922, 1923). Hardy and Bainbridge have reported sagittae taking cirripede larvae. Ussing (1938) states that in polar waters *Clione* preys largely on the shelled pteropods. Owing to the economic importance of fish larvae, perhaps rather more is known of the diet of these carnivores than of other predaceous forms. Most fish larvae feed mainly on copepods but Wiborg has shown that cod larvae of different ages consume different species and stages of copepods. He suggests that the breadth of mouth of the fish larva is an important factor in the selection of food. Lebour (1918, 1919) also investigated the food of many species of fish larvae. Although phytoplankton might be taken to a small extent, the main food for most larval teleosts consisted of the common copepods, chiefly *Pseudocalanus*, *Temora*, *Acartia*, *Calanus* and *Oithona*. Cladocera were readily eaten when available, and balanid nauplii and larval molluscs were also taken. The diet was influenced largely by the abundance of the food species, but there was evidence of some selection due mainly to the size of mouth of the fish larva or post-larva in relation to the size of the prey. Possibly more active selection occurred, however. Lebour noted for instance that very few decapod larvae were eaten by young fish, and the amphipod *Hyperia* was not taken even though readily available. That dietary requirements change with age in fish larvae is illustrated by the extensive investigations of Hardy (1924) on the food of the herring. Figure 17.1 illustrates that there is a degree of selection and this changes with age. Thus larval herring, like many other teleost larvae, though essentially carnivorous, appear to take phytoplankton food as well as larval molluscs and young copepods at a very early stage. According to Lebour (1921) phytoplankton is apparently not eaten after the disappearance of the yolk sac. Following this change to animal diet, there is still some selec-

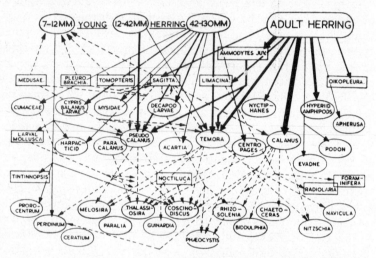

FIG. 17.1 The food of the herring (Hardy, 1924).

tion: larval molluscs are less important and *Pseudocalanus* becomes the chief food. Only older post-larvae will take larger copepods. Plaice larvae take phytoplankton food and later, copepod nauplii and mollusc larvae. Shelbourne's (1953) investigations suggest that *Oikopleura* is a particularly important food after the earliest stages. The degree of selection in the diet may be largely determined by the vulnerability of the prey. Marak (1960) concludes that there is very little selection, apart from size, in the feeding of larvae of the gadoids, cod, haddock and coalfish. Small larvae subsisted mainly on larval copepods; larger post-larvae on adult copepods, while the largest post-larvae could feed to some extent on young euphausids and amphipods, as well as on the copepods. *Centropages, Pseudocalanus, Paracalanus, Calanus, Temora* and *Tortanus* were all used as food; provided they were suitable in size, the larval fish fed on the most abundant species.

Investigations on the food of some carnivorous members of the zooplankton have shown that they may feed on species which are themselves carnivorous. In this way second-stage predators can be present in the zooplankton. Pelagic heteropods, for example, feed partly on copepods but to a large extent on chaetognaths. Medusae and ctenophores will feed on sagittae as do many fish larvae (Lebour, 1923). The ctenophore *Beroe cucumis* has been observed to feed on *Pleurobrachia*; in Russian waters, according to Kamshilov (1955), it feeds exclusively on the ctenophore *Bolinopsis infundibulum*, so that its presence could be beneficial rather than harmful to young fish. Studies by Wiborg (1948a, b, 1949) have demonstrated that cod larvae may consume euphausids, decapod larvae and other crustaceans which are themselves partly carnivorous. Cod fry may also feed occasionally on other fish larvae. Recently, Wiborg (1960) has reported haddock fry in one locality feeding on medusae.

The predominantly herbivorous groups of the zooplankton include the copepods, cladocerans, euphausids and some other crustaceans, together with the appendicularians and the shelled pteropods. The larvae of most of the bottom invertebrates, such as veligers, trochophores, nauplii and the larvae of echinoderms feed generally on phytoplankton, as do the younger stages of many holoplanktonic animals.

Of the herbivores, the copepods have perhaps been most studied and diatoms are usually regarded as the most important food. This is probably true, especially of polar regions, where vast diatom blooms occur. In the Antarctic, euphausids as well as the commoner copepods appear to live almost exclusively on the great concentrations of diatoms, and in more temperate regions the investigations of Esterly, Dakin, Marshall and others have shown that diatoms usually are the chief food of copepods. Dakin (1908) recorded only phytoplankton, chiefly diatoms, but also peridinians and unidentified micro-algae, from the guts of *Calanus finmarchicus*. Esterly (1916), however, from an examination of *Gaidius* and *Undeuchaeta*, found that copepod remains as well as phytoplankton occurred in the gut contents, indicating a mixed diet. In *Scottocalanus* (*Scolecithrix*) *persecans* Esterly found abundant copepod remains. Undoubtedly even in such a predominantly herbivorous group as the copepods, carnivorous forms such as *Euchaeta* and *Scottocalanus* also occur. Ussing (1938) points out that other species such as the deep sea copepods *Bathycalanus*, *Megacalanus* and *Valdiviella* are almost certainly animal feeders. They live on other copepods, particularly those that tend to drift down from the upper layers. The mouth parts of *Euchaeta* in particular are relatively coarse in texture, and it is doubtful whether they could retain much typical phytoplankton food (cf. Conover, 1960). Laboratory experiments strongly suggest that *Euchaeta* will not take phytoplankton. Not all the carnivorous copepods are deep-living, however. *Tortanus discaudatus* is a surface living copepod off North America which has been suggested (cf. Raymont, 1959) as being exclusively carnivorous, and Wickstead (1959) has recently reported that the copepod *Candacia bradyi* is predaceous on chaetognaths. Lebour (1922) also considered that *Anomalocera* and *Labidocera* are mainly predatory. In addition there appear to be a number of copepods such as *Temora* and *Centropages*, which, though they can be fed in the laboratory on phytoplankton, appear from the work of Lebour and others to exist under natural conditions on a mixed diet of phytoplankton and animal food. Observations by Lance (1960) and others have shown that the copepods *Acartia* and *Centropages* may sometimes consume younger stages of other copepods. Many copepods probably consume detritus and tend towards an omnivorous diet. The taking of animal food may be particularly important during the period of winter scarcity at high latitudes. Ussing (1938) in his investigations in polar waters, considered that copepods might become partly carnivorous during the winter, though his examination of the guts of the animals gave little support to the theory. Digby (1954) also believes that *Calanus* must be partly carnivorous over the winter period. In a somewhat similar manner, the meagre supply of food in deep water makes it likely that a number of deeper living copepod species must be partly carnivorous.

This variation in the diet of particular species is probably true of other groups of zooplankton, though copepods have received most study. Some euphausids are undoubtedly herbivorous; the Antarctic *Euphausia superba* appears to feed exclusively on the rich blooms of diatoms. Barkley (1940) concludes that there is some selection in the species of diatom used as food; *Fragilariopsis antarctica* is most generally consumed, and other relatively small and smooth-celled species are also widely eaten. According to Barkley, no organisms apart from diatoms appear to be of any nutritional significance to *E. superba*. Lebour (1924) found that *Nyctiphanes couchi* fed on phytoplankton, mostly diatoms, but there was some unidentifiable debris which might indicate detrital feeding. Animal food was occasionally taken. On the other hand, Hickling (1925) claimed that euphausids were feeding on detritus and some earlier investigators regarded them as carnivorous. Ussing (1938) stated that euphausids occurring off East Greenland were carnivorous, and Einarsson (1945) considered that for *Thysanoessa* spp., *Meganyctiphanes norvegica* and *Thysanopoda acutifrons*, phytoplankton food was unimportant, detritus and some zooplankton being eaten. Macdonald (1927) investigated the feeding of *Meganyctiphanes norvegica* in the Clyde Area. He observed that diatoms and micro-plankton formed part of the food of this euphausid, particularly of the younger stages, but that detritus, including some of terrestrial origin, bulked very largely in the food. Macdonald also noted that the largest *Meganyctiphanes* were carnivorous to a considerable extent, feeding on copepods such as *Calanus* and *Euchaeta*. A recent re-investigation of the food of the same euphausid by Fisher and Goldie (1959) confirms that detritus is an important constituent of the regular diet. Phytoplankton is of less importance though dinoflagellates and some diatoms are eaten. Crustacea, including copepods and Eucarida, are taken to a considerable extent. Mauchline (1959) considers that the smallest *Meganyctiphanes* are mainly filter feeders while the largest are mainly carnivorous. Crustacea remains bulk largest of the animal food taken; *Euchaeta* and *Sagitta* are important in the diet and the amount increases with the size of *Meganyctiphanes*. Mauchline agrees with other authors that detritus and filamentous algae are taken to a considerable extent as food. Of the phytoplankton consumed, dinoflagellates are of more significance than diatoms.

Ponomareva (1955) has investigated the food of *Thysanoessa inermis*, *Th. raschii*, *Th. longipes* and *Euphausia pacifica* in the Sea of Japan. She emphasizes the importance of examining the contents of the thoracic "basket" between the legs as well as the stomach material, since hard portions of the food such as chitinous and siliceous skeletons are apparently held back in the "basket" to a large extent. All the species except *Th. longipes* will feed on phytoplankton, filtering usually the most abundant species in spring; all take detritus to some extent. The lack of phytoplankton feeding exhibited by *Th. longipes* may perhaps be associated with its somewhat deeper living habit. However, while *Th. raschii* takes only some eggs and nauplii of copepods, apart from phytoplankton and detritus, the other three euphausids are more obviously carnivorous on the zooplankton. Molluscs, amphipods and *Oikopleura*, and, at times of scarcity of larger zooplankton, tintinnids and *Globigerina*, are all consumed. But the chief animal food comes from copepods. Euphausids also appear to feed on each other to some degree. There is some selection with regard to the copepod diet; *Metridia pacifica* and *Calanus tonsus* are most commonly eaten, though they are not always the most abundant in the plankton. While copepods such as *Eucalanus bungii* and *Pareuchaeta japonica* may be too large, it is surprising that the common small copepod, *Oithona similis*, is rarely taken. It is certain that deeper living species must rely mainly on animal food and upon detritus.

Some species of mysids undoubtedly filter phytoplankton effectively (cf. Lucas, 1936), but Tattersall and Tattersall (1951) suggest that many species supplement their food with animal tissue. Zenkevitch and Birstein (1956) state that the deep-living mysid *Gnathophausia gigas* and the euphausid, *Bentheuphausia amblyops*, while essentially carnivorous, may feed by filtration and that they utilize the faecal pellets of other plankton. The ostracods appear to furnish yet another example of differences in the diet of various species. Cannon's (1931) investigations on *Cypridina levis* indicate that the animal feeds by filtering particles. On the other hand, his study (Cannon, 1940) of *Gigantocypris mulleri* shows that this species is apparently predaceous on sagittae, copepods and even fish larvae, despite its comparatively poor swimming powers.

Our knowledge of specific dietary requirements is thus fragmentary. Nevertheless, much information is available for certain groups, especially copepods. Although such species as *Acartia*, *Temora* and *Centropages* are omnivorous, they usually graze extensively on phytoplankton. Similarly, though *Calanus* may take some animal food in times of scarcity, this species as well as such common forms as *Rhincalanus*, *Pseudocalanus*, *Paracalanus* and *Metridia* are essentially herbivorous in their feeding. Studies on the food of *Calanus finmarchicus* have been excellently summarized in the work of Marshall and Orr (1955). It can feed on a wide variety of diatoms, including some of the largest forms like *Coscinodiscus* and *Ditylum brightwelli*. At the other extreme it will readily graze on small species of *Chaetoceros* and especially on *Skeletonema costatum*, which, in the Clyde and other areas, is one of the main spring diatoms. *Calanus* will take even the very small *Nitzschia closterium* var. *minutissima* (= *Phaeodactylum*). Harvey (1937b) suggested, however, that there is some selectivity in the diet. He fed *Calanus* with a mixture of *Chaetoceros* and *Lauderia* and showed that although *Chaetoceros* was hardly eaten, the second of the two diatoms was readily consumed. Again, with a mixture of *Lauderia* and *Nitzschia*, Harvey found a larger volume swept clear for the former species. *Calanus* may also feed on dinoflagellates. Field examinations and laboratory experiments have demonstrated that such species as *Prorocentrum*, *Peridinium*, *Gymnodinium* and *Syracosphaera* are readily utilized by *Calanus*, but some powers of selection may once more be apparent. Marshall found that silicoflagellates and coccolithophores did not form an important part of the diet, and *Ceratium*, though often very abundant in the seas, is comparatively rarely eaten by *Calanus*. Small flagellates included in the nannoplankton such as *Dicrateria*, *Pyramimonas* and *Chlamydomonas* were shown by Raymont and Gross (1942) to be grazed by this copepod. Ussing had previously questioned whether *Calanus* could filter small flagellates. He based his suggestion on an examination of the distance between the setules of the feeding appendages, and thought that organisms below a diameter of $4-5\,\mu$ might pass through the filter. Marshall and Orr's (1956) measurements gave the smallest distance as $2-3\,\mu$. This would support the view that many flagellates can be filtered, though extremely small forms (e.g. *Nannochloris oculata*) may not be retained (Fig. 17.2).

But size may not be the only important factor in feeding. There was some suggestion from earlier work that *Chlamydomonas* was more suitable as food than algae of similar size. Marshall and Orr (1952) have examined the effects of different foods on *Calanus* in more detail. They found that starvation caused a marked reduction in egg laying, and egg production was therefore used as a criterion of the suitability of organisms as food. All diatoms tested (*Lauderia*, *Chaetoceros*, *Coscinodiscus*, *Skeletonema*, *Rhizosolenia*, *Ditylum*) were shown to be suitable food material causing oviposition, as were some dinoflagellates (*Peridinium*, *Syracosphaera* and *Gymnodinium*). Some flagellates such as *Chlamydomonas* (*Dunaliella*) and an un-identified Chrysomonad were satisfactory foods, but others (*Dicrateria*, *Hemiselmis* and *Chlorella*) though ingested, did not cause any increase in egg production as compared with starved copepods. *Chlorella* indeed appeared to pass through the gut almost unchanged. Some phytoplankton species are known to be toxic and are presumably avoided by herbivores. There is some evidence that other phytoplankton species in really high concentrations are avoided by zooplankton; Bainbridge (1953) observed this behaviour with very high concentrations of two species of flagellate. There would thus appear to be a whole range of algal species extending from definitely harmful, through useless to edible species of differing suitabilities.

To this complex picture of specific adult food requirements must be added the differing demands of the various stages of copepods. It would seem probable that the younger stages of *Calanus* would be restricted to smaller algae. Marshall and Orr (1955a) suggested

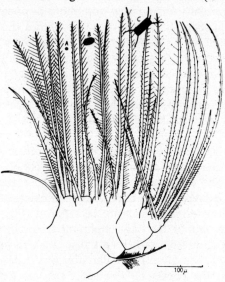

FIG. 17.2 The left maxilla of *Calanus helgolandicus*. A = *Nannochloris oculata;* B = *Syracosphaera elongata;* C = *Chaetoceros decipiens* (from Marshall and Orr, 1956).

that the younger nauplii might consume organisms only up to 10 μ in diameter, although the older stages might feed on a considerable variety of algae. Later work by Marshall and Orr (1956) showed that Nauplius I and II stages did not feed at all, but that Nauplius III could eat phytoplankton, both flagellates and diatoms, measuring up to approximately 20 μ in diameter. Moreover, the distance between the setules of the filtering apparatus did not appear to vary much with age in *Calanus*, so that there is no very marked selectivity on account of size. Young copepodites can unquestionably feed on a large range of phytoplankton cells, since the strong mouth parts can crush relatively large algae.

Clarke and Gellis (1935) considered whether *Calanus* might use bacteria as food. The later work of Fuller and Clarke (1936), however, demonstrated clearly that these micro-organisms cannot be regarded as a food source. High concentrations of bacteria, far greater than those present in the sea, failed to increase the survival of copepods. *Calanus* appears, therefore, to feed on a considerable variety of phytoplankton, ranging greatly in size; not all species, however, meet the dietary demands equally.

Far less detailed information is available on the specific food requirements of copepods other than *Calanus finmarchicus*, though evidence suggests that they feed generally on the same types of phytoplankton. A study of gut contents suggests that a wide variety of diatoms and of other plankton algae may be taken by most copepods. Beklemishev (1954) investigated the gut contents of several calanoids in Pacific waters, *Calanus* spp., *Metridia* spp., and *Eucalanus bungii*. He found that diatoms predominated in the diet in more northern waters, many of the larger diatom species being of considerable importance. The larger cells are partly broken before being swallowed, but smaller diatoms are eaten whole. There was evidence that comparatively deeper living copepods, *Gaidius* sp. and *Gaetanus minor*, also consumed large diatoms such as *Coscinodiscus oculus-iridis*. In warmer areas Beklemishev found that the copepods consumed a greater proportion of *Exuviella*, coccolithophores and peridinians; he believes that dinoflagellates and other flagellates are of importance in providing nutriment over the summer in temperate waters when diatoms are less abundant. All the copepods are carnivorous to some degree, especially over the winter. Deep living species are often predatory, and the structure of the mandibles in such carnivorous forms as *Euchaeta* and *Bathycalanus* is associated with the predatory habit (cf. Bogorov, 1958c). Conover (1960) also believes that these deep living copepods as well as species such as *Euchirella rostrata* are at least partially carnivorous, but on the other hand he has demonstrated that the deep living *Calanus hyperboreus* is a herbivore. As a result of laboratory experiment Clarke and Gellis (1935) showed that the smaller calanoids *Centropages*, *Acartia* and *Labidocera* showed some improvement in survival when fed on the flagellates *Chlamydomonas*, *Dunaliella* and *Carteria* as well as on the diatom *Nitzschia*. Gauld (1953) was able to keep several small copepods (*Temora*, *Pseudocalanus* and *Centropages*) on cultures of *Chlamydomonas* and *Skeletonema* while studying the feeding rates of the copepods. Conover (1956) has compared the feeding of two species of *Acartia*, *A. clausi* and *A. tonsa*. He suggests that although *Acartia* can live on a wide variety of diatom and flagellate foods, the setae of the feeding appendages are rather coarse and *Acartia* tends to be a "wasteful" feeder as compared with other copepods of similar size. Raymont (1959) showed that flagellates, mostly *Dunaliella* and *Dicrateria*, are filtered extensively by several copepods including *Centropages hamatus*, *Eurytemora herdmani*, *Pseudocalanus minutus*, *Temora longicornis* and *Metridia lucens*. There was some suggestion that *Centropages hamatus* did not always feed as readily on phytoplankton as the other species. This might confirm earlier suggestions from field observations that *Centropages* feeds on a mixture of plant and animal food. In some of these experiments nauplii were produced from eggs laid by the copepods. This would suggest that the food filtered was suitable. However, no detailed observations on the effect of different types of food on smaller copepods similar to those of Marshall and Orr on *Calanus* have yet been made. The unpublished results of Gross and Clarke's work on the fertilization of sea water in enclosed tanks at Woods Hole, support the general view that smaller copepods feed on a wide range of algae. In these tank experiments a considerable variety of diatom and other phytoplankton forms were observed. This mixed phytoplankton supported remarkably dense populations of the copepod, *Tisbe furcata*, as well as some calanoid forms, mainly *Pseudocalanus minutus*. These results can be supplemented by those of Raymont and Miller (1962) also from tank fertilization experiments at Woods Hole. Although a variety of diatoms and μ-flagellates occurred in these cultures early in the experiments, there was a very marked tendency for only one or two species of phytoplankton to predominate, mainly *Exuviella marina*, *Nannochloris* sp. and *Nitzschia closterium*. Several small species of copepods, *Paracalanus crassirostris*, *Eurytemora hirundoides*, *Oithona brevicornis* and especially *Acartia tonsa*, flourished and passed through several reproductive cycles in the tanks. They must therefore have fed almost exclusively on these few species of phytoplankton, but utilized them successfully for egg production and for naupliar development. The real suitability of these algae as food is apparent from the very high densities of zooplankton which were obtained in the experiments.

The problem of the nutritional value of different algae to various species of the zooplankton may be even more complicated if the

investigations of Provasoli and his colleagues (e.g. Shiraishi and Provasoli, 1959) on the harpacticoid copepod *Tigriopus japonicus* are
applicable to marine calanoids. These workers have demonstrated
that *Tigriopus* may be grown on many different bacterial-free algal
cultures, but that growth and the reproductive capacity of the animals
vary greatly. Some algal foods, for example, do not promote egg
production; others allow a limited number of generations, whereas
some food species permit apparently continuous reproduction. The
presence of bacteria may modify the effect of an algal food, suggesting that vitamins or other growth factors are involved.

Few studies have been made on specific food requirements of zooplankton other than copepods. The larvae of several species of bivalves have been fed on algal cultures by Loosanoff and his associates.
The larvae of *Venus mercenaria*, for example, have been grown on
Chlorella and sulphur bacteria cultures, as well as on detrital suspen-
sions (cf. Loosanoff, Miller and Smith, 1951). The economic importance of the oyster has focused attention on the dietary requirements of the larvae of this lamellibranch. Many workers (Cole,
Korringa, Loosanoff, Nelson, Bruce, Knight and Parke) have stressed
the necessity of providing food of suitable size for young larval
stages. Algal cells exceeding $10\,\mu$ in diameter cannot be ingested.
The μ-flagellates are, therefore, particularly useful as a source of
food for oyster larvae, but the work of Bruce, Knight and Parke
(1940) suggested that not all algae of suitable size were equally effective as food. This work has been carried further by Davis (1953) who
investigated the food of the larvae of the American oyster, *Crasso-
strea virginica*). Davis showed that while the size of food particles
was of great importance it was not the only significant factor determining whether an organism would serve as food. Earlier work
demonstrated that four species of bacteria and three flagellate species
would not promote good growth, and that detritus was also ineffective as a food source. Later, Davis showed that nine different
species of bacteria and one species of chrysomonad failed to meet
the dietary demands of oyster larvae, but five species of μ-flagellate
(*Dicrateria inornata*, *Hemiselmis rufescens*, *Isochrysis galbana*,
Chromulina pleiades, *Pyramimonas grossii*) all gave very good growth,
as did a "mixed *Chlorella*" culture (cf. Fig. 17.3). There was some
indication that the suitability of the various food organisms changed
with growth of the larvae. The youngest oyster larvae could not
utilize pure *Chlorella* cultures, whereas older larvae were capable

of growth on *Chlorella* (cf. Marshall and Orr's results for *Calanus*). Davis did not obtain strong evidence for interaction between different algal food species, but Bruce, Knight and Parke (1940) suggested that with *Ostrea edulis* larvae, *Pyramimonas* and *Chromulina* fed together were more effective as a food supply. There is some evidence

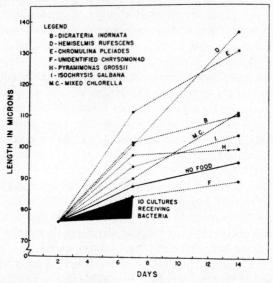

FIG. 17.3 Growth of oyster larvae on different diets (from Davis, 1953).

that excessive food concentrations may prove harmful as for copepods.

With regard to the food of other zooplankton, the cirripede larvae *Balanus balanoides*, *Verruca stroemia* and *Chthamalus stellatus* have been reared through a series of moults by Bassindale (1936) on a culture of *Nitzschia closterium*. Certain other algae appeared in some of the cultures however, and growth was not followed by settlement. Lochhead (1936) investigated the size of particles taken by nauplii of *Balanus perforatus* and claimed that cells exceeding 6 μ in diameter could not be swallowed, though the length of cells could be considerably greater. He included Protozoa, small diatoms, filamentous algae and especially small flagellates in the diet. Many other workers have shown that cirripede nauplii can filter small phytoplankton cells including both diatoms and flagellates. Lochhead held that there was no selection of food apart from size, but that *B. perforatus* nauplii could not masticate larger diatoms. There seems little doubt, however, that a wide variety of food organisms can be utilized by cirripede larvae. Soares (1957) showed that diatoms as large as *Coscinodiscus* can be broken up and eaten by the nauplii of *Elminius modestus*, yet both *E. modestus* and *Balanus crenatus* larvae filtered flagellates of the size of *Dunaliella* and the small diatom *Nitzschia closterium*. Barnes holds that growth of cirripede larvae in the Clyde Area is promoted by the spring phytoplankton increase which is dominated by diatoms, especially *Skeletonema costatum*. Hudinaga and Kasahara (1941) were able to rear *B. amphitrite* var. *hawaiiensis* on *Skeletonema*.

Perhaps the most successful rearing of cirripedes on known diets has been achieved by Costlow and Bookhout (1957, 1958). Nauplii of *Balanus eburneus* and of *B. amphitrite* var. *denticulata* were reared to the cyprid stage and through metamorphosis to the settled adult on *Chlamydomonas* sp. culture to which some developing *Arbacia* eggs were added. There was a suggestion that development was not successful on pure *Chlamydomonas* diet. The dietary value of other species of flagellate and of diatoms would be of considerable interest.

An example of a member of the zooplankton exhibiting marked selection in feeding comes from the field studies of Bainbridge (1958), who analysed the food of the marine cladoceran *Evadne nordmanni*. This crustacean appears to become abundant in the Clyde Area mainly when certain types of phytoplankton, peridinians and tintinnids, are plentiful. Examination of gut contents and of the food held by feeding appendages confirmed that *Evadne* is a very selective feeder. *Peridinium* spp., *Ceratium furca* and probably other peridinians are eaten, though even other species of *Ceratium* appear to be neglected (cf. Table 17.1). Tintinnids are also eaten but diatoms tend to be unimportant. It seems likely that *Evadne* actively seizes particles and does not filter its food. Many workers have suggested however, that active grasping of particulate food as well as filtration may go on in many crustaceans including copepods and mysids. Harvey (1939) suggested this for *Calanus*, and Cushing has put forward the theory that calanoids may sense the presence of diatoms by means of the antennules; the algae are then actively seized.

Studies on the rearing of polychaete and echinoderm larvae (cf. Wilson) on algal cultures such as *Nitzschia* and various flagellates demonstrate that, as with lamellibranchs, the smaller phytoplankton species can be utilized as food. There is little information, however, as to whether larvae are selective and whether some foods differ in their suitability for full development. There is even less certainty on the nutritive requirement of zooplankton demanding animal food. The pioneer work of Lebour (1928) showed that various species

TABLE 17.1 The percentage composition of organisms held by preserved *Evadne*

(The percentages for 17 and 18 October 1951 are compared with the percentage composition of the microplankton at 1 m.) (from Bainbridge, 1958).

	Organisms held by *Evadne* 17 and 18 October 1951	Microplankton 17 and 18 October 1951
Phytoplankton		
Diatoms	—	0.03
Peridinium spp.	20.9	3.0
Peridinium spp. fragments	1.6	—
Ceratium furca	56.4	34.6
C. furca fragments	15.0	—
Ceratium spp. less *C. furca*	—	55.1
Other dinoflagellates	1.6	6.6
Zooplankton		
Tintinnopsis spp.	1.6	0.06
Tintinnopsis spp. fragments	—	—
Small copepod eggs	3.2	0.5
Copepod egg membranes	—	—
Copepod nauplii	—	—
Larval lamellibranchs	—	—
Unidentified debris	—	—
Number of microplankton organisms examined	62	—
Mean number of organisms per litre	—	12,760

of crab larvae would feed on *Nitzschia* and other algae, but needed animal food to complete a series of moults. Oyster larvae and the young stages of other benthic animals were consumed, together with mussel flesh in the megalopa stages. Costlow and Bookhout (1959) used *Arbacia* eggs and *Artemia* nauplii, supplemented by beef liver, to rear *Callinectes sapidus* in the laboratory. Broad (1957) investigated the rearing of two species of *Palaemonetes* using algal cultures (*Nitzschia, Chlamydomonas, Thorocomonas, Nannochloris, Porphyri-*

dium and *Pyramimonas*), and also animal food including *Artemia* nauplii, chaetognaths and other zooplankton. Differences in survival, frequency of moulting and rate of development were associated with the amount of food available. Broad's work supports Lebour's view that some animal food is necessary, since he found that unialgal cultures or mixtures of algae failed to permit the survival of larvae. The best results were obtained by feeding *Artemia* nauplii. These larvae and mussel flesh have been used in feeding other zooplankton (e.g. lobster larvae), but there is little precise knowledge of the requirements of carnivorous forms. Rochford has recently re-emphasized the role of detritus in the feeding of some zooplankton species. Although Zobell lists a variety of animals which may feed on marine bacteria, the low density of these micro-organisms in the pelagic zone suggests that they are unimportant in the nutrition of plankton.

Apart from specific food requirements, the problem of the feeding of the zooplankton must also involve the amount of food necessary for maintenance and for growth. Although copepods may seize food particles, automatic filtration is the more normal method for food collection. Other feeders on small particles such as many mysids and euphausids may employ filtration. Investigations on the amount of food required by zooplankton animals have been almost confined to filtration rates. In the great majority of cases, a species of copepod, in particular *Calanus finmarchicus*, has been studied.

Filtration in calanoids, although apparently largely automatic, may cease voluntarily and its rate is dependent on physical and chemical factors. There is general agreement that filtration rate increases with a rise of temperature (cf. Fuller, 1937). Food concentration appears to have little effect on feeding rate, though very high concentrations of algae often depress filtration. Feeding may even cease; possibly the feeding appendages become clogged. Fuller (1937) obtained some slight evidence of a diurnal rhythm in feeding, and considered that light might lower the feeding intensity. Wimpenny (1938) also believed, as a result of field observations, that *Calanus* and some smaller calanoids showed some diurnal feeding rhythm. Gauld (1953), however, observed *Calanus* both in the field and in the laboratory, and demonstrated that no feeding rhythm existed. The copepods could have full guts at all hours of the day and could feed continuously over long periods. Differences in feeding between copepods living in the surface and deeper water layers might appear owing to the relative abundance of phytoplankton in the different water layers.

As a result of feeding experiments on Stage V *Calanus finmarchicus*, Fuller and Clarke (1936) obtained a filtration rate for the diatom *Nitzschia closterium* of 5–6 c.c. water swept clear per day. Later rates given by Fuller were somewhat lower. Fuller and Clarke then calculated the amount of food needed by Stage V *Calanus*, on the basis of the oxygen requirements as determined by Marshall, Nicholls and Orr (1935), to satisfy daily maintenance requirements. From an examination of the concentrations of phytoplankton in the seas off the north east coast of North America, Fuller and Clarke showed that about 100 c.c. of water containing diatoms, or 300 c.c. containing flagellates, would need to be filtered daily. Taking all types of phytoplankton, they calculated that a filtration rate of about 70 c.c. per day was essential for maintenance alone. Although it is now known that greater densities of nannoplankton may be available which would reduce the daily volume to be filtered, the discrepancy between the clearance found experimentally and that which appears to be required is very large. Harvey (1937b), working also with *Calanus finmarchicus*, found much higher clearance rates, though some of his experiments covered shorter periods. He suggests for the diatom *Lauderia* a mean clearance rate of 3 c.c. per hour, but with *Ditylum*, rates of 7 and even 10 c.c. per hour were obtained. These values would correspond to approximately 70 c.c. per day for *Lauderia*; the mean rate for *Ditylum* would be 200 c.c. per day. The marked difference between Fuller's and Harvey's estimates may possibly be explained by the fact that in Fuller's experiment the copepods were confined in very small volumes of water and filtration was greatly depressed by these conditions. Possibly also *Nitzschia* is less actively filtered than the larger diatoms. It is doubtful whether the highest rates recorded by Harvey would hold over a 24 hr period. The two experiments on *Ditylum* ran for only 7 hours though *Ditylum* may be exceptionally well filtered in view of its large size. There is little doubt, however, from Harvey's work that rates of the order of 70 c.c./day are real for a 24-hour period. This would agree with the results of Gauld (1951) who, working with *Calanus* Stage V, obtained filtration rates varying from 40–100 c.c./day, with a mean of *ca.* 70 c.c./day. Gauld's experiments lasted for 18–24 hr. He emphasizes the point that the copepods were behaving as filter feeders. The rate of filtration was independent of the food concentration as Fuller and Clarke had found, though possibly the copepods fed only intermittently. These relatively high clearance rates were obtained by Gauld using *Chla-*

mydomonas as food. This flagellate, though slightly larger than *Nitzschia*, does not reach the dimensions of *Chaetoceros*. But the filtering rates for *Chlamydomonas* are far higher than for this diatom. Selection in feeding is apparently not merely a matter of size of food particle. Marshall and Orr (1955b) suggest indeed that with diatoms, the size of cell has no effect on feeding rate. These workers obtained only slight evidence, however, for selection of food species by *Calanus*. Both the experiments by Harvey and those of Gauld would indicate that filtration rates for *Calanus* can cover the calculated food requirements. But the calculations made by Fuller and Clarke were made for water fairly rich in phytoplankton. Over considerable periods of the year the plant cells are much less abundant. Moreover, even when the phytoplankton is rich, the high densities are confined to the surface layers. As *Calanus* and other copepods spend a considerable portion of the day below the surface, they must be capable of filtering much larger quantities of water in order to obtain food sufficient for growth, maintenance and reproduction. The danger of starvation looms particularly large for copepods which, at a certain stage in the life history, migrate for long periods to deep water. The difficulty may be increased if, as Marshall and Orr (1955b) suggest for *Calanus* Stage V, overwintering copepods do not feed so actively.

Marshall and Orr (1955b), in considering the food requirements of *Calanus* have determined filtration rates with the aid of ^{32}P. A large variety of diatoms, dinoflagellates and of flagellates belonging to the Chlorophyceae, Chrysophyceae and Cryptophyceae were grown in culture with radioactive phosphorus. *Calanus* were then fed on these cultures, and the volume of culture cleared estimated from the radioactivity of the bodies of the copepods, due consideration being paid to the activity of faeces and eggs produced. Although almost all cultures were freely filtered, including *Prymnesium parvum* which is known to be toxic to fish, there was an extraordinary range in feeding rates, even when the same food organism was used. Rates were somewhat lower in the highest food concentrations, but as other workers have suggested, apart from this effect, there is little relation between concentration and rate of filtration. Individual copepods were remarkably variable, however, in their feeding. In the same experiment some would feed very actively and others would cease feeding altogether, though all the animals appeared healthy. Probably the state of maturity, and other factors affecting the physiology of the animal influence the filtration rate. The time of year as well as the age both of food culture and of the grazers are other factors which Marshall and Orr believe may play some part. These authors confirmed Gauld's observation that calanoids are apparently not automatic feeders in the sense that they must ingest food all the time that their locomotory organs are moving; the copepods may cease filtering. At high food concentrations they suggest that *Calanus* is unable to ingest so much food, rather than experiencing any inhibitory effect from the algae. Faecal pellet production gave a reasonably quantitative estimation of the feeding rate, but Marshall and Orr find that at high concentrations, the number of faecal pellets does not increase regularly with the food concentration.

One of the most surprising results of this more recent work was the high percentage of algal cells digested by *Calanus*. Most earlier work had suggested that copepods frequently feed to excess, certainly in laboratory experiment, and sometimes in the sea. Marshall and Orr's results indicated that while a few organisms, including the flagellates *Dicrateria inornata*, *Chromulina pusilla* and *Chlorella stigmatophora*, were not being digested efficiently, for the great majority of phytoplankton some 70–80% of the cells were digested. Variation occurred even with the same food organisms but where the food was obviously being utilized, the extreme variation ranged between 50 and over 90%. This high degree of utilization is all the more remarkable as Marshall and Orr themselves found very high rates of faecal pellet production; at its maximum one faecal pellet could occur every five or seven minutes. However, even at these rates there appears to be a high percentage of digestion. The authors suggest that the viable cells which most investigators have noted in faecal pellets amount to only a small percentage of the material.

Phosphorus is known to be labile in part in algae and it appeared possible that a fraction of the phosphorus might be adsorbed on the copepods or on the faecal pellets. This would give rise to incorrectly high digestion figures. Further experiments by Marshall and Orr (1955c) using cultures of *Skeletonema costatum*, *Cryptomonas* sp. and *Syracosphaera carterae* labelled with ^{14}C, however, confirmed high values for digestion by *Calanus*. The values for *Syracosphaera* were slightly below those for ^{32}P culture but for all the cultures, digestion ranged from 50–80%. The experimental work of Marshall and Orr therefore suggests that most of the food ingested by copepods, even when feeding rapidly, is digested. This leaves open, however, the important problem that there appears to be a considerable gap between the amount of water which a copepod can clear under experimental conditions, and the volume necessary for growth and maintenance. Marshall and Orr point out that concentrations of several thousand phytoplankton cells per c.c. occur in the sea for only very short periods; normally the concentrations are far lower. The volumes filtered as determined by ^{32}P and ^{14}C techniques were much lower than those obtained by Gauld and Harvey. Marshall and Orr's values ranged from less than 1 c.c. per *Calanus* per day to about 40 c.c/day; only very rarely were higher filtration rates obtained. For much of the year therefore *Calanus* would appear to be obtaining

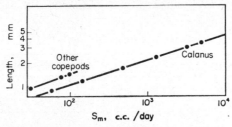

FIG. 17.4 "Mechanical grazing rates" (S_m) for *Calanus* and "other copepods" (from Cushing, 1959).

only a few hundred cells per day under natural conditions. But perhaps grazing rates as determined by ^{32}P methods are too low. Some preliminary experiments by Conover, Marshall and Orr (1959) on *Calanus finmarchicus* and *Acartia clausi* suggest very tentatively that there may be a constant discrepancy between rates as determined by cell counts and as measured by ^{32}P uptake.

Using the carbon content of *Calanus*, Riley, and later Cushing have calculated the amount of water that the copepod must filter to supply minimal needs. The value approaches 70 c.c./day. Cushing, however, has recently advanced the view that the "encounter theory" of grazing (cf. p. 515), will enable a copepod to sweep clear a much increased volume of water. The diatoms are sensed by the tactile hairs on the extended antennules and then eaten. Cushing has calculated from the size of copepods, their antennule length and the distribution of hairs, the volume which might be swept clear at different swimming speeds. Allowing time for the seizing of the cells, he has calculated that *Calanus* may sweep far more than 1000 c.c./day (cf. Fig. 17.4). Cushing has also observed a very sharp reduction in algal numbers in the North Sea which, if caused by grazing by the known density of copepods, would indicate clearances of considerably more than 1000 c.c./day. To a considerable extent the calculation of the volumes cleared by a copepod must depend not only on the precise distribution of the antennal hairs but on the angles which they maintain during locomotion. And if such volumes can be swept clear, it seems curious that these high rates have not been obtained by experiment. Cushing, however, claims that the size of experimental vessel is a most important factor. With *Temora longicornis*, he has shown that the volume cleared increases with the capacity of the container, so that with a vessel of 500 c.c., this relatively small copepod can filter even 150 c.c./day (Table 17.2). For the larger copepod

TABLE 17.2 (from Cushing, 1959)

Volume of vessel	5 c.c.	25 c.c.	100 c.c.	500 c.c.
Volume swept clear by *Temora longicornis* in one day	6 c.c.	13 c.c.	26 c.c.	150 c.c.

Anomalocera patersoni, he claims a grazing rate of approximately 1000 c.c./day when large flasks are used. It would appear necessary to check these very high filtration rates with other zooplankton. Corner (1961) has recently reported feeding rates for female *Calanus helgolandicus* using a constant flow method. Preliminary estimates show a mean filtration rate of 21.5 c.c./day during summer months. With the amount of particulate matter then available for food, it would appear that this rate was more than sufficient to supply the animal's metabolic needs. The average amount of food consumed was 25% of the dry body weight, which is a remarkably high value. It is still unknown whether these rates of feeding will hold over other months of the year.

Very little information is available on the filtering rates of copepods other than late stage *Calanus finmarchicus*. Gauld (1951) shows that for St. IV *Calanus* the rate is reduced to·37 c.c./day, and for St. III copepodites to only 22 c.c./day. For the smaller copepods, *Pseudocalanus minutus*, *Temora longicornis* and *Centropages hamatus*, the rates range from 4–13 c.c./day (Table 17.3). Gauld considers that the rate is roughly proportional to the square of the linear dimensions of the copepod. Cushing has calculated, employing his "encounter theory", the volumes cleared by the various copepodite stages of *Calanus* at different food cell concentrations (Fig. 17.5). Marshall and Orr (1956) using the ^{32}P method, show a rise in filtration rate with the developmental stage for *Calanus*. Nauplius III, for example, has a maximum rate of about 1 c.c./day as against a maximal rate

TABLE 17.3 (modified from Gauld, 1951)

Species	No. of copepods per vessel	Volume of vessel (c.c.)	Duration (hr)	Tempera-ture (°C)	Mean volume swept clear per copepod (c.c.)
Pseudocalanus minutus	1	10	24	10	4.28
Temora longicornis	10	150	24	10	8.38
Centropages hamatus	10	150	24	10	12.99
Calanus finmarchicus Stage V*	1	100	24	12.5	64.36
C. finmarchicus Stage V*	1	100	18	17	71.03
C. finmarchicus Stage IV	2	100	18	17	36.65
C. finmarchicus Stage III	3	100	18	17	22.24

* Two series of experiments.

of 9 c.c./day for Copepodite III. Conover (1956) studied the feeding rates of *Acartia tonsa* and *A. clausi*. A range in clearance rate of 6 to > 20 c.c./copepod/day was found for *A. tonsa* at temperatures from 10–20 °C when the copepod was fed on *Skeletonema costatum*. The rate appeared to depend on the age of the food culture (Fig. 17.6). At 10 °C the values given by Conover are from 6–12 c.c./day. *A. tonsa* would appear to be about the same length as the small calanoids investigated by Gauld, and the grazing rates found by these two investigators agree closely. Conover found that temperature had a marked effect on filtration rate as other observers had noted. Conover's work, however, included a comparison of the filtration efficiencies of the two closely related species at various temperatures. His results indicated that some conditioning to temperature might occur. In early January grazing rate was about linear with respect to temperature;

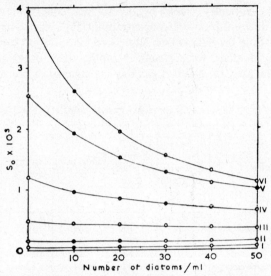

FIG. 17.5 Relationship between operational volume swept clear (So)
and the density of diatom food culture for the six copepodite
stages of *Calanus* (from Cushing, 1959).

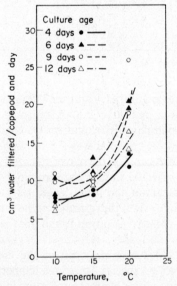

FIG. 17.6 The grazing rates of *Acartia tonsa* on *Skeletonema costatum*
culture of different ages (from Conover, 1956).

in February filtration rates declined at temperatures exceeding 15 °C (cf. Fig. 17.7). Exceedingly few attempts have been made to determine the grazing rates of zooplankton other than copepods. Some experiments have been carried out with mysids and euphausids. Raymont and Conover (1961) found rates varying from 25–62 c.c./day in very

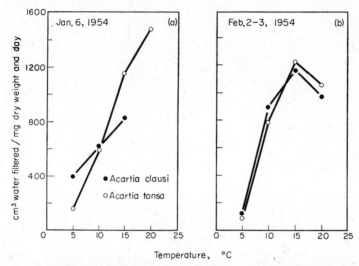

FIG. 17.7 Seasonal change in the relationship between temperature and filtration rate in two species of *Acartia* (from Conover, 1956).

preliminary experiments with the euphausids *Meganyctiphanes norvegica* and *Thysanoessa* sp. Euphausids are notoriously difficult to maintain under laboratory conditions, however, and in view of the relatively large size of these animals, much higher rates may be expected under natural conditions. Even for copepods, the rates found generally by experiment appear to be distinctly low in view of the animals' requirements. The much greater filtration volumes which Cushing has suggested would allow copepods sufficient food for growth as well as for maintenance.

Interest in the respiration of zooplankton has arisen mainly from its connection with food requirements. The values obtained by Putter for the respiration of the smaller calanoids, were certainly far too high (cf. Krogh, 1931). The studies by Marshall, Nicholls and Orr (1935) suggested that at a temperature of 15 °C Stage V *Calanus finmarchicus* required about 0.4–0.5 μl O_2/copepod/hr. Clarke and

Bonnet (1939) obtained somewhat higher values for Stage V *Calanus*, ranging fom 0.5 to nearly 1.0 μl O₂/copepod/hr, for experiments at 15–17 °C. Raymont and Gauld (1951) give a mean figure of 0.5 μl O₂/copepod/hr for Stage V *Calanus* which agrees well with that of Marshall, Nicholls and Orr. Clarke and Bonnet obtained similar results in their experiments whether they followed the Winkler technique, as employed by Marshall *et al.*, or the Dixon-Haldane

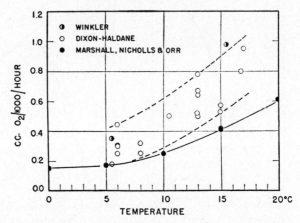

FIG. 17.8 The relation between oxygen consumption and temperature for Stage V *Calanus* (Dashed lines give limits for all determinations with Dixon-Haldane respirometer)
(from Clarke and Bonnet, 1939).

constant pressure respirometer method, which Raymont and Gauld used. Differences in the results cannot therefore be ascribed to the use of varying methods. Conover (1960) has demonstrated higher respiratory rates for *Calanus* from Georges Bank than for those from the Gulf of Maine. There are certain discrepancies between the results of Marshall *et al.* for the respiration of adult *Calanus* and those of Raymont and Gauld. Marshall *et al.* found 0.6 μl O₂/copepod/hr was required by female *C. finmarchicus* as against Raymont and Gauld's figure of 0.86 μl O₂/copepod/hr. It is doubtful, however, whether these differences have very much significance, as all investigators have found considerable variation in respiratory rates in series of experiments (cf. Fig. 17.8, 17.9).

Temperature has a very marked effect on the respiration of *Calanus*. The rate roughly doubles with a rise in temperature from 0–10 °C but there is an even steeper rise with further increase in temperature. With Stage V *Calanus* the rate at 10 °C is nearly 0.25 μl O$_2$/copepod/hr, but at 20 °C it exceeds 0.6 μl O$_2$/hr (Fig. 17.9).

Very little is known about the respiration of young stages of copepods apart from the work of Marshall and Orr (1958). They carried out a few experiments with copepodites and nauplii of *Calanus finmarchicus*. For Copepodite IV their mean value is 0.13 μl O$_2$/*Calanus*/hr.

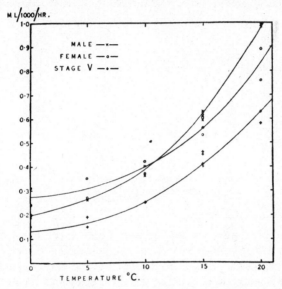

FIG. 17.9 The respiration of *Calanus* (Marshall and Orr, 1955).

Raymont and Gauld (1951) obtained a rate of 0.25 μl O$_2$/hr for Copepodite IV, but these experiments were carried out at 17 °C whereas Marshall and Orr's results refer to a temperature of 10 °C. There appears to be a fairly sharp drop in respiratory rate in Copepodite III according to Marshall and Orr's results; their mean value is only 0.06 μl O$_2$/*Calanus*/hr. At successively younger stages of development, there is a fairly steady fall in respiration, with the youngest nauplii respiring at a rate approximating to 0.002 μl O$_2$/*Calanus*/hr (Fig. 17.10).

Comparatively little work has been done on the respiration of copepods other than *Calanus finmarchicus*. Beklemishev (1954) quotes results obtained by Vinogradov suggesting that *Calanus tonsus*

Stage V had a respiratory rate of about 0.53 μl O_2/copepod/hr at a temperature of 6 °C. The much larger *C. cristatus* had an uptake of 0.84 μl O_2/copepod/hr at approximately the same temperature. Raymont and Gauld (1951) and Gauld and Raymont (1953) have examined the respiration of small species such as *Centropages hamatus*, *Acartia clausi* and *Temora longicornis*. They found that at 17 °C the rate was about 0.08 μl O_2/copepod/hr for *Centropages hamatus* and *Acartia clausi*, and a little higher (*ca.* 0.11 μl O_2/copepod/hr) for

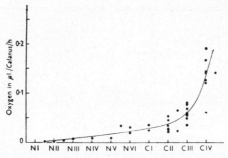

FIG. 17.10 The oxygen consumption of the early stages of *Calanus* (from Marshall and Orr, 1958).

Temora. Centropages typicus, which is larger than *C. hamatus*, had a considerably larger oxygen uptake. Some experiments with the large copepod, *Euchaeta norvegica*, gave much higher rates (e.g. ♀♀, 4.28 μl/copepod/hr; Stage V 2.23 μl/copepod/hr). Raymont and Gauld (1951) suggested that for several species and stages of copepods respiratory rate was related to surface area. It was closely proportional to: (cephalothorax length)$^{2.2}$. Further studies by Raymont (1959) on American calanoids have shown a reasonable measure of agreement between oxygen uptake and surface. Attention must be paid to marked variations in shape of cephalothorax as, for example, in *Eurytemora herdmani*. When allowance is made for differences in size of American and British forms of species such as *Centropages hamatus* and *Temora longicornis*, the respiratory rates are similar for the copepods from the eastern and western Atlantic. This does not appear to hold for *Acartia clausi*, however; Conover (1956) obtained lower values from Long Island Sound (U.S.A.) than those obtained by Gauld and Raymont for British waters. Despite some difference in average length of the specimens, there appeared to be a significant difference in the respiration of *A. clausi* from the two sea areas. Conover (1959) believes as a result of investigations on the respiration of four species of *Acartia* and other small calanoids that respiratory rate is more closely related to dry weight than to surface. Nevertheless, a marked difference in the respiration of *Acartia clausi* from U.S.A. and from English waters still holds.

Temperature affects the respiration of copepods other than *Calanus finmarchicus*. This has been shown for *Temora longicornis*, *Centropages*

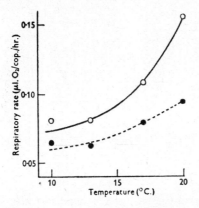

Fig. 17.11 The respiration of *Temora longicornis* o———o, and of *Acartia clausi* ●···········● (from Gauld and Raymont, 1953).

hamatus and *Acartia clausi* by Gauld and Raymont (1953) (Fig. 17.11) and for *Acartia tonsa* and *A. clausi* by Conover (1956) (cf. Fig. 17.11.1). Other factors apart from temperature and size, however, may affect respiratory rates. Gauld and Raymont obtained some evidence that different generations in *Centropages hamatus* had differing rates of oxygen uptake. Conover (1956) considered that some seasonal adaptation occurred in *Acartia clausi* (cf. Fig. 17.11.1). These differences appeared to hold, irrespective of changes in length of the copepods with the season, and quite apart from temperature variations. Raymont (unpublished) found that the respiration of *Centropages hamatus* and of *Acartia* spp. tended to fall during winter, irrespective of temperature, and Conover (1959) obtained strong evidence for a seasonal decline in respiration with several calanoids, especially in *Acartia discaudata* (cf. Fig. 17.12). Marshall and Orr (1957) also reported seasonal changes in the respiratory rates of *Centropages hamatus*, *Temora longicornis* and possibly of *Pseudocalanus minutus*, the main change being a rise in early spring and a subsequent decline in early summer. Their investigations (Marshall and Orr, 1958) showed that seasonal variations were also true of *Calanus finmarchicus*. Length alone was insufficient to account for the differences in respiratory rate. Thus over-wintering Stage V copepodites may have

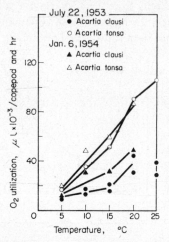

FIG. 17.11.1 The relationship between respiration and temperature for *Acartia* spp. on two dates (summer and winter) to show seasonal change in respiration (from Conover, 1956).

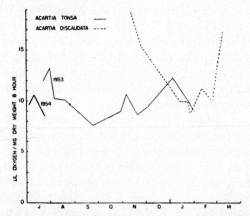

FIG. 17.12 Seasonal variation in respiratory rate for *Acartia tonsa* from Long Island Sound, U.S.A. (1953/54), and for *Acartia discaudata* from Southampton, England (1954/55); Temperature 20 °C (from Conover, 1959).

a rate approximately only one half that of spring and summer broods. The state of sexual maturity may also influence respiration: ripe female *Calanus* have a markedly higher respiratory rate than unripe specimens of the same size.

Among many other factors which may affect respiration are light, food and salinity. Bright light increases the respiratory rate, at least in *Calanus finmarchicus*, and presumably there will be increased oxygen uptake when these copepods swarm near the surface of the sea. On the other hand, Conover obtained very little effect of light on respiration for *Acartia tonsa*. Starvation has been shown to depress respiration in *Calanus* (Marshall and Orr, 1955a), in *Acartia* spp. (Conover, 1956) and in *Centropages hamatus* and *Tortanus discaudatus* (Raymont, 1959). The experiments on *Tortanus* are of interest since this copepod has a higher respiratory rate than might be expected from its size. The fall in respiration with lack of food is, however, very marked. Raymont has suggested that this may be associated with the carnivorous habit of this species (cf. also Conover, 1960). With regard to salinity, the position is not very clear. Marshall and Orr found a reduced respiratory rate with lowered salinities for *C. finmarchicus*, but Lance (1960) obtained a rise in respiration with reduction of salinity for *Acartia* spp. Over most of the seas, omitting estuaries, variation in salinity is probably too slight to affect respiration materially. Little information is available on the effect of lowered oxygen on respiratory uptake except for some experiments on *Calanus* by Marshall and Orr which suggested that at 15 °C the oxygen consumption showed a rapid fall when the oxygen tension fell below 3 c.c. of oxygen/l. As Marshall and Orr point out, *Calanus* may be abundant in places where the oxygen content is of the order of 2 c.c. oxygen/l. It is surprising if this fall in respiration with lowered oxygen tension holds generally, for much greater deficiencies of oxygen are experienced in the minimum oxygen zone, particularly in the Pacific; yet healthy populations of zooplankton appear to exist there. Zeuthen found a depression of respiration with zooplankton only at considerably reduced oxygen tensions. He believed that generally over the seas, oxygen content had little effect on respiration. There is considerable agreement that the interpretation of laboratory experiments on the respiration of zooplankton is difficult since the animals are often strongly affected by laboratory conditions. Some workers find that the respiratory rate of many plankton animals is abnormally high shortly after their capture.

There are unfortunately few data on the respiration of members of the zooplankton other than copepods. Zeuthen (1947) included a very few experiments on molluscan and polychaete larvae in his studies on metabolic rate. For polychaete trochophores of length 0.6–0.9 mm he obtained rates of about 0.03 μl O_2/animal/hr; for gastropod larvae (length 0.4 mm) the rate approached 0.02 μl O_2/animal/hr, and for lamellibranch larvae of 0.2 mm length the respiration could be as low as 0.0001 μl O_2/larva/hr. Zeuthen emphasizes that these are preliminary figures only; rates varied greatly according to the activity of the larvae. Krishnaswamy (1959) has recently obtained some data on the respiration of *Pleurobrachia pileus*. There was an enormous range in oxygen uptake depending partly on the size of animal, but when reckoned on a dry weight basis, the rate varied from 0.8–8.0 μl O_2/mg dry wt/hr at 10 °C. This may be compared with Conover's data for *Acartia* spp. His mean rate at 10 °C approached 4 μl O_2/mg dry wt/hr. Preliminary experiments have been carried out by Raymont and Conover (1961) on the respiration of some larger planktonic crustaceans. For the euphausid, *Nematoscelis megalops*, they suggest a mean rate of 5 μl O_2/animal/hr, and for the mysid, *Neomysis americana*, ca. 2 μl O_2/animal/hr. Reckoning the dry weight of these crustaceans as some 20% of the wet weight, the respiration rates would approximate to 0.6 μl O_2/mg dry wt/hr for *Nematoscelis* and to 1.6 μl O_2/mg dry wt/hr for *Neomysis*. Conover (1960) has investigated the respiratory rates of a number of zooplankton species and has demonstrated the close relationship between size and respiration. Among other forms, he has included respiratory rates for some planktonic amphipods. For *Euthemisto compressa* the suggested mean rate is 3.5 μl O_2/animal/hr, or 0.7 μl O_2/mg dry wt/hr; for *Hyperia galba* the corresponding values are 3.3 μl O_2/animal/hr or 0.5 μl O_2/mg dry wt/hr.

Detailed information on the metabolism of zooplankton is lacking. Gardiner (1937) made the important discovery that a variety of zooplankton animals could excrete significant quantities of phosphate in a matter of a few hours. More recently, Conover, Marshall and Orr, and also Cushing have suggested that there is a considerable turnover of soluble phosphorus when zooplankton graze actively. Marshall and Orr, as a result of their ^{32}P studies on *Calanus finmarchicus*, made the significant discovery that a considerable amount of the ingested phosphorus is distributed rapidly to the body tissues. In females a high proportion goes to the ovary, or to the eggs in actively laying females. In Stage V copepodites, a much larger proportion is present in the fat. Males had a surprisingly small amount in the reproductive system, a fair quantity in the fat, and slightly more in the musculature than either females or Stage V. However, very little is known concerning metabolic pathways in zooplankton. There is also little information on the chemical composition. Earlier studies were made mostly on mixed catches, but there was the suggestion that the protein content was high. For "copepods", Brandt (1898) suggested

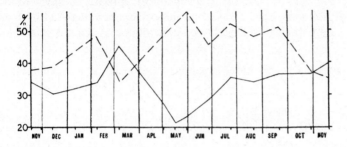

FIG. 17.13 The percentage of fat (———) and of protein (– – – –) in Stage V *Calanus* (from Orr, 1934).

average values of 59% protein, 7% fat, 20% carbohydrate, 5% chitin, 9% ash. The investigations of Orr (1934a, b) dealt with analyses of single species of copepods. Orr showed that the fat content of *Calanus finmarchicus* was higher than that suggested by Brandt. Stage V copepodites had a higher fat content than the adult copepods. The mean value for Stage V was about 30% of the dry weight but a fluctuation of 20% occurred with the seasons (cf. Fig. 17.13). The percentage of fat in female *C. finmarchicus* ranged from about 13–30%. Marshall and Orr attribute the lower fat content of females to the production of eggs. Orr's results suggest that there is only a very minor reduction in the fat content of Stage V *Calanus* during overwintering, so that the copepods would not appear to be living on the fat reserves significantly. There appears to be rather less variation in the protein content of *C. finmarchicus* (cf. Fig. 17.13). Stage V gave mean protein values of about 50%, adult females being somewhat richer in protein. However, these values are lower than those for mixed copepods obtained by Brandt. Orr's values for chitin (3%) and for ash (3–4%) are also lower than Brandt's. For *Euchaeta norvegica*

Orr has obtained fat and protein values of the same order as for *Calanus*.

One of the most interesting biochemical studies on plankton has been that of Kon, Fisher and their colleagues on vitamin A reserves (e.g. Kon, 1958; Fisher and Kon, 1959; Fisher and Goldie, 1959). Early interest in the vitamin A content of plankton stemmed from the large amounts of this vitamin in fish and whale oils (cf. Drummond and Gunther, 1934). Recent work has confirmed earlier findings, however, that *Calanus finmarchicus* appears to have no vitamin A. Of more than twenty species of copepod analysed by Fisher *et al.*, only three were found to contain vitamin A. On the other hand,

TABLE 17.4 Organic content of plankton (dry weight) (after Walford, 1958)

	Protein %	Fat %	Carbo-hydrate %	Ash %	P_2O_5%	Nitro-gen %
Copepods	70.9–77.0	4.6–19.2	0–4.4	4.2–6.4	0.9–2.6	11.1–12.0
Sagittae	69.6	1.9	13.9	16.3	3.6	10.9
Diatoms	24.0–48.1	2.0–10.4	0–30.7	30.4–59.0	0.9–3.7	3.8–7.5
Dino-flagellates	40.9–66.2	2.4–6.0	5.9–36.1	12.2–26.5	0.7–2.9	6.4–10.3

euphausids, show relatively large quantities of the vitamin, the highest content occurring in the eyes. The authors believe that the source of vitamin A for the euphausid *Meganyctiphanes norvegica* is from β-carotene derived from organic debris near the bottom and from carotenes contained in dinoflagellates and diatoms. Vitamin A in the eyes of other Eucarida eaten as food formed another source. Possibly astaxanthin found generally in crustaceans, including copepods, may be another precursor.

There is a marked need for further studies on the composition of zooplankton other than copepods. The summary given by Walford (1958) of Krey's data indicates that there are considerable differences between the composition of sagittae and copepods (Table 17.4). Raymont and Krishnaswamy (1960) examined the carbohydrate content of some planktonic animals. *Calanus finmarchicus*, *Neomysis integer* and *Pleurobrachia pileus* have very little carbohydrate amounting to only 0.4, 1.3 and 0.2% respectively of the dry body weight. Feeding appeared to increase the amount of carbohydrate only to a limited extent. More recently, Raymont and Conover (1961) have examined eleven species of zooplankton and shown that the carbohydrate content is extremely low. For copepods the content was similar to that already given for *C. finmarchicus*; euphausids appeared to have even less carbohydrate. Although feeding caused an alteration in carbohydrate level, at least in *C. finmarchicus*, it seems extremely unlikely that sufficient carbohydrate is obtained to meet the nutritional demands if carbohydrate is the chief energy source. How far inter-conversion of fat and carbohydrate occurs is unknown.

Information on food reserves, however, even if limited, is of value in considering plankton food cycles in the sea. Probably the most reliable figures available are those for Stage V *C. finmarchicus*. Marshall and Orr have shown that the basic food requirements estimated as carbohydrate for Stage V during winter would appear to be of the order of 0.006 mg/individual/day, and in summer, 0.013 mg/day. Reckoned as fat the values would be 0.002 mg/day in winter and 0.005 mg/day in summer. For Stage V, therefore, the amount of food required daily during winter is between 1.5 and 3.5% of the dry body weight. In summer, rather higher amounts varying between 1.5 and 4.5% of the body weight are necessary. Vinogradov's results suggest that *Calanus tonsus* requires about 4.5% of the body weight per day for basal metabolism at a temperature of 6 °C. *Calanus cristatus* requires some 2% per day at a rather higher temperature (10 °C). These values are of the same order as for *C. finmarchicus* and they are very much lower than those put forward by Putter, where requirements of the order of 40% of the body weight per day were suggested. The reduction in oxygen uptake which now appears to hold during winter will help to reduce food requirements. Nevertheless, there would appear to be a gap between the amount of food present during the winter in most seas and that necessary for maintenance. More detailed information on the metabolism of copepods and of other zooplankton might help to solve this problem.

Information at present available on the physiology of zooplankton, however, has enabled some investigators to suggest theoretical methods for analysing the changes in zooplankton populations, using field data in addition. Riley (1947b), for example, has put forward a method which may be applied to a limited area such as Georges Bank. He employs equations similar to those used for phytoplankton production The size of the herbivore population (*H*) which constitutes the bulk of the zooplankton, at time t may be expressed by the equation:

$$H_t = H_0 e^{(A-R-C-D)t}$$

where A = rate of assimilation of food by herbivores
R = herbivore respiration rate
C = rate of consumption of herbivores by predators
D = herbivore death rate

An estimate of the rate of assimilation may be deduced indirectly from the amount of phytoplankton produced per day per unit area

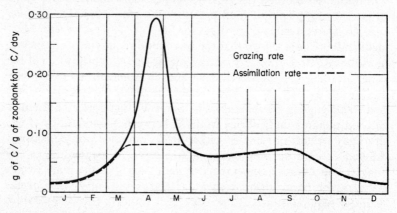

FIG. 17.14 Estimated rates of grazing and of assimilation of phytoplankton food by zooplankton on Georges Bank (from Riley, 1947).

of water, and from the known grazing rates of copepods. Over the period of the spring increase, however, allowance must be made for excessive grazing by the copepods (Fig. 17.14). Experimental results on the respiration of *Calanus* give an indication of the loss of matter due to respiration, due regard being paid to the effect of temperature. Riley uses the seasonal changes in the population of *Sagitta elegans*, which he regards as the main zooplankton predator on Georges Bank (Fig. 17.15), to estimate the rate of predation. He deduces also a death rate which includes natural death, predation other than that due to sagittae, and dilution. Figure 17.16a gives the seasonal rate of change of the herbivorous zooplankton on Georges Bank due to the operation of these various factors. Riley emphasizes the need for more detailed information on assimilation, respiration and other aspects of the physiology of both the herbivorous and carnivorous plankton. Nevertheless, the value of the use of such mathematical tools with experimental data in estimating seasonal changes in zooplankton is obvious. Figure 17.16b indicates a remarkably close agreement between the calculated and observed populations on Georges Bank.

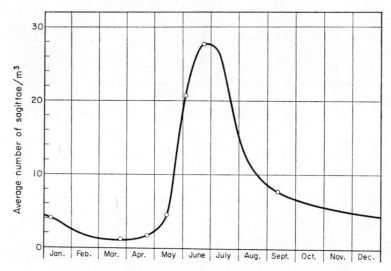

FIG. 17.15 Seasonal variation in the *Sagitta* population on Georges Bank (from Riley, 1947).

Somewhat similar theoretical models have been used by other authors, notably Cushing (1959a), to assess the conversion of algal material into zooplankton substance. Cushing deduces an algal reproductive rate from the light energy available at various depths over the first six months of the year (cf. Chapter X). Grazing rate is estimated partly from the minimal food requirements necessary for survival, together with the initial population and rate of increase of the herbivorous copepods. Cushing estimates this rate of increase from data on egg production of *Calanus* in relation to food concentration (Fig. 17.17). He also takes into consideration the mean mortality rates for the juvenile copepodite stages of *Calanus* (Table 17.5) and the mortality of adults due to various causes. Figure 17.18 indicates the results obtained by the operation of such

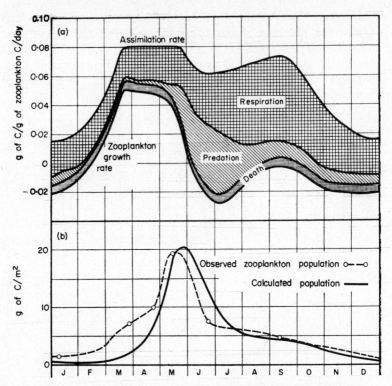

FIG. 17.16 (a) The rate of growth of the zooplankton on Georges Bank.
(b) Calculated and observed seasonal variations in zooplankton density on Georges Bank (from Riley, 1947).

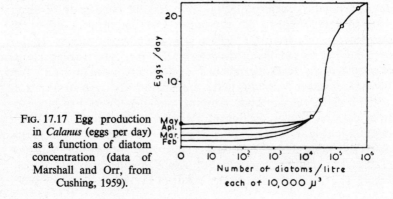

FIG. 17.17 Egg production
in *Calanus* (eggs per day)
as a function of diatom
concentration (data of
Marshall and Orr, from
Cushing, 1959).

TABLE 17.5 Estimated percentage mortality for juvenile *Calanus* in weekly periods (after Cushing, 1959).

Months:	February				March				April			
Weeks	1	2	3	4	1	2	3	4	1	2	3	4
%	80	80	80	80	80	80	83	86	87	90	93	97

Months:	May				June							
Weeks	1	2	3	4	1	2	3	4				
%	97	97	97	97	97	97	97	97				

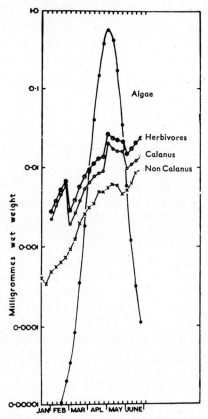

FIG. 17.18 The theoretical production of algae, and of *Calanus* and "other copepods" as mg wet weight per litre for the period January to June (from Cushing, 1959).

a theoretical model. The seasonal change in the weight of *Calanus*, the dominant grazer, and of other smaller copepods (e.g. *Pseudocalanus, Oithona*) is seen, together with the total production of herbivores in relation to the theoretical production of phytoplankton. The total quantity grazed over the 6-month period is practically equal to the theoretical production of algae so that the final algal standing crop is very small (cf. Chapter X, Fig. 10.13). The total amount of herbivore produced is approximately one seventh of the algal production (cf. Table 17.6). Figure 17.19 indicates that the

TABLE 17.6 Quantities of production from January to June (after Cushing, 1959).

	Per unit volume mg/l wet weight	Beneath unit surface gC/m²	Average daily rate gC/m² daily
Algal production (P_R)	1.78*	6.08	0.034
Quantity of algae grazed (P_G)	1.78*	6.11	0.034
Calanus production (P_H^1)	0.179	0.61	0.0034
"Other copepod" production (P_H^2)	0.077	0.264	0.0015

* These values are the same because the final value of algal standing stock is very small compared with the total production.

copepods appear to be undernourished during the first few months of the year but they feed to excess over the main spring increase. This material is not wasted since it may serve as food for the benthos. However, there would still appear to be marked under-nourishment of the plankton during winter. The use of food reserves, a lowered metabolic rate and a partial change to an omnivorous diet may all assist copepods in tiding over these months of scarcity.

The value of operating mathematical models in estimating population changes which can then be followed in the field is clear. But it is obvious that better results from the use of models in plankton analysis can be achieved only with a greater accumulation of precise knowledge of the physiology of zooplankton. Moreover, the food chains in the plankton are too complex to treat all members of the zooplankton as statistical units. Information on the metabolism of individual species is essential, not only for its own sake, but for a fuller understanding of energy flow in the oceans.

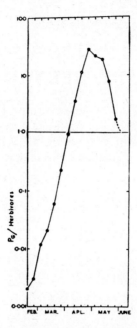

FIG. 17.19 The ratio of quantity of algae grazed to the weight of herbivores (from Cushing, 1959).

CHAPTER XVIII

FOOD CYCLES – BOTTOM FAUNA AND NEKTON

FOOD cycles in the oceans commence with the synthesis of organic material by the phytoplankton. At the next stage, herbivorous members of the zooplankton feeding on the algae assimilate this organic substance. The plankton community is subject to death, after which

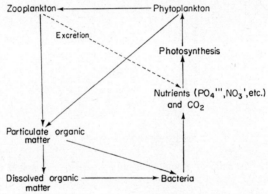

FIG. 18.1 The organic cycle in the plankton of the oceans.

the animals and plants decompose mainly owing to bacterial action, and nitrates, phosphates and other mineral nutrients are finally regenerated to complete the biological cycle (Fig. 18.1). This simplified outline is deceptive, however, in that it fails to take account of other trophic relationships which exist in the sea and which together constitute an extremely intricate food web (cf. Fig. 18.40). Any survey of the productivity of the oceans at various trophic levels must, therefore, include some account of the biology of marine communities other than the plankton.

Even in the plankton, there is a remarkable complexity of feeding patterns (cf. Chapter XVII) and our knowledge of trophic relationships within the plankton is still very incomplete. This is especially true of carnivorous and omnivorous species and of deep living forms. There is little precise information on the dietary requirements of whole groups of bathypelagic plankton (e.g. hyperiid amphipods, Acanthephyridae), but detritus arising from the decay of plankton is likely to make a substantial contribution to their nutrition (cf. Bogorov, 1958 b). Indeed, relatively few living algae may be expected to escape capture far below the surface. In open tropical oceans, Steemann Nielsen and Aabye Jensen (1957) suggest that even more than 95% of the living algae consumed are eaten in the upper 200 m. Krey (1961) has called attention to the relatively large quantities of detritus present in some sea areas (cf. p. 502). How far dissolved organic matter and bacteria may be utilized by deep sea species is still not known but the possibility exists.

However much the deeper living zooplankton feeds on material drifting down from the upper layers, some of the plant and animal plankton, either as living matter or as detritus, falls slowly out of the pelagic zone and reaches the sea floor. This particulate matter there serves as food for the vast variety of animals which live either in or on the substratun, and are collectively termed the benthos or bottom fauna. A fair amount of particulate detritus originates from land, and recent work, particularly from the Galathea Expedition, has demonstrated that terrestrial detritus may be carried to great distances in oceanic areas. A recent interesting observation by McAllister, Parsons and Strickland (1960) suggests that a considerable quantity of detritus, representing some 80–90% of the total particulate matter, and amounting to ca. 125 mg carbon/m³, occurs in the euphotic zone in oceanic waters of the north-east Pacific. A fair amount of detritus is also present at depths of at least 1000 m. Although much of the detritus is probably of planktonic origin, the presence of cellulose fibres suggests a terrestrial source for some of the detritus, probably drifting wood. The detritus is comparatively rich in protein and to a lesser extent in carbohydrate. A bottom fauna thus exists even in the deepest trenches of the oceans at depths exceeding 10,000 m (cf. Wolff, 1960). Actinians, polychaetes, holothurians, isopods and amphipods, molluscs, as well as certain Echiuroidea and Pogonophora, all obtain nourishment at these excessive depths. In some trenches, Wolff suggests that the biomass exceeds 10 gm/m².

Although detritus other than that arising from plankton may contribute to the particulate matter over oceanic depths, nevertheless it appears that most of the primary food matter on which the bottom fauna lives must be derived ultimately from the plankton. Although in coastal areas benthic algae and other fixed plants may contribute to some limited extent to the food supply, it is the annual crop of plankton which must determine the density of the animal population living on the bottom. This is, however, extremely difficult to demonstrate in any detailed and precise study. Harvey (1950) discussed this problem for the English Channel, and suggested that with a mean

TABLE 18.1 Comparison of mean annual standing crops and organic production (g organic matter/m²) in the English Channel (EC) and Central Long Island Sound (LIS) (modified from Riley, 1956).

	Standing Crop		Daily Production	
	EC	LIS	EC	LIS
Phytoplankton	4	16	—	3.2*
		—	0.4–0.5†	1.07†
Zooplankton	1.5	2	0.15	—
Pelagic fish	1.8	—	0.0016	—
Demersal fish	1–1.25	—	0.001	—
Epi- and in-fauna	17	9	0.03	—
Bacteria	0.1	—	—	—

* Photosynthetic glucose production.
† Phytoplankton production in excess of respiratory requirement.

standing crop of phytoplankton of *ca.* 4 g/m² as dry organic matter the bottom fauna biomass amounted to *ca.* 17 g/m² (dry organic matter). But the daily rate of production of the relatively slow growing benthos was much smaller (less than one tenth) than that of the phytoplankton (Table 18.1).

Following investigations of the oceanography of Long Island Sound, Riley (1956) has attempted a comparison between the crop in that area with that of the English Channel (Table 18.1). Riley (1956) suggests that despite the greater amount of nutrients in Long Island Sound and the higher crop of phytoplankton, zooplankton production is only slightly greater than in the English Channel. In the shallower waters of Long Island Sound a large amount of phytoplankton and detritus should, therefore, be available to the benthos and a very much richer bottom fauna might be expected. The preliminary values given for the standing crop of benthos in Long Island Sound (cf. Table 18.1) do not support this theory, but later figures given by Sanders suggest that the bottom fauna density in Long Island Sound is really much greater (cf. p. 591). Such comparisons illustrate the difficulties in relating plankton production to crop of benthos. An interesting observation is that of Longhurst (1959) who has assessed the richness of the benthos in different areas off the coast of West Africa. In determining the richness of the fauna, biomass, the number of individuals per m^2, and the number of species per sample have all been used. Longhurst concludes that the Guinea shelf area is poorer generally than comparable parts of the Senegal area. He associates this difference with the different productivities of the overlying waters. The Canary Current influencing Senegal is a comparatively cool water mass, fairly rich in plankton; the Guinea coast is mainly influenced by the warm and generally unproductive Guinea Current.

The difficulties encountered in deeper sea investigations of this type are even greater. Bogorov (1958a, b) emphasizes the much greater richness of zooplankton in boreal as compared with tropical Pacific waters and states that this difference holds for the whole water column to the bottom. The carbon production is also much higher in boreal waters. Later, Bogorov (1959) gives some figures for the biomass of benthos in tropical and subtropical regions of the Central Pacific. Apart from neritic areas, the crop of benthos is low throughout the tropical zone, but there is some increase in subtropical areas. There is considerably greater variability in the production of plankton in the surface waters, however, and it appears difficult to relate benthos directly to the mass of plankton. The variable quantities of the deeper-living and larger pelagic animals might be responsible for some of the apparent discrepancies. The smaller biomass of plankton in tropical seas may also be reckoned against the greater number of generations in warm waters. Cushing (1959a) has attempted a comparison of the standing crops of animals in the English Channel and in the Sargasso Sea (Table 18.2). He has suggested that perhaps the deep scattering layer animals in oceanic regions replace ecologically the bottom fauna of continental shelves. Some strict estimates of bottom fauna densities in the Sargasso Sea and in other oceanic regions are essential, however, before these comparisons can be examined critically.

Even in temperate regions, it is difficult to account for considerable differences in richness of the fauna (in density as opposed to species) between one area of the sea bed and another. Undoubtedly one of the major problems is that currents are constantly carrying the overlying water masses away from the area of substratum under investigation so that the two zones (pelagic and benthic) may show little clear relationship. In particular, the regular passage of water past the bottom permits filter-feeding animals of the bottom fauna to draw their food supply from a relatively enormous and changing volume of seawater. Except in very enclosed areas, the benthos need not rely solely on the crop of plankton of the overlying water

TABLE 18.2 Standing stocks in the English Channel and in the Sargasso Sea in g dry weight/m² (from Cushing, 1959).

	Phyto-plankton	Zoo-plankton	Macro-plankton	Pelagic fish	Benthos	Demersal fish
English Channel	4	1.5	–	1.8	17	1.125
Sargasso Sea	0.36–2.32 0.60–8.32	2.2–3.5	1.58	5–10		–

mass for its whole food supply. Despite the operation of such complex factors, over broad regions of the oceans the richer areas of plankton production are usually the areas of denser bottom faunas. One of the best examples is the Antarctic where very rich benthos is present. More generally, continental shelves and slopes are characterized by a much higher density of bottom animals than are abyssal ocean beds, in agreement with the generally greater crop of plankton in shallower waters. Zenkevitch and Birstein (1956) show that in the northern Pacific, whereas some hundreds of grams of benthos per m² occur on the shallow continental shelf areas, the biomass of benthos decreases with depth and also regularly with distance from land (Fig. 18.2). A comparison of the biomass of benthos from shallow seas with that in the deepest regions suggests a reduction of the order of at least one thousand times. The authors relate the poverty of the deep sea benthos to the lessened food supply. They point out that the biomass of plankton also decreases with depth. It diminishes with distance from the coast, although there may be oceanic zones of relative abundance as for instance when warm and cold currents meet (Fig. 18.2). Zenkevitch (1961) has recently re-emphasized the dependence of the biomass of benthos on plankton production. From investigations in the Pacific and Indian Oceans he claims that the density of the benthos drops from a kilogram or so per m² along the coasts to as little as 50 mg/m² (in places even less) on the abyssal ocean floor. Recent investigations in the Atlantic confirm the very sharp fall in density of benthos in abyssal depths. The reduction in biomass from shallow coastal waters to oceanic depths is of the order of 10^6 for the benthos; for the plankton, however, it approaches 10^4.

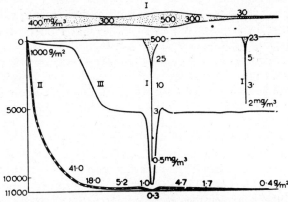

FIG. 18.2 The biomass of plankton (I) and of benthos (II) in relation to distance from land and in relation to depth for Pacific waters. (The section (III) crosses the Kurile Trench.) (from Zenkevitch and Birstein, 1956).

A somewhat similar observation is that of Savilov (1957) from the north Okhotsk Sea. Savilov identified five major biological zones; in any one zone, though the most abundant species might vary, they were similar in biological characters, possessing the same adaptive characters and leading a similar type of life on the bottom. The first zone, in shallow coastal areas, was characterized generally by a hard substratum and an abundance of sessile and encrusting benthic animals. These were mainly suspension feeders, utilizing the rich plankton and detrital food. In the next zone further offshore were extensive sandy areas with filter-feeding bivalves. This zone was succeeded by more muddy-sand regions marked by benthos using more finely divided detritus as food. With increasingly softer deposits and more silt, small bivalves, polychaetes and ophiurans were commonest. In the deepest areas, the bottom deposit was a soft ooze, inhabited mostly by polychaetes and large echinoderms, which fed unselectively on the bottom deposit. Savilov concluded that although many irregularities of distribution occurred, the five major zones followed successively outwards from the coast; moreover, the general total biomass of benthos decreased with increasing depth and distance from shore. Thus, inshore the hard substratum had an average biomass of 732 g/m², as against < 25 g/m² (in places < 5 g/m²) for the deepest central area. Savilov attributes the differences in richness of benthos chiefly to the available food supply (plankton and detritus), which generally decreases with distance from land. Areas characterized by major mixing of water masses, even over deep water, might, however, possess a rich bottom fauna.

There are some other detailed examples of the varying densities of benthos from different areas of the sea bottom, drawn mainly from investigations in shallower seas. With amphipod communities, Petersen (1918) described a *Haploops* community where there could be four to five thousand amphipods/m², as well as a few other organisms, and an even greater density has been recorded for a comparable *Ampelisca* community (cf. Thorson, 1957) with numbers exceeding 14,000/m². Smidt (1951) has described in the Danish Waddensea, communities of small **bivalves** amounting to several thousand/m². Some of the high **densities recorded** for various animals of intertidal mud communities are listed by Raymont (1955). Beyond the intertidal zone, Vevers (1952) has described parts of the sea bottom off Plymouth where even hundreds of ophiuroids can occur in a square metre so that the bottom appears to be covered by a pavement of their radiating arms. Petersen (1918) found fairly large numbers of ophiuroids characteristic of the *Amphiura* community in Danish waters. On the other hand, there are extremely poor parts of the sea bottom where fewer than half a dozen animals may be present per square metre. Vevers' work furnishes a striking illustration in that only a few miles away from his dense ophiuroid beds, there are areas which show no animals existing above the substratum.

Numbers of animals on the sea floor may give a very misleading impression, however, of the real richness of the standing crop of bottom fauna; the weight of the animal population in a given area (or biomass) is usually a better criterion. The weight of a few thousand amphipods, for example, may be very little compared with a few hundred polychaetes or large bivalves. Moreover, where some thousands of young bivalves or polychaetes may occur after a recent dense settlement, their weight may be much less than that of the standing

population of older organisms. Smidt (1951) showed that vast numbers of young polychaetes, such as *Pygospio elegans*, of gastropods
such as *Hydrobia ulvae*, and of bivalves such as *Cardium edule* and
Macoma baltica, may settle on a small area of mud-flats immediately
following a spawning, but he also demonstrated that mortality may be
extremely heavy, resulting in much reduced populations after a few
months. Davis (1923) investigated *Spisula* and *Mactra* beds in the
North Sea. Over a very large area where *Spisula* tended to be the
abundant species, there was an average population approaching
3000 bivalves per m². The dominance of the young 0-group was,
however, very obvious; some 2500 bivalves per m² were of this age
group, as against 300 Group-I, and the Group-II *Spisula* amounted
to only 5–6 bivalves/m². Although patches of higher density were
found, they also were dominated by young *Spisula*. One area showed
8250 0-Group *Spisula*/m² but the density of the Group-I bivalves
was only about 1000/m². Davis concludes that an average mortality
of 90% per annum occurs with *Spisula* on the Dogger Bank area
(Fig. 18.3). Boysen-Jensen (1919) has similarly drawn attention to the

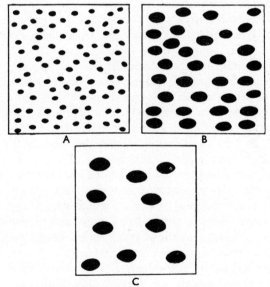

FIG. 18.3 Density of *Spisula subtruncata* on the Dogger Bank 1922. Each
square represents ¹⁄₁₀₀m².
A = 0-gp bivalves in October; B = 0-gp in June; C = I-group in
October (from Cole ed. Graham, 1956).

low density of the large-sized spawning stock as compared with the high density of the young age groups for several species of bivalves and polychaetes. Total weight or biomass must take account of the different densities and weights of both young and old individuals.

Before examining further the fluctuations in density of species of bottom fauna inhabiting different parts of the sea floor, it is essential to question how far animal communities are really characteristic of different bottom areas. The idea of animal communities applied to the sea bottom may be attributed largely to the work of Petersen (1918) in the shallow Danish fjords. Petersen first identified as the *epifauna* those animals living either upon or in association with coarse gravel, rocks, stones, piling and vegetation. Obvious examples are mussels, a variety of gastropods such as *Nassarius*, *Gibbula*, *Littorina*, *Rissoa*, *Nucella* and barnacles, ascidians, polyzoans, hydroids, corals, most sponges, and many other animals. Secondly he distinguished the *infauna* – i.e. those animals which inhabit the sandy or muddy upper layers of the sea bottom, where the bottom deposit is composed of small particles. The substratum is reasonably soft so that the animals can live partially buried in the deposit, or they may construct burrows or tubes so that they may exist at a depth of several inches from the surface (e.g. *Mya*, *Pinna*, *Echinocardium*) (Fig. 18.4). These animals which include, above all, lamellibranchs, many polychaetes, irregular echinoids and holothurians, either feed on the suspended detritus and plankton particles brought by the surrounding water, or on the organic matter in the bottom deposit (Fig. 18.5). With the infauna there may be considerable variety of micro-habitat, including holes and crevices between rocks and in coral reefs, as well as all grades of sand and mud. In the shallowest parts of the marine zone, a multiplicity of niches exist amongst seaweeds and *Zostera*. The fauna therefore tends to be diverse, though vast areas of similar sand or mud may show little variety. As regards the epifauna, the variation in habitat would appear to be considerable also. But Thorson (1957) has convincingly demonstrated the much more stringent conditions which such a fauna has to undergo than has the corresponding infauna in the colder seas. He has shown that the abundance of individuals and of species of the epifauna increases greatly towards the tropics (Fig. 18.6); in the coldest marine areas, on the other hand, the epifauna is extremely sparse. As regards the infauna, conditions in the sea are much more uniform even over vast distances and thus the infauna does not show this great

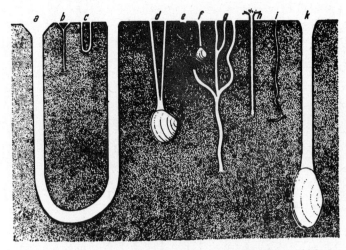

FIG. 18.4 The infauna of sand and mudflats showing depths to which some species burrow. Total thickness about 30 cm; a = *Arenicola marina*; b = *Pygospio elegans*; c = *Corophium volutator*; d = *Scrobicularia plana*; e = *Cardium edule*; f = *Macoma baltica*; g = *Nereis diversicolor*; h = *Lanice conchilega*; i = *Heteromastus filiformis*; k = *Mya arenaria* (after Remane, 1940).

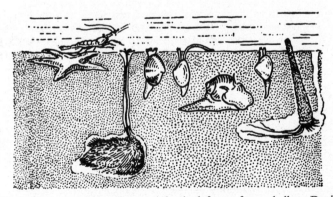

FIG. 18.5 A typical north-east Atlantic infauna from shallow Danish waters. Animals include *Astropecten, Leander, Echinocardium, Venus, Tellina, Spisula, Natica* and *Pectinaria* (after Thorson, 1957).

increase in abundance in the warmest seas. Away from the coasts the number of microhabitats is far fewer for the infaunal population; the ecological conditions are relatively very stable, and it is to be expected that here marine communities might be more definitely delimited.

Even in relatively shallow waters, Petersen showed by quantitative sampling that the larger animals living in a unit area of the sea

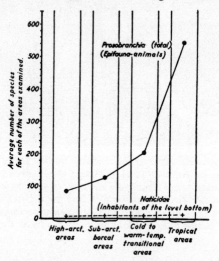

Fig. 18.6 Increase in numbers of epifauna, represented by prosobranchs, from Arctic to tropics. The average numbers of species from equally large coastal areas at the various latitudes are given. Note the lack of increase in Naticidae (level bottom forms) (from Thorson, 1957).

bottom varied in the abundance of particular species from one area to another. He, therefore, attempted to characterize especially the infauna as particular communities, though he meant no more in the first place by these "communities" than a description of statistical units. For example, he demonstrated that in very shallow waters from the tidal zone downwards, particularly under estuarine conditions, a generally muddy sea bottom was characterized by *Macoma baltica*, together with some four or five other fairly common species. By contrast, an offshore sandy sea bed tended to be dominated by the bivalve *Venus gallina* with certain other associated species. These communities could occur over wide areas, and later work showed similar lists of species were characteristic of many parts of the world, sometimes with closely related species, giving as it were "parallel" communities.

Further offshore, in somewhat deeper waters, the sea floor is usually mud or a mixture of mud and sand, but occasionally coarser deposits are encountered. Petersen suggested that each type of bottom had its own characteristic fauna. The change from one type of fauna to another on the sea bed is, however, extremely slow and gradual, and this has led many ecologists to doubt the validity of communities in the marine benthos. All workers are agreed that there are variations in the *precise* assemblages of animals seen on one particular type of bottom deposit under similar marine conditions, i.e. different "facies" exist of the one community. Here we are probably dealing with microhabitats which can occur on the same broad type of bottom, e.g. small irregularities in the bottom; biological and micro-chemical differences in the overlying water; small chemical variations in the deposit and in food supply. The problem, therefore, arises whether the assemblage of animals seen on one type of sea floor is the result of fortuitous circumstances, or whether the animals (and in shallow water the plants too) are linked together from an eco-logical point of view so that a true biocoenosis exists. There is little doubt, as Jones (1950) and also Thorson (1957) pointed out, that Petersen when describing his communities, originally looked on them as descriptive statistical units. But however much overlapping dis-tributions occur, and though different facies undoubtedly exist, true ecological communities are probably present. Modern study of marine communities will have to take into account not only the commoner and more obvious animals, but also the micro-faunal inhabitants. The amount of organic matter and inorganic detritus and all the complex variety of physical, chemical and biological factors which are concerned with the settlement and survival of the fauna must also be investigated. This is indeed a difficult and complex task, but if all factors could be fully studied it would seem likely that the sort of assemblages of animals described originally by Petersen would be found to be real communities. MacGinitie (1939) probably implies this when he defines a marine bottom community as "an assemblage of animals living in a common locality under similar conditions of environment and with some apparent association of activities and habits". At the same time MacGinitie deprecates an over-emphasis on the dominant members of marine bottom communities. He suggests that the species revealed in Petersen's investigations were mainly surface living or shallow burrowing forms, and that the deep living species were not sampled. He also emphasizes the importance of regarding marine communities as changing and not static assemblages of animals. Where populations of certain species of benthos occur fairly regularly together, part of the association is dependent on common ecological requirements such as food, shelter and type of bottom deposit. If this were all, such a collection of benthic species would be an extremely loose type of community, but it is difficult to believe that more definite ecological relationships such as predator/prey, symbiotic and parasitic relationships, do not play some part. Jones (1950) considered which physico-chemical factors on the one hand, and which biological factors on the other, were important in controlling the composition of a marine benthic community. Under physico-chemical factors he quoted temperature, salinity, exposure to desiccation, oxygen, currents and tides, possibly light, but above all, bottom deposit. It was difficult to assess the importance of wave action apart from its enormous influence on the composition of the bottom deposit. Under biological factors Jones considered that suitable food organisms, as well as the occurrence of parasites and commensals, must play a direct part in community life. The interplay of the reproductive habits of the different species will presumably also have an effect. At the same time, in marine bottom communities biological factors are probably of less importance than physical ones.

Of the physical factors, temperature, salinity and the composition of the bottom deposit are of the greatest importance. In really deep water these three factors as well as most others are exceedingly constant, and it is not surprising that with this relative uniformity of ecological conditions deep benthic populations may appear similar over wide areas. With moderately deep water, salinity and bottom deposit may show relatively little variation so that temperature as between, for example, polar regions and the tropics becomes of much greater significance in affecting distribution. Even so, it is possible, as Thorson (1957) has pointed out, for species which are dominant in shallow waters of the Arctic, such as *Pecten groenlandicus* and *Natica groenlandica* to occur on similar bottoms in the deep colder water of warm temperate regions.

Although low temperatures may greatly affect the distribution of benthic species, cold water areas may have a remarkably large stand-

ing crop of animals. Vibe (1939) investigated coastal areas of Greenland, and commented that although the number of species tends
to be low, the number of individuals and the average weight of the
population may be very high. In *Macoma calcarea* communities
living on sand, there were frequently weights exceeding 1 kg (wet
weight) per m², with large numbers of *Owenia fusiformis* and *Macoma*
making total populations of between 3500 and 5500 animals/m².
The largest samples found by Vibe came from a sandy clay area.
Here the fauna consisted mainly of *Cardium groenlandicum*, a very
slow growing species with a life span of more than a dozen years,
and *Pectinaria granulata*. The greatest weight recorded from this
fauna ranged from 3.4 to 3.9 kg/m². Filatova (1957) has also noted
that in the Arctic and sub-Arctic seas in the northern U.S.S.R, although
relatively few species of bivalves occur, those which are present
can be very abundant and have a very high biomass. Apart from the
littoral and uppermost sublittoral areas of the Murman coast in the
Barents Sea, where beds of *Mytilus edulis* can attain such a remarkable maximum biomass as 25 kg/m², shallow areas in the south-east
Barents Sea may show a total bivalve biomass of up to 700 g/m².
A *Modiolus/Pecten islandicus* community in one of the sublittoral
areas of the Barents Sea reached even 1500 g/m². At the opposite
extreme, the deepest and poorest areas in the Barents and Kara Seas
have benthic populations with a biomass of even below 1 g/m².
Filatova points out that the very cold East Siberian Sea may have
very rich bivalve populations (up to 700 g/m²). Generally in these
northern seas, bivalves are richest in the shallow regions where food
conditions are favourable; with increasing depth the contribution
to the total biomass from lamellibranchs becomes less and less important. Thorson (1957) has pointed out that very rich areas of
bottom (i.e. with a high standing crop) may be characteristic of cold,
Arctic bottom communities. The dominant species are very slow
growing and have such a long life span that different generations
overlap to a remarkable degree. Rates of production, in contrast to the
large standing crop, are low, and changes in the composition of the
bottom fauna tend to be extremely slow, so that such benthic communities are frequently very uniform.

If we now confine our attention to more boreal and temperate
waters such as round the British coasts, temperature though somewhat variable, is more limited in its range; 3–16 °C is a reasonable
estimate, but in any event variation decreases rapidly with depth, so

that temperature becomes of rather lesser significance in limiting bottom communities. Salinity may vary considerably, and in very shallow and especially in intertidal waters, there may be an appreciable range even over 24 hours. But in general the bottom deposit becomes the most fundamental physical factor affecting the different communities over a more limited marine region. We shall look at some half dozen of these boreal benthic communities; for a fuller treatment and classification of the various types, reference should be made to Jones (1950) or to Thorson (1957).

1. The *Tellina tenuis* shallow sand community.

This assemblage of animals is characteristic of rather exposed sandy shores and may occur from the tidal zone to a depth of per-

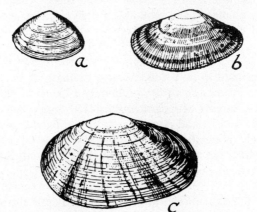

FIG. 18.7 Bivalves from sandy shores. a = *Tellina tenuis*; b = **Donax** *vittatus*; c = *Gari depressa* (from Yonge, 1949).

haps 10 m. It is dominated by *Tellina tenuis* but occurring also is *Donax vittatus* (Fig. 18.7), the polychaetes *Nephthys caeca* and sometimes *N. hombergi* and *Arenicola marina*, and the echinoderm *Astropecten irregularis*. Of amphipods *Bathyporeia pelagica* is common (Fig. 18.8). Where a slight mixture of silt is present *Tellina fabula* occurs and may become more important than *Tellina tenuis*. In Stephen's studies (1930, 1932) this occurred in slightly deeper water with *Tellina fabula* and *Echinocardium cordatum* as the chief species. This community really grades into the offshore sand communities.

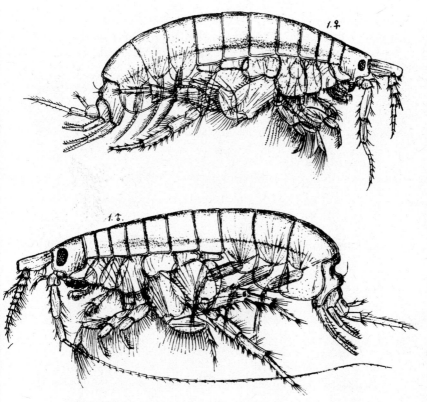

FIG. 18.8 *Bathyporeia pelagica* (♂ and ♀) (from Sars, 1895).

2. *Venus* communities.

In slightly more open sea conditions, on sandy bottoms occurring to a depth of perhaps 50 m are communities of animals which are largely dominated by the lamellibranch *Venus*. One of the commonest is the *Venus gallina* community described by Petersen (1918) from Danish waters (Fig. 18.9). The characteristic animals are bivalves such as *Venus gallina*, *Spisula* spp. and sometimes *Mactra* and *Psammobia*; the polychaetes *Nephthys*, *Ophelia* and sometimes *Pectinaria*, and the echinoderms *Echinocardium* or *Spatangus purpureus*. Amphipods (e.g. *Ampelisca*) and other animals such as *Natica* and *Astropecten* often occur. With rather more loose sand, *Spisula* can become a dominant organism, and although the community can fluctuate in abundance from year to year, there can be a very high standing crop. According to Davis (1923) *Spisula* reaches maturity after one year at a mean size of 13 mm on the Dogger Bank so that a fairly rapid production of benthos can occur. Off Plymouth, Ford (1923)

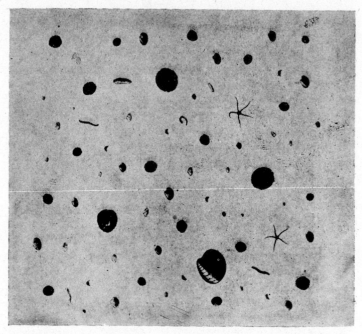

FIG. 18.9 A *Venus* community with *Echinocardium* (Petersen, 1918). (In this and succeeding plates from Petersen's work the animals illustrated are represented as occurring in an area of bottom of $\frac{1}{4}$ m².)

identified *Venus* communities, but *V. gallina* was less abundant than in the Danish waters, and with more silt *Abra* (*Syndosmya*) became important (Fig. 18.10). Where the sands are harder, species of *Tellina* can enter the community and *Ophiothrix fragilis* may be common. Ford showed that a *Venus* community is also typical of a coarser deposit which is really a shell gravel. This shell gravel community which was also described by Smith (1932) tends to hold larger, more solid bivalves such as *Venus fasciata*, *Glycymeris glycymeris*, *Ensis arcuata*, *Tellina crassa*, and the two echinoderms *Spatangus* and *Echinocardium flavescens*, with characteristic species like *Branchio-*

stoma (*Amphioxus*), *Echinocyamus* and *Polygordius* (Fig. 18.11). Polychaetes such as *Glycera*, *Lumbriconereis* and *Nephthys* occur in the Venus communities.

FIG. 18.10 An *Echinocardium cordatum/Venus gallina* type of community off Plymouth, dominated by the bivalve *Syndosmya* (*Abra*) *alba* (Area represents $\frac{1}{10}$ m²) (from Ford, 1923).

3. The *Macoma baltica* shallow mud community.

This community which was also described by Petersen from Danish waters is perhaps one of the best known communities of north west European waters (Fig. 18.12). The characteristic animal is *Macoma baltica*, together with *Mya arenaria*, *Cardium edule*, *Arenicola marina*, *Hydrobia ulvae* and *Corophium volutator*. This is a

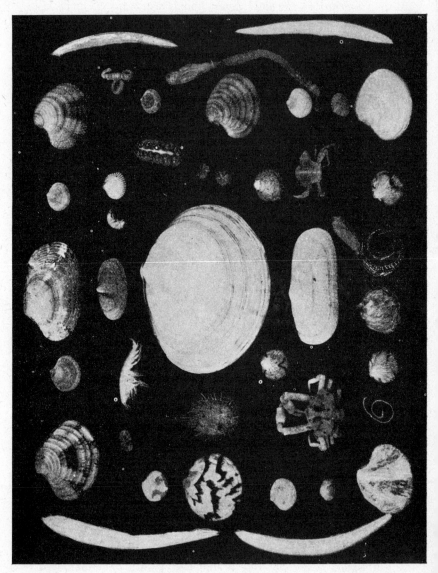

FIG. 18.11 *A Spatangus/Venus fasciata* community found on shell gravel near the Eddystone, Plymouth $\left(\text{Area represents } \frac{1}{10} \text{ m}^2\right)$ (after Ford, 1923).

shallow water community extending from the tidal zone to about
10 m depth, but occurring somewhat deeper in Baltic areas. The
bottom is usually muddy but can vary to quite a considerable extent
in texture. Where there tends to be rather more clay and silt, the bivalve

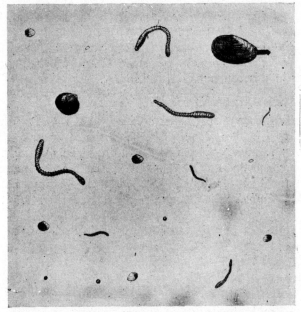

FIG. 18.12 *Macoma baltica* community (after Petersen, 1918).

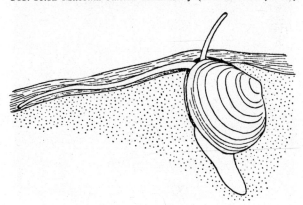

FIG. 18.13 *Scrobicularia plana* showing method of feeding. Bivalve is
normally at a depth of 6–8″ (after Yonge, 1949).

Scrobicularia plana may occur (Fig. 18.13) (Holme, 1949; Green, 1957); with a greater admixture of sand there is often a preponderance of *Cardium*. Smidt (1951) in examining this community off W. Jutland, and others who have investigated *Macoma* communities elsewhere, have found locally great abundance of such species as *Pygospio elegans* and *Nereis diversicolor*, together with the epifaunal forms *Mytilus edulis* and *Littorina littorea*. As both *Macoma* and *Cardium* have a fairly long life expectancy (about 3 years for *Macoma*) and as even *Hydrobia ulvae* normally persists for about two years, the rate of turnover in this community is rather low.

4. The *Syndosmya* (*Abra*) community.

This assemblage of species has been described from Danish waters and occurs in shallow depths in rather sheltered areas. The bottom is usually a muddy-sand, fairly rich in organic material; conditions are sometimes rather estuarine. Lamellibranchs are especially important, notably *Syndosmya* (*Abra*) *alba* and *S. prismatica*, *Cultellus pellucidus*, *Corbula gibba*, and *Nucula turgida* (Fig. 18.14). Other

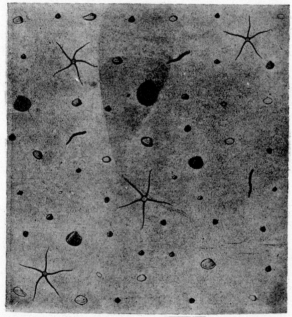

FIG. 18.14 *Syndosmya* (*Abra*) and *Echinocardium* community (after Petersen, 1918).

common species include the polychaetes *Pectinaria auricoma*, *Nephthys* spp., *Scalibregma inflatum* and *Glycera* spp., and the echinoderms *Ophiura texturata* and *Echinocardium cordatum*. Boysen-Jensen who studied a *Syndosmya* community in the Limfjord, Denmark, showed that the standing crop is relatively short-lived, *Syndosmya* itself being a rapidly growing lamellibranch. The age groups of this and

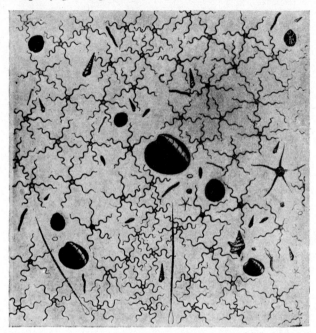

FIG. 18.15 *Echinocardium cordatum/Amphiura filiformis* community (from Petersen, 1918).

almost all the other common species are important as fish food. Blegvad (1925) also regarded this community as a rich feeding ground owing to the abundance of small, thin-shelled bivalves and polychaetes.

In Jones' view, the *Syndosmya* (*Abra*) community is one of the offshore muddy-sand animal associations, and it may grade into a community dominated by the brittle star, *Amphiura filiformis*, and by *Echinocardium cordatum* (Petersen's community Fig. 18.15). Other common animals in these muddy-sand environments are *Turritella communis* (Fig. 18.16), *Aporrhais pes-pelicani*, and *Philine aperta*.

FIG. 18.16 A *Venus gallina* type of community on a more muddy bottom dominated by *Turritella communis* $\left(\text{Area represents } \frac{1}{10}\,\text{m}^2\right)$ (from Ford, 1923).

5. Deeper mud communities.

Usually somewhat deeper than the sandy-mud areas, occurs a soft mud bottom. Petersen (1918) found a community characterized by *Amphiura chiajei* with the echinoid *Brissopsis lyrifera* (Fig. 18.17). *Syndosmya prismatica* and *S. nitida* with *Nucula* spp. are fairly evident, together with many polychaetes such as *Nephthys incisa*, *Glycera rouxi*, *Lumbriconereis impatiens* and some sedentary worms (e.g. Maldanids and Capitellids).

Grading from this association into slightly deeper water is the somewhat similar community described by Petersen with *Ophiura sarsi* and *Brissopsis lyrifera* as conspicuous species (Fig. 18.18). Jones points out that this deep mud environment is subject to very small temperature variations. Species encountered in the slightly shallower mud zones also occur here, together with a number of other sedentary polychaetes such as *Terebellides stroemi*, *Chaetozone setosa* and *Melinna cristata*.

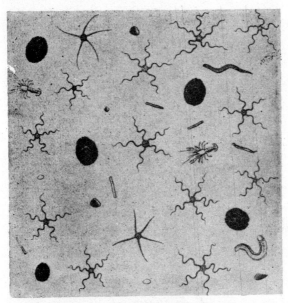

FIG. 18.17 *Brissopsis/chiajei* community (Petersen, 1918).

Other benthic communities may be briefly mentioned. Where a rocky bottom occurs in shallow water, an epifauna may be present with several of those animals found abundantly between tidemarks such as *Mytilus edulis*, *Littorina* spp., *Nucella lapillus* and *Balanus balanoides*. A rather peculiar community described by Petersen (1918) over a small area in Danish waters was characterized by an abundance of the amphipod *Haploops tubicola* (Fig. 18.19). The particular area studied had a rather stiff clay mud bottom, but Thorson (1957) points out that similar communities on softer deposits and with somewhat estuarine conditions have been described elsewhere. Apart from the dominant amphipod species *Haploops*, some bivalves (e.g. *Pecten septemradiatus*) occurred, together with a number of polychaetes such as *Eumenia crassa* and *Aphrodite aculeata*. The

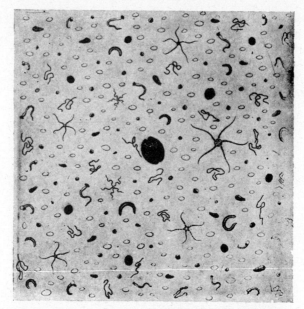

FIG. 18.18 *Brissopsis/sarsii* community (Petersen, 1918).

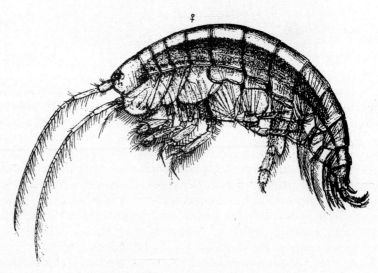

FIG. 18.19 *Haploops tubicola* (♀) (from Sars, 1895).

weight of animals present, despite the very high numbers of amphipods, was low. Nevertheless, the amphipods breed comparatively quickly and have a short life, so that the weight of the annual crop may be considerable. Another different type of community on a sandy bottom has recently been described by Sanders (1958) where again the association was dominated by amphipods, including *Ampelisca* spp. (Fig. 18.20).

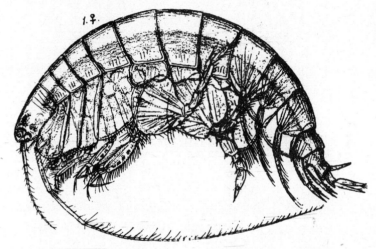

FIG. 18.20 *Ampelisca tenuicornis* (♀) (from Sars, 1895).

A few of the commoner communities such as the *Macoma* community appear to be true not only of boreal regions but more widely throughout the world. Thorson (1957) has shown that communities similar to *M. baltica* with different species of *Macoma*, and comparable species of *Cardium*, *Mya* and *Arenicola* are typical of the Arctic and of the North-East Pacific, and there is a suggestion of a similar community occurring in tropical waters (cf. Fig. 18.21). Parallel communities are also known for sandy substrata (*Venus* communities), and on muds (*Amphiura* communities) (cf. Thorson, 1958).

The existence of such parallel marine bottom communities lends support to the view that assemblages of benthic animals are to some extent bound together by both physico-chemical and biotic factors. Moreover, investigations suggest that communities seem to be relatively permanent. Holme (1950) showed for West Bay, Devon, that the *Spisula* and *Turritella* beds which had been described some 30 years before by Ford were still present in the same regions. There may be large fluctuations in abundance of the main species from year to year, however, as shown by Davis (1923) for *Spisula* and *Mactra* beds near the Dogger Bank.

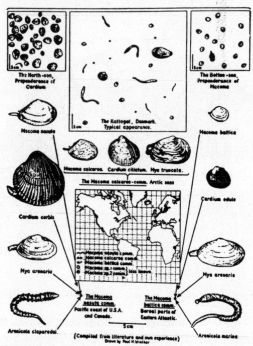

FIG. 18.21 Parallelism exhibited between Arctic, boreal, and N.E. Pacific *Macoma* communities (from Thorson, 1957).

We have already emphasized the importance of the bottom deposit to boreal benthic communities, but we must now discuss how this and other factors may affect the distribution of particular species. Salinity is unquestionably one of the controlling factors in seas such as the Baltic, and the habitable shallower areas of the Black Sea, and above all, in estuaries. Not only are there marked specific differences in relation to salinity, but the total number of benthic species is greatly reduced in comparison with typical marine environments. Whole major groupings such as the echinoderms may be virtually un-represented. In the Baltic, Ekman (1953) gives the number of invertebrates as between 200 and 300. Species such as *Metridium dianthus* and many other typically marine forms do not penetrate further than the Danish islands; *Asterias, Arenicola* and *Ophiura albida* a little further; *Scoloplos* and *Terebellides* reach the vicinity of Gotland; while among those which penetrate the more brackish regions are *Cardium, Mya, Mytilus* and *Macoma,* with *Corophium* and *Nereis diversicolor.* For the Black Sea, Caspers (1957) lists just over 1000 zoobenthic species as against more than 5000 for the Mediterranean.

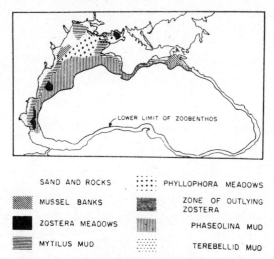

FIG. 18.22 The limit of the benthos in the Black Sea and the distribution of some of the benthic complexes in the northern areas (from Caspers, 1957).

A special condition holds in addition for the Black Sea, where with the extensive deoxygenation, much of the central region is azoic (cf. Fig. 18.22). Under brackish conditions (e.g. Baltic) some species may survive as adult animals but are unable to breed, or the larval stages are less viable. Barnes (1953) as a result of his work on barnacle nauplii, considered that the relative abilities of the larvae of different species to withstand lowered salinities was likely to be an important factor in the distribution of the adults. It is also well known that the ability of an animal to withstand salinity fluctuations is often influenced by temperature. Thus Costlow and Bookhout (1959) investigated the effects of temperature and salinity on several species of crab larvae. Large variations caused mortality, but with lesser changes in the environmental conditions, both the duration of individual larval stages and the time required for complete development were increased. While salinity appeared to have a somewhat greater effect than temperature, the combined effects of the two factors definitely influenced survival. Nikitin and Turpaeva (1957) have also demonstrated the effects of lowered salinity on the deve-

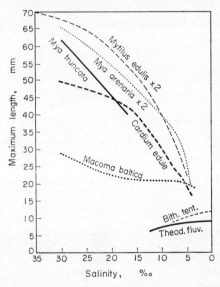

FIG. 18.23 Suggested relationship between the maximal length and salinity for certain molluscs (after Remane, 1940).

lopment of certain molluscs (e.g. *Mactra subtruncata, Venus gallina, Nassa reticulata*) and crabs (*Portunus* spp.) from the Black Sea. They found that though both adults and larvae could live at salinities of the order of $17^o/_{oo}$ or below, the lowest limit for larval development for each species was slightly higher than that for adult survival. Moreover, reduced salinity prolonged larval development. Amemiya (1926) found retardation and abnormal development with lowered salinity in oyster larvae; the American oyster could develop at a salinity of $15^o/_{oo}$ (optimum $25-29^o/_{oo}$) but European oyster larvae did not survive salinities below $24^o/_{oo}$ (optimum $31-35^o/_{oo}$). Salinity also affects the rate of growth after metamorphosis in many marine animals, so that with a lowering of salinity, the average size of the animal is reduced (cf. Fig. 18.23).

If we may turn for a moment to nektonic animals, salinity differences have been put forward as influencing the success or failure of developing broods of teleost fishes. The teleost larva must presumably constantly maintain its internal fluid against water loss to the surrounding seawater. Shelbourne (1957) has pointed to the difficulty encountered by young plaice larvae in maintaining this osmotic regulation before the impermeable integument and regulatory mechanisms of the adult fish have developed. He suggested that lack of food may so intensify the difficulty of osmotic stress as to cause marked mortality. On the other hand, with herring larvae which frequently occur in areas of lowered salinity, Holliday and Blaxter (1960) have demonstrated that a wide range of salinity is tolerated. A fairly efficient regulatory mechanism exists in the larvae, maintaining the blood hypotonic to that of normal seawater, and considerable regulation took place in response to changes in concentration of the external environment. Lasker and Theilacker (1962) have also shown that embryos and larvae of the Pacific sardine (*Sardinops caerulea*) are able to maintain an internal concentration markedly hypotonic to seawater. Salinity is probably therefore not a major factor in the survival of larvae of these teleosts, but with many species osmotic stress may well be a factor in larval survival.

In any event, in the open sea, salinity will be a less important limiting factor than temperature. With widely distributed benthic species the temperature limits may show differences in the northern and southern extremes of the range. Often, too, in boreal regions the essentially cold water species breed during the colder months of the year, while the warmer Mediterranean forms do so in summer. This has been demonstrated for such widely different groups as fishes (Table 12.3), bivalves, barnacles and gastropods (cf. Qasim, 1956; Crisp, 1954; Patel and Crisp, 1960). It is well known that the larval stages of many animals are more restricted in their temperature range than are the adults. The larvae of species of *Teredo* are less resistant to low temperature than are the adults. Similarly oyster larvae are more susceptible to low temperatures. This holds for both the European and American species. Thus in North America the oyster cannot normally breed north of Cape Cod (Massachusetts) although limited breeding occurs with a more northern variety. However, oysters are regularly transported north of the Cape and grow very successfully there as post-larval stages. Turner (1953) discusses the ecological distribution of several other molluscs over the east coast of N. America, and emphasizes the importance of temperature in restricting the spread of the warmer species into colder northern waters. Conversely, he shows that warm waters may limit the extension southwards of colder species. *Pecten grandis* is an oceanic species, confined to deep waters south of Massachusetts apparently owing to the high inshore temperatures, whereas to the north, in the cooler waters, the species may occur more inshore. It is the spawning of some invertebrates as well as larval development which is especially temperature dependent, and which therefore limits the distribution of many benthic species. Stephen (1938) gives the lower temperature limit for spawning of the American oyster as 20 °C, for the European oyster as 18 °C, and for *Cardium edule* as 12 °C, though comparatively few strict temperature limits are quoted in the literature for benthic species. The work of Loosanoff and his colleagues (e.g. Loosanoff and Davis, 1950, 1951) has yielded considerable information on the relationship between temperature and spawning for lamellibranchs. Working first on oysters, and then on *Venus mercenaria*, Loosanoff *et al.* showed the dependence of successful spawning on the attainment of a minimum temperature; for example, for *Venus mercenaria* the temperature limit appears to be about 23 °C. These investigators have shown that a number of species can be caused to spawn in the laboratory, provided the temperature is raised to the correct critical level. This relationship has been demonstrated not only for a number of bivalves but for a gastropod and for *Asterias*. Low temperature may thus delay spawning, but even when spawning occurs, Loosanoff, Miller and Smith (1951) showed that for *Venus mercenaria* the growth of the larvae was generally more rapid at higher temperatures, at least between 18 and 30 °C. In this way lower temperatures delay the onset of metamorphosis. Larvae which were exposed to temperatures below 15 °C were virtually inhibited in growth. Although temperature therefore may have its most conspicuous effects on spawning and larval development, it is possible to show that it has also a direct effect on growth after metamorphosis, at least on some bottom invertebrates. Turner (1953) showed that the rate of growth of *Mya* became reduced as one passed northwards into colder waters, and the work of Pratt and Campbell (1956) suggests that in *Venus mercenaria* the rate of growth is negligible below 10 °C but increases with a rise in temperature at least to 23 °C. The reverse relationship may be seen in what may be called cold adapted species; for example, the sea scallop, *Pecten grandis*, which has already been described as a cold species, grows best at temperatures of 10 °C or lower, and the growth rate decreases as the temperature is raised until the animals are killed at a temperature of about 22 °C. The effect of temperature on growth, at least in some species of bivalve, may perhaps be associated with filtration rates. Verwey (1952) states that while *Venus mercenaria* and *Ostrea* spp. tend to close their shells at temperatures approaching 3°C, *Mytilus edulis* remains active, though the feeding rate is reduced. *Ostrea edulis* exhibits a clear reduction in filtering activity with a fall in temperature from 20–10 °C; there is some decline in rate with *Mytilus*, but the two lamellibranchs *Spisula solida* and *Cultellus pellucidus* are apparently unaffected in their filtration rate by the same drop in temperature.

Closely allied species may also show differences in their breeding cycles and in the average number of young produced per brood according to the temperature. In the wood-boring isopod genus *Limnoria*, for instance, *L. tripunctata*, a warm water species, produces few and small broods at moderate temperatures and ceases to breed altogether in boreal waters. *L. quadripunctata* breeds successfully in the moderately warm waters of the English Channel, whereas *L. lignorum*, a boreal species, is most successful in colder waters (cf. Jones, 1960).

Although some species of benthic animals are adapted to breed at any of the temperatures found in the whole marine environment, it must be remembered, as Thorson (1950) has pointed out, that low temperature will tend to slow down development so that the period of larval life may be lengthened. He suggests three weeks as the average life for free swimming planktonic larvae such as those of lamellibranchs and polychaetes. But in Arctic waters an increased duration of larval existence must occur and this will be dangerous, since the larvae are subject all the time to the predations of carnivorous species. The prevalence of direct development or of short-lived larval stages in extreme northern waters is thus of survival value, and contrasts sharply with the large proportion of planktonic larvae produced by bottom animals in warm tropical waters (Fig. 18.24).

We know very little at present about the precise effect of substratum on species of animals, though some information is available. According to Jones (1950) *Turritella communis* becomes smothered in bottom deposits that are too soft; *Aporrhais ceresiana*, because of the shape of the shell, resists being smothered in a very soft deposit and therefore can compete successfully with *Aporrhais pes-pelicani*. Again *Corbula gibba* can live successfully in a fairly muddy sand

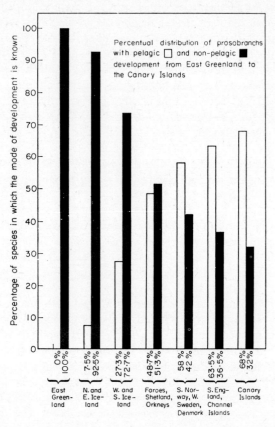

FIG. 18.24 Relations between pelagic and non-pelagic larval development for prosobranchs in the North Atlantic (from Thorson, 1950).

provided there is some attachment, such as a small stone to which it can anchor its single byssus thread. The type of deposit is not necessarily a very important factor limiting the distribution of all benthic species, however. Smidt (1951) points out for the *Macoma* community that species such as *Macoma* and *Hydrobia* seem to be more or less indifferent to the deposit itself but are strongly influenced by the sheltered conditions. On the other hand, *Arenicola* and *Pygospio* are confined to muddy-sand areas; *Nephthys hombergi* occurs on more sandy deposits, whereas *Scrobicularia* inhabits muds only. As regards *Arenicola*, many workers have agreed that it cannot occur on mud but must have a mixture of sand. This restriction is probably due to the need for the production of a firm burrow into which the worm can retire without the walls collapsing. Pratt and Campbell (1956) claim a reduction in growth rate for the clam *Venus mercenaria* in sediments with a high silt-clay fraction. Among other effects, clogging of the burrow and reduced filtration may occur with sedimentation. The depths of burrowing may be considerably influenced by the grade of the deposit.

Particle size of the deposit may itself be of direct importance to animals. But particle size is a reflection of the degree of movement of water and this may affect some species more strongly. There seems to be general agreement with Smidt's view that *Macoma* occurs in sheltered, often estuarine, areas but can live in more sandy stretches of shore as well as on muds (cf. Petersen, Stephen, Rees). Spooner and Moore (1940) believe that *Nereis diversicolor* is also much more affected by the degree of shelter than by the amount of fine grade deposits, and Beanland (1940) stresses the need of quiet water to *Corophium*. Sanders (1958) has given a new view on this problem of direct and indirect effects of substratum from his investigations of animal populations in Buzzards Bay, near Woods Hole. He states that while the distribution and abundance of certain species would appear to be closely associated with sands of a particular grade, this is partly a reflection of the degree of water movement which enables the animals to feed sufficiently. This would apply particularly to suspension feeders. A well sorted deposit but one that is sufficiently stable will provide a suitable environment for such bottom animals. Very fine deposits with small average particle size will be associated with more mud of high organic content, and this may be of greater significance for those benthic animals which are deposit feeders.

While both *Cardium* and *Macoma* are somewhat indifferent to the type of deposit, *Cardium* tends to be the commoner bivalve on more sandy shores since it is a suspension feeder. Spooner and Moore (1940) have suggested that in intertidal areas the distribution of *Cardium* is largely determined by the time during which it is submerged. Only over this period can it feed. *Macoma*, common in sheltered situations, is not so strictly limited since it feeds with its

long siphons on the surface of the muddy deposit. *Scrobicularia*
(Fig. 18.13) also tends to feed on the surface layer of ooze between
the mud and the overlying water, where bottom diatoms as well as
detritus will provide an abundant food supply. This species is however confined to mud deposits. How far chemical factors of the
bottom deposit can directly affect the viability of a species is not

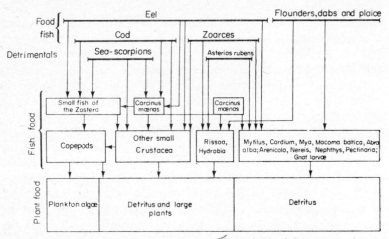

FIG. 18.25 Diagrammatic representation of the food of fishes and other
principal animals in Nyborg Fjord (from Blegvad, 1916).

known, but it is not unreasonable to believe that inorganic and
organic micro-nutrients may prove to be of significance. We shall
return to the problem of how far such factors influence the settlement of larvae of benthic animals.

Apart from salinity, temperature and substrate, a most important
factor in distribution of bottom faunas is food supply. It has
been suggested that the plankton provides the bulk of the food.
From a series of studies made in Danish waters, however, Blegvad
(1914) emphasized the great importance of detritus, particularly
that derived from fixed algae and *Zostera* (Fig. 18.25). He listed bivalves and ascidians as among the most important detritus feeders,
and regarded planktonic diatoms as of little significance in their
food supply. Blegvad divided the benthos into herbivores, detritus
eaters and carnivores, and discussed some of the methods of taking
food, a subject which was reviewed later in greater detail by Yonge
(1928). The work of Hunt (1925), however, and the results of more

recent investigations show that the phytoplankton, both as living and as dead matter, is of the greatest significance as food for the benthos, and that in most areas, detritus derived from fixed weeds plays a much smaller part. There may be very considerable variety in food organisms. Hunt showed, particularly for *Pecten opercularis*, that the food taken is to some extent a reflection of the abundant food species available and may thus show seasonal fluctuations. Nevertheless benthic animals, just as any other group of organisms, are selective to some degree. Feeding mechanisms and habits, size of food, as well as more subtle factors, all restrict the type of food consumed. Verwey (1952) dealing with lamellibranchs, points out that although selective mechanisms are employed in feeding, most bivalves appear to take in a considerable variety of organisms as well as organic detritus. However, not all the stomach contents necessarily serve as food. Many dinoflagellates taken by the Californian mussel, for example, are not apparently digested; pseudofaeces from several species of lamellibranch have been shown to include living organisms. Bivalves almost certainly differ in their ability to digest organic detritus also; Verwey suggests for instance that mussels utilize it to a greater extent than do oysters.

Food must therefore limit the distribution of species. For example, those animals that are algal feeders, such as many smaller gastropods, must obviously be restricted to fairly shallow water where they can feed on seaweeds; similarly browsers on *Zostera* will be limited to comparatively inshore areas. A number of bottom animals also feed on the diatoms and possibly debris on the fronds of seaweeds and must therefore be confined to the shallow algal zone.

Hunt found that Blegvad's division into herbivores and detritus feeders was not applicable, however, to animals living below the narrow algal fringes of the coast. In muds and sands animals may select from the surrounding water suspended particles, including micro-organisms such as plankton, and detritus. This usually involves the use of a sieve mechanism such as cilia or setae, and often a feeding current is employed (e.g. bivalves, ascidians, serpulids and sabellids, sponges, bryozoans). These animals have been termed suspension feeders. On the other hand, many animals feed on the micro-organisms and especially the detritus in and on the bottom deposit (deposit feeders). It is a fair generalization that deposit feeders are commoner in the softer deposits whereas suspension feeders predominate on the shells and gravels.

Sanders (1956) has further divided deposit feeders into those that feed discriminately on or in the sediment ("selective deposit feeders") including the bivalves *Macoma* and *Nucula*, polychaetes such as *Melinna*, *Pista*, and *Flabelligera*, and the amphipods *Amphithoe* and *Erichthonius*, and those animals that are non-selective deposit feeders (e.g. *Ophelia*, *Scalibregma* and many Maldanids). In addition, there are the predatory species which tend to roam more widely over various types of bottom since most predaceous forms are somewhat unrestricted in their prey. Predatory forms, therefore, particularly relatively fast moving species, are generally less clear indicators of communities.

The slower rates of growth of invertebrates in colder seas and the relatively small proportion of meroplanktonic larvae may contribute to fairly stable bottom populations. It is rather more difficult to see how bottom communities have remained recognisable and reasonably stable in temperate and warm water regions in view of the wealth of planktonic larvae and the considerable proportion of rapidly breeding forms (cf. Fig. 18.24). One might expect that dense and often fairly short-lived settlements of particular species would produce instability of the bottom fauna. In temperate waters the sudden appearance of dense settlements of recently metamorphosed ("0-year-group") polychaetes, barnacles, ascidians and mussels is a common experience. Many such organisms are of great significance in the fouling of shore installations. There is often an enormous mortality amongst such young benthic animals, so that the appearance of the bottom fauna changes rapidly. Workers in such areas as the Limfjord, Dogger Bank and Waddensea, have been impressed with the very high numbers of young bivalves and polychaetes which can settle suddenly on the bottom. But investigators such as Thamdrup (1935) and Smidt have commented also on the enormous mortality and rapid disappearance of the young spat. Marked variations in spat settlement from one year to another can therefore lead to great differences in the success of particular year broods. This has been observed in inter-tidal areas for bivalves such as *Cardium*, *Macoma* and *Mytilus* (cf. Stephen, 1931, 1932, 1938; Raymont, 1955). Boysen-Jensen (1919) has investigated the same problem in shallow inshore waters and agrees that, especially with relatively rapid breeding and short lived species, there can be very great differences in standing crop from one year to another (cf. Fig. 18.26). The investigation of year broods in those waters beyond low tide level is undoubtedly more difficult but Sanders (1956) indi-cates the variable strength of broods in some polychaetes (e.g. *Nephthys, Cistenoides*) and in lamellibranchs. Not only is the rate of breeding significant but rate of growth will affect the standing crop (cf. Fig. 18.27). The increase in weight of various species of the

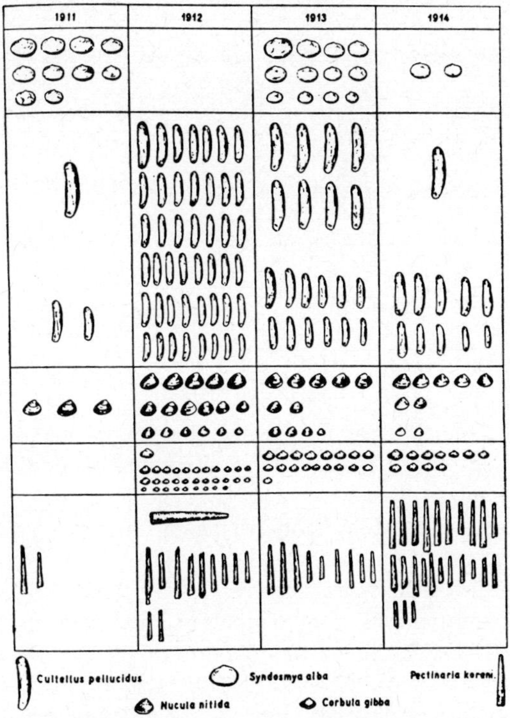

FIG. 18.26 Yearly fluctuations in the abundance of certain species in the *Syndosmya* (*Abra*) *alba* community from the western Limfjord (from Boysen-Jensen, 1919).

benthos is shown in Fig. 18.28. Jones (1956) has also examined the growth of certain molluscs and echinoderms. He concludes that a species such as *Cardium scabrum* is virtually an annual, probably due in part to breeding habits and partly to the intense depredations by fish (e.g. haddock). Thus its density on the bottom will tend to vary greatly. *Ophiura affinis* and *Abra prismatica*, which probably breed twice per year, are similar. On the other hand, such species as *Turritella communis, Corbula gibba* and *Ophiura albida* are longer lived and less liable to such marked fluctuations (Fig. 18.28.1). In more temperate regions therefore, bottom communities, despite variations in the density of species, will have some continuity. As Boysen-Jensen has pointed out, even with the marked differences in success of year broods in the shorter lived species, the most essential requirement for the preservation of the community is the maintenance

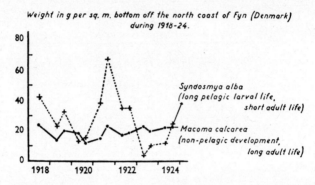

FIG. 18.27 The large fluctuations in *Syndosmya alba*, with a long pelagic larval life, and the small fluctuations in *Macoma calcarea* (non-pelagic development) (from Thorson, 1957).

of a small spawning stock from which by intense reproduction recruitment can occur.

An added difficulty arises, however, in the problem of the stability of benthic communities. If in temperate areas bottom animals are largely propagated by planktonic larvae, there must be tremendous competition and almost haphazard settlement of these larvae from the plankton on the bottom. Indeed, until comparatively recently, the recruitment of the benthos was regarded in this light. Of the hordes of meroplanktonic larvae about to metamorphose, the great majority will be carried to environments which are unsuitable, and these larvae perish. Numbers are sufficient, however, for dense settlements to occur by chance in suitable areas where heavy depredation and other factors causing mortality further reduce the stock. Undoubtedly larvae may frequently be carried to unsuitable habitats and mortality may be heavy. But increasing knowledge of the behaviour of planktonic larvae suggests that settlement is not quite so haphazard as was at one time thought. In general, meroplanktonic larvae tend to be positively phototactic when young and to become negative to light when older, so that they tend to seek the bottom when they are ready to metamorphose. However, Thorson (1957) describes certain very shallow water species (*Pygospio*, *Pomatoceros*, *Asterias*, *Balanus*

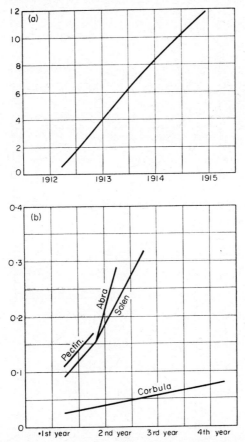

Fig. 18.28 Rates of growth for *Echinocardium cordatum* (a) and for *Syndosmya* (*Abra*), *Solen*, *Corbula* and *Pectinaria* (b) (from Boysen-Jensen, 1919).

and *Mytilus*) as positively phototactic even when they are ready to metamorphose; this enables them to crowd in the upper layers and to settle in shallow waters, even in the intertidal zone.

A complication arises when such surface-loving larvae encounter water layers of lowered salinity as in estuaries. The larvae of *Asterias*

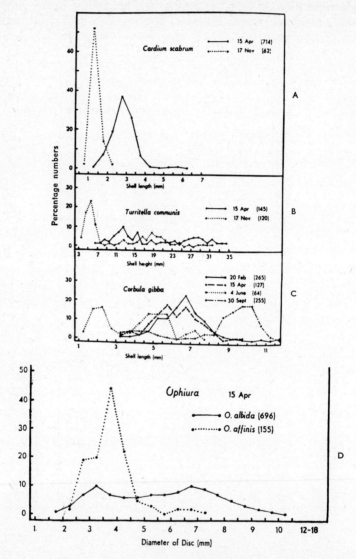

FIG. 18.28.1 Size distribution curves for some benthic species. A = *Cardium scabrum*; B = *Turritella communis*; C = *Corbula gibba*; D = *Ophiura* spp. (from Jones, 1956).

and *Pomatoceros*, for instance, though positively phototactic, will remain below water of lowered salinity and will tend to be carried into the slightly less shallow areas of the shore. It is likely that the various species of meroplanktonic larvae have different limiting salinity values beyond which they will not migrate into the upper water layers (cf. Davis, 1958, for lamellibranchs). A particularly clear example of the limiting effects of salinity on positively phototactic

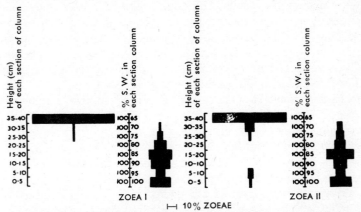

ZOEA I   ⊢ 10% ZOEAE   ZOEA II

FIG. 18.28.2 The distribution of *Porcellana* zoeas under the influence of light from above in salinity gradients. For each zoeal stage, the figure on the left indicates distribution in a column of normal seawater; that on the right, in a salinity gradient (from Lance, 1960).

behaviour is seen in the work of Lance (1960) on *Porcellana* zoeas. In normal seawater they are intensely positively phototactic, but an upper stratum of low salinity seawater prevents their upward migration (cf. Fig. 18.28.2). Earlier investigations suggest that salinity may even reverse the phototactic sign in some planktonic forms. Other environmental factors may modify the behavioural patterns of meroplanktonic larvae so that their distribution at metamorphosis is not merely haphazard.

During the past 25 years the effect of the bottom itself has been shown to be of importance. The work especially of Wilson (1937, 1948) has suggested, mainly for polychaete larvae, that metamorphosis could be delayed for a short period if the larvae touched areas of bottom which were unsuitable for the adults. Although particle size and shape was at one time considered as the specific stimulus, this now seems less likely. The physical size and nature of the surface for attachment may have some effect (cf. Barnes and Powell, 1950), but Wilson (1953) has shown that organic matter, both living and dead, is a factor influencing settlement. Whatever the stimulus, it appears as if some species of larvae, swimming near the bottom as they approach metamorphosis, can, as it were, "sample" the substratum, occasionally touching the mud or sand surface and then swimming on again. Any tactile or chemoreceptors possessed by the animal are likely to be involved in this kind of "positive selection" of substratum. Apart from polychaete larvae, some molluscs are reported to exhibit such selection. *Teredo*, for example, selects wood surfaces in preference to stone or metallic substrata; there is even a suggestion that the larvae select spring rather than the harder wood (cf. Lane, 1959). Carriker reported a transitional phase in the settling of *Venus mercenaria*, during which both the swimming organ and the foot were present, when it appeared as if types of substratum were tested. Among other animals, *Protodrilus* is also said to be influenced in its metamorphosis by a chemical effect of the shell-gravel substratum. The specific stimuli associated with the bottom are undoubtedly extremely subtle. The bacterial flora associated with mud particles has been considered by Walne (1958) as a factor in the culture of oyster larvae. Wilson and Armstrong's (1958) results on the development of *Echinus esculentus* gave little support to the view that bacterial action on the seawater affected development, but it could be a factor in settlement. Wilson's results (1954) suggest that *Ophelia bicornis* larvae positively select substrata with certain micro-organisms, including flagellates. Presumably other types of micro-organisms may be distasteful. Organisms, and organic and inorganic substances in extraordinarily low concentration, derived from the bottom deposit, may all be effective in influencing metamorphosis.

Of great interest are the experiments of Knight-Jones and his colleagues on the gregariousness witnessed in the settlement of larvae of such different animals as barnacles, *Spirorbis* and oysters (e.g. Knight-Jones and Stevenson 1950; Knight-Jones, 1953). Settling larvae definitely seem to favour surfaces on which other members of the same species have previously settled. Knight-Jones (1951, 1955) has even shown an apparent discrimination between *Spirorbis borealis* and *S. pagenstecheri*, and also between areas which have been settled by *Balanus* and by the barnacle, *Verruca*. One is again tempted to think of chemical trace substances which are present on the settled areas and which induce the settlement of the same species. Such an idea receives some support from the demonstration by Crisp and by Barnes (e.g. Crisp and Spencer, 1958; Barnes and Barnes, 1959) of the existence of substances promoting hatching in barnacles. Crisp and Spencer's results suggest that an adult ripe barnacle, under the stimulus of feeding, will secrete an active substance into the mantle cavity which promotes liberation of nauplii. If organic substances in very low concentrations can induce hatching, others may presumably affect settlement.

Most of the work on gregariousness concerns inshore species of bottom animals. How far such factors operate more offshore is doubtful. Thorson (1957) suggests that a tendency for young spat to settle in great numbers on previously colonized areas in offshore bottom communities is deleterious for the species as a whole. He maintains, by contrast, that a species like *Spisula*, which is very sensitive to large amounts of silt and detritus, may rather be prevented from settling in areas which have already been extensively colonized by older individuals. Perhaps the presence of a quantity of faecal material from *Spisula* beds might deter the young spat so that they would colonize only the more barren areas where the sand is purer. This may account for the remarkable patchiness of *Spisula* populations, for instance in the North Sea. The importance of the substratum, however, is evident. Indeed it may be regarded as the most potent single factor determining the stability and continuance of bottom communities. Thorson (1955) has pointed out that this is true also for the predator species of benthic communities (cf. Loosanoff *et al.*, 1955). The metamorphosing larvae of benthic predators are influenced by the substratum far more than by the presence of their prey. Marine communities are, therefore, not entirely haphazard assemblages, though it may be a long time before we discover the specific factors which limit one species to a particular type of substratum.

It is more difficult to explain the extraordinary differences in density of total bottom fauna which may be seen between sea floors of apparently similar nature. It is common experience that in areas of the sea bottom separated by only comparatively short distances, marked variations in biomass can exist. Sometimes there are reasonably obvious explanations—a deep pocket of a sea floor may have a very low oxygen content and may be practically azoic; close inshore, pounding surf may restrict life; further offshore, areas may occur with great tidal scour and the resulting constantly shifting coarse deposit is rather unfavourable to life. However, one must be cautious in assessing the effects of environmental factors; some degree of movement of water is favourable for suspension feeders. But leaving aside obvious cases where a poor benthos may be expected, there still remain many puzzling examples of sea areas where the bottom fauna density is remarkably poor.

The number of animals existing in a unit area of sea bottom may give a very misleading indication of its richness owing to the great variation in size of animals. The living or wet weight of organisms/m² in the community under study is a much better index. But we encounter an enormous variation in the wet weight of material on various sea floors. Petersen and Boysen-Jensen (1911) record animal communities with several hundred grams wet weight of benthos per square metre, and at the other extreme, very poor areas where only a few grams of living matter were present (Fig. 18.29). Demel and Mulicki (1958) have recently given values for the biomass of the benthos in parts of the Baltic. Bivalves appear to be the most important animals contributing to the total biomass. But very considerable variations can occur; *Macoma baltica* averaged 3.9 g/m², but in places reached as high a figure as 24 g/m²; *Astarte borealis* reached even 100 g/m². The total standing crop of the benthos ranged from 3.5 g/m² to more than 170 g/m². This range omits the relatively enormous biomass which may be experienced with dense beds of the mussel, *Mytilus edulis*. Demel and Mulicki recorded values from mussel beds as high as > 3 kg/m². Greater variations than those recorded by Demel and Mulicki have been previously noted however, even apart from mussel beds. Blegvad (1925, 1928) records on certain rare occasions 200 to 300 g/m² of bivalves alone in certain areas of the Limfjord. Although this was probably mainly a result of a sudden spat-fall, very large weights of benthos can occur more permanently, especially in colder seas. But wet weights may also be misleading; a more significant index of richness of the bottom fauna is the dry organic matter present per unit area of bottom. Petersen and his colleagues recognized this in their early work. For example, they showed that polychaetes might have some 16–20% dry organic matter, whereas, at the other extreme, echinoderms might have only 1–3%. Thorson (1957) has given some average figures for dry organic matter and suggests that most polychaetes and crustaceans have about 20% dry organic matter, whereas lamellibranchs and echinoderms, with the relatively large amount of

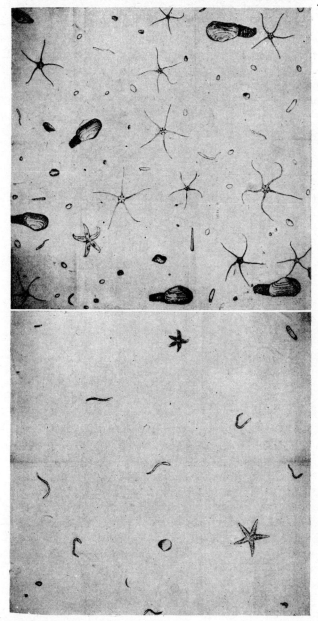

FIG.18.29 Rich (upper) and poor (lower) benthic communities from Danish waters. Each square represents an area of 0.25 m² (Petersen and Boysen-Jensen, 1911).

calcium carbonate, may have only 6–7% (cf. Fig. 18.30). These are most useful figures for converting wet weight to dry organic matter, though all authors recognize that even in the same group of animals, species can vary greatly. Animals at different stages of growth may also show differences. Enormous variations remain, however, in the standing crop reckoned on a dry organic weight basis between one region and another. Harvey (1950) suggests that areas exist with bottom faunas as rich as 200 g/m² of dry organic matter, whereas,

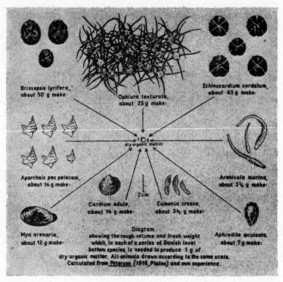

FIG. 18.30 Diagram to illustrate the rough volume and wet weight for a number of Danish benthic species which would yield 1 gram dry organic matter (from Thorson, 1957).

at the other extreme, some sea bottoms have less than 5 g/m². Raymont (1947) has shown the wide range which can exist in the dry weight of the benthos even in a very small inshore area. Part of the difficulty in seeking an explanation arises no doubt from the comparatively small number of quantitative investigations of bottom faunas. Particularly striking is the very great lack of information on seasonal variations and fluctuations from year to year. Most quantitative investigations have been conducted over a comparatively short period of time, and the few investigations which have been continued for a longer period have been confined to shallow inshore waters. Until research on bottom faunas can give us accurate information on yearly fluctuations, comparisons of biomass between one area and another are bound to be regarded with some uncertainty.

In attempting to compare the richness of one sea bottom with another, there is also the difficulty of determining how far predators should be included in the total biomass. The weight of predators can show wide variations between areas. In one survey by Petersen (1918) some communities had as little as 10% of the biomass (wet weight) as predatory species, and 70% or more consisted of small bivalves and polychaetes useful as fish food. On the other hand, some areas had only 40% of useful fish food with relatively higher quantities of predatory forms. In accordance with Elton's theory of the pyramid of numbers, there is a limit to the density of predators which can be supported by an area of sea. Nevertheless, predators are unusually mobile and can range over the sea bottom; they are also usually less specialized in their food requirements than detritus and suspension feeders. Thus their density may not be a fair index of the standing crop of benthos.

The depredations of these predaceous carnivores on the bottom fauna might be of such magnitude as to cause marked depletion of the benthos. Differences in bottom fauna densities could therefore be in part a reflection of the feeding intensities of predatory populations. Members of the nekton such as demersal fishes can make extremely heavy inroads on the stock of benthos, but members of the benthos itself such as asteroids, and some ophiuroids and gastropods are also voracious predators on the bottom fauna. Indeed Thorson (1958) summarizes the scant data available on the amount of food consumed by marine predators by suggesting that carnivorous invertebrates eat considerably more food than fishes on a body weight basis. Some species (e.g. *Amphiura*) may feed on detritus to a considerable extent but they can become predatory species when an abundance of prey is present. Sanders (1956) has shown that *Nephthys incisa*, hitherto regarded as carnivorous, may also feed on detritus when necessary. It may be that there are a number of primarily predaceous benthic animals which can vary their feeding habits. When prey is abundant such species may become of considerable significance in causing large variations in the density of bottom faunas. On some areas of sea bottom with enormous populations of such voracious animals as ophiuroids, it is indeed difficult to see how the non-predatory species can survive. But the settlement and survival of this benthos would not appear to be quite haphazard. Thorson (1955, 1958) has shown that ophiuroids, asteroids, some gastropods and other carnivores are prevented from preying extensively on recently metamorphosed larvae and spat just settled on the bottom. During this period of settlement many of the carnivores are also breeding. Ophiuroids, carnivorous gastropods and asteroids apparently do not feed at this time; there is considerable evidence that for approximately a month beforehand, while the gonads are enlarging, very little feeding takes place, and that immediately following spawning, when in many cases some deterioration of the gut occurs, the animals also take very little food. In this way, for two or three months in the year bivalves and other bottom living forms can settle on the bottom and become established, even though a heavy predator population exists.

Some of the differences in richness of the benthos may be more apparent than real. Sanders (1956) has pointed out that some of the discrepancies may be attributed to the varying methods and techniques employed by different investigators. He obtains less variability between sampling at any one station by excluding the larger and rarer animals and believes that still greater uniformity can be achieved if only the in-fauna is compared. Comparisons of the biomass of bottom fauna from various regions are given in Fig. 18.31. Long Island Sound appears to be much richer than other regions such as Plymouth when comparisons are made on this (dry organic weight) basis. Riley (1955) has also commented on the greater richness of the benthos of Long Island Sound as compared with the English Channel. Long Island Sound is even richer than the fertilized area of Loch Craiglin. Yet on a numerical density basis, Loch Craiglin seems to be equally as rich as Long Island Sound. At Plymouth, the benthos is certainly not as rich numerically, especially as regards the smaller-sized species, but the difference is not so striking as when dry organic weights of the benthos are compared. The criterion on which richness of the bottom fauna is assessed is, therefore, of the utmost importance.

Although attention to standardizing techniques may assist in evaluating bottom fauna densities more accurately, real and marked differences in biomass still occur and demand explanation. Apart from severe depredations by carnivorous species, extreme climatic conditions may be important in their long-term effects on the bottom fauna. For example, very cold winters in the North Sea have been held to be responsible for the failure of certain bivalve broods. In the shallow waters of intertidal and nearshore areas, Danish investigations have shown that the bottom fauna may be extensively killed during a severe winter. Raymont (1947, 1950, 1955) has also suggested that in the shallower parts of Loch Sween the density of the benthos is markedly affected by frosts. In deeper waters, however, the greater

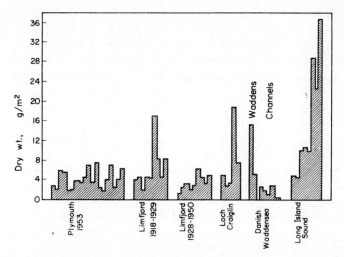

FIG. 18.31 Comparison of the weight of bottom fauna from several shallow sea areas (from Sanders, 1956).

stability of the environmental conditions largely preclude this effect of climate on the bottom fauna.

The difference in standing crop between one area and another may presumably be correlated with food supply. Since many of the bottom community are detritus feeders, the food available should be reflected in the amount of organic matter in the bottom deposit. There have been comparatively few determinations on the organic matter, but investigations such as those of Mare (1942) and Jones (1956) suggest that the amount present in most bottom deposits is very large as compared with the weight of bottom fauna. However, much of this organic matter is in a relatively stable chemical form which apparently detritus feeders cannot assimilate. Some of the material is too deep in the deposit to be accessible to the majority of bottom animals. Many authors have suggested that bacteria form a considerable portion of the food of bottom feeders, and Fox and his collaborators believe that excessively fine particulate or even colloidal organic matter is an important source of food. Nevertheless it appears that in the majority of muddy deposits from inshore regions a large percentage of the general organic matter is not used as food.

On the other hand, the density of the benthos in the ocean deeps appears to be far less than that of shallower regions such as continental shelves and slopes (cf. Zenkevitch and Birstein, 1956). Admittedly the results of some of the more recent deep sea expeditions suggest that the bottom fauna in abyssal depths may be considerably greater than had been once envisaged; densities at the bottom of the deep oceans with a biomass approaching 1–2 g/m^2 have been mentioned by Sparck (1951). But these values are far less than the standing crop of benthos found in many shallow areas. Moreover, the amount of dry organic matter in most deep sea faunas is extremely low. There is therefore a very slow turn-over of the organic matter in deep sea regions. Without doubt this very low rate must be associated with the extraordinarily small amount of detritus and other food reaching the bottom at great depths (cf. also Zenkevitch, 1961).

The low temperatures prevalent in ocean abysses will reduce the respiratory rate of the sluggish and sessile benthos; maintenance demands in terms of food supply are therefore low. Even in inshore regions the respiration of the generally rather slow-moving bottom fauna is relatively low in comparison with pelagic animals. The rate of growth of the bottom fauna is also low as compared with other members of the marine environment. But the daily food demand of the benthos on the plankton is considerable. This is mainly a reflection of the relatively large standing crop of bottom fauna present in a typical shallow marine community. In the balance sheet which Harvey (1950) attempted to produce for the English Channel, he suggested that of some 0.4 g of dry organic matter produced by the phytoplankton daily beneath a square metre of sea surface, approximately one half is taken by the zooplankton community. But one half of the phytoplankton daily production (i.e. 0.2 g/m^2), in addition to 0.12 g of zooplankton organic matter/m^2, goes to nourish the bottom fauna. This is a very considerable demand. Although there appear to be large quantities of organic matter present in bottom muds, this richness is misleading, and the benthos is very much dependent on the plankton supply from the waters above.

In enclosed waters such as Long Island Sound, Riley has been able to demonstrate this relationship. Open oceans present a much more difficult problem. Another method of demonstrating the relationship between basic productivity and benthos is by artificially raising the productivity of a limited area by the addition of limiting nutrients. The experiments which have been done on the fertilization of marine areas at Loch Sween (Raymont, 1947, 1950) show that there is a very slow increase in the biomass of the bottom fauna accompanying a rapid marked increase in plankton production.

So far discussion of the bottom fauna has been centred on the more readily recognized animals ranging in size from the large members of the community to those of only a few millimetres in length. Thousands of organisms of much smaller dimensions including those just exceeding one millimetre down to those of bacterial size also occur in the bottom deposit. Comparatively few studies have been made on this minute fauna and flora. Mare (1942) divided the benthos into three groups largely on size and weight. She also recognized the great range in generation time of these benthic animal groups, though for many of the species the details of reproduction are unknown. Mare emphasized that the three divisions are not sharply separated and are therefore to some extent artificial. The first group (the macrobenthos) is the usual macrofauna which alone is normally analysed in most studies of the bottom (Fig. 18.32). It consists of those animals which are generally retained by a sieve of 1 mm mesh and whose live weight may approach a minimum of 1 mg. The largest animals may weigh several grams by contrast. The second group is termed the meiobenthos (Fig. 18.32) and comprises relatively minute animals including very small crustaceans such as harpacticoid copepods, cumaceans and ostracods, as well as nematodes, turbellarians, and the very smallest polychaetes and bivalves. These animals are normally retained by an 0.1 mm mesh sieve and their weight may vary from 0.05 to less than 0.001 mg. Included in the meiobenthos also are Foraminifera which in some areas can be very abundant. A brief reference to considerable densities of Foraminifera is made by Smidt (1951) for shallow muddy-sands on the Danish coast. In the relatively shallow tropical waters of the Great Barrier Reef lagoon Collins (1958) found a large and varied assemblage of Foraminifera. In cold waters, as in the Antarctic, the number of species may be more limited but an abundance of foraminiferans may be found. As regards overall density, Earland (1933, 1934) states that

Antarctic material is usually dominated by arenaceous foraminiferans. Some of the larger arenaceous Foraminifera such as *Astrorhiza limicola*, may, however, be large enough to be included in macrobenthic

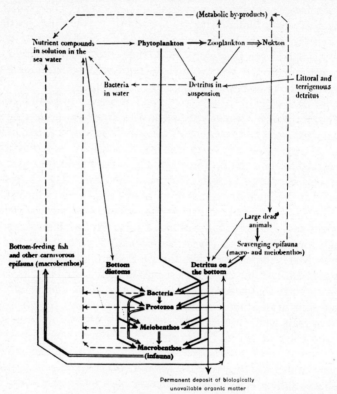

FIG. 18.32 Diagram of the main phases of the marine food cycle. Above are stages occurring in the water; below are those taking place at the surface of the bottom and in the bottom deposit (from Mare, 1942).

studies. Thorson (1957) speaks of Foraminifera communities, but the densities of these foraminiferans are not comparable to those usually included in meiobenthic studies. Buchanan (1958) also found larger foraminiferans in silty sand deposits off Accra which formed part of the normal benthos, and in a more recent investigation off the Northumberland coast, Buchanan and Hedley (1960) found *Astrorhiza limicola*, but only in moderate densities (mean 53 animals/m²).

Although the groups of benthos are not sharply separated, there-fore, a third category may be recognized — the microbenthos. This group consists mainly of ciliates, amoebae, flagellates and bacteria. In shallow water, bottom diatoms must also be included (Fig.18.32). Microbenthic organisms are of excessively small size: their weight may vary from about 1×10^{-4} to 1×10^{-9} mg. It is very difficult to assess them numerically except by special techniques such as culture methods. Dead and dying organisms, contributing to the detritus, occur with the microbenthos. In relatively shallow mud bottoms, pelagic diatoms are most numerous amongst these dying organisms, but a number of living planktonic diatoms also are present, though these cannot be part of the true micro-benthos. The immediate mud surface appears to be by far the richest layer for all groups of microbenthos; the density of organisms is appreciably less even at a depth of 1–2 cm. Mare suggests that in waters off Plymouth of the order of 40 m depth, the planktonic diatoms contribute by far the greatest weight of living matter to the surface layer. They form therefore an important source of food for the detritus eaters. Bottom diatoms can be important, particularly in winter, in these shallow waters, but bacteria, Protozoa and the bottom diatoms contribute far less than the planktonic species. Mare estimates that only a very small amount, probably less than 0.5%, of the total organic carbon in the mud is due to the true micro-benthos, but the planktonic diatoms at their maximum can possibly contribute about 2.5% to the total organic carbon.

Of the microbenthic community, the bacteria are of profound significance in marine food chains. Apart from their activities in releasing inorganic phosphates, nitrates and other plant nutrients, they decompose resistant detritus and convert part of this into the living protoplasm of their bodies. Bacteria feed upon the dissolved organic matter also and convert this into living particulate sub-stance. A special case is that of the Black Sea where, with the extensive deoxygenation and H_2S production, life in the deeper waters is restricted to microorganisms. However, Kriss (1959) points out that the considerable variety and the great abundance of bacteria in the deep layers causes the microbial biomass beneath a square metre of surface to approach $1\frac{1}{2}$ times that of the biomass of the phytoplankton and zooplankton. Kriss claims, therefore, a very appreciable synthesis of organic matter by the exceptionally rich bacterial flora. More generally in marine environments, Zobell has emphasized that bacteria form a most essential link in the food chain, converting dissolved and detrital material, often unavailable to other organisms, into a particulate form which animals can assimilate. The Protozoa of the microbenthos undoubtedly play a large part in feeding on, and thus controlling, the rich bacterial populations. In shallow waters, ciliates, amoebae and the larger flagellates, while feeding to some extent on bacteria, feed also according to Mare on the decomposing diatom cells arising from the plankton (Fig. 18.33). In deeper waters only more limited detritus will be available. The smaller flagellates and amoebae are mainly bacterial-feeding but undoubtedly many flagellates can exist on dissolved organic matter. In all probability a number of Protozoa can vary their diet to some degree. Not only the bacteria, therefore, but the whole microbenthos is of importance in that it converts detritus and dissolved organic matter into particulate living material. Its significance is out of all proportion to its extremely small biomass. All stages in complex food chains may involve a loss of organic matter, lowering the efficiency of the energy flow. Some of the more resistant particulate material is not utilized by bacteria or other marine micro-organisms and accumulates as marine humus (Fig. 18.33). The slow and steady deposition contributes to the large amount of non-living organic substance in most marine muds.

While muds may have large microbenthic populations, the results of Mare's analyses of much coarser shell gravel deposits near Plymouth show far lower populations. The smaller densities are true of all groups of the microbenthos. However, an appreciable deposition of planktonic diatoms was encountered on these gravels. In general, the coarser deposits appear to have far less available food than the richer organic muds. But almost all investigators, working in both intertidal areas and offshore, have found a disproportionately large amount of organic matter to benthos. Part of this deposit may represent compacted faecal pellets which are not readily taken by deposit feeders, and in which any residual organic matter is resistant to digestion. Moore (1931) has demonstrated that a large proportion of a marine mud consisted of faeces, especially those of bivalves and of polychaetes such as Maldanidae. These faecal pellets appear to be remarkably resistant to further breakdown.

The upper layers of mud deposits are the most densely populated by the meiobenthic fauna. According to Mare (1942) the uppermost stratum to a depth of 0.5 cm is the richest, and only nematodes and a few polychaetes occur below this layer. This conclusion is in broad agreement with those of Krogh and Sparck (1936) for Danish waters, and of Moore (1931) for the Clyde, though Moore found that whereas harpacticoid copepods and ostracods were very sharply restricted to the uppermost layer, the nematodes could penetrate a little deeper, and reached their maximum density at a depth of 1–2 cm. This may

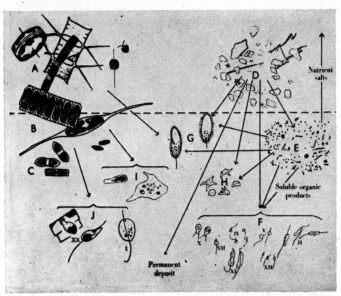

Fig. 18.33 Food chains in the microbenthos. Probable food relationships between supplies dropping from the water and organisms on the surface of the mud.
A = Phytoplankton; B = Tychopelagic diatoms; C = bottom diatoms; D = Detritus; E = Bacteria; F = small colourless flagellates; G = ciliates, H = small amoebae; I = larger amoebae; J = large colourless flagellates (from Mare, 1942).

be associated with the greater ability of nematodes to live under conditions of lowered oxygen tension (cf. Fig. 18.34). Very few meiobenthic animals appear to live deeper than 10 cm.

The work of Smidt (1951) on the Danish waddens indicates that inter-tidal muds are much richer in meiobenthos than deeper waters, a conclusion which is supported by the work of Moore, Barnett (1959) and others. Rees (1940) obtained the extraordinary density of between 11 and 12 million animals/m², consisting of nematodes, copepods and ostracods, for the estuarine muds of the Bristol Channel. Smidt also emphasized the importance of these three groups of meiobenthos. The results of both investigations showed that the top 1 cm layer was richest. It is likely that the densities of some animals have been under-estimated. Thus Barnett obtained more than 1 million harpacticoids/m² in one sampling from Southampton Water although most investigators have quoted much lower densities (cf. Table 18.3). Many of the harpacticoids were naupliar stages and there was a very rich population of other meiobenthic animals, especially nematodes and small polychaetes.

The meiobenthos of sub-littoral regions is related to the so-called interstitial fauna of sandy beaches. This fauna is, however, restricted to inter-tidal areas and to somewhat coarse deposits. The problems concerning its biology are therefore somewhat different from those

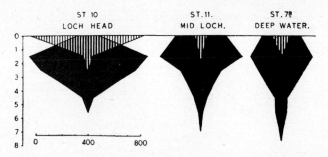

FIG. 18.34 Distribution of nematodes (black) and copepods (shaded) in relation to depth (in cm). 3 stations are given: all muddy deposit. Numbers of individuals in column of 100 cm² surface area (from Moore, 1931).

TABLE 18.3 (from Smidt, 1951)

	Nematodes per m²	Copepoda per m²	Ostracoda per m²
Rees 1940 (tidal area in Bristol Channel)	10,400,000	500,000	790,000
Moore 1931 (Loch Head, Clyde Sea area, 24 m)	251,500	69,700	12,500
Mare 1942 (at Plymouth, 45 m)	116,000	32,000	6000
Krogh and Sparck 1936 (the Sound, 17 m)	87,000	14,500	1600
Bougis 1946 (Lion Bay, 200 m)	888,000	136,000	19,000
Purasjoki 1945 (Tvaerminne, Finland, salinity 0.5⁰/₀₀)	58,120	4,840	37,360

affecting the meiobenthos of muds, and only comparatively brief reference will be made to such investigations. Nicholls, Pearse, Remane, Deboutteville, Krishnaswamy and many others have noted the large populations of animals of microscopic size which live permanently between the sand grains of beaches. The fauna appears to be more varied than the mud meiobenthos, though copepods,

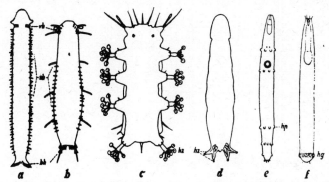

FIG. 18.35 Animals from various phyla occurring as interstitial fauna of sands (not drawn to same scale). Note attachment organs a = *Turbanella cornuta*; b = *Thaumastoderma heideri*; c = *Batillipes mirus*; d = *Diurodrilus minimus*; e = *Cicerina remanei*; f = *Rhinepera remanei* (from Remane, 1933).

especially harpacticoids, and nematodes may be especially abundant (cf. Renaud-Debyser, 1959). Many other animal groups including ostracods, turbellarians, gastrotrichs, archiannelids, polychaetes, oligochaetes, nemertines, kinorhynchs, tardigrades, foraminiferans, as well as cnidarians such as *Psammohydra* and *Halammohydra*, may all be represented (cf. Remane, 1933, 1959). The fauna often shows conspicuous structural adaptations for life in the interstices of the sand (cf. Fig. 18.35, 18.36, 18.37). Swedmark (1959) has also commented on special adaptations in connection with reproduction. The fauna penetrates considerably further into the substratum (> 50 cm) than the meiofauna of muds. As the animals are intertidal, diatoms and other micro-algae are available as food, but the fauna feeds extensively on the detritus in the bottom deposit. Predaceous species also exist.

With regard to the mud meiobenthos below low tide level, the animals must be dependent on the microbenthos (bacteria and protozoans) and on detritus for their food supply. In shallower

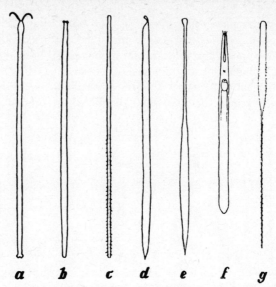

FIG. 18.36 Similarity of body form in various animals of the interstitial sand fauna (not drawn to same scale) a = *Protodrilus chaetifer*; b = *Coelogynopera* sp.;   c = *Michaelsena* sp.;   d = ciliate; e = *Trachelocerca* sp.; f = *Proschizorhynchus oculatus*; g = *Urodasys mirabilis* (from Remane, 1933).

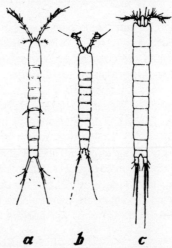

FIG. 18.37 The elongate body form shown by three copepods of the interstitial sands. a = *Leptastacus macronyx*; b = *Evansula incerta*; c = *Ectinosoma leptoderma* (from Remane, 1933).

waters where sufficient light penetrates, micro-algae may also be eaten (cf. Mare). Turbellarians and many of the nematodes in the meiobenthos have been regarded as carnivorous, but in a recent study Wieser (1960) considers that many species of nematode, previously stated to be predators, feed essentially on the deposit. Although far too little is known of the precise feeding habits of the macro-fauna, it is probable that the meiobenthos forms an important constituent of the diet of many of the larger bottom feeders. Smidt found that young flatfish and small fish such as gobies fed extensively on harpacticoids. *Crangon*, mysids and other crustaceans also fed on these copepods. Many other macrofaunal species are undoubtedly omnivorous, and include microscopic animals in their diet. In this way the meiobenthos forms a most important link in the exceedingly complex food net from dissolved organic matter and detritus on the one hand to the larger benthos on the other (cf. Fig. 18.32).

The significance of the meiobenthos is out of all proportion to its biomass. Mare (1942) considered that the total meiobenthic fauna amounted to little more than 1 g/m², though in numbers the density approached 150,000 animals/m². This estimate of biomass is in fair agreement with the investigations of Wieser (1960) working in somewhat coarser deposits, who obtained larger populations ranging from 169,000–1,861,000/m², but with a weight of 0.4–2.5 g/m². The larger populations found at some stations by Wieser may probably be attributed to finer sampling methods. He and other workers agree that greater densities of animals are found in the finer mud deposits where presumably more detrital food is available. Wieser's results suggest that the bottom deposit exerts an influence on the faunal composition also. Nematodes were overwhelmingly dominant at all stations, but the most abundant species of nematode and the particular species of other animals such as kinorhynchs present, varied with the type of bottom.

Comparison of the numbers of meiobenthos and of macrofauna suggest that the meiofauna may be 100 times more abundant. Mare cites a mean macrofaunal population of 2300/m² as against a meiobenthos of 150,000/m². Wieser (1960) quotes a meiofaunal density of 170,000–1,861,000/m² in comparison with a macrobenthos ranging from 5000–13,000 animals/m². The microfauna is in turn overwhelmingly richer numerically than the meiobenthos. Reliable values for density of the microfauna cannot be quoted in terms of numbers per square metre. However, Mare (1942) suggests populations of

710,000 bacteria and 57,000 Protozoa/g of dry mud in the uppermost layer. Zobell gives densities for bacteria alone ranging from 9×10^3 to 9×10^8 per gram of mud. The significance of these enormous densities of micro- and meio-fauna is not properly appreciated if too much attention is given to biomass alone. Figure 18.38 summarizes Mare's conclusions, regarding the biomass of the various constituents of the benthos off Plymouth. Mare emphasizes that the total amount of living matter in the bottom deposit is very small (approximately 1%). Although some of the rarer bottom animals may have been excluded

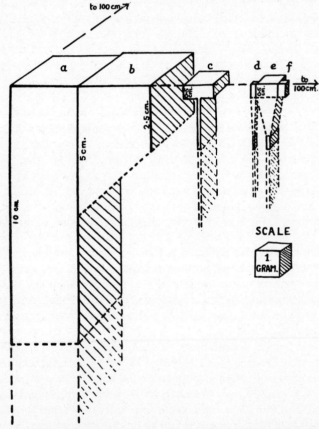

FIG. 18.38 The total amount of living matter in 1 m² of Rame (Plymouth) mud. a = large macrobenthos; b = small macrobenthos; c = meiobenthos; d–f = microbenthos; d = protozoans; e = bacteria; f = bottom diatoms (from Mare, 1942).

from her analyses, Mare's estimate is of the same magnitude as that of Jones (1956). The weight of living macrofauna just exceeds 100 g/m², while that of the meiobenthos amounts to 1 g/m², and the microfauna, excluding pelagic diatoms, to *ca.* 0.5 g/m². Thus the meiobenthos is approximately 1% and the microbenthos only 0.5% of the weight of the total living organic matter. But numbers rather than weight of the standing crop acquire a special significance when the rate of reproduction of the microscopic fauna is considered. For the microfauna of muds off Plymouth, Mare has estimated that the bacteria may divide once in two hours and small ciliates once in fifteen hours. Zobell has also emphasized the relatively large amount of bacterial substance which may be synthesized every day owing to the large densities and the high reproductive rate of the bacteria in the upper centimetre of mud. The contribution to the diet of benthic animals may not then be so inconsiderable; it is the turnover rather than the size of standing crop of microfauna which is important. Zobell (1946) has mentioned that even as much as 10 g dry weight of bacterial substance may be produced per day in a cubic foot of shallow marine mud. In deeper waters, production must be far less but the food forms an important supply for meiobenthic animals such as nematodes and copepods in addition to Protozoa. There is considerable evidence for believing that macrobenthic animals (mussels, gephyreans, tubeworms) also feed extensively on bacteria in the bottom deposit, so that in deep water, deposit feeders may obtain a considerable proportion of their food from bacteria. How far the macrofauna may utilize dissolved organic substances for food as Putter suggested is unknown, though recent work suggests that this is likely for some species.

Though little is known of the reproduction of the meiobenthos, a high rate is suspected. Laboratory studies on the harpacticoids *Tisbe* and *Tigriopus* show that very large populations may be built up rapidly. Barnett's (1959) investigations suggest that on inter-tidal mud flats high densities of the harpacticoid *Platychelipus* may be attained very quickly. It is logical to expect that harpacticoids and other meiofauna from deeper water can reproduce rapidly. In this way a considerable production of organic matter serving as food for the macrobenthos may accrue from the meiobenthos, despite its small standing crop.

The biomass of the macrofauna is far greater than that of the microscopic fauna (cf. Fig. 18.38 and 18.39) but its rate of turn-over of material is generally low. Many of the macrobenthos are carnivorous; Mare has estimated that some 25% of the species in the Rame (Plymouth) mud are predators. Some animals such as starfish are seldom eaten by other organisms so that a large biomass accumulates. Where the macrobenthos includes a large proportion of smaller species the rate of turn-over may be higher. Mare emphasized the importance of the smaller polychaetes (e.g. *Scalibregma*), and Sanders has also stressed the significance of the smaller macro-

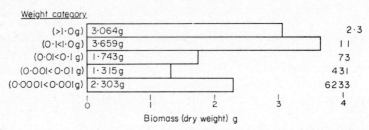

FIG. 18.39 The relationship between the various sizes of benthic animals (expressed as weight categories) and their contribution to the total biomass (as dry weight) at one station. Average numbers of the various groups of animals are shown on the right (from Sanders, 1960—slightly altered).

benthos. It is the large and slow growing benthic species which usually give a very small annual production. Even here, however, the benthos may contribute greatly to the food chain in producing very large broods. The young (0-group) of bivalves, gastropods and worms can show sudden and large increases in density (Boysen-Jensen, 1919; Thamdrup, 1935; Wohlenberg, 1937; Stephen, 1938). The subsequent rapid decline in numbers is frequently due in part to the eager feeding of young fishes (cf. Smidt, 1951). The turn-over of organic material in such examples is fairly rapid.

The bottom fauna includes in itself some exceedingly complex food chains, of which some animals (e.g. ascidians and starfish) may represent end links. More generally perhaps the end links are to be found in the nekton, represented particularly by the fishes (cf. Fig. 18.25). The feeding habits of fish are infinitely varied, and no exhaustive review of this topic will be attempted; only the role of fishes and other members of the nekton in important food chains in the marine environment will be discussed. For fuller treatment of the great science of fisheries, the reader should consult such volumes as Graham (1956), Hardy (1960) and the Buckland lectures, as well as original papers, especially those published by the International Council for the Exploration of the Sea, and by the Norwegian, Danish, German and British fisheries laboratories.

The first group of fishes which may be classed together on feeding habits are those which consume small food particles—mostly planktonic animals and plants. There are relatively few marine fish feeding largely on phytoplankton. Examples include the pilchard and the menhaden, a fish occurring in large numbers off the east coast of N. America. Two important British food fishes, the herring and mackerel, feed on zooplankton. The mackerel is essentially a feeder on copepods such as *Calanus* and *Pseudocalanus*. One of the earliest correlations found between zooplankton abundance and fishery catches was established by Allen for the mackerel fishery in the English Channel. The work of Hardy on the food of the herring has already been mentioned (cf. Fig. 17.1). Young larval herring feed to some extent on phytoplankton and the somewhat older stages feed on small zooplankton, especially on copepods such as *Pseudocalanus* and *Temora*. Although adult herring may also take the smaller copepods, they tend to feed extensively on *Calanus*. The important series of investigations involving the use of the Hardy Plankton Indicator in the North Sea has demonstrated the correlation between abundance of *Calanus* and the herring shoals. Although undoubtedly herring feed extensively by straining the zooplankton from the water, they appear to be capable of considerable selection in their feeding. Figure 17.1 indicates that herring take euphausids, amphipods and sand eels to a considerable extent as well as copepods. The work of Lebour indicates that larval fishes of many species which feed on plankton may show considerable selectivity. Apart from the mackerel and herring, there are some high seas fishes which feed on plankton. Even the sun fish, despite its large size, feeds mainly on medusae, leptocephali and crustaceans in the plankton. The huge manta rays and basking sharks are mainly plankton feeders. The great majority of fishes, however, including most of our chief food fishes, are demersal in habit. They feed on the animals of the benthos, especially on bivalves, worms and crustaceans (cf. Fig. 18.40). Some species of fish, including many of the highly modified abyssal forms as well as most sharks, prey mainly on other species of fish which themselves feed on the bottom invertebrate fauna. Some predaceous species on the other hand prey chiefly on pelagic fishes.

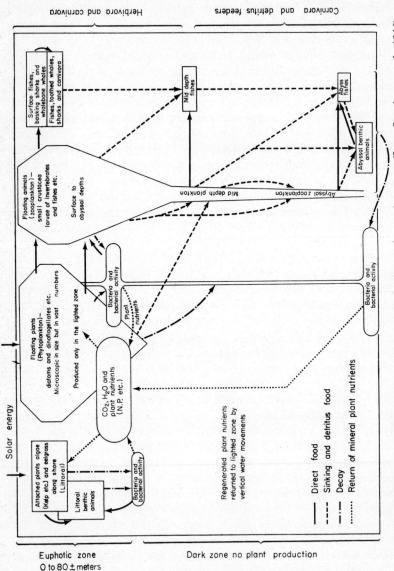

Herbivora and carnivora

Carnivora and detritus feeders

Surface fishes, basking sharks and whalebone whales
Fishes, toothed whales, sharks and carnivora

Mid depth fishes

Abyss fishes

Abyssal benthic animals

Floating animals (zooplankton)—small crustacea larvae of invertebrates and fishes etc.

Surface to abyssal depths

Mid depth plankton

Abyssal zooplankton

Bacteria and bacterial activity

Plant nutrients

Floating plants (Phytoplankton)—diatoms and dinoflagellates etc. Microscopic in size but in vast numbers

Produced only in the lighted zone

Bacteria and bacterial activity

CO_2, H_2O and plant nutrients (N.P. etc.)

Solar energy

Attached plants algae (Kelp etc.) and eelgrass along shore (Littoral)

Litoral benthic animals

Bacteria and bacterial activity

Regenerated plant nutrients returned to lighted zone by vertical water movements

———— Direct food
– – – – Sinking and detritus food
–·–·– Decay
·········· Return of mineral plant nutrients

Euphotic zone
0 to 80 ± meters

Dark zone no plant production

FIG. 18.40 Main inter-relationships between organisms in the marine environment (from Sverdrup et al., 1946).

Hickling (1935) found that the hake fed partly on euphausids and cephalopods, but to a large extent on such active pelagic fish as mackerel, blue whiting, horse mackerel and herring.

Probably the feeding habits of the demersal food fishes are best known. Smaller gadoids like the whiting feed extensively on crustaceans such as shrimps and prawns, as well as on polychaetes and fish. Menon (1950) found that *Gadus minutus* fed mainly on crustaceans though some fish were eaten. Larger fishes may take large thick-shelled molluscs, as well as echinoderms and crustaceans. The haddock obtains its food mainly from the bottom, feeding on echinoderms, polychaetes, bivalves and crustaceans, but feeds only to a small extent on fish. Dogfish eat larger crustaceans, *Buccinum* and poly-chaetes, as well as fish (Eales, 1949). The habits of the prey and of the predator must play a large part in determining the food selected. Thus Steven (1930) claimed that the gurnard *Trigla lineata* failed to capture the more rapidly-moving crustaceans and worms, as it relied mainly on touch and smell in hunting its prey, whereas other species of gurnard, with better vision, captured these animals successfully. The diet may also change with age. Cod take a variety of bottom invertebrates during the "codling" stage but later live increasingly on fish, especially herring. Most workers (e.g. Blegvad, 1916; Steven, 1930) are agreed, however, that to a large extent demersal fish will feed on whatever bottom fauna is easily available and abundant, provided it is of the right size and consistency. The food taken, therefore, reflects to a considerable degree the type of bottom fauna. Nevertheless, the extent of the gape of the predator imposes an upper size limit on the prey. This is particularly well exemplified by flatfishes. The extensive investigations which have been undertaken on the feeding of fishes such as plaice, dab and flounder, especially by Danish and British workers, have shown conclusively that these relatively small-mouthed feeders take mainly small thin-shelled bivalves, as well as polychaetes and small crustaceans. Steven (1930) considers that the lemon sole (*Pleuronectes microcephalus = Microstomus kitt*) is even more restricted to a diet of polychaetes.

Although some bottom invertebrates especially species of asteroids, ophiuroids and ascidians may be largely immune from the attacks of demersal fishes, it is clear that most of the bottom fauna is preyed upon by some species owing to the variety of their feeding habits. But there may be several further links in the food chain with fishes feeding on other fish species (cf. Fig. 18.40). In general, it is the fishes with large mouths and well developed teeth which are predaceous on other members of the fish population (cf. Fig. 18.41). But this cannot be accepted as a rule. For example, the wolf fish, *Anarrhichas*

A C.H.

FIG. 18.41 Fish from oceanic deep water. 1 = *Parabrotula plagiophthalmus*; 2 and 3 = young and mature *Lampanyetus pusillus*; 4 = *Gonostoma bathyphilum*; 5 = *Saccopharynx johnsoni*; 6 = *Melanocetus johnsoni* (from Hardy, 1956).

lupus, with a very remarkable tooth armature, is predominantly a mollusc feeder. Most demersal fish, especially those feeding partly on other fishes, show a considerable lack of selectivity in the diet and this enables these species to compete successfully.

The broad pattern of feeding relationships between the plankton, benthos and nekton is illustrated in Fig. 18.40. The real intricacy of the food web, however, is revealed only by detailed consideration of the food habits of individual species at all levels. But this complexity of feeding relationships, and the general tendency in the sea for the food chains to include numerous links does not lead to a high level of efficiency in organic production. With an increasing number of links in the complex food chain, efficiency falls. Every additional stage leads to a loss of organic material (cf. Fig. 18.42, 18.43). Both

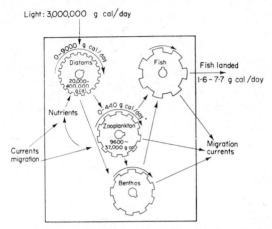

FIG. 18.42 Schematic representation of production on Georges Bank. The values given are the averages for the whole Bank per m² of sea surface. Maximum and minimum values in the cog wheels represent standing crop; those over the cog wheels are for net production rate. Yield is indicated on the right (from Clarke, 1946).

Harvey (1950) and Cooper (1948b) have shown that the return of organic matter from the sea, for instance as demersal fish, is very small (cf. Fig. 16.1). Whatever the precise trophic level of the particular species of fish captured, the overall efficiency of production of fish flesh in relation to the amount of sunlight energy falling on the sea surface, and to the amount of phytoplankton synthesized, is very low. Despite this low efficiency of production, these demersal fisheries, operated over the broad continental shelves, where the biomass of plankton and bottom fauna is generally high, are the major fisheries of the world. Considerable wastage of organic material appears to be inevitable in these fisheries. A comparison of the efficiency of a pelagic high seas fishery (e.g. tuna) would be of interest.

Apart from fishes, there are included in the nekton fast moving cephalopods which appear to be relatively common in the high seas. The recent review by Fisher and Kon (1959) suggests that many cephalopods feed on euphausids, the common planktonic inhabitants of the open oceans, though some squids undoubtedly feed on fish as well. Cephalopods may represent the final link in one of the more direct food chains in the sea. However, some species of cephalopod

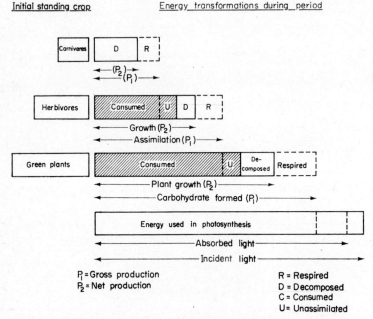

P_1 = Gross production
P_2 = Net production

R = Respired
D = Decomposed
C = Consumed
U = Unassimilated

Fig. 18.43 Diagram illustrating qualitatively the trophic relations in a production pyramid involving no net increase or decrease (from Clarke, 1946).

are preyed on by seals and by sperm whales which grow fast and lay down considerable stores of fat on this nutritious diet.

The whale-bone whales, among the nekton, exhibit a remarkably high rate of growth, and demonstrate one of the few direct food chains in the marine environment. The Mystacoceti include the largest of all vertebrates, yet these animals gain their food from the zoo-plankton. The northern whale-bone whales feed on a rather more varied diet than the Antarctic forms. They will take euphausids, especially *Meganyctiphanes norvegica*, copepods such as *Calanus*, pteropods, and at times, small fishes (Fig. 18.44). In the Antarctic, however, investigations over the last 30 years especially of the Discovery

Committee, have shown that the southern whalebone whales feed almost exclusively on *Euphausia superba* (Fig. 18.45). This zooplankton animal indeed appears to hold a key position in the trophic relationships of Antarctic waters; it is a common food for a variety of larger marine animals (cf. Fig. 18.46). *Euphausia superba* appears

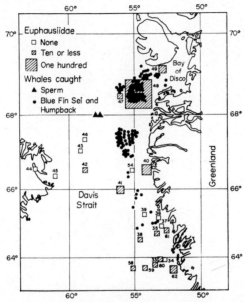

FIG. 18.44 Correlation between abundance of whales west of Greenland as revealed by catches, and concentration of euphausids (from Sverdrup *et al.*, 1946).

to confine its food to the rich phytoplankton of the area. The food chain to whales is, therefore, remarkably direct, the organic matter synthesized by the phytoplankton passing through only one intermediate animal. The rate of growth of whales is exceptionally high. The largest species, the blue whale, exceeds 20 feet at birth, and may reach a length of about 55 feet after one year (Fig. 18.47). At sexual maturity, which is attained in about four years, the average length is 70 ft. The greatest length given for a blue whale (cf. Mackintosh, 1946) is of the order of 93 feet. Since these whale-bone whales can produce a calf every second year, the vast conversion of organic matter represented by phytoplankton and then zooplankton into whale flesh is really extraordinary. Sverdrup *et al.* (1946) suggest that a blue whale at birth may weigh of the order of 2 tons; at weaning, which occurs some seven months after birth, the weight is over 20 tons. At sexual maturity, in a further 3 to 4 years, the whale may weigh over 70 tons. This rapid conversion of organic matter to whale flesh is, therefore, a notable exception to the generally low rate of

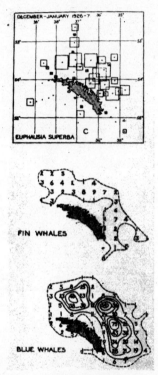

FIG. 18.45 Correlation between the abundance of whales and the concentration of *Euphausia superba* near South Georgia in December, 1926 (from Hardy and Gunther, 1936).

return of organic material from the sea. The poor return experienced in the majority of fisheries is all the more remarkable in view of the enormous basic production of living matter over the oceans (cf. Steemann Nielsen, 1952). It may prove possible in the future to utilize some intermediate links in the complex and intricate food web in the sea and thereby save some of the loss of organic material (cf. Walford, 1958). Direct harvesting of plankton, the farming of fishes and of shellfish are among the possibilities which are now being studied in an attempt to increase the efficiency of the return of organic matter from the oceans.

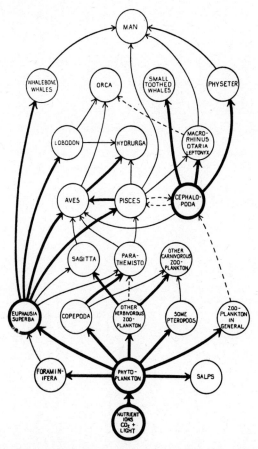

FIG. 18.46 Diagram illustrating some of the more important food relations in Antarctic seas (from Hart, 1942).

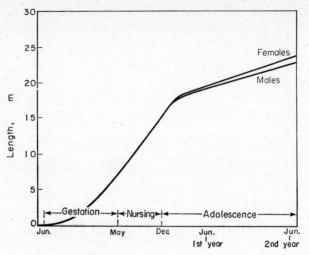

FIG. 18.47 Estimated mean curve of growth for blue whales (modified from Mackintosh and Wheeler, 1929).

REFERENCES

ABBOTT, B. C., and D. BALLANTINE (1957) The toxin from *Gymnodinium veneficum* Ballantine. *J. Mar. Biol. Ass.* **36**, 169–189.

ADLER, G., and P. JESPERSEN (1920) Variations saisonnières chez quelques copépodes planctoniques marins. *Medd. Komm. Havund. Ser. Plankton* **2**, 1–45.

ALEEM, A. A. (1950) The diatom community inhabiting the mud-flats at Whitstable. *New Phytol.* **49**, 174–188.

ALEEM, A. A. (1950) Distribution and ecology of British marine littoral diatoms. *J. Ecol.* **38**, 75–106.

ALEXANDER, W. B., B. A. SOUTHGATE, and R. BASSINDALE (1935) Survey of the River Tees. Pt. II The Estuary—Chemical and Biological. D.S.I.R. Water Pollution Research, H. M. Stat. Office. Tech. Pap. No. 5, 171 pp.

ALLEN, E. J., and E. W. NELSON (1910) On the artificial culture of marine plankton organisms. *J. Mar. Biol. Ass.* **8**, 421–474.

AMEMIYA, I. (1926) Notes on experiments on the early developmental stages of the Portuguese, American and English native oysters, with special reference to the effect of varying salinity. *J. Mar. Biol. Ass.* **14**, 161–175.

ARMSTRONG, F. A. J. (1954) Phosphorus and silicon in sea water off Plymouth during the years 1950 to 1953. *J. Mar. Biol. Ass.* **33**, 381–392.

ARMSTRONG, F. A. J. (1957) The iron content of sea water. *J. Mar. Biol. Ass.* **36**, 509–517.

ARMSTRONG, F. A. J. (1958) Inorganic suspended matter in sea water. *J. Mar. Res. Thompson Anniversary Volume* **17**, 23–34.

ATKINS, W. R. G. (1926) The phosphate content of sea water in relation to the growth of the algal plankton, Part. III. *J. Mar. Biol. Ass.* **14**, 447–467.

ATKINS, W. R. G. (1953) The seasonal variation in the copper content of sea water. *J. Mar. Biol. Ass.* **31**, 493–494.

ATKINS, W. R. G., and H. H. POOLE (1940) A cubical photometer for studying the angular distribution of submarine daylight. *J. Mar. Biol. Ass.* **24**, 271–281.

ATKINS, W. R. G., and H. H. POOLE (1958) Cube photometer measurements of the angular distribution of submarine daylight and the total submarine illumination. *J. Cons. Int. Explor. Mer.* **23**, 327–336.

AUSTIN, T. S., and V. E. BROCK (1959) Meridional variations in some oceanographic and marine biological factors in the Central Pacific. Int. Ocean. Congress Preprints. A.A.A.S. Washington, 130–131.

AURICH, H. J. (1949) Die Verbreitung des Nannoplanktons im Oberflächenwasser vor der Nordfriesischen Küste. *Ber. Dtsch. Komm. Meeresforsch.* **11**, 403–405.

BAINBRIDGE, R. (1953) Studies on the interrelationships of zooplankton and phytoplankton. *J. Mar. Biol. Ass.* **32**, 385–445.

BAINBRIDGE, R. (1957) The size, shape and density of marine phytoplankton concentrations. *Biol. Rev.* **32**, 91–115.

BAINBRIDGE, V. (1958) Some observations on *Evadne nordmanni* Lovén. *J. Mar. Biol. Ass.* **37**, 349–370.

BAKER, A. DE C. (1959) The distribution and life history of *Euphausia triacantha* Holt and Tattersall. *Discovery Repts.* **29**, 311–339.

BANSE, K. (1956) Über den Transport von meroplanktischer Larven aus dem Kattegat in die Kieler Bucht. *Ber. Dtsch. Komm. Meeresforsch.* **14**, 147–164.

BANSE, K. (1957) Über das Verhalten von Copepoden in geschichteten Wasser. *Verh. Dtsch. Zool. Ges., Zool. Anz.* **20**, Suppl.-Bd., 435–444.

BARGMANN, H. E. (1945) The development and life history of adolescent and adult krill *Euphausia superba. Discovery Repts.* **23**, 105–176.

BARKER, H. A. (1935a) Photosynthesis in diatoms. *Arch. Mikrobiol.* **6**, 141–156.

BARKER, H. A. (1935b) The culture and physiology of marine dinoflagellates. *Arch. Mikrobiol.* **6**, 157–181.

BARKLEY, E. (1940) Nahrung und Filterapparat des Walkrebschens *Euphausia superba* Dana. *Z. Fisch.* **1**(i), 65–156.

BARLOW, J. P. (1955) Physical and biological processes determining the distribution of zooplankton in a tidal estuary. *Biol. Bull. Woods Hole* **109**, 211–225.

BARNES, H. (1953) The effect of lowered salinity on some barnacle nauplii. *J. Anim. Ecol.* **22**, 328–330.

BARNES, H. (1957a) Nutrient elements. Chapter 11 in *Treatise on Marine Ecology and Paleoecology.* Vol I. Ecology Ed. J. W. HEDGPETH. Geol. Soc. Amer. Memoir **67**, 297–344.

BARNES, H. (1957b) Processes of restoration and synchronization in marine ecology. The diatom increase and the "spawning" of the common barnacle, *Balanus balanoides* (L). *Année Biologique* **33**, 1–2, 67–85.

BARNES, H., and M. BARNES (1958) The rate of development of *Balanus balanoides* larvae. *Limnol. and Oceanogr.* **3**, 29–32.

BARNES, H., and M. BARNES (1959) Note on stimulation of cirripede nauplii. *Oikos* **10**, 19–23.

BARNES, H., and H. T. POWELL (1950) Some observations on the effect of fibrous glass surfaces upon the settlement of certain sedentary marine organisms. *J. Mar. Biol. Ass.* **29**, 299–302.

BARNETT, P. R. O. (1959) The ecology of harpacticoids on a mudflat with particular reference to *Platychelipus*. Ph. D. Thesis. University of Southampton.

BARY, B. Mc. K. (1959) Biogeographic boundaries: The use of temperature–salinity–plankton diagrams. Int. Ocean. Congress Preprints. A.A.A.S. Washington. 132–133.

BASSINDALE, R. (1936) The developmental stages of three English barnacles, *Balanus balanoides* (Linn.), *Chthalamus stellatus* (Poli) and *Verruca stroemia* (O. F. Müller). *Proc. Zool. Soc. Lond.* **106**, 57–74.

BEANLAND, F. L. (1940) Sand and mud communities in the Dovey Estuary. *J. Mar. Biol. Ass.* **24**, 589–611.

BEEBE, W. (1935) *Half Mile Down.* John Lane The Bodley Head. London. 344 pp.

BEKLEMISHEV, K. V. (1954) Feeding of some common plankton copepods in far eastern seas. *Zool. J. Inst. Oceanol. Acad. Sci. U.S.S.R.* **33**, 1210–1229.

BEKLEMISHEV, K. V. (1957) The spatial interrelationships of marine zoo- and phytoplankton. *Trans. Inst. Oceanol. Acad. Sci. U.S.S.R.* **20**, 253–278.

BELSER, W. L. (1959) Bioassay of organic materials in sea water. Int. Ocean. Congress Preprints A.A.A.S. Washington. 908–909.

BENTLEY, J. A. (1960) Plant hormones in marine phytoplankton, zooplankton and sea water. *J. Mar. Biol. Ass.* **39**, 433–444.

BERNARD, F. (1939) E'tude sur les variations de fertilité des eaux méditerranéennes. *J. Cons. Int. Explor. Mer.* **14**, 228–241.

BERNARD, F. (1948) Recherches sur le cycle du *Coccolithus fragilis* Lohm., Flagellé dominant des mers chaudes. *J. Cons. Int. Explor. Mer.* **15**, 177–188.

BERNARD, F. (1953) Rôles des Flagellés calcaires dans la fertilité et la sédimentation en mer profonde. *Deep Sea Res.* **1**, 34–46.

BERNARD, F. (1958) Données récentes sur la fertilité elémentaire en méditerranée. *Rapp Proc.-Verb Cons. Int. Explor. Mer.* **144**, 103–108.

BIGELOW, H. B. (1926) Plankton of the offshore waters of the Gulf of Maine. *Bull. U.S. Bur. Fish.* **40**, II, 1–507.

BIGELOW, H. B. (1938) Plankton of the Bermuda Oceanographic Expeditions VIII. Medusae taken during the years 1929 and 1930. *Zoologica*, New York. **23**, 99–189.

BIGELOW, H. B., and M. SEARS (1939) Studies of the waters of the continental shelf, Cape Cod to Chesapeake Bay. III. A volumetric study of the zooplankton. *Mem. Mus. Comp. Zool.* (*Harvard*), **54**, 183–378.

BIGELOW, H. B., L. LILLICK and M. SEARS (1940) Phytoplankton and planktonic Protozoa of the offshore waters of the Gulf of Maine. Part I. Numerical distribution. *Trans. Amer. Phil. Soc.* **31**, 149–191.

BLEGVAD, H. (1914) Food and the conditions of nourishment among the communities of invertebrate animals found on or in the sea bottom in Danish waters. *Rept. Dan. Biol. Stat.* **22**, 41–78.

BLEGVAD, H. (1916) On the food of fish in the Danish waters within the Skaw. *Rept. Dan. Biol. Stat.* **24**, 17–72.

BLEGVAD, H. (1925) Continued studies on the quantity of fish food in the sea bottom. *Rept. Dan. Biol. Stat.* **31**, 27–56 .

BLEGVAD, H. (1928) Quantitative investigations of bottom invertebrates in the Limfjord 1910–27, with special reference to plaice food. *Rept. Dan. Biol. Stat.* **34**, 33–52.

BODEN, B. P. (1954) The euphausiid crustaceans of southern African waters. *Trans. Roy. Soc. S.A.* **34**, 181–243.

BODEN, B. P., and E. BRINTON (1957) The euphausiid crustaceans *Thysanopoda aequalis* Hansen and *Thysanopoda subaequalis* Boden their taxonomy and distribution in the Pacific. *Limnol. & Oceanogr.* **2**, 337–341.

BODEN, B. P., M. W. JOHNSON and E. BRINTON (1955). The Euphausiacea (Crustacea) of the North Pacific. *Bull. Scripps Inst. Oćeanogr.* **6**, 287–400.

BODEN, B. P., and E. M. KAMPA (1953) Winter cascading from an oceanic island and its biological implications. *Nature, Lond.* **171**, 426–427.

BOGOROV, B. G. (1934) Seasonal changes in biomass of *Calanus finmarchicus* in the Plymouth area in 1930. *J. Mar. Biol. Ass.* **19**, 585–612.

BOGOROV, B. G. (1946) Peculiarities of diurnal vertical migration of zooplankton in Polar Seas. *J. Mar. Res.* **6**, 25–32.

BOGOROV, B. G. (1958a) Estimates of primary production in biogeographical regionization of the ocean. *Rapp. Proc.-Verb. Cons. Int. Explor. Mer.* **144**, 117–121.

BOGOROV, B. G. (1958b) Biogeographical regions of the plankton of the North-Western Pacific Ocean and their influence on the deep sea. *Deep Sea Res.* **5**, 149–161.

BOGOROV, B. G. (1958c) Perspectives in the study of seasonal changes of plankton and of the number of generations at different latitudes. *Perspectives in Marine Biology.* Ed. BUZZATI-TRAVERSO. Univ. of California Press. Berkeley and Los Angeles. 145–158.

BOGOROV, B. G. (1959) Geographical zonation in the Central Pacific. Int. Ocean. Congress Preprints. A.A.A.S. Washington. 139–140.

BOSSANYI, J. (1957) A preliminary survey of the small natant fauna in the vicinity of the sea floor off Blyth, Northumberland. *J. Anim. Ecol.* **26**, 353–368.

BOWEN, V. T., and D. SUTTON (1951) Comparative studies of mineral constituents of marine sponges. I. *J. Mar. Res.* **10**, 153–167.

BOYSEN-JENSEN, P. (1919) Valuation of the Limfjord I. Studies on fish food in the Limfjord 1909–17. *Rept. Dan. Biol. Stat.* **26**, 1–44.

BRAARUD, T. (1935) The Øst Expedition to the Denmark Strait 1929. II. Phyto-plankton and its conditions of growth. *Hval. Skr.* Nr. 10, 1–173.

BRAARUD, T. (1939) Microspores in diatoms. *Nature, Lond.* **143**, 899.

BRAARUD, T. (1961) Cultivation of marine organisms as a means of understanding environmental influences on populations. *In* Oceanography. Public. No. 67, A.A.A.S. Washington, D.C. ed. M. Sears; 271–298.

BRAARUD, T., and A. KLEM (1931) Hydrographical and chemical investigations in the coastal waters off Møre and in the Romsdalsfjord. *Hval. Skr.* Nr. 1, 1–88.

BRAARUD, T., K. R. GAARDER and J. GRØNTVED (1953) The phytoplankton of the North Sea and adjacent waters in May 1948. *Rapp. Proc.-Verb. Cons. Int. Explor. Mer.* **133**, 1–89.

VON BRAND, T., N. W. RAKESTRAW and C. E. RENN (1937) The experimental decomposition and regeneration of nitrogenous organic matter in sea water. *Biol. Bull. Woods Hole* **72**, 165–175.

von BRAND, T., N. W. RAKESTRAW and C. E. RENN (1939) Further experiments on the decomposition and regeneration of nitrogenous organic matter in sea water. *Biol. Bull. Woods Hole* **77**, 285–296.

von BRAND, T., and N. W. RAKESTRAW (1941) The determination of dissolved organic nitrogen in sea water. *J. Mar. Res.* **4**, 76–80.

von BRAND, T., and N. W. RAKESTRAW (1937–47) Decomposition and regeneration of nitrogenous organic matter in sea water. Parts I–VI. *Biol. Bull. Woods Hole* **72, 77, 79, 81, 83, 92.**

BRANDHORST, W. (1958) Nitrite accumulation in the North-East tropical Pacific. *Nature, Lond.* **182**, 679.

BRANDHORST, W. (1959) Nitrification and denitrification in the eastern tropical North Pacific. *J. Cons. Int. Explor. Mer.* **25**, 3–20.

BRANDT, K. (1898) Beiträge zur Kenntnis der chemischen Zusammensetzung des Planktons. *Wiss. Meeresuntersuch., Abt. Kiel, N.F.* **3**, 43–90.

BROAD, A. C. (1957) The relationship between diet and larval development of Palaemonetes. *Biol. Bull. Woods Hole* **112**, 162–170.

BRODSKY, K. A. (1959) Zoogeographical zones of the South Pacific and bipolar distribution of some calanoids, Int. Ocean. Congress Preprints. A.A.A.S. Washington. 145–147.

BRONGERSMA-SANDERS, M. (1957) Mass mortality in the sea. Chapter 29 in *Treatise on Marine Ecology and Paleoecology* Vol I. Ecology. Ed. J. W. HEDG-PETH. Geol. Soc. Amer. Memoir **67**, 941–1010.

BROWN, M. E. (Ed.) (1957) *The Physiology of Fishes* Vol. I Metabolism. Academic Press. N.Y. 447 pp.

BRUCE, J. R., M. KNIGHT and M. W. PARKE (1940) The rearing of oyster larvae on an algal diet. *J. Mar. Biol. Ass.* **24**, 337–374.

BRUNS, E. (1958) *Ozeanologie.* Band I. VEB Deutsch. Verlag der Wissensch. Berlin. 420 pp.

BRUUN, A. F. (1957) Deep sea and abyssal depths. Chapter 22 in *Treatise on Marine Ecology and Paleoecology* Vol. I Ecology. Ed. J. W. HEDGPETH. Geol. Soc. Amer. Memoir **67**, 641–672.

BSHARAH, L. (1957) Plankton of the Florida current V. *Bull. Mar. Sci. Gulf and Caribb.* **7**, 201–251.

BUCHANAN, J. B. (1958) The bottom fauna communities across the Continental Shelf off Accra Ghana (Gold Coast). *Proc. Zool. Soc. Lond.* **130**, 1–56.

BUCHANAN, J. B. and R. H. HEDLEY (1960) A contribution to the biology of *Astrorhiza limicola* (Foraminifera). *J. Mar. Biol. Ass.* **39**, 549–560.

BURKHOLDER, P. R., and L. M. BURKHOLDER (1956) Vitamin B_{12} in suspended solids and marsh muds collected along the coast of Georgia. *Limnol. & Oceanogr.* **1**, 202–208.

BURKHOLDER, P. R. (1959) Vitamin-producing bacteria in the sea. Int. Ocean. Congress Preprints. A.A.A.S. Washington 912–913.

BURLEW, J. S. (1953) Algal culture from laboratory to pilot plant. Carnegie. Inst. Washington. Publ. 600. 357 pp.

BUYS, M. E. L. (1959) The South African pilchard (*Sardinops ocellata*) and Maasbanker (*Trachurus trachurus*). Hydrographical environment and the commercial catches, 1950–57. Investigational Report No. 37, Division of Fisheries, Union of South Africa, Pretoria. 176 pp.

CANNON, H. G. (1931) On the anatomy of a marine ostracod, *Cypridina* (*Doloria*) *levis* Skogsberg. *Discovery Repts.* **2**, 435–482.

CANNON, H. G. (1940) On the anatomy of *Gigantocypris mülleri. Discovery Repts.* **19**, 185–224.

CAREY, C. L. (1938) The occurrence and distribution of nitrifying bacteria in the sea. *J. Mar. Res.* **1**, 291–304.

CARRIKER, M. R. (1951) Ecological observations on the distribution of oyster larvae in New Jersey estuaries. *Ecol. Monogr.* **21**, 19–38.

CASPERS, H. (1957) Black Sea and Sea of Azov. Chapter 25 in *Treatise on Marine Ecology and Paleoecology* Vol. I. Ecology. Ed. J. W. HEDGPETH. Geol. Soc. Amer. Memoir **67**, 801–890.

CHADEFAUD, M., and L. EMBERGER (1960) *Traité de Botanique systematique* Tome 1. Masson et Cie. Paris. 1016 pp.

CHENG, C. (1947) On the fertility of marine Cladocera with a note on the formation of the resting egg in *Evadne nordmanni* Lovén and *Podon intermedius* Lilljeborg. *J. Mar. Biol. Ass.* **26**, 551–561.

CHOW, T. J., and T. G. THOMPSON (1952) The determination and distribution of copper in sea water. Part I. *J. Mar. Res.* **11**, 124–138.

CHOW, T. J., and T. G. THOMPSON (1954) Seasonal variation in the concentration of copper in the surface waters of San Juan Channel, Washington. *J. Mar. Res.* **13**, 233–244.

CLARKE, G. L. (1930) Change of phototropic and geotropic signs in *Daphnia* induced by changes of light intensity. *J. Exp. Biol.* **7**, 109–131.

CLARKE, G. L. (1933) Diurnal migration of plankton in the Gulf of Maine and its correlation with changes in submarine irradiation. *Biol. Bull. Woods Hole* **65**, 402–436.

CLARKE, G. L. (1934) Further observations on the diurnal migration of copepods in the Gulf of Maine. *Biol. Bull. Woods Hole* **67**, 432–448.

CLARKE, G. L. (1936) Light penetration in the Western North Atlantic and its application to biological problems. *Rapp. Proc.-Verb. Cons. Int. Explor. Mer.* **101**, 3–12.

CLARKE, G. L. (1939a) The utilization of solar energy by aquatic organisms. *Problems in Lake Biology*. Publ. Amer. Assoc. Advanc. Sci. **10**, 27–38.

CLARKE, G. L. (1939b) The relation between diatoms and copepods as a factor in the productivity of the sea. *Quart. Rev. Biol.* **14**, 60–64.

CLARKE, G. L. (1940) Comparative richness of zooplankton in coastal and offshore areas of the Atlantic. *Biol. Bull. Woods Hole* **78**, 226–255.

CLARKE, G. L. (1946) Dynamics of production in a marine area. *Ecol. Monogr.* **16**, 323–335.

CLARKE, G. L. (1954) *Elements of Ecology*. John Wiley, New York. 534 pp.

CLARKE, G. L., and S. S. GELLIS (1935) Nutrition of copepods in relation to the food-cycle of the sea. *Biol. Bull. Woods Hole* **68**, 231–245.

CLARKE, G. L., and D. D. BONNET (1939) Influence of temperature on the survival, growth and respiration of *Calanus finmarchicus*. *Biol. Bull. Woods Hole* **76**, 371–383.

CLARKE, G. L., E. L. PIERCE and D. F. BUMPUS (1943) The distribution and reproduction of *Sagitta elegans* on Georges Bank in relation to the hydrographical conditions. *Biol. Bull. Woods Hole* **85**, 201–226.

CLARKE, G. L., and R. H. BACKUS (1956) Measurements of light penetration in relation to vertical migration and records of luminescence of deep-sea animals. *Deep Sea Res.* **4**, 1–14.

CLARKE, G. L., and G. K. WERTHEIM (1956) Measurements of illumination at great depths and at night in the Atlantic Ocean by means of a new bathyphotometer. *Deep Sea Res.* **3**, 189–205.

CLARKE, G. L., and C. J. HUBBARD (1959) Quantitative records of the luminescent flashing of oceanic animals at great depths. *Limnol. & Oceanogr.* **4**, 163–180.

CLOWES, A. J. (1938) Phosphate and silicate in the Southern Ocean. *Discovery Repts.* **19**, 1–20.

CLOWES, A. J. (1950) An introduction to the hydrology of South African waters. Investigational Report No. 12. Division of Fisheries, Union of South Africa, Pretoria. 42 pp.

CLOWES, A. J. (1954) The South African pilchard (*Sardinops ocellata*). The temperature, salinity and inorganic phosphate content of the surface layer near St. Helena Bay, 1950–52. Investigational Report No. 16. Division of Fisheries, Union of South Africa, Pretoria. 47 pp.

COE, W. R. (1936) Plankton of the Bermuda Oceanographic Expeditions. VI. Bathypelagic nemerteans taken in the years 1929, 1930 and 1931. *Zoologica*. N.Y. **21**, 97–113.

COLE, H. A. (1956) Benthos and the shellfish of commerce in *Sea Fisheries, their Investigation in the United Kingdom*. Edward Arnold, London. 487 pp.

COLMAN, J. S., and F. SEGROVE (1955) Tidal plankton over Stoupe Beck Sands, Robin Hood's Bay. *J. Anim. Ecol.* **24**, 445–462.

COLLIER, A. (1953) The significance of organic compounds in sea water. *Trans. N. Amer. Wildl. Conf. March* **18**, 463–472.

COLLIER, A. (1958) Some biochemical aspects of red tides and related oceanographic problems. *Limnol. & Oceanogr.* **3**, 33–39.

COLLIER, A., S. RAY and W. B. WILSON (1956) Some effects of specific organic compounds on marine organisms. *Science* **124**, 220.

COLLINS, A. C. (1958) Foraminifera. *Gt. Barrier Reef. Exped. Sci. Repts. B.M. (N.H.)* **6**, 335–437

CONOVER, R. J. (1956) Oceanography of Long Island Sound. 1952–1954. VI. Biology of *Acartia clausi* and *A. tonsa. Bull. Bingham Oceanogr. Coll.* **15**, 156–233.

CONOVER, R. J. (1959) Regional and seasonal variation in the respiratory rate of marine copepods. *Limnol. & Oceanogr.* **4**, 259–268.

CONOVER, R. J. (1960) The feeding, behaviour and respiration of some marine planktonic Crustacea. *Biol. Bull. Woods Hole* **119**, 399–415.

CONOVER, R. J., S. M. MARSHALL and A. P. ORR (1959) Feeding and excretion of *Calanus finmarchicus* with reference to the possible role of the zooplankton in the mineralization of organic matter. Ref. No. 59–32. Woods Hole Ocean. Inst. unpubl. manuscript. 1–12.

CONOVER, S. A. M. (1956) Oceanography of Long Island Sound, 1952–1954. IV. Phytoplankton. *Bull. Bingham Oceanogr. Coll.* **15**, 62–112.

COOPER, L. H. N. (1933) Chemical constituents of biological importance in the English Channel. Nov. 1930 to Jan. 1932. Part I. Phosphate, silicate, nitrate and ammonia. *J. Mar. Biol. Ass.* **18**, 677–728.

COOPER, L. H. N. (1934) The variation of excess base with depth in the English Channel with reference to the seasonal consumption of calcium by plankton. *J. Mar. Biol. Ass.* **19**, 747–754.

COOPER, L. H. N. (1935a) Iron in the sea and in marine plankton. *Proc. Roy. Soc.* B **118**, 419–438.

COOPER, L. H. N. (1935b) The rate of liberation of phosphate in sea water by the breakdown of plankton organisms. *J. Mar. Biol. Ass.* **20**, 197–200.

COOPER, L. H. N. (1937) The nitrogen cycle in the sea. *J. Mar. Biol. Ass.* **22**, 183–204.

COOPER, L. H. N. (1938) Phosphate in the English Channel, 1933–38, with a comparison with earlier years, 1916 and 1923–32. *J. Mar. Biol. Ass.* **23**, 181–195.

COOPER, L. H. N. (1948a) The distribution of iron in the waters of the Western English Channel. *J. Mar. Biol. Ass.* **27**, 279–313.

COOPER, L. H. N. (1948b) Phosphate and fisheries. *J. Mar. Biol. Ass.* **27**, 326–336.

COOPER, L. H. N. (1951) Chemical properties of the sea water in the neighbourhood of the Labadie Bank. *J. Mar. Biol. Ass.* **30**, 21–26.

COOPER, L. H. N. (1952a) Processes of enrichment of surface water with nutrients due to strong winds blowing on to a continental slope. *J. Mar. Biol. Ass.* **30**, 453–464.

COOPER, L. H. N. (1952b) Factors affecting the distribution of silicate in the North Atlantic Ocean and the formation of North Atlantic deep water. *J. Mar. Biol. Ass.* **30**, 511–526.

COOPER, L. H. N. (1952c) The physical and chemical oceanography of the waters bathing the continental slope of the Celtic Sea. *J. Mar. Biol. Ass.* **30**, 465–510.

COOPER, L. H. N. (1956) On assessing the age of deep oceanic water by carbon – 14. *J. Mar. Biol. Ass.* **35**, 341–354.

COOPER, L. H. N. (1961) Vertical and horizontal movements in the ocean. In *Oceanography*. Public. No. 67. A.A.A.S. Washington D.C. ed. M. Sears; 599–621.

COOPER, L. H. N.. and D. VAUX (1949) Cascading over the continental slope of water from the Celtic Sea. *J. Mar. Biol. Ass.* **28**, 719–750.

CORLETT, J. (1953) Net phytoplankton at ocean weather stations "I" and "J" *J. Cons. Int. Explor. Mer.* **19**, 178–190.

CORNER, E. D. S. (1961) On the nutrition and metabolism of zooplankton. I. *J. Mar. Biol. Ass.* **41**, 5–16.

CORNISH, V. (1910) *Waves of the Sea and other Water Waves.* T. Fisher Unwin. London. 374 pp.

COSTLOW, J. D., and C. G. BOOKHOUT (1957) Larval development of *Balanus eburneus* in the laboratory. *Biol. Bull. Woods Hole* **112**, 313–324.

COSTLOW, J. D., and C. G. BOOKHOUT (1958) Larval development of *Balanus amphitrite var. denticulata* Broch reared in the laboratory. *Biol. Bull. Woods Hole* **114**, 284–295.

COSTLOW, J. D., and C. G. BOOKHOUT (1959) The effects of salinity and temperature on larval development of Brachyura reared in the laboratory. Int. Ocean. Congress Preprints A.A.A.S. Washington. 228–229.

COWEY, C. B. (1956) A preliminary investigation of the variation of vitamin B_{12} in oceanic and coastal waters. *J. Mar. Biol. Ass.* **35**, 609–620.

CREITZ, G. I., and F. A. RICHARDS (1955) The estimation and characterization of plankton populations by pigment analysis. III. *J. Mar. Res.* **14**, 211–216.

CRISP, D. J. (1954) The breeding of *Balanus porcatus* (da Costa) in the Irish Sea. *J. Mar. Biol. Ass.* **33**, 473–496.

CRISP, D. J., and C. P. SPENCER (1958) The control of hatching process in barnacles. *Proc. Roy. Soc.* B**148**, 278–299.

CROMWELL, T. (1953) Circulation in a meridional plane in the Central Equatorial Pacific. *J. Mar. Res.* **12**, 196–213.

CURL, H. C. (1960) Primary production measurements in the north coastal waters of South America. *Deep Sea Res.* **7**, 183–189.

CURRIE, R. I. (1953) Upwelling in the Benguela current. *Nature Lond.* **171**, 497–500.

CURRIE, R. I. (1958) Some observations on organic production in the North-East Atlantic. *Rapp. Proc.-Verb. Cons. Int. Explor. Mer.* **144**, 96–102.

CUSHING, D. H. (1951) The vertical migration of planktonic Crustacea. *Biol. Rev.* **26**, 158–192.

CUSHING, D. H. (1953) Studies on plankton populations. *J. Cons. Int. Explor. Mer.* **19**, 3–22.

CUSHING, D. H. (1955) Some experiments on the vertical migration of zooplankton. *J. Anim. Ecol.* **24**, 137–166.

CUSHING, D. H. (1958) The estimation of carbon in phytoplankton. *Rapp. Proc.-Verb. Cons. Int. Explor. Mer.* **144**, 32–33.

CUSHING, D. H. (1959a) On the nature of production in the sea. *Fish. Invest. Lond.* Series II. **22**, No. 6, 1–40.

CUSHING, D. H. (1959b) The seasonal variation in oceanic production as a problem in population dynamics. *J. Cons. Int. Explor. Mer.* **24**, 455–464.

DAISLEY, K. W., and L. R. FISHER (1958) Vertical distribution of vitamin B_{12} in the sea. *J. Mar. Biol. Ass.* **37**, 683–686.

DAKIN, W. J. (1908) Notes on the alimentary canal and food of the Copepoda. *Int. Rev. ges. Hydrobiol. Hydrogr.* **1**, 772–782.

DAKIN, W. J., and A. N. COLEFAX (1935) Observations on the seasonal changes in temperatures, salinity, phosphates and nitrates, nitrogen and oxygen of the ocean waters on the continental shelf off New South Wales, and the relationship to plankton production. *Proc. Linn. Soc. N.S.W.* **60**, 303–314.

DAKIN, W. J., and A. N. COLEFAX (1940) *The plankton of the Australian coastal waters off New South Wales* Pt. I. Public. Univ. Sydney. Monograph No. I. Dept. of Zoology, 1–215.

DAMAS, D. (1905) Notes biologiques sur les Copépodes de la Mer Norvégienne. *Public. de Circonst.* No. 22. Copenhagen: 1–23.

DAVIS, F. M. (1923) Quantitative studies on the fauna of the sea bottom No. 1. *Fish. Invest. Lond.* Ser. II, **6**, 1–54.

DAVIS, H. C. (1953) On food and feeding of larvae of the American oyster, *C. virginica. Biol. Bull. Woods Hole* **104**, 334–350.

DAVIS, H. C. (1958) Survival and growth of clam and oyster larvae at different salinities. *Biol. Bull. Woods Hole* **114**, 296–307.

DAVID, P. M. (1958) The distribution of the Chaetognatha of the Southern Ocean. *Discovery Repts.* **29**, 199–228.

DAVID, P. M. (1961) The influence of vertical migration on speciation in the oceanic plankton. *System. Zool.* **10**, 10–16.

DEACON, G. E. R. (1933) A general account of the hydrology of the South Atlantic Ocean. *Discovery Repts.* **7**, 173–238.

DEACON, G. E. R. (1937) The hydrology of the Southern Ocean. *Discovery Repts.* **15**, 1–124.

DEEVEY, G. B. (1948) Zooplankton of Tisbury Great Pond. *Bull. Bingham Oceanogr. Coll.* **12**, 1–44.

DEEVEY, G. B. (1952) A survey of the zooplankton of Block Island Sound 1943–1946. *Bull. Bingham Oceanogr. Coll.* **13**, 65–119.

DEEVEY, G. B. (1956) Oceanography of Long Island Sound 1952–1954. V. Zooplankton. *Bull. Bingham Oceanogr. Coll.* **15**, 113–155.

DEMEL, K., and Z. MULICKI (1958) The zoobenthic biomass in the Southern Baltic. *J. Cons. Int. Explor. Mer.* **24**, 43–54.

DENTON, E. J. and T. I. SHAW (1962) The buoyancy of gelatinous marine animals. *J. Physiol.* **161**, 14–15 P.

DIGBY, P. S. B. (1950) The biology of the small planktonic copepods of Plymouth. *J. Mar. Biol. Ass.* **29**, 393–438.

DIGBY, P. S. B. (1953) Plankton production in Scoresby Sound, East Greenland. *J. Anim. Ecol.* **22**, 289–322.

DIGBY, P. S. B. (1954) Biology of the marine planktonic copepods of Scoresby Sound, East Greenland. *J. Anim. Ecol.* **23**, 298–338.

DROOP, M. R. (1957) Auxotrophy and organic compounds in the nutrition of marine phytoplankton. *J. Gen. Microbiol.* **16**, 286–293.

DROOP, M. R. (1958) Requirement for thiamine among some marine and supralittoral Protista. *J. Mar. Biol. Ass.* **37**, 323–329.

DRUMMOND, J. C., and E. R. GUNTHER (1934) Observations on fatty constituents of marine plankton. III Vitamin A and D content of oils. *J. Exp. Biol.* **11**, 203–209.

DOTY, M. S., and M. OGURI (1957) Evidence for a photosynthetic daily periodicity. *Limnol. & Oceanogr.* **2**, 37–40.

DUNBAR, M. J. (1940) On the size, distribution and breeding cycles of four marine planktonic animals from the Arctic. *J. Anim. Ecol.* **9**, 215–226.

DUNBAR, M. J. (1946) On *Themisto libellula* in Baffin Island coastal waters. *J. Fish. Res. Bd. Canada* **6**, 419–434.

EALES, N. B. (1949) The food of the dogfish, *Scyliorhinus caniculus* L. *J. Mar. Biol. Ass.* **28**, 791–793.

EARLAND, A. (1933) Foraminifera. Part II South Georgia. *Discovery Repts.* **7**, 27–138.

EARLAND, A. (1934) Foraminifera. Part III The Falklands Sector of the Antarctic (excluding South Georgia). *Discovery Repts.* **10** 1–208.

EINARSSON, H. (1945) Euphausiacea. I. Northern Atlantic Species. *Dana Repts.* **27**, Copenhagen, 1–185.

EKMAN, S. (1953) *Zoogeography of the Sea.* Sidgwick and Jackson Ltd. London. 417 pp.

EMERY, K. O. (1956) Deep standing internal waves in California basins. *Limnol. & Oceanogr.* **1**, 35–41.

ESTERLY, C. O. (1912) The occurrence and vertical distribution of the Copepoda of the San Diego region with particular reference to nineteen species. *Univ. Calif. Publ. Zool.* **9**, 253–340.

ESTERLY, C. O. (1916) The feeding habits and food of pelagic copepods and the question of nutrition by organic substances in solution in the water. *Univ. Calif. Publ. Zool.* **16**, 171–184.

ESTERLY, C. O. (1917) Occurrence of a rhythm in the geotropism of two species of plankton copepods when certain recurring external conditions are absent. *Univ. Calif. Publ. Zool.* **16**, 393–400.

ESTERLY, C. O. (1919) Reactions of various plankton animals with reference to their diurnal migrations. *Univ. Calif. Publ. Zool.* **19**, 1–83.

EVANS, R. G. (1948) The lethal temperatures of some common British littoral molluscs. *J. Anim. Ecol.* **17**, 165–173.

EWALD, W. F. (1912) On artificial modification of light reactions and the influence of electrolytes on phototaxis. *J. Exp. Zool.* **13**, 591–612.

EYDEN, D. (1923) Specific gravity as a factor in the vertical distribution of plankton. *Proc. Camb. Phil. Soc. Biol. Sci.* **1**, 49–55.

FARRAN, G. P. (1947) Vertical distribution of plankton (*Sagitta, Calanus* and *Metridia*) off the South Coast of Ireland. *Proc. Roy. Irish. Acad.* **51** B, 121–136.

FARRAN, G. P. (1949) The seasonal and vertical distribution of the Copepoda. *Gt. Barrier Reef Exped. Sci. Repts. B.M. (N.H.)* **2**, 291–312.

FILATOVA, Z. A. (1957) General review of the bivalve molluscs of the Northern Seas of the U.S.S.R. *Trans. Inst. Oceanol. Acad. Sci. U.S.S.R.* **20**, 3–59.

FISH, C. J. (1925) Seasonal distribution of the plankton of the Woods Hole Region. *Bull. U.S. Bur. Fish.* **41**, 91–179.

FISH, C. J. (1936a) The biology of *Calanus finmarchicus* in the Gulf of Maine and Bay of Fundy. *Biol. Bull. Woods Hole* **70**, 118–142.

FISH, C. J. (1936b) The biology of *Pseudocalanus minutus* in the Gulf of Maine and Bay of Fundy. *Biol. Bull. Woods Hole* **70**, 193–215.

FISH, C. J. (1936c) The biology of *Oithona similis* in the Gulf of Maine and Bay of Fundy. *Biol. Bull. Woods Hole* **71**, 168–187.

FISH, C. J. (1954) Preliminary observations on the biology of boreo-arctic and subtropical oceanic zooplankton populations. *Symposium on Marine and Fresh-water Plankton in the Indo-Pacific.* Bangkok, 3–9.

FISH, C. J., and M. W. JOHNSON (1937) The biology of the zooplankton population in the Bay of Fundy and Gulf of Maine with special reference to production and distribution. *J. Biol. Bd. Canada* **3**, 189–321.

FISHER, L. R., and E. H. GOLDIE (1959) The food of *Meganyctiphanes norvegica* (M. Sars) with an assessment of the contributions of its components to the vitamin A reserves of the animal. *J. Mar. Biol. Ass.* **38**, 291–312.

FISHER, L. R., and S. K. KON (1959) Vitamin A in the invertebrates. *Biol. Rev.* **34**, 1–36.

FLEMING, R. H. (1939) The control of diatom populations by grazing. *J. Cons. Int. Explor. Mer.* **14**, 210–227.

FLEMING, R. H. (1957) General features of the oceans. Chapter 5 in *Treatise on Marine Ecology and Paleoecology*, Vol. I. Ecology, Ed. J. W. HEDGPETH. Geol. Soc. Amer. Memoir **67**, 87–108.

FOGG, G. E. (1953) *The Metabolism of Algae.* Methuen. London and N.Y. 149 pp.

FORD, E. (1923) Animal communities of the level sea-bottom in the waters adjacent to Plymouth. *J. Mar. Biol. Ass.* **13**, 164–224.

FOX, D. L. (1957) Particulate organic detritus. Chapter 14 in *Treatise on Marine Ecology & Paleoecology.* Vol. I. Ecology, Ed. J. W. Hedgpeth. Geol. Soc. Amer. Memoir **67**, 383–389.

FOX, D. L., J. D. ISAACS and E. F. CORCORAN (1952) Marine Leptopel, its recovery, measurement and distribution. *J. Mar. Res.* **11**, 29–46.

FOXTON, P. (1956) Standing crop of zooplankton in the Southern Ocean. *Discovery Repts.* **28**, 193–235.

FRASER, F. C. (1936) On the development and distribution of the young stages of krill (*Euphausia superba*). *Discovery Repts.* **14**, 3–192.

FRASER, J. H. (1939) Distribution of Chaetognatha in Scottish waters in 1937. *J. Cons. Int. Explor. Mer.* **14**, 25–34.

FRASER, J. H. (1947) Fiches d'Identification du Zooplancton. Nos. 9 and 10. Thaliacea I and II. *Cons. Inter. Explor. Mer.* Copenhagen.

FRASER, J. H. (1952) The Chaetognatha and other zooplankton of the Scottish area and their value as biological indicators of hydrographical conditions. *Mar. Res. Scot.* 1952, No. 2, 1–52.

FRASER, J. H. (1955) The plankton of the waters approaching the British Isles in 1953. *Mar. Res. Scot.* 1955, No. 1, 1–12.

FRASER, J. H. (1961) The survival of larval fish in the northern North Sea according to the quality of the water. *J. Mar. Biol. Ass.* **41**, 305–312.

FRITSCH, F. E. (1948) *The Structure and Reproduction of the Algae.* 1. Cambridge University Press. 791 pp.

FULLER, J. L. (1937) Feeding rate of *Calanus finmarchicus* in relation to environmental conditions. *Biol. Bull. Woods Hole* **72**, 233–246.

FULLER, J. L., and G. L. CLARKE (1936) Further experiments on the feeding of *Calanus finmarchicus. Biol. Bull. Woods Hole* **70**, 308–320.

GAARDER, T., and H. H. GRAN (1927) Investigations of the production of plankton in the Oslo Fjord. *Rapp. Proc.-Verb. Cons. Int. Explor. Mer.* **42**, 1–48.

GAARDER, T., and R. SPARCK (1931) Biochemical and biological investigations of the variations in the productivity of the West Norwegian Oyster Pools. *Rapp. Proc.-Verb. Cons. Int. Explor. Mer.* **75**, 47–58.

GARDINER, A. C. (1933) Vertical distribution in *Calanus finmorchicus. J. Mar. Biol. Ass.* **18**, 575–610.

GARDINER, A. C. (1937) Phosphate production by planktonic animals. *J. Cons. Int. Explor. Mer.* **12**, 144–146.

GAULD, D. T. (1950) A fish cultivation experiment in an arm of a sea-loch. III The plankton of Kyle Scotnish. *Proc. Roy. Soc. Edinb.* B **64**, 36–64.

GAULD, D. T. (1951) The grazing rate of planktonic copepods. *J. Mar. Biol. Ass.* **29**, 695–706.

GAULD, D. T. (1953) Diurnal variations in the grazing of planktonic copepods. *J. Mar. Biol. Ass.* **31**, 461–474.

GAULD, D. T., and J. E. G. RAYMONT (1953) The respiration of some planktonic copepods. II. The effect of temperature. *J. Mar. Biol. Ass.* **31**, 447-460.

GEORGE, P. C. (1953) The marine plankton of the coastal waters of Calicut with observations on the hydrological conditions. *J. Zool. Soc. India* **5**, 76–107.

GILLBRICHT, M. (1952) Die Planktonverteilung in der Irminger See im Juni 1955. *Ber. Dtsch. Komm. Meeresforsch.* **15**, 260–275.

GLOVER, R. S. (1961) Biogeographical boundaries: The shapes of distributions. In *Oceanography* Public. No. 67. A.A.A.S. Washington D.C. ed. M. Sears, 201–228.

GOLDBERG, E. D. (1957) Biogeochemistry of trace metals. Chapter 12 in *Treatise on Marine Ecology & Paleoecology.* Vol. I. Ecology, Ed. J. W. HEDGPETH. Geol. Soc. Amer. Memoir **67**, 345–358.

GOLDBERG, E. D., M. BAKER and D. L. FOX (1952) Microfiltration in oceanographic research I. *J. Mar. Res.* **11**, 194–204.

GOLDBERG, E. D., W. MCBLAIR and K. M. TAYLOR (1951) The uptake of vanadium by tunicates. *Biol. Bull. Woods Hole* **101**, 84–94.

GRAHAM, M. (1956) (Ed.) *Sea Fisheries, their Investigation in the United Kingdom.* Edward Arnold. London. 487 pp.

GRAINGER, E. H. (1959) The annual oceanographic cycle at Igloolik in the Canadian Arctic I. *J. Fish. Res. Bd. Canada.* **16**, 453–501.

GRAN, H. H. (1912) Pelagic plant life. Chapter 6 in *Depths of the Ocean*, Ed. Murray and Hjort. MacMillan and Co., London, 821 pp.

GRAN, H. H. (1927) The production of plankton in the coastal waters off Bergen March–April 1922. *Rept. Norweg. Fish. Mar. Invest.* **3**(8), 1–74.

GRAN, H. H. (1929a) Quantitative plankton investigations carried out during the expedition with the *Michael Sars*, July–Sept. 1924. *Rapp. Proc.-Verb. Cons. Int. Explor. Mer.* **56**(5), 1–50.

GRAN, H. H. (1929b) Investigation of the production of plankton outside the Romsdalsfjord 1926–1927. *Rapp. Proc.-Verb. Cons. Int. Explor. Mer.* **56**(6), 1–112.

GRAN, H. H. (1931) On the conditions for the production of plankton in the sea. *Rapp. Proc.-Verb. Cons. Int. Explor. Mer.* **75**, 37–46.

GRAN, H. H., and T. BRAARUD (1935) A quantitative study of the phytoplankton in the Bay of Fundy and the Gulf of Maine (including observations on hydrography, chemistry and turbidity). *J. Biol. Bd. Canada.* **1**, 279–467.

GREEN, J. (1957) Growth of *Scrobicularia plana* (da Costa) in the Gwendraeth estuary. *J. Mar. Biol. Ass.* **36**, 41–47.

GRØNTVED, J. (1952) Investigations on the phytoplankton in the Southern North Sea in May 1947. *Medd. Komm. Dan. Fisk. Havund. Ser. Plankton* **5**, No. 5, 1–49.

GRØNTVED, J. (1957) A sampler for underwater macro-vegetation in shallow waters. *J. Cons. Int. Explor. Mer.* **22**, 293–297.

GRØNTVED, J. (1958) Underwater macrovegetation in shallow coastal waters. *J. Cons. Int. Explor. Mer.* **24**, 32–42.

GROSS, F. (1937a) The life history of some marine plankton diatoms. *Phil. Trans.* B **228**, 1–47.

GROSS, F. (1937b) Notes on the culture of some marine plankton organisms. *J. Mar. Biol. Ass.* **21**, 753–768.

GROSS, F. (1940) The osmotic relations of the plankton diatom *Ditylum brightwelli* (West). *J. Mar. Biol. Ass.* **24**, 381–415.

GROSS, F., S. M. MARSHALL, A. P. ORR and J. E. G. RAYMONT (1947) An experiment in marine fish cultivation. 1–V. *Proc. Roy. Soc. Edinb.* B **63**, 1–95.

GROSS, F., and E. ZEUTHEN (1948) The buoyancy of plankton diatoms: a problem of cell physiology. *Proc. Roy. Soc.* B **135**, 382–389.

GROSS, F., S. R. NUTMAN, D. T. GAULD and J. E. G. RAYMONT (1950) A fish cultivation experiment in an arm of a sea-loch. I–V. *Proc. Roy. Soc. Edinb.* B **64**, 1–135.

GUELIN, A. (1954) La contamination des poissons et le problème des eaux polluées. *Ann. Inst. Pasteur.* **86**, 303–308.

GUELIN, A. (1955) Bactériophages typhiques à grandes et à petites plages des eaux polluées et leur photosensibilité. *Ann. Inst. Pasteur.* **88**, 576–590.

GUILLARD, R. R. L., and P. J. WANGERSKY (1958) The production of extracellular carbohydrates by some marine flagellates. *Limnol. & Oceanogr.* **3**, 449–454.

GUNTER, G. (1957) Temperature. Chapter 8 in *Treatise on Marine Ecology and Paleoecology.* Vol I Ecology. Ed. J. W. HEDGPETH, Geol. Soc. Amer. Memoir **67**, 159–184.

GUNTER, G., R. H. WILLIAMS, C. C. DAVIS and F. G. WALTON SMITH (1948) Catastrophic mass mortality of marine animals and coincident phytoplankton bloom on the west coast of Florida, Nov. 1946 to August 1947. *Ecol. Monogr.* **18**, 310–324.

GUNTHER, E. R. (1934) Observations on the fatty constituents of marine plankton. I. Biology of the plankton. *J. Exp. Biol.* **11**, 173–197.

GUNTHER, E. R. (1936) A report on oceanographical investigations in the Peru coastal current. *Discovery Repts.* **13**, 109–276.

HAECKEL, E. (1881) *Monographie der Medusen* (Vol. 2). Gustav Fischer, Jena. 205 pp.

HANSEN, K. V. (1951) On the diurnal migration of zooplankton in relation to the discontinuity layer. *J. Cons. Int. Explor. Mer.* **17**, 231–241.

HANSEN, V. K. (1959) Investigations of the primary production and the quantitative and qualitative distribution of macroplankton in the North Atlantic. Int. Ocean. Congress Preprints. A.A.A.S. Washington, 308–309.

HARDER, W. (1952) Über das Verhalten von Zooplankton in geschichtetem Wasser. Kurze Mitt. fischereibiol. Abt. Max-Pl.-Inst. Meeresbiol. Wilhelmshaven. 1, 28–34.

HARDER, W. (1957) Verhalten von Organismen gegenüber Sprungschichten. Ann. Biol. 33, 227–232.

HARDY, A. C. (1924) The herring in relation to its animate environment, Part I. The food and feeding habits of the herring. Fish. Invest. Lond. Ser. II, 7, No. 3, 1–53.

HARDY, A. C. (1956) The Open Sea, its Natural History: The World of Plankton. Collins, London. 355 pp.

HARDY, A. C. (1960) The Open Sea: its Natural History II Fish and Fisheries. Collins, London. 322 pp.

HARDY, A. C., and R. BAINBRIDGE (1954) Experimental observations on vertical migrations of plankton animals. J. Mar. Biol. Ass. 33, 409–448.

HARDY, A. C., and E. R. GUNTHER (1936) Plankton of the South Georgia whaling grounds and adjacent waters, 1926–1927. Discovery Repts. 11, 1–456.

HARDY, A. C., and W. N. PATON (1947) Experiments on vertical migration of plankton animals. J. Mar. Biol. Ass. 26, 467–526.

HARRIS, E. (1959) The nitrogen cycle in Long Island Sound. Bull. Bingham Oceanogr. Coll. 17, 31–65.

HARRIS, J. E. (1953) Physical factors involved in the vertical migration of plankton. Quart. J. Micr. Sci. 94, 537–550.

HART, T. J. (1934) On the phytoplankton of the South-West Atlantic and the Bellingshausen Sea, 1929–1931. Discovery Repts. 8, 1–268.

HART, T. J. (1942) Phytoplankton periodicity in Antarctic surface waters. Discovery Repts. 21, 263–348.

HART, T. J. (1953) Plankton of Benguela current. Nature, Lond. 171, 631–634.

HART, T. J., and R. I. CURRIE (1960) The Benguela current. Discovery Repts. 31, 123–298.

HARTMAN, O., and K. O. EMERY (1956) Bathypelagic coelenterates. Limnol. & Oceanogr. 1, 304–312.

HARVEY, H. W. (1926) Nitrate in the sea. J. Mar. Biol. Ass. 14, 71–88.

HARVEY, H. W. (1928) Biological Chemistry and Physics of Sea Water. Cambridge Comp. Physiol. Cambridge University Press 194 pp.

HARVEY, H. W. (1934) Measurement of phytoplankton population. J. Mar. Biol. Ass. 19, 761–773.

HARVEY, H. W. (1937a) The supply of iron to diatoms. J. Mar. Biol. Ass. 22, 205–220.

HARVEY, H. W. (1937b) Notes on selective feeding by Calanus. J. Mar. Biol. Ass. 22, 97–100.

HARVEY, H. W. (1942) Production of life in the sea. Biol. Rev. 17, 221–246.

HARVEY, H. W. (1945) Recent Advances in the Chemistry and Biology of Sea Water. Cambridge University Press. 164 pp.

HARVEY, H. W. (1947) Manganese and the growth of phytoplankton. J. Mar. Biol. Ass. 26, 562–579.

HARVEY, H. W. (1949) On manganese in sea and freshwaters. *J. Mar. Biol. Ass.* **28**, 155–164.

HARVEY, H. W. (1950) On the production of living matter in the sea. *J. Mar. Biol. Ass.* **29**, 97–136.

HARVEY, H. W. (1955) *The Chemistry and Fertility of Seawaters.* Cambridge University Press 224 pp.

HARVEY, H. W., L. H. N. COOPER, M. V. LEBOUR and F. S. RUSSELL (1935) Plankton production and its control. *J. Mar. Biol. Ass.* **20**, 407–441.

HASLE, G. R. (1959) A quantitative study of phytoplankton from the equatorial Pacific. *Deep Sea Res.* **6**, 38–59.

HEILBRUNN, L. V. (1952) *An Outline of General Physiology* (3rd Edn.). W. B. Saunders Co. Philadelphia and London. 818 pp.

HEINRICH, A. K. (1962) The life histories of plankton animals and seasonal cycles of plankton communities in the oceans. *J. Cons. Int. Explor. Mer.* **27**, 15–24.

HENDEY, N. I. (1959) The structure of the diatom cell wall as revealed by the electron microscope. *J. Quekett Micro. Club*, Ser. 4, **5**, 147–175.

HENTSCHEL, E., and H. WATTENBERG (1930) Plankton und Phosphat in der Oberflächenschicht des Südatlantischen Ozeans. *Ann. Hydrogr.* Berlin. **58**, 273–277.

HICKLING, C. F. (1925) Notes on euphausiids. *J. Mar. Biol. Ass.* **13**, 735–745.

HICKLING, C. F. (1935) *The Hake and the Hake Fishery.* Buckland Lectures for 1934. Edward Arnold and Co. London. 142 pp.

HOCK, C. W. (1941) Marine chitin-decomposing bacteria. *J. Mar. Res.* **4**, 99–106.

HOFFMAN, C. (1956) Untersuchungen über die Remineralisation des Phosphors im Plankton. *Kieler Meeresforsch.* **12**, 25–36.

HOLLIDAY, F. G. T., and J. H. S. BLAXTER (1960) The effects of salinity on the developing eggs and larvae of the herring. *J. Mar. Biol. Ass.* **39**, 591–603.

HOLME, N. A. (1949) The fauna of sand and mud banks near the mouth of the Exe estuary. *J. Mar. Biol. Ass.* **28**, 189–237.

HOLME, N. A. (1950) The bottom fauna of Great West Bay. *J. Mar. Biol. Ass.* **29**, 163–183.

HOLMES, R. W. (1958) Surface chlorophyll "A", surface primary production and zooplankton volumes in the eastern Pacific Ocean. *Rapp. Proc.-Verb. Cons. Int. Explor. Mer.* **144**, 109–116.

HUDINAGA, M., and H. KASAHARA (1941) On the rearing and metamorphosis of *Balanus amphitrite hawaiiensis* Broh. [English Summary only.] *Zool. Mag. (Tokyo)* **54**, 108–118.

HULBERT, E. M., J. H. RYTHER and R. R. L. GUILLARD (1960) The phytoplankton of the Sargasso Sea off Bermuda. *J. Cons. Int. Explor. Mer.* **25**, 115–128.

HUNT, O. D. (1925) The food of the bottom fauna of the Plymouth fishing grounds. *J. Mar. Biol. Ass.* **13**, 560–599.

HYMAN, L. H. (1940, 1951) *The Invertebrates*, Vols. I & II. McGraw-Hill N.Y. and London. 726 and 550 pp.

ISELIN, C. O'D. (1939) Some physical factors which may influence the productivity of New England's coastal waters. *J. Mar. Res.* **2**, 75–85.

JENKIN, P. M. (1937) Oxygen production by the diatom *Coscinodiscus excentricus* Ehr. in relation to submarine illumination in the English Channel. *J. Mar. Biol. Ass.* **22**, 301–343.

JERLOV, N. G. (1951) Optical studies of ocean waters. *Repts. Swedish Deep Sea Expdn.* Vol 3, Physics and Chemistry No. 1, 1–59.

JERLOV, N. G., and F. KOCZY (1951) Photographic measurements of daylight in deep water. *Repts. Swedish Deep Sea Expdn.* Vol. 3, Physics and Chemistry No. 2, 61–69.

JESPERSEN, P. (1924) On the quantity of macroplankton in the Mediterranean and Atlantic. *Int. Rev. ges. Hydrobiol. Hydrogr.* **12**, 102–115.

JESPERSEN, P. (1935) Quantitative investigations on the distribution of macroplankton in different oceanic regions. *Dana Rept.* No. 7, 1–44.

JESPERSEN, P. (1939) The zoology of East Greenland. Copepods. *Medd. Grønland.* **121**(3), 1–66.

JESPERSEN, P. (1940) Investigations on the quantity and distribution of zooplankton in Icelandic waters. *Medd. Komm. Dan. Fisk. Havund. Ser. Plankton.* **3**(5), 1–77.

JESPERSEN, P. (1944) Investigations on the food of the herring and the macroplankton in the waters around the Faroes. *Medd. Komm. Dan. Fisk. Havund. Ser. Plankton.* **3**(7), 1–44.

JOHN, D. D. (1936) The southern species of the genus *Euphausia. Discovery Repts.* **14**, 193–324.

JOHNSON, M. W. (1958) Observations on inshore plankton collected during summer 1957 at Point Barrow, Alaska. *J. Mar. Res. Thompson Anniversary Volume.* **17**, 272–281.

JOHNSON, W. H. (1938) Effect of light on vertical movements of *Acartia clausi* (Giesbrecht). *Biol. Bull. Woods Hole* **75**, 106–118.

JOHNSON, W. H., and J. E. G. RAYMONT (1939) The reactions of the planktonic copepod, *Centropages typicus* to light and gravity. *Biol. Bull. Woods Hole* **77**, 200–215.

JOHNSTON, R. (1955) Biologically active compounds in the sea. *J. Mar. Biol. Ass.* **34**, 185–195.

JOHNSTON, R. (1959) Antimetabolites and marine algae. Int. Ocean. Congress Preprints. A.A.A.S. Washington, 918–919.

JOHNSTONE, J., A. SCOTT and H. C. CHADWICK (1924) *The Marine Plankton.* Univ. Press of Liverpool. Hodder and Stoughton. London. 194 pp.

JONES, G. E. (1959) Biologically active organic substances in sea water. Int. Ocean. Congress Preprints. A.A.A.S. Washington, 921–922.

JONES, L. T. (1960) A comparative study of three species of the wood-boring isopod *Limnoria.* Ph. D. Thesis. University of Southampton.

JONES, N. S. (1950) Marine bottom communities. *Biol. Rev.* **25**, 283–313.

JONES, N. S. (1956) The fauna and biomass of a muddy sand deposit off Port Erin, I.O.M. *J. Anim. Ecol.* **25**, 217–252.

JORGENSEN, E. G., and E. STEEMANN NIELSEN (1959) Effect of filtrates from cultures of unicellular algae on the growth of *Staphylococcus aureus.* Int. Ocean. Congress Preprints A.A.A.S. Washington, 923.

KAIN, J. M., and G. E. FOGG (1958) Studies on the growth of marine phytoplankton. II *Isochrysis galbana* Parke. *J. Mar. Biol. Ass.* **37**, 781–788.

KALLE, K. (1953) Der Einfluß des englischen Küstenwassers auf den Chemismus der Wasserkörper in der südlichen Nordsee. *Ber. Dtsch. Komm. Meeresforsch.* **13**, 130–135.

KALLE, K. (1957) Chemische Untersuchungen in der Irminger See im Juni 1955. *Ber. Dtsch. Komm. Meeresforsch.* **14**, 313–328.

KAMPA, E. M., and B. P. BODEN (1956) Light generation in a ionic-scattering layer. *Deep Sea Res.* **4**, 73–92.

KAMSHILOV, M. M. (1955) The nutrition of ctenophore *Beroë cucumis* Fab. (Seen in abstract only). *Dokl. Akad. Nauk S.S.S.R.* **102**, 399–405.

KANDLER, R. I. (1950) Jahreszeitliches Vorkommen und unperiodisches Auftreten von Fischbrut, Medusen und Dekapod-Larven im Fehmarnbelt in den Jahren 1934–1943. *Ber. Dtsch. Komm. Meeresforsch.* **12**, 47–85.

KETCHUM, B. H. (1939) The absorption of phosphate and nitrate by illuminated cultures of *Nitzschia closterium*. *Amer. J. Bot.* **26**, 399–407.

KETCHUM, B. H. (1947) Biochemical relations between marine organisms and their environment. *Ecol. Monogr.* **17**, 309–315.

KETCHUM, B. H. (1954) Relation between circulation and planktonic populations in estuaries. *Ecology* **35**, 191–200.

KETCHUM, B. H. (1957) The effects of the ecological system on the transport of elements in the sea. *Publ. Nation. Acad. Sci. Nation. Res. Counc.* No. 551, 52–59.

KETCHUM, B. H., and A. C. REDFIELD (1949) Some physical and chemical characteristics of algae growth in mass culture. *J. Cell. Comp. Physiol.* **33**, 281–299.

KETCHUM, B. H., and D. J. KEEN (1948) Unusual phosphorus concentrations in the Florida "red tide" sea water. *J. Mar. Res.* **7**, 17–21.

KETCHUM, B. H., C. L. CAREY and M. BRIGGS (1949) Preliminary studies on the viability and dispersal of coliform bacteria in the sea. Limnol. Aspects of Water Supply and Waste Disposal. Published by A.A.A.S. 64–73.

KETCHUM, B. H., J. C. AYERS and R. F. VACCARO (1952) Processes contributing to the decrease of coliform bacteria in a tidal estuary. *Ecology* **33**, 247–258.

KETCHUM, B. H., N. CORWIN and D. J. KEEN (1955) The significance of organic phosphorus determinations in ocean waters. *Deep Sea Res.* **2**, 172–181.

KETCHUM, B. H., J. H. RYTHER, C. S. YENTSCH and N. CORWIN (1958) Productivity in relation to nutrients. *Rapp. Proc.-Verb. Cons. Int. Explor. Mer.* **144**, 132–140.

KEYS, A., E. H. CHRISTENSEN and A. KROGH (1935) The organic metabolism of sea-water with special reference to the ultimate food cycle in the sea. *J. Mar. Biol. Ass.* **20**, 181–196.

KIELHORN, W. V. (1952) The biology of the surface zone zooplankton of a Boreo-Arctic Atlantic Ocean area. *J. Fish. Res. Bd. Canada.* **9**, 223–264.

KIKUCHI, K. (1930) Diurnal migration of plankton Crustacea. *Quart. Rev. Biol.* **5**, 189–206.

KING, J. E., and J. DEMOND (1953) Zooplankton abundance in the Central Pacific. *U.S. Fish and Wildlife Service, Fish Bull.* **54**, 111–144.

KING, J. E., and T. S. HIDA (1957) Zooplankton abundance in the Central Pacific. Pt. II. *U.S. Fish and Wildlife Service, Fish. Bull.* **57**, 365–395.

KLIE, W. (1943) Fiches d'Identification du Zooplancton. No. 4. Copepoda-I. Sub-order: Harpacticoida. *Cons. Inter. Explor. Mer.* Copenhagen.

KNIGHT-JONES, E. W. (1951) Gregariousness and some other aspects of the setting behaviour of *Spirorbis*. *J. Mar. Biol. Ass.* **30**, 201–222.

KNIGHT-JONES, E. W. (1953) Decreased discrimination during setting after prolonged planktonic life in larvae of *Spirorbis borealis* (Serpulidae). *J. Mar. Biol. Ass.* **32**, 337–345.

KNIGHT-JONES, E. W. (1955) The gregarious setting reaction of barnacles as a measure of systematic affinity. *Nature, Lond.* **175**, 266.

KNIGHT-JONES, E. W., and S. Z. QASIM (1955) Responses of some marine plankton animals to changes in hydrostatic pressure. *Nature, Lond.* **175**, 941.

KNIGHT-JONES, E. W., and J. P. STEVENSON (1950) Gregariousness during settlement in the barnacle *Elminius modestus* Darwin. *J. Mar. Biol. Ass.* **29**, 281–297.

KOHN, A. J., and P. HELFRICH (1957) Primary organic productivity of a Hawaiian coral reef. *Limnol. & Oceanogr.* **2**, 241–251.

KON, S. K. (1958) Some thoughts on biochemical perspectives in marine biology *Perspectives in Marine Biology* Ed. Buzzati-Traverso, Univ. of California Press. Berkeley and Los Angeles 283–296.

KORNMANN, P. (1955) Beobachtungen an *Phaeocystis*-Kulturen. *Helgoländ. Wiss. Meeresunters.* **5**, 218–233.

KREPS, E., and N. VERJBINSKAYA (1930) Seasonal changes in the phosphate and nitrate content and in hydrogen ion concentration in the Barents Sea. *J. Cons. Int. Explor. Mer.* **5**, 327–346.

KREPS, E., and N. VERJBINSKAYA (1932) The consumption of nutrient salts in the Barents Sea. *J. Cons. Int. Explor. Mer.* **7**, 25–46.

KREY, J. (1958a) Chemical methods of estimating standing crop of phytoplankton *Rapp. Proc.-Verb. Cons. Int. Explor. Mer.* **144**, 20–27.

KREY, J. (1958b) Chemical determinations of net plankton, with special reference to equivalent albumin content. *J. Mar. Res. Thompson Anniversary Volume* **17**, 312–324.

KREY, J. (1961) Der Detritus im Meere. *J. Cons. Int. Explor. Mer.* **26**, 263–280.

KRISHNASWAMY, S. (1959) Metabolic studies on marine parasitic copepods and on certain zooplankton species. Ph. D. Thesis, University of Southampton.

KRISS, A. E. (1959) Microbiology and the chief problems in the Black Sea. *Deep Sea Res.* **5**, 193–200.

KRISS, A. E., I. N. MITZKEVICH, I. E. MISHUSTINA and S. S. ABYZOV (1961) Microorganisms as hydrological indicators in seas and oceans IV. *Deep Sea Res.* **7**, 225–236.

KRISS, A. E., and E. A. RUKINA (1952) Biomass of micro-organisms and their rates of reproduction in oceanic depths. *Zh. Obshch. Biol.* [seen in summary only] **12**, 349–362.

KROGH, A. (1931) Dissolved substances as food of aquatic organisms. *Biol. Rev.* **6**, 412–442.

KROGH, A. (1934) Conditions of life in the ocean. *Ecol. Monogr.* **4**, 421–429.

KROGH, A. (1934) Life at great depths in the ocean. *Ecol. Monogr.* **4**, 430–439.

KROGH, A. (1939) *Osmotic regulation in aquatic animals.* Cambridge University Press. 242 pp.

KROGH, A., and R. SPARCK (1936) On a new bottom-sampler for investigation of the micro-fauna of the sea bottom. *Kgl. Danske Vidensk. Selsk. Biol. Medd.* **13**, 1–12.

KUENZLER, E. J. (1961) Phosphorus budget of a mussel population. *Limnol. & Oceanogr.* **6**, 400–415.

KUNNE, C. (1950) Die Nahrung der Meerestiere II. Das Plankton. In *Handbuch der Seefischerei Nordeuropas*. Schweiz. Verlag. Stuttgart.

LACKEY, J. B. (1940) Some new flagellates from the Woods Hole Area. *Amer. Midl. Nat.* 23, 463–471.

LANCE, J. (1960) Effects of water of reduced salinity on the zooplankton of Southampton Water, with special reference to calanoid copepods. Ph. D. Thesis. University of Southampton.

LANE, C. E. (1959) Some aspects of the general biology of *Teredo*: in *Marine Boring and Fouling Organisms*. Ed. D. L. Ray. Friday Harbour Symposia. Univ. Washington Press. Seattle. 137–144.

LASKER, R., and G. H. THEILACKER (1962). Oxygen consumption and osmoregulation by single Pacific sardine eggs and larvae (*Sardinops caerulea* Girard) *J. Cons Int. Explor. Mer.* 27, 25–33.

LEAVITT, B. B. (1935) A quantitative study of the vertical distribution of the larger zooplankton in deep water. *Biol. Bull. Woods Hole* 68, 115–130.

LEAVITT, B. B. (1938) The quantitative vertical distribution of macrozooplankton in the Atlantic Ocean basin. *Biol. Bull. Woods Hole* 74, 376–394.

LEBOUR, M. V. (1918a) Food of post-larval fish. *J. Mar. Biol. Ass.* 11, 433–469.

LEBOUR, M. V. (1918b) Food of post-larval fish No. II. *J. Mar. Biol. Ass.* 12, 22–47.

LEBOUR, M. V. (1919) Food of young fish No. III. *J. Mar. Biol. Ass.* 12, 261–324.

LEBOUR, M. V. (1921) The food of young clupeoids. *J. Mar. Biol. Ass.* 12, 458–467.

LEBOUR, M. V. (1922) Food of plankton organisms. *J. Mar. Biol. Ass.* 12, 644–677.

LEBOUR, M. V. (1923) Food of plankton organisms II. *J. Mar. Biol. Ass.* 13, 70–92.

LEBOUR, M. V. (1924) The Euphausiideae in the neighbourhood of Plymouth and their importance as herring food. *J. Mar. Biol. Ass.* 13, 402–420.

LEBOUR, M. V. (1925) *The Dinoflagellates of Northern Seas*. Mar. Biol. Assoc. U.K. 250 pp.

LEBOUR, M. V. (1928) Larval stages of the Plymouth Brachyura. *Proc. Zool. Soc. London* 98, 473–556.

LEBOUR, M. V. (1930) *The Planktonic Diatoms of Northern Seas*. Ray Society. London, 244 pp.

LEWIN, J. C., and R. A. LEWIN (1959) Auxotrophy and heterotrophy in marine littoral diatoms. Int. Ocean. Congress Preprints, A.A.A.S. Washington. 928–929.

LILLICK, L. C. (1938) Preliminary report on the phytoplankton of the Gulf of Maine. *Amer. Midl. Nat.* 20, 624–640.

LILLICK, L. C. (1940) Phytoplankton and planktonic Protozoa of the offshore waters of the Gulf of Maine. Part II. *Trans. Amer. Phil. Soc.* 31, 193–237.

LOCHHEAD, J. H. (1936) On the feeding mechanism of the nauplius of *Balanus perforatus* Brugiere. *J. Linn. Soc. (Zool.)* 39, 429–441.

LOCHHEAD, J. H. (1954) On the distribution of a marine cladoceran, *Penilia avirostris* Dana (Crustacea, Branchiopoda), with a note on its bioluminescence. *Biol. Bull. Woods Hole* 107, 92–105.

LOHMANN, H. (1908) Untersuchungen zur Feststellung des vollständigen Gehaltes des Meeres an Plankton. *Wiss. Meeresuntersuch. Abt. Kiel* N.F. 10, 129–370.

LOHMANN, H. (1911) Über das Nannoplankton und die Zentrifugierung. *Int. Rev. ges. Hydrobiol. Hydrogr.* 4, 1–38.

LONGHURST, A. R. (1959) Benthos densities off tropical West Africa. *J. Cons. Int. Explor. Mer.* 25, 21–28.

LOOSANOFF, V. L., and H. C. DAVIS (1950) Conditioning *Venus mercenaria* for spawning in winter and breeding its larvae in the laboratory. *Biol. Bull. Woods Hole* **98**, 60–65.

LOOSANOFF, V. L., and H. C. DAVIS (1951) Delayed spawning of lamellibranchs by low temperature. *J. Mar. Res.* **10**, 197–202.

LOOSANOFF, V. L., W. S. MILLER and P. B. SMITH (1951) Growth and setting of larvae of *Venus mercenaria* in relation to temperature. *J. Mar. Res.* **10**, 59–81.

LOOSANOFF, V. L., J. B. ENGLE and C. A. NOMEJKO (1955) Differences in intensity of setting of oysters and starfish. *Biol. Bull. Woods Hole* **109**, 75–81.

LUCAS, C. E. (1936) On certain inter-relations between phytoplankton and zooplankton under experimental conditions. *J. Cons. Int. Explor. Mer.* **11**, 343–361.

LUCAS, C. E. (1938) Some aspects of integration in plankton communities. *J. Cons. Int. Explor. Mer.* **13**, 309–321.

LUCAS, C. E. (1941) Continuous plankton records: phytoplankton in the North Sea, 1938–39. Part I–Diatoms. *Hull Bull. Mar. Ecol.* **2**, No. 8, 19–46.

LUCAS, C. E. (1942) Continuous plankton records: phytoplankton in the North Sea, 1938–39. Part II–Dinoflagellates, Phaeocystis, etc. *Hull Bull. Mar. Ecol.* **2**, No. 9, 47–70.

LUCAS, C. E. (1947) Ecological effects of external metabolites. *Biol. Rev.* **22**, 270–295.

LUCAS, C. E. (1955) External metabolites in the sea. *Pap. Mar. Biol. & Oceanogr. Deep Sea Res. Suppl.* **3**, 139–148.

LUCAS, C. E. (1956) Plankton and basic production in *Sea Fisheries, their Investigation in the United Kingdom*. Edward Arnold. London. 487 pp.

LUCAS, C. E. (1961) Interrelationships between aquatic organisms mediated by external metabolites. In *Oceanography* Public. No. 67, A.A.A.S. Washington, D.C. ed. M. Sears 499–517.

LUCAS, C. E., and H. G. STUBBINGS (1948) Continuous plankton records: Size variations in diatoms and their ecological significance. *Hull Bull. Mar. Ecol.* **2**, No. 12, 133–171.

MCALLISTER, C. D., T. R. PARSONS and J. D. H. STRICKLAND (1960) Primary productivity and fertility at Station "P" in the North-East Pacific Ocean. *J. Cons. Int. Explor. Mer.* **25**, 240–259.

MCHUGH, J. L. (1954) Distribution and abundance of the diatom *Ethmodiscus rex* off the West coast of North America. *Deep Sea Res.* **1**, 216–222.

MACDONALD, R. (1927) Food and habits of *Meganyctiphanes norvegica. J. Mar. Biol. Ass.* **14**, 753–784.

MACGINITIE, G. E. (1939) Littoral marine communities. *Amer. Midl. Nat.* **21**, 28–55.

MACKINTOSH, N. A. (1934) Distribution of the macroplankton in the Atlantic sector of the Antarctic. *Discovery Repts.* **9**, 67–158.

MACKINTOSH, N. A. (1937) Seasonal circulation of the Antarctic macroplankton. *Discovery Repts.* **16**, 367–412.

MACKINTOSH, N. A. (1946) The natural history of whalebone whales. *Biol. Rev.* **21**, 60–74.

MACKINTOSH, N. A., and J. F. G. WHEELER (1929) Southern blue and fin whales. *Discovery Repts.* **1**, 259–539.

MARAK, R. R. (1960) Food habits of larval cod, haddock, and coalfish in the Gulf of Maine and Georges Bank Area. *J. Cons. Int. Explor. Mer.* **25**, 147–157.

MARE, M. F. (1940) Plankton production off Plymouth and the mouth of the English Channel in 1939. *J. Mar. Biol. Ass.* **24**, 461–482.

MARE, M. F. (1942) A study of a marine benthic community with special reference to the micro-organisms. *J. Mar. Biol. Ass.* **25**, 517–554.

MARGALEF, R. (1958) Temporal succession and spatial heterogeneity in phytoplankton. *Perspectives in Marine Biology* Ed. Buzzati-Traverso. Univ. of California Press. Berkeley and Los Angeles, 323–347.

MARSHALL, N. B. (1954) *Aspects of Deep Sea Biology*, Hutchinson. London, 380 pp.

MARSHALL, P. T. (1958) Primary production in the Arctic. *J. Cons. Int. Explor. Mer.* **23**, 173–177.

MARSHALL, S. M. (1933) The production of microplankton in the Great Barrier Reef region. *Gt. Barrier Reef Exped. Sci. Repts. B.M. (N.H.)* **2**, 111–158.

MARSHALL, S. M. (1949) On the biology of the small copepods in Loch Striven. *J. Mar. Biol. Ass.* **28**, 45–122.

MARSHALL, S. M., and A. P. ORR (1927) The relation of the plankton to some chemical and physical factors in the Clyde sea area. *J. Mar. Biol. Ass.* **14**, 837–868.

MARSHALL, S. M., and A. P. ORR (1928) The photosynthesis of diatom cultures in the sea. *J. Mar. Biol. Ass.* **15**, 321–360.

MARSHALL, S. M., and A. P. ORR (1930). A study of the spring diatom increase in Loch Striven. *J. Mar. Biol. Ass.* **16**, 853-878.

MARSHALL, S. M., and A. P. ORR (1948). Further experiments on the fertilization of a sea loch (Loch Craiglin). *J. Mar. Biol. Ass.* **27**, 360-379.

MARSHALL, S. M., and A. P. ORR (1952) On the biology of *Calanus finmarchicus* VII. Factors affecting egg production. *J. Mar. Biol. Ass.* **30**, 527–547.

MARSHALL, S. M., and A. P. ORR (1955a) *The Biology of a Marine Copepod. Calanus finmarchicus.* (Gunnerus). Oliver and Boyd. Edinburgh and London. 188 pp.

MARSHALL, S. M., and A. P. ORR (1955b) On the biology of *Calanus finmarchicus* VIII. Food uptake, assimilation and excretion in adult and Stage V *Calanus*. *J. Mar. Biol. Ass.* **34**, 495–529.

MARSHALL, S. M., and A. P. ORR (1955c) Experimental feeding of the copepod *Calanus finmarchicus* (Gunner) on phytoplankton cultures labelled with radioactive carbon (^{14}C). *Pap. Mar. Biol. & Oceanogr. Deep Sea Res. Suppl.* **3**, 110–114.

MARSHALL, S. M., and A. P. ORR (1956) On the biology of *Calanus finmarchicus* IX. Feeding and digestion in the young stages. *J. Mar. Biol. Ass.* **35**, 587-603.

MARSHALL, S. M., and A. P. ORR (1957) A preliminary note on seasonal changes in respiration of copepods. *Ann. Biol.* **33**, 221–224.

MARSHALL, S. M., and A. P. ORR (1958) On the biology of *Calanus finmarchicus* X. Seasonal changes in oxygen consumption. *J. Mar. Biol. Ass.* **37**, 459–472.

MARSHALL, S. M., and A. P. ORR (1960) On the biology of *Calanus finmarchicus* XI. Observations on vertical migration especially in female *Calanus*. *J. Mar. Biol. Ass.* **39**, 135–147.

MARSHALL, S. M., and A. P. ORR (1961) Studies on the biology of *Calanus finmarchicus* XII. *J. Mar. Biol. Ass..* **41**, 463–488.

MARSHALL, S. M., A. G. NICHOLLS and A. P. ORR (1933–34) On the biology of *Calanus finmarchicus* Parts I–V. *J. Mar. Biol. Ass.* **19–20**.

MARSHALL, S. M., A. G. NICHOLLS and A. P. ORR (1935) On the biology of *Calanus finmarchicus*. VI. Oxygen consumption in relation to environmental conditions. *J. Mar. Biol. Ass.* **20**, 1–28.

MAUCHLINE, J. (1959) The biology of the Euphausiid crustacean *Meganyctiphanes norvegica* (M. Sars). *Proc. Roy. Soc. Edinb.* **67**B, 141–179.

MAYER, A. G. (1910) Medusae of the World. Vols. I–III. *Carnegie Inst. Washington. Public. No. 109.*

MENON, M. A. S. (1945) Observations on the seasonal distribution of the plankton of the Trivandram coast. *Proc. Indian Acad. Sci.* **22**B, 31–62.

MENON, M. D. (1950) Bionomics of the poor-cod (*Gadus minutus* L.) in the Plymouth area. *J. Mar. Biol. Ass.* **29**, 185–239.

MENZEL, D. W., and J. H. RYTHER (1960) The annual cycle of primary production in the Sargasso Sea off Bermuda. *Deep Sea Res.* **6**, 351–367.

MENZEL, D. W., and J. H. RYTHER (1961) Nutrients limiting the production of phytoplankton in the Sargasso Sea, with special reference to iron. *Deep Sea Res.* **7**, 276–281.

MENZEL, D. W., and J. H. RYTHER (1961) Zooplankton in the Sargasso Sea off Bermuda and its relation to organic production. *J. Cons. Int. Explor Mer.* **26**, 250–258.

MICHAEL, E. L. (1911) Classification and vertical distribution of the Chaetognatha of the San Diego region, including redescriptions of some doubtful species of the group. *Univ. Calif. Publ. Zoology*, **8**, 21–186.

MIYAKE, Y., and K. SARUHASHI (1956) On the vertical distribution of the dissolved oxygen in the ocean. *Deep Sea Res.* **3**, 242–247.

MOBERG, E. G. (1926) Chemical composition of marine plankton. *Proc. 3rd Pan-Pacific Sci. Congr. Tokyo*, 233–236.

MOORE, H. B. (1930) The muds of the Clyde sea area. I. Phosphate and nitrogen contents. *J. Mar. Biol. Ass.* **16**, 595–607.

MOORE, H. B. (1931) The muds of the Clyde sea area. III. Chemical and physical conditions; rate and nature of sedimentation; and fauna. *J. Mar. Biol. Ass.* **17**, 325–358.

MOORE, H. B. (1949) The zooplankton of the upper waters of the Bermuda area of the North Atlantic. *Bull. Bingham Oceanogr. Coll.* **12**, 1–97.

MOORE, H. B. (1950) The relation between the scattering layer and the Euphausiacea. *Biol. Bull. Woods Hole* **99**, 181–212.

MOORE, H. B. (1952) Physical factors affecting the distribution of euphausids in the North Atlantic. *Bull. Mar. Sci. Gulf and Caribb.* **1**, 278–305.

MOORE, H. B., and E. G. CORWIN (1956) The effects of temperature, illumination and pressure on the vertical distribution of zooplankton. *Bull. Mar. Sci. Gulf and Caribb..* **6**, 273–287.

MURRAY, J., and J. HJORT (1912) *Depths of the Ocean.* MacMillan and Co. London: 821 pp.

NICHOLLS, A. G. (1933a) On the biology of *Calanus finmarchicus*. I. Reproduction and seasonal distribution in the Clyde sea area during 1932. *J. Mar. Biol. Ass.* **19**, 83–110.

NICHOLLS, A. G. (1933b) On the biology of *Calanus finmarchicus*. III. Vertical distribution and diurnal migration in the Clyde sea area. *J. Mar. Biol. Ass.* **19**, 139–164.

NICHOLLS, G. D., H. CURL and V. T. BOWEN (1959) Spectrographic analyses of marine plankton. *Limnol. & Oceanogr.* **4**, 472–478.

NIKITIN, V. N., and E. P. TURPAEVA (1957) The euryhalinity of some species of the Black Sea benthos and the possibility of their settlement in the Sea of Azov. *Trans. Inst. Oceanol. Acad. Sci. U.S.S.R.* **20**, 60–87.

ODUM, H. T. (1957) Primary production measurements in eleven Florida springs and a marine turtle-grass community. *Limnol. & Oceanogr.* **2**, 85–97.

OMMANEY, F. D. (1936) *Rhincalanus gigas* (Brady) a copepod of the southern macroplankton. *Discovery Repts.* **13**, 277–384.

ORR, A. P. (1934a) On the biology of *Calanus finmarchicus*. IV. Seasonal changes in the weight and chemical composition in Loch Fyne. *J. Mar. Biol. Ass.* **19**, 613–632

ORR, A. P. (1934b) The weight and chemical composition of *Euchaeta norvegica* Boeck. *Proc. Roy. Soc. Edinb.* **54**B, 51–55.

ORR, A. P. (1947) An experiment in marine fish cultivation II. Some physical and chemical conditions in a fertilized sea loch. *Proc. Roy Soc. Edinb.* B **63**, 3–20.

ORR, A. P., and F. W. MOORHOUSE (1933) Physical and chemical conditions in mangrove swamps. *Gt. Barrier Reef Exped. Sci. Repts. B.M. (N.H.)* **2**, 102–110.

ORTON, J. H. (1920) Sea temperature, breeding and distribution in marine animals. *J. Mar. Biol. Ass.* **12**, 339–366.

ORTON, J. H. (1923) Some experiments on rate of growth in a polar region (Spitzbergen) and in England. *Nature, Lond.* **111**, 146–148.

OSTER, R. H., and G. L. CLARKE (1935) The penetration of the red, green and violet components of daylight into Atlantic waters. *J. Optic. Soc. Amer.* **25**, 84–91.

PARKE, M. (1949) Studies on marine flagellates. *J. Mar. Biol. Ass.* **28**, 255–286.

PARKE, M., I. MANTON and B. CLARKE (1955) Studies on marine flagellates II. *J. Mar. Biol. Ass.* **34**, 579–609.

PARKE, M., I. MANTON and B. CLARKE (1956) Studies on marine flagellates III. *J. Mar. Biol. Ass.* **35**, 387–414.

PARKE, M., I. MANTON and B. CLARKE (1959) Studies on marine flagellates V. *J. Mar. Biol. Ass.* **38**, 169–188.

PARKE, M., and I. ADAMS (1960) The motile (*Crystallolithus hyalinus* Gaarder and Markali) and non-motile phases in the life history of *Coccolithus pelagicus* (Wallich) Schiller. *J. Mar. Biol. Ass.* **39**, 263–274.

PARKER, G. H. (1902) The reactions of copepods to various stimuli, and the bearing of this on the daily depth migrations. *Bull. U.S. Fish. Comm.* **21**, 103–123.

PATEL, B., and D. J. CRISP (1960) Rates of development of the embryos of several species of barnacles. *Physiol. Zool.* **33**, 104–119.

PAULSEN, O. (1906) Studies in the biology of *Calanus finmarchicus* in the waters round Iceland. *Medd. Komm. Havund. Ser. Plankton* **1**, 1–21.

PETERSEN, C. G. J. (1918) The sea bottom and its production of fish-food. (A survey of the work done in connection with valuation of the Danish waters from 1883–1917.) *Rept. Dan. Biol. Stat.* **25**, 1–62.

PETERSEN, C. G. J., and P. BOYSEN-JENSEN (1911) Valuation of the sea. I. Animal life of the sea bottom, its food and quantity. *Rept. Dan. Biol. Stat.* **20**, 1–79.

638   PLANKTON AND PRODUCTIVITY IN THE OCEANS

PIERCE, E. L. (1941) The occurrence and breeding of *Sagitta elegans* Verrill and *Sagitta setosa* J. Müller in parts of the Irish Sea. *J. Mar. Biol. Ass.* **25**, 113–124.

PLUNKETT, M. A., and N. W. RAKESTRAW (1955) Dissolved organic matter in the sea. *Pap. Mar. Biol. & Oceanogr. Deep Sea Res. Suppl.* **3**, 12–14.

POMEROY, L. R., and F. M. BUSH (1959) Regeneration of phosphate by marine animals. Int. Ocean. Congress Preprints A.A.A.S. Washington, 893–894.

PONOMAREVA, L. A. (1955) Nutrition and distribution of euphausids in the Sea of Japan. *Zoolog. Zh.* **34**, 85–97.

PONOMAREVA, L. A. (1957) Zooplankton of the West Kara Sea and Baidaratskaya Bay. *Trans. Inst. Oceanol. Acad. Sci. U.S.S.R.* **20**, 228–245.

POWELL, W. M., and G. L. CLARKE (1936) The reflection and absorption of daylight at the surface of the ocean. *J. Optic. Soc. Amer.* **26**, 111–120.

PRASAD, R. R. (1954) Observations on the distribution and fluctuation of planktonic larvae off Mandapan. *Symposium on Marine and Freshwater Plankton in the Indo-Pacific.* Bangkok, 21–34.

PRATT, D. M. (1949) Experiments in the fertilization of a salt water pond. *J. Mar. Res.* **8**, 36–59.

PRATT, D. M. (1950) Experimental study of the phosphorus cycle in fertilized salt water. *J. Mar. Res.* **9**, 29–54.

PRATT, D. M., and D. A. CAMPBELL (1956) Environmental factors affecting growth in *Venus mercenaria*. *Limnol. & Oceanogr.* **1**, 2–17.

PROCTOR, V. W. (1957) Studies of algal antibiosis using *Hematococcus* and *Chlamydomonas*. *Limnol. & Oceanogr.* **2**, 125–139.

PROSSER, C. L. (Ed.) (1950) *Comparative Animal Physiology*, W. B. Saunders Co., Philadelphia and London. 888 pp.

PROVASOLI, L. (1958) Growth factors in unicellular marine algae. *Perspectives in Marine Biology* Ed. BUZZATI-TRAVERSO, Univ. of California Press. Berkeley and Los Angeles. 385–403.

PROVASOLI, L., J. J. A. MCLAUGHLIN and M. R. DROOP (1957) The development of artificial media for marine algae. *Arch. Mikrobiol.* **25**, 392–428.

PUTTER, A. (1909) *Die Ernährung der Wassertiere und der Stoffhaushalt der Gewässer.* J. Fischer. Jena. 168 pp.

PUTTER, A. (1925) Die Ernährung der Copepoden. *Arch. Hydrobiol.* **15**, 70–117.

PYEFINCH, K. A. (1948) Notes on the biology of cirripedes. *J. Mar. Biol. Ass.* **27**, 464–503.

QASIM, S. Z. (1956) Time and duration of the spawning season in some marine teleosts in relation to their distribution. *J. Cons. Int. Explor. Mer.* **21**, 144–155.

RAE, K. M. (1950) The continuous plankton recorder survey; the plankton round the north of the British Isles in 1950. *Ann. Biol.* **7**, 72–76.

RAE, K. M. (1958) Parameters of the marine environment. *Perspectives in Marine Biology* Ed. BUZZATI-TRAVERSO. Univ. of California Press. Berkeley and Los Angeles, 3–14.

RAE, K. M., and J. H. FRASER (1941) Ecological investigations with the continuous plankton recorder: The Copepoda of the Southern North Sea, 1932–1937. *Hull Bull. Mar. Ecol.* **1**, No. 4, 171–238.

RAE, K. M., and C. B. REES (1947) Continuous plankton records: The Copepoda in the North Sea, 1938–1939. *Hull Bull. Mar. Ecol.* **2**, No. 11, 95–132.

RAKESTRAW, N. W. (1936) The occurrence and significance of nitrite in the sea. *Biol. Bull. Woods Hole* **71**, 133–167.

RAKESTRAW, N. W., and D. E. CARRITT (1948) Some seasonal chemical changes in the open ocean. *J. Mar. Res.* **7**, 362–369.

RAMMNER, W. (1939) Fiches d'Identification du Zooplancton. No. 3. Cladocera. *Cons. Inter. Explor. Mer.* Copenhagen.

RAYMONT, J. E. G. (1947) An experiment in marine fish cultivation. IV. The bottom fauna and the food of flatfishes in a fertilized sea-loch (Loch Craiglin). *Proc. Roy. Soc. Edinb.* B **63**, 34–55.

RAYMONT, J. E. G. (1950) A fish cultivation experiment in an arm of a sea-loch. IV. The bottom fauna of Kyle Scotnish. *Proc. Roy. Soc. Edinb.* B **64**, 65–108.

RAYMONT, J. E. G. (1955) The fauna of an inter-tidal mud flat. *Pap. Mar. Biol. & Oceanogr. Deep Sea Res. Suppl.* **3**, 178–203.

RAYMONT, J. E. G. (1959) The respiration of some planktonic copepods. III. The oxygen requirements of some American species. *Limnol. & Oceanogr.* **4**, 479–491.

RAYMONT, J. E. G., and F. GROSS (1942) On the feeding and breeding of *Calanus finmarchicus* under laboratory conditions. *Proc. Roy. Soc. Edinb.* B **61**, 267–287.

RAYMONT, J. E. G., and D. T. GAULD (1951) The respiration of some planktonic copepods. *J. Mar. Biol. Ass.* **29**, 681–693.

RAYMONT, J. E. G., and M. N. E. ADAMS (1958) Studies on the mass culture of *Phaeodactylum. Limnol. & Oceanogr.* **3**, 119–136.

RAYMONT, J. E. G., and B. G. A. CARRIE (1959) The zooplankton of Southampton Water. *Int. Ocean. Congress Preprints A.A.A.S.* Washington. 320–321.

RAYMONT, J. E. G., and S. KRISHNASWAMY (1960) Carbohydrates in some marine planktonic animals. *J. Mar. Biol. Ass.* **39**, 239–248.

RAYMONT, J. E. G., and R. J. CONOVER (1961) Further investigations on the carbohydrate content of marine zooplankton. *Limnol. & Oceanogr.* **6**, 154–164.

RAYMONT, J. E. G., and R. S. MILLER (1962). Production of marine zooplankton with fertilization in an enclosed body of sea water. *Int. Revue ges. Hydrobiol.* **47**, 169–209.

REDFIELD, A. C. (1939) The history of a population of *Limacina retroversa* during its drift across the Gulf of Maine. *Biol. Bull. Woods Hole* **76**, 26–47.

REDFIELD, A. C. (1941) The effect of circulation of water on the distribution of the calanoid community in the Gulf of Maine. *Biol. Bull. Woods Hole* **80**, 86–110.

REDFIELD, A. C. (1958) The biological control of chemical factors in the environment. *Amer. Scientist.* **46**, 205–221.

REDFIELD, A. C., H. P. SMITH and B. H. KETCHUM (1937) The cycle of organic phosphorus in the Gulf of Maine. *Biol. Bull. Woods Hole* **73**, 421–443.

REDFIELD, A. C., and A. B. KEYS (1938) The distribution of ammonia in the waters of the Gulf of Maine. *Biol. Bull. Woods Hole* **74**, 83–92.

REDFIELD, A. C., and A. BEALE (1940) Factors determining the distribution of populations of chaetognaths in the Gulf of Maine. *Biol. Bull. Woods Hole* **79**, 459–487.

REES, C. B. (1939) The plankton of the upper reaches of the Bristol Channel. *J. Mar. Biol. Ass.* **23**, 397–425.

REES, C. B. (1940) A preliminary study of the ecology of a mud-flat. *J. Mar. Biol. Ass.* **24**, 185–199.

REMANE, A. (1933) Verteilung und Organisation der benthonischen Mikrofauna der Kieler Bucht. *Wiss. Meeresuntersuch. Abt. Kiel* **21**, 161–221.

REMANE, A. (1940) Einführung in die zoologische Ökologie der Nord- und Ostsee. In *Die Tierwelt der Nord- und Ostsee*. Ed. GRIMPE and WAGLER. Akad. Verlags. Becker & Erler. Leipzig. Bd. 1, 1–238.

REMANE, A. (1959) Die interstitielle Fauna des Meeressandes. *Proc. 15th Internat. Congr. Zool.* London, 320–323.

RENAUD-DEBYSER, J. (1959) Contribution à l'étude de la faune interstitielle du bassin d'Arcachon. *Proc. 15th Internat. Congr. Zool.* London, 322–325.

REUSZER, H. W. (1933) Marine bacteria and their role in the cycle of life in the sea. III. Distribution of bacteria in the ocean waters and muds about Cape Cod. *Biol. Bull. Woods Hole* **65**, 480–497.

RICE, T. R. (1954) Biotic influences affecting population growth of planktonic algae. *Fish. Bull. U.S. Fish and Wildlife. Serv.* **54**, 227–245.

RICHARDS, F. A. (1957a) Oxygen in the Ocean. Chapter 9 in *Treatise on Marine Ecology and Paleoecology*. Vol. 1. Ecology. Ed. J. W. HEDGPETH Geol. Soc. Amer. Memoir **67**, 185–238.

RICHARDS, F. A. (1957b) Some current aspects of chemical oceanography. In *Progress in Physics and Chemistry of the Earth* (Pergamon Press, London) Vol 2, No. 4, 77–128.

RICHARDS, F. A., and B. B. BENSON (1961) Nitrogen/argon and nitrogen isotope ratios in two anaerobic environments, the Cariaco Trench in the Caribbean Sea and Dramsfjord, Norway. *Deep Sea Res.* **7**, 254–264.

RICHARDS, F. A., and T. G. THOMPSON (1952) The estimation and characterization of plankton populations by pigment analyses II. *J. Mar. Res.* **11**, 156–172.

RICHARDS, F. A., and R. F. VACCARO (1956) The Cariaco Trench, an anaerobic basin in the Caribbean Sea. *Deep Sea Res.* **3**, 214–228.

RILEY, G. A. (1937) Significance of the Mississippi River drainage for biological conditions in the northern Gulf of Mexico. *J. Mar. Res.* **1**, 60–74.

RILEY, G. A. (1939) Plankton studies. II, The western North Atlantic, May–June 1939. *J. Mar. Res.* **2**, 145–162.

RILEY, G. A. (1941) Plankton studies. V. Regional summary. *J. Mar. Res.* **4**, 162–171.

RILEY, G. A. (1942) The relationship of vertical turbulence and spring diatom flowerings. *J. Mar. Res.* **5**, 67–87.

RILEY, G. A. (1946) Factors controlling phytoplankton populations on Georges Bank. *J. Mar. Res.* **6**, 54–73.

RILEY, G. A. (1947a) Seasonal fluctuations of the phytoplankton population in New England coastal waters. *J. Mar. Res.* **6**, 114–125.

RILEY, G. A. (1947b) A theoretical analysis of the zooplankton population of Georges Bank. *J. Mar. Res.* **6**, 104–113.

RILEY, G. A. (1953) Letter to the editor. *J. Cons. Int. Explor. Mer.* **19**, 85–89.

RILEY, G. A. (1955) Review of the oceanography of Long Island Sound. *Pap. Mar. Biol. & Oceanogr. Deep Sea Res. Suppl.* **3**, 224–238.

RILEY, G. A. (1956) Oceanography of Long Island Sound, 1952–1954. IX. Production and utilization of organic matter. *Bull. Bingham Oceanogr. Coll.* **15**, 324–344.

RILEY, G. A. (1957) Phytoplankton of the North Central Sargasso Sea. *Limnol. & Oceanogr.* **2**, 252–270.

RILEY, G. A. (1959) Note on particulate matter in Long Island Sound. *Bull. Bingham Oceanogr. Coll.* **17**, 83–85.

RILEY, G. A., and D. F. BUMPUS (1946) Phytoplankton–zooplankton relationships on Georges Bank. *J. Mar. Res.* **6**, 33–47.

RILEY, G. A., H. STOMMEL and D. F. BUMPUS (1949) Quantitative ecology of the plankton of the Western North Atlantic. *Bull. Bingham Oceanogr. Coll.* **12**, 1–169.

RILEY, G. A., and S. A. M. CONOVER (1956) Oceanography of Long Island Sound, 1952–54. III. Chemical oceanography. *Bull. Bingham Oceanogr. Coll.* **15**, 47–61.

ROBERTSON, J. D. (1957) *Recent Advances in Invertebrate Physiology.* Ed. SCHEER, BULLOCK, KLEINHOLZ and MARTIN. Univ. of Oregon Publication. Eugene. 304 pp.

ROBINSON, R. J., and H. E. WIRTH (1934a) Report on the free ammonia, albuminoid nitrogen and organic nitrogen in the waters of the Puget Sound area, during the summers of 1931 and 1932. *J. Cons. Int. Explor. Mer.* **9**, 15–27.

ROBINSON, R. J., and H. E. WIRTH (1934b) Free ammonia, albuminoid nitrogen and organic nitrogen in waters of the Pacific Ocean off the coasts of Washington and Vancouver Island. *J. Cons. Int. Explor. Mer.* **9**, 187–195.

ROCHFORD, D. J. (1960) The intermediate depth waters of the Tasman and Coral Seas I. *Aust. J. Mar. & Freshw. Res.* **11**, 127–147.

ROSE, M. (1925) Contributions à l'étude de la biologie du plankton. Le problème des migrations verticales journalières. *Arch. Zool. Exp. Gén.* **64**, 387–542.

ROSE, M. (1933) *Faune de France* 26. Copépodes pélagiques. Lechevalier. Paris. 374 pp.

RUSSELL, F. S. (1925–1934) The vertical distribution of marine macroplankton I–XII. *J. Mar. Biol. Ass.* **13–19**.

RUSSELL, F. S. (1927) The vertical distribution of plankton in the sea. *Biol. Rev.* **2**, 213–256.

RUSSELL, F. S. (1928) The vertical distribution of marine macroplankton. VII. Observations on the behaviour of *Calanus finmarchicus. J. Mar. Biol. Ass.* **15**, 429–454.

RUSSELL, F. S. (1930–1947) On the seasonal abundance of young fish I–VIII. *J. Mar. Biol. Ass.* **16–26**.

RUSSELL, F. S. (1931) The vertical distribution of marine macroplankton. X. Notes on the behaviour of Sagitta in the Plymouth area. *J. Mar. Biol. Ass.* **17**, 391–414.

RUSSELL, F. S. (1932) On the biology of Sagitta. The breeding and growth of *Sagitta elegans* Verrill in the Plymouth area, 1930–1931. *J. Mar. Biol. Ass.* **18**, 131–146.

RUSSELL, F. S. (1933) On the biology of Sagitta. III. A further observation on the growth and breeding of *Sagitta setosa* in the Plymouth area. IV. Observations on the natural history of *Sagitta elegans* Verrill and *Sagitta setosa*. J. Müller in the Plymouth area. *J. Mar. Biol. Ass.* **18**, 555–558 and 559–574.

RUSSELL, F. S. (1934a) On the occurrence of the siphonophores *Muggiaea atlantica* Cunningham and *Muggiaea kochi* (Will) in the English Channel. *J. Mar. Biol. Ass.* **19**, 555–558.

RUSSELL, F. S. (1934b) The zooplankton III. *Gt. Barrier Reef Exped. Sci. Repts. B.M. (N.H.)* **2**, 176–201.

RUSSELL, F. S. (1934c) The vertical distribution of marine macroplankton. XII. Some observations on the vertical distribution of *Calanus finmarchicus* in relation to light intensity. *J. Mar. Biol. Ass.* **19**, 569–584.

RUSSELL, F. S. (1935a) A review of some aspects of zooplankton research. *Rapp. Proc.-Verb. Cons. Int. Explor. Mer.* **95**, 5–30.

RUSSELL, F. S. (1935b) On the value of certain plankton animals as indicators of water movements in the English Channel and North Sea. *J. Mar. Biol. Ass.* **20**, 309–332.

RUSSELL, F. S. (1935c) The seasonal abundance and distribution of the pelagic young of teleostean fishes caught in the ring-trawl in offshore waters in the Plymouth area. Part II. *J. Mar. Biol. Ass.* **20**, 147–179.

RUSSELL, F. S. (1936) Observations on the distribution of plankton animal indicators made on Col. E. T. Peel's yacht *St. George* in the mouth of the English Channel, July 1935. *J. Mar. Biol. Ass.* **20**, 507–522.

RUSSELL, F. S. (1939) Fiches d'Identification du Zooplancton. No. 1. Chaetognatha. *Cons. Inter. Explor. Mer.* Copenhagen.

RUSSELL, F. S. (1939) Hydrographical and biological conditions in the North Sea as indicated by plankton organisms. *J. Cons. Int. Explor. Mer.* **14**, 171–192.

RUSSELL, F. S. (1953) *The Medusae of the British Isles.* Cambridge University Press. 530 pp.

RUSSELL, F. S., and J. S. COLMAN (1934) The zooplankton II. *Gt. Barrier Reef Exped. Sci. Repts. B.M. (N.H.)* **2**, 159–176.

RUSSELL, F. S., and J. S. COLMAN (1935) The zooplankton IV. *Gt. Barrier Reef Exped. Sci. Repts. B.M. (N.H.)* **2**, 203–276.

RUSSELL, R. C. M., and D. H. MACMILLAN (1952) *Waves and Tides,* Hutchinson's Sci. & Techn. Publications London, 348 pp.

RUSTAD, E. (1946) Experiments on photosynthesis and respiration at different depths in the Oslo Fjord. *Nytt. Mag. Naturvid.* **85**, 223–229.

RUUD, J. T. (1929) On the biology of copepods off Möre 1925–1927. *Rapp. Proc.-Verb. Cons. Int. Explor. Mer.* **56** (8), 1–84.

RYTHER, J. H. (1954a) Inhibitory effects of phytoplankton upon the feeding of *Daphnia magna* with reference to growth, reproduction and survival. *Ecology* **35**, 522–533.

RYTHER, J. H. (1954b) Ecology of phytoplankton blooms in Moriches Bay and Great South Bay, Long Island, N. Y. *Biol. Bull. Woods Hole* **106**, 198–209.

RYTHER, J. H. (1956) Photosynthesis in the ocean as a function of light intensity. *Limnol. & Oceanogr.* **1**, 61–70.

RYTHER, J. H., and R. F. VACCARO (1954) Comparison of the oxygen and ^{14}C methods of measuring marine photosynthesis. *J. Cons. Int. Explor. Mer.* **20**, 25–34.

RYTHER, J. H., and C. S. YENTSCH (1957) Estimation of phytoplankton production in the ocean from chlorophyll and light data. *Limnol. & Oceanogr.* **2**, 281–286.

RYTHER, J. H., and C. S. YENTSCH (1958) Primary production of continental shelf waters off New York. *Limnol. & Oceanogr.* **3**, 327–335.

RYTHER, J. H., and D. W. MENZEL (1960) The seasonal and geographical range of primary production in the Western Sargasso Sea. *Deep Sea Res.* **6**, 235–238.

SANDERS, H. L. (1956) Oceanography of Long Island Sound, 1952–1954. X. Biology of marine bottom communities. *Bull. Bingham Oceanogr. Coll.* **15**, 345–414.

SANDERS, H. L. (1958) Benthic studies in Buzzards Bay. I. Animal-sediment relationships. *Limnol. & Oceanogr.* **3**, 245–258.

SANDERS, H. L. (1960) Benthic studies in Buzzards Bay. III. *Limnol. & Oceanogr.* **5**, 138–153.

SARS, G. O. (1895–1903) *An Account of the Crustancea of Norway.* Vols. I, III and IV. Bergen Museum.

SAVILOV, A. I. (1957) Biological aspect of the bottom fauna groupings of the North Okhotsk Sea. *Trans. Inst. Oceanol. Acad. Sci. U.S.S.R.* **20**, 88–170.

SCHALLEK, W. (1942) The vertical migration of the copepod *Acartia tonsa* under controlled illumination. *Biol. Bull. Woods Hole* **82**, 112–126.

SCHALLEK, W. (1943) The reaction of certain Crustacea to direct and to diffuse light. *Biol. Bull. Woods Hole* **84**, 98–105.

SCHOLANDER, P. F., L. VAN DAM, J. W. KANWISHER, H. T. HAMMEL and M. S GORDON (1957) Supercooling and osmoregulation in Arctic fish. *J. Cell & Comp. Physiol.* **49**, 5–24.

SEARS, M. (1954) Notes on the Peruvian coastal current. I. An introduction to the ecology of Pisco Bay. *Deep Sea Res.* **1**, 141–169.

SEIWELL, G. E. (1935) Note on iron analyses of Atlantic coastal waters. *Ecology* **16**, 663–664.

SEIWELL, H. R. (1935) The annual organic production and nutrient phosphorus requirement in the tropical Western North Atlantic. *J. Cons. Int. Explor. Mer.* **10**, 20–32.

SEIWELL, H. R. (1939) Daily temperature variations in the Western North Atlantic. *J. Cons. Int. Explor. Mer.* **14**, 357–369.

SEIWELL, H. R. (1942) An analysis of vertical oscillations in the Southern North Atlantic. *Trans. Amer. Phil. Soc.* **85**, 136–158.

SEWELL, R. B. S. (1929) Geographic and oceanographic research in Indian waters. V. *Mem. Asia Soc. Bengal.* **9**, 207–356.

SEWELL, R. B. S. (1948) The free swimming planktonic Copepoda-geographical distribution. *John Murray Expdn. 1933–34, Sci. Repts. B.M. (N.H.)* **8**, 321–592.

SHELBOURNE, J. E. (1953) The feeding habits of plaice post-larvae in the Southern Bight. *J. Mar. Biol. Ass.* **32**, 149–159.

SHELBOURNE, J. E. (1957) The feeding and condition of plaice larvae in good and bad plankton patches. *J. Mar. Biol. Ass.* **36**, 539–552.

SHIRAISHI, K., and L. PROVASOLI (1959) Growth factors as supplements to inadequate algal food for *Tigriopus japonicus.* Int. Ocean. Congress Preprints. A.A.A.S. Washington, 951–952.

SIEBURTH, J. MC. N., and P. R. BURKHOLDER (1959) Antibiotic activity of Antarctic phytoplankton. Int. Ocean. Congress Preprints. A.A.A.S. Washington, 933–934.

SMAYDA, T. J. (1958) Biogeographical studies of marine phytoplankton. *Oikos* **9**, 158–191.

SMIDT, E. L. B. (1951) Animal production in the Danish Waddensea. *Medd. Komm. Dan. Fisk. Havund. Ser. Fiskeri* **11** (6), 1–151.

SMITH, J. E. (1932) The shell gravel deposits, and the infauna of the Eddystone grounds. *J. Mar. Biol. Ass.* **18**, 243–278.

SMYTH, J. C. (1955) A study of the benthic diatoms of Loch Sween (Argyll). *J. Ecology* **43**, 149–171.

SOARES, M. (1957) A study of the distribution and abundance of cirripede larvae in Southampton Water. M. Sc. Thesis, University of Southampton.

SØMME, J. D. (1934) Animal plankton of the Norwegian coast waters and the open sea. I. Production of *Calanus finmarchicus* (Gunner) and *Calanus hyperboreus* (Krøyer) in the Lofoten Area. *Rep. Norweg. Fish. & Mar. Invest.* **4** (9), 1–163.

SOUTHWARD, A. J. (1961) The distribution of some plankton animals in the English Channel and Western Approaches I. *J. Mar. Biol. Ass.* **41**, 17–35.

SOUTHWARD, A. J. (1962) The distribution of some plankton animals in the English Channel and approaches II. *J. Mar. Biol. Ass.* **42**, 275–375.

SPARCK, R. (1951) Density of bottom animals on the ocean floor. *Nature, Lond.* **168**, 112–113.

SPENCER, C. P. (1954) Studies on the culture of a marine diatom. *J. Mar. Biol. Ass.* **33**, 265–290.

SPENCER, C. P. (1956) The bacterial oxidation of ammonia in the sea. *J. Mar. Biol. Ass.* **35**, 621–630.

SPOONER, G. M. (1933) Observations on the reactions of marine plankton to light. *J. Mar. Biol. Ass.* **19**, 385–438.

SPOONER, G. M., and H. B. MOORE (1940) The ecology of the Tamar estuary. (VI) An account of the macrofauna of the intertidal muds. *J. Mar. Biol. Ass.* **24**, 283–330.

STANBURY, F. A. (1931) The effect of light of different intensities reduced selectively and non-selectively, upon the rate of growth of *Nitzschia closterium*. *J. Mar. Biol. Ass.* **17**, 633–653.

STARR, T. J., M. E. JONES and D. MARTINEZ (1957) The production of vitamin B_{12}-active substances by marine bacteria. *Limnol. & Oceanogr.* **2**, 114–119.

STEELE, J. H. (1956) Plant production on the Fladen Ground. *J. Mar. Biol. Ass.* **35**, 1–33.

STEELE, J. H. (1958) Production studies in the Northern North Sea. *Rapp. Proc.-Verb. Cons. Int. Explor. Mer.* **144**, 79–84.

STEELE, J. H. (1959) The quantitative ecology of marine phytoplankton. *Biol. Rev.* **34**, 129–158.

STEEMANN NIELSEN, E. (1935) The production of phytoplankton at the Faroe Isles, Iceland, E. Greenland and in the waters around. *Medd. Komm. Dan. Fisk. Havund. Ser. Plankton* **3** (1), 1–93.

STEEMANN NIELSEN, E. (1937a) The annual amount of organic matter produced by the phytoplankton in the Sound off Helsingor. *Medd. Komm. Dan. Fisk. Havund. Ser. Plankton* **3** (3), 1–37.

STEEMANN NIELSEN, E. (1937b) On the relation between the quantities of phytoplankton and zooplankton in the sea. *J. Cons. Int. Explor. Mer.* **12**, 147–153.

STEEMANN NIELSEN, E. (1940) Die Produktionsbedingungen des Phytoplanktons in Übergangsgebiet zwischen der Nord- und Ostsee. *Medd. Komm. Dan. Fisk. Havund. Ser. Plankton* **3** (4), 1–55.

STEEMANN NIELSEN, E. (1951) The marine vegetation of the Isefjord—A study of ecology and production. *Medd. Komm. Dan. Fisk. Havund. Ser. Plankton* **5** (4), 1–114.

STEEMANN NIELSEN, E. (1952) Use of radio-active carbon (C^{14}) for measuring organic production in the sea. *J. Cons. Int. Explor. Mer.* **18**, 117–140.

STEEMANN NIELSEN, E. (1954) On organic production in the oceans. *J. Cons. Int. Explor. Mer.* **19**, 309–328.

STEEMANN NIELSEN, E. (1958a) The balance between phytoplankton and zooplankton in the sea. *J. Cons. Int. Explor. Mer.* **23**, 178–198.

STEEMANN NIELSEN, E. (1958b) A survey of recent Danish measurements of the organic productivity in the sea. *Rapp. Proc.-Verb. Cons. Int. Explor. Mer.* **144**, 92–95.

STEEMANN NIELSEN, E. (1958c) Experimental methods for measuring organic production in the sea. *Rapp. Proc.-Verb. Cons. Int. Explor. Mer.* **144**, 38–46.

STEEMANN NIELSEN, E., and E. AABYE JENSEN (1957) Primary oceanic production. The autotrophic production of organic matter in the oceans. *Galathea Rept.* **1**, 49–136.

STEEMANN NIELSEN, E., and V. K. HANSEN (1959) Light adaptation in marine phytoplankton populations and its interrelation with temperature. *Physiologia Plantarum* **12**, 353–370.

STEPHEN, A. C. (1930) Studies on the Scottish marine fauna: Additional observations on the fauna of the sandy and muddy areas of the tidal zone. *Trans. Roy. Soc. Edinb.* B **56**, 521–535.

STEPHEN, A. C. (1931) Notes on the biology of some lamellibranchs on the Scottish coast. *J. Mar. Biol. Ass.* **17**, 277–300.

STEPHEN, A. C. (1932) Notes on the biology of some lamellibranchs in the Clyde area. *J. Mar. Biol. Ass.* **18**, 51–68.

STEPHEN, A. C. (1938) Production of large broods in certain marine lamellibranchs with a possible relation to weather conditions. *J. Anim. Ecol.* **7**, 130–143.

STEPHENSON, W. (1949) Certain effects of agitation upon the release of phosphate from mud. *J. Mar. Biol. Ass.* **28**, 371–380.

STEVEN, G. A. (1930) Bottom fauna and the food of fishes. *J. Mar. Biol. Ass.* **16**, 677–706.

STOMMEL, H. (1958) *The Gulf Stream.* University of California Press, Berkeley and Los Angeles. Cambridge Univ. Press, London. 202 pp.

STRØM, K. M. (1936) Land-locked waters. Hydrography and bottom deposits in badly ventilated Norwegian fjords with remarks on sedimentation under anaerobic conditions. *Norske Vidensk.-Akad. Oslo Mat.-Nat. Kl.* No. 7, 1–85.

SUBRAHMANYAN, R. (1959) Studies on the phytoplankton of the West Coast of India. Part I. *Proc. Indian Acad. Sci.* B. **50**, 113–187.

SVERDRUP, H. U. (1953) On conditions for the vernal blooming of phytoplankton. *J. Cons. Int. Explor. Mer.* **18**, 287–295.

SVERDRUP, H. U., and W. E. ALLEN (1939) Distribution of diatoms in relation to the character of water masses and currents off Southern California in 1938. *J. Mar. Res.* **2**, 131–144.

SVERDRUP, H. U., M. W. JOHNSON and R. H. FLEMING (1946) *The Oceans their Physics, Chemistry and General Biology.* Prentice-Hall, New York, 1087 pp.

SWALLOW, J. C. (1957) Some further deep current measurements using neutrally buoyant floats. *Deep Sea Res.* **4**, 93–104.

SWALLOW, J. C., and L. V. WORTHINGTON (1961) An observation of a deep countercurrent in the Western North Atlantic. *Deep Sea Res.* **8**, 1–19.

SWEDMARK, B. (1959) On the biology of sexual reproduction of the interstitial fauna of marine sand. *Proc. 15th Internat. Congr. Zool. London,* 327–329.

TALLING, J. F. (1957) The growth of two plankton diatoms in mixed cultures. *Physiologia Plantarum* **10**, 215–223.

TALLING, J. F. (1960) Comparative laboratory and field studies of photosynthesis by a marine planktonic diatom. *Limnol. & Oceanogr.* **5**, 62–77.

TATTERSALL, W. M., and O. S. TATTERSALL (1951) *The British Mysidacea.* Ray Soc. Lond. 460 pp.

TESCH, J. J. (1947) Fiches d'Identification du Zooplancton. No. 8. Pteropoda Thecosomata. *Cons. Inter. Explor. Mer.* Copenhagen.

THAMDRUP, H. M. (1935) Beiträge zur Ökologie der Wattenfauna. *Medd. Komm. Dan. Fisk. Havund. Ser. Fiskeri* **10**, No. 2, 1–125.

THOMPSON, T. G. and R. W. BREMNER (1935) The occurrence of iron in the water of the N. E. Pacific Ocean. *J. Cons. Int. Explor. Mer.* **10**, 39–47.

THOMPSON, E. F., and H. C. GILSON (1937) Chemical and physical investigations. *John Murray Expdn. 1933–34, Sci. Repts. B.M. (N.H.)* **2**, 15–81.

THORSON, G. (1950) Reproductive and larval ecology of marine bottom invertebrates. *Biol. Rev.* **25**, 1–45.

THORSON, G. (1955) Modern aspects of marine level-bottom animal communities. *J. Mar. Res.* **14**, 387–397.

THORSON, G. (1957) Bottom communities. Chap. 17 in *Treatise on Marine Ecology and Paleoecology.* Vol. I. Ecology, Ed. J. W. HEDGPETH Geol. Soc. Amer. Memoir **67**, 461–534.

THORSON, G. (1958) Parallel level-bottom communities, their temperature adaptation, and their "balance" between predators and food animals. *Perspectives in Marine Biology.* Ed. BUZZATI-TRAVERSO. Univ. of California Press. Berkeley and Los Angeles, 67–82.

TURNER, H. J. (1953) A review of the biology of some commercial molluscs of the east coast of North America. 6th Rept. Invest., Shellfish Mass. Div. Mar. Fish Dept. Conserv. Mass. Boston, 39–74.

USSING, H. H. (1938) The biology of some important plankton animals in the fjords of East Greenland. *Medd. Grønland* **100**, 1–108.

VACCARO, R. F., and J. H. RYTHER (1960) Marine phytoplankton and the distribution of nitrite in the sea. *J. Cons. Int. Explor. Mer.* **25**, 260–271.

VERJBINSKAYA, N. (1932) Observations on the nitrite changes in the Barents Sea. *J. Cons. Int. Explor. Mer..* **7**, 47–52.

VERWEY, J. (1952) On the ecology of distribution of cockle and mussel in the Dutch Waddensea. Their role in sedimentation and the source of their food supply. With a short review of the feeding behaviour of bivalve molluscs. *Arch. Néerland. Zool.* **10**, 171–239.

VEVERS, H. G. (1952) A photographic survey of certain areas of sea floor near Plymouth. *J. Mar. Biol. Ass.* **31**, 215–221.

VIBE, C. (1939) Preliminary investigations on shallow water animal communities in the Upernavik- and Thule- districts (Northwest Greenland). *Medd. Grønland* **124**, 1–42.

VINOGRADOV, A. P. (1953) The elementary chemical composition of marine organisms. *Sears Foundation Mar. Res. Mem.* **2**. (New Haven), 647 pp.

VINOGRADOVA, N. G. (1959) The zoogeographical distribution of the deep-water bottom fauna in the abyssal zone of the ocean. *Deep Sea Res.* **5**, 205–208.

WAKSMAN, S. A. (1933) On the distribution of organic matter in the sea bottom and the chemical nature and origin of marine humus. *Soil Science* **36**, 125–147.

WAKSMAN, S. A., C. L. CAREY and H. W. REUSZER (1933) Marine bacteria and their role in the cycle of life in the sea. I Decomposition of marine plant and animal residues by bacteria. *Biol. Bull. Woods Hole* **65**, 57–79.

WAKSMAN, S. A., H. W. REUSZER, C. L. CAREY, M. HOTCHKISS and C. E. RENN (1933) Studies on the biology and chemistry of the Gulf of Maine. III Bacteriological investigations of the sea water and marine bottoms. *Biol. Bull. Woods Hole* **64**, 183–205.

WAKSMAN, S. A., and C. L. CAREY (1935) Decomposition of organic matter in sea water by bacteria. *J. Bact.* **29**, 531–543.

WAKSMAN, S. A., and C. E. RENN (1936) Decomposition of organic matter in sea water III. *Biol. Bull. Woods Hole* **70**, 472–483.

WAKSMAN, S. A., and M. HOTCHKISS (1937) Viability of bacteria in sea water. *J. Bact.* **33**, 389–400.

WAKSMAN, S. A., and U. VARTIOVAARA (1938) The adsorption of bacteria by marine bottom. *Biol. Bull. Woods Hole* **74**, 56–63.

WALFORD, L. A. (1958) *Living Resources of the Sea; Opportunities for Research and Expansion.* Ronald Press. New York. 321 pp.

WALKER, F. T. (1947) Sub-littoral seaweed survey. *J. Ecol.* **35**, 166–185.

WALKER, F. T. (1954) Distribution of Laminariacaea around Scotland. *J. Cons. Int. Explor. Mer.* **20**, 160–166.

WALKER, F. T., and W. D. RICHARDSON (1957) Perennial changes of *Laminaria cloustoni* Edm. on the coasts of Scotland. *J. Cons. Int. Explor. Mer.* **22**, 298–308.

WALNE, P. R. (1958) The importance of bacteria in laboratory experiments on rearing the larvae of *Ostrea edulis* (L). *J. Mar. Biol. Ass.* **37**, 415–425.

WANGERSKY, P. J. (1952) Isolation of ascorbic acid and rhamnosides from sea water. *Science* **115**, 685.

WANGERSKY, P. J. (1959) Dissolved carbohydrates in Long Island Sound 1956–1958. *Bull. Bingham Oceanogr. Coll.* **17**, 87–94.

WATERMAN, T. H., R. F. NUNNEMACHER, F. A. CHACE and G. L. CLARKE (1939) Diurnal vertical migrations of deep-water plankton. *Biol. Bull. Woods Hole* **76**, 256–279.

WEBB, D. A. (1939) Observations on the blood of certain ascidians, with special reference to the biochemistry of vanadium. *J. Exp. Biol.* **16**, 499–522.

WHEELER, J. F. G. (1934) Nemerteans from the South Atlantic and Southern Oceans. *Discovery Repts.* **9**, 217–294.

WHITELEY, G. C. (1948) The distribution of larger planktonic Crustacea on Georges Bank. *Ecol. Monogr.* **18**, 234–264.

WIBORG, K. F. (1948a) Investigations on cod larvae in the coastal waters of Northern Norway. *Rep. Norweg. Fish & Mar. Invest.* **9**, No. 3, 1–27.

WIBORG, K. F. (1948b) Some observations of the food of cod (*Gadus callarias* L.) of the 0-II-group from deep water and the littoral zone in Northern Norway and from deep water at Spitzbergen. *Rep. Norweg. Fish & Mar. Invest.* **9**, No. 4, 1–17.

WIBORG, K. F. (1949) Food of cod of 0-II-group from deep water in some fjords of Northern Norway. *Rep. Norweg. Fish & Mar. Invest.* **9**, No. 8, 1–27.

648   PLANKTON AND PRODUCTIVITY IN THE OCEANS

WIBORG, K. F. (1954) Investigations on zooplankton in coastal and offshore waters of western and northwestern Norway. *Rep. Norweg. Fish & Mar. Invest.* **11**, No. 1, 1–246.

WIBORG, K. F. (1955) Zooplankton in relation to hydrography in the Norwegian Sea. *Rep. Norweg. Fish & Mar. Invest.* **11**, No. 4, 1–66.

WIBORG, K. F. (1960) Investigations on pelagic fry of cod and haddock in coastal and offshore areas of Northern Norway in July-August 1957. *Rep. Norweg. Fish & Mar. Invest.* **12**, No. 8, 1–18.

WICKSTEAD, J. H. (1958) A survey of the larger zooplankton of Singapore Straits. *J. Cons. Int. Explor. Mer.* **23**, 341–353.

WICKSTEAD, J. H. (1959) A predatory copepod. *J. Anim. Ecol.* **28**, 69–72.

WIESER, W. (1960) Benthic studies in Buzzards Bay. II The Meiofauna. *Limnol. & Oceanogr.* **5**, 121–137.

WILSON, C. B. (1932) The Copepods of the Woods Hole region Massachusetts. *Bulletin 158. U.S. Nat. Mus.* Washington, 635 pp.

WILSON, D. P. (1937) The influence of the substratum on the metamorphosis of *Notomastus* larvae. *J. Mar. Biol. Ass.* **22**, 227–243.

WILSON, D. P. (1948) The relation of the substratum to the metamorphosis of *Ophelia* larvae. *J. Mar. Biol. Ass.* **27**, 723–760.

WILSON, D. P. (1953) The settlement of *Ophelia bicornis* Savigny larvae. The 1951 experiments. *J. Mar. Biol. Ass.* **31**, 413–438.

WILSON, D. P. (1954) The attractive factor in the settlement of *Ophelia bicornis* Savigny. *J. Mar. Biol. Ass.* **33**, 361–380.

WILSON, D. P., and F. A. J. ARMSTRONG (1958) Biological differences between sea waters: experiments in 1954 and 1955. *J. Mar. Biol. Ass.* **37**, 331–348.

WIMPENNY, R. S. (1936a) The size of diatoms I. *J. Mar. Biol. Ass.* **21**, 29–60.

WIMPENNY, R. S. (1936b) The distribution, breeding and feeding of some important plankton organisms of the south-west North Sea in 1934 Pt. I. *Fish. Invest. Lond.* Ser. II, **15** (3), 1–53.

WIMPENNY, R. S. (1938) Diurnal variation in the feeding and breeding of zooplankton related to the numerical balance of the zoo- phyto-plankton community. *J. Cons. Int. Explor. Mer.* **13**, 323–336.

WIMPENNY, R. S. (1946) The size of diatoms II. *J. Mar. Biol. Ass.* **26**, 271–284.

WIMPENNY R. S. (1958) Carbon production in the sea at the Smith's Knoll Lightvessel. *Rapp. Proc.-Verb. Cons. Int. Explor. Mer.* **144**, 70–72.

WISEMAN, J. D. H., and N. I. HENDEY (1953) The significance and diatom content of a deep-sea floor sample from the neighbourhood of the greatest oceanic depth. *Deep Sea Res.* **1**, 47–59.

WOHLENBERG, E. (1937) Die Wattenmeer-Lebensgemeinschaften im Königshafen von Sylt. *Helgoländ. Wiss. Meeresunters.* **1**, No. 1, 1–92.

WOLFF, T. (1960) The hadal community an introduction. *Deep Sea Res.* **6**, 95–124.

WOOD, E. J. F. (1950) Investigations of underwater fouling. 1. The role of bacteria in the early stages of fouling. *Aust. J. Mar. Freshw. Res.* **1**, 85–91.

WOOD, E. J. F. (1953) Heterotrophic bacteria in marine environments of Eastern Australia. *Aust. J. Mar. Freshw. Res.* **4**, 160–200.

WOODMANSEE, R. A. (1958) The seasonal distribution of the zooplankton off Chicken Key in Biscayne Bay, Florida. *Ecology* **39**, 247–262.

WORTHINGTON, L. V. (1954) A preliminary note on the time scale in North Atlantic circulation. *Deep Sea Res..* **1**, 244–251.

Wust, G. (1930) Meridionale Schichtung und Tiefenzirkulation in den West-hälften der drei Ozeane. *J. Cons. Int. Explor. Mer.* **5**, 7–21.

Wust, G., W. Brogmus and E. N. Noodt (1954) Die zonale Verteilung von Salz-gehalt, Niederschlag, Verdunstung, Temperatur und Dichte an der Ober-fläche der Ozeane. *Kieler Meeresforsch.* **10**, 137–161.

Wyrtki, K. (1961) The thermohaline circulation in relation to the general cir-culation in the oceans. *Deep Sea Res.* **8**, 39–64.

Yentsch, C. S., and R. F. Scagel (1958) Diurnal study of phytoplankton pigments, an *in situ* study in East Sound, Washington. *J. Mar. Res. Thompson Anni-versary Volume* **17**, 567–583.

Yentsch, C. S., and J. H. Ryther (1959) Relative significance of the net phyto-plankton and nanoplankton in the waters of Vineyard Sound. *J. Cons. Int. Explor. Mer.* **24**, 231–238.

Yonge, C. M. (1928) Feeding mechanisms in the invertebrates. *Biol. Rev.* **3**, 21–76.

Yonge, C. M., M. J. Yonge and A. G. Nicholls (1932) Studies on the physiology of corals. VI. *Gt. Barrier Reef Exped. Sci. Repts. B.M. (N.H.)* **1**, 213–251.

Zenkevitch, L. A. (1961) Certain quantitative characteristics of the pelagic and bottom life of the ocean. In *Oceanography.* Public. No. 67, A.A.A.S. Washing-ton D.C. ed. M. Sears; 323–335.

Zenkevitch, L. A., and J. A. Birstein (1956) Studies of the deep water fauna and related problems. *Deep Sea Res.* **4**, 54–64.

Zeuthen, E. (1947) Body size and metabolic rate in the animal kingdom with special regard to the marine micro-fauna. *C. R. Lab. Carlsberg, Ser. Chim.* **26**, 17–161.

Zobell, C. E. (1946) *Marine Microbiology.* Chronica Botanica Co. Waltham Mass. 240 pp..

Zobell, C. E. (1957) Marine Bacteria in *Treatise on Marine Ecology and Paleo-ecology.* Vol. I. Ecology. Ed. J. W. Hedgpeth. Geol. Soc. Amer. Memoir **67**, 1035–1040.

Zobell, C. E., and D. Q. Anderson (1936) Observations on the multiplication of bacteria in different volumes of stored seawater and the influence of oxygen tension and solid surfaces. *Biol. Bull. Woods Hole* **71**, 324–342.

Zobell, C. E., and F. H. Johnson (1949) The influence of hydrostatic pressure on the growth and viability of terrestrial and marine bacteria. *J. Bact.* **57**, 179–189.

Additional References added in Proof

GRAINGER, E. H. (1961) The copepods *Calanus glacialis* Jaschnov and *Calanus finmarchicus* (Gunnerus) in Canadian arctic-subarctic waters. *J. Fish. Res. Bd. Canada* Vol. 18, pp. 663–678.

MENZEL D. W., and J. P. SPAETH (1962 a) Occurrence of iron in the Sargasso Sea off Bermuda. *Limnol. & Oceanogr.* Vol. 7, pp. 155–158.

MENZEL, D. W., and J. P. SPAETH (1962 b) Occurrence of vitamin B_{12} in the Sargasso Sea. *Limnol. & Oceanogr.* Vol. 7, pp. 151–154.

Note: Reference may be made to the comprehensive treatise *Physical Oceanography* Vols. I & II by A. Defant, Pergamon Press Limited, 1961. This work appeared while this volume was in preparation.

GENERAL INDEX

(Bold page numbers refer to figures)

651